PHILIP'S

STREET ATLAS

Cornwall

First published in 2003 by

Philip's, a division of
Octopus Publishing Group Ltd
2-4 Heron Quays, London E14 4JP

First edition 2003
Third impression 2004

ISBN 0-540-08328-3 (spiral)

© Philip's 2004

Ordnance Survey®

This product includes mapping data licensed from Ordnance Survey® with the permission of the Controller of Her Majesty's Stationery Office. © Crown copyright 2004. All rights reserved. Licence number 100011710.

Printed and bound in Spain
by Cayfosa-Quebecor

Contents

II **Key to map pages**

IV **Route planning**

VIII **Administrative and Postcode boundaries**

1 **Key to map symbols**

2 **Street maps** at 1¾ inches to 1 mile

104 **Street maps** at 3½ inches to 1 mile

148 **Street map of Plymouth city centre** at 7 inches to 1 mile

150 **Index** of towns and villages

152 **Index** of streets, hospitals, industrial estates, railway stations, schools, shopping centres, universities and places of interest

Digital Data

The exceptionally high-quality mapping found in this atlas is available as digital data in TIFF format, which is easily convertible to other bitmapped (raster) image formats.

The index is also available in digital form as a standard database table. It contains all the details found in the printed index together with the National Grid reference for the map square in which each entry is named.

For further information and to discuss your requirements, please contact Philip's on 020 7644 6932 or james.mann@philips-maps.co.uk

Key to map pages

149	Map pages at 7 inches to 1 mile
128	Map pages at 3½ inches to 1 mile
100	Map pages at 1¾ inches to 1 mile

Scale

0　5　10　15　20　25 km

0　　5　　　10　　　15 miles

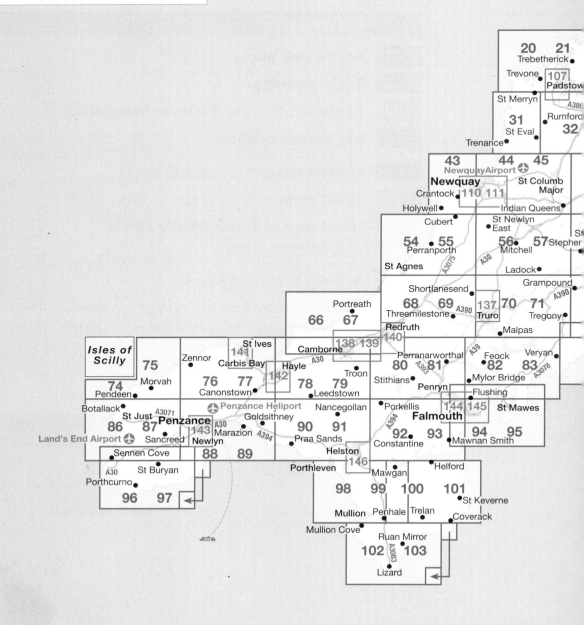

20 **21** Trebetherick

Trevone **107** Padstow

St Merryn A389

31 Rumford **32**
St Eval

Trenance

43 **44** **45**
Newquay Airport St Columb Major
Newquay **110 111**
Crantock Indian Queens
Holywell St Newlyn East
Cubert **56** **57** St Stepher
54 **55** Mitchell
Perranporth Ladock
St Agnes Grampound

Shortlanesend **70** **71**
68 **69** A390 **137** Tregony
Threemilestone **Truro**
Redruth Malpas
Portreath **140**

66 **67** **138 139** Perranarworthal Feock Veryan
Camborne **80** A393 **81** **82** **83**
St Ives **141** Stithians Mylor Bridge A3078
Carbis Bay **142** Troon Penryn Flushing
Zennor **Hayle** **78** **79** Leedstown **144 145** St Mawes
Isles of Scilly **75** **76** **77** Nancegollan Porkellis **Falmouth**
74 Morvah Canonstown **90** **91** **92** **93** **94** **95**
Pendeen Goldsithney Constantine Mawnan Smith
Botallack Penzance Heliport Praa Sands
St Just A3071 **Penzance** A30 Nancegollan Helston
86 **87** **143** Marazion A394 **146**
Land's End Airport Sancreed Newlyn **88** **89** Porthleven
Sennen Cove A30 Helford
St Buryan Mawgan Helford
Porthcurno **98** **99** **100** **101**
96 **97** Mullion Penhale Trelan St Keverne
Mullion Cove Coverack
Ruan Mirror
102 A3083 **103**
Lizard

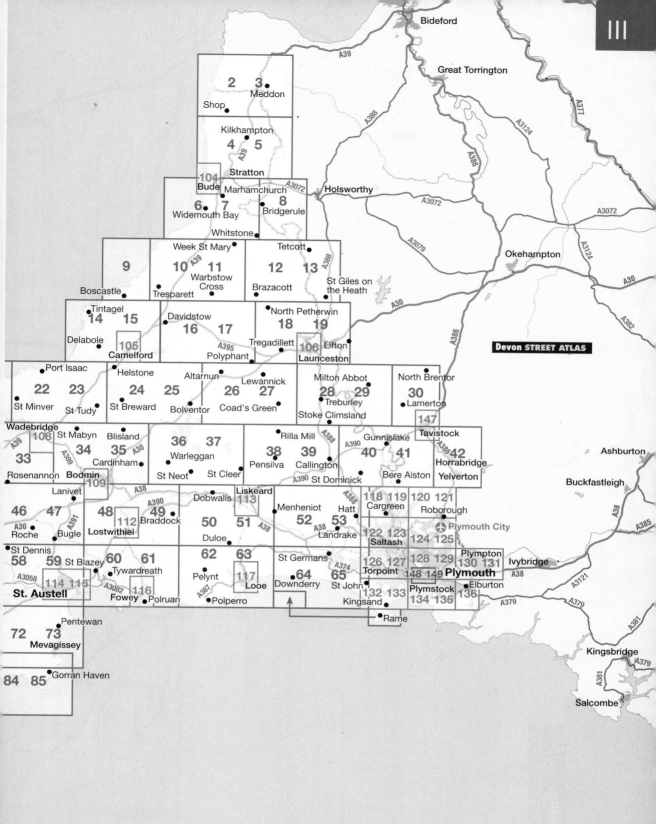

Bideford

Great Torrington

Holsworthy

Okehampton

Devon STREET ATLAS

Ashburton

Buckfastleigh

Ivybridge

Kingsbridge

Salcombe

2 3 Meddon

Shop

Kilkhampton

4 5

Stratton

104
Bude Marhamchurch

6 7 Bridgerule 8
Widemouth Bay

Whitstone

Week St Mary   Tetcott

9   10 11   12 13
    Warbstow
    Cross   Brazacott   St Giles on
Boscastle   the Heath
    Tresparrett

    Tintagel   North Petherwin
14 15   Davidstow   18 19
    16 17   Tregadillett   Lifton
Delabole   Polyphant   106
    105   Altarnun   Launceston
    Camelford   Lewannick   Milton Abbot   North Brentor
Port Isaac   Helstone   28 29   30
22 23   24 25   26 27   Treburley   Lamerton
St Minver   Bolventor   Coad's Green   Stoke Climsland
    St Tudy   St Breward   147
Wadebridge   Tavistock
108   St Mabyn   Blisland   Rilla Mill   Gunnislake
33 34 35   36 37   38 39   40 41   42
Rosenannon   Cardinham   Warleggan   Pensilva   Callington   Bere Alston   Horrabridge
Bodmin   St Neot   St Cleer   St Dominick   Yelverton
109   Lanivet   Liskeard   118 119   120 121
    Dobwalls   113   Menheniot   Cargreen   Roborough
46 47   48 49   50 51   52 53   122 123   124 125
Roche   Braddock   Duloe   Landrake   Saltash   Plymouth City
St Dennis   Bugle   Lostwithiel   62 63   St Germans   126 127   128 129   Plympton
58 59   60 61   Pelynt   117   64 65   Torpoint   148 149   Plymouth
St Blazey   Tywardreath   116   Looe   Downderry   St John   132 133   Plymstock
114 115   Fowey Polruan   Polperro   Kingsand   134 135   136
St. Austell   Rame   Elburton
    Pentewan
72 73
Mevagissey
84 85   Gorran Haven

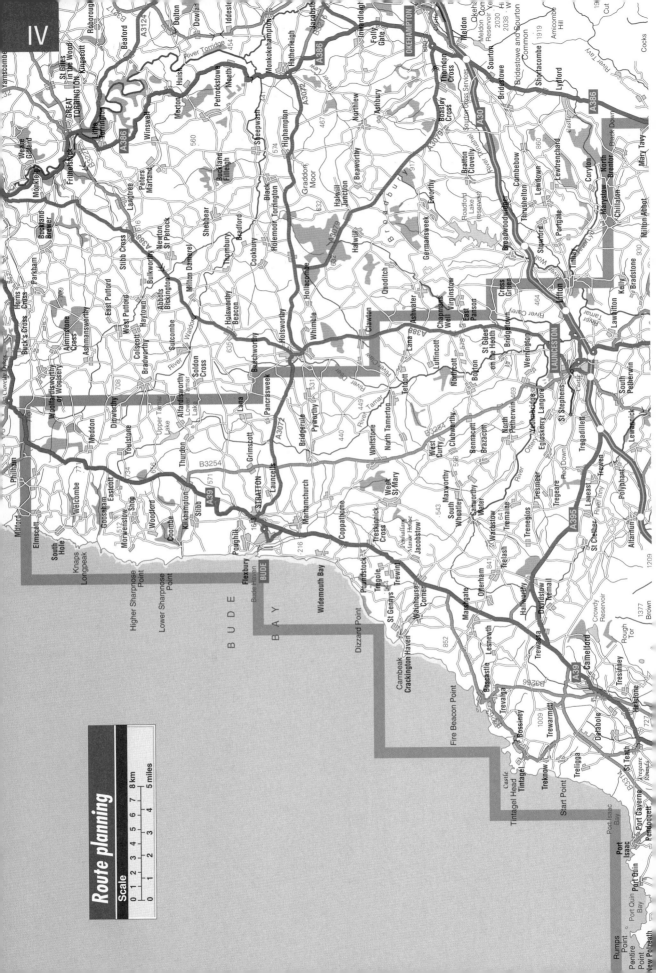

Route planning

Scale

0	1	2	3	4	5	6	7	8 km
0		1	2	3	4	5 miles

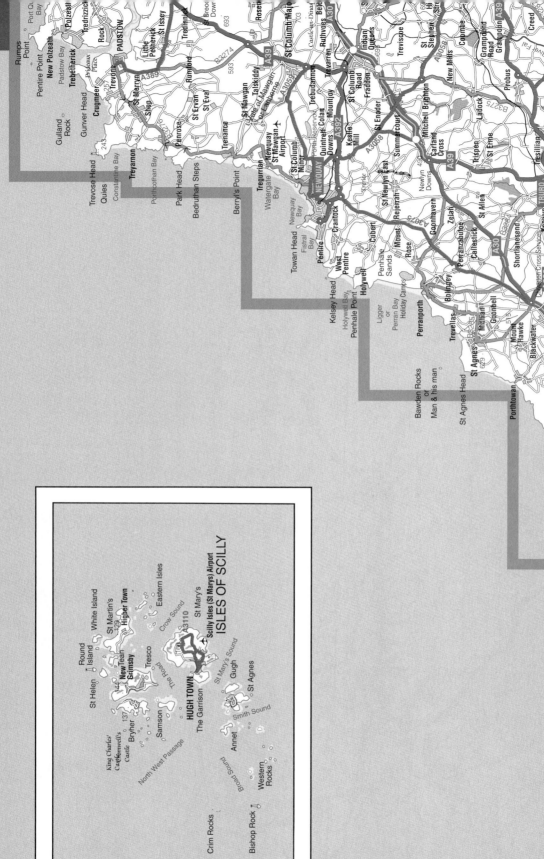

Major administrative and Postcode boundaries

Scale

| 0 | 5 | 10 | 15 | 20 | 25 | 30 km |
| 0 | 5 | 10 | 15 | 20 miles |

County and unitary authority boundaries
District boundaries
Postcode boundaries
Area covered by this atlas

SS
SX
SW
SX
SW

Devon

City of Plymouth

Cornwall

North Cornwall

Caradon

Restormel

Carrick

Kerrier

Penwith

EX39 EX22 EX23 EX21 EX35

PL19 PL16 PL15 PL17 PL20 PL18 PL6 PL7 PL8
PL5 PL9 PL1 PL2 PL3 PL4
PL11 PL10 PL12 PL13 PL14 PL22 PL23 PL24 PL25 PL26 PL27 PL28 PL29 PL30 PL31 PL32 PL33 PL34 PL35

TR1 TR2 TR3 TR4 TR5 TR6 TR7 TR8 TR9 TR10 TR11 TR12 TR13 TR14 TR15 TR16 TR17 TR18 TR19 TR20 TR26 TR27

Shop Stratton Bude Week St Mary Launceston Tavistock Callington Plymouth Saltash Torpoint Kingsand Boscastle Tintagel Camelford Delabole St Tudy St Cleer Liskeard Looe Fowey Lostwithiel St Austell Sticker Mevagissey Portloe Bodmin Port Isaac Padstow Wadebridge St Columb Major Newquay St Newlyn East Truro Tregony Portscatho Falmouth Penryn Feock Perranporth Redruth Camborne Portreath Helford Lizard Helston Porthleven Mullion Hayle St Ives Penzance Newlyn St Just Land's End Porthcurno

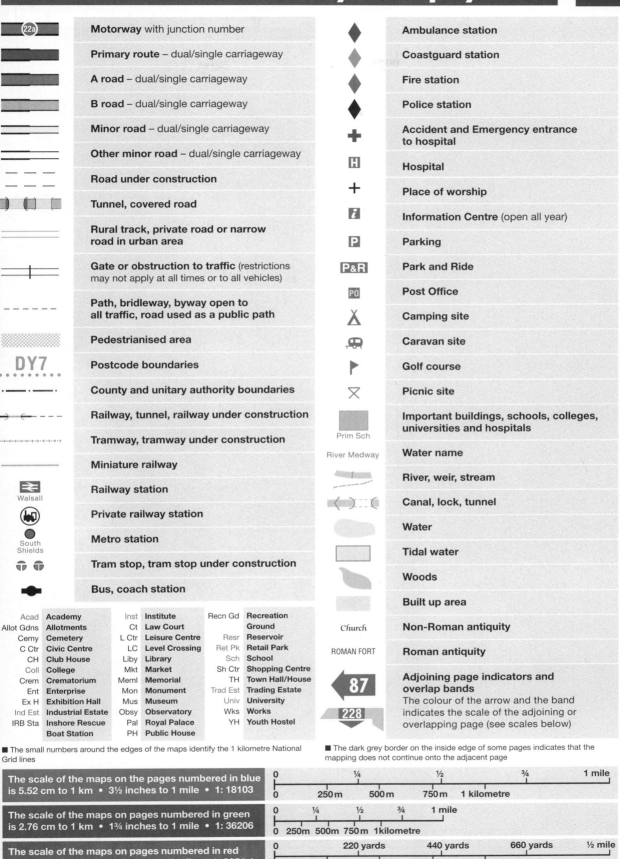

Motorway with junction number	Ambulance station
Primary route – dual/single carriageway	Coastguard station
A road – dual/single carriageway	Fire station
B road – dual/single carriageway	Police station
Minor road – dual/single carriageway	Accident and Emergency entrance to hospital
Other minor road – dual/single carriageway	Hospital
Road under construction	Place of worship
Tunnel, covered road	Information Centre (open all year)
Rural track, private road or narrow road in urban area	Parking
Gate or obstruction to traffic (restrictions may not apply at all times or to all vehicles)	Park and Ride
Path, bridleway, byway open to all traffic, road used as a public path	Post Office
Pedestrianised area	Camping site
Postcode boundaries	Caravan site
County and unitary authority boundaries	Golf course
Railway, tunnel, railway under construction	Picnic site
Tramway, tramway under construction	Important buildings, schools, colleges, universities and hospitals
Miniature railway	Water name
Railway station	River, weir, stream
Private railway station	Canal, lock, tunnel
Metro station	Water
Tram stop, tram stop under construction	Tidal water
Bus, coach station	Woods

Prim Sch

River Medway

Church

ROMAN FORT

Built up area

Non-Roman antiquity

Roman antiquity

Adjoining page indicators and overlap bands
The colour of the arrow and the band indicates the scale of the adjoining or overlapping page (see scales below)

Acad	Academy	Inst	Institute	Recn Gd	Recreation Ground		
Allot Gdns	Allotments	Ct	Law Court				
Cemy	Cemetery	L Ctr	Leisure Centre	Resr	Reservoir		
C Ctr	Civic Centre	LC	Level Crossing	Ret Pk	Retail Park		
CH	Club House	Liby	Library	Sch	School		
Coll	College	Mkt	Market	Sh Ctr	Shopping Centre		
Crem	Crematorium	Meml	Memorial	TH	Town Hall/House		
Ent	Enterprise	Mon	Monument	Trad Est	Trading Estate		
Ex H	Exhibition Hall	Mus	Museum	Univ	University		
Ind Est	Industrial Estate	Obsy	Observatory	Wks	Works		
IRB Sta	Inshore Rescue Boat Station	Pal	Royal Palace	YH	Youth Hostel		
		PH	Public House				

■ The small numbers around the edges of the maps identify the 1 kilometre National Grid lines

■ The dark grey border on the inside edge of some pages indicates that the mapping does not continue onto the adjacent page

The scale of the maps on the pages numbered in blue is 5.52 cm to 1 km • 3½ inches to 1 mile • 1: 18103	0 ¼ ½ ¾ 1 mile 0 250 m 500 m 750 m 1 kilometre
The scale of the maps on pages numbered in green is 2.76 cm to 1 km • 1¾ inches to 1 mile • 1: 36206	0 ¼ ½ ¾ 1 mile 0 250m 500m 750m 1kilometre
The scale of the maps on pages numbered in red is 11.04 cm to 1 km • 7 inches to 1 mile • 1: 9051.4	0 220 yards 440 yards 660 yards ½ mile 0 125 m 250 m 375 m ½ kilometre

Scale: 1¾ inches to 1 mile
0   ¼   ½ mile
0   250m   500m   750m   1 km

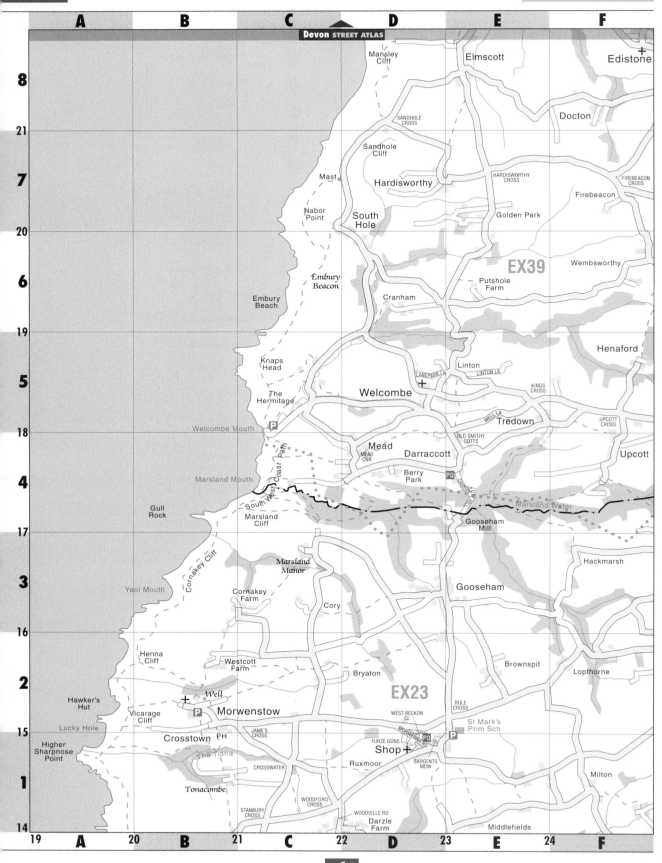

Edistone

Elmscott

Mansley Cliff

Docton

SANDHOLE CROSS

Sandhole Cliff

Mast

Hardisworthy

HARDISWORTHY CROSS

FIREBEACON CROSS

Nabor Point

South Hole

Golden Park

Firebeacon

EX39

Embury Beacon

Putshole Farm

Wembsworthy

Embury Beach

Cranham

Knaps Head

Linton

LINTON LA

Henaford

LANE PARK LA

Welcombe

KINGS CROSS

The Hermitage

WELL LA

Tredown

UPCOTT CROSS

Welcombe Mouth

OLD SMITHY COTTS

Upcott

Mead

Darraccott

MEAD CNR

Berry Park

PO

Marsland Mouth

Gull Rock

Marsland Cliff

Gooseham Mill

Marsland Water

DARRACOTT HILL

Cornakey Cliff

Marsland Manor

Hackmarsh

Yeol Mouth

Cornakey Farm

Gooseham

Cory

Henna Cliff

Westcott Farm

Bryaton

Brownspit

Lopthorne

EX23

RULE CROSS

Hawker's Hut

Well

WEST BECKON CL

St Mark's Prim Sch

Vicarage Cliff

P

Morwenstow

JAME'S CROSS

PO

P

Lucky Hole

Crosstown

PH

FURZE GDNS

MORWENNA RD

Higher Sharpnose Point

The Tidna

Shop

Ruxmoor

SARGENTS MDW

Milton

CROSSWATER

STANBURY CROSS

Tonacombe

WOODFORD CROSS

WOODVILLE RD

Middlefields

Darzle Farm

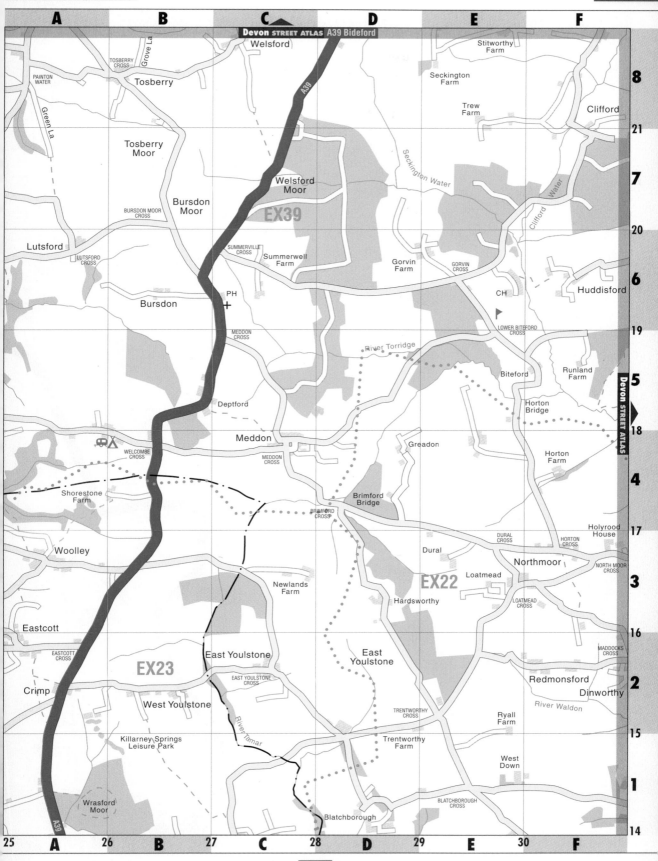

Devon STREET ATLAS A39 Bideford

Welsford

Stitworthy
Farm

Seckington
Farm

Trew
Farm

Clifford

PAINTON
WATER

TOSBERRY
CROSS

Grove La

Tosberry

Green La

Tosberry
Moor

Welsford
Moor

Seckington Water

Clifford Water

EX39

Bursdon
Moor

BURSDON MOOR
CROSS

Bursdon
Moor

SUMMERVILLE
CROSS

Summerwell
Farm

Gorvin
Farm

Gorvin
Cross

CH

Huddisford

Lutsford

LUTSFORD
CROSS

PH
✛

MEDDON
CROSS

River Torridge

LOWER BITEFORD
CROSS

Bursdon

Deptford

Biteford

Runland
Farm

Horton
Bridge

Meddon

MEDDON
CROSS

Greadon

Horton
Farm

WELCOMBE
CROSS

Shorestone
Farm

BRIMFORD
CROSS

Brimford
Bridge

Dural
Cross

Horton
Cross

Holyrood
House

Woolley

Newlands
Farm

Dural

Northmoor

NORTH MOOR
CROSS

EX22

Loatmead

Eastcott

EASTCOTT
CROSS

EX23

East Youlstone

EAST YOULSTONE
CROSS

Hardsworthy

East
Youlstone

LOATMEAD
CROSS

MADDOCKS
CROSS

Redmonsford

Dinworthy

Crimp

West Youlstone

River Tamar

TRENTWORTHY
CROSS

River Waldon

Killarney Springs
Leisure Park

Trentworthy
Farm

Ryall
Farm

West
Down

Wrasford
Moor

Blatchborough

BLATCHBOROUGH
CROSS

A39

A   B   C   D   E   F

8
21
7
20
6
19
5
18
4
17
3
16
2
15
1
14

25   A   26   B   27   C   28   D   29   E   30   F

5

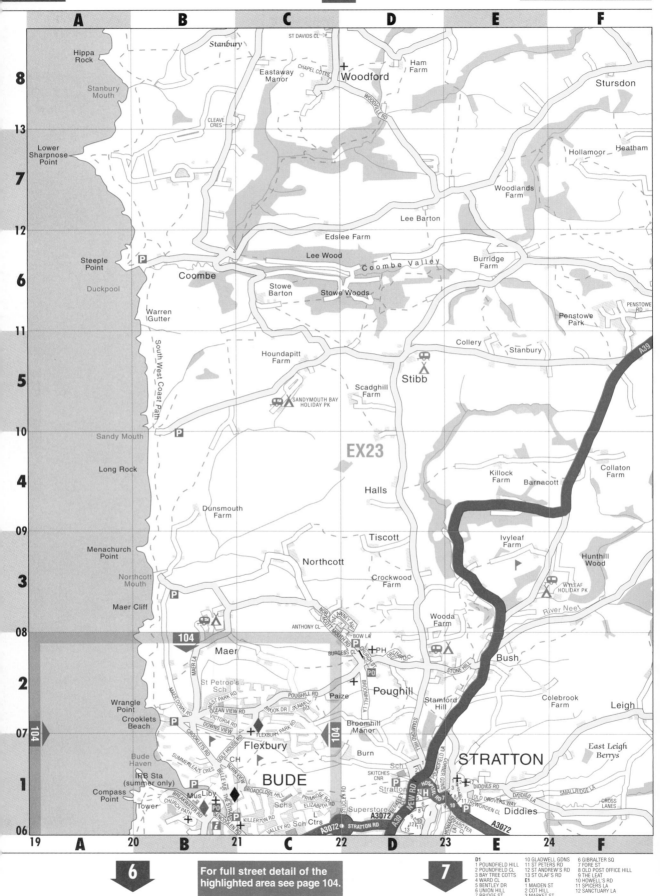

Scale: 1¾ inches to 1 mile

0   ¼   ½ mile

0   250m   500m   750m   1 km

A   B   C   D   E   F

Stanbury

St Davids Cl

Chapel Cotts

Eastaway Manor

Woodford

Ham Farm

Stursdon

Hippa Rock

Stanbury Mouth

Cleave Cres

Woodville Rd

Lower Sharpnose Point

Woodlands Farm

Lee Barton

Hollamoor

Heatham

Steeple Point

Coombe

Edslee Farm

Lee Wood

Coombe Valley

Burridge Farm

Penstowe Rd

Duckpool

Warren Gutter

Stowe Barton

Stowe Woods

Penstowe Park

South West Coast Path

Houndapitt Farm

Collery

Stanbury

Sandymouth Bay Holiday Pk

Scadghill Farm

Stibb

A39

Sandy Mouth

EX23

Long Rock

Killock Farm

Barnacott

Collaton Farm

Dunsmouth Farm

Halls

Menachurch Point

Tiscott

Ivyleaf Farm

Hunthill Wood

Northcott Mouth

Northcott

Crockwood Farm

River Neet

Wyleaf Holiday Pk

Maer Cliff

104

Wooda Farm

Bush

Maer

Maer La

Anthony Cl

Bow La

Burgess Cl

Church La

Orchard Cl

PH

PO

Poughill

Stamford Hill

Colebrook Farm

Leigh

Wrangle Point

Crooklets Beach

St Petroc's Sch

West Park Rd

Ocean View Rd

Victoria Rd

Downs View

Poughill Rd

Brook Dr

Seaview Rd

Paize

Broomhill La

Stone Hill

Maer Down Rd

Crooklets Rd

Golf House Rd

Flexbury Park Rd

Flexbury

104

Broomhill Manor

Burn

Stamford Hill

Sch

Stratton

Superstore

STRATTON

East Leigh Berrys

Bude Haven

Summerleaze Cres

Belle Vue

Burn View

CH

BUDE

Skitches Cnr

Conner Gdns

Stamford Hill

Kew Rd

Diddies Rd

Diddies La

Old Drovers Way

Spicers La

Smallridge La

Cross Lanes

Compass Point

Tower

Church Path

Breakwater Rd

Mus

Liby

PO

Benson Dr

Killerton Rd

Schs

Broadclose Hill

Primrose Rd

Elizabeth Rd

Valley Rd

Sch Ctrs

L Ctrs

Stucley Rd

A3072

STRATTON RD

A39

Church Per

Berkeley Rd

Howell's Rd

Treworden Cl

Sanctuary La

Diddies

A3072

19   A   20   B   21   C   22   D   23   E   24   F

8   13   7   12   6   11   5   10   4   09   3   08   2   07   1   06

For full street detail of the highlighted area see page 104.

D1		
1 POUNDFIELD HILL	10 GLADWELL GDNS	6 GIBRALTER SQ
2 POUNDFIELD CL	11 ST PETERS RD	7 FORE ST
3 BAY TREE COTTS	12 ST ANDREW'S RD	8 OLD POST OFFICE HILL
4 WARD CL	13 ST OLAF'S RD	9 THE LEAT
5 BENTLEY DR	E1	10 HOWELL'S RD
6 UNION HILL	1 MAIDEN ST	11 SPICERS LA
7 BRIDGE ST	2 COT HILL	12 SANCTUARY LA
8 WOODLEY CL	3 MARKET ST	
9 ST MICHAEL'S RD	4 CHURCH SQ	
	5 CHURCH ST	

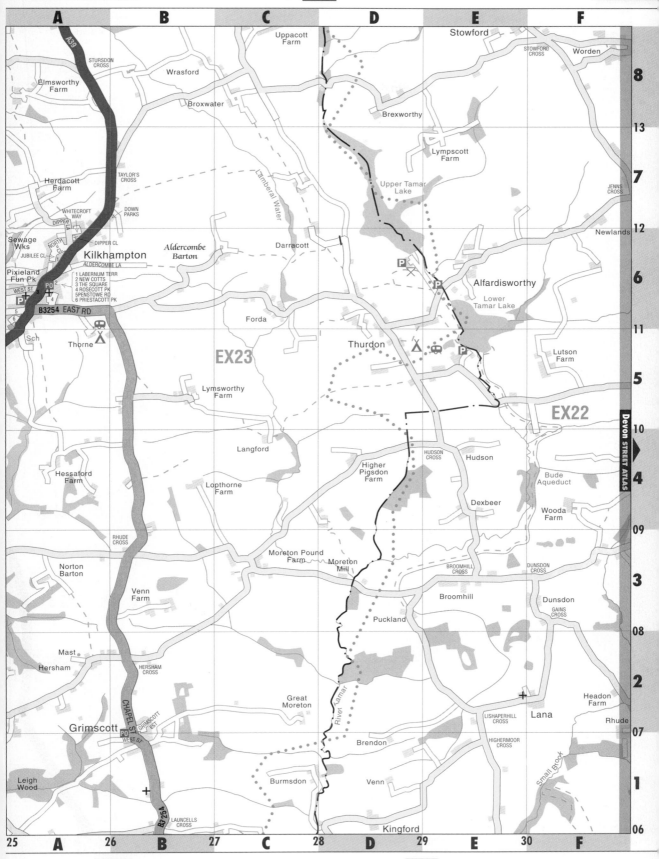

For full street detail of the highlighted area see page 104.

Scale: 1¾ inches to 1 mile

0   ¼   ½ mile
0   250m   500m   750m   1 km

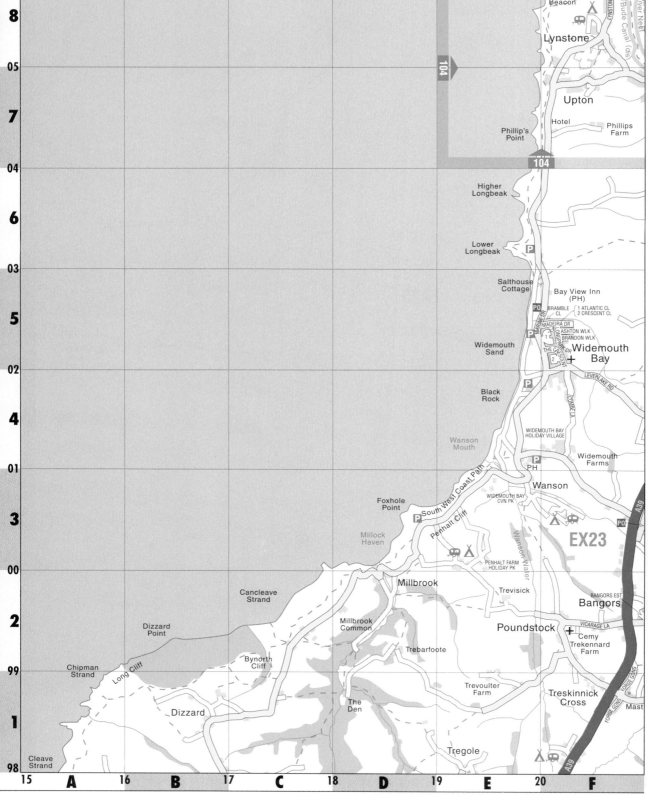

Ebbingford Manor

Efford Beacon

Lynstone

Upton

Hotel

Phillips Farm

Phillip's Point

Higher Longbeak

Lower Longbeak

Salthouse Cottage

Bay View Inn (PH)

BRAMBLE CL

1 ATLANTIC CL
2 CRESCENT CL

MADEIRA DR
ASHTON WLK
BRANDON WLK

Widemouth Sand

THE CRESCENT

Widemouth Bay

LEVERLAKE RD

Black Rock

WIDEMOUTH BAY HOLIDAY VILLAGE

Wanson Mouth

Widemouth Farms

South West Coast Path

WIDEMOUTH BAY CVN PK

Wanson

Foxhole Point

Penhalt Cliff

Wanson Water

EX23

Millock Haven

PENHALT FARM HOLIDAY PK

Bangors Est

Millbrook

Trevisick

Bangors

Cancleave Strand

Millbrook Common

Poundstock

VICARAGE LA

Cemy Trekennard Farm

Dizzard Point

Trebarfoote

Bynorth Cliff

Chipman Strand

Long Cliff

Trevoulter Farm

Treskinnick Cross

Dizzard

The Den

Mast

Cleave Strand

Tregole

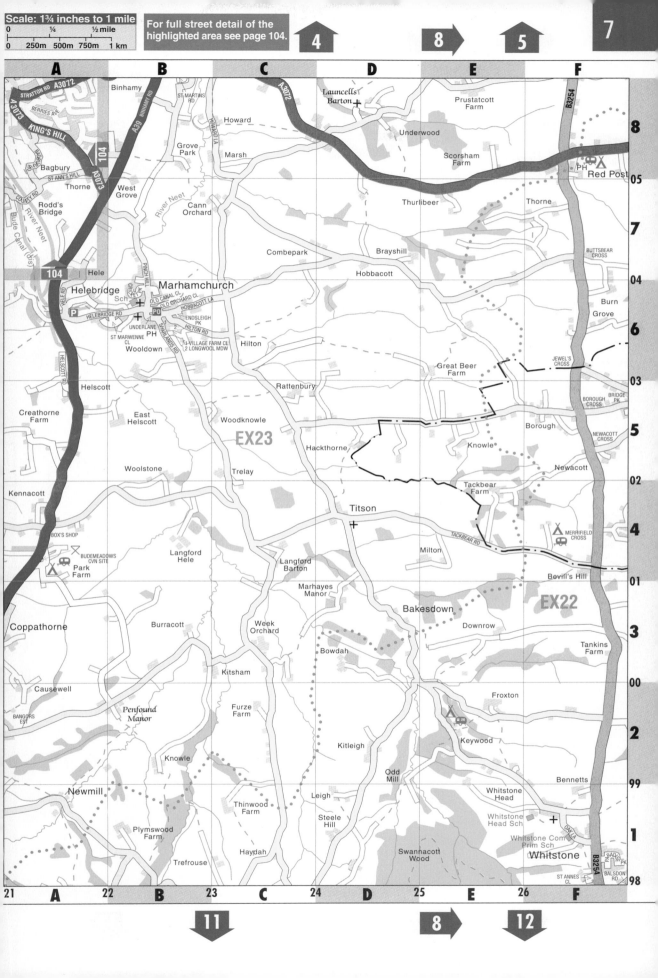

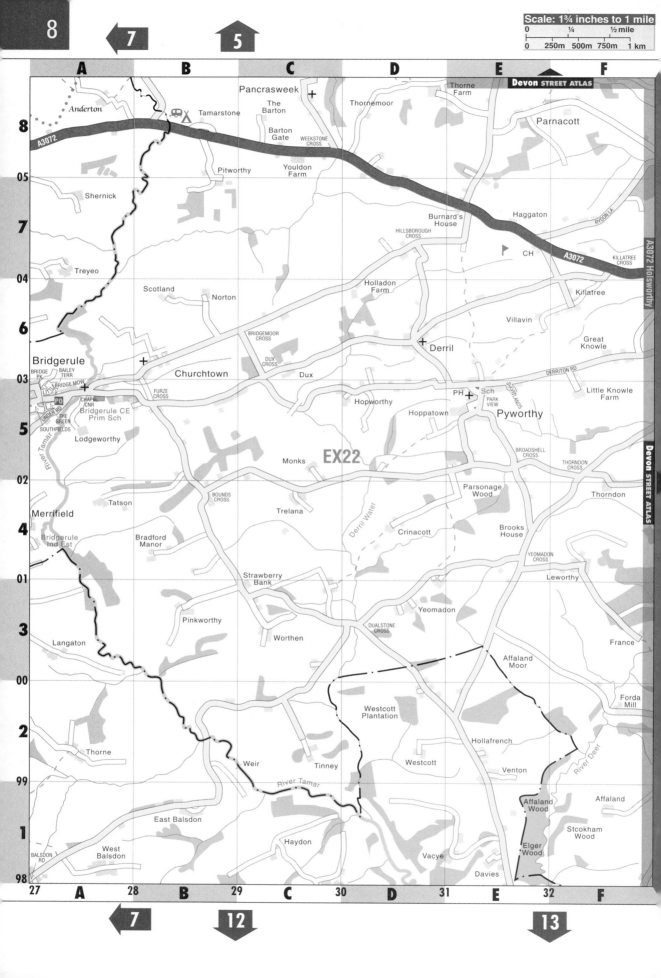

A   B   C   D   E   F

8

97

7

96

6

95

5

94

4

93

3

92

2

91

1

90

Cambeak

High Cliff

Voter Run   **EX23**

Rusey Cliff

Buckator

Gull Rock

Beeny Sisters

Fire Beacon Point

Seals Hole

South West Coast Path

Beeny

Beeny Cliff

Trebyla Farm

B3263

Pentargon

Hillsborough

Tremorle

Trewannett

PL35

Tresuck

Newmills

Trefalger

Meachard

Penally Hill

Valency Row

Penally House

River Valency

Trebiffin

Penally Point

Harbour

YH

Mus

PENALLY HILL

MARINE TERR

P

Visitor Ctr

PENALLY CT
C1
1 PENTARGON RD
2 EGLOS VIEW
3 TREFLEUR CL
4 LANGFORDS MDW
5 FORRABURY HILL
6 CLOVER LANE CL
7 WHITE SMOCK MDW
8 DOCTORS HILL
9 GUNPOOL LA
10 DUNN ST

Willapark

NEW RD

Forrabury

Mast

B3263

PO   Sch

FORE ST

BUTTS

Home Farm

Trewold

Short Island

Firebeacon Hill

Ladies Window

Boscastle

CAMBERAY

GREEN LA

UNDER RD

HIGH ST

B3266

Mount Pleasant

Long Island

Welltown Manor

TINTAGEL RD

BARN PARK RD

PARADISE RD

Paradise House

B3266

Trevalga

B3263

07   A   08   B   09   C   10   D   11   E   12   F

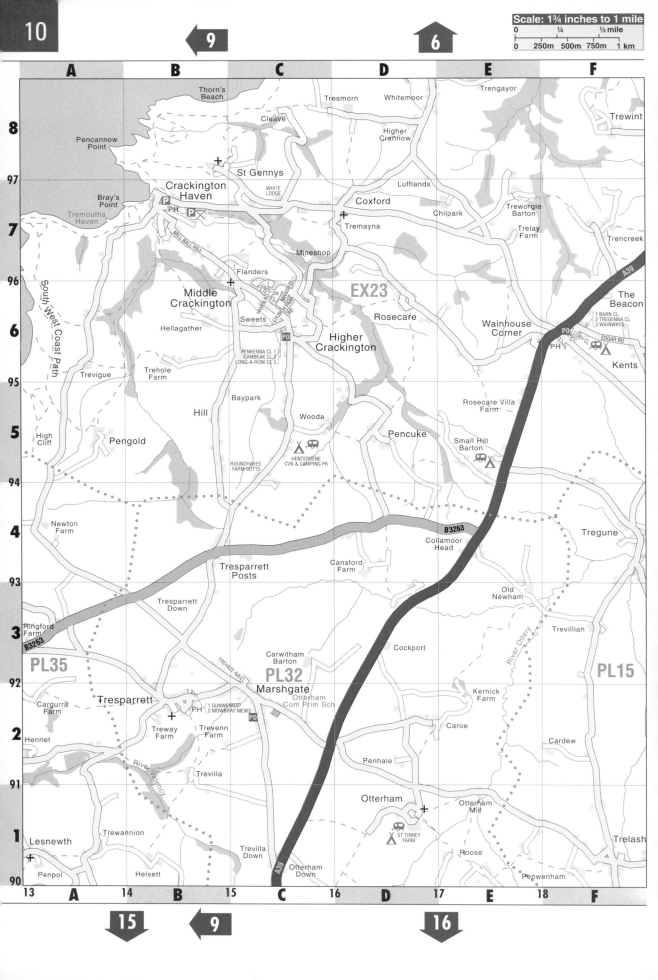

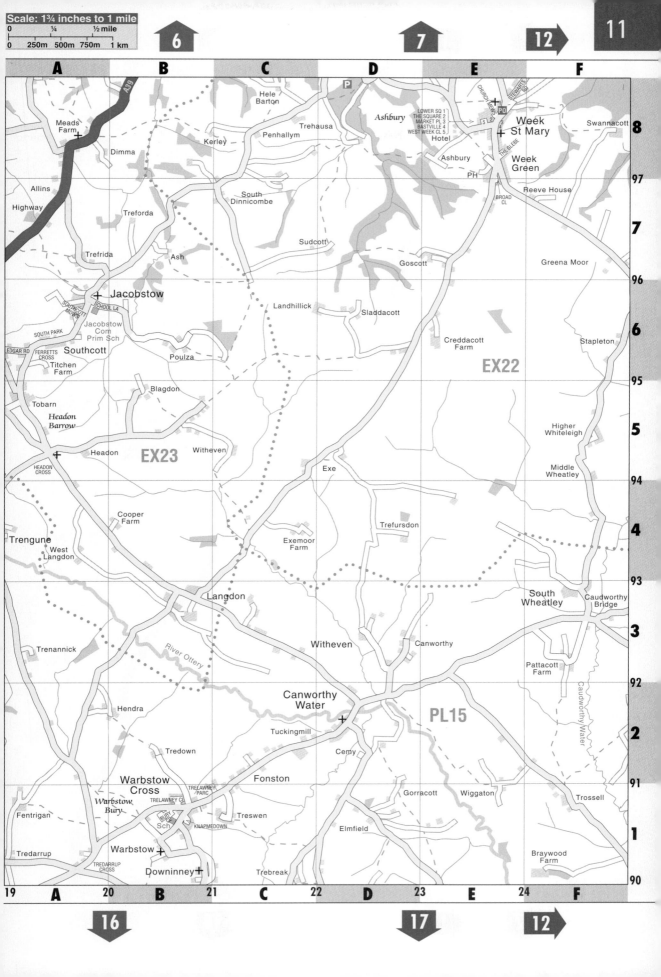

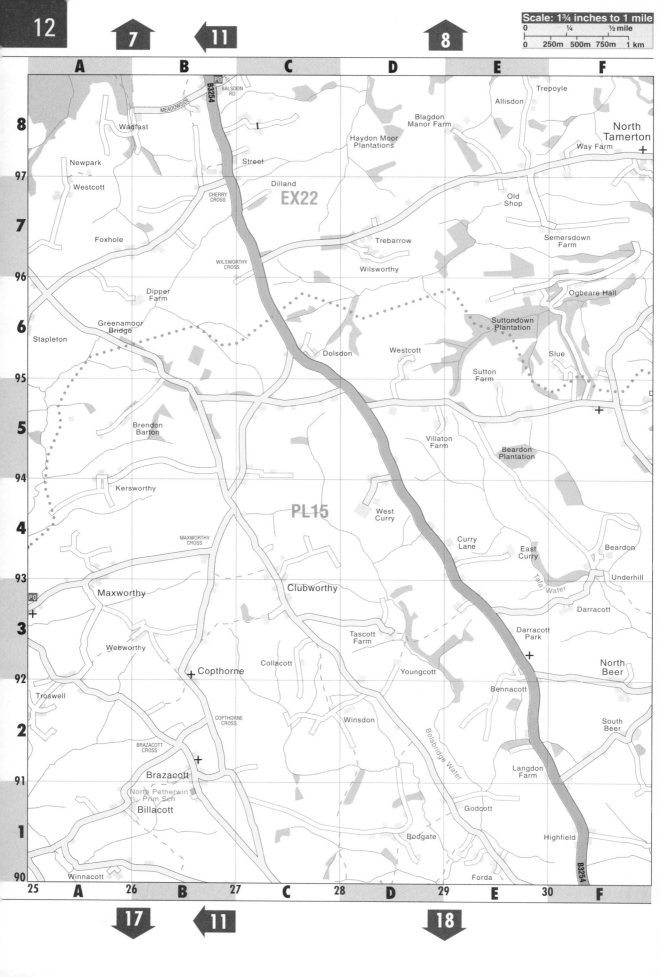

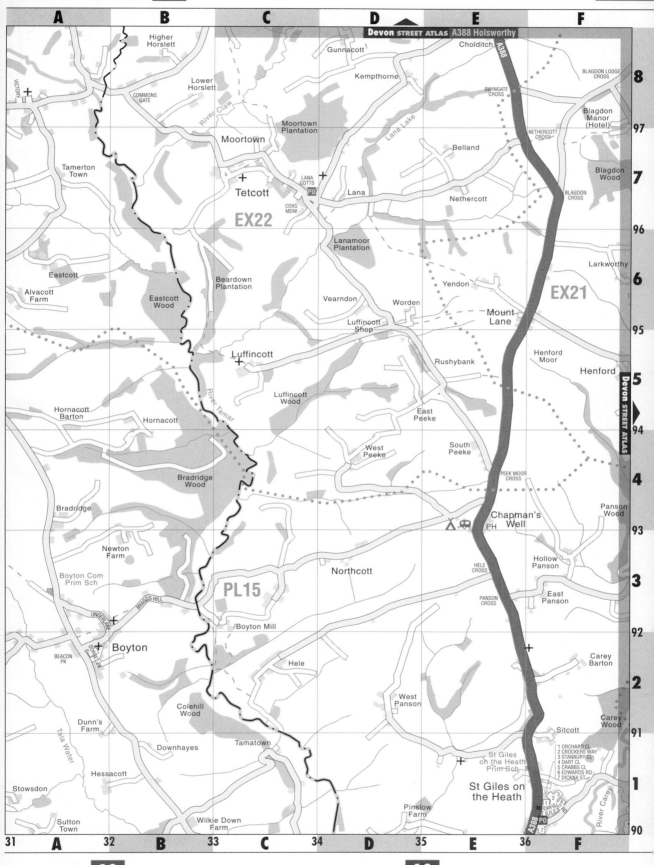

Scale: 1¾ inches to 1 mile

0   ¼   ½ mile
0 250m 500m 750m 1 km

8

Devon STREET ATLAS

18   **19**

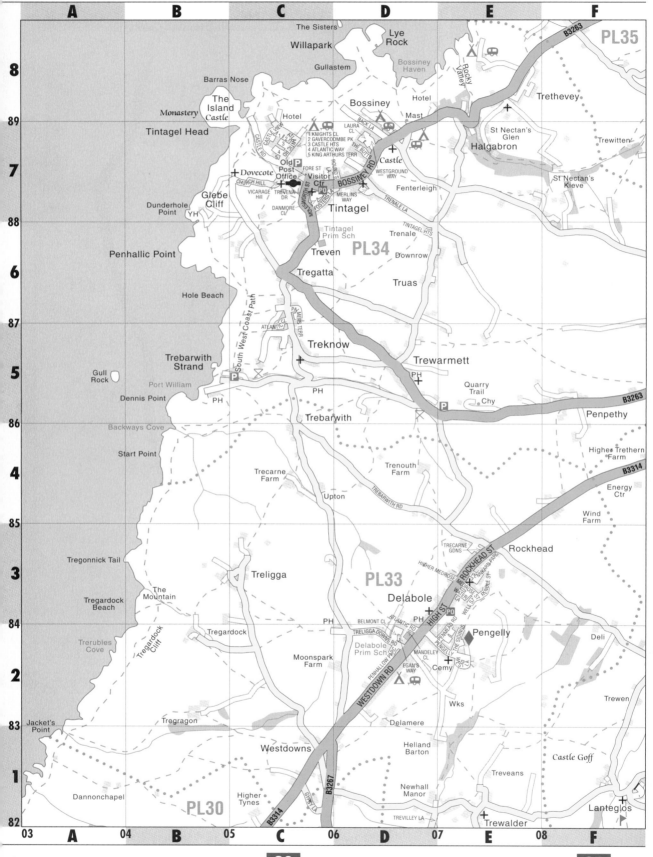

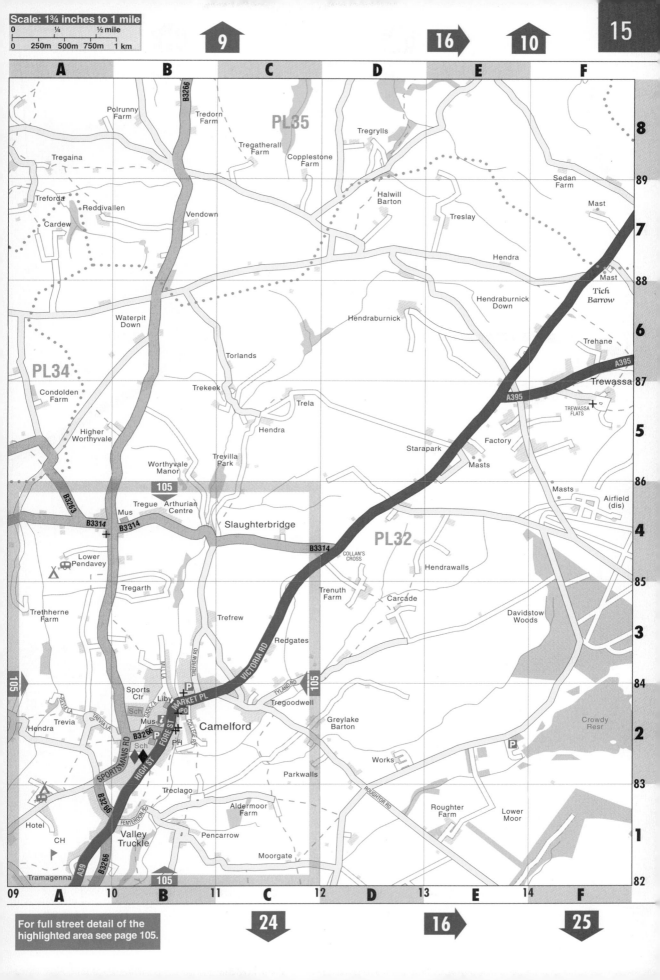

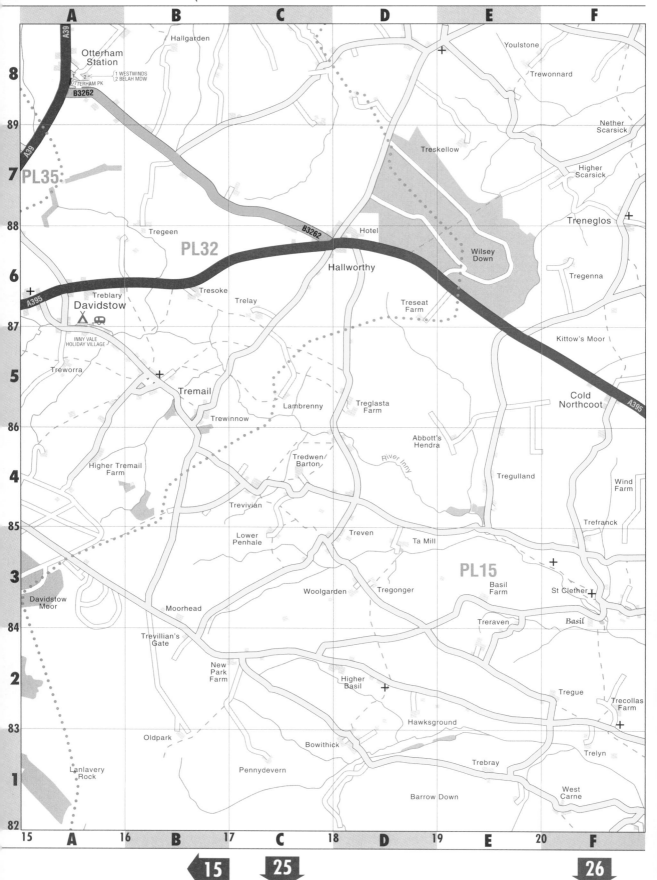

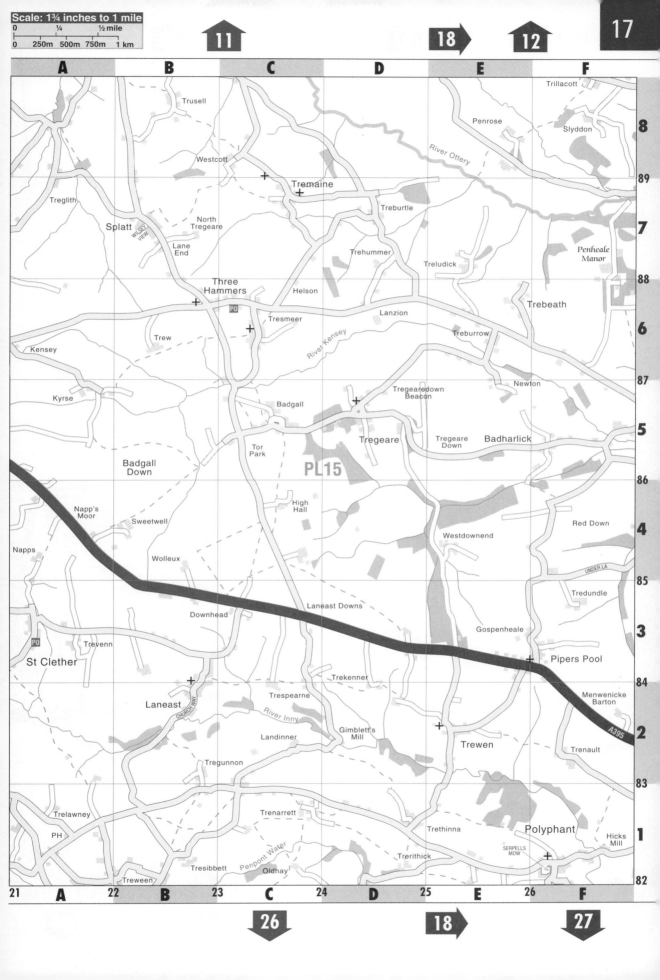

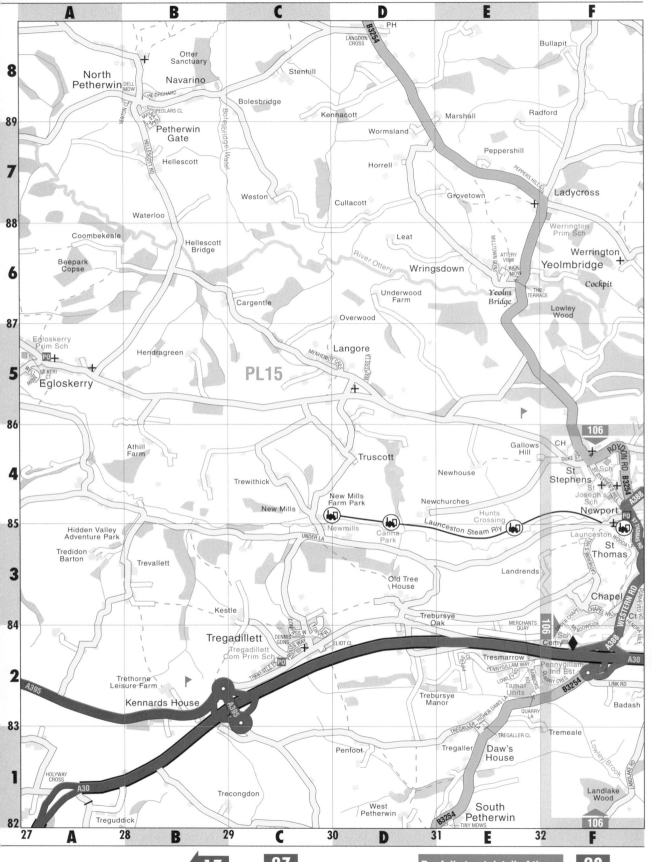

Scale: 1¾ inches to 1 mile
0   ¼   ½ mile
0   250m 500m 750m 1 km

A B C D E F

8

LANGDON CROSS
B3254
PH
Bullapit

North Petherwin
DELL MDW
Otter Sanctuary
Navarino
Stenhill
Radford
Marshall

89

THE ORCHARD
PEDLARS CL
Petherwin Gate
Bolesbridge
Kennacott
Wormsland
Peppershill

7

Hellescott
HELLESCOTT RD
Bolesbridge Water
Horrell
PEPPERS HILL CL
Ladycross

Weston
Cullacott
Grovetown
Werrington Prim Sch

88

Waterloo
Werrington
Yeolmbridge

Coombekeale
Hellescott Bridge
Leat
MILLTOWN GDNS
ATTERY VIEW
RICK MDW
Cockpit

6

Beepark Copse
River Ottery
Wringsdown
Yeolm Bridge
THE TERRACE
Lowley Wood

Cargentle
Overwood
Underwood Farm

87

Egloskerry Prim Sch
PO
Hendragreen
Langore
MENHENIOT CRES
WALKERS LA

5

WELL MDW
ST KERI CT
Egloskerry
PL15

86

Athill Farm
Truscott
Gallows Hill
CH
106
DUKE ST
ROYDON RD
B3254

4

Hidden Valley Adventure Park
Trewithick
Newhouse
St Stephens
ST STEPHENS HILL
Sch
St Joseph's Sch
Newport
A388

New Mills
Newchurches
Hunts Crossing
PO

85

Tredidon Barton
Newmills
Canna Park
UNDER LA
Launceston Steam Rly
Landrends
St Thomas
CLATHER'S LA

Trevallett
Old Tree House

3

Kestle
Treburyse Oak
Chapel
WESTERN RD
CHAPEL HILL
UPPER CHAPEL
A388

84

Tregadillett
COMPASS W
Tregadillett Com Prim Sch
PO
DENNIS GDNS
PROULE'S WAY
ELIOT CL
MERCHANTS QUAY
Cemy
Pennygillam Ind Est
106
A30

Trethorne Leisure Farm
TREKESTILE LA
Tresmarrow
PENNYGILLAM WAY
LOWLEY CL
BANGORS RD
Tamar Units
QUARRY CRES
LINK RD
Badash

2

A395
Kennards House
A395
Treburyse Manor
HIGHER DAWS LA
QUARRY LA
B3254
Tremeale

83

Penfoot
Tregaller
TREGALLER CL
Daw's House
LOWLEY BROOK
LANDLAKE RD

1

HOLYWAY CROSS
A30
Trecongdon
Tregaller
Landlake Wood
106

82

Treguddick
West Petherwin
B3254
South Petherwin
TINY MDWS

27 A 28 B 29 C 30 D 31 E 32 F

For full street detail of the highlighted area see page 106.

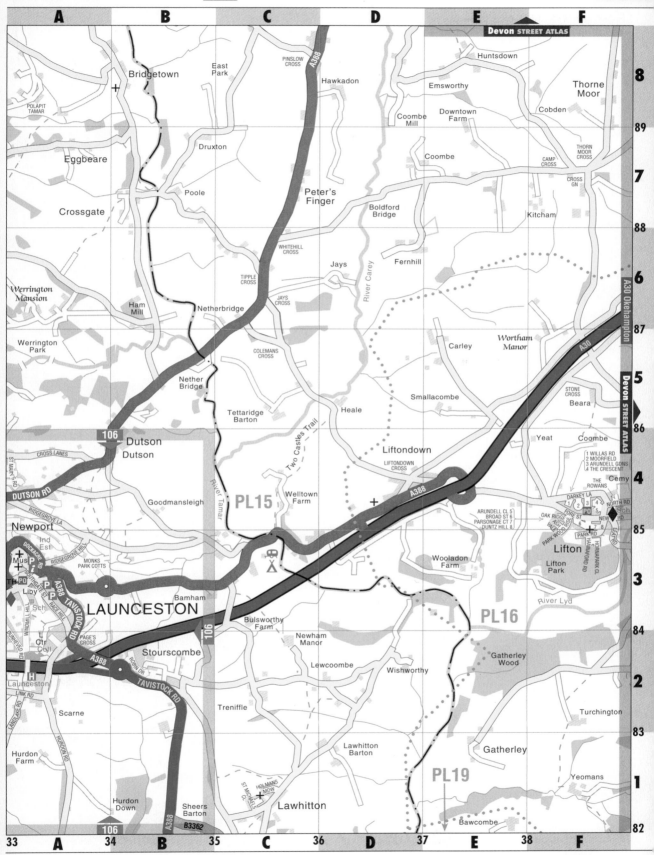

13

Devon STREET ATLAS

8

89

7

88

6

87

5

86

4

85

3

84

2

83

1

82

A30 Okehampton

Devon STREET ATLAS

Bridgetown

East Park

PINSLOW CROSS

A388

Hawkadon

Huntsdown

Emsworthy

Thorne Moor

POLAPIT TAMAR

Druxton

Coombe Mill

Downtown Farm

Cobden

THORN MOOR CROSS

Eggbeare

Coombe

CAMP CROSS

CROSS GN

Poole

Peter's Finger

Crossgate

Boldford Bridge

Kitcham

Werrington Mansion

WHITEHILL CROSS

Jays

Fernhill

River Carey

Ham Mill

TIPPLE CROSS

Netherbridge

JAYS CROSS

Carley

Wortham Manor

Werrington Park

COLEMANS CROSS

Nether Bridge

Smallacombe

STONE CROSS

Beara

CROSS LANES

ST MARY'S RD

106

Dutson
Dutson

Tettaridge Barton

Heale

Liftondown

Yeat

Coombe

1 WILLAS RD
2 MOORFIELD
3 ARUNDELL GDNS
4 THE CRESCENT

DUTSON RD

RIDGEGROVE LA

Goodmansleigh

River Tamar

PL15

Welltown Farm

Two Castles Trail

LIFTONDOWN CROSS

A388

THE ROWANS

DARKEY LA

FORE ST

NORTH RD

Cemy

Newport

Ind Est

RIDGEGROVE HILL

MONKS PARK COTTS

ARUNDELL CL 5
BROAD ST 6
PARSONAGE CT 7
DUNTZ HILL 8

OAK RIDGE

PARK RD

NEW RD

Mus

DOCKACRE RD

PP

A388

Bamham

Wooladon Farm

Lifton

PARK WOOD RISE

HORNAPARK CL

HAINAFORD RD

TH

Liby

P

SOUTHGATE ST

RACE HILL

TAVISTOCK RD

LAUNCESTON

Bulsworthy Farm

Lifton Park

River Lyd

WINDMILL HILL

Sch

106

PAGE'S CROSS

Stourscombe

Newham Manor

PL16

L Ctr Coll

DUNHEVED RD

A388

ROBIN DR

TAVISTOCK RD

Lewcoombe

Wishworthy

Gatherley Wood

LINK RD

H
Launceston

Scarne

Treniffle

Turchington

LANDLAKE RD

HURDON RD

Lawhitton Barton

Gatherley

Hurdon Farm

PL19

Yeomans

Hurdon Down

ST MICHAELS CL

HOLMANS MDW

Lawhitton

Bawcombe

Sheers Barton

106

A388

B3362

33   34   35   36   37   38

A   B   C   D   E   F

28

29

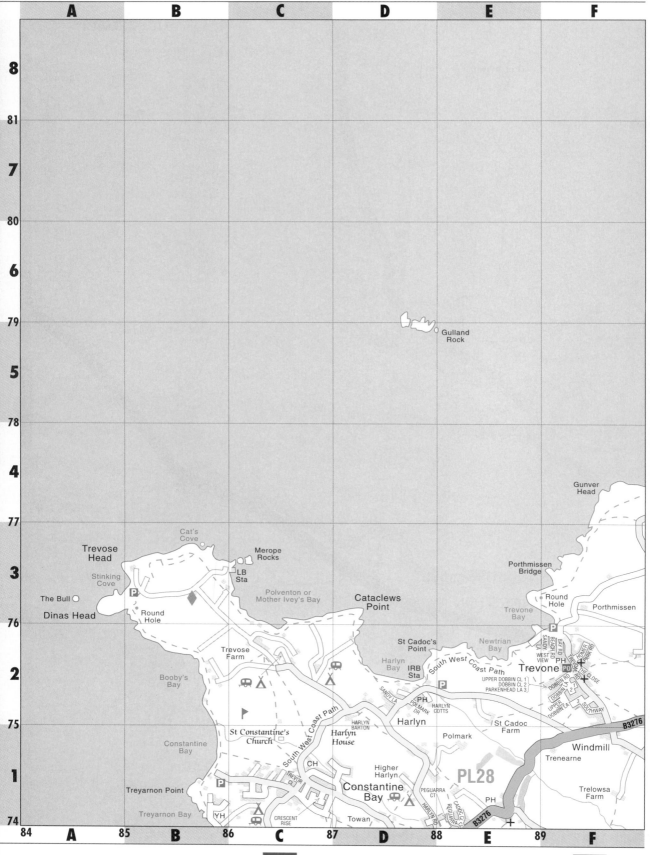

A B C D E F

8

81

7

80

6

79

Gulland
Rock

5

78

4

77

Gunver
Head

Trevose
Head

Cat's
Cove

Merope
Rocks

Porthmissen
Bridge

3

Stinking
Cove

LB
Sta

Polventon or
Mother Ivey's Bay

Cataclews
Point

Round
Hole

Porthmissen

The Bull

Dinas Head

Round
Hole

Trevone
Bay

76

St Cadoc's
Point

Newtrian
Bay

BAY RD
BEACH RD
SANDY

TOWER PARK RD

Trevose
Farm

Harlyn
Bay

IRB
Sta

South West Coast Path

Trevone

WEST END
VIEW

THE CLOSE

Booby's
Bay

SANDY LA

FOX MARK
DR

PH

HARLYN
COTTS

P

UPPER DOBBIN CL 1
DOBBIN CL 2
PARKENHEAD LA 3

DOBBIN RD

DOBBIN LA

2

UPPER
DOBBIN LA

SOUTHWAY

St Constantine's
Church

South West Coast Path

Harlyn
BARTON

Harlyn
House

Harlyn

St Cadoc
Farm

B3276

75

Constantine
Bay

CH

Polmark

Windmill

PL28

Trenearne

1

Treyarnon Point

TREVUR
CL

Higher
Harlyn

PEGUARRA
CT

CADOC CL
PEGUARRA

Trelowsa
Farm

Constantine
Bay

Treyarnon Bay

YH

CRESCENT
RISE

Towan

HARLYN RD

PH

B3276

74

84 A 85 B 86 C 87 D 88 E 89 F

31

32

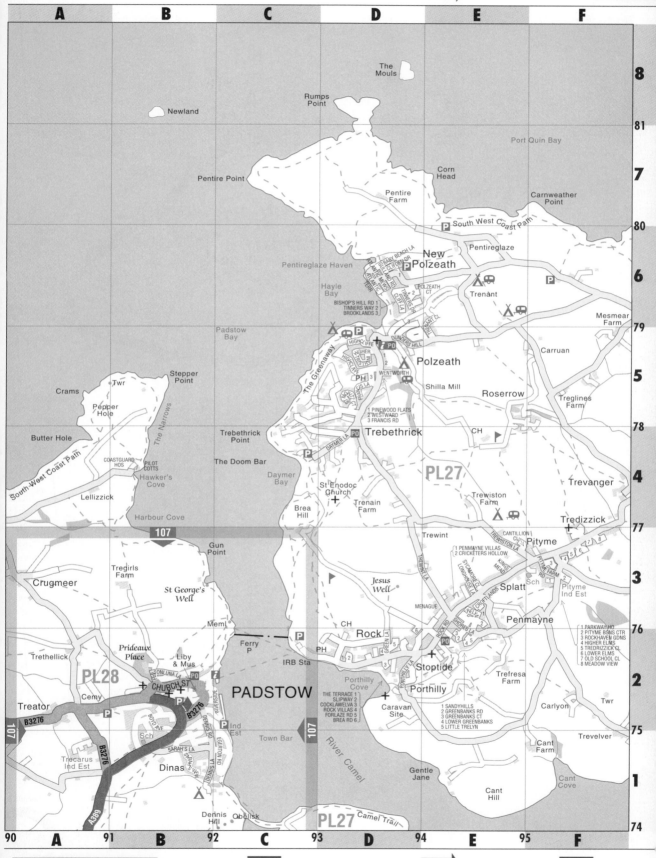

22

A B C D E F

8
81
7
80
6
79
5
78
4
77
3
76
2
75
1
74

The Mouls

Newland

Rumps Point

Port Quin Bay

Pentire Point

Corn Head

Pentire Farm

Carnweather Point

South West Coast Path

New Polzeath

Pentireglaze

Pentireglaze Haven

Hayle Bay

BISHOP'S HILL RD 1
TINNERS WAY 2
BROOKLANDS 3

Padstow Bay

POLZEATH CT

Trenant

Mesmear Farm

The Greenaway

Polzeath

Carruan

Shilla Mill

Roserrow

Carrua n

Treglines Farm

WENTWORTH

1 PINEWOOD FLATS
2 WESTWARD
3 FRANCIS RD

Trebethrick

PL27

Trevanger

Crams

Twr

Stepper Point

Pepper Hole

The Narrows

Trebethrick Point

CH

Tredizzick

Butter Hole

COASTGUARD HOS

PILOT COTTS

The Doom Bar

Daymer Bay

St Enodoc Church

Trewiston Farm

Trenain Farm

Trewint

South-West Coast Path

Hawker's Cove

Lellizzick

Harbour Cove

Brea Hill

CANTILLION CL

Trewint

1 PENMAYNE VILLAS
2 CRICKETERS HOLLOW

Pityme

107

Gun Point

Jesus Well

KINGS MEAD

Splatt

Pityme Ind Est

Crugmeer

Tregirls Farm

St George's Well

MENAGUE

Penmayne

1 PARKWAY HO
2 PITYME BSNS CTR
3 ROCKHAVEN GDNS
4 HIGHER ELMS
5 TREDRIZZICK CL
6 LOWER ELMS
7 OLD SCHOOL CL
8 MEADOW VIEW

Meml

CH

Rock

PH

Stoptide

Trefresa Farm

Trethellick

Prideaux Place

Liby & Mus

Ferry P

IRB Sta

Porthilly Cove

Porthilly

PL28

PADSTOW

THE TERRACE 1
SLIPWAY 2
COCKLAWELVA 3
ROCK VILLAS 4
FORLAZE RD 5
BREA RD 6

Carlyon

Twr

Treator

Cemy

B3276

CHURCH ST

Town Bar

Caravan Site

1 SANDYHILLS
2 GREENBANKS RD
3 GREENBANKS CT
4 LOWER GREENBANKS
5 LITTLE TRELYN

Trevelver

Cant Farm

107

B3276

Sch

Ind Est

Gentle Jane

Cant Hill

Cant Cove

Trecarus Ind Est

Dinas

SARAH'S LA

River Camel

A389

Dennis Hill

Obelisk

Camel Trail

PL27

90 A 91 B 92 C 93 D 94 E 95 F

For full street detail of the highlighted area see page 107.

32

22

33

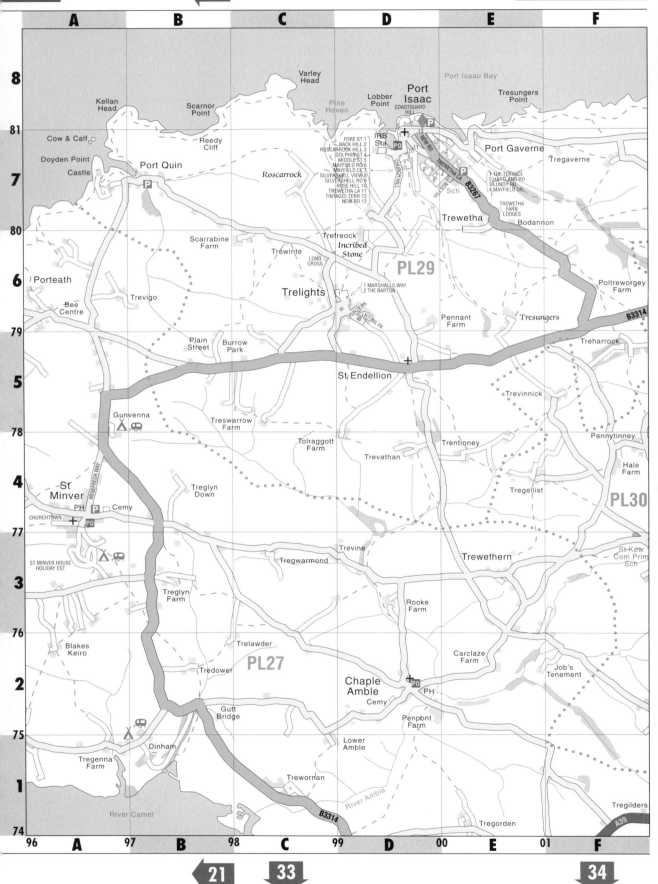

Scale: 1¾ inches to 1 mile

0   ¼   ½ mile

0   250m   500m   750m   1 km

A **B** **C** **D** **E** **F**

8

Port Isaac Bay

Varley
Head

Kellan
Head

Scarnor
Point

Pine
Haven

Lobber
Point

**Port
Isaac**

COASTGUARD
HILL

Tresungers
Point

81

Cow & Calf

Reedy
Cliff

IRB
Sta

FORE ST 1
BACK HILL 2
ROSCARROCK HILL 3
DOLPHIN ST 4
MIDDLE ST 5
MAYFIELD RD 6
MAYFIELD CL 7
SILVERSHELL VIEW 8
SILVERSHELL RD 9
ROSE HILL 10
TREWETHA LA 11
TINTAGEL TERR 12
NEW RD 13

Port Gaverne

Tregaverne

Doyden Point
Castle

Port Quin

Roscarrock

NEW RD

TREWETHA LA

HILLSON

Sch

1 THE TERRACE
2 HARTLAND RD
3 LUNDY RD
4 MAYFIELD DR.

7

B3267

CHURCH HILL

TREWETHA
FARN
LODGES

Trewetha

Bodannon

80

Scarrabine
Farm

Trewinte

Trefreock

LONG
CROSS

Incribed
Stone

PL29

6

Porteath

Trevigo

Trelights

1 MARSHALLS WAY
2 THE BARTON

PURTE PK

BRENTONS PK

Pennant
Farm

Tresungers

Poltreworgey
Farm

Bee
Centre

79

B3314

Plain
Street

Burrow
Park

St Endellion

Treharrock.

5

Gunvenna

Treswarrow
Farm

Trevinnick

78

Tolraggott
Farm

Trevathan

Trentinney

Pennytinney

4

**St
Minver**

MENEFREDA WAY

Treglyn
Down

Hale
Farm

PL30

CHURCHTOWN

PH   Cemy

PO

Tregellist

77

St Endellion

ST MINVER HOUSE
HOLIDAY EST

Trevine

Tregwarmond

Trewethern

St Kew
Com Prim
Sch

3

Treglyn
Farm

Rooke
Farm

76

Blakes
Keiro

Trelawder

PL27

Carclaze
Farm

Job's
Tenement

2

Tredower

**Chaple
Amble**

PO
PH

Penpont
Farm

Gutt
Bridge

Cemy

75

Dinham

Lower
Amble

1

Tregenna
Farm

Trewornan

River Amble

Tregilders

74

River Camel

B3314

Tregorden

A39

96   **A**   97   **B**   98   **C**   99   **D**   00   **E**   01   **F**

Scale: 1¾ inches to 1 mile

0   ¼   ½ mile
0   250m   500m   750m   1 km

A   B   C   D   E   F

Barrett's Zawn
Ranie Point
West Co
South ast Path
Bourds Cliff

PL29

Treore Farm

PH
Treore Cl

Pendoggett

Tregildren House

Trewiggett

Tregeare Rounds

Hendra

Dinnabroad

Lower Tynes

B3314

Benbole

B3267

Lanagan

Trewennan

PL33

Bodulgate

Trevilley La

Trevilley Farm

Treroosel Rd

Treroosel

Sch

St Teath

The Meadows
North Rd
Tethadene
Fore St
PO
B3267

Knightsmill

A39

Tregreenwell

Cemy
Eglos Ct

1 THE SQUARE
2 BRYNY CL
3 VALLEY VIEW
4 TREHANNICK CL

Suffenton

Whitewell

Carkeen

Treveighan

Chapel La
Folders Cl

Trevilla Cl

Tredarrup

Trekee

Treburgett

Trewethen

Trevorrian

Trehannick Farm

Tregawn

Trenewth

Trevenning

Pengenna

Trewane

Poltreworgey

Cemy

Trelill

PL30

Polshea

Michaelstow Holiday Village

Pennytinney

Lanow Farm

Penvose Farm

Lamellen

B3266

Bokelly

PH
St Kew

Trequite

Trewen Farm

Lanterrick

Tremeer

Wadebridge Rd
Bodinnick Rd
Tremer La
Glebe Parc
PH
Hengar La

St Tudy

PO
Sch

Tregarrick

Maidenland

Great Brighter Farm

River Allen

Meadowside Cl

Tretawn Farm

Kellygreen

JORYS MDW 1
BODINNICK PARC 2
MORMAN'S WAY 3
MAYMEAR TERR 4
CHAPEL RD 5
CHURCH RD 6

Wetherham

Redvale Rd
Wetherham La

Tregooden

Tinten Manor

Loskeyle Farm

St Kew Highway

PH
Syms Cl
Allen Pk

1
2
3
4
5

1 WHITEHALL BGWS
2 WHITEHALL EST
3 KENWYN PK
4 LEMELLEN GDNS
5 TRETAWN CL

Hendra

CH

Benbole

Trethevan Farm

Hotel

Trevisquite Manor

Tamsquite

Penhale

Leeches

Tregilders

Cross Hill

Polglaze

Tresquare

B3266

El Sub Sta

8
81
7
80
6
79
5
78
4
77
3
76
2
75
1
74

02   03   04   05   06   07

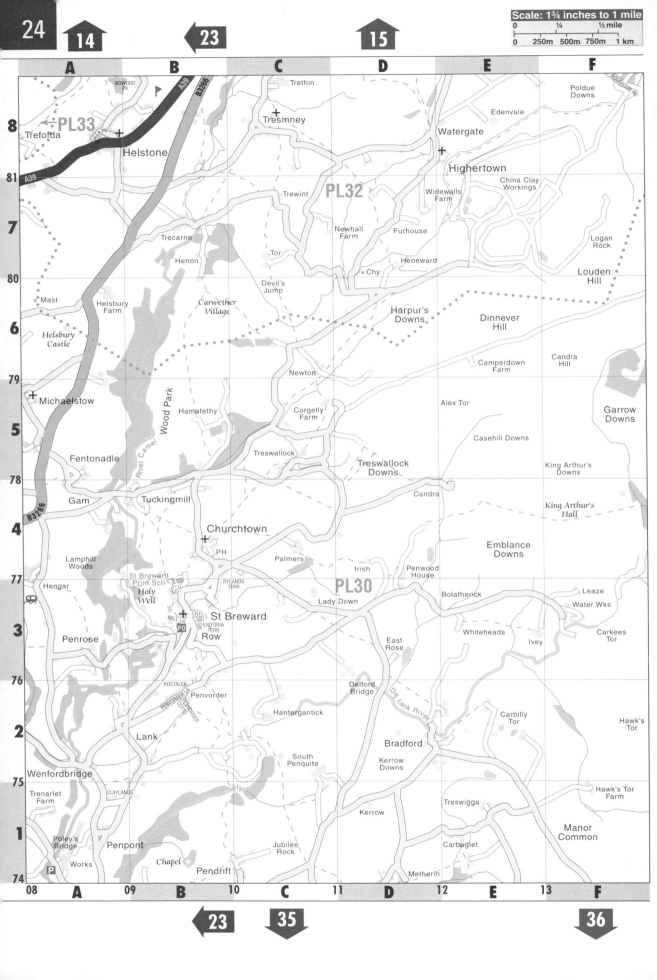

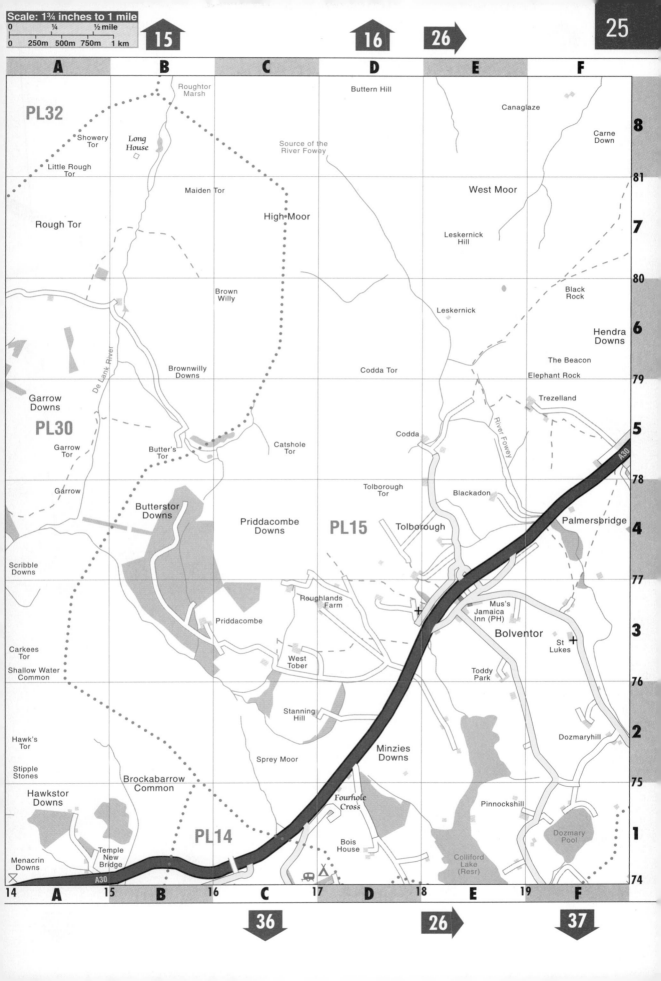

A B C D E F

8
81
7
80
6
79
5
78
4
77
3
76
2
75
1
74

PL32

Showery Tor

Long House

Roughtor Marsh

Buttern Hill

Canaglaze

Carne Down

Little Rough Tor

Source of the River Fowey

Maiden Tor

West Moor

Rough Tor

High Moor

Leskernick Hill

Brown Willy

Leskernick

Black Rock

De Lank River

Brownwilly Downs

Codda Tor

Hendra Downs

The Beacon

Elephant Rock

Garrow Downs

Trezelland

PL30

Butter's Tor

Catshole Tor

Codda

River Fowey

Garrow Tor

Tolborough Tor

Blackadon

Garrow

Butterstor Downs

Priddacombe Downs

PL15

Tolborough

Palmersbridge

Scribble Downs

A30

Roughlands Farm

Mus's Jamaica Inn (PH)

Carkees Tor

Priddacombe

Bolventor

St Lukes

Shallow Water Common

West Tober

Toddy Park

Hawk's Tor

Stanning Hill

Dozmaryhill

Stipple Stones

Minzies Downs

Sprey Moor

Brockabarrow Common

Hawkstor Downs

Fourhole Cross

Pinnockshill

Dozmary Pool

PL14

Bois House

Colliford Lake (Resr)

Menacrin Downs

Temple New Bridge

A30

14 A 15 B 16 C 17 D 18 E 19 F

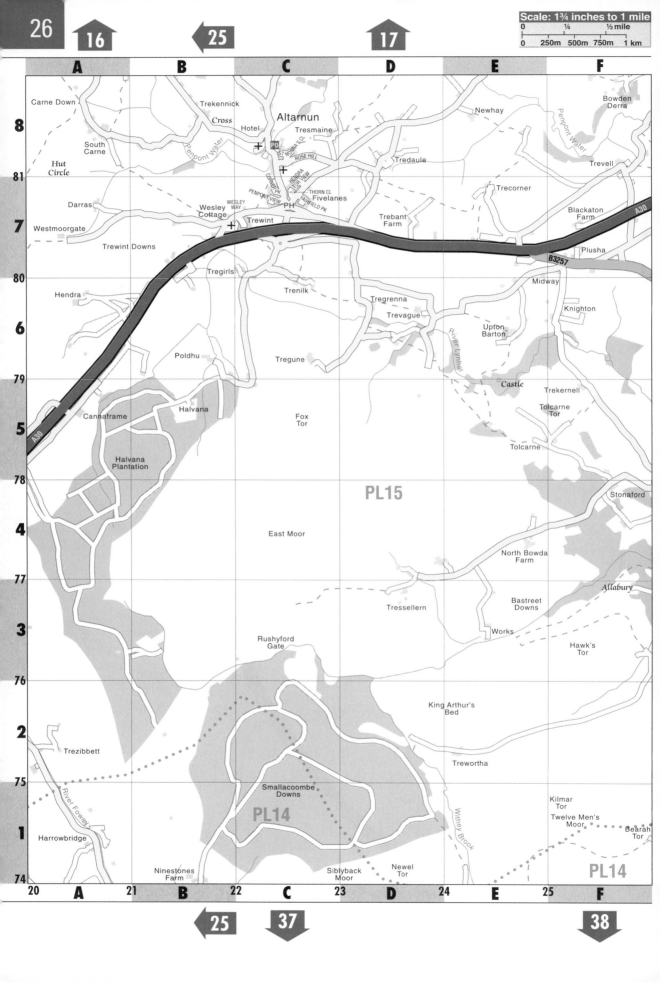

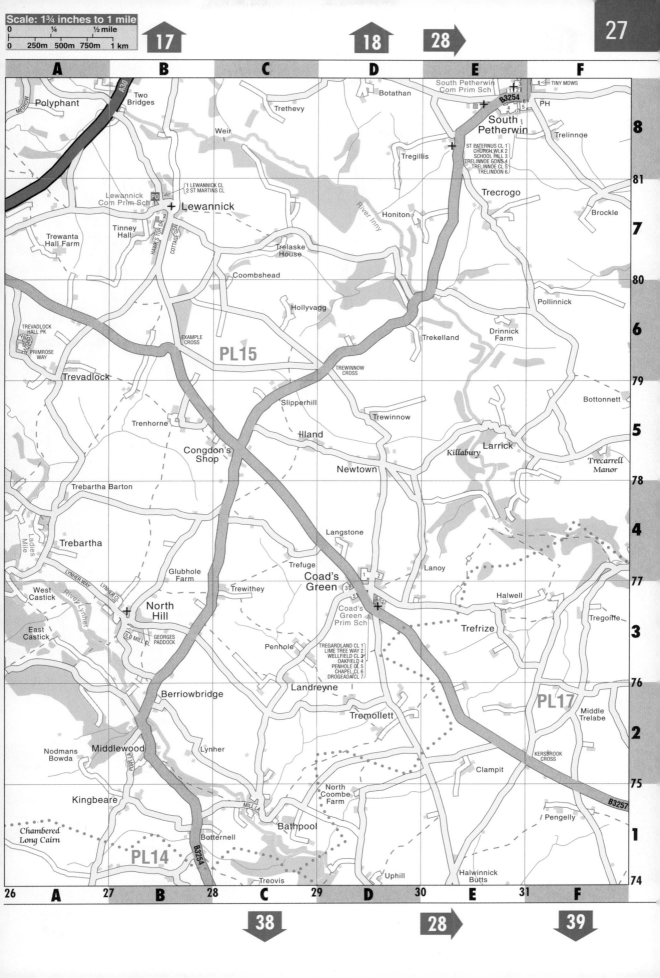

A   B   C   D   E   F

Polyphant
Two Bridges
A30
MEDROW

Trethevy
Botathan

South Petherwin
Com Prim Sch
B3254
PH

Weir

Tregillis

Trelinnoe

8

ST PATERNUS CL 1
CHURCH WLK 2
SCHOOL HILL 3
TRELINNOE GDNS 4
TRELINNOE CL 5
TRELINDON 6

81

1 LEWANNICK CL
2 ST MARTINS CL

Lewannick
Com Prim Sch
PO
Lewannick

Trecrogo

Brockle

7

Trewanta
Hall Farm

Tinney
Hall

HAWK'S TOR DR
COTTAGE COM

River Inny

Honiton

Trelaske
House

Pollinnick

80

Coombshead

6

TREVADLOCK
HALL PK
PRIMROSE WAY

Example Cross

Hollyvagg

Trekelland

Drinnick
Farm

PL15

79

Trevadlock

Trewinnow
Cross

Bottonnett

Trenhorne

Slipperhill

Trewinnow

5

Congdon's
Shop

Illand

Killabury

Larrick

Trecarrell
Manor

78

Trebartha Barton

Newtown

Trebartha

Langstone

4

LYNHER WAY
LYNHER CL

Glubhole
Farm

Trefuge

Trewithey

Coad's
Green

Lanoy

Halwell

77

West
Castick

River Lynher

North
Hill

OLD MILL CL
GEORGES
PADDOCK

Coad's
Green
Prim Sch

Trefrize

Tregoiffe

East
Castick

Penhole

TREGARDLAND CL 1
LIME TREE WAY 2
WELLFIELD CL 3
OAKFIELD 4
PENHOLE CL 5
CHAPEL CL 6
DROGEADA CL 7

3

Berriowbridge

Landreyne

PL17

Middle
Trelabe

76

Tremollett

Nodmans
Bowda

Middlewood
PORK LA

Lynher

Kersbrook
Cross

Clampit

2

75

Kingbeare

MILL LA

North
Coombe
Farm

Pengelly

B3257

Chambered
Long Cairn

Bathpool

1

PL14
B3254

Botternell

Treovis

Uphill

Halwinnick
Butts

74

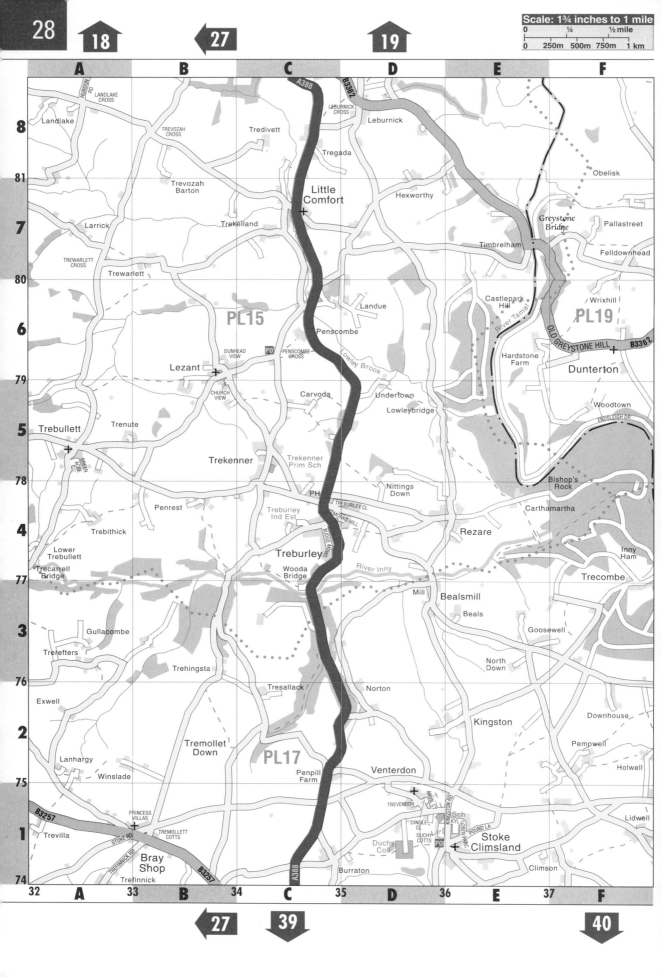

A   B   C   D   E   F

8

81

7

80

6

79

5

78

4

77

3

76

2

75

1

74

HURDON RD
LANDLAKE CROSS
Landlake
TREVOZAH CROSS
Trevozah Barton
TREDIVETT
Larrick
Trekelland
TREWARLETT CROSS
Trewarlett

PL15

Lezant
DUNHEAD VIEW
PO
PENSCOMBE CROSS
CHURCH VIEW
Carvoda

Trenute

Trekenner
Trekenner Prim Sch

Trebullett
GREEN ACRE

Penrest
Trebithick
Lower Trebullett

Trecarrell Bridge

Gullacombe
Trerefters
Exwell

Trehingsta

Lanhargy
Winslade
Tremollet Down

PL17

Penpill Farm

B3257
Trevilla
PRINCESS VILLAS
Tremollett Cotts
STOKE RD
TREFINNICK RD
Bray Shop
Trefinnick
B3257

A388

B3362
LEBURNICK CROSS
Leburnick
Tregada
Hexworthy

Little Comfort

Landue
Penscombe
Lowley Brook
Undertown
Lowleybridge

PH
TREBURLEY CL
MONKS HILL

Nittings Down

Treburley Ind Est
BRIDGE RD
Treburley
Wooda Bridge
River Inny

Tresallack
Norton
Venterdon

TREVENDON
ANVIL RD
BRISMISH RD
DINGLE CL
DUCHY COTTS
Sch
KYL
OVER PARC
POUND LA
PO
Duchy Coll

Burraton

A388

Timbrelham

Castlepark Hill
River Tamar
Hardstone Farm
HARDSTONE
OLD GREYSTONE HILL
Greystone Bridge
Obelisk
Wrixhill
PL19
Dunterton
Pallastreet
Felldownhead
Woodtown
ENDSLEIGH DR
Bishop's Rock
Carthamartha
Rezare
Inny Ham
Trecombe
Bealsmill
Beals
Goosewell
North Down
Kingston
Downhouse
Pempwell
Holwell
Lidwell
Stoke Climsland
Climson

Mill

B3362

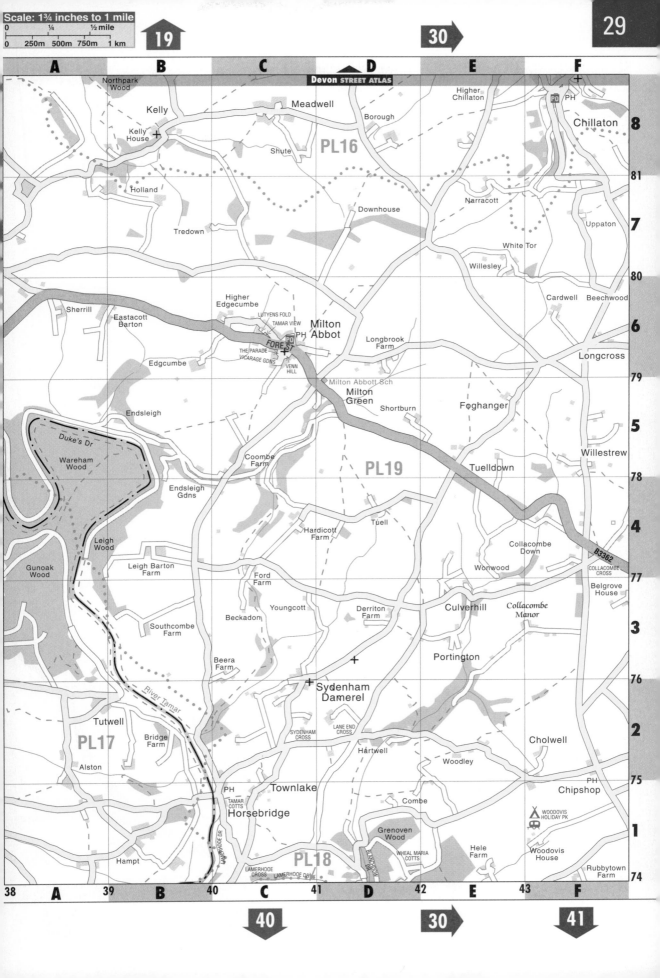

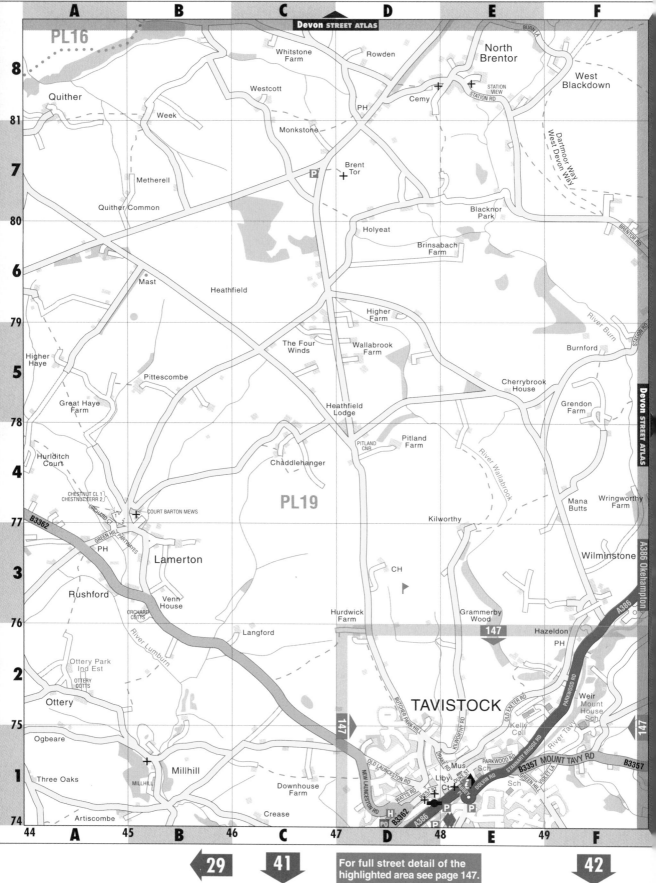

Scale: 1¾ inches to 1 mile

0   ¼   ½ mile

0   250m 500m 750m 1 km

PL16

Devon STREET ATLAS

8

Quither

Whitstone
Farm

Rowden

North
Brentor

West
Blackdown

Westcott

Week

81

Cemy

STATION
VIEW

Monkstone

PH

STATION RD

STATION RD

Metherell

7

P

Brent
Tor

Quither Common

Blacknor
Park

Dartmoor Way
West Devon Way

BRENTOR RD

80

Holyeat

Brinsabach
Farm

6

Mast

Heathfield

Higher
Farm

River Burn

Higher
Haye

The Four
Winds

Wallabrook
Farm

Burnford

5

Pittescombe

Cherrybrook
House

Grendon
Farm

Great Haye
Farm

Heathfield
Lodge

78

Hurlditch
Court

Chaddlehanger

PITLAND
CNR

Pitland
Farm

Pitland
Farm

River Wallabrook

Mana
Butts

Wringworthy
Farm

4

CHESTNUT CL 1
CHESTNUT TERR 2

COURT BARTON MEWS

Kilworthy

77

B3362

ORCHARD CL

GREEN HILL

PARTWAYES

2

Lamerton

CH

Wilminstone

A386 Okehampton

3

PH

Rushford

Venn
House

Hurdwick
Farm

Grammerby
Wood

Hazeldon

PH

147

A386

ORCHARD
COTTS

76

River Lumburn

Langford

TAVISTOCK

BUTCHER PARK HILL

2

Ottery Park
Ind Est

OTTERY
COTTS

OLD EXETER RD

PARKWOOD RD

Weir
Mount
House
Sch

River Tavy

147

Ottery

Kelly
Coll

75

Ogbeare

KILWORTHY RD

PARKWOOD RD

Sch

B3357 MOUNT TAVY RD

B3357

147

Three Oaks

MILLHILL

Millhill

Downhouse
Farm

NEW LAUNCESTON RD

WATTS RD

OLD LAUNCESTON RD

Mus

A386

DRAKE RD

Liby

Ct

DOLVIN RD

GREEN HILL

MORET LA

STANNARY BRIDGE RD

Sch

1

Artiscombe

Crease

H

PO

B3362

WEST ST

P

P

P

74

For full street detail of the
highlighted area see page 147.

PL19

Scale: 1¾ inches to 1 mile

0   ¼   ½ mile

0   250m 500m 750m 1 km

20
32
44
32
45

Trethias Island
Treyarnon
Trevear
St Merryn Prim Sch
PH
PO
B3276
St Merryn
Hotel
Pepper Cove
Trethias Farm
Tatan CT
Shop
1 TREVITHICK CL
2 PARC EGLOS
3 HARLYN RD
4 TRELANTIS EST
Warren Cove
Trehemborne
Kerketh Farm
Higher Trevorgus
Fox Cove
Carnevas
PL28
Minnows Islands
Trevoyan
Tregolds
St Merryn Holiday Village
Will's Rock
Trevorrick
Trevean
MARIBOU CT
Porthcothan Bay
Trescore Islands
P   PH
Porthcothan
Trevethan
Furze Park
Trevio
POINT CURLEW COUNTRY HOLIDAY EST
Porth Mear
Airfield (disused)
Trevemedar
Lewidden
Park Head
Pentire Farm
P
Penrose
PO
Cow & Calf
Pentire Steps
Treburrick
Efflins
Trevorgey
Cemy
Diggory's Island
Trethewell Farm
Queen Bess Rock
Tregona
Engollan
Trerair Farm
PL27
Redcliff Castle
Trembleathe Barton
Pendarves Island
Bedruthan Steps
Trevisker Farm
F3
1 BOTHA RD
2 WELLINGTON RD
3 MOSQUITO CRES
4 LIBERATOR ROW
5 WARWICK CRES
6 LINCOLN ROW
7 WILDEBEEST RD
8 BEAUFORT AVE
9 SHACKLETON CRES
Carnewas Island
Hotel
Carnewas
Downhill
St Eval Airfield (disused)
St Eval
South West Coast Path
Trerathick Point
Sch
PO
High Cove
Higher Lanherne
Trenance Point
Trenance Rock
Trenance
CH
Trevilledor
GWEL-AN-MOR 1
TREDRAGON CL 2
SANDY CT 3
EUROPA CT 4
Hotel
Merlin Farm
Lower Lanherne
Dayman's Farm
Berryl's Point
Mawgan Porth
Hotel PH
P
TR8
The Beacon
Gluvian Farm
Retorrick Mill
Lower Denzell
Beacon Cove
Vale of Mawgan
Griffin's Point
Trevarrian
Trevedras
PH
Stem Point
B3276
Tolcarne Merock
Polgreen
Bolingey

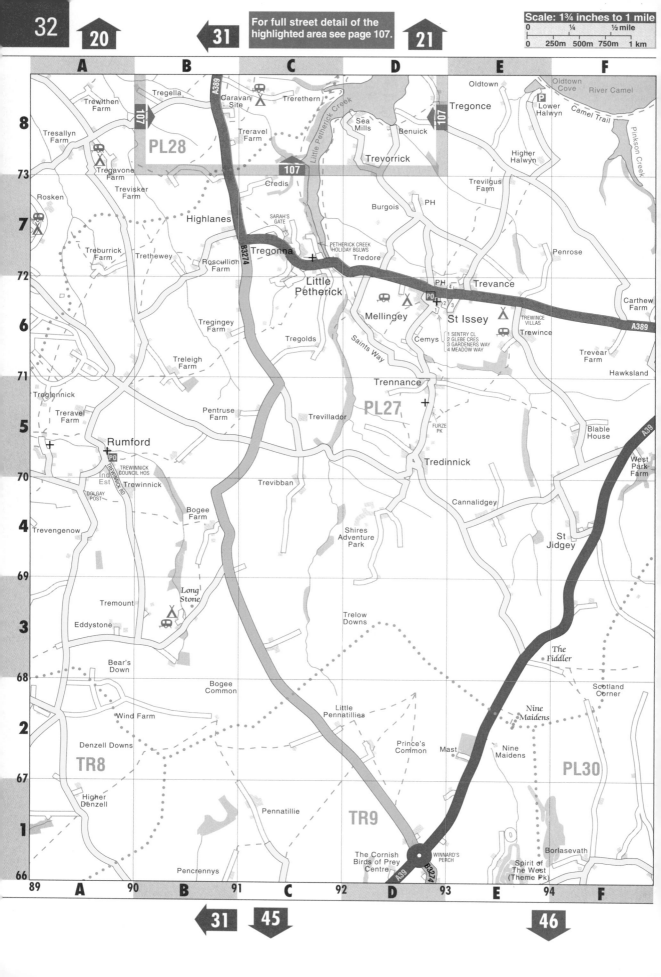

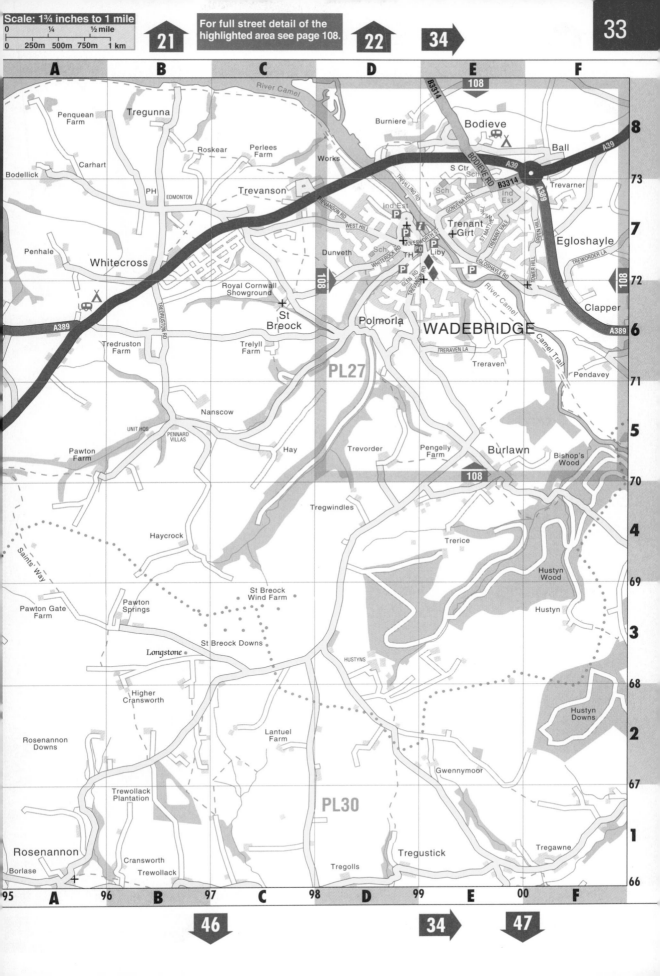

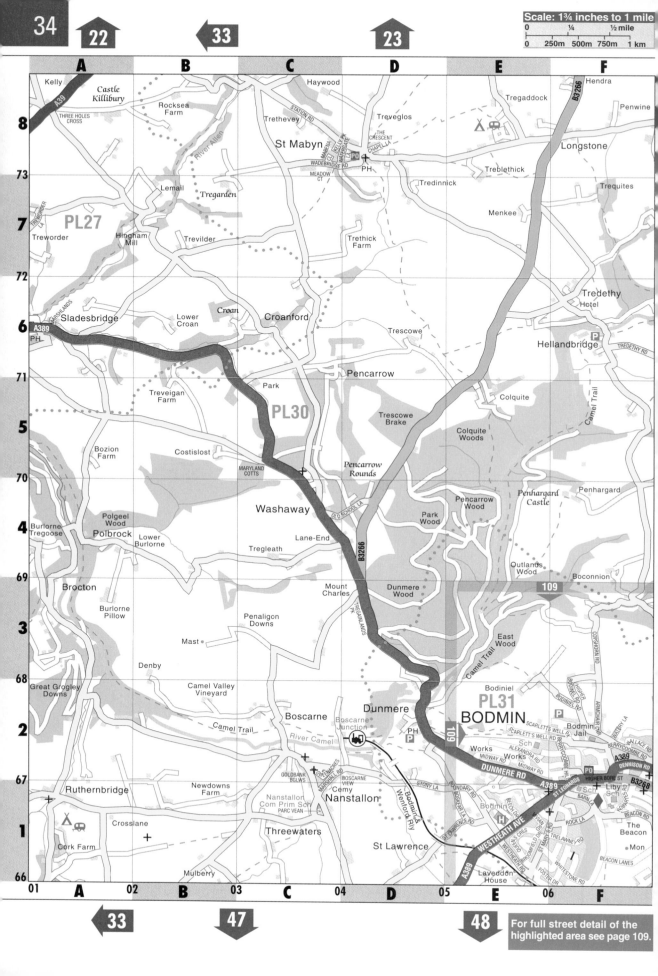

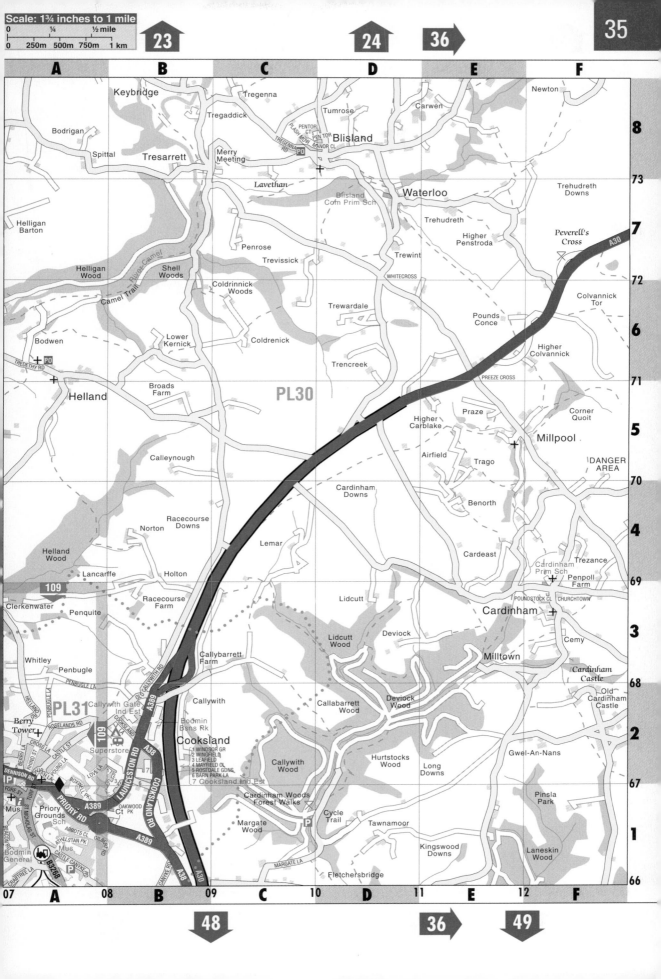

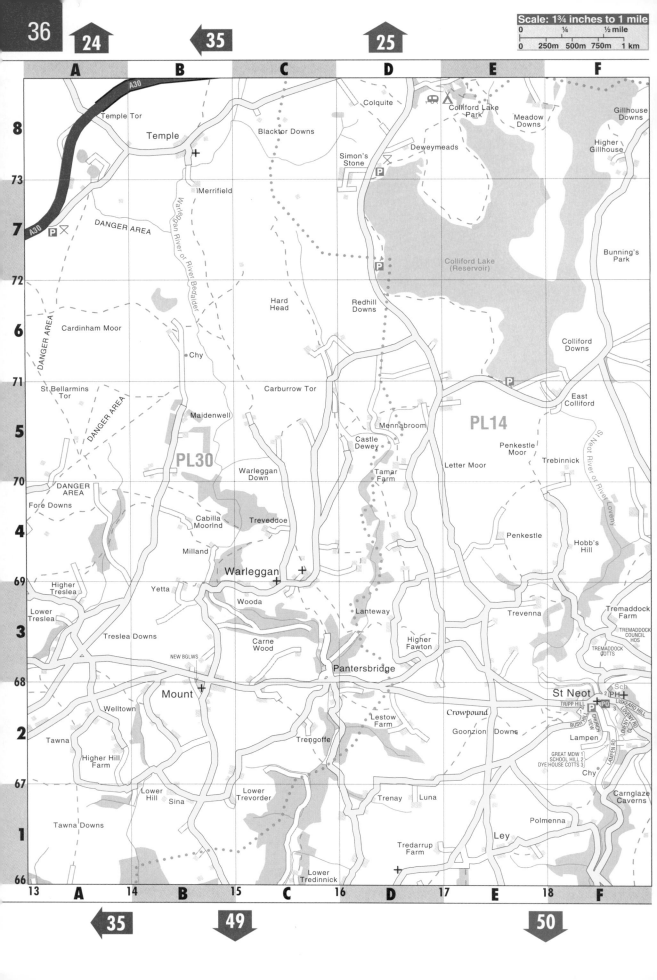

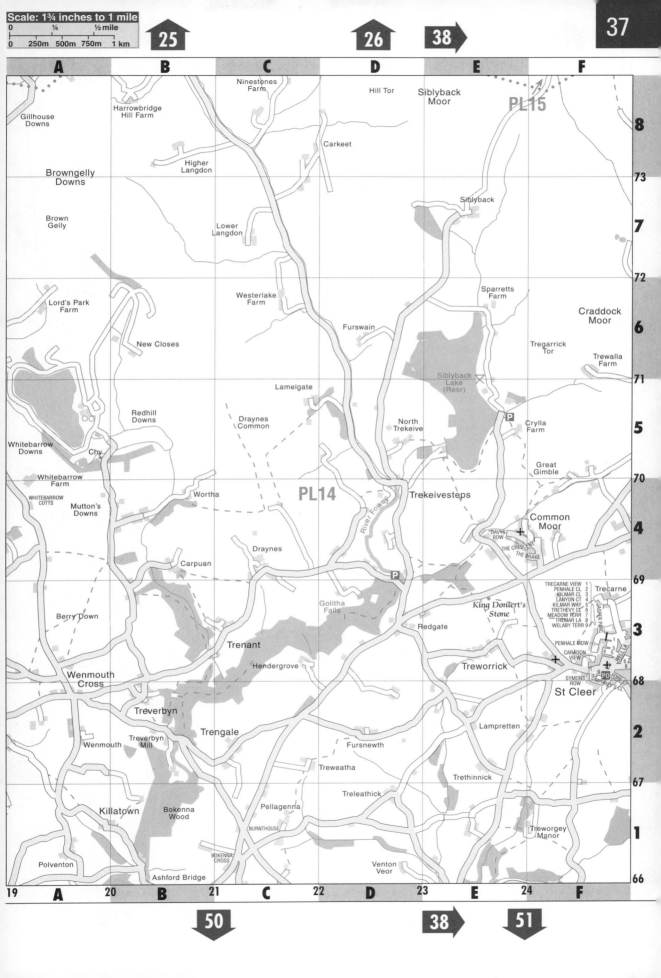

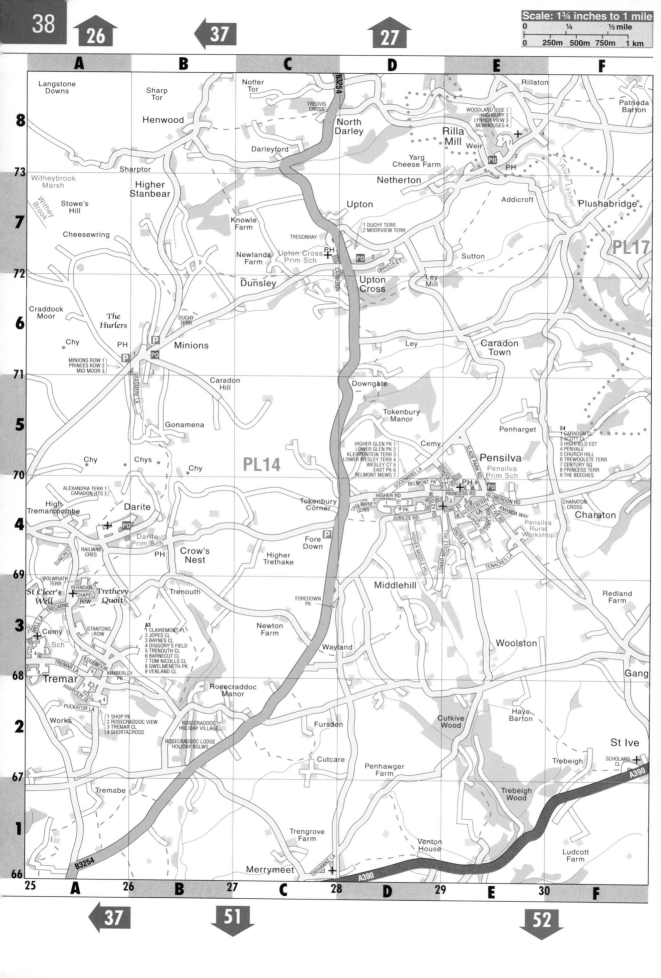

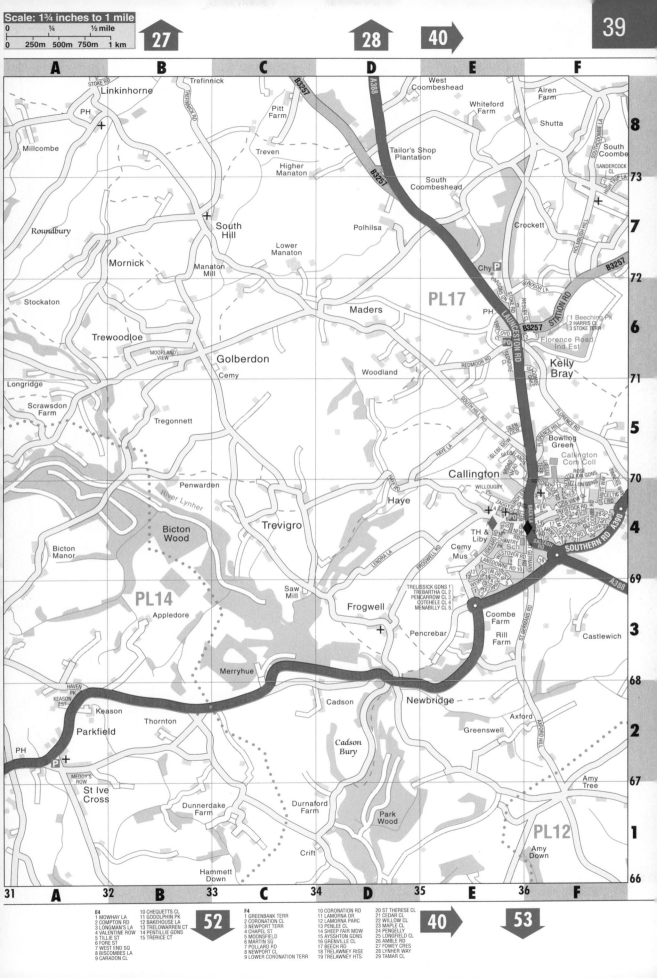

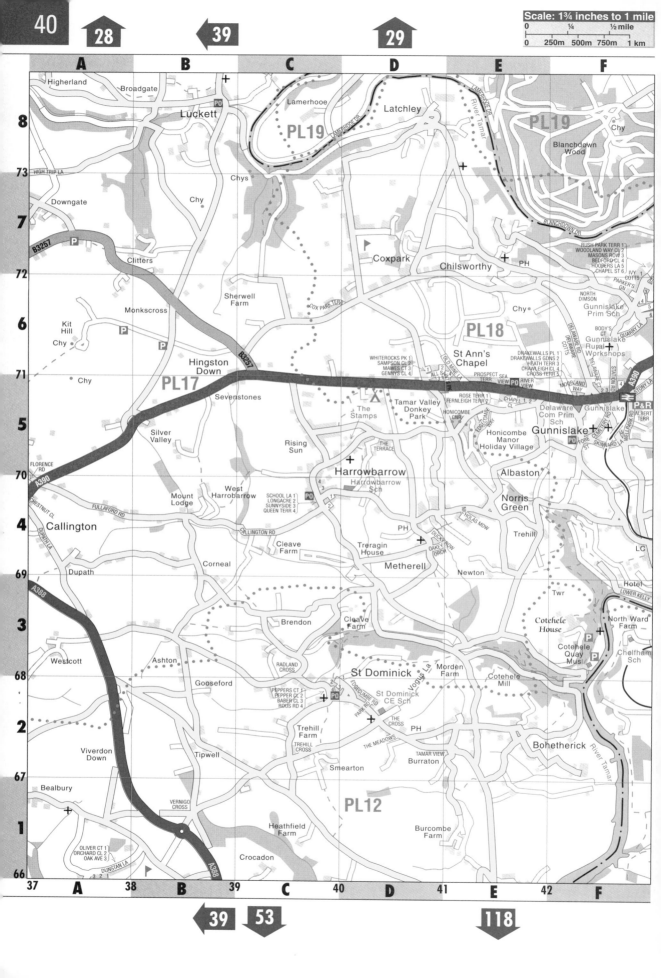

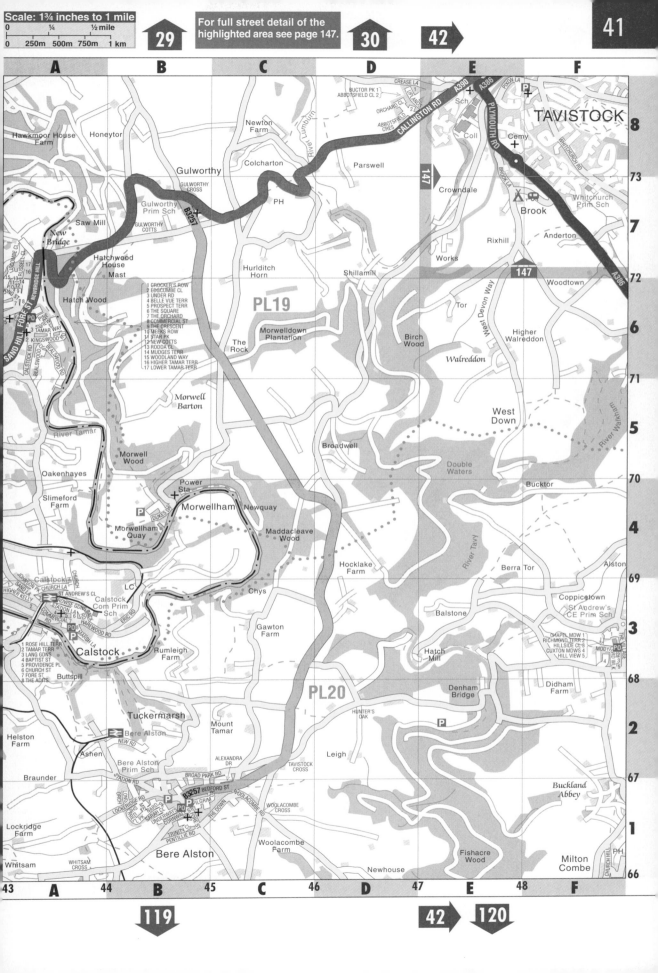

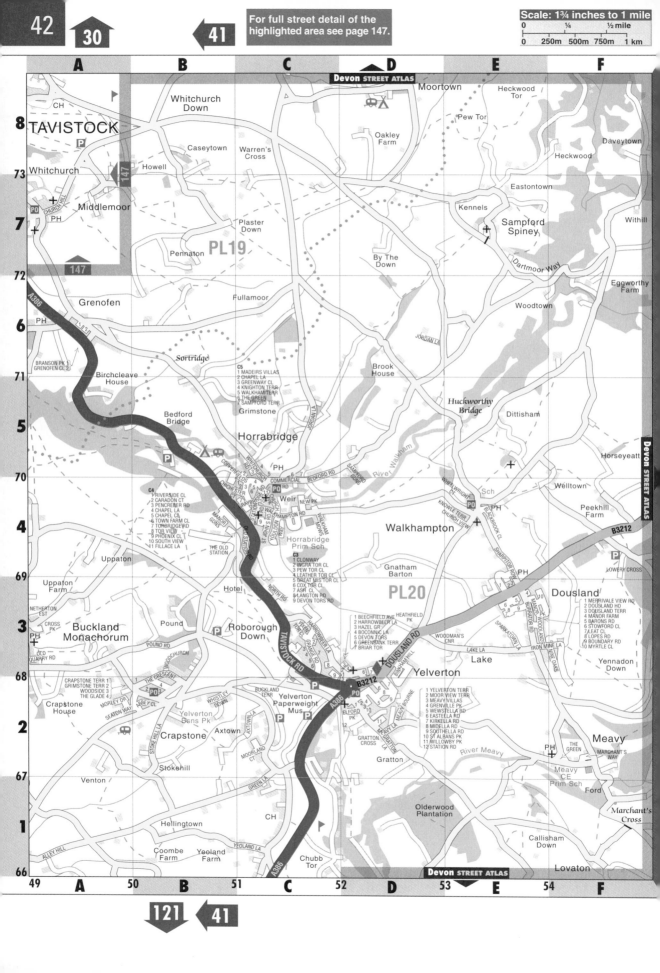

A B C D E F

8

65

7

64

6

Towan Head

110

63

P Gazzle

5

Hotel

HEADLAND RD DANE RD

Fistral
Bay

Fistral
Beach

P

62

LB Sta

NEWQUAY

CH

South West Coast Path

ESPLANADE RD

The
Goose

Cemy

TR7

CRANTOCK ST

4

Pentire
Point East

PENTIRE AVE

PENTIRE RD

PO

MOUNT WISE

Pentire

P

PENTIRE CRES

PENMERE DR

A392

Pentire
Point West

Ferry P
(summer only)

TREVEAN WAY

CHYNANCE DR

61

The
Chick

Vugga
Cove

Crantock
Beach

110

A392

Kelsey
Head

Porth
Joke

Hotel

West
Pentire

Crantock

BEACH RD

PH

Penpol

The
Gannel

3

GREEN LA

GOSPORTH HILL

PENPOL HILL

South West Coast Path

WEST PENTIRE RD

GUSTORY RD

TREVELLICK RD

Trevella

Cave

South West Coast Path

Treago
Farm

ST
CARANTOC
WAY

HALWYN RD

Treringey

60

PO

The
Kelseys

P

Trevowah

Trevella
Park

2

Carter's or
Gull Rocks

Holywell
Bay

Holywell
Beach

Cubert
Common

TR8

Penhale
Point

Dunes

Lewannick

Carines

110

59

Treworgans

Penhale
Camp

RHUBARB HILL

CH

PH

Fun
Park

Carevick

Treworthal

1

Cave

GUN HILL RD

CENTRAL GDNS

Trevornick

Tresean

Cemy

Hoblyn's
Cove

TREGUTH
CL

TREVAIL
COTTS

Trevail

Cubert
Prim Sch

Trenissick

Ligger
Point

DANGER
AREA

CHYNOWEN
PARC

CHYNOWEN LA

PH

A3075

58

75 A 76 B 77 C 78 D 79 E 80 F

55 ↓ **44** ↓ For full street detail of the
highlighted area see page
110.

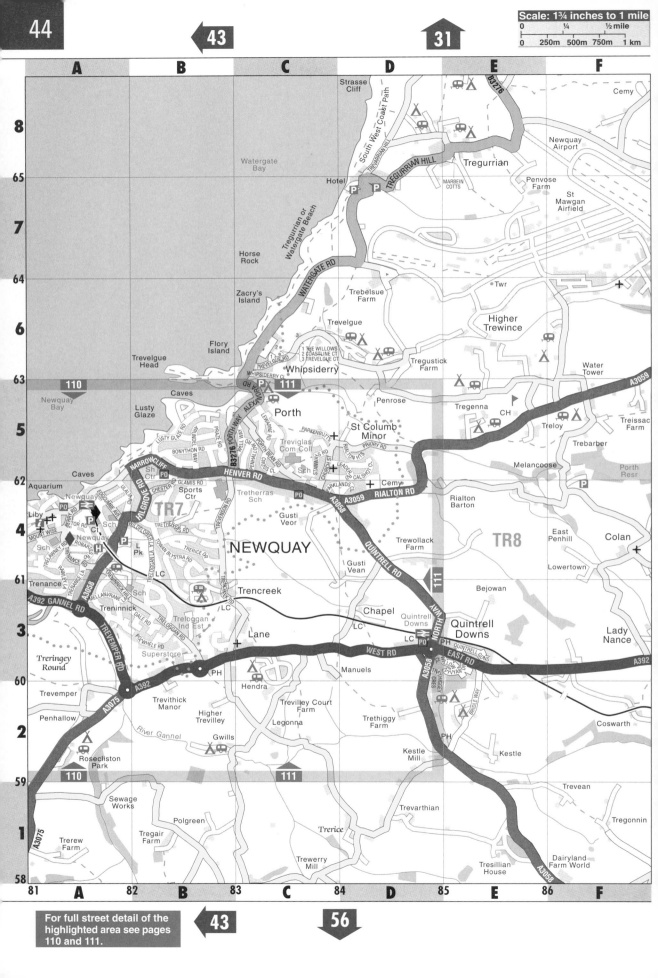

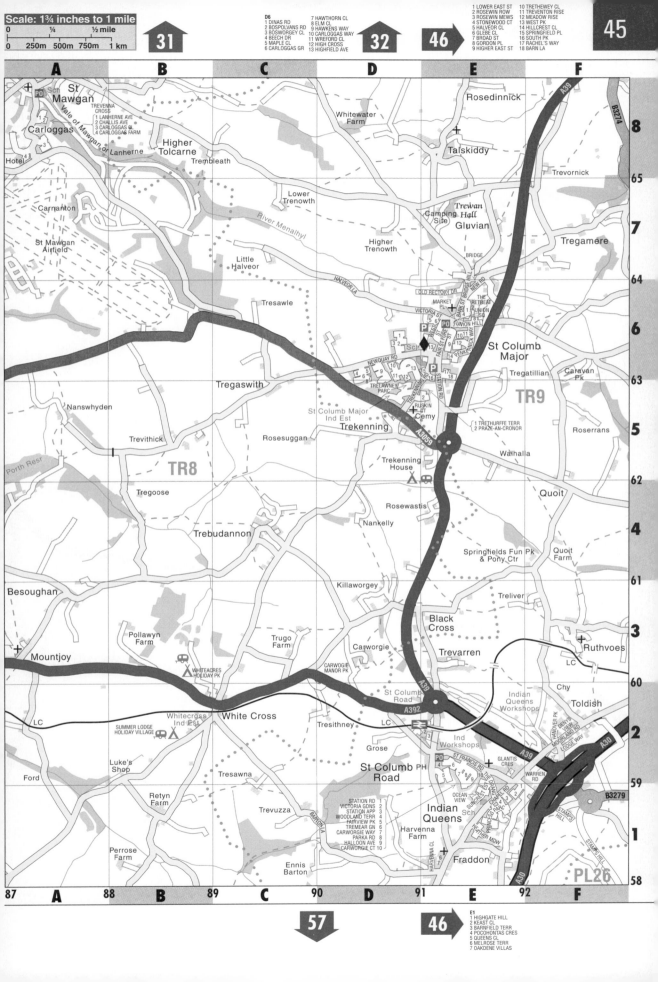

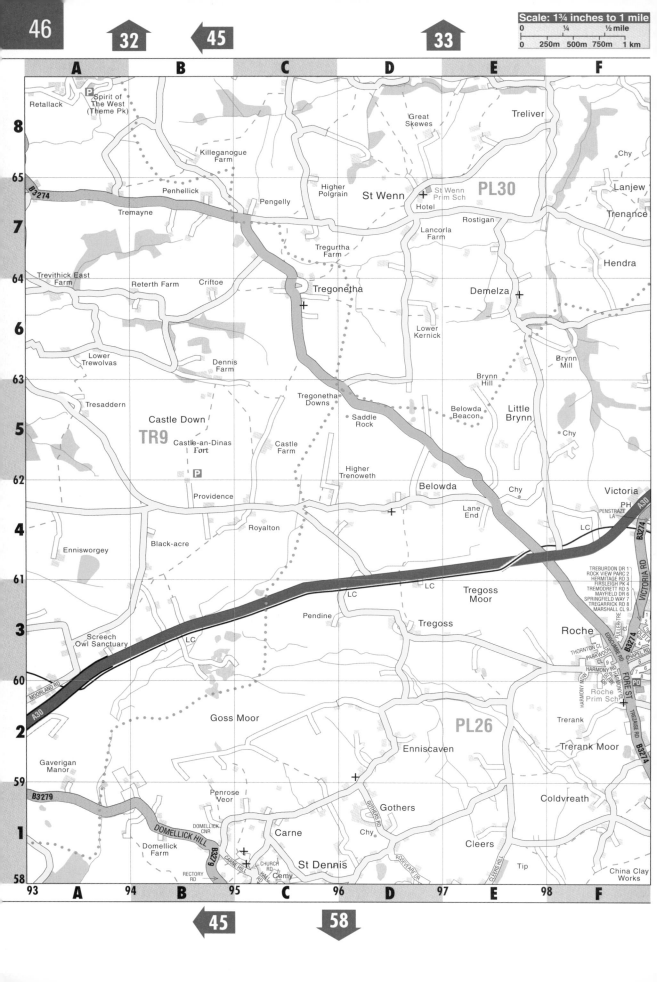

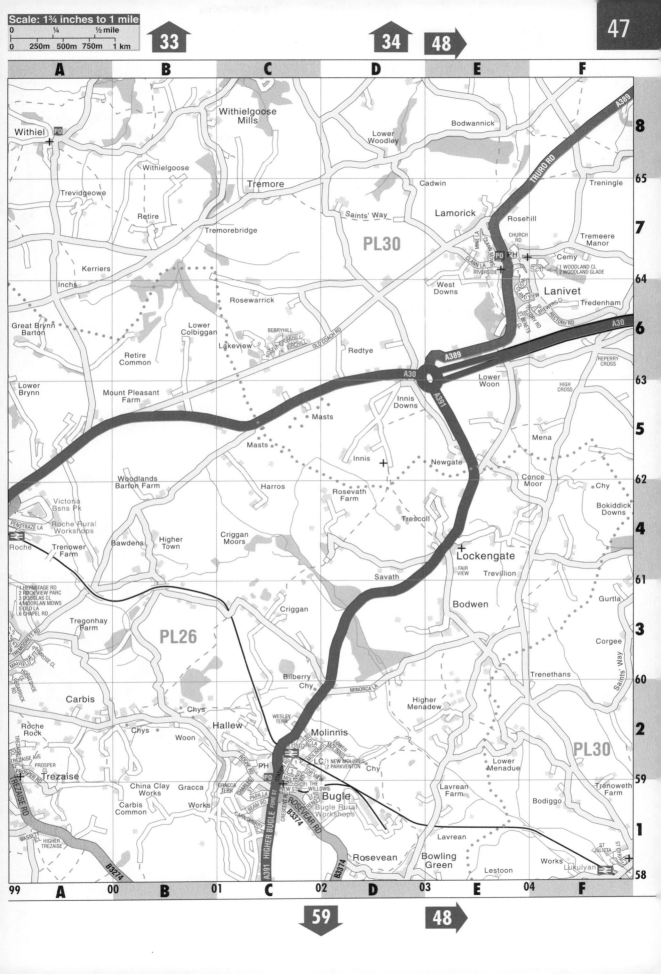

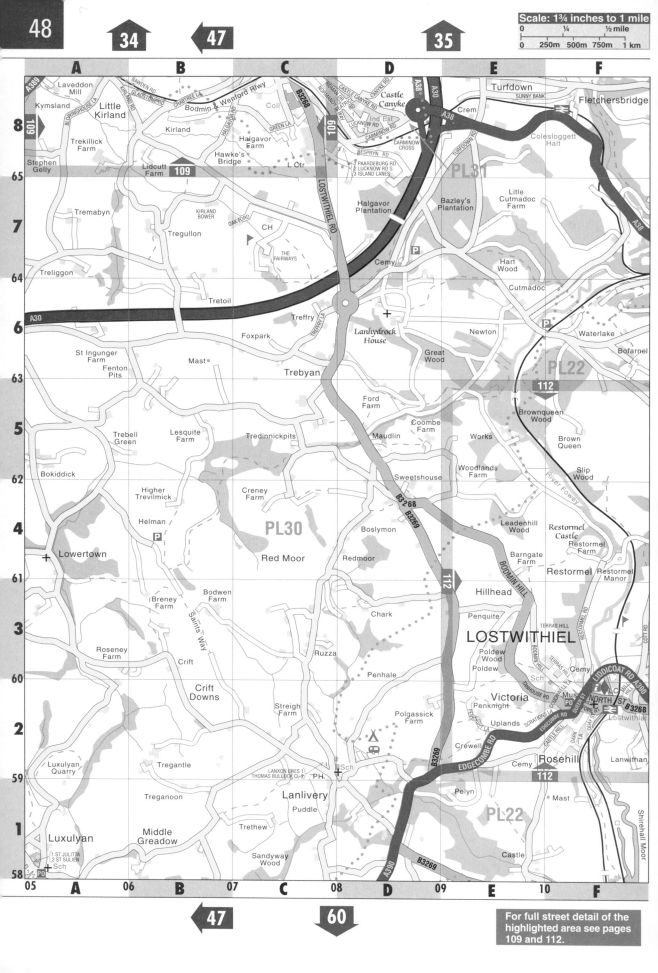

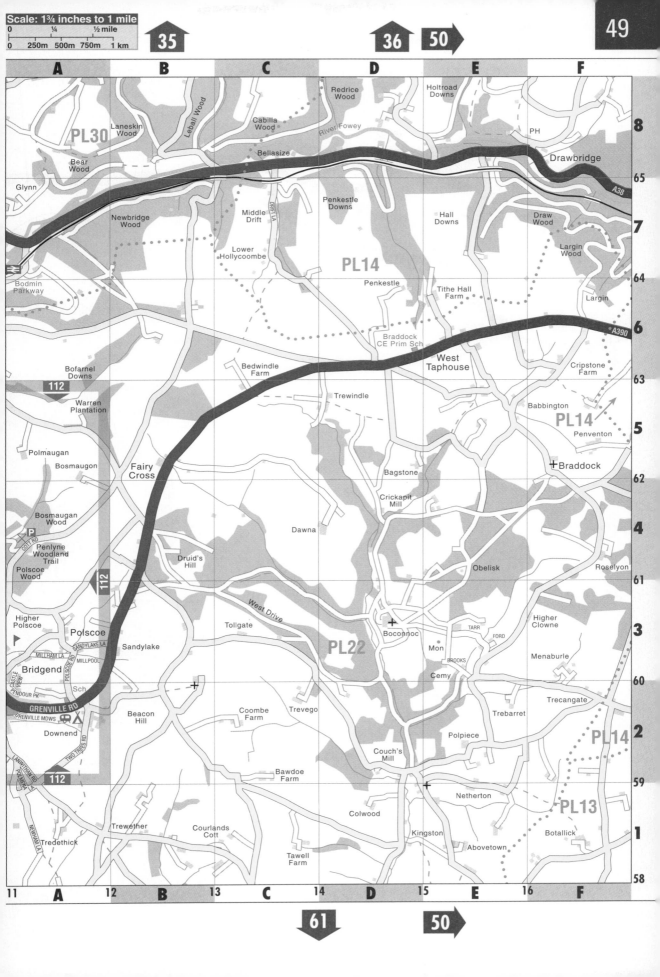

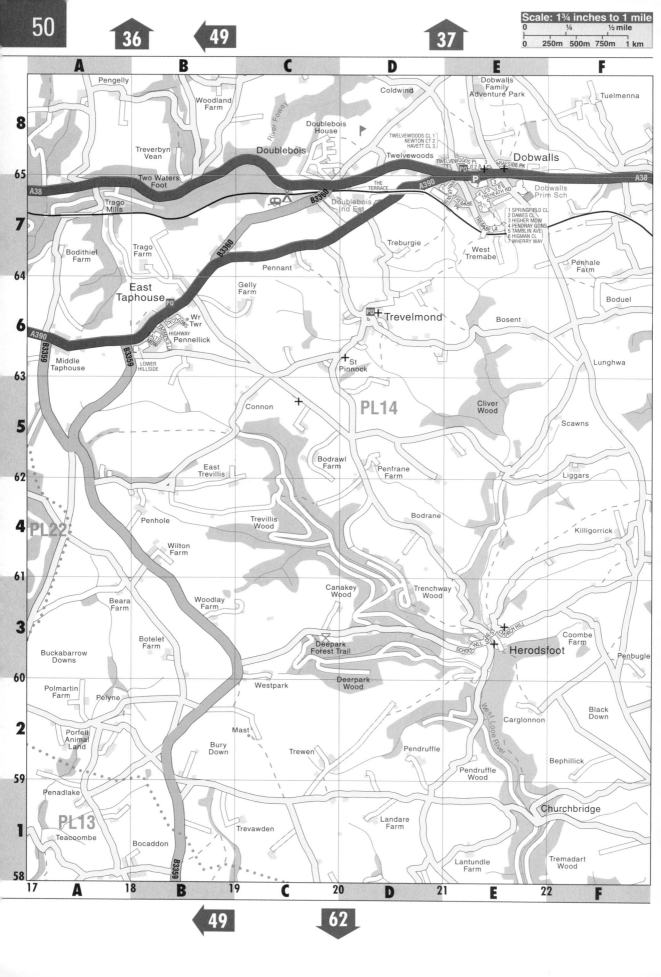

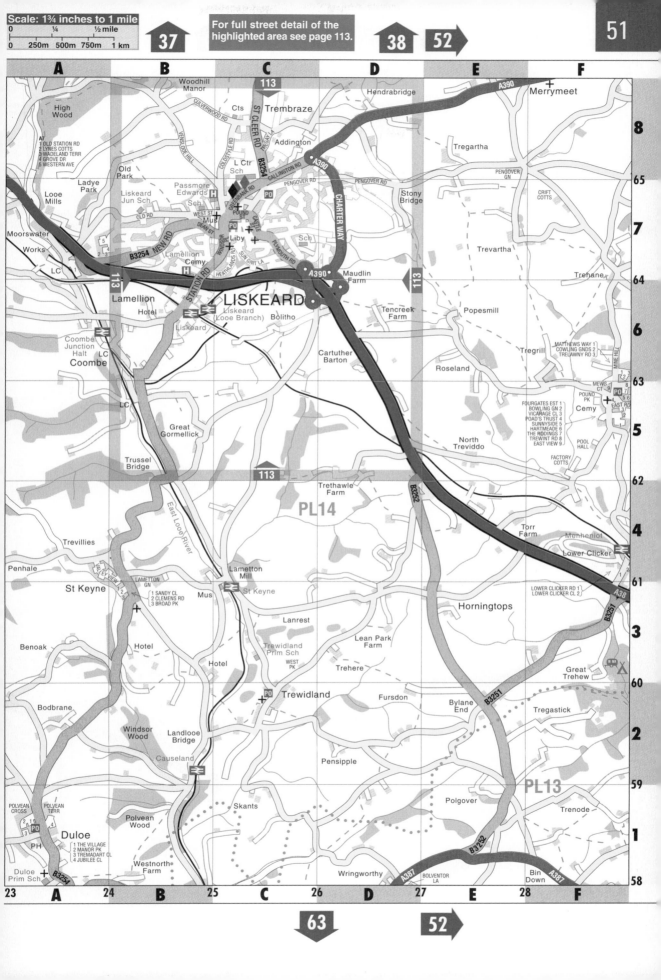

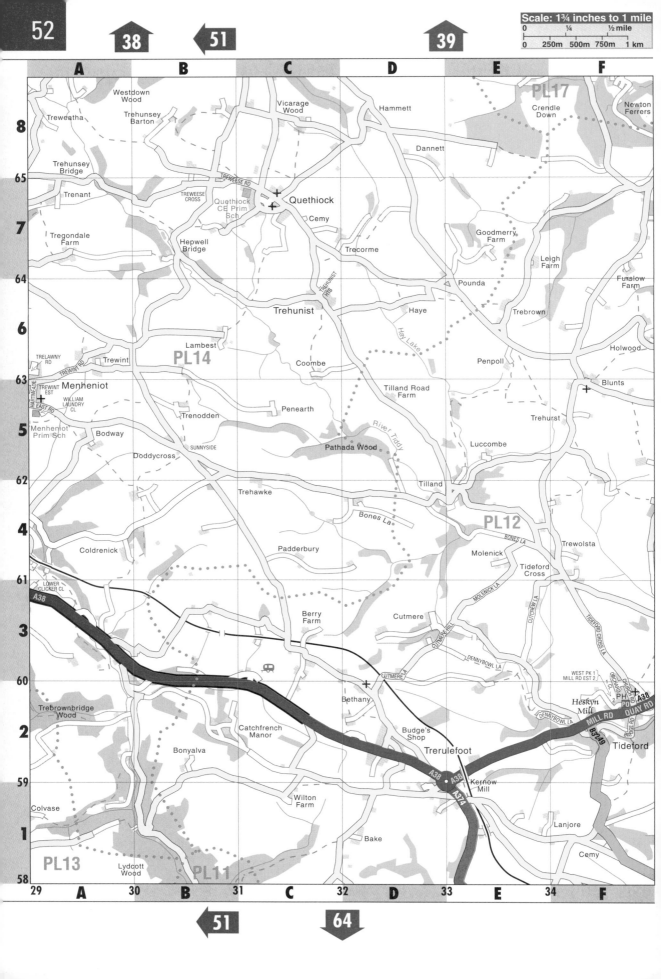

Scale: 1¾ inches to 1 mile

0   ¼   ½ mile
0   250m   500m   750m   1 km

PL17

8

Westdown Wood

Treweatha

Trehunsey Barton

Vicarage Wood

Hammett

Crendle Down

Newton Ferrers

Dannett

65

Trehunsey Bridge

TREWEESE RD

Quethiock

Trenant

TREWEESE CROSS

Quethiock CE Prim Sch

Goodmerry Farm

7

Tregondale Farm

Hepwell Bridge

Cemy

Trecorme

Leigh Farm

64

TREHUNIST RDS

Pounda

Furslow Farm

Trehunist

Haye

Trebrown

6

Lambest

Coombe

Holwood

TRELAWNY RD

PL14

Hay Lake

Penpoll

63

TREWINT RD

Trewint

Tilland Road Farm

Blunts

TREWINT EST

Menheniot

HARTMEADE

WILLIAM LAUNDRY CL

Penearth

River Tiddy

Trehurst

EAST RD

5

Menheniot Prim Sch

Bodway

Trenodden

Luccombe

SUNNYSIDE

Pathada Wood

62

Doddycross

Tilland

Trehawke

4

Coldrenick

Padderbury

Bones La

PL12

BONES LA

Trewolsta

Molenick

Tideford Cross

61

LOWER CLICKER CL

MOLENICK LA

CUTCARW LA

TIDEFORD CROSS LA

A38

Berry Farm

Cutmere

3

DENNYBOWL LA

CUTMERE HILL

CUTMERE LA

WEST PK 1
MILL RD EST 2

60

Bethany

ORCHARD CL

PH

A38

Heskyn Mill

Trebrownbridge Wood

Catchfrench Manor

Budge's Shop

MILL RD

POOL RD

QUAY RD

2

Bonyalva

Trerulefoot

DENNYBOWL LA

B3249

Tideford

A38

SHOE RD

59

A38

Kernow Mill

A374

Colvase

Wilton Farm

Lanjore

1

Bake

Cemy

58

PL13

Lydcott Wood

PL11

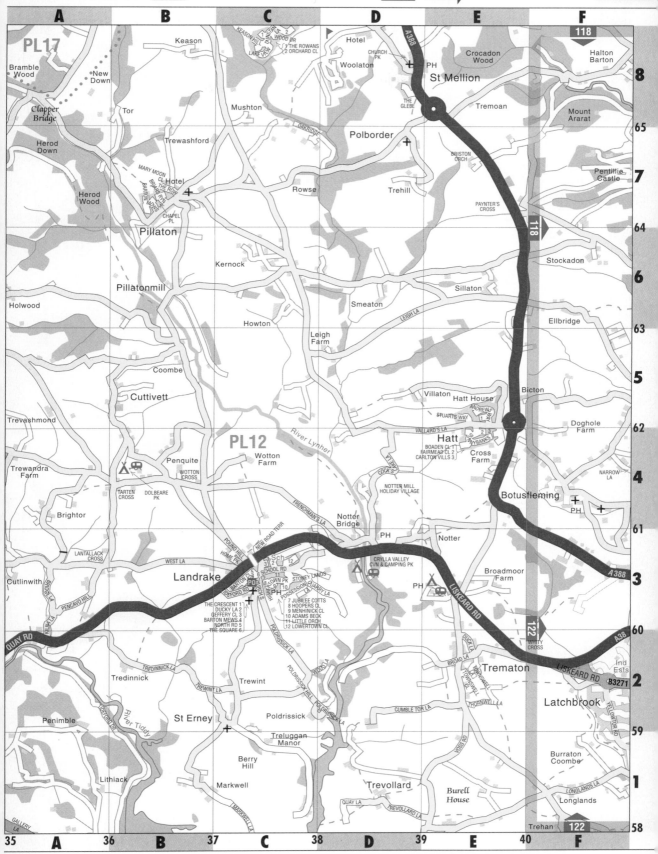

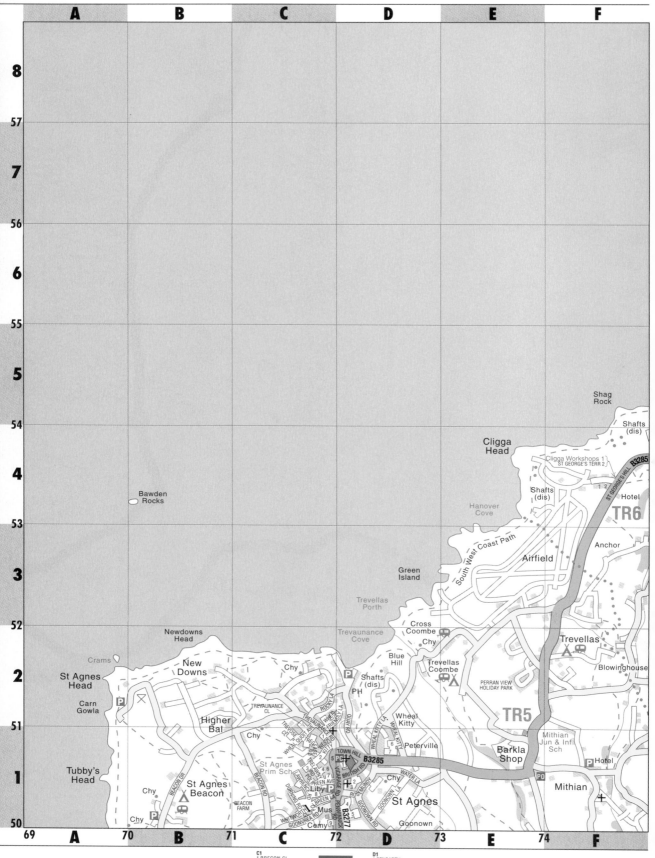

St Agnes Head

St Agnes
Head

Carn
Gowla

Crams

New
Downs

Newdowns
Head

Tubby's
Head

Bawden
Rocks

Chy

Chy

Chy

Higher
Bal

Chy

St Agnes
Prim Sch

St Agnes
Beacon

BEACON
FARM

Liby

Mus

Cemy

Chy

Trevaunance
CL

Chy

Trevaunance
Cove

Trevellas
Porth

Green
Island

Blue
Hill

Shafts
(dis)

PH

Cross
Coombe

Chy

Trevellas
Coombe

St Agnes

Goonown

Chy

Wheal
Kitty

Peterville

WATER LA

B3285

B3277

Hanover
Cove

Cligga
Head

South West Coast Path

Airfield

Shafts
(dis)

Shafts
(dis)

Shag
Rock

Cligga Workshops 1
ST GEORGE'S TERR 2

ST GEORGE'S HILL

B3285

Hotel

TR6

Anchor

Trevellas

Blowinghouse

PERRAN VIEW
HOLIDAY PARK

TR5

Barkla
Shop

Mithian

Mithian
Jun & Inf
Sch

Hotel

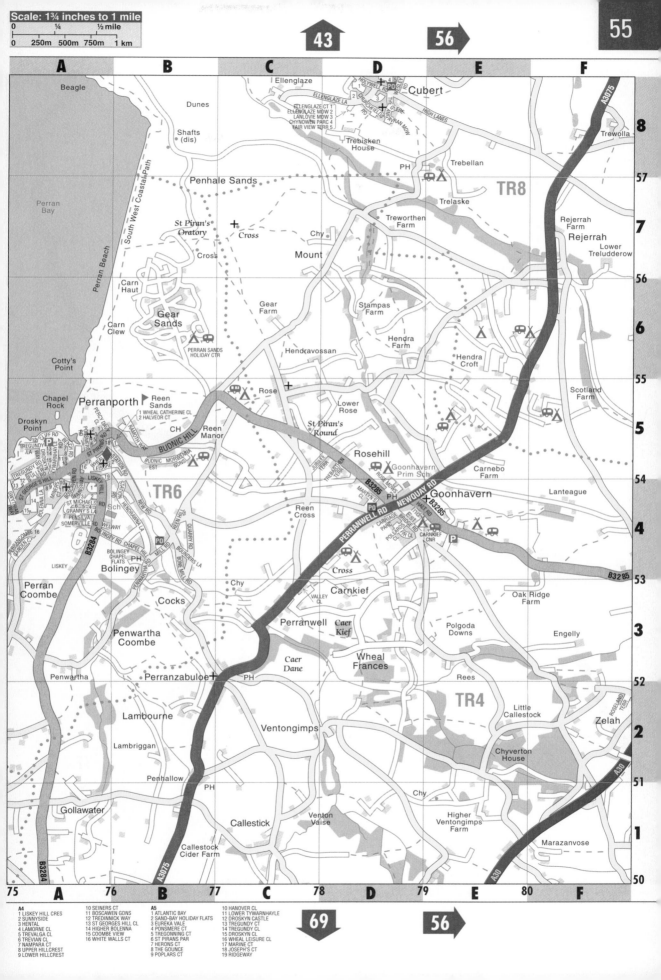

Beagle

Dunes

Shafts (dis)

Ellenglaze

Cubert

ELLENGLAZE CT 1
ELLENGLAZE MDW 2
LANLOVIE MDW 3
CHYNOWEN PARC 4
FAIR VIEW TERR 5

HOLYWELL RD
CHURCHFIELD RD
THE CLEZE
THE MORAN MDW
HIGH LANES

Trebisken House

Trewolla

Penhale Sands

PH

Trelaske

TR8

57

Perran Bay

St Piran's Oratory

Cross

Cross

Cross

Chy

Mount

Treworthen Farm

Rejerrah Farm

Rejerrah

Lower Treludderow

7

Perran Beach

South West Coastal Path

Carn Haut

Carn Clew

Gear Sands

Gear Farm

Stampas Farm

56

Hendra Farm

6

Cotty's Point

PERRAN SANDS HOLIDAY CTR

Hendravossan

Hendra Croft

55

Chapel Rock

Perranporth

Reen Sands

1 WHEAL CATHERINE CL
2 HALVEOR CT

Rose

St Piran's Round

Lower Rose

Scotland Farm

5

Droskyn Point

CH

Reen Manor

Rosehill

Carnebo Farm

Lanteague

BUDNIC HILL

BUDNIC MORWENNA GDNS EST

Goonhavern Prim Sch

TR6

St Michaels Rd Sch

JUBILEE TERR
TREBARTHEN
ROSE MDW
MARTY'S CL

PERRANWELL RD

NEWQUAY RD

B3285

HALT RD

Goonhavern

B3285

54

Granny's La
Pensilva
Somerville Rd

Welway

Reen Cross

PH

CARRIAGE PARC
BRIDGE RD
POL GARDS
CTR CL

CARNKIEF CNR

P

CARNKIEF

Oak Ridge Farm

53

Bolingey

Chapel Flats

PH

Chy

Cross

Carnkief

VALLEY CL

4

Perran Coombe

Cocks

Perranwell

Caer Kief

Polgoda Downs

Engelly

3

Penwartha Coombe

Caer Dane

Wheal Frances

Rees

52

Perranzabuloe

PH

TR4

Little Callestock

Zelah

2

Penwartha

Lambourne

Ventongimps

Chyverton House

Lambriggan

Penhallow

PH

Chy

51

Gollawater

Callestick

Venton Vaise

Higher Ventongimps Farm

Marazanvose

1

Callestock Cider Farm

A3075

A30

50

A4
1 LISKEY HILL CRES
2 SUNNYSIDE
3 HENTAL
4 LAMORNE CL
5 TREVALGA CL
6 TREVIAN CL
7 NAMPARA CT
8 UPPER HILLCREST
9 LOWER HILLCREST

10 SEINERS CT
11 BOSCAWEN GDNS
12 TREDINNICK WAY
13 ST GEORGES HILL CL
14 HIGHER BOLENNA
15 COOMBE VIEW
16 WHITE WALLS CT

A5
1 ATLANTIC BAY
2 SAND-BAY HOLIDAY FLATS
3 EUREKA VALE
4 PONSMERE CT
5 TREGONNING CT
6 ST PIRANS PAR
7 HERONS CT
8 THE GOUNCE
9 POPLARS CT

10 HANOVER CL
11 LOWER TYWARNHAYLE
12 DROSKYN CASTLE
13 TREGUNDY CT
14 TREGUNDY CL
15 DROSKYN CL
16 WHEAL LEISURE CL
17 MARINE CT
18 JOSEPH'S CT
19 RIDGEWAY

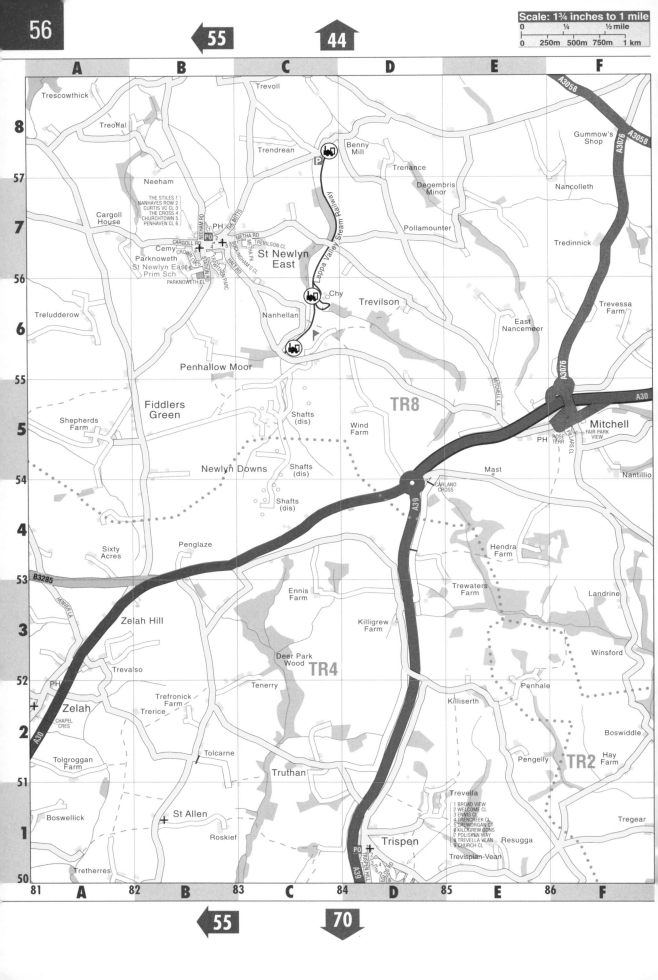

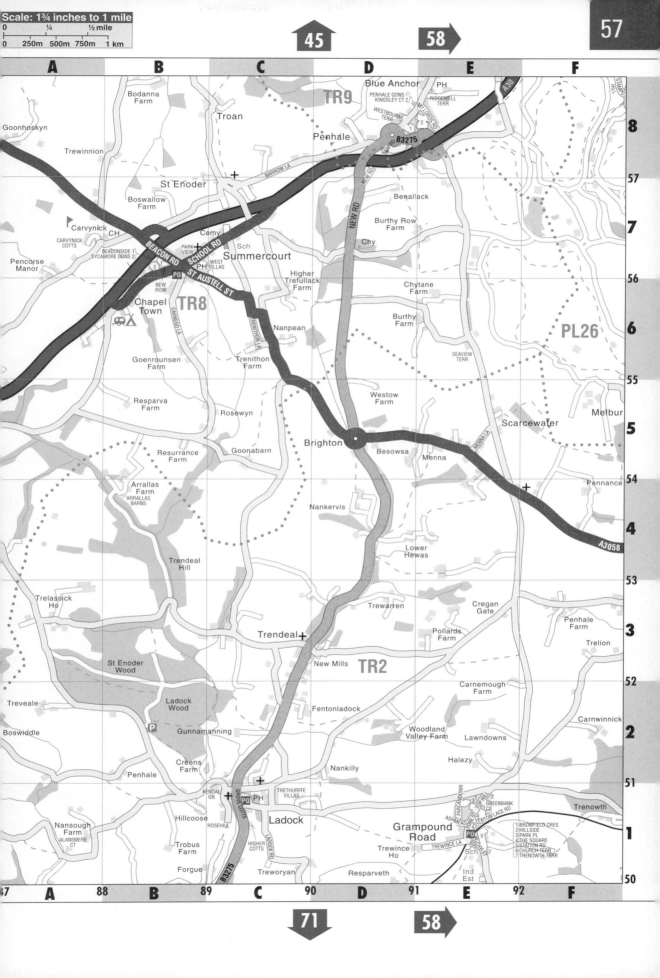

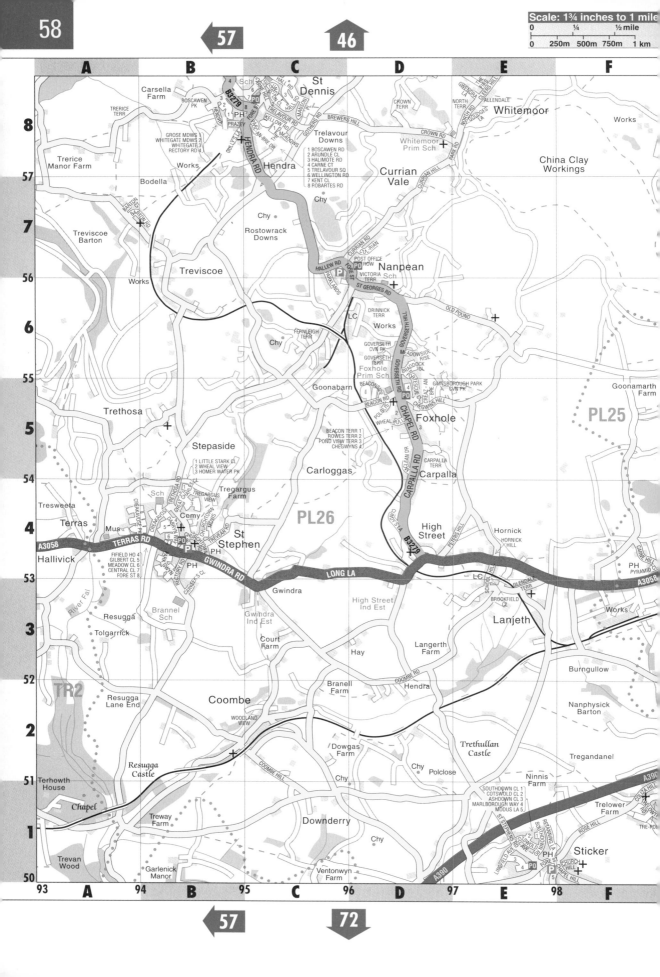

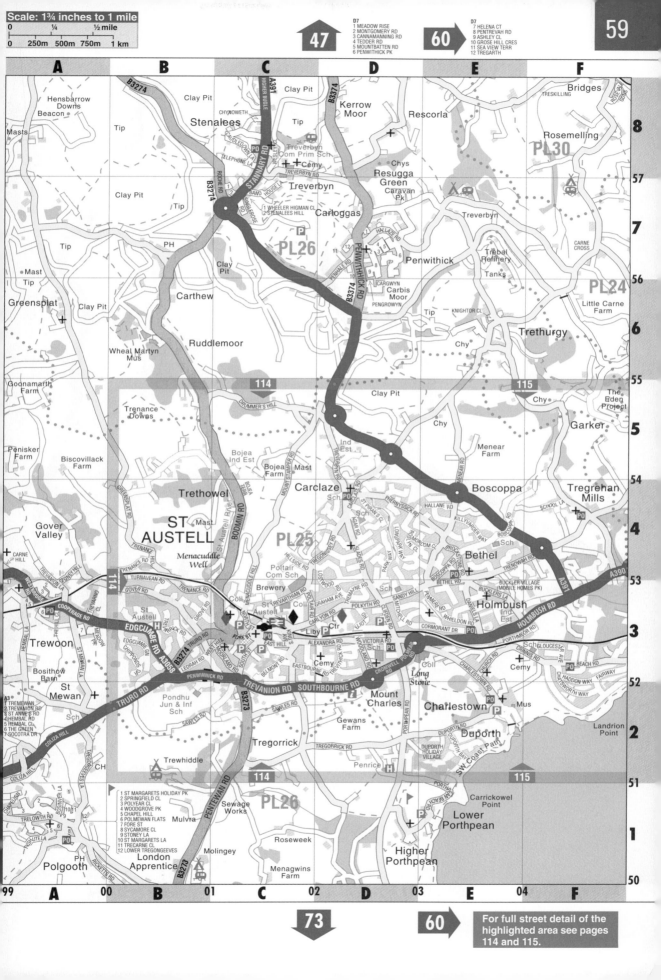

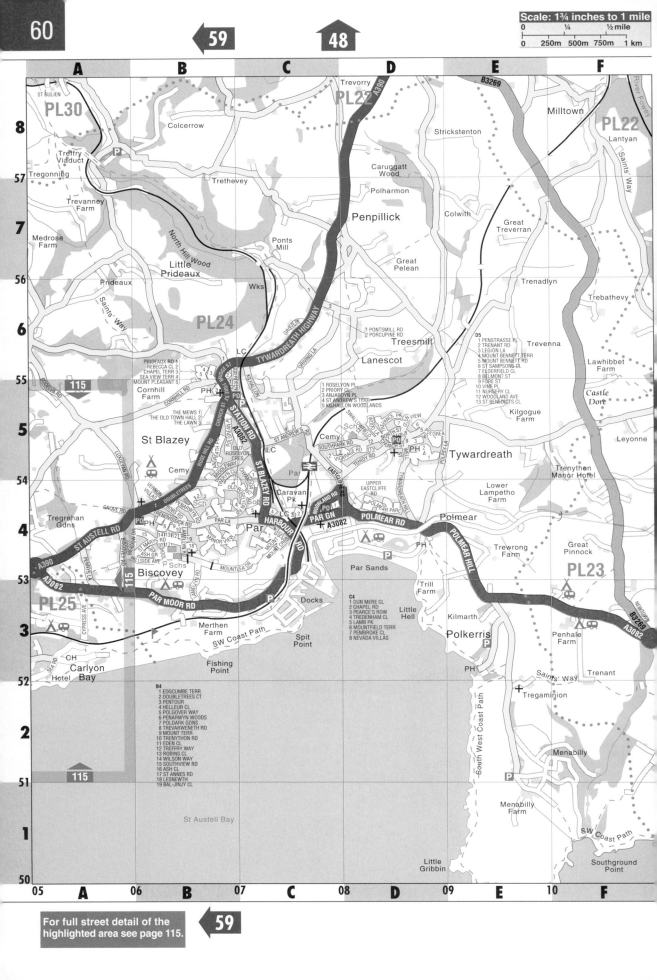

Scale: 1¾ inches to 1 mile

0   ¼   ½ mile

0   250m 500m 750m 1 km

8

57

7

56

6

55

5

54

4

53

3

52

2

51

1

50

A   B   C   D   E   F

St SULIEN

PL30

Treffry Viaduct

Tregonning

Trevanney Farm

Medrose Farm

Prideaux

Saints' Way

Colcerrow

North Hill Wood

Little Prideaux

Trethevey

Ponts Mill

Wks

PL24

TYWARDREATH HIGHWAY

GROVER LA

DRUVING LA

Trevorry

PL22

Penpillick

Polharmon

Caruggatt Wood

Great Pelean

Treesmill

Lanescot

Strickstenton

Colwith

Trenadlyn

Great Treverran

Trevenna

Milltown

PL22

Lantyan

Saints' Way

Trebathevy

Lawhibbet Farm

Castle Dore

Leyonne

1 PONTSMILL RD
2 PORCUPINE RD

D5
1 PENSTRASSE PL
2 TRENANT RD
3 LEGION LA
4 MOUNT BENNETT TERR
5 MOUNT BENNETT RD
6 ST SAMPSONS CL
7 ELDERFIELD CL
8 BELMONT ST
9 FORE ST
10 VINE PL
11 NURSERY CL
12 WOODLAND AVE
13 ST BENEDICTS CL

Kilgogue Farm

PRIDEAUX RD 1
REBECCA CL 2
CHAPEL TERR 3
SEA VIEW TERR 4
MOUNT PLEASANT 5

Cornhill Farm

THE MEWS 1
THE OLD TOWN HALL 2
THE LAWN 3

St Blazey

Cemy

Tregrehan Gdns

PL25

A390

A3082

Biscovey

PAR MOOR RD

Merthen Farm

SW Coast Path

Fishing Point

Carlyon Bay

Hotel

CH

SEA RD

CYPRESS AVE

St Austell Bay

115

1 ROSELYON PL
2 PRIORY CL
3 ANJARDYN PL
4 ST ANDREW'S TERR
5 KILHALLON WOODLANDS

Schsfield

ST ANDREW ST

Cemy

SOUTHPARK RD

VICARAGE RD

TEHIDY RD

NORTH ST

CHURCH ST

POLKERRIS

POLCAREA

Tywardreath

Trenython Manor Hotel

Lower Lampetho Farm

Polmear

POLMEAR RD

POLMEAR HILL

Par

Caravan Pk

HARBOUR RD

MOORLAND RD

PAR GN

A3082

EASTCLIFFE RD

UPPER EASTCLIFFE RD

POLMEAR PARC

Par Sands

Docks

Spit Point

Little Hell

C4
1 DUN MERE CL
2 CHAPEL RD
3 PEARCE'S ROW
4 TREDENHAM CL
5 LAMB PK
6 MOUNTFIELD TERR
7 PEMBROKE CL
8 NEVADA VILLAS

Trill Farm

Kilmarth

Polkerris

PH

Trewrong Farm

Great Pinnock

PL23

B3269

A3082

Penhale Farm

Trenant

Saints' Way

Tregaminion

Menabilly

Menabilly Farm

South West Coast Path

Little Gribbin

Southground Point

SW Coast Path

B4
1 EDGCUMBE TERR
2 DOUBLETREES CT
3 PENTOUR
4 HELLEUR CL
5 POLGOVER WAY
6 PENARWYN WOODS
7 POLDARK GDNS
8 TREVARWENETH RD
9 MOUNT TERR
10 TRENYTHON RD
11 EDEN CL
12 TREFFRY WAY
13 ROBINS CL
14 WILSON WAY
15 SOUTHVIEW RD
16 ASH CL
17 ST ANNES RD
18 LESNEWTH
19 BAL-JINJY CL

05   A   06   B   07   C   08   D   09   E   10   F

For full street detail of the highlighted area see page 115.

59

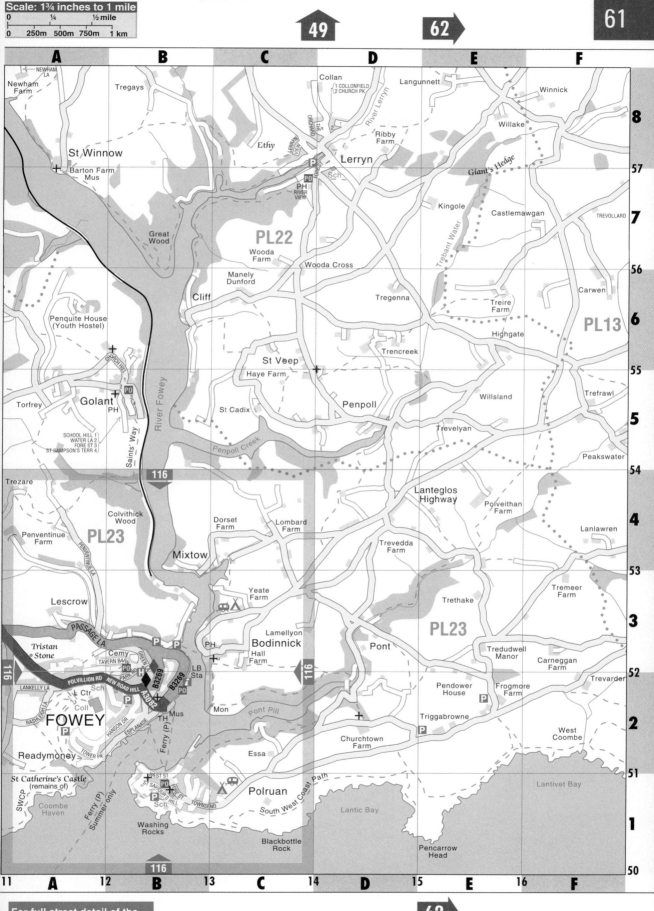

A   B   C   D   E   F

NEWHAM LA

Newham Farm

Tregays

Collan
1 COLLONFIELD
2 CHURCH PK

Langunnett

Winnick

8

St Winnow

Ethy

Lerryn

Willake

57

+ Barton Farm
Mus

LERRYN VIEW

River Lerryn

Ribby Farm

Sch

Giant's Hedge

Kingole

Castlemawgan

TREVOLLARD

7

PO
PH
RIVER VIEW

PL22

Wooda Farm

Trebant Water

56

Great Wood

Wooda Cross

Manely Dunford

Tregenna

Treire Farm

Carwen

PL13

6

Penquite House
(Youth Hostel)

Cliff

Highgate

+

Trencreek

St Veep

55

CHURCH HILL

+

Haye Farm

Penpoll

Willsland

Trefrawl

Torfrey

Golant

PO

PH

St Cadix

Trevelyan

5

SCHOOL HILL 1
WATER LA 2
FORE ST 3
ST SAMPSON'S TERR 4

River Fowey

Penpoll Creek

Peakswater

Saints' Way

116

Lanteglos Highway

Polveithan Farm

54

Trezare

Colvithick Wood

Dorset Farm

Lombard Farm

4

Penventinue Farm

PL23

PENVENTINUE LA

Mixtow

Trevedda Farm

Lanlawren

53

Lescrow

Yeate Farm

Trethake

Tremeer Farm

3

PASSAGE LA

Lamellyon

Bodinnick

Pont

PL23

Tristan Stone

Cemy

P   P

PH

Hall Farm

Tredudwell Manor

Carneggan Farm

Trevarder

52

TAVERN BARN

PO

H

B3269

B3269

LB Sta

Pendower House

Frogmore Farm

POLVILLION RD

NEW ROAD HILL

A3082

Sch

Mus

Mon

P

Triggabrowne

West Coombe

2

LANKELLY LA

Ctr

Coll

TH (P)

Ferry (P)

Churchtown Farm

FOWEY

ESPLANADE

Essa

HANSON DR

Readymoney

TOWER PK

WEST ST

PO

Pont Pill

St Catherine's Castle
(remains of)

SAULS HILL

TOWNSEND

Polruan

Lantivet Bay

51

SWCP

Ferry (P)
Summer only

Sch

South West Coast Path

Lantic Bay

Coombe Haven

Washing Rocks

Blackbottle Rock

Pencarrow Head

1

116

50

11   A   12   B   13   C   14   D   15   E   16   F

For full street detail of the highlighted area see page116.

62

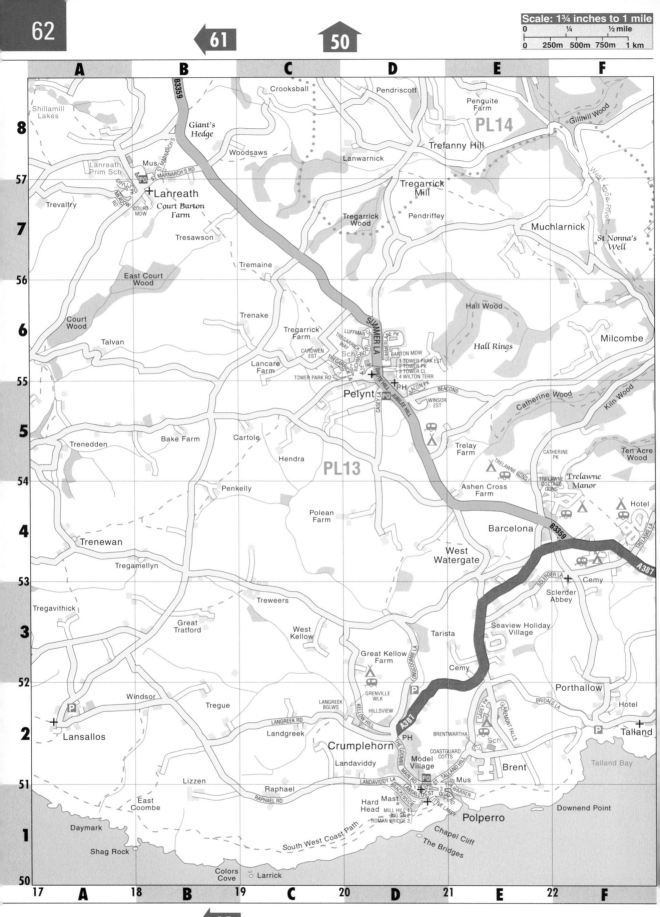

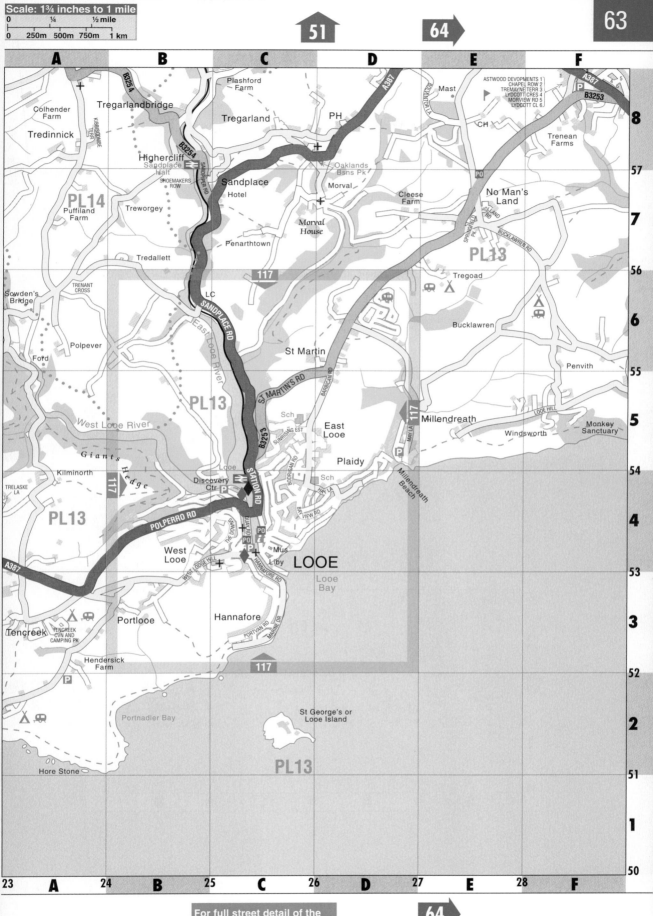

A B C D E F

8
57
7
56
6
55
5
54
4
53
3
52
2
51
1
50

Tregarlandbridge
Colhender Farm
Tredinnick
B3254
Plashford Farm
Tregarland
Tregarland
PH
Mast
ASTWOOD DEVOPMENTS 1
CHAPEL ROW 2
TREMAYNE TERR 3
LYDCOTT CRES 4
MORVIEW RD 5
LYDCOTT CL 6.
B3253
P
5
5

Highercliff
Sandplace Halt
B3254
SHOEMAKERS ROW
Sandplace
Hotel
Oaklands Bsns Pk
Morval
CH
No Man's Land
Trenean Farms

PL14
Puffiland Farm
Treworgey
SANDPIPER RD
Morval House
Cleese Farm
PO
PL13
BUCKLAWREN RD
SPRINGFIELD
HOLLAND RD

Tredallett
Penarthtown
117
Tregoad
Bucklawren

Sowden's Bridge
TRENANT CROSS
LC
SANDPLACE RD
East Looe River
Penvith

Polpever
Ford
St Martin
ST MARTIN'S RD
BABBACH RD
LOOE HILL
Millendreath
Windsworth
Monkey Sanctuary

Giants Hedge
Kilminorth
117
TRELASKE LA
West Looe River
B3253
SUNRISING EST
Sch
East Looe
117
MAY LA
Millendreath

PL13
Looe
Discovery Ctr
P
STATION RD
BODRIGAN RD
Sch
Plaidy
Millendreath Beach

POLPERRO RD
QUAY RD
PO
i
P
PO
BULLER ST
BAY VIEW RD
HA LA
Looe Bay

A387
West Looe
WEST LODGE WLL
Mus
Lby
HANNAFORE RD
LOOE

Tencreek
TENCREEK CVN AND CAMPING PK
Portlooe
Hannafore
PORTVAN RD
MARINE DR

Hendersick Farm
P
117

Portnadler Bay
St George's or Looe Island

Hore Stone
PL13

23 A 24 B 25 C 26 D 27 E 28 F

For full street detail of the highlighted area see page 117.

64

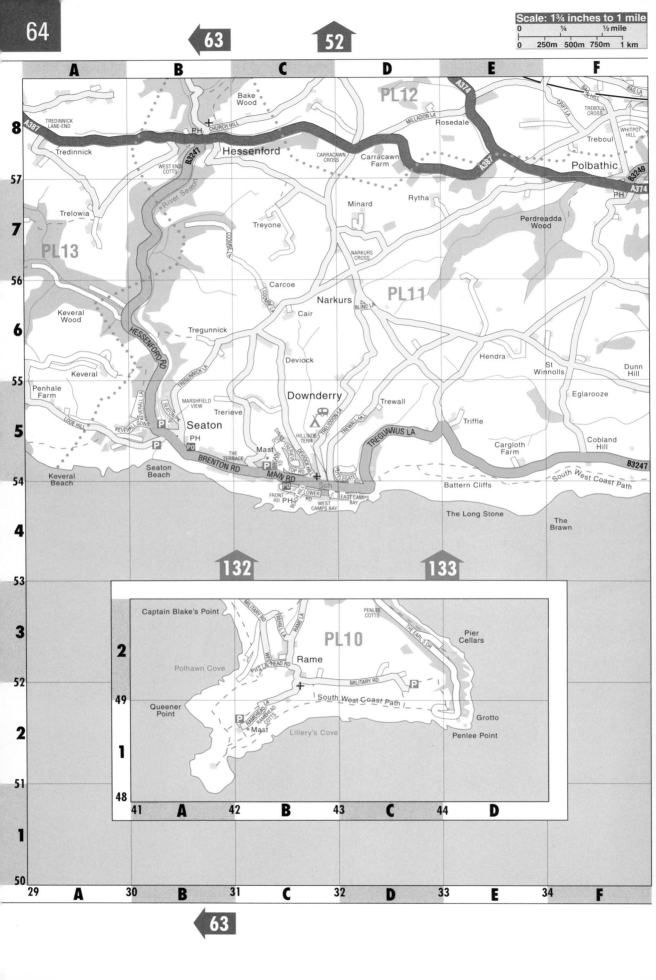

St Germans

B3249
GALLERY LA
BAG LA
NEWPORT
FORE ST
ELDERBERRY DR
CHURCH ST
Port Eliot House
QUARRY ST 1
QUARRY LA 2
GAYS LA 3
MILL LA 4
THE S/R WILLIAMS 5
MOYLES ALMSHOUSES
Sch
FAIRFIELD
LOWER FAIRFIELD
Haparanda
OLD QUAY LA

1 TIDDY CL
2 TREBOUL WAY
3 ELIOT DR
4 TREGALISTER GDNS
5 SUDDENBEAKE TERR
6 NUT TREE HILL

St Germans Quay

Grove

MARWELL LA

ELMGATE CROSSWAYS

Elm Gate

Trehan

126

PL12

Mon

Wivelscombe

Shillingham Manor

8

Hotel

KELLOW PK

Ince Castle

57

7

Trewin

Tredis

Sheviock Wood

Black Rock

St Germans or Lynher River

126

Bulland Quay

56

PL11

Haye

HAY LA

Sheviock

GEORGES LA

CHURCH ROW

Berry Down

Erth Hill

Erth Barton

Clift Quay

Clift

6

Dunn Hill

Tredrossel

B3247

HORSEPOOL LA
HORSEPOOL RD

SHEVIOCK LA

A374

55

Trewrickle Farm

The Beacon

KIMBERLEY FOSTER CL 1
WEST LA 2
DAWNAY TERR 3
THE TERR 4

CROSS PK

B3247

Crafthole

COOMBE LA

Trethill

TRETHILL LA

CROOKEDOR LA

Scraesdon Fort

HOLLONG PK

PH

ANTONY HILL

Antony

Sch

ABBOTS...

PO

Cemy

5

PH

Hotel

Hotel

Wolsdon House

54

Old Coastguard Cotts

THE TERR

FINNYGOOK LA

WHITSAND BAY VIEW

CAREW CL

BURNS VIEW

PO

Cross

Portwrinkle

P

CH

Trethill Cliffs

Blerrick

B3247

Lower Tregantle

SUNWELL LA

JACK'S LA

ST JOHNS LA

PH

MOWHAY MDW 1
CHURCH LA 2

4

DANGER AREA

Tregantle Fort

OLDAPPLE LA

Ranges

53

Higher Tregantle Farm

B3247

PL10

WITHNOE LA

BRAKE LA

Tregantle Cliff

P

Freathy

Withnoe

3

Sharrow Point

132

CLIFF LA

Tregonhawke

52

MILITARY RD

Mon

2

Whitsand Bay

51

1

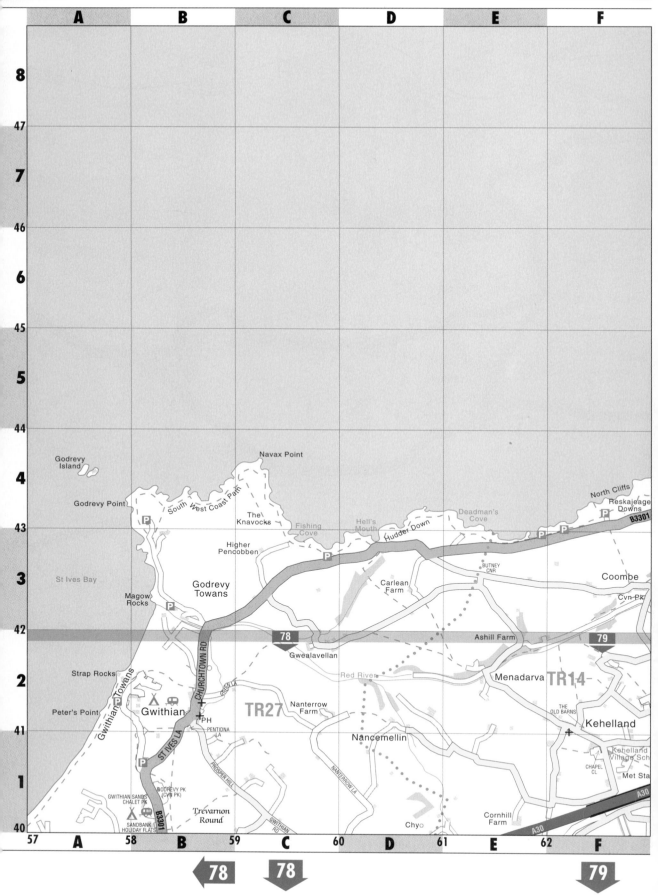

Godrevy
Island

Navax Point

Godrevy Point

South West Coast Path

The Knavocks

Fishing Cove

Hell's Mouth

Hudder Down

Deadman's Cove

North Cliffs
Reskajeage Downs

B3301

St Ives Bay

Higher Pencobben

Godrevy Towans

Butney CNR

Carlean Farm

Coombe

Cvn Pk

Magow Rocks

78

Gwealavellan

Ashill Farm

79

Menadarva

TR14

Strap Rocks

Red River

TR27

Nanterrow Farm

THE OLD BARNS

Kehelland

Peter's Point

Gwithian Towans

Gwithian

PH

PENTIDNA LA

GREEN LA

CHURCHTOWN RD

Nancemellin

CHAPEL CL

Kehelland Village Sch

Met Sta

ST IVES LA

PROSPER HILL

NANTERROW LA

Godrevy Pk (Cvn Pk)

Gwithian Sands Chalet Pk

B3301

Trevarnon Round

GWITHIAN RD

Chyo

Cornhill Farm

Sandbank Holiday Flats

A30

57   A   58   B   59   C   60   D   61   E   62   F

78   78   79

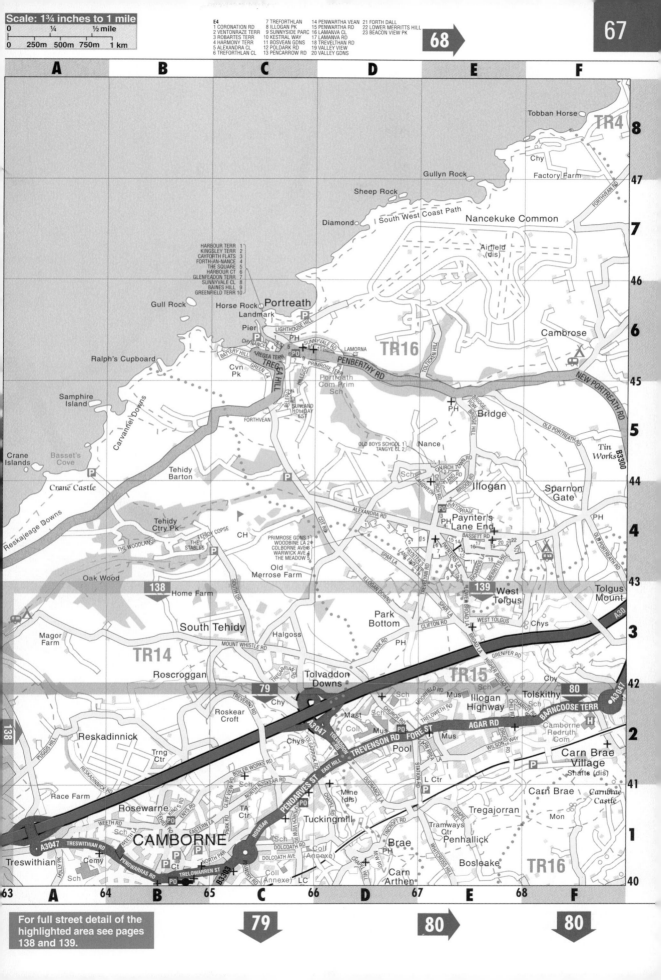

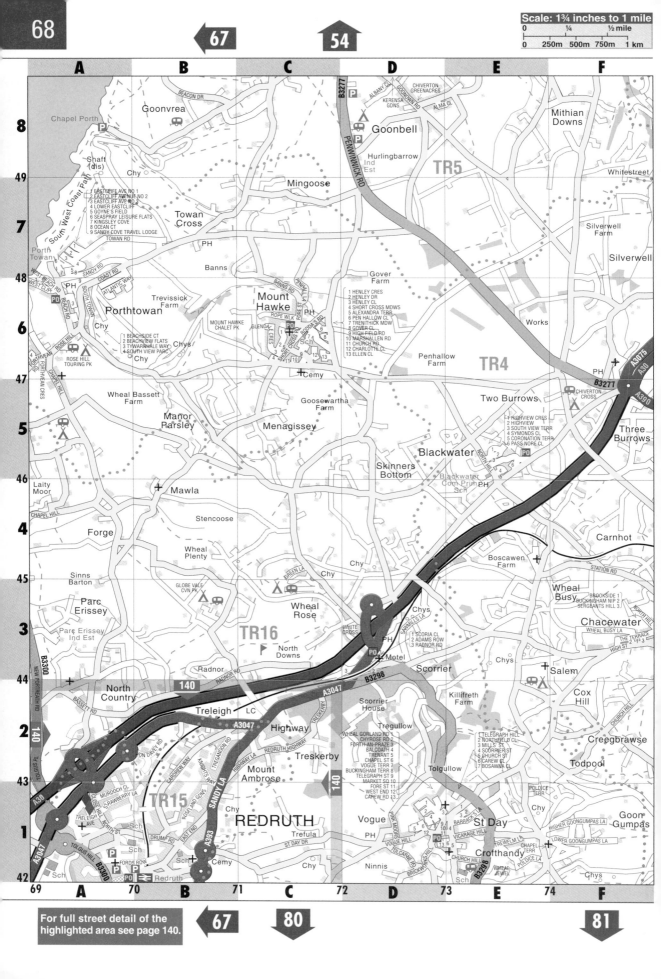

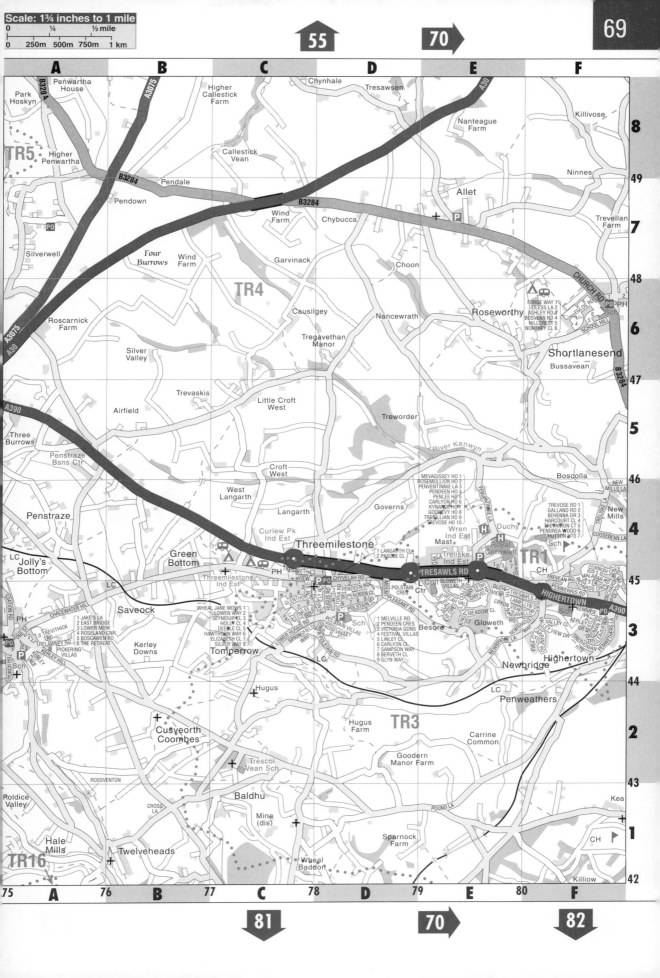

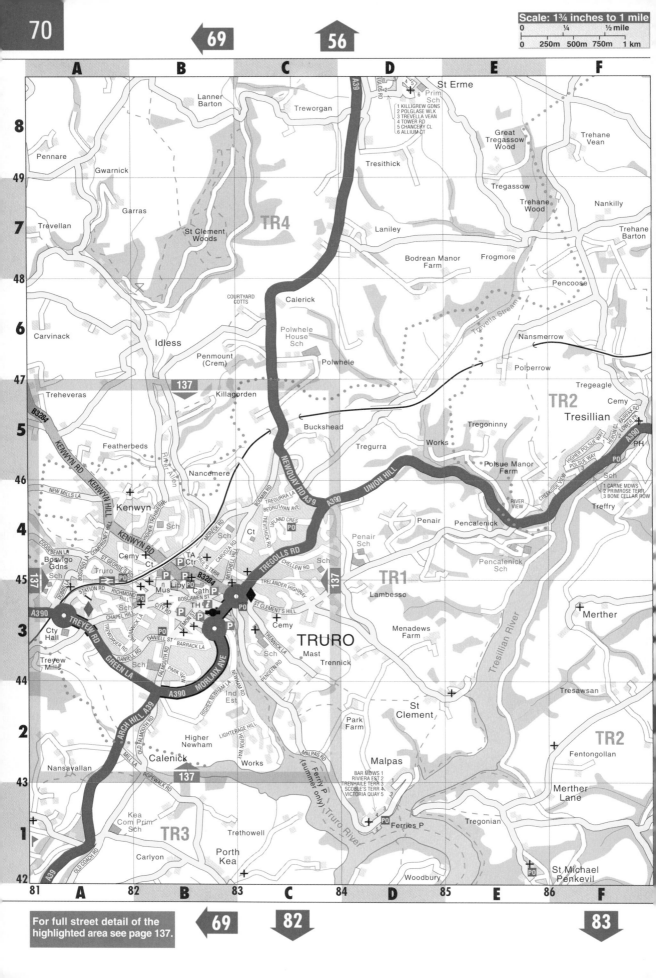

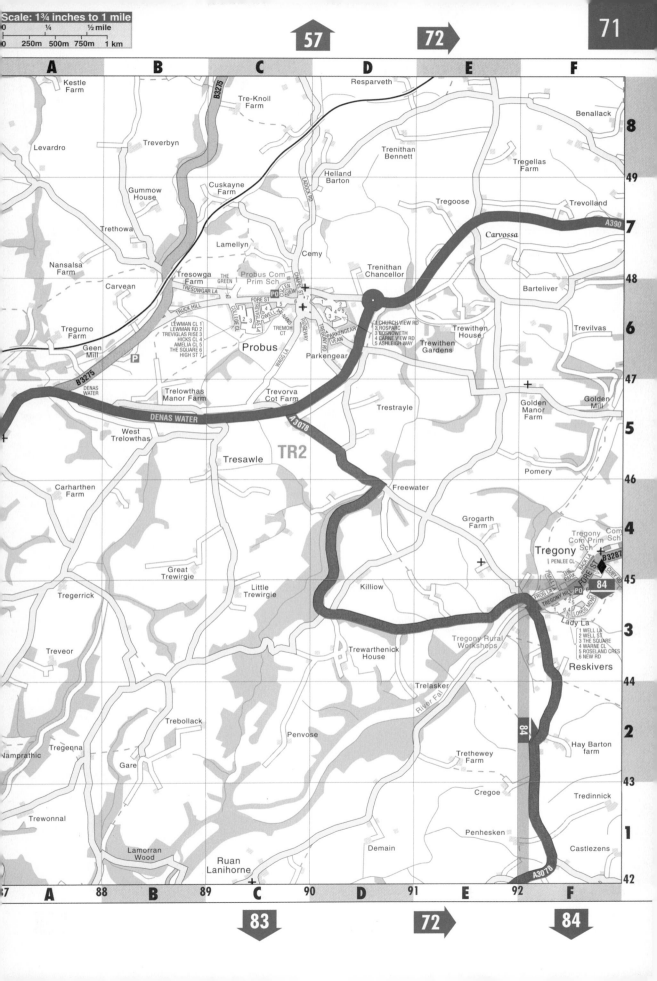

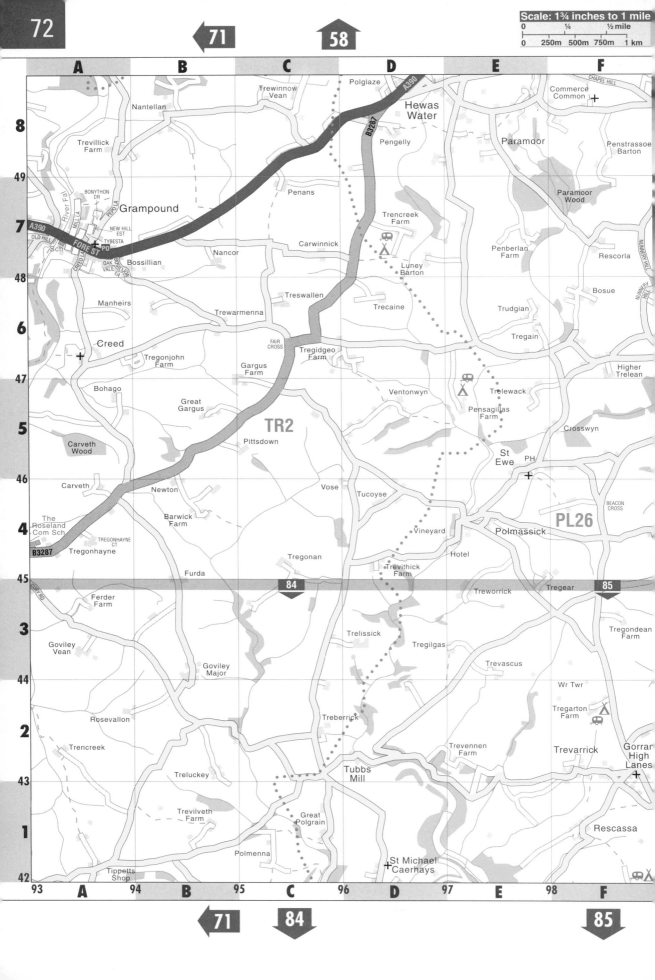

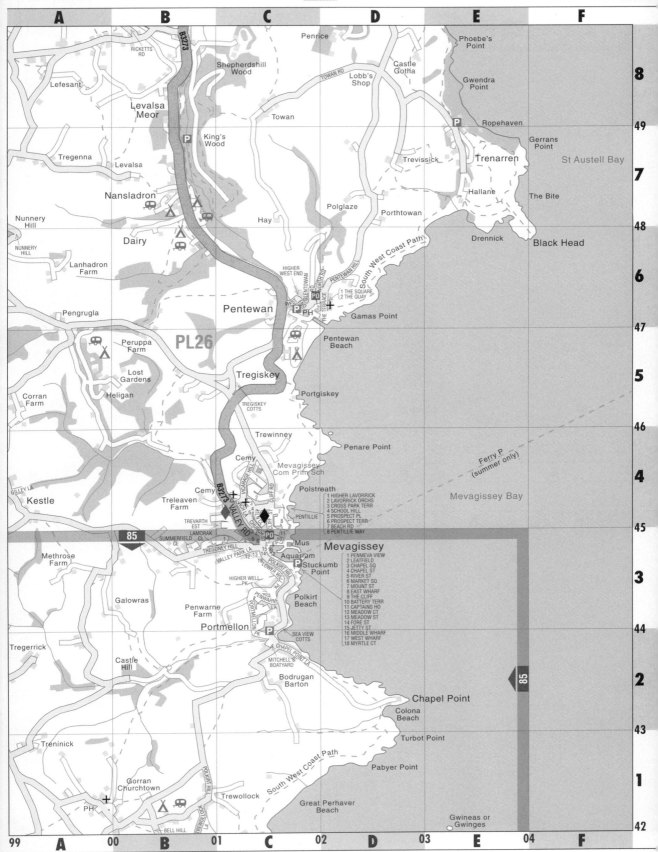

Scale: 1¾ inches to 1 mile

0 ¼ ½ mile
0 250m 500m 750m 1 km

	A	B	C	D	E	F

RICKETTS RD

B3273

Penrice

Shepherdshill Wood

Phoebe's Point

Lefesant

Levalsa Meor

King's Wood

TOWAN RD

Castle Gotha

Gwendra Point

8

Tregenna

Levalsa

Towan

Trevissick

Trenarren

Ropehaven

Gerrans Point

St Austell Bay

49

7

Nansladron

Hay

Polglaze

Porthtowan

Hallane

The Bite

Nunnery Hill

NUNNERY HILL

Dairy

Drennick

Black Head

48

Lanhadron Farm

HIGHER WEST END

PENTEWAN HILL

NORTH RD

South West Coast Path

6

Pengrugla

Pentewan

WEST END

GLENTOWAN

PD

PH

P

THE TERRACE

1 THE SQUARE
2 THE QUAY

PL26

Pentewan Beach

Gamas Point

47

Peruppa Farm

Tregiskey

Portgiskey

5

Corran Farm

Lost Gardens

Heligan

TREGISKEY COTTS

Trewinney

Penare Point

46

Cemy

Mevagissey Com Prim Sch

Polstreath

1 HIGHER LAVORRICK
2 LAVORRICK ORCHS
3 CROSS PARK TERR
4 SCHOOL HILL
5 PROSPECT PL
6 PROSPECT TERR
7 BEACH RD
8 PENTILLIE WAY

Ferry P (summer only)

Mevagissey Bay

4

Kestle

GILLEY LA

B3273

Cemy

VICARAGE HILL

CLIFF RD

PENTILLIE

45

Treleaven Farm

TREVARTH EST

VALLEY RD

CHURCH ST

PD

Mus

85

SUMMERFIELD CL

LAMORAK CL

TREGONEY HILL

VALLEY PARK LA

POLKIRT HILL

Mevagissey

Aquarium

Stuckumb Point

P

1 PENMEVA VIEW
2 LEATFIELD
3 CHAPEL SQ
4 CHAPEL ST
5 RIVER ST
6 MARKET SQ
7 MOUNT ST
8 EAST WHARF
9 THE CLIFF
10 BATTERY TERR
11 CAPTAINS HO
12 MEADOW CT
13 MEADOW ST
14 FORE ST
15 JETTY ST
16 MIDDLE WHARF
17 WEST WHARF
18 MYRTLE CT

3

Methrose Farm

Galowras

HIGHER WELL PK

PENWARNE LA

PORTMELLON PK

Polkirt Beach

Penwarne Farm

Portmellon

P

SEA VIEW COTTS

44

Tregerrick

Castle Hill

CHAPEL POINT LA

MITCHELL'S BOATYARD

Bodrugan Barton

85

Chapel Point

Colona Beach

2

43

Treninick

POLKIRT HILL

THREWOLLOCK

Gorran Churchtown

PH

Trewollock

South West Coast Path

Great Perhaver Beach

Turbot Point

Pabyer Point

Gwineas or Gwinges

1

BELL HILL

42

Scale: 4 miles to 1 inch

0   1   2   3   4 miles
0 1 2 3 4 5 6 7 km

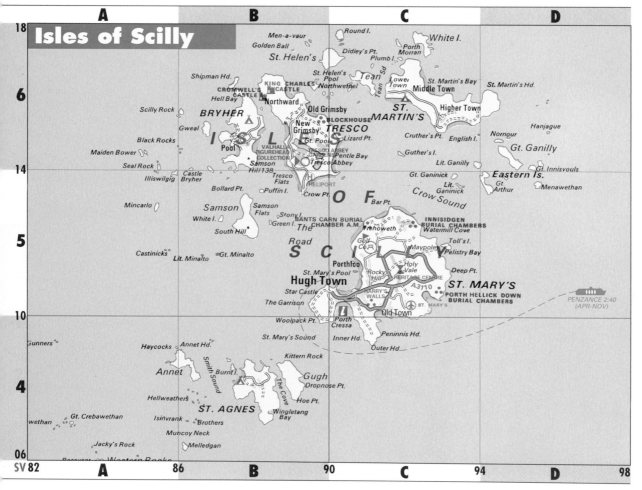

Isles of Scilly

Men-a-vaur · Round I. · White I.
Golden Ball · Didley's Pt. · Porth Morran
St. Helen's · Plumb I.
Shipman Hd. · St. Helen's Pool · Northwethel · Tean Sd. · Lower Town · St. Martin's Bay · St. Martin's Hd.
KING CHARLES CASTLE · Middle Town
CROMWELL'S CASTLE · Northward · Old Grimsby · ST. MARTIN'S · Higher Town
Hell Bay · BLOCKHOUSE
Scilly Rock · BRYHER · New Grimsby · TRESCO
Gweal · Lizard Pt. · Cruther's Pt. · English I. · Hanjague
Black Rocks · ISLES · Gt. Pool · Pentle Bay · Guther's I. · Norngur · Gt. Ganilly
Maiden Bower · VALHALLA FIGUREHEAD COLLECTION · TRESCO ABBEY GARDENS · Lit. Ganilly · Gt. Innisvouls · Eastern Is.
Seal Rock · Samson Hill 138 · Tresco Abbey · Gt. Arthur · Menawethan
Illiswillig · Castle Bryher · Tresco Flats · HELIPORT · Gt. Ganinick · Lit. Ganinick · Gt.
Mincarlo · Bollard Pt. · Puffin I. · Crow Pt. · OF · Bar Pt. · Crow Sound
Samson · White I. · Samson Flats · Stony I. · BANTS CARN BURIAL CHAMBER A.M. · Treboweth · INNISIDGEN BURIAL CHAMBERS
Castinicks · Lit. Minalto · Gt. Minalto · Green I. · The · Golf Co. · Watermill Cove · Toll's I. · Pelistry Bay
SCILLY · Road · Porthloo · Maypole · Deep Pt.
St. Mary's Pool · Rocky Hill · Holy Vale · HERITAGE CENTRE
Hugh Town · A.3710 · ST. MARY'S
Star Castle · HARRY'S WALLS · PORTH HELLICK DOWN BURIAL CHAMBERS
The Garrison · ST. MARY'S · PENZANCE 2:40 (APR-NOV)
Woolpack Pt. · Porth Cressa · Old Town
Gunners · St. Mary's Sound · Inner Hd. · Peninnis Hd.
Haycocks · Annet Hd. · Kittern Rock · Outer Hd.
Annet · Smith Sound · Burnt I. · Gugh · Dropnose Pt.
Hellweathers · The Cove · Hoe Pt. · Wingletang Bay
wethan · Gt. Crebawethan · Isinvrank · ST. AGNES
· Brothers
Muncoy Neck · Melledgan
Jacky's Rock · Western Rocks
Beacon

SV 82 · A · 86 · B · 90 · C · 94 · D · 98

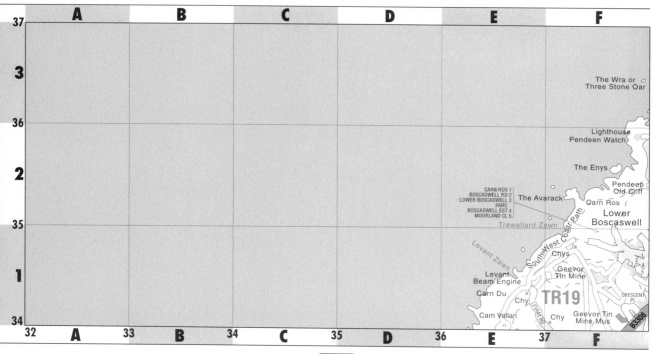

The Wra or Three Stone Oar

Lighthouse Pendeen Watch

The Enys

Pendeen Old Cliff

CARN ROS 1
BOSCASWELL RD 2
LOWER BOSCASWELL 3
PARC
BOSCASWELL EST 4
MOORLAND CL 5.
· The Avarack · Carn Ros · Lower Boscaswell

Trewellard Zawn

Levant Zawn · South West Coast Path · Chys

Levant Beam Engine · Geevor Tin Mine
Carn Du · Chy · TR19 · CRESCENT PL
Carn Vellan · Chy · Geevor Tin Mine Mus · B3306

32 · A · 33 · B · 34 · C · 35 · D · 36 · E · 37 · F

Scale: 1¾ inches to 1 mile

0   ¼   ½ mile
0 250m 500m 750m 1 km

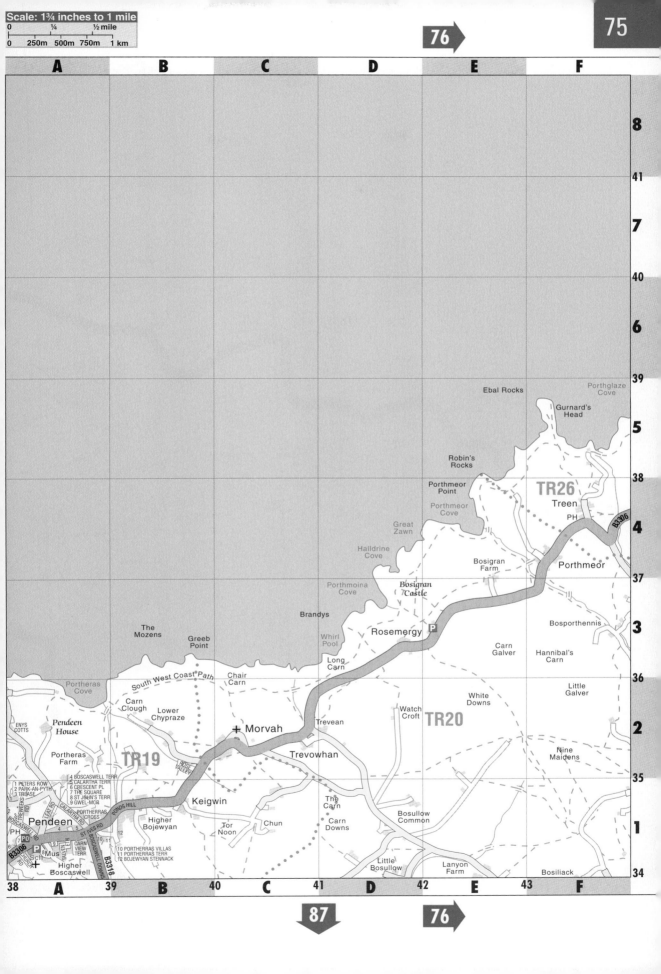

A B C D E F

8

41

7

40

6

39

Porthglaze
Cove

Ebal Rocks

Gurnard's
Head

5

Robin's
Rocks

Porthmeor
Point

TR26

Treen

38

PH

Porthmeor
Cove

B3306

4

Great
Zawn

Porthmeor

Halldrine
Cove

Bosigran
Farm

37

Porthmoina
Cove

Bosigran
Castle

Bosporthennis

Brandys

3

The
Mozens

Whirl
Pool

Rosemergy

P

Carn
Galver

Hannibal's
Carn

Greeb
Point

Long
Carn

Portheras
Cove

South West Coast Path

Chair
Carn

Little
Galver

36

Carn
Clough

Watch
Croft

White
Downs

Pendeen
House

Lower
Chypraze

TR20

2

ENYS
COTTS

Morvah

Trevean

Portheras
Farm

TR19

Trevowhan

Nine
Maidens

35

1 Peters Row
2 Park-an-Pyth
3 Trease

4 Boscaswell Terr.
5 Calartha Terr
6 Crescent Pl
7 The Square
8 St John's Terr
9 Gwel-Mor

ROSE VALLEY

Keigwin

The
Carn

Bosullow
Common

Pendeen

PH

PO

Higher
Bojewyan

PONDS HILL

Tor
Noon

Chun

Carn
Downs

1

PORTHERAS CROSS

ST IVES RD

10 Portheras Villas
11 Portheras Terr
12 Bojewyan Stennack

Little
Bosullow

Lanyon
Farm

Bosiliack

P

Mus

B3306

Higher
Boscaswell

B3318

34

38 A 39 B 40 C 41 D 42 E 43 F

Scale: 1¾ inches to 1 mile

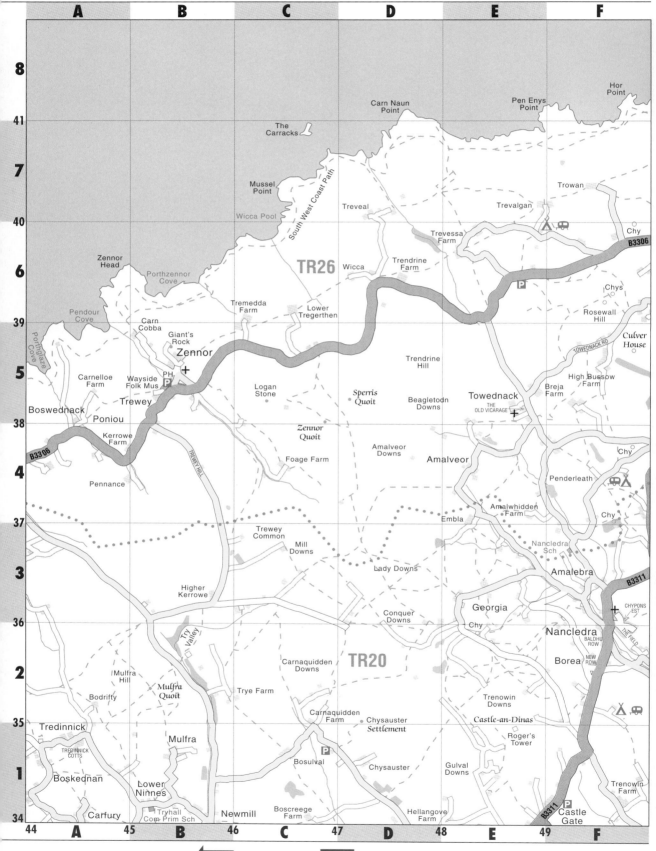

Carn Naun Point

Pen Enys Point

Hor Point

The Carracks

Trowan

Mussel Point

Trevalgan

Chy

B3306

Wicca Pool

South West Coast Path

TR26

Treveal

Trevessa Farm

Chys

Zennor Head

Wicca

Trendrine Farm

Rosewall Hill

Porthzennor Cove

Tremedda Farm

Lower Tregerthen

TOWEDNACK RD

Culver House

Pendour Cove

Carn Cobba

Giant's Rock

Trendrine Hill

High Bussow Farm

Porthglaze Cove

Zennor

Towednack
THE OLD VICARAGE

Breja Farm

Carnelloe Farm

Wayside Folk Mus
PH

Logan Stone

Sperris Quoit

Beagletodn Downs

Chy

Boswednack

Trewey

Poniou

Zennor Quoit

Amalveor Downs

Amalveor

Penderleath

Kerrowe Farm

Foage Farm

Chy

B3306

Pennance

Amalwhidden Farm

Embla

Nancledra Sch

Trewey Common

Mill Downs

Lady Downs

Amalebra

B3311

Higher Kerrowe

Conquer Downs

Georgia

CHYPONS EST

Try Valley

Chy

Nancledra

BALDHU ROW

TR20

Borea

THE FIELD

NEW ROW

Mulfra Hill

Mulfra Quoit

Carnaquidden Downs

Bodrifty

Trye Farm

Trenowin Downs

Castle-an-Dinas

Tredinnick

Carnaquidden Farm

Chysauster Settlement

Roger's Tower

Trenowin Farm

TREDINNICK COTTS

Mulfra

Bosulval

Chysauster

Gulval Downs

Boskednan

Lower Ninnes

Boscreege Farm

Hellangove Farm

B3311

Castle Gate

Carfury

Tryhall Com Prim Sch

Newmill

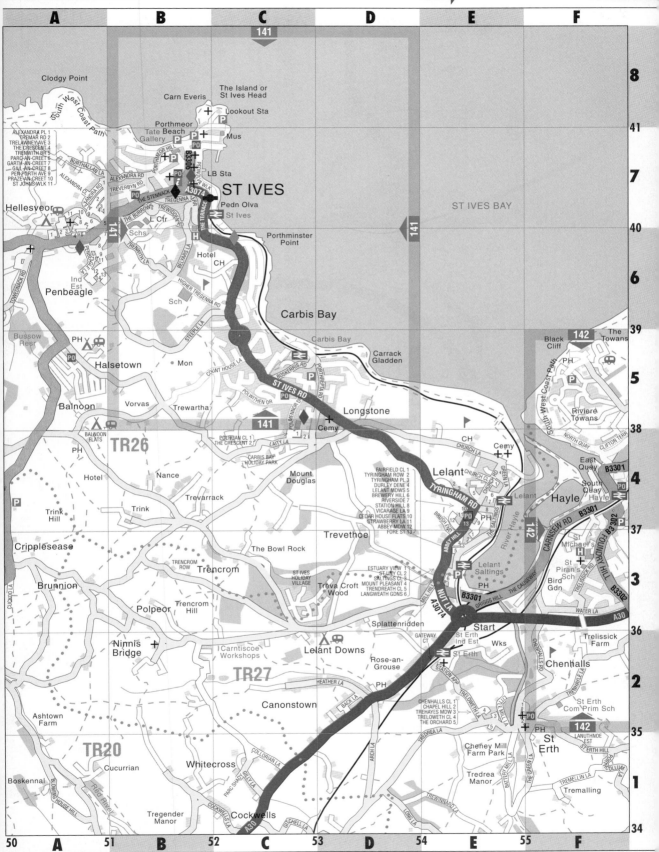

A   B   C   D   E   F

141

8

Clodgy Point

South West Coast Path

41

Carn Everis

The Island or
St Ives Head

Lookout Sta

Porthmeor
Tate Beach
Gallery

Mus

ALEXANDRA PL 1
TREMAR RD 2
TRELAWNEY AVE 3
THE CRESCENT 4
TRENWITH BR 5
PARC-AN-CREET 6
GARTH-AN-CREET 7
GILL-AN-CREET 8
PEN-FORTH AVE 9
PRAZE-VAN-CREET 10
ST JOHNS WLK 11

7

BURTHALLAN LA

PO

ALEXANDRA RD

TREVERBYN RD

PORTHMEOR HILL

B3306

PENOLVA WLK

LB Sta

Hellesveor

ALEXANDRA CT

TRENWITH LA

THE STENNACK

TREGENNA

A3074

PO

ST IVES

Pedn Olva

St Ives

40

141

ST IVES BAY

Penbeagle

Ind
Est

THE BURROWS

THE TERRACE

Porthminster
Point

Hotel
CH

HIGHER TREGENNA RD

Sch

6

Bussow
Resr

PH

Halsetown

STEEP LA

Mon

COUNT HOUSE LA

Carbis Bay

Carbis Bay

Carrack
Gladden

Black
Cliff

142

The
Towans

39

PH

P

PO

Balnoon

Vorvas

Trewartha

BOSKERRIS RD

ST IVES RD

PORTHREPTA RD

PO

Longstone

POLWITHEN DR

141

Cemy

North Quay

Riviere
Towans

South-West Coast Path

CLIFTON TERR

5

38

TR26

BALNOON
FLATS

PH

Hotel

Nance

Trevarrack

POLRUAN CL 1
THE CRESCENT 2

LAITY LA

CARBIS BAY
HOLIDAY PARK

Mount
Douglas

FAIRFIELD CL 1
TYRINGHAM ROW 2
TYRINGHAM PL 3
DURLEY DENE 4
LELANT MDWS 5
BREWERY HILL 6
RIVERSIDE 7
STATION HILL 8
VICARAGE LA 9
CEDAR HOUSE FLATS 10
STRAWBERRY LA 11
ABBEY MDW 12
FORE ST 13

CHURCH LA

Lelant

TYRINGHAM RD

Cemy

CH

CHURCH RD

GREEN LA

Lelant

East
Quay

South
Quay

B3301

Hayle
Hayle

B3301

B3302

P

4

37

Cripplesease

Trink
Hill

Trink

Trevethoe

THE BOWL ROCK

TRENCROM
ROW

Trencrom
Hill

St Ives
Holiday
Village

Treva Croft
Wood

ESTUARY VIEW
ST UNY CL 2
SALTINGS CL 3
MOUNT PLEASANT 4
TRENDREATH CL 5
LANGWEATH GDNS 6

River Hayle

ABBEY HILL

BRUSH END

Lelant
Saltings

PH

THE CAUSEWAY

CARNSEW RD

142

FOUNDRY HILL

St
Michael's

St
Piran's
Sch

Bird
Gdn

TRELISSICK RD

B3302

WATER LA

A30

3

Brunnion

Polpeor

Trencrom

Splattenridden

P

B3301

GRIGGS HILL

NUT LA

Start

St Erth
Ind Est

Wks

Trelissick
Farm

Chenhalls

36

Ninnis
Bridge

Carntiscoe
Workshops

Lelant Downs

Rose-an-
Grouse

PH

GATEWAY
CT

STATION APP

St Erth

CHENHALLS RD

St Erth
Com Prim Sch

TR27

HEATHER LA

BACK LA

CHENHALLS CL 1
CHAPEL HILL 2
TREHAYES MDW 3
TRELOWETH CL 4
THE ORCHARD 5

GREEN LA

St Erth

PH

PO

142

2

Ashtown
Farm

TR20

Cucurrian

Canonstown

COLLORIAN LA

PARC-SHADY GILLY LA

Whitecross

TREDREA LA

ARCH LA

LONG LA

TREWINNARD RD

PH

Cheney Mill
Farm Park

Tredrea
Manor

St
Erth

LANUTHNOE
EST

St Erth
Hill

GREEN LA

COLLUM

35

Boskennal

BUSSOW HOUSE HILL

Red River

Tregender
Manor

Cockwells

COCKWELLS LA

CHAPEL LA

A30

Tremalling

TREMELLIN LA

BITTERN MILL LA

1

34

50   A   51   B   52   C   53   D   54   E   55   F

89

78

For full street detail of the
highlighted area see pages
141 and 142.

A6
1 CHY-AN-DOUR CL
2 HELLESVEAN
3 HELLESVEAN CL
4 PARC-AN-STAMPS
5 CROWS-AN-EGLOS
6 PARC-AN-FORTH
7 PENBEAGLE TERR
8 PENBEAGLE CRES
9 CORVA RD
10 PRIORS CL
11 CORVA RD
12 PORTHIA RD
13 CARNSTABBA RD
14 ALAN HARVEY CL

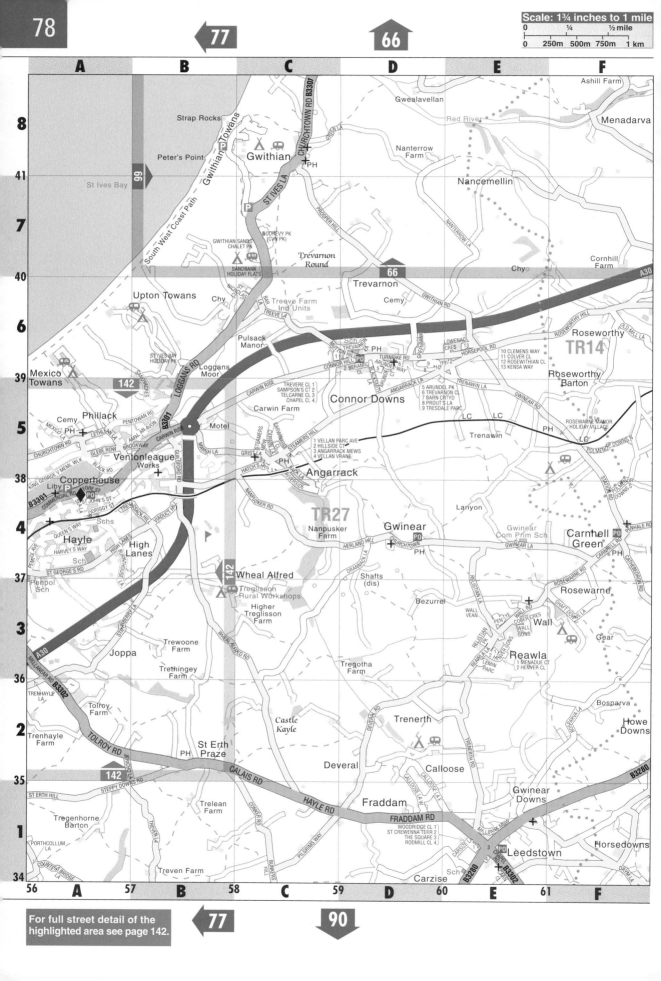

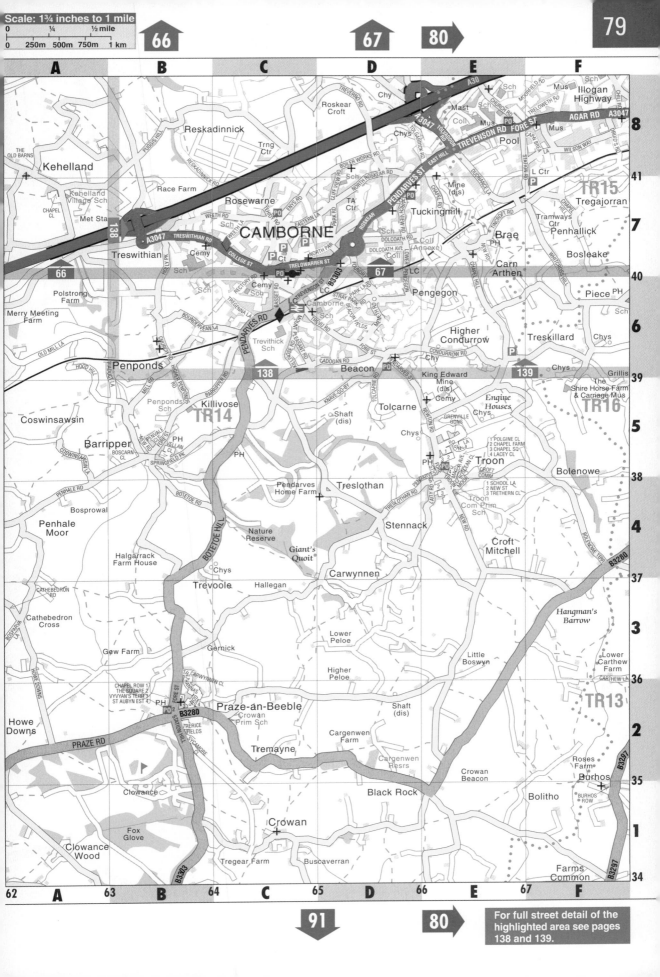

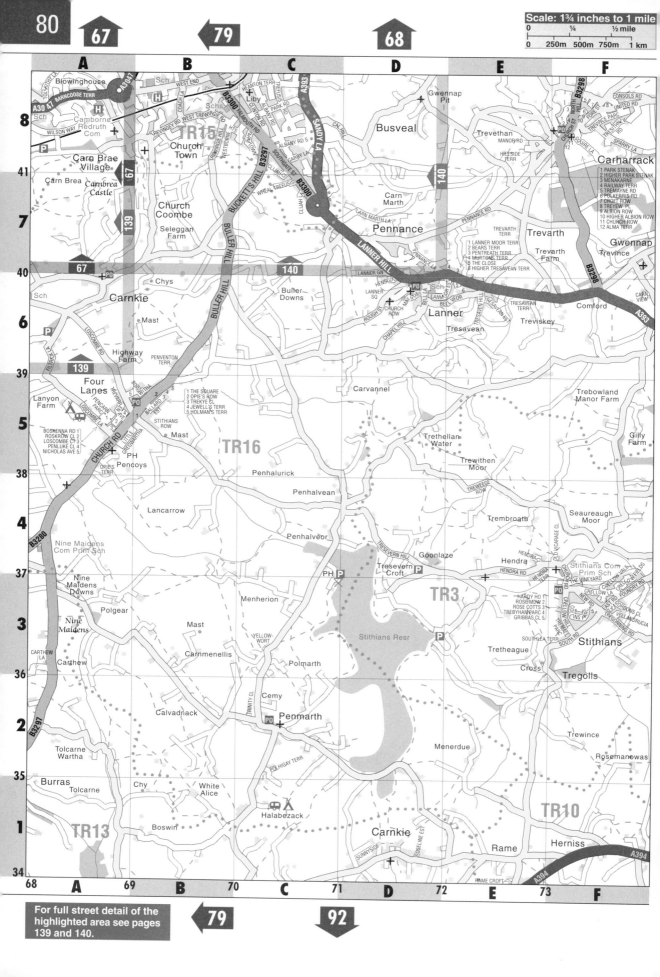

Scale: 1¾ inches to 1 mile

For full street detail of the
highlighted area see pages
139 and 140.

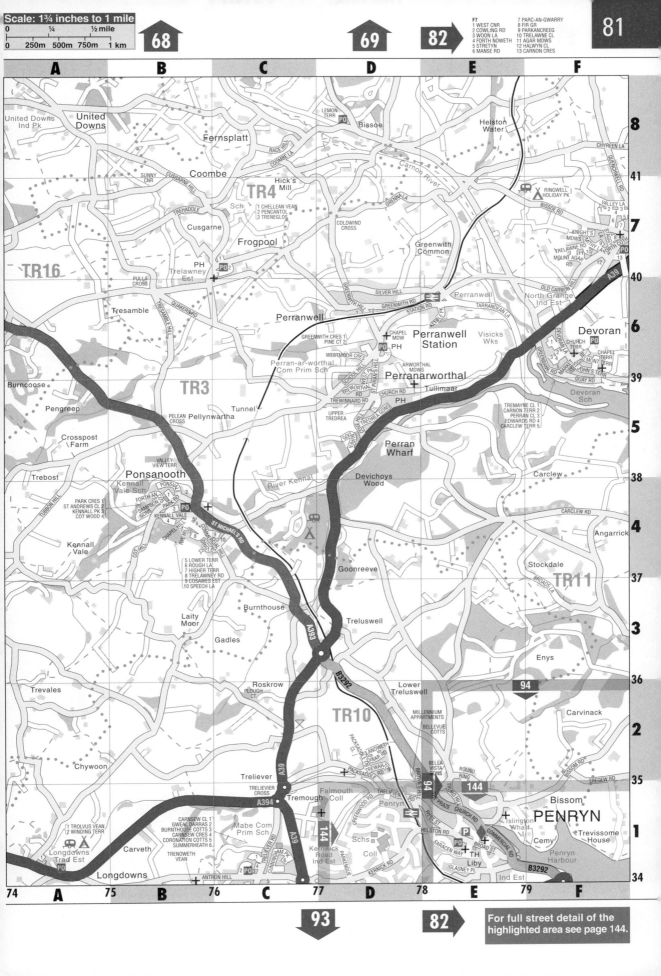

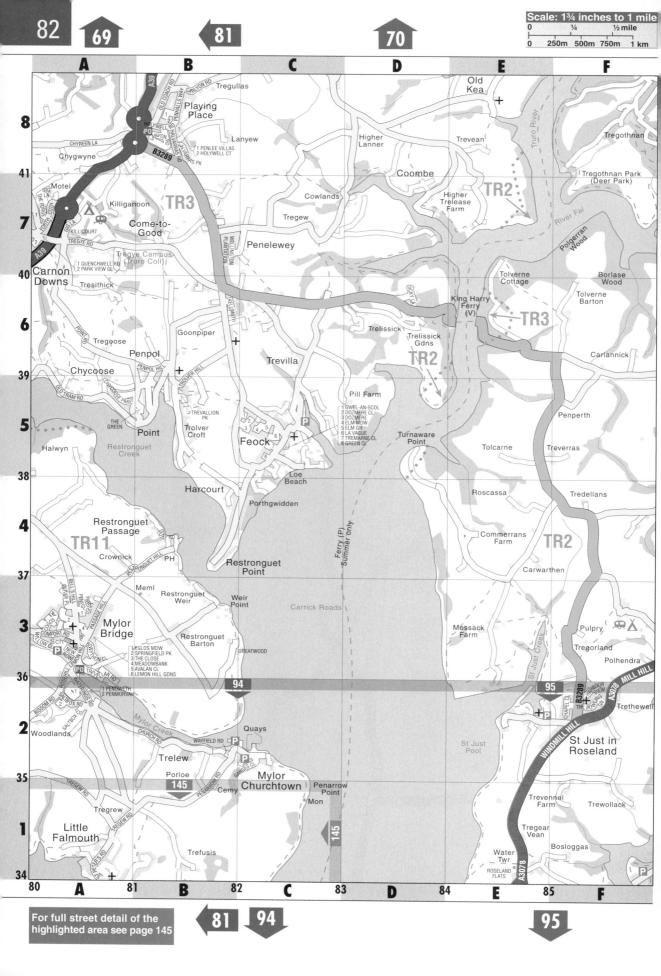

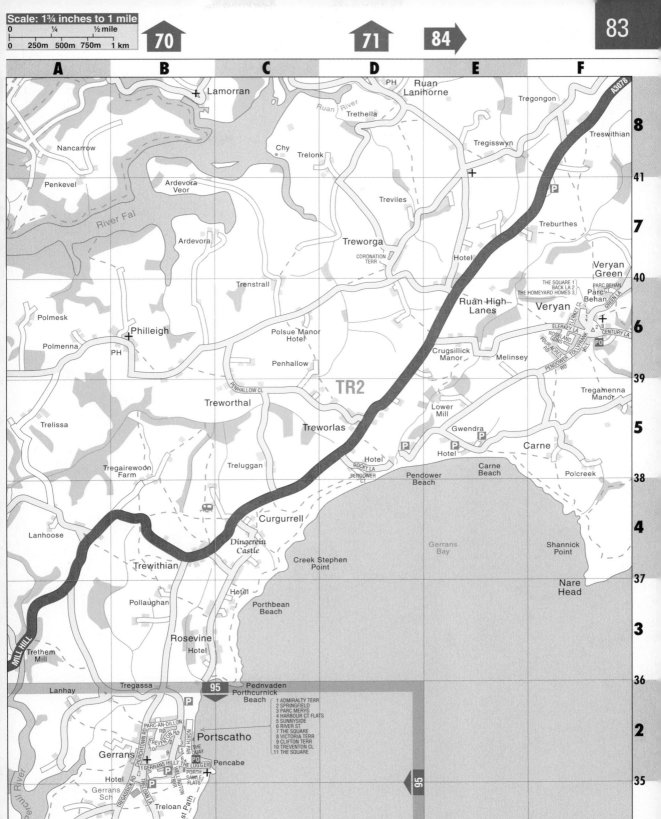

Lamorran

Nancarrow

Penkevel

Ardevora Veor

Ardevora

River Fal

Polmesk

Polmenna

Philleigh

PH

Trelissa

Tregairewoon Farm

Trewithian

Lanhoose

MILL HILL

Trethem Mill

Lanhay

Tregassa

Gerrans

Hotel

Gerrans Sch

Tregassick

PH

Ruan Lanihorne

Trethella

Chy

Trelonk

Trelonk

Trentrall

Treworga

CORONATION TERR

Polsue Manor Hotel

Penhallow

PENHALLOW CL

Treworthal

Treworlas

Treluggan

Dingerein Castle

Pollaughan

Rosevine

Hotel

PARC-AN-DILLON RD

TREVERTON RD

NORTH PAR

CHURCHTOWN RD

WELLINGTON TERR

TREGASSICK RD

TRELOELLA

Portscatho

PO

THE LUGGER

PORTH SAWLE FLATS

Pencabe

Treloan

South West Coast Path

Tregisswyn

Treviles

Hotel

Ruan High Lanes

Crugsillick Manor

Lower Mill

Hotel

ROCKY LA

Hotel

PENDOWER CL

Curgurrell

Creek Stephen Point

Hotel

Porthbean Beach

Pednvaden

Porthcurnick Beach

95

1 ADMIRALTY TERR
2 SPRINGFIELD
3 PARC MERYS
4 HARBOUR CT FLATS
5 SUNNYSIDE
6 RIVER ST
7 THE SQUARE
8 VICTORIA TERR
9 CLIFTON TERR
10 TREVENTON CL
11 THE SQUARE

Tregongon

Treswithian

Treburthes

Veryan Green

Parc Behan

PARC BEHAN

THE SQUARE 1
BACK LA 2
THE HOMEYARD HOMES 3

Veryan

ELERKEY CL

ROSELAND GDNS

FOUR ACRES RD

PENDOWER RD

TOLLYBRANK

CENTURY LA

GREEN LA

MILL RD

PO

Melinsey

Tregamenna Manor

Gwendra

Carne

Carne Beach

Polcreek

Pendower Beach

Gerrans Bay

Shannick Point

Nare Head

TR2

A3078

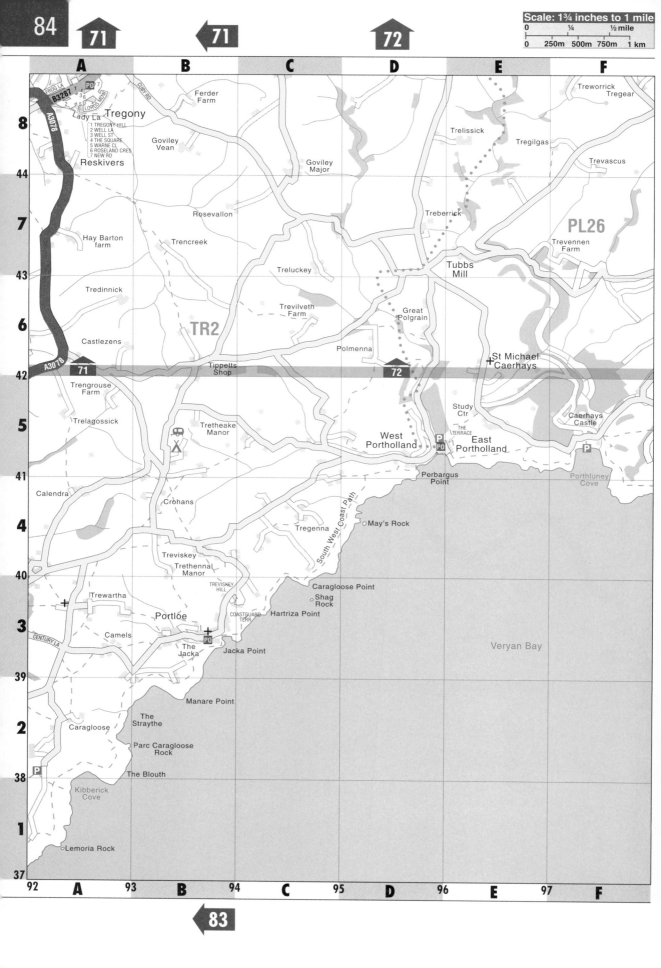

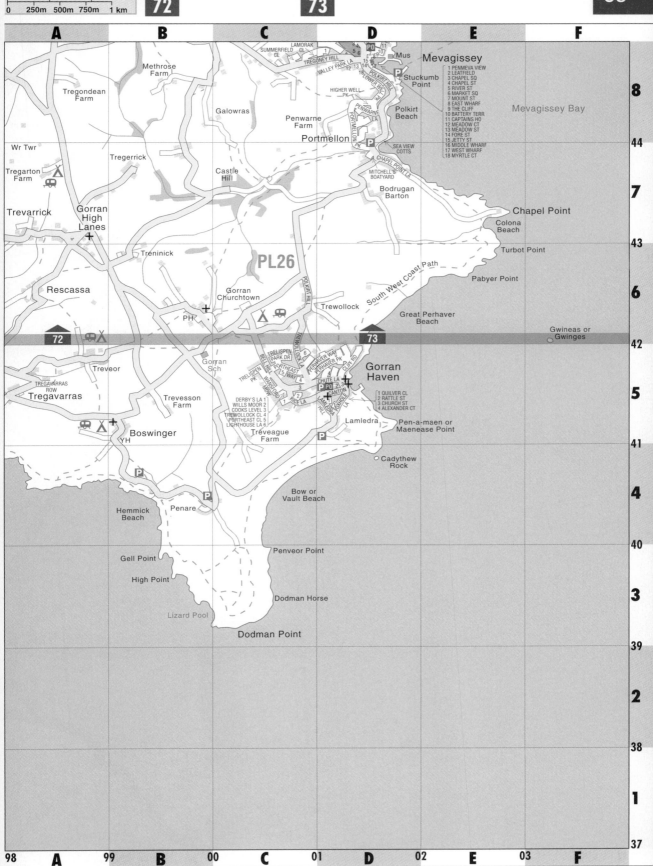

Mevagissey

1 PENMEVA VIEW
2 LEATFIELD
3 CHAPEL SQ
4 CHAPEL ST
5 RIVER SQ
6 MARKET SQ
7 MOUNT ST
8 EAST WHARF
9 THE CLIFF
10 BATTERY TERR
11 CAPTAINS HO
12 MEADOW CT
13 MEADOW ST
14 FORE ST
15 JETTY ST
16 MIDDLE WHARF
17 WEST WHARF
18 MYRTLE CT

Tregondean Farm
Methrose Farm
Galowras
Penwarne Farm
Wr Twr
Tregarton Farm
Tregerrick
Castle Hill
Portmellon
Stuckumb Point
Polkirt Beach
Mus
SEA VIEW COTTS
Mevagissey Bay

Trevarrick
Gorran High Lanes
Treninick
PL26
Bodrugan Barton
Chapel Point
Colona Beach
Turbot Point

Rescassa
Gorran Churchtown
Trewollock
MITCHELL'S BOATYARD
South West Coast Path
Pabyer Point
Great Perhaver Beach

PH
Gorran Sch
Trelispen Park Dr
Gorran Haven
Gwineas or Gwinges

Treveor
Tregavarras Row
Tregavarras
Trevesson Farm
Trévéague Farm
Lamledra
1 QUILVER CL
2 RATTLE ST
3 CHURCH ST
4 ALEXANDER CT
Pen-a-maen or Maenease Point

Boswinger
YH
Cadythew Rock

Hemmick Beach
Penare
Bow or Vault Beach

Gell Point
Penveor Point

High Point
Dodman Horse
Lizard Pool
Dodman Point

Scale: 1¾ inches to 1 mile

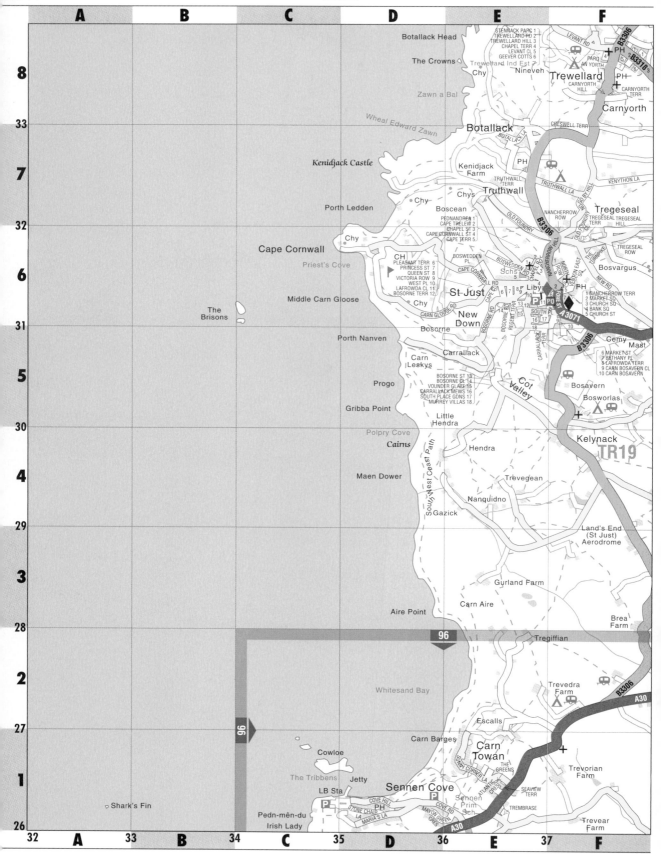

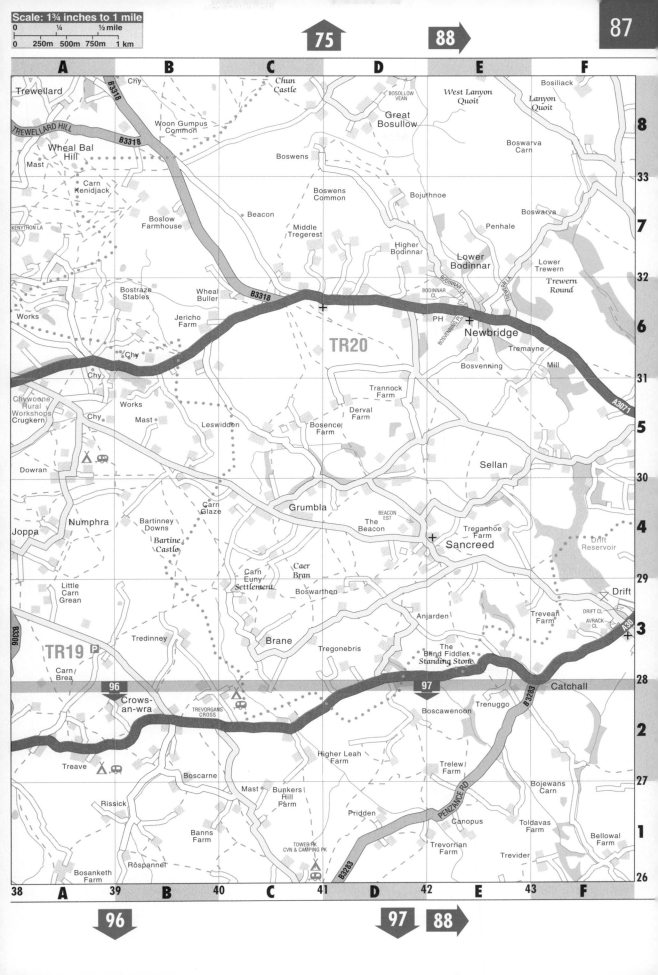

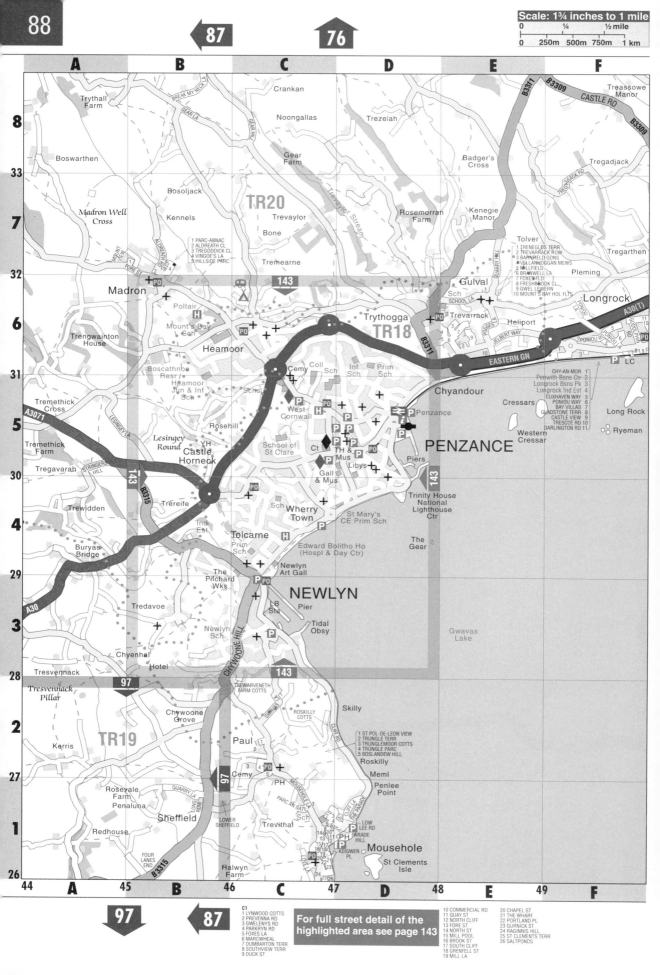

Scale: 1¾ inches to 1 mile
0   ¼   ½ mile
0   250m   500m 750m   1 km

A   B   C   D   E   F

8
Trythall Farm
Crankan
Noongallas
Trezelah
Treassowe Manor
B3311 B3309 CASTLE RD
B3309
Tregadjack

33
Boswarthen
Bosoljack
Gear Farm
Badger's Cross
TREGOSACK RD

7
Madron Well Cross
Kennels
TR20
Trevaylor
Rosemorran Farm
Kenegie Manor
Tregarthen
Tolver
1 TRENEGLOS TERR   1
2 TREVARRACK ROW   2
3 BARNFIELD GDNS   3
4 VELLANHOGGAN MEWS 4
5 MILLFIELD   5
6 BRANWELL LA   6
7 FOXEYELD   7
8 FRESHBROOK CL   8
9 GWEL LOWERN   9
10 MOUNT'S BAY HOL FLTS 10
Pleming
Bone
Tremearne

32
MOUNT VIEW
FORE ST
ALDREATH RD
1 PARC-ABNAC
2 ALDREATH CL
3 TREGODDICK CL
4 VINGOE'S LA
5 HILLSIDE PARC
Madron
PO
143
Gulval
School La
Sch
PO
Longrock
A30(T)

6
Trengwainton House
Poltair
Mount's Bay Sch
H
PO
Heamoor
Trythogga
TR18
B3311
Trevarrack
Heliport
QUARRY HILL
JELBERT WAY
POSES
ALBERT WAY
PONIOU RD
PONIOU
LA
PONIOU RD

31
Tremethick Cross
Boscathnoe Resr
Cemy
Coll
Sch
Heamoor Jun & Inf Sch
Inf Sch
Prim Sch
EASTERN GN
Chyandour
Cressars
CHY-AN-MOR   1
Penwith Bsns Ctr   2
Longrock Bsns Pk   3
Longrock Ind Est   4
CUXHAVEN WAY   5
PONIOU WAY   6
GLADSTONE TERR   7
BAY VILLAS   8
CASTLE VIEW   9
TRESCOE RD   10
DARLINGTON RD   11
Long Rock
P
LC

5
A3071
Tremethick Farm
LESINGEY LA
Rosehill
West Cornwall
H
P
School of St Clare
TH & Mus
P
Penzance
P
PENZANCE
Western Cressar
Ryeman

30
Tregavarah
STRINGERS HILL
143
B3315
Trereife
YH
Castle Horneck
Lesingey Round
Ct
Gall & Mus
Libys
Piers
143
Trinity House National Lighthouse Ctr

4
Buryas Bridge
Trewidden
Ind Est
Sch
Tolcarne
Prim Sch
H
Wherry Town
St Mary's CE Prim Sch
Edward Bolitho Ho (Hospl & Day Ctr)
The Gear

29
A30
Tredavoe
The Pilchard Wks
Newlyn Art Gall
P
PO
NEWLYN
Gwavas Lake

3
Newlyn Sch
CHYWOONE HILL
P
LB Sta
Pier
Tidal Obsy
Chyenhal
Hotel

28
Tresvennack
97
Trewarveneth Farm Cotts
143

2
Tresvennack Pillar
TR19
Karris
Chywoone Grove
GWAVAS
Paul
Roskilly Cotts
Skilly
CLIFF RD
1 ST POL-DE-LEON VIEW
2 TRUNGLE TERR
3 TRUNGLEMOOR COTTS
4 TRUNGLE PARC
5 BOSLANDEW HILL
Roskilly
Meml
Penlee Point

27
Roseyale Farm Penaluna
QUARRY LA
LONG ROW
97
Cemy
PO
PH
PARC AN GATE
Sch
MOUSEHOLE LA
CLIFF LA
THE PARADE

1
Redhouse
Sheffield
LOWER SHEFFIELD
Trevithal
FOUR LANES END
Low Lee Rd
Parade Hill
PH
P
Keigwen Pl
Mousehole
St Clements Isle

26
B3315
Halwyn Farm
FORE ST

44   45   46   47   48   49

For full street detail of the highlighted area see page 143

C1
1 LYNWOOD COTTS
2 PREVENNA RD
3 GWELENYS RD
4 PARKRYN RD
5 FOXES LA
6 MARCWHEAL
7 DUMBARTON TERR
8 SOUTHVIEW TERR
9 DUCK ST
10 COMMERCIAL RD
11 QUAY ST
12 NORTH CLIFF
13 FORE ST
14 NORTH ST
15 MILL POOL
16 BROOK ST
17 SOUTH CLIFF
18 GRENFELL ST
19 MILL LA
20 CHAPEL ST
21 THE WHARF
22 PORTLAND PL
23 GURNICK ST
24 RAGINNIS HILL
25 ST CLEMENTS TERR
26 SALTPONDS

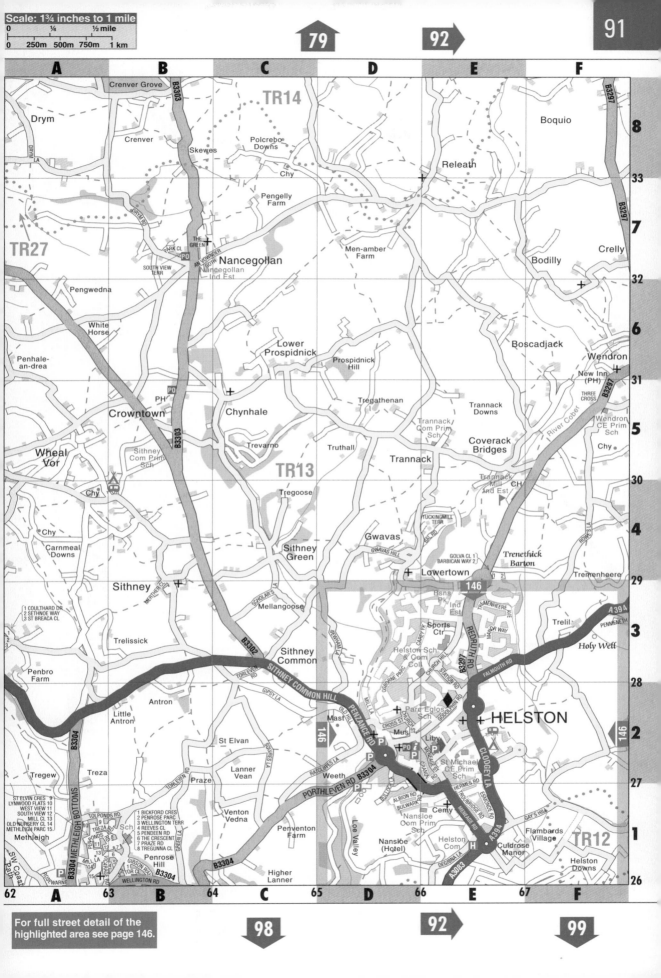

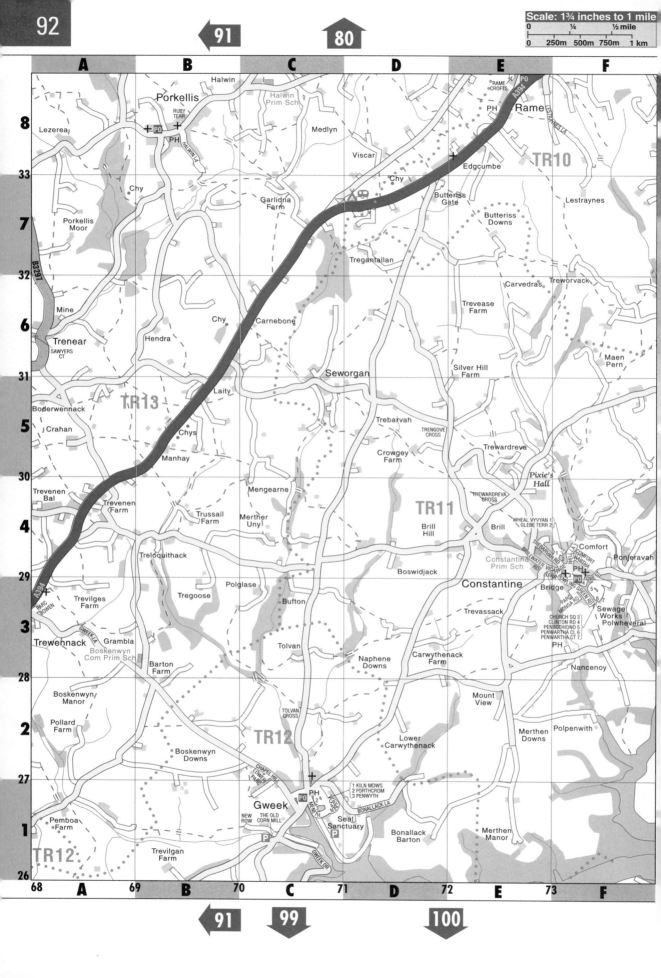

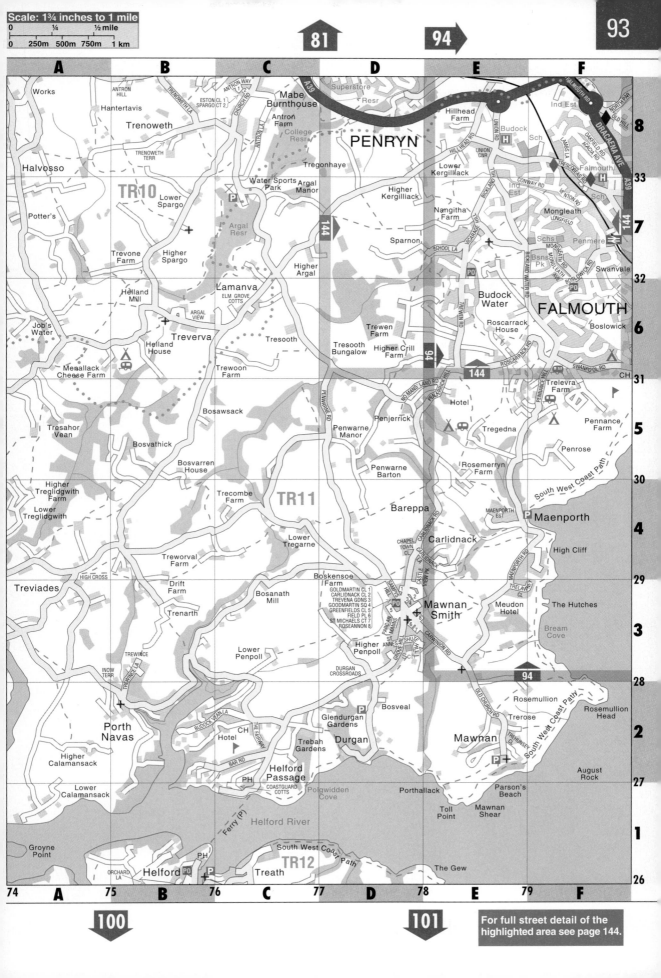

A   B   C   D   E   F

Works

Hantertavis

Trenoweth

ANTRON HILL

TRENOWETH LA

CHURCH RD

ANTRON WAY

ESTON CL 1
SPARGO CT 2

Mabe
Burnthouse

A39

Superstore
Resr

Hillhead
Farm

Ind Est

Halvosso

TR10

Lower
Spargo

Trenoweth
Terr

Antron
Farm

College
Resr

Tregonhaye

PENRYN

UNION
RD

H

Budock

Sch

Lower
Kergillack

HILL HEAD RD

UNION
CNR

FALMOUTH RD

DRACAENA AVE

OLD HILL

NORTHYAR

A39

Falmouth

OAKFIELD RD
AGAR RD

TRESCOBEAS RD

33

A39

144

Potter's

Trevone
Farm

Higher
Spargo

Water Sports
Park

P

Argal
Manor

Higher
Kergilliack

Nangitha
Farm

VICARAGE

SCHOOL LA

Sparnon

BICKLAND

Ind
Est

CONWAY RD

NEWTON RD

Mongleath

LONGFIELD

Schs

Bsns
Pk

MOOR LEATH RD
MONGLEATH AVE

BOSLOWICK RD

Penmere

Penmere

144

7

Argal
Resr

BICKLAND WATER RD

PO

32

Job's
Water

Helland
Mnl

Lamanva

ELM GROVE
COTTS

Higher
Argal

TREVEN RD

Budock
Water

Roscarrack
House

PO

FALMOUTH

Boslowick

6

Menallack
Cheese Farm

ARGAL
VIEW

Treverva

Helland
House

Tresooth

Trewen
Farm

Tresooth
Bungalow

Higher Crill
Farm

94

ROSCARRACK RD

SWANPOOL RD

144

CH

31

Trewoon
Farm

Bosawsack

PENWARNE RD

NO MANS LAND RD

PEARSACK RD

Penjerrick

Hotel

PENNANCE HILL

Trelevra
Farm

Pennance
Farm

5

Tresahor
Vean

Bosvathick

Penwarne
Manor

Penwarne
Barton

Tregedna

Rosemerryn
Farm

Penrose

Bosvarren
House

Lower
Treglidgwith

Higher
Treglidgwith
Farm

Trecombe
Farm

TR11

Barreppa

South West Coast Path

MAENPORTH
EST

P

Maenporth

30

Lower
Tregarne

CARLIDNACK RD

Carlidnack

MAENPORTH RD

High Cliff

4

Treviades

Treworval
Farm

HIGH CROSS

Drift
Farm

Trenarth

Bosanath
Mill

Boskensoe
Farm

GOLDMARTIN CL 1
CARLIDNACK CL 2
TREVENA GDNS 3
GOODMARTIN SQ 4
GREENFIELDS CL 5
FIELD PL 6
ST MICHAELS CT 7
ROSEANNON 8

SAMPYS HILL

CHAPEL
TOWN
CL

CASTLE VIEW LA

Mawnan
Smith

TRELAWNE
CL

Meudon
Hotel

The Hutches

Bream
Cove

29

3

TREWINCE LA

TREWINCE LA

INOW
TERR

Trenarth

Lower
Penpoll

Lower
Penpoll

PARCAN MAINS

GROVE HILL

ST
ANNES CL

SHUTE HILL

Higher
Penpoll

DURGAN
CROSSROADS

PARSONS RD

CARWINION RD

Bosveal

OLD CHURCH RD

THEHUNSEY CL

TREHUNSEY CL

Mawnan

Rosemullion

Trerose

South West Coast Path

Rosemullion
Head

2

Porth
Navas

BUDOCK VEAN LA

CH

Hotel

THE FAIRWAY

Glendurgan
Gardens

Trebah
Gardens

Durgan

P

P

August
Rock

Higher
Calamansack

BAR RD

PH

Helford
Passage

COASTGUARD
COTTS

Polgwidden
Cove

Porthallack

Toll
Point

Parson's
Beach

Mawnan
Shear

27

Lower
Calamansack

Ferry (P)

Helford River

South West Coast Path

TR12

The Gew

1

Groyne
Point

ORCHARD
LA

PH

Helford

PO

P

Treath

74   A   75   B   76   C   77   D   78   E   79   F

100

101

For full street detail of the
highlighted area see page 144.

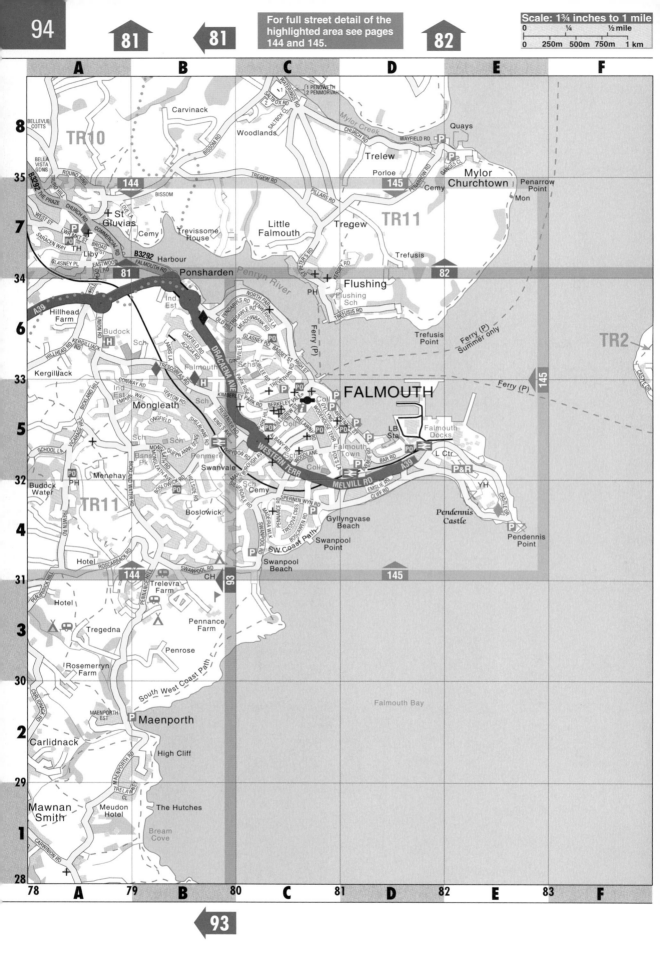

A   B   C   D   E   F

Trethewell
Lanhay
Tregassa
Pednvadan
Porthcurnick Beach
Portscatho

1 ADMIRALTY TERR
2 SPRINGFIELD
3 PARC MERYS
4 HARBOUR CT FLATS
5 SUNNYSIDE
6 RIVER ST
7 THE SQUARE
8 VICTORIA TERR
9 CLIFTON TERR
10 TREVENTON CL
11 THE SQUARE

St Just in Roseland

St Just Pool

Gerrans

PARC-AN-DILLON RD
TREVENTON
CHURCHTOWN RD
GERRANS HILL
THE QUAY
Pencabe

Hotel
Gerrans Sch

PORTH SAWLE FLATS

Trevennel Farm
Trewollack

Tregear Vean

Tregassick

Treloan

Bosloggas

Water Twr

ROSELAND FLATS

TR2

Percuil

South West Coast Path

Treanale

82
83

St Mawes

Trewince

UPPER CASTLE RD
POLVARTH RD
TREDENHAM RD
A3078

1 PORTH VIEW
2 PERCUIL VIEW
3 PEN BREA CL

Percuil River

Quay

TREWINCE MANOR

Froe

Rosteague

Greeb Point

Castle Point

St Mawes Harbour

Porth Farm

Towan Beach

Ferry P (summer only)

Bohortha

St Anthony

Killigerran Head

Carricknath Point

A6
1 MANOR CT
2 ST AUSTELL ROW
3 THE SQUARE
4 KINGS RD
5 COMMERCIAL RD
6 GIBRALTAR TERR
7 CHURCH HILL
8 PEN-EGLOE
9 THE ROPE WLK
10 CHAPEL TERR
11 SEA VIEW CRES
12 SEA VIEW RD
13 NEWTON PK
14 HANCOCK LA
15 PLACE VIEW RD
16 KENNERLEY TERR
17 BROOKLYN TERR
18 BROOKLYN FLATS
19 BEECH HALL FLATS
20 BOHELLA RD

Place House

Place Barton

Porthbeor Beach

Porthmellin Head

MILITARY RD

St Anthony Head

Zone Point

84   A   85   B   86   C   87   D   88   E   89   F

8
35
7
34
6
33
5
32
4
31
3
30
2
29
1
28

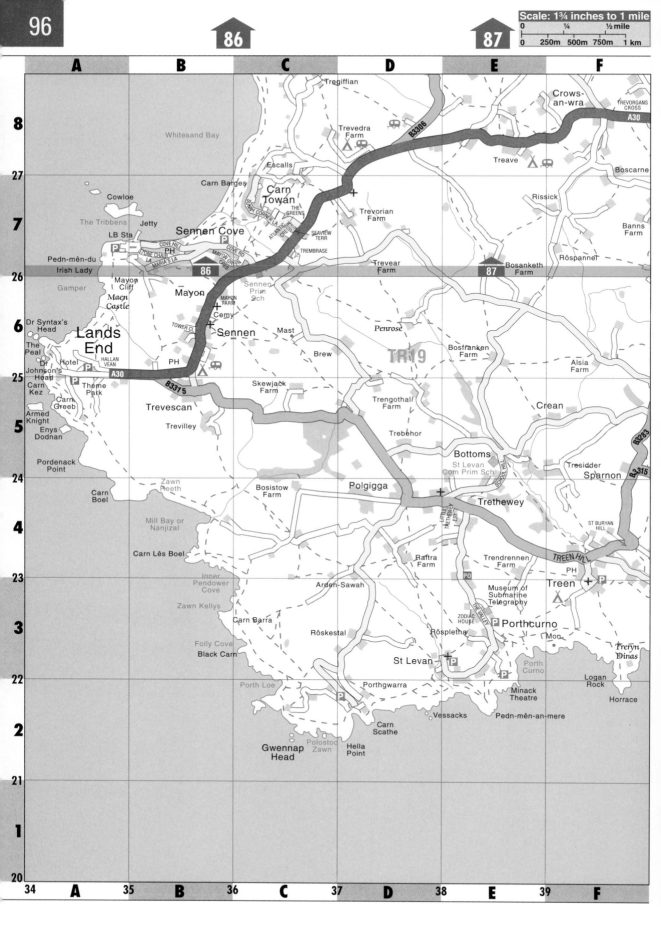

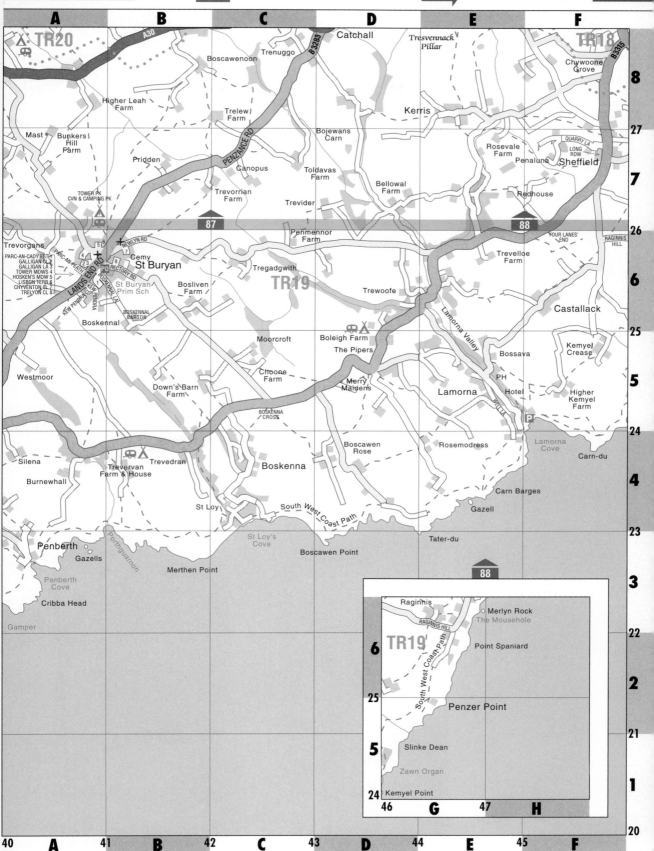

Scale: 1¾ inches to 1 mile

0   ¼   ½ mile
0 250m 500m 750m 1 km

87 →

88 →

| A | B | C | D | E | F |

TR20

A30

Catchall

Tresvennack Pillar

TR18

Chywoone Grove

8

Boscawenoon

Trenuggo

B3283

27

Higher Leah Farm

Trelew Farm

Kerris

PENZANCE RD

Bojewans Carn

Rosevale Farm

Penaluna

QUARRY LA

LONG ROW

Sheffield

7

Mast

Bunkers Hill Farm

Pridden

Canopus

Toldavas Farm

Bellowal Farm

Redhouse

B3315

TOWER PK CVN & CAMPING PK

Trevorrian Farm

Trevider

Penmennor Farm

87

88

26

Trevorgans

NEWLYN RD

PARC-AN-CADY EST 1
GALLIGAN CL 2
GALLIGAN LA 3
HOSKEN'S MDW 4
TOWER MDWS 5
LISBON TERR 6
CHYVENTON CL 7
TRELYON CL 8

PARC-AN-PEATH

Cemy

St Buryan

Tregadgwith

TR19

Trevelloe Farm

FOUR LANES' END

RAGINNIS HILL

6

LANDS END RD

KEW PENDRA

RECTORY RD

BOSKENNAL LA

PO

St Buryan Prim Sch

Bosliven Farm

Trewoofe

Castallack

Boskennal

BOSKENNAL BARTON

Moorcroft

Boleigh Farm

The Pipers

Lamorna Valley

Bossava

Kemyel Crease

25

Westmoor

Down's Barn Farm

Choone Farm

Merry Maidens

Lamorna

PH

Hotel

Higher Kemyel Farm

5

BOSKENNA CROSS

VELLA

P

Silena

Trevervan Farm & House

Trevedran

Boskenna

Boscawen Rose

Rosemodress

Lamorna Cove

Carn-du

4

Burnewhall

St Loy

Carn Barges

South West Coast Path

Gazell

Penberth

Gazells

St Loy's Cove

Boscawen Point

Tater-du

23

Merthen Point

Penberth Cove

Porthguarnon

88

3

Cribba Head

Raginnis

Merlyn Rock

The Mousehole

22

Gamper

RAGINNIS HILL

South West Coast Path

TR19

Point Spaniard

2

6

25

Penzer Point

21

5

Slinke Dean

Zawn Organ

1

24

Kemyel Point

46 G 47 H

20

| A | B | C | D | E | F |
40 41 42 43 44 45

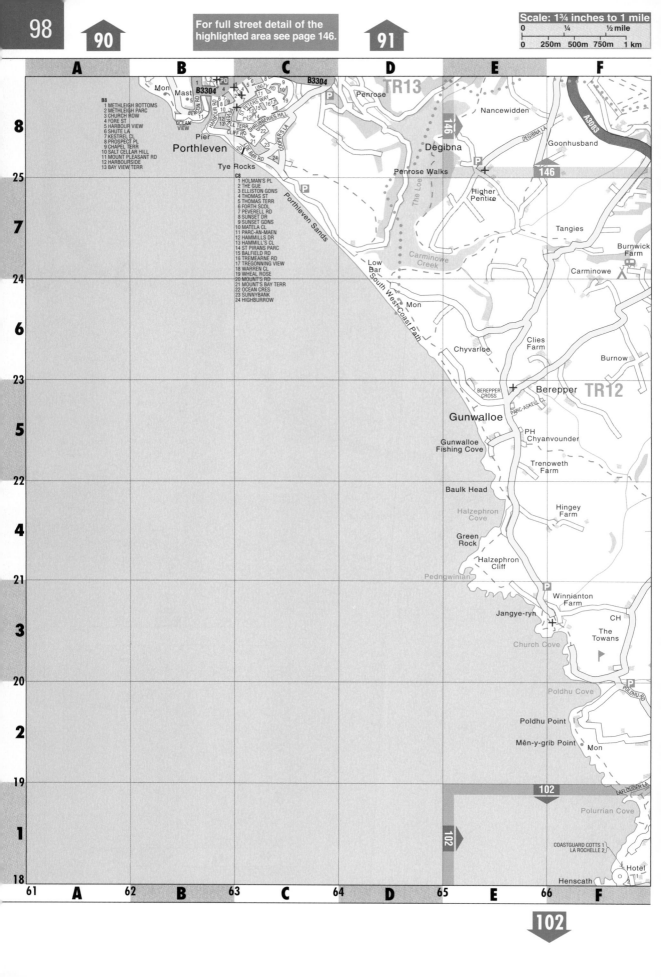

90

91

For full street detail of the highlighted area see page 146.

Scale: 1¾ inches to 1 mile
0   ¼   ½ mile
0   250m 500m 750m 1 km

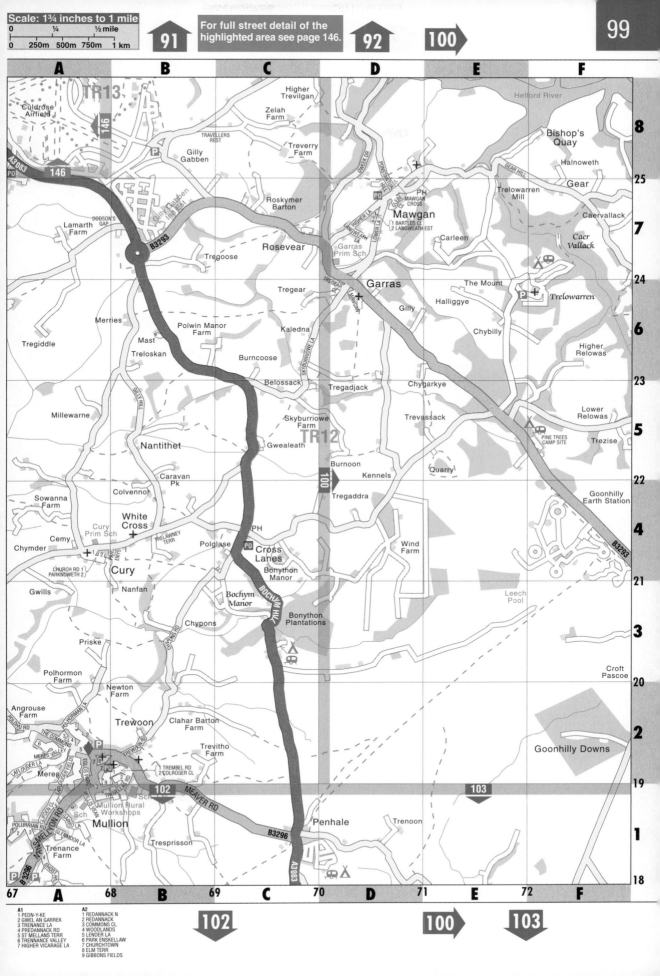

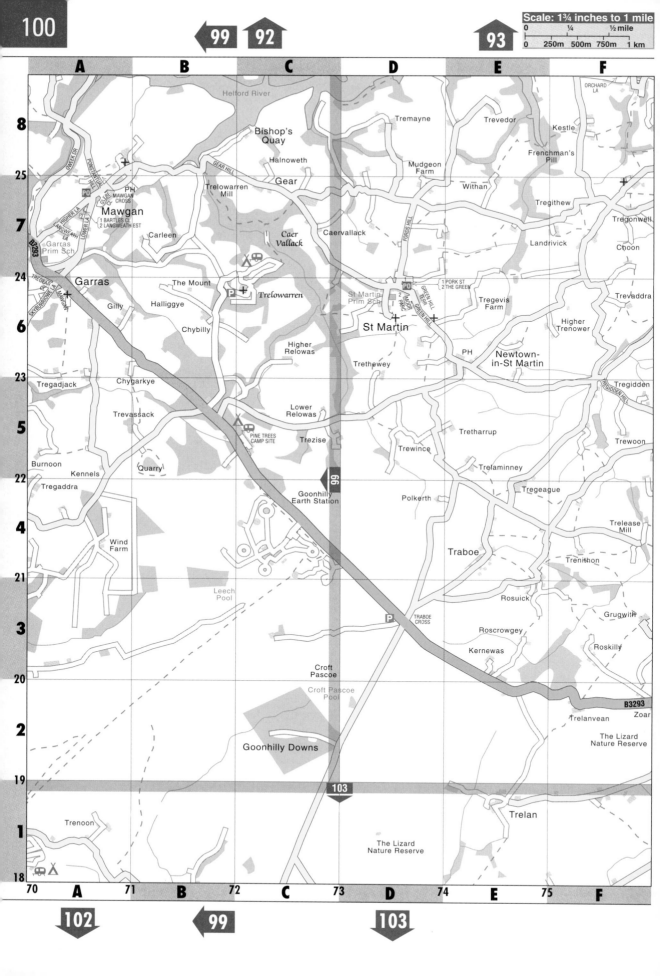

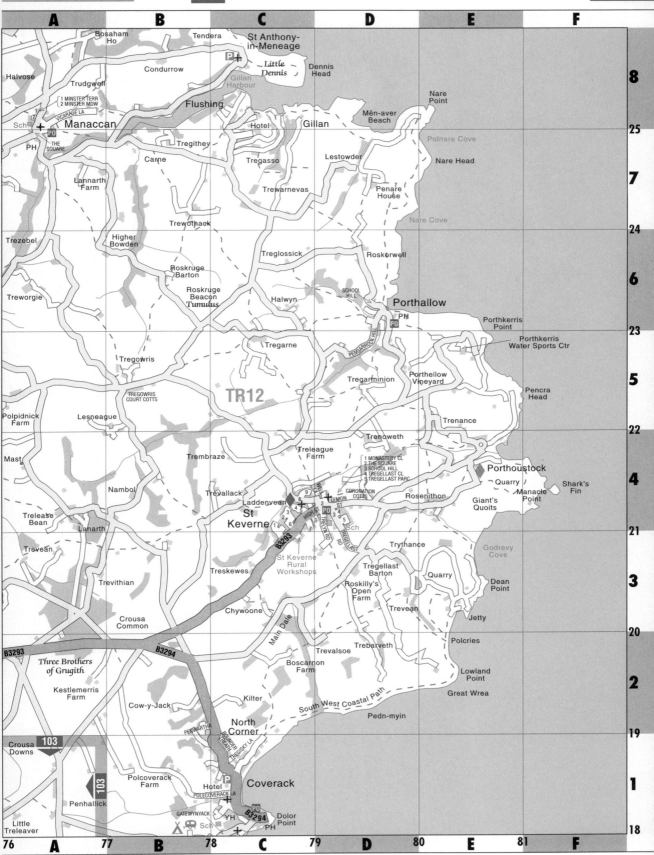

A B C D E F

8
25
7
24
6
23
5
22
4
21
3
20
2
19
1
18

Bosaham Ho
Tendera
St Anthony-in-Meneage
Little Dennis
Dennis Head
Halvose
Trudgwell
Condurrow
Gillan Harbour
Flushing
Nare Point
Mên-aver Beach
1 MINSTER TERR
2 MINSTER MDW
Sch
Manaccan
PO
THE SQUARE
VICARAGE LA
PH
Gillan
Hotel
Polnare Cove
Tregithey
Carne
Tregasso
Lestowder
Nare Head
Lannarth Farm
Trewarnevas
Penare House
Trezebel
Higher Bowden
Trewothack
Treglossick
Roskorwell
Nare Cove
Roskruge Barton
Halwyn
SCHOOL HILL
Porthallow
Treworgie
Roskruge Beacon Tumulus
PH
PO
Porthkerris Point
PENARROCK HILL
Porthkerris Water Sports Ctr
Tregowris
Tregarne
Tregarminion
Porthellow Vineyard
TR12
TREGOWRIS COURT COTTS
Pencra Head
Polpidnick Farm
Lesneague
Trenoweth
Trenance
Mast
Trembraze
Treleague Farm
1 MONASTERY CL
2 THE SQUARE
3 SCHOOL HILL
4 TREGELLAST CL
5 TREGELLAST PARC
Porthoustock
Quarry
Shark's Fin
Nambol
Trevallack
9
WEL
CORONATION COTTS
Rosenithon
Giant's Quoits
Manacle Point
Laddenvean
LEMON ST
PO
Sch
St Keverne
HIGH ST
TRELYN RD
TREGELLAST RD
Treduder
Trelease Bean
Lanarth
B3293
St Keverne Rural Workshops
Trythance
Godrevy Cove
Trevean
Treskewes
Tregellast Barton
Quarry
Dean Point
Trevithian
Roskilly's Open Farm
Chywoone
Trevean
Jetty
Crousa Common
Main Dale
Trevalsoe
Trebarveth
Polcries
B3293
B3294
Boscarnon Farm
Lowland Point
Three Brothers of Grugith
Kestlemerris Farm
Kilter
Great Wrea
Cow-y-Jack
South West Coastal Path
Pedn-myin
103
Crousa Downs
PENWARTHIN
North Corner
103
TREGISKY LA
Polcoverack Farm
Penhallick
P
Hotel
POLCOVERACK LA
Coverack
GATEWYNYACK
YH
PH
Dolor Point
Little Treleaver
Sch
B3294

76   A   77   B   78   C   79   D   80   E   81   F

C4
1 TRESKEWES EST
2 TREVALLACK VIEW
3 TREVALLACK PARC
4 LANHEVERNE PARC
5 DOCTORS HILL
6 POLVENTON PARC
7 PENMENNER EST
8 COMMERCIAL RD
9 TREGONNING PARC

Scale: 1¾ inches to 1 mile

0   ¼   ½ mile
0   250m   500m   750m   1 km

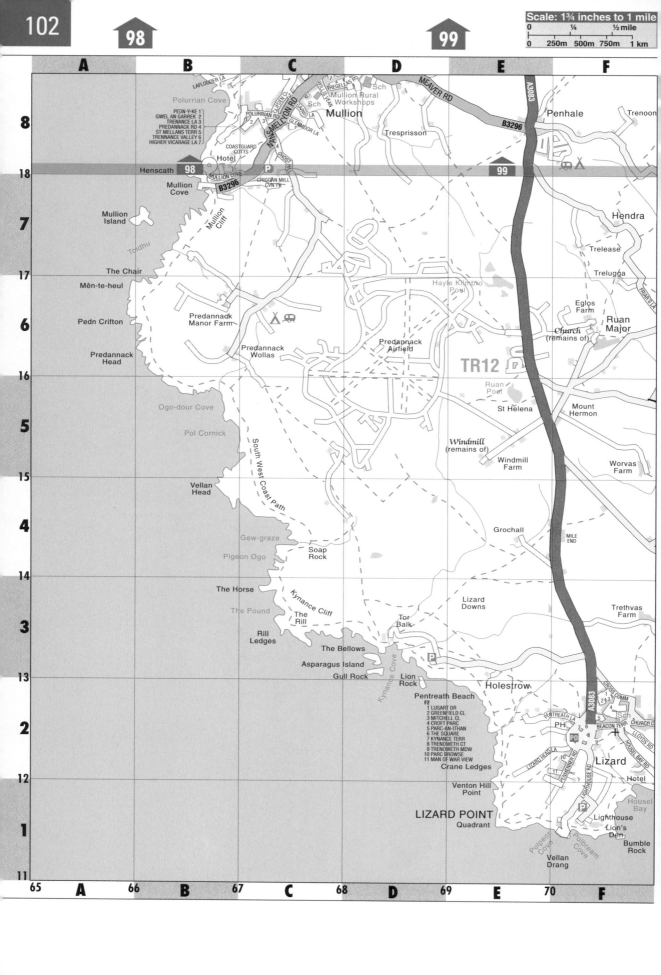

LAFLOUDER LA
Polurrian Cove
PEDN-Y-KE 1
GWEL AN GARREK 2
TRENANCE LA 3
PREDANNACK RD 4
ST MELLANS TERR 5
TRENNANCE VALLEY 6
HIGHER VICARAGE LA 7

KYREGELLAS RD
Mullion Rural Workshops
Sch
Sch
Mullion

MEAVER RD
B3296
Penhale
Trenoon

POLURRIAN RD
GAMELLYON RD
QUEEN CL
GARRO LA
GLENMOOR LA
Tresprisson

A3083

Henscath   **98**
Hotel
COASTGUARD COTTS
P
GHOST HILL
99

Mullion Cove
B3296
CRIGGAN MILL CVN PK

Hendra

Mullion Island
Totdhu
Mullion Cliff

Trelease

The Chair

Trelugga

Mên-te-heul
Hayle Kimbro Pool

Eglos Farm

Pedn Crifton
Predannack Manor Farm
Church (remains of)
Ruan Major

Predannack Wollas
Predannack Airfield
TR12

Predannack Head
Ruan Pool

South West Coast Path
St Helena
Mount Hermon

Ogo-dour Cove

Pol Cornick
Windmill (remains of)
Windmill Farm

Worvas Farm

Vellan Head

Gew-graze
Soap Rock
Grochall
MILE END

Pigeon Ogo

The Horse
Kynance Cliff
Lizard Downs
Trethvas Farm

The Pound
The Rill

Rill Ledges
Tor Balk

The Bellows
P
Asparagus Island
Lion Rock
Holestrow
A3083
CROSS COMM

Gull Rock
Kynance Cove
Pentreath Beach
Sch
CHURCH C

1 LUSART DR
2 GREENFIELD CL
3 MITCHELL CL
4 CROFT PARC
5 PARC-AN-ITHAN
6 THE SQUARE
7 KYNANCE TERR
8 TRENOWETH CT
9 TRENOWETH MDW
10 PARC BROWSE
11 MAN OF WAR VIEW
Crane Ledges

PENTREATH LA
PH
PO
BEACON TERR
PENROSENWEN RD
LIGHTHOUSE RD
LLOYDS RD
HOUSEL BAY RD

Lizard
Hotel

Venton Hill Point

LIZARD HEAD LA
Housel Bay

LIZARD POINT
Quadrant
P
Lighthouse
Lion's Den

Polpeor Cove
Polbream Cove
Bumble Rock

Vellan Drang

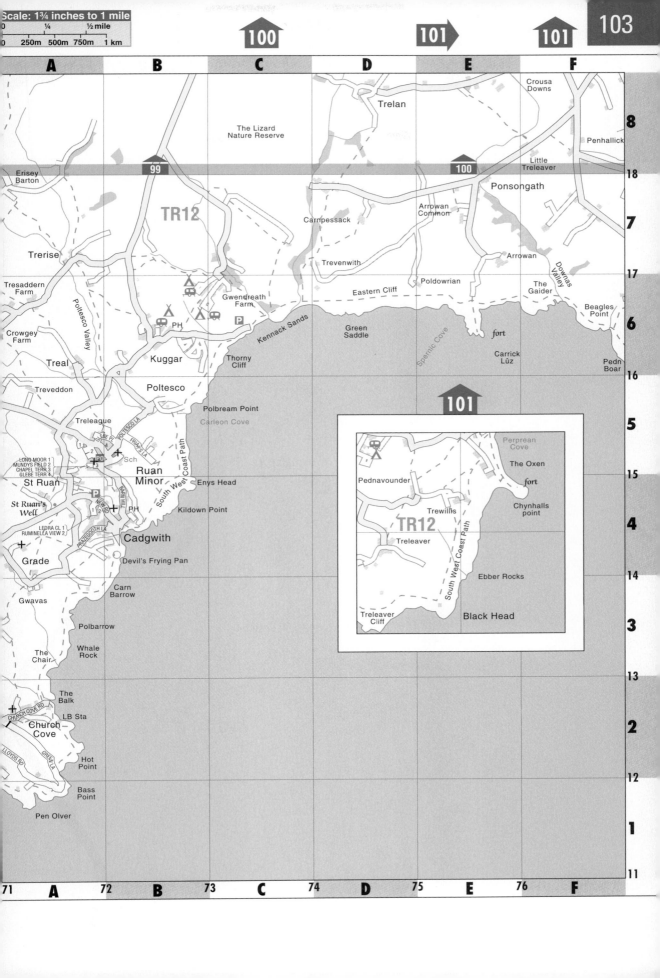

A B C D E F

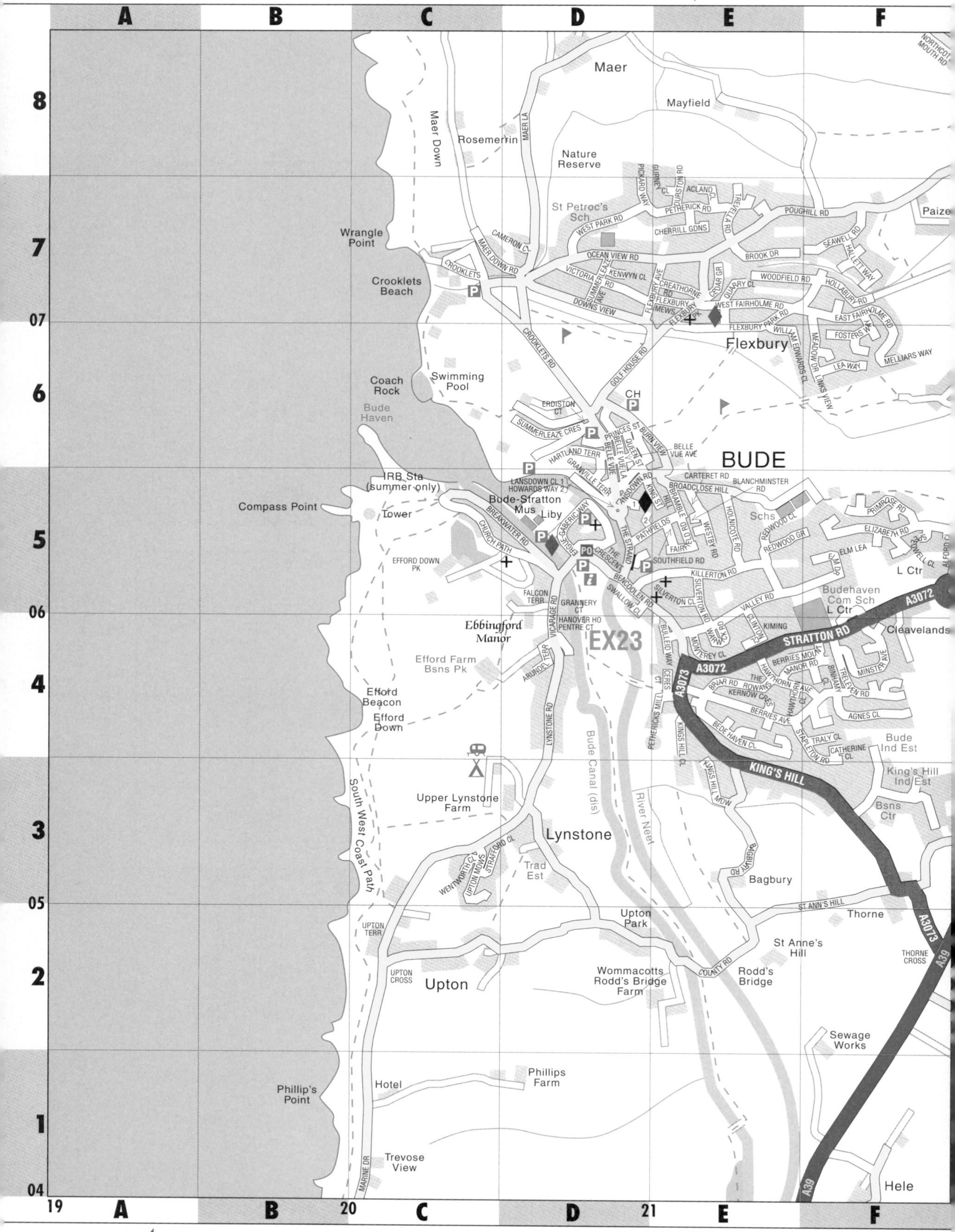

8

Maer
Mayfield
Rosemerrin
Nature Reserve
St Petroc's Sch

7
Wrangle Point
Crooklets Beach
Maer Down
Cameron Cl
Crooklets
Ocean View Rd
Victoria Rd
Downs View
Flexbury
BUDE
Poughill Rd
Paize

07
Coach Rock
Swimming Pool
Bude Haven
IRB Sta (summer only)
Erdiston Ct
Summerleaze Cres
Hartland Terr
Granville Terr
CH

6
Compass Point
Tower
Bude-Stratton Mus
Liby
Belle Vue Ave
Carteret Rd
Broadclose Hill
Blanchminster Rd
Schs

5
Efford Down Pk
Church Path
Breakwater Rd
Falcon Terr
PO
Southfield Rd
Killerton Rd
Silverton Rd
Redwood Gr
L Ctr
Budehaven Com Sch L Ctr
Cleavelands

06
Ebbingford Manor
Grannery Ct
Hanover Ho
Pentre Ct
Vicarage Rd
Lynstone Rd
EX23
STRATTON RD
A3072
Bude Ind Est

4
Efford Beacon
Efford Down
Efford Farm Bsns Pk
Arundel
Bude Canal (dis)
River Neet
A3073
King's Hill
KING'S HILL
King's Hill Ind Est
Bsns Ctr

3
South West Coast Path
Upper Lynstone Farm
Trad Est
Lynstone
Bagbury
Thorne

05
Upton Terr
Upton Park
St Ann's Hill
Thorne Cross

2
Upton Cross
Upton
Wommacotts
Rodd's Bridge Farm
Rodd's Bridge
St Anne's Hill
A39
Sewage Works

1
Phillip's Point
Hotel
Phillips Farm
Marine Dr

04
Trevose View
Hele

19 A B 20 C D 21 E F

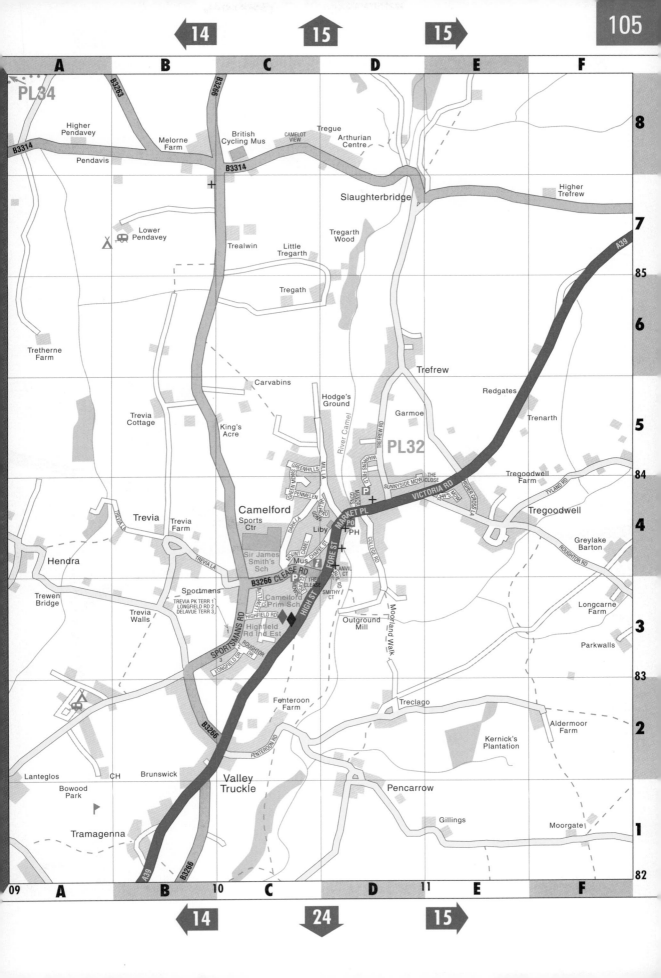

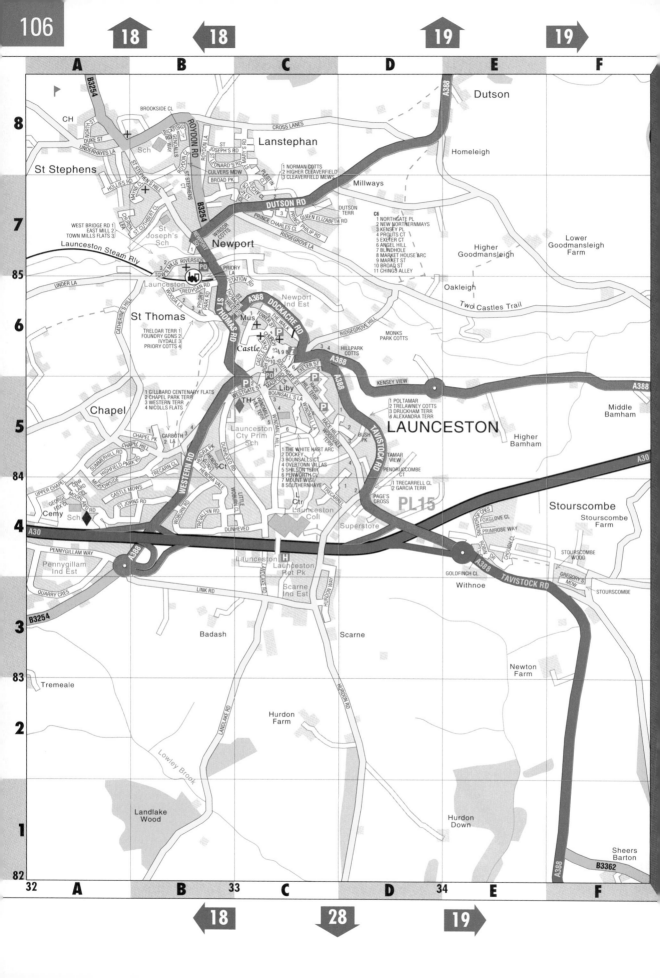

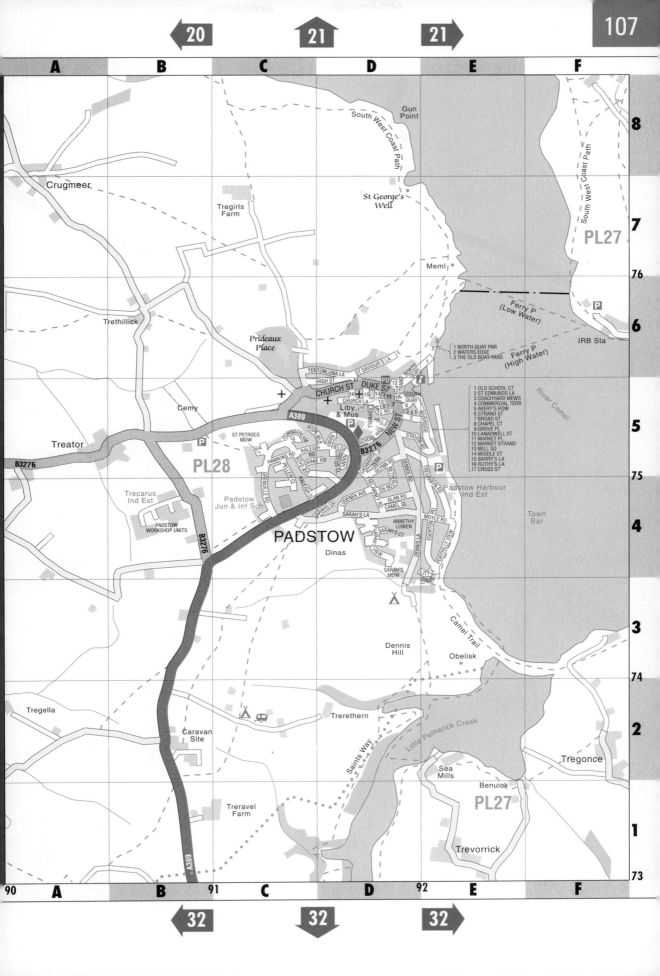

20 21 21

A B C D E F

8

7

PL27

76

Gun Point

South West Coast Path

South West Coast Path

Crugmeer

St George's Well

Tregirls Farm

Meml

Ferry P (Low Water)

6

IRB Sta

Trethillick

Prideaux Place

1 NORTH QUAY PAR
2 WATERS EDGE
3 THE OLD BOAT-YARD

Ferry P (High Water)

River Camel

Treator

Cemy

FENTONLUNA LA
ST SAVIOUR'S LA
HIGH ST
CHURCH ST
DUKE ST
CHURCH LA
Liby & Mus

NORTH QUAY
SOUTH QUAY
RIVERSIDE

1 OLD SCHOOL CT
2 ST EDMUNDS LA
3 COACHYARD MEWS
4 COMMERCIAL TERR
5 AVERY'S ROW
6 STRAND ST
7 BROAD ST
8 CHAPEL CT
9 GROVE PL
10 LANADWELL ST
11 MARKET PL
12 MARKET STRAND
13 MILL SQ
14 MIDDLE ST
15 BARRY'S LA
16 RUTHY'S LA
17 CROSS ST

5

B3276

ST PETROCS MDW

PL28

DOWNSTREAM
ROPE WLK
RALEIGH RD
DRAKE RD
HAWKINS RD
PELLEW CL
BOYD AVE
GRENVILLE RD
MALEIGH CL

SCHOOL HILL
HILL ST
CASWARN
FIELDS
RAINS
STATION RD

Padstow Harbour Ind Est

Town Bar

75

Trecarus Ind Est

Padstow Jun & Inf Sch

PADSTOW

Padstow Workshop Units

Dinas

LOSENEK AVE
GLYNN RD
TREFRESA RD
FREEWIND RD
DENNIS RD

ALAN RD
CAMEL CL
SARAH'S LA
SARAH'S CT
ANNETHY LOWEN
SARAH'S VIEW

DENNIS LA
EGERTON RD
MOYLE RD
TRE-PEN-POL RD
PORTHILLY VIEW

4

Camel Trail

Sarah's Mdw

3

Tregella

Dennis Hill

Obelisk

74

Camel Trail

Caravan Site

Trerethern

Little Petherick Creek

Tregonce

2

Saints Way

Sea Mills

Benuick

PL27

Treravel Farm

Trevorrick

1

73

32 32 32

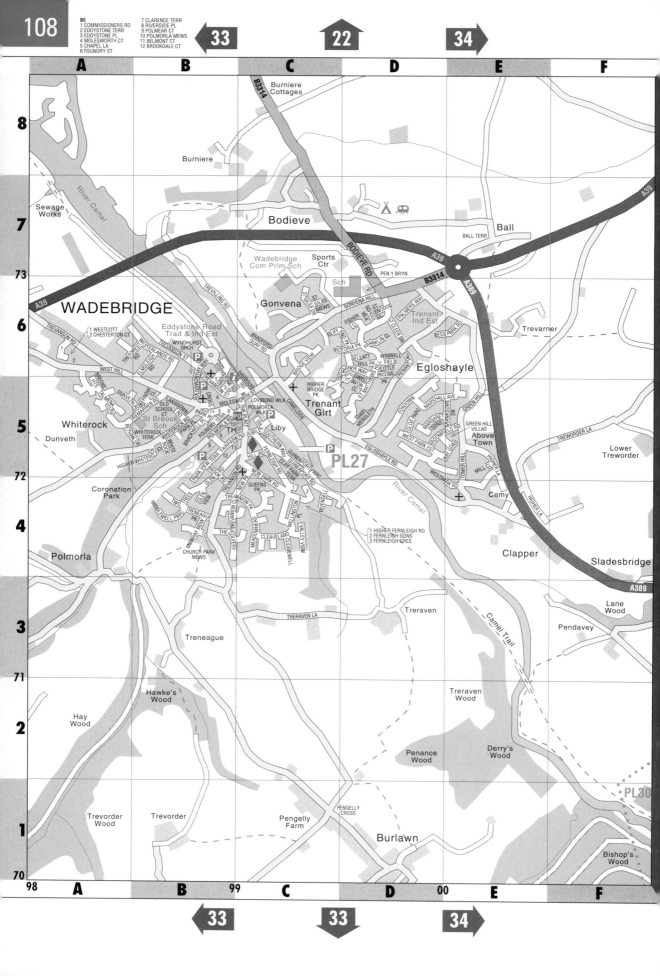

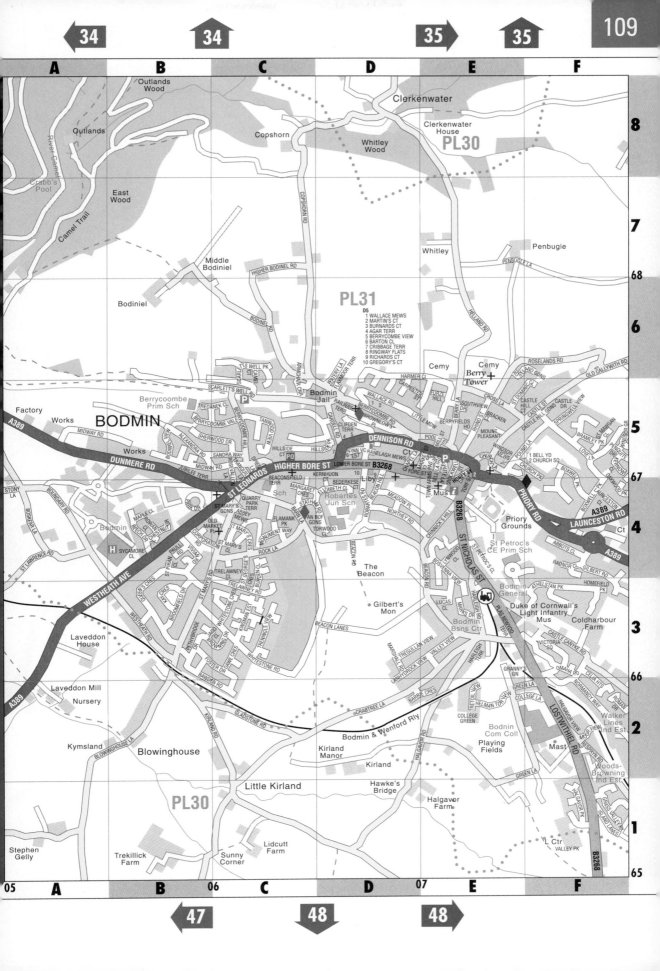

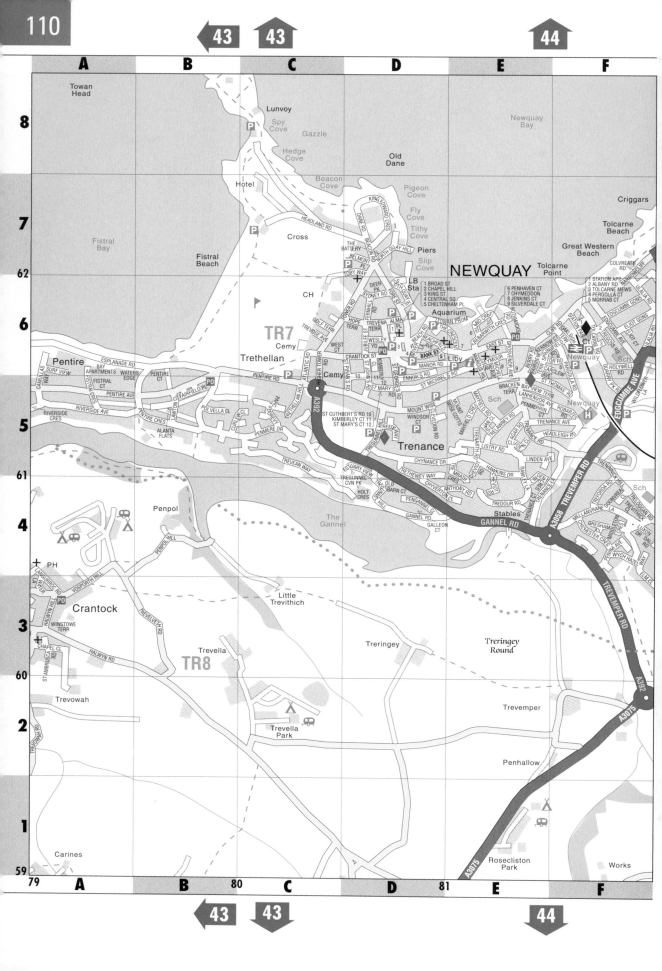

A B C D E F

8

Towan
Head

Lunvoy
Spy
Cove
Gazzle
Hedge
Cove
Beacon
Cove
Old
Dane
Pigeon
Cove
Fly
Cove
Tithy
Cove
Newquay
Bay
Criggars
Tolcarne
Beach

7

Fistral
Bay
Fistral
Beach
Hotel
HEADLAND RD
KING EDWARD CRES
DANE RD
BEACON RD
NORTH QUAY HILL
Cross
THE
BATTERY
BELMONT
Piers
Slip
Cove
Tolcarne
Point
Great Western
Beach
COLVREATH
RD
NARROWCLIFF

62

TR7
Cemy
Trethellan
Trevena
TERR
ALMA
PL
Aquarium
TOWAN PROM
NEWQUAY
1 BROAD ST
2 CHAPEL HILL
3 KING ST
4 CENTRAL SQ
5 CHELTENHAM PL
6 PENHAVEN CT
7 CHYMEDDON
8 JENKINS CT
9 SILVERDALE CT
1 STATION APP
2 ALBANY RD
3 TOLCARNE MEWS
4 PERGOLLA CT
5 MORRAB CT
STATION RD
Newquay
Sch
H

6

Pentire
ESPLANADE RD
SURF VIEW
BAY
APARTMENTS
WATERS
EDGE
PENTIRE
CT
GOLF TERR
TREVOSE AVE
HOPE
TERR
WEST
CT
DEER
PK
SYDNEY RD
TOWER RD
JUBILEE ST
Cemy
BANK ST
EAST ST
Liby
EDGCUMBE AVE

5

CAMILLA S
FISTRAL
CRES
RIVERSIDE AVE
PENTIRE AVE
PENTIRE CRES
ALANTA
FLATS
FAIRFIELD RD
PARC
SPREDY
POL VELLA CL
CURLEW
CL
PENMERE DR
PENTIRE RD
TRETHELLAN HILL
HIGHER TOWER
RD
ATLANTIC RD
FERNHILL
ST PIRAN S RD
ST MARY S
RD
CRANTOCK ST
KIMBERLEY
ST GEORGES RD
ST MICHAEL S RD
ENNOR S RD
MOUNT WISE
CLEVEDON RD
WINDSOR
RD
ST CUTHBERT'S RD 10
KIMBERLEY CT 11
ST MARY'S CT 12
Trenance
TR7
MAYFIELD RD
TRENANCE AVE
HEADLEIGH RD
BRACKEN
TERR
BAY VIEW TERR
LANHENVOR AVE
ROBARTES
PENMERIN
CT
PENMERE
MANOR RD

61

RIVERSIDE
CRES
Penpol
TREVEAN WAY
TREGUNNEL
CVN PK
HOLT
CRES
ESTUARY VIEW
TRETHEWEY WAY
CHYVERTON CL
ANTHONY RD
GANNEL RD
TREDOUR RD
Stables
GANNEL RD
LINDEN AVE
LISTRY RD
A3058 TREVEMPER RD
Sch

4

Penpol
PENPOL HILL
The
Gannel
GALLEON
CT
TREVEMPER RD
TREVITHICK
LUXON
DR
WYCH HAZEL

PH
LANGURROC RD
VOSPORTH HILL
Little
Trevithich
A392
A3075

3

Crantock
TREVELVE RD
WINSTOWE
TERR
HALWYN RD
Trevella
TR8
Treringey
Treringey
Round

60

ST AMBRUSCA
CHAPEL CL
RD
HALWYN RD
Trevowah
Trevella
Park
Trevemper

2

TREGURRIAN RD
Penhallow

1

Carines
Rosecliston
Park
Works

59

79 A B 80 C D 81 E F

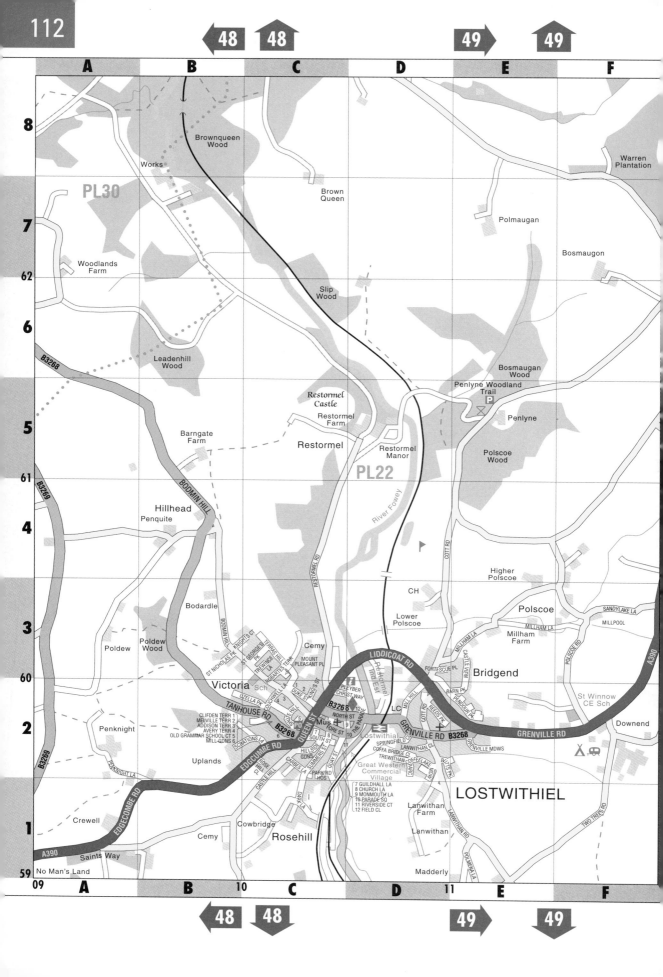

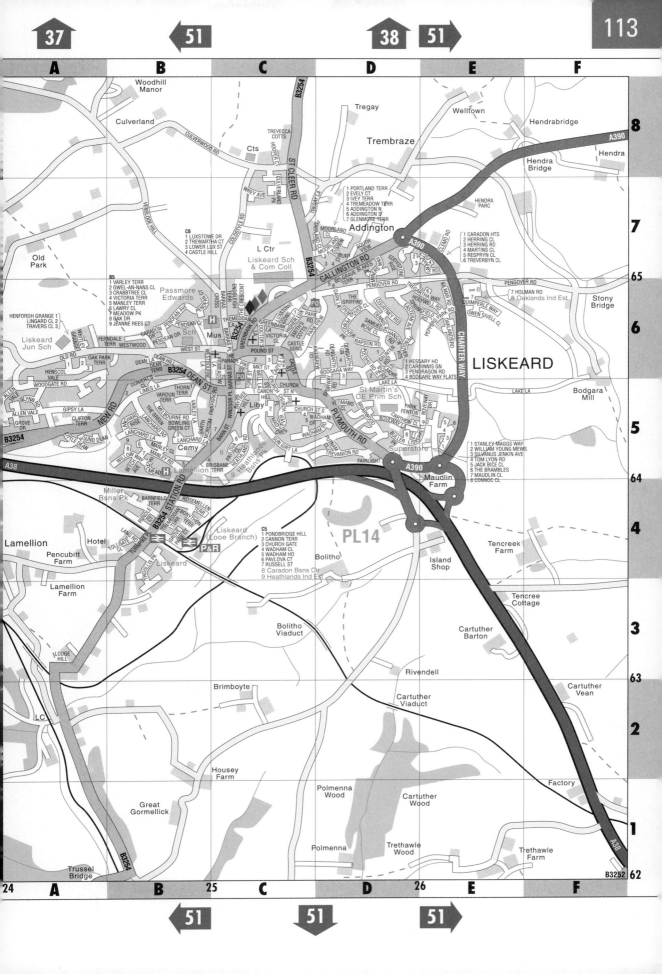

A B C D E F

8

Woodhill Manor
Culverland
Tregay
Welltown
Hendrabridge
A390
Hendra
Hendra Bridge
CULVERWOOD RD
TREVECCA COTTS
Cts
Trembraze
Hendra Parc

7
C6
1 LUXSTOWE DR
2 TREWARTHA CT
3 LOWER LUX ST
4 CASTLE HILL
L Ctr
Liskeard Sch & Com Coll
Addington
1 PORTLAND TERR
2 EVELY CT
3 IVEY TERR
4 TREMEADOW TERR
5 ADDINGTON N
6 ADDINGTON S
7 GLENMORE TERR
1 CARADON HTS
2 HERRING CL
3 HERRING RD
4 MARTINS CL
5 RESPRYN CL
6 TREVERBYN CL
7 HOLMAN RD
8 Oaklands Ind Est
PENGOVER RD
65
Stony Bridge

Old Park
B5
1 VARLEY TERR
2 GWEL-AN-NANS CL
3 CRABBTREE CL
4 VICTORIA TERR
5 MANLEY TERR
6 MEADOW PK
7 OAK DR
8 JEANNE REES CT
Passmore Edwards
THE CRESCENT
The Griffins
Pengover Rd
QUIMPERLE WAY
OWEN SIVELL CL
CHARTER WAY
LISKEARD
6
Henfordh Grange 1
Lingard Cl 2
Travers Cl 3
Liskeard Jun Sch
H Mus
Sch
1 HESSARY HO
2 CARDINNIS GN
3 PENDRAGON RD
4 BODGARE WAY FLATS
Bodgara Mill

Old Rd
DEAN ST
Liby
PLYMOUTH RD
St Martin's CE Prim Sch
Park Fenton
LAKE LA
5
B3254
NEW RD
Cemy
Liskeard Superstore
A390
1 STANLEY MAGGS WAY
2 WILLIAM YOUNG MEWS
3 SILVANUS JENKIN AVE
4 TOM LYON RD
5 JACK BICE CL
6 THE BRAMBLES
7 MAUDLIN CL
8 CONNOC CL

A38
Miller Bsns Pk
H Lamellion
STATION RD
Maudlin Farm
64

Lamellion
Hotel
Liskeard (Looe Branch)
P&R
C5
1 PONDBRIDGE HILL
2 CANNON TERR
3 CHURCH GATE
4 WADHAM CL
5 WADHAM HO
6 PAVLOVA CT
7 RUSSELL ST
8 Caradon Bsns Ctr
9 Heathlands Ind Est
PL14
Island Shop
Tencreek Farm
4
Pencubitt Farm
Bolitho
Tencree Cottage

Lamellion Farm
Cartuther Barton
Cartuther Vean
3
Lodge Hill
Bolitho Viaduct
Rivendell
63

Brimboyte
Cartuther Viaduct
2
LC

Housey Farm
Polmenna Wood
Cartuther Wood
Factory

Great Gormellick
1
Polmenna
Trethawle Wood
Trethawle Farm

Trussel Bridge
B3254
A38
B3252
62

59
59

A B C D E F

8

Trenance Downs

Lansalson Farm

Colchester House

PL26

Scredda

PL26

Clay Pit
Carclaze Downs

DRUMMER'S HILL

B3274

7

Sunny Corner

Works (dis)

Palace Close Farm

Bojea Ind Est

Mount Stamper Farm

Carclaze Ind Est

54

Bojea Farm

Mast

Carwollen

Carclaze

Jeryon Cl 1
Ropehaven Cl 2
Pridmouth Rd 3
Sylvan Cl 4
Tregonissy La End 5

GRIBBEN

Sch

6

Trethowel

Mast

PL25

BODMIN RD

Menacuddle Farm

John Keay House

ST PIRAN'S CL

St AUSTELL RIVER

BOJEA TERR

MOUNT STAMPER RD

Sch

PO

MEMBILLY RD

ROPEHAVEN RD

AGAR RD

CARCLAZE RD

CENTURY CL

EMLYN FIELDS

PHERNYSSICK RD

MEADOW

CLANBORNE

POLMARTH CL

HAWTHORN CL

ROSLYN

LANDREW

MORCOM

FRANKLYN

THE COPSE

SPRINGFIELD CL

5

ST AUSTELL

Menacuddle Well

Trenance Farm

TRENANCE HILL

TRENANCE RD

Resr

Watersedge Cl 1
Trenance Pl 2
Blowing House La 3
Trenance Pl 4
Blowing House Cl 5

1 Blowing House Hill
2 Market Hill
3 Elm Terr
4 Trevarthian Rd
5 The Sycamore

Brewery

HILLSIDE RD

Poltair Com Sch

PRINCE CHARLES RD

PRINCE CHARLES HO

PRINCE CHARLES PK

CENTRAL AVE

ROBARTES GDNS FLATS

ROBARTES PL

ROBARTES GDNS

TRELAWNEY RD

SYCAMORE RD

THORNPARK RD

GWALLON RD

EDDYSTONE RD

COURTENAY RD

BAY VW PK

PARK WAY

MANOR CL

CASTFIELD CL

AVALON WAY

BROOKSIDE

Sch

Sandy Bottom

BRAY'S PL

53

TURNAVEAN RD

TREMBEAR RD

GOVER RD

GROSVENOR PL

SPARNON RD

TRENANCE RD

ORCHARD GR

STONE LA

TIMBER CL

GROVE RD

Coll

TREMENA GDNS

TREMENA RD

MEYLAND RD

HIGHER TREMENA RD

MENACUDDLE LA

N NRTH HILL PK

TREVARTHIAN RD

St Austell Coll

POLTAIR CRES

POLTAIR AVE

POLTAIR CT

GRAHAM RD

CARNSMERRY CRES

POLTAIR RD

DOBEL

TREWYNE RD

POLKYTH RD

CHOUGH CRES

TREVERBYN GDNS

SANDY HILL

MITCHEL CRES

LYTTON PL

GANNET DR

4

A3058

EDGCUMBE RD

LOWER WOODSIDE

SCHOOL RD

HIGHER WOODSIDE

TRENOWTH DR

TREVARRICK RD

Gover Stream

TRELAC RD

CLARENCE RD

LEWINGTON CL

PRIORY RD

COACH LA

NORTH ST

TREGATHE RD

St Austell

Cemy

BEECH

HIGH ST

PALACE RD

Liby

L Ctr Mount Charles

CARLYON RD

ORCHARD CL

ELIOT RD

BRAE LEY

BRILL

RASHLEIGH CL

FAIRBOURNE RD

CLIFDEN RD

BRIDGE

KERVOR CL

H

St Austell

THE OAKS

ROBERT ELIOT CT

PARK RD

WEST HILL

COLLEGE GN

SOUTH ST

TRINITY ST

FORE ST

10
11
12 13
14 15

CHANDOS PL

EAST HILL

EAST HILL

HIGHFIELD AVE

ALEXANDRA RD

QUEENS RD

MOUNT CHARLES RD

VICTORIA RD

WESLEY PL

MORVEN PL

Mount Charles Trad Est

CHARLES CL 1
BOSCARNE CRES 2

PO

3

CHAPEL RD

MOUNT STEPHEN

CLINTON RD

WEST HILL RD

EDGCUMBE GN

MOUNTFIELD DR

MENEAGE VILLAS

LEDRAH RD

OLD LAWN RD

BRENTON

PRIVET GR

GLEN RD

MORELAND RD

PONDHU RD

COURT GDNS

BELMONT RD

BOSINNEY RD

BOCONNOC

PENWINNICK RD

TREWHIDDLE RD

CLEMO RD

ALBERT RD

COLENSO

HIGHFIELD RD

EASTBOURNE RD

PASY VIA

TREVANION RD

TREVERY CL

WATKINS HILL RD

Cemy

TOLCARNE CL

ELIZABETH CL

WOODLAND CL

MARGARET AVE

EASTBOURNE CL

Mount Charles Jun & Inf Est Sch

B3274

A3058

TRURO RD

52

TRURO RD

A390

PENWINNICK RD

DITHMARSCHEN WAY

B3273

TREVANION RD

SOUTHBOURNE RD

1 Beech La
2 Cherry Tree Mews
3 Carvath Ho
4 Chisholme Cl
5 Chisholme Ct
6 Horsley Rise

CROMWELL RD

POLMEAR RD

A390

Long Stone

Superstore

2

A390

Sch

Trewhiddle Farm

SAWLES RD

SAWLES RD

PENTEWAN RD

Gewans Farm

PORTHPEAN RD

DUPORTH RD

PL26

PENSCOT LA

BRIDGEMEAD RD

Tregorrick

Tregorrick Farm

TREGORRICK RD

Rugby Football Gd

Penrice

H

RIDGEWOOD CL

PORTHPEAN BEACH RD

1

Trewhiddle House

White House Cottage

St Austell River

B3273

51

00 A B 01 C D 02 E F

C3
1 MOORLAND CT
2 GRENVILLE CT
3 SAVOY BLDG
4 GRANT'S WLK
5 BIDDICK'S CT
6 MARKET ST
7 CROSS LA
8 CHURCH ST
9 VICTORIA PL
10 VICARAGE HILL
11 OLD VICARAGE PL
12 CHANDOS PL
13 AYLMER PL
14 AYLMER SQ
15 LOWER AYLMER SQ

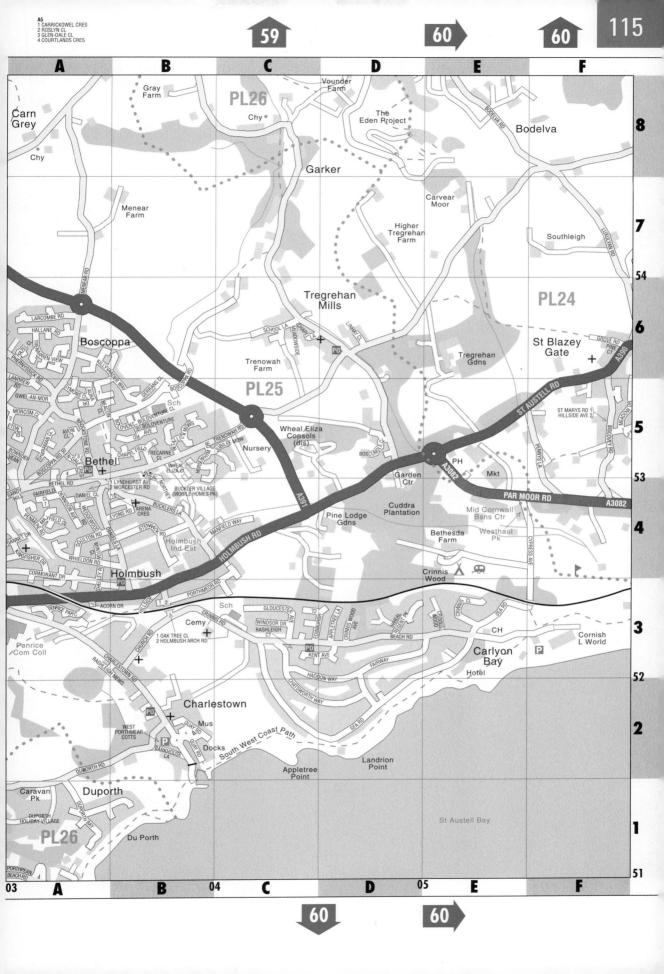

A5
1 CARRICKOWEL CRES
2 ROSLYN CL
3 GLEN-DALE CL
4 COURTLANDS CRES

A   B   C   D   E   F

PL26

Carn Grey

Chy

Gray Farm

Chy

Vounder Farm

The Eden Project

Bodelva

Garker

Carvear Moor

Menear Farm

Higher Tregrehan Farm

Southleigh

BODELVA RD

LUVUTAN RD

Tregrehan Mills

PL24

MENEAR RD

LARCOMBE RD
HALLANE RD

Boscoppa

SCHOOL LA
MEADOWSIDE
CHAPEL LA

PO

LINHAY CL

St Blazey Gate

GROVE RD
PINE CT
A390

Trenowah Farm

Tregrehan Gdns

PL25

ST AUSTELL RD

ST MARYS RD 1
HILLSIDE AVE 2

BISCOVEY RD
MEADOW DR

Wheal Eliza Consols (dis)

Nursery

BOSCUNDLE CL

Bethel

PO

Wheal Eliza Cl

Garden Ctr

A3082

PH

Mkt

PENWIS LA

53

BUCKLER VILLAGE (MOBILE HOMES PK)

Cuddra Plantation

PAR MOOR RD
A3082

BUCKLERS LA

Pine Lodge Gdns

Mid Cornwall Bsns Ctr

Holmbush Ind Est

MANFIELD WAY

Bethesda Farm

Westhaul Pk

CYPRESS AVE

Holmbush

PO

HOLMBUSH RD

PORTHMEOR RD

Crinnis Wood

ACORN DR

HILLSIDE

Sch

GLOUCESTER AVE

CRINNIS WOOD AVE

Wheal Regent Pk

CRINNIS CL

SEA RD

CH

Cornish L World

Penrice Com Coll

Cemy

CRINNIS RD

Windsor Dr
RASHLEIGH CT

EDINBURGH

APPLETREE LA

BEACH RD

P

Carlyon Bay

Hotel

RASHLEIGH MEWS

CHURCH RD

1 OAK TREE CL
2 HOLMBUSH ARCH RD

PO
KENT AVE

FAIRWAY

Charlestown

CHATSWORTH WAY

HADDON WAY

PO

Mus

QUAY RD

SEA RD

WEST PORTHMEAR COTTS

P

BARKHOUSE LA

Docks

Appletree Point

Landrion Point

South West Coast Path

Caravan Pk

Duporth

DUPORTH RD

St Austell Bay

PL26

Du Porth

PORTHPEAN BEACH RD

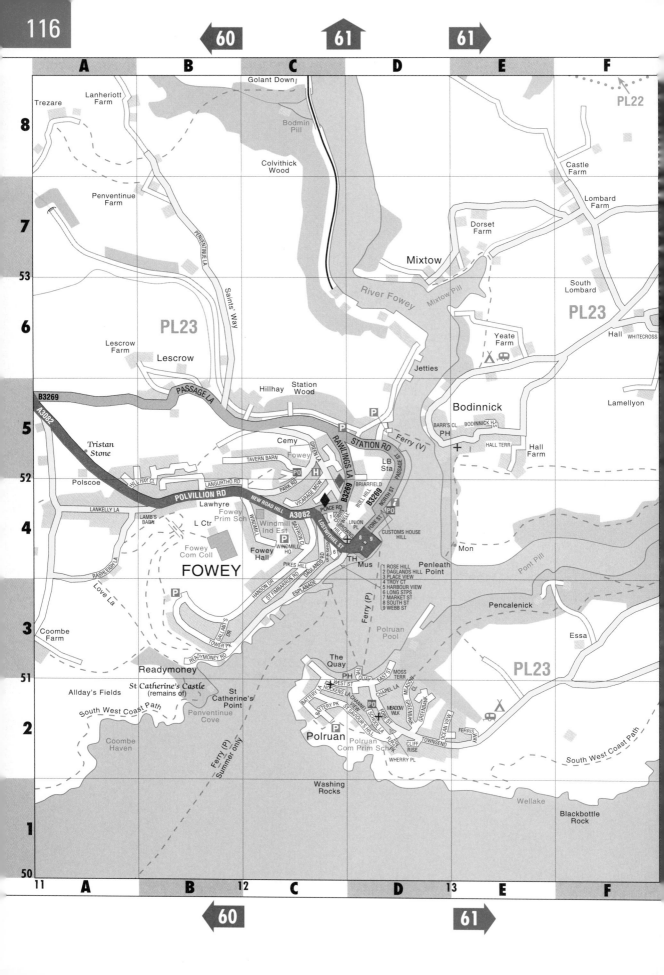

PL22

Trezare
Lanheriott Farm
Golant Down

Bodmin Pill

Castle Farm

Colvithick Wood

Penventinue Farm

PENVENTINUE LA

Lombard Farm

Dorset Farm

Mixtow

River Fowey
Mixtow Pill

South Lombard

PL23

Saints' Way

PL23

Hall WHITECROSS

Lescrow Farm

Lescrow

PASSAGE LA

Station Wood

Hillhay

Jetties

Yeate Farm

Bodinnick

Lamellyon

B3269
A3082

Tristan Stone

Cemy

Fowey
GREEN LA

RAWLINGS LA
STATION RD

Ferry (V)

BARR'S CL
PH
BODINNICK H

HALL TERR

Hall Farm

Polscoe
HILL HAY CL
TAVERN BARN
LANGURTHO RD
PARK RD
PO
H
B3269
BRIARFIELD
LB Sta
PASSAGE LA
NORTH ST

POLVILLION RD
NEW ROAD HILL
VICARAGE MDW
BULL HILL
B3269
FORE ST

Lawhyre
LANKELLY LA
LAMB'S BARN
L Ctr
SAFFRON CL
A3082
PLACE RD
PO
i

Hall TERR

Mon

Fowey Prim Sch
WINDMILL
Fowey Hall
WINDMILL HQ
Windmill Ind Est

UNION PL
CUSTOMS HOUSE HILL

RASHLEIGH LA

Love La

FOWEY
PIKES HILL
HANSON DR
ST FIMBARROS RD
DAGLANDS RD
ESPLANADE

TH
Mus

Penleath Point

1 ROSE HILL
2 DAGLANDS HILL
3 PLACE VIEW
4 TROY CT
5 HARBOUR VIEW
6 LONG STPS
7 MARKET ST
8 SOUTH ST
9 WEBB ST

Pencalenick

Coombe Farm

GALLANTS
TOWER PK
READYMONEY RD

Ferry (P)
Polruan Pool

PL23

Essa

Readymoney

St Catherine's Castle
(remains of)

St Catherine's Point

Penventinue Cove

The Quay

WEST ST
PH
THE QUAY
EAST ST
MOSS TERR
CHAPEL LA
MEADOW
GREENBANK

Allday's Fields

South West Coast Path

Ferry (P)
Summer only

BATTERY LA
HOCKENS LA
CHANNEL VIEW
BATTERY PK
ST SAVIOUR'S HILL
PO
FORE ST
SCHOOL LA
PLACE ST

OCEAN VIEW
FERRIS WAY

Pencalenick

Coombe Haven

Polruan
Polruan Com Prim Sch
CLIFF RISE
TOWNSEND
WHERRY PL

South West Coast Path

Washing Rocks

Wellake

Blackbottle Rock

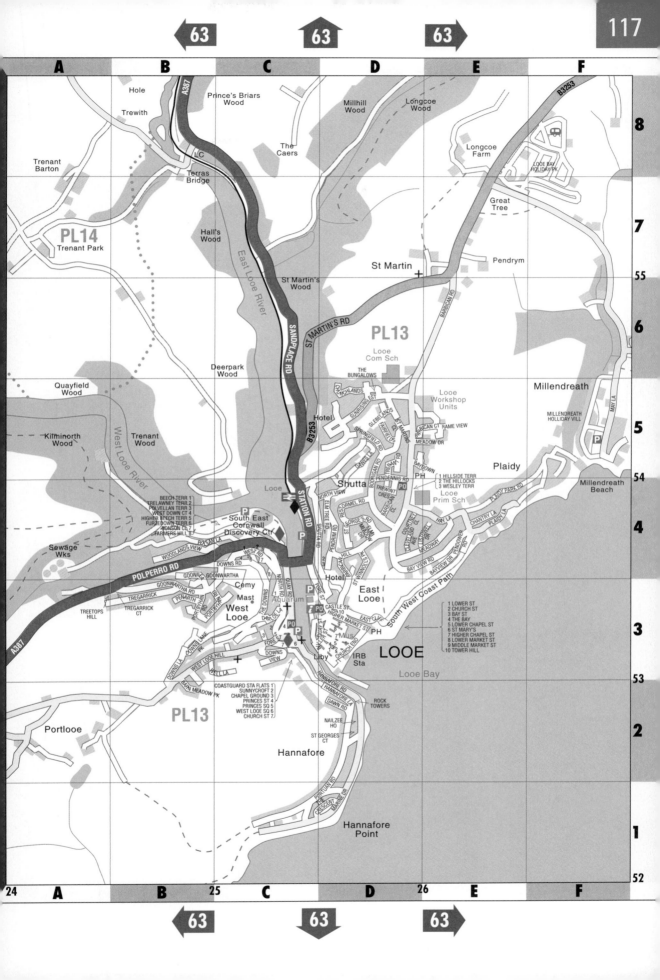

63 63 63

A B C D E F

8 7 55 6 54 4 3 53 2 1 52

Hole

Trewith

Trenant Barton

Prince's Briars Wood

The Caers

Millhill Wood

Longcoe Wood

Longcoe Farm

Looe Bay Holiday Pk

Great Tree

B3253

A387

LC

Terras Bridge

PL14
Trenant Park

Hall's Wood

East Looe River

St Martin's Wood

St Martin

Pendrym

PL13

Deerpark Wood

SANDPLACE RD

ST MARTIN'S RD

BARBICAN RD

B3253

Looe Com Sch

THE BUNGALOWS

Looe Workshop Units

Millendreath

MILLENDREATH HOLLIDAY VILL

Quayfield Wood

Kilminorth Wood

West Looe River

Trenant Wood

Hotel

ROCHLANDS

SUNRISING EST

GLEBELANDS

FAIRFIELDS

ST MARTINS

SPRINGFIELD RD

DAVIS LA

BODRIGAN RD

TRELAWNY RD

RAME VIEW

MEADOW DR

BARBICAN CT

Plaidy

MAY LA

Millendreath Beach

MILLENDREATH HOLLIDAY VILL

Looe

Shutta

Looe Prim Sch

1 HILLSIDE TERR
2 THE HILLOCKS
3 WESLEY TERR

PLAIDY PARK RD

CHANTRY LA

PLAIDY LA

STATION RD

P

BEECH TERR 1
TRELAWNEY TERR 2
POLVELLAN TERR 3
WEST DOWN CT 4
HIGHER BEECH TERR 5
FURZEDOWN TERR 6
BONSON CL 7
FARMERS HILL 8

South East Cornwall Discovery Ctr

P

Sewage Wks

WOODLANDS VIEW

POLPERRO RD

DOWNS RD

GOONWARTHA RD

GOONWARTHA

GOONR

Cemy

Mast

West Looe

WEST RD

THE DOWNS

NORTH RD

QUAY LA

NORTH VIEW

ELM TREE RD

PENDRIM RD

SHUTTA RD

ST GEORGE'S RD

CORMEL RD

PORTUAN HILL

ST WINNOLS PK

MEADOW

BAY VIEW RD

ST MARTINS

PENDENNIS RD

TREWINT CRESC

BARBICAN CL

COURTENAY RD

CLEVELAND CL

RUSSELL CT

MEADOWAY

BAYVIEW RD

BAYVIEW DR

PENDOWER RD

Hotel

East Looe

EAST CLIFF

South West Coast Path

Aquarium

TREGARRICK

TREGARRICK CT

PENARTH

PORTBYHAN

TREVORNA

A387

TREETOPS HILL

DOWNS LA

WEST LOOE HILL

WELL LA

DOWNS VIEW

FORE ST

BARN MEADOW PK

DOWNS LANE

COASTGUARD STA FLATS 1
SUNNYCROFT 2
CHAPEL GROUND 3
PRINCES ST 4
PRINCES SQ 5
WEST LOOE SQ 6
CHURCH ST 7

CASTLE ST

HIGHER MARKET ST

QUAY ST

FORE ST

Mus

CHURCH END

1 LOWER ST
2 CHURCH ST
3 BAY ST
4 THE BAY
5 LOWER CHAPEL ST
6 ST MARY'S
7 HIGHER CHAPEL ST
8 LOWER MARKET ST
9 MIDDLE MARKET ST
10 TOWER HILL

PH

LOOE

Looe Bay

Liby

IRB Sta

HANNAFORE RD

HANNAFORE A

DAWN RD

ROCK TOWERS

NAILZEE HO

ST GEORGES CT

PL13

Portlooe

Hannafore

PORTUAN RD

CRESCENT

MARINE DR

Hannafore Point

24 A B 25 C D 26 E F

63 63 63

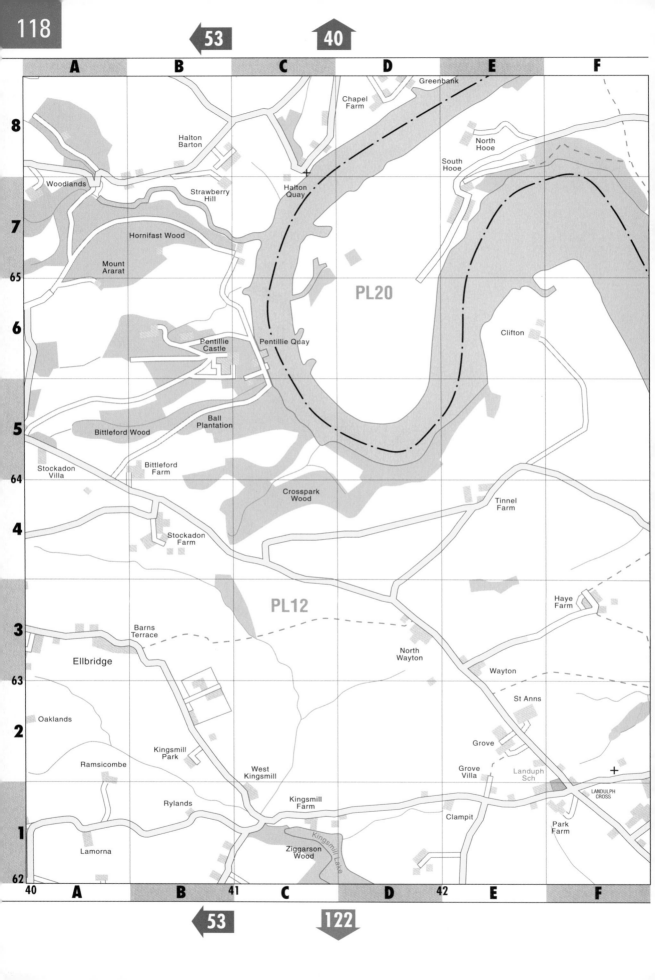

53
40

A **B** **C** **D** **E** **F**

8

Greenbank
Chapel Farm
Halton Barton
North Hooe
Woodlands
South Hooe
Strawberry Hill
Halton Quay

7

Hornifast Wood

65

Mount Ararat

PL20

6

Clifton
Pentillie Castle
Pentillie Quay

5

Ball Plantation
Bittleford Wood

64

Stockadon Villa
Bittleford Farm
Crosspark Wood
Tinnel Farm

4

Stockadon Farm

PL12

Haye Farm

3

Barns Terrace
North Wayton
Wayton
Ellbridge

63

St Anns
Oaklands

2

Grove
Kingsmill Park
Grove Villa
Landuph Sch
Ramsicombe
West Kingsmill
LANDULPH CROSS
Rylands
Kingsmill Farm
Clampit
Park Farm

1

Lamorna
Ziggarson Wood
Kingsmill Lake

62

40 **A** **B** 41 **C** **D** 42 **E** **F**

53
122

A B C D E F

8

Wottons Farm

Well Farm

Higher Birch

Down Farm

HOLE CROSS

Hewton

Cotts

Down Wood

Hole's Hole

7

Leeches

65

Hole Farm

Quay

Weir Quay

Shangri-La

6

Cleave Farm

LEY LA

Clamoak

Clamoak Poll Wood

Tuckham Bridge

Ley Farm

5

Clamoak Quay

Fairway

Shutecombe

64

Ormonde House

Parsonage Farm

HENSBURY LA

4

Liphil Quay

New Park Farm

PL20

Greystone

TREVITHAIN PK

PO

FORE ST

PH

SILVER ST

Bere Ferrers

Bere Ferrers

STATION RD

Bere Barton

3

63

Thorn Point

2

Cargreen

COOMBE LA

COOMBE DR

HOOPERS WAY

PH

Hall

CLOAKE PL

FORE ST

Quays

New Barn Farm

MILL GDNS

CHURCH LA

Penyoke

PL12

Pennard's Point

River Tavy

1

62

43 A B 44 C D 45 E F

River Tamar

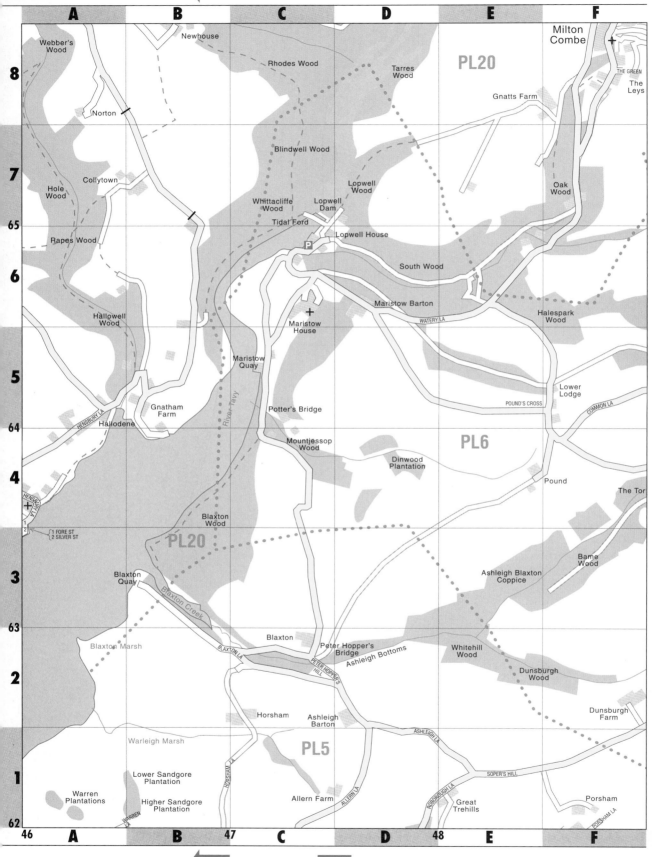

Uphill

Morey House

MOORLAND CL

Hotel

PL20

Dashel

Bickham

Bickham

Upper Road Plantation

Charity Bickham

Bulteel Bickham

Webbers

COMMON LA

Middlelodge Plantation

The Wilderness

Higher Park

Commonlane Plantation

Middle Lodge

LEG LANE DR

Henshears

Higher Lodge

PL6

Combe Park Farm

Little Down

Lower Upperton

ROBOROUGH DOWN LA

Welltown Bridge

Marrowpark Plantation

UPPERTON LA

North Broadley

Coppers

Haxter Lodge

Roborough Farm

Roborough Plantation

Leigh

LITTLE DOWN LA

Broadley

Broadley Ind Pk

BROADLEY CT

PARKWOOD CL

BROADLEY PARK RD

Roborough House

TAMERTON RD

LEIGH LA

Vicarage

HELE LA

Coombe Barton

NEW RD

Haxter Wood

PORSHAM CL

HAXTER CL

BELLIVER WAY

LOPES DR 1
VILLAGE DR 2

PH

TAVISTOCK RD

LEATSIDE

LEAF WK

CARSON LA

BLACKEVEN HILL

Roborough

Coombe Wood

Porsham Plantation

Belliver Ind Est

CRAMBER CL 3
STAPLE CL 4

HESSARY DR

JUMP CL

BLACKEVEN CL

BICKLEIGH DOWN RD

Hursley Bsns Pk

A386

PL5

Ten Acre Brake

A   B   C   D   E   F

8
Cross Park Farm
Rumbullion Farm
Sladeland
Marraborough
Colloggett Hill
PL12

7
Botusfleming
+ PH
+
Clark's Lake
NARROW LA
Moditonham House
Moditonham Quay
Colloggett Quay
Marsh Farm
Holy Well
The Marsh
Smallacombe
The Marsh

61
A388
Kingsmill Lake

6
Woodside Racing Stables
Atuba
East Town Farm
Carkeel
Burrhills Farm
Burrhills Quay
South Down
Hole Wood
Skinham Creek
Chine Fleet Country Club

5
Broadmoor Wood
DIRTY LA
Carkeel Farm
Saltash Service Area
A388
RIVER CT
FOSCUMBE RD
PRIDEAUX CL
KINGSMILL RD
Tamar View Ind Est
AVERY WAY
PL12
Quarryfield Coppice
Tamar Park

60
Peninsular Pk
Saltash Bsns Pk
FORGE LA
CANNON RD
B3271
Gwel Avon Bsns Pk
Saltash
MORTAIN RD
GILSTON RD
BRUNEL
CASTLE IND EST
LYNDON CT
BADGERS WLK
GOLDFINCH GR
MYRTLES CT
THE WAY
Pill Farm
PILL LA
Mill Park
BEAUMONT TERR

4
A38 LISKEARD RD
B3271
WHITY CROSS
Saltash Parkway Ind Est
LONG ACRE
LONG LONG RD
WOOD ACRE
Moorlands Trad Est
BURRATON RD
CALLINGTON RD
PILLMERE DR
HONEYSUCKLE
HAREBELL CL
BLUEBELL CL
MEADOW DR
OAK APPLE CL
CAMPION CL
GRASSMERE
CRESTWAY
DARTMOOR VIEW
GOLDFINCH CRES
PADDOCK CL
Burraton
CAREY CT
ROGERS DR
BROOKS HILL
POLLARDS WAY
HESSARY VIEW
BROCKDOWN
CARBADON TERR
Saltmill Creek
P
B3271

3
Latchbrook
BARROW DOWN
LISKEARD RD
PH
SMITHS WAY
BUTTERDOWN 1
SMITHFIELD DR 2
HIGHFIELD PK 3
PONDFIELD RD
HEART RD
PLOUGH GN
GRENFELL GDNS
FEARNSIDE WAY
GRENFELL AVE
WARRATON LA 1
WARRATON GN 2
WARRATON RD
Sch
FRITH RD
WINE'S RD
ST GEORGES RD
LONGVIEW RD
CUNINGHAM
CALLINGTON RD
CLEAR VIEW
CONCORD
ADIT LA
JACKSON WAY
HILLSIDE RD
DEER PK
NEW RD
Westbourne
NORTH RD B3271

59
FOXGLOVE WAY 4
THE HEDGEROWS 5
Latchbrook Leat
Wadgeworthy Farm
GALLACHER WAY
PROSPECT LA
HERITAGE
THORN LA
THE CLOSE
PORTER WAY
HOBBS CT
BROOKING WAY
RUSSELL CT
OAKLANDS DR
OAKLANDS GN
HOWARD CL
TORBRIDGE RD
CASTLEMEAD DR
MORTIMORE CL
BURNETT CL
6 LANGERWELL 13
7 PROSPECT WLK
8 THE GREEN
9 ELM COTTS
10 THE SQUARE
11 SOUTHFIELD
12 HODGE CL
CAS LEMEAD
SHANLANE
JUBILEE
CLEAR VIEW
South Pill
Saltash Leisure Ctr
Liby
Brunel Prim Sch
WINDSOR LA
GLEBE AVE
FENTEN
P
PO
Regal CT
WESLEY ST
FORE ST
CULVER

2
Burraton Coombe
TOWER CT 13 16
CASTLE CT 14
YELLOW TOR CT 15
POLLARD CL 16
LINNET
ROWAN
YELLOW TOR LA
HAWKS PK
WENTWORTH
WILLOW GN
MANOR PK
FAIRWAY
MAYBROOK DR
HOLCROFT CL
BROOM HILL
Saltash Coll
SWARRATON RD
STEPHENS RD
HAWTH
HIGHER PORT VIEW
HARBOUR VIEW
LOVE LA
LOWER PORT VIEW
VALLEY RD
TRELAWNEY RD
Wearde
VINCENT WAY
St Barnabas
VICTORIA RD
ESSA RD

1
Wadgeworthy Farm
Longlands
LONGLANDS LA
TOR LA
SALTASH
Cross
MEADOWSWEET
NANCARROWS 1
TANNERY CT 2
CARNOUSTIE DR 3
BIRKDALE CL 4
SUMMERFIELDS
BARKER'S HILL
HEWITT CL
Sch
DOWN
WENTWORTH
ST ANDREWS
BRIANSWAY
CHURCHTOWN VALE
PARKESWAY
St Stephens
F Ed
BROAD WLK
WEARDE RD
KILGREW AVE
TOWER VIEW
UPLANDS
BROAD WLK
COWDRAY TERR
PO
BERRY RD
COURTLANDS
LYNHER DR
CHURCHILL WLK
DEACON DR
Bishop Cornish CE Prim Sch
1 BABIS FARM MEWS
2 BABIS FARM CT
3 BABIS FARM ROW

58
Trehan
Little Trehan Farm
FAYRE VIEW
RIVERSIDE COTT
CASTLE HILL
GERALDINE TERR
Forder
ST STEPHEN'S HILL
House on the Hill
Saltash Com Sch

40   A   B   41   C   D   42   E   F

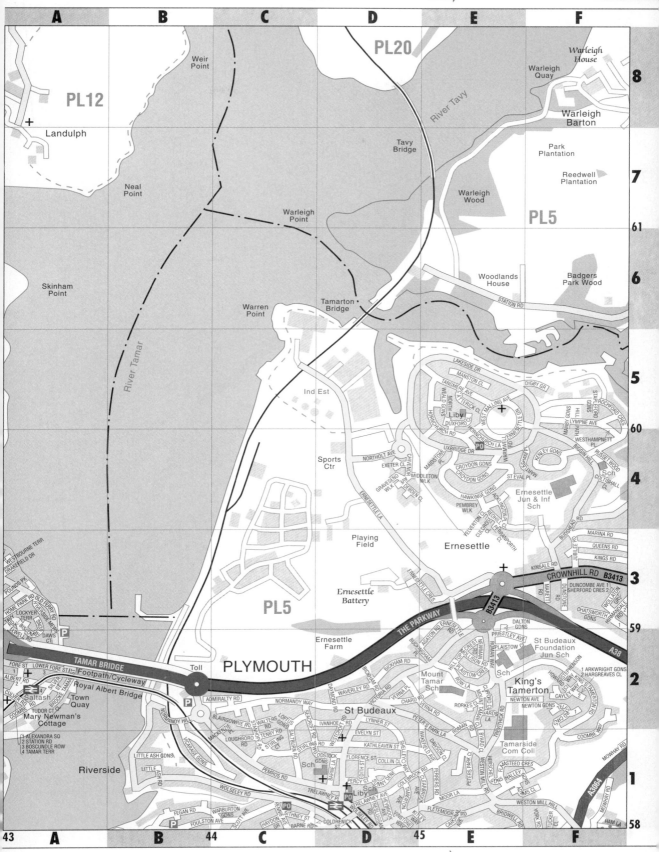

A   B   C   D   E   F

PL20

Weir Point

PL12

Landulph

River Tavy

Tavy Bridge

Warleigh House

Warleigh Quay

8

Warleigh Barton

Neal Point

Warleigh Point

Park Plantation

Reedwell Plantation

7

Warleigh Wood

PL5

61

Skinham Point

Warren Point

Tamarton Bridge

Woodlands House

Badgers Park Wood

6

STATION RD

River Tamar

Ind Est

LAKESIDE DR

MANSTON CL

TANGMERE AVE

WEALD GDNS

NORTH HORNCHURCH RD

ATTERICK CL

MANSTON CL

DUXFORD

Liby

WEST TAMAR LING AVE

DIGBY GR

STARCHFORD CRES

STARCHFORD GDNS

MANBY GDNS

LYMPNE AVE

HILL

RUSSEL WOOD

5

Sports Ctr

NORTHOLT AVE

EXETER CL

MAIDSTONE PL

UXBRIDGE DR

CHIVENOR

PO

TERNESTILE RD

KENLEY GDNS

WESTHAMPNETT PL

60

GRAVESEND WLK

DESDEN PL

MIDDLETON WLK

JNV

CROYDON GDNS

CROYDON GDNS

ST EVAL PL

BIGGIN HILL

Sch

COLTISHALL CL

4

ERNESETTLE LA

HAWKINGE GDNS

PEMBREY WLK

VELVERTON GDNS

CULSWORTHY

ACKLINGTON DR

FARRANFORTH

Ernesettle Jun & Inf Sch

BUDSHEAD RD

MARINA RD

QUEENS RD

KINGS RD

Playing Field

Ernesettle

Ernesettle Battery

ERNESETTLE CRES

KINSALE RD

CROWNHILL RD   B3413

3

MARETTI

DUNSTONE

CHATSWORTH GDNS

59

PL5

THE PARKWAY

B3413

DALTON GDNS

PRIESTLEY AVE

St Budeaux Foundation Jun Sch

A38

Ernesettle Farm

AGATON RD

BUDSHEAD RD

Sch

ROMAN WAY

PLAISTOW CL

King's Tamerton

2

TAMAR BRIDGE

Toll

PLYMOUTH

BICKHAM RD

ADMIRALTY RD

Mount Tamar Sch

NEWTON GDNS

Footpath/Cycleway

Royal Albert Bridge

Town Quay

Mary Newman's Cottage

St Budeaux

Tamarside Com Coll

1

Riverside

Liby

PO

58

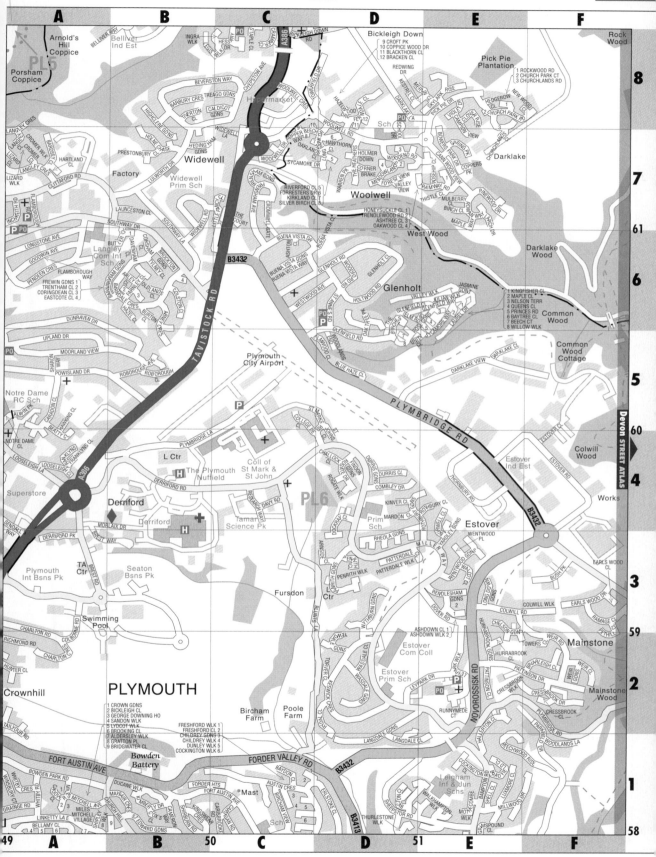

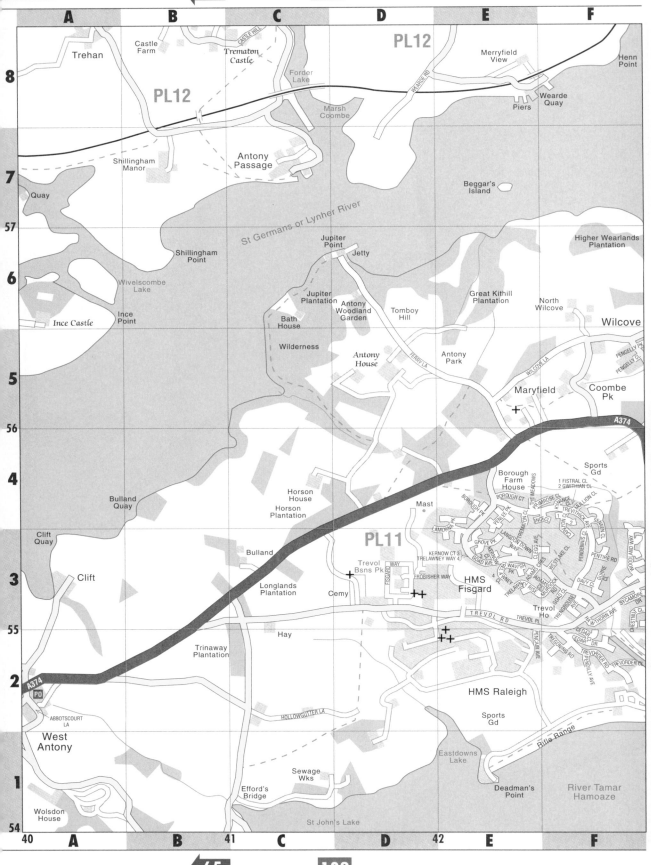

PL12

A B C D E F

8 Trehan

Castle Farm

Castle Hill

Trematon Castle

Forder Lake

PL12

Merryfield View

Henn Point

Wearde Rd

Piers

Wearde Quay

7 PL12

Shillingham Manor

Antony Passage

Marsh Coombe

Quay

St Germans or Lynher River

Beggar's Island

57

Shillingham Point

Jupiter Point

Jetty

Higher Wearlands Plantation

6 Wivelscombe Lake

Jupiter Plantation

Antony Woodland Garden

Bath House

Great Kithill Plantation

North Wilcove

Wilcove

Ince Castle

Ince Point

Wilderness

Antony House

Tomboy Hill

Antony Park

Ferry La

Wilcove La

Pengelly Pk

Pengelly Cl

5

Maryfield

Coombe Pk

56

Bulland Quay

Horson House

Horson Plantation

A374

Borough Farm House

Sports Gd

1 Fistral Cl
2 Gwithian Cl

4

Clift Quay

Mast

PL11

Borough Pk

Borough Ct

The Meadows

Primrose Cl

Grange

Trevithick Ave

Seaver Cl

Pentire Rd

Penlee Pk

Kynance

Trevithick Cl

Ince Cl

3 Clift

Longlands Plantation

Bulland

Trevol Bsns Pk

Cemy

Way

Fisgard

Frobisher Way

Trelawney Way 4
Kernow Ct 3

Grove Pk

Kernow Pk

Cleggs

Langdon Down Way

Goad Ave

Adams Cl

Trelawney Rise

Wavish Pk

Westlake Cl

Murdock

Penderths Cl

Davy Cl

Gurne Cl

HMS Fisgard

Trevol Ho

Sycamore

Hawthorn Ave

Chestnut Cl

55

Hay

Trevol Rd

Trevol Pl

Cedar Dr

Tregoning Rd

Trevorder Rd

Trepenruly Ave

Trevorder Cl

2

A374

PO

Abbotscourt La

Trinaway Plantation

Hollowgutter La

HMS Raleigh

Sports Gd

Pencar Ave

Tregonning Rd

West Antony

Eastdowns Lake

Rifle Range

1

Efford's Bridge

Sewage Wks

Deadman's Point

River Tamar Hamoaze

Wolsdon House

St John's Lake

54

40 A B 41 C D 42 E F

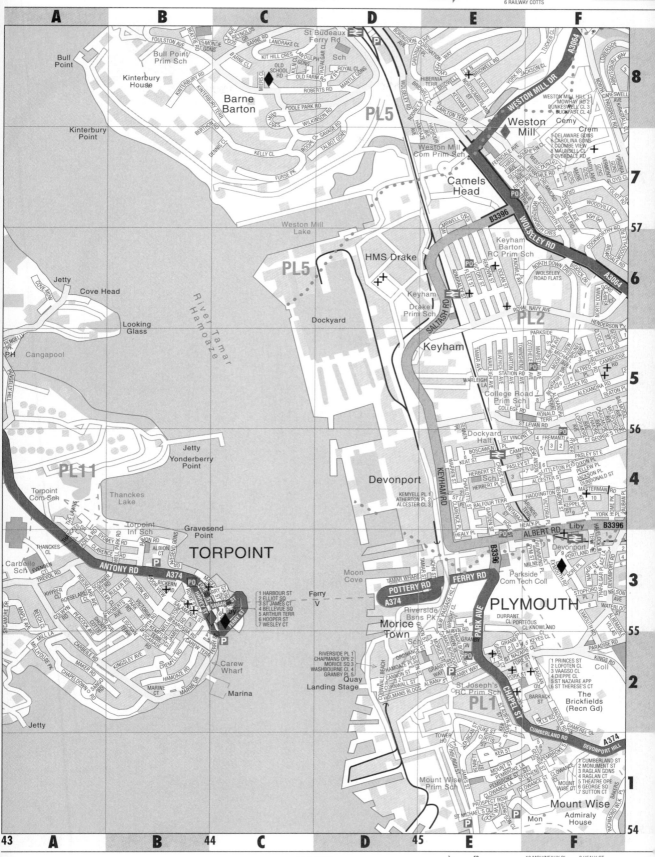

F5
1 NEPEAN ST
2 ADELAIDE ST
3 BRUNEL TERR
4 EPWORTH TERR
5 SUSSEX TERR
6 RAILWAY COTTS
7 YORK TERR
8 ST MAWES TERR

1 HARBOUR ST
2 ELLIOT SQ
3 ST JAMES CT
4 BELLEVUE SQ
5 ARTHUR TERR
6 HOOPER ST
7 WESLEY CT

RIVERSIDE PL 1
CHAPMANS OPE 2
MORICE SQ 3
WASHBOURNE CL 4
WESTBOURNE PL 5

1 PRINCES ST
2 LOFOTEN CL
3 VAAGSO CL
4 DIEPPE CL
5 ST NAZAIRE APP
6 ST THERESE'S CT

1 CUMBERLAND ST
2 MONUMENT ST
3 RAGLAN GDNS
4 RAGLAN CT
5 THEATRE OPE
6 GEORGE SQ
7 SUTTON CT

KEMYELL PL 1
ATHERTON PL 2
ALCESTER CL 3

WESTON MILL HILL 1
MOWHAY RD 2
DUNKESWELL CL 3
BUCKFAST CL 4

5 DELAWARE GDNS
6 CAROLINA GDNS
7 COOMBE VIEW
8 MAUNSELL CL
9 OVERDALE RD

43   44   45   54

133   128

F3
1 CLARENDON HO
2 GARFIELD TERR
3 TRAFALGAR PL
4 THE MEWS
5 NELSON GDNS
6 BEYROUT PL
7 ST MICHAEL'S CT
8 ST MICHAEL'S TERR
9 PORTLAND CT
10 MOLYNEAUX PL
F4
1 ST GEORGES CT
2 HORNBY ST
3 PHILLIMORE ST
4 FREMANTLE GDNS
5 FAIRFAX TERR
6 HARGOOD TERR
7 HARRISON ST
8 KEPPEL TERR
9 HEALY CT
10 BRUNSWICK PL

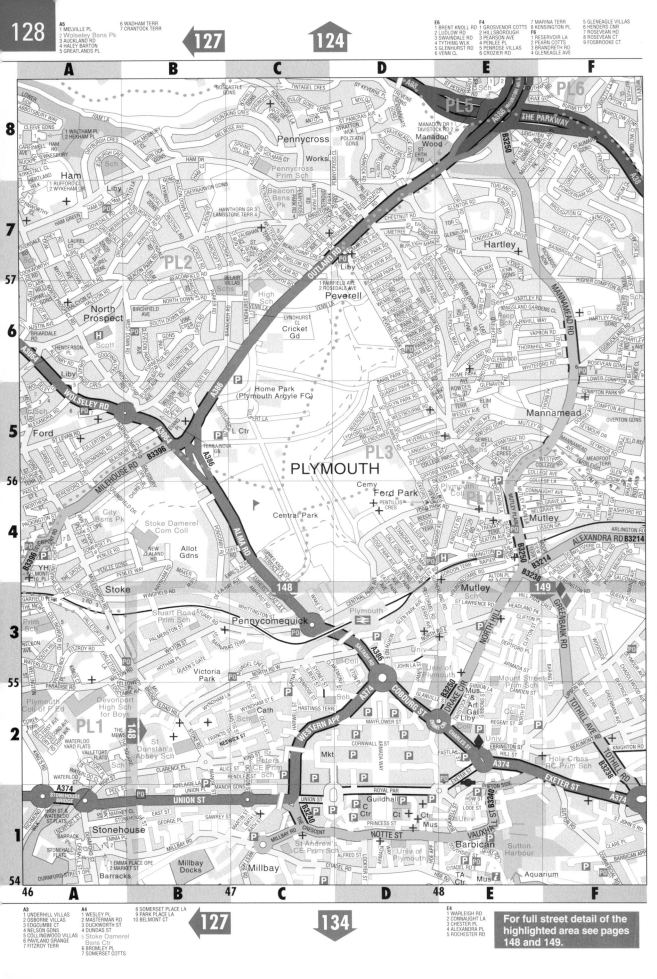

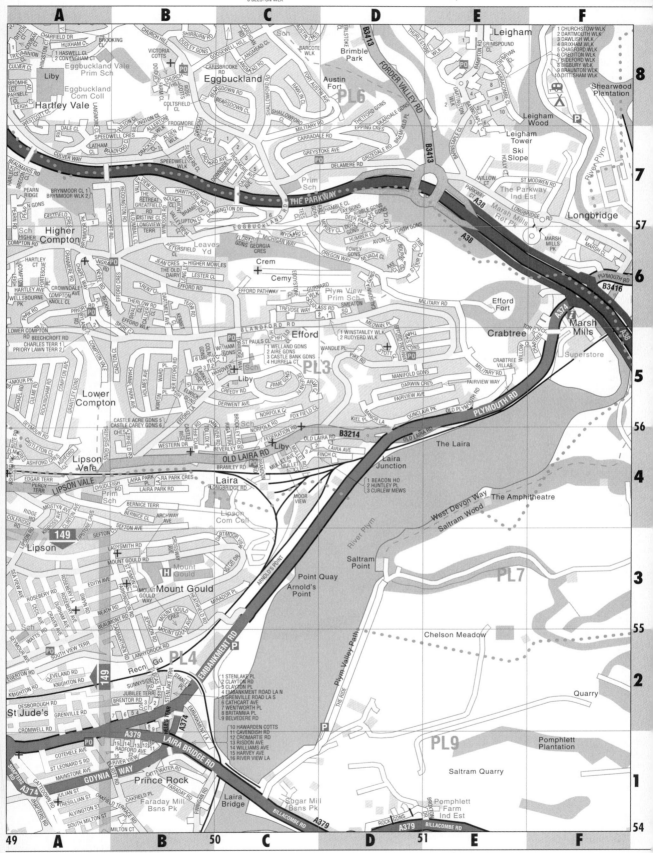

C7
1 BRAMBLE WLK
2 BOWHAYS WLK
3 BRISMAR WLK
4 MOORFIELD AVE
5 BEAUDYN WLK
6 BEESTON WLK

125

130

1 CHURCHSTOW WLK
2 DARTMOUTH WLK
3 DAWLISH WLK
4 BRIXHAM WLK
5 CHAGFORD WLK
6 CREDITON WLK
7 BIDEFORD WLK
8 BIGBURY WLK
9 BRAUNTON WLK
10 DITTISHAM WLK

For full street detail of the highlighted area see page 149.

135

130

129

E7
1 PERSEVERANCE COTTS
2 BLANCHARD PL

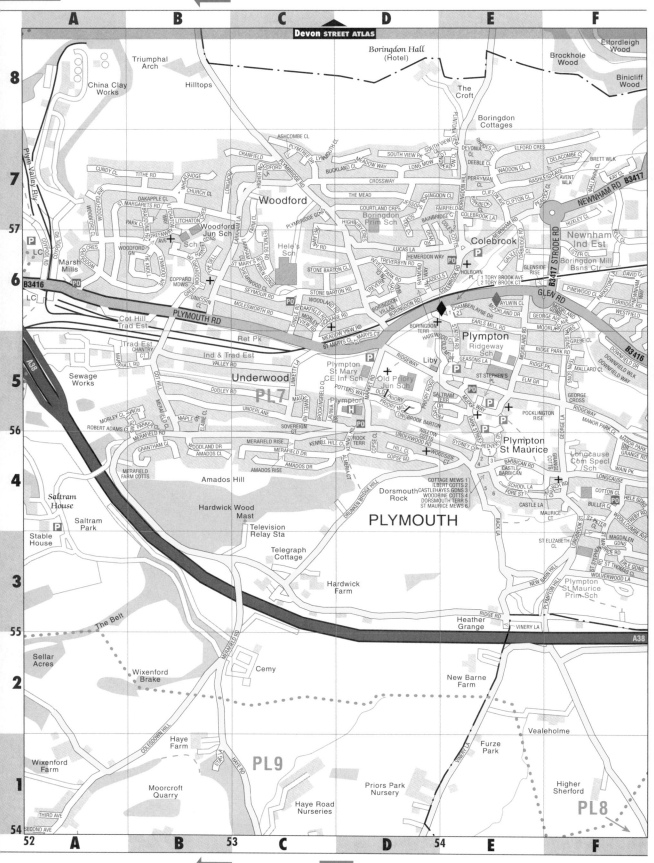

Devon STREET ATLAS

A B C D E F

Devon STREET ATLAS

8

Sparkwell Farm

Newnham Park

Furzeacre Wood

Windwhistle

Sparkwell CE Prim Sch

B3417

Furzeacre Bridge

Beechwood Cross

Beechwood

Holly Wood

Lowdamoor

Hemerdon

Hemerdon House

Old Newnham Farm

Hemerdon Farm

Miners' Arms (PH)

Lodge

7

Old Newnham

WEST PARK HILL

Sherwell

NEWNHAM RD

CORNFIELD GDNS

Lodge

BIRCHWOOD GDNS
NEWNHAM
COMPASS DR

UPPER

LOWER GRIDINGS

Sparkwell Bridge

57

Newnham Ind Est

FACEACRE CL

BRIDLE LA

Moor Bridge

STOGGY LA

6

HEMERDON HTS

GREENWOOD PARK CL

GREENWOOD PARK RD

WESTMOOR CL

GLENAVEN CL

LANGAGE CROSS

WALDON CL

TORRIDGE RD

TORRIDGE RD

HEMERDON HTS

ALMOND DR

OAKFIELD CL

GREENVILLE CT

ROBECLAVE

WESTFIELD

WESTRO

Chaddlewood

LEIGH

GILBERT

OAKWOOD

Langage Science Pk

KINGSTON CL

POULTNEY CL

COUNTY CL

DENGIE CL

POPLAR CL

FERN CL

BARNFIELD DR

WESTERN WOOD WAY

BEECHWOOD WAY

Higher Langage

Schs

BROOKFIELD

SPRUCE GDNS

JUNIPER WAY

BAKER

DOWNS

Combe Farm

5

NASH CL

ROWAN CL

HICKORY DR

JASMINE GDNS

PERIWINKLE DR

WALNUT

GLEN RD

Lower Langage

HILLCREST CL

HORSWELL CHADDLEWOOD HO

CLEMENT

ST MARNARDE CL

CELANDINE DR

HOLLAND RD

SUMMER LANDS CL

Applethorn Slade

DEVERY CL

MOULTON CL

FLANDERS GDNS

56

KENMARE DR

WENSUM CL

LITTLEWOOD CL

EDWARDS CL

CARDIFF CL

KNOWLE CL

EAGLE RD

EASTERN WOOD RD

GARDEN CL

CHADDLEWOOD CL

LONGWOOD CL

SPARKE CL

POLE DR

TOTNES DR

DUNSTER CL

ASHLEIGH WAY

Langage Ind Est

MEADOW CL

MANOR PARK DR

THE SPINNEY

OKEHAMPTON CL

BELLINGHAM CRES

TREGANTLE

SANDY RD

Langage Pk

PL7

BARN CL

4

GRANGE RD

WAGGON HILL

NEW PARK RD

WALLACE RD

CORNWOOD RD

ST MAURICE VIEW

GRIGGS CL

RIDGEWAY

BRAEMAR CL

HELE CL

YEALMPSTONE DR

HERON CL

Ley Farm

CHERRY TREE LA

LOWER FARM

YEALMPSTONE DR

MADDOCK DR

NEAL CL

DANUM DR

HARESTON CL

Voss

BROADLANDS RD

COLLARD RD

BRAMBLE

HIGHER PARK CL

The Lyneham Inn (PH)

3

ERLE GDNS

PK

ONE CL

CANHAYE CL

MEADOWFIELD PL

CANEFIELDS AVE

GREENLEES DR

TUXTOM CL

WOLVERWOOD CL

A38

Yealmpstone Farm Prim Sch

AYCLIFFE GDNS

ATELANDS CL

WOLVERWOOD LA

DEEP LA

B3416

SPRINGWOOD CL

BROOK CL

55

DEEP LA

Battisford

Wiverton House

Butlas Farm

Tuxton Farm

Tuxton Wood

2

Wiverton Acre

PL8

Blackpool

1

East Sherford

Devon STREET ATLAS

A38 Exeter, M5

Devon STREET ATLAS

54

55 A B 56 C D 57 E F

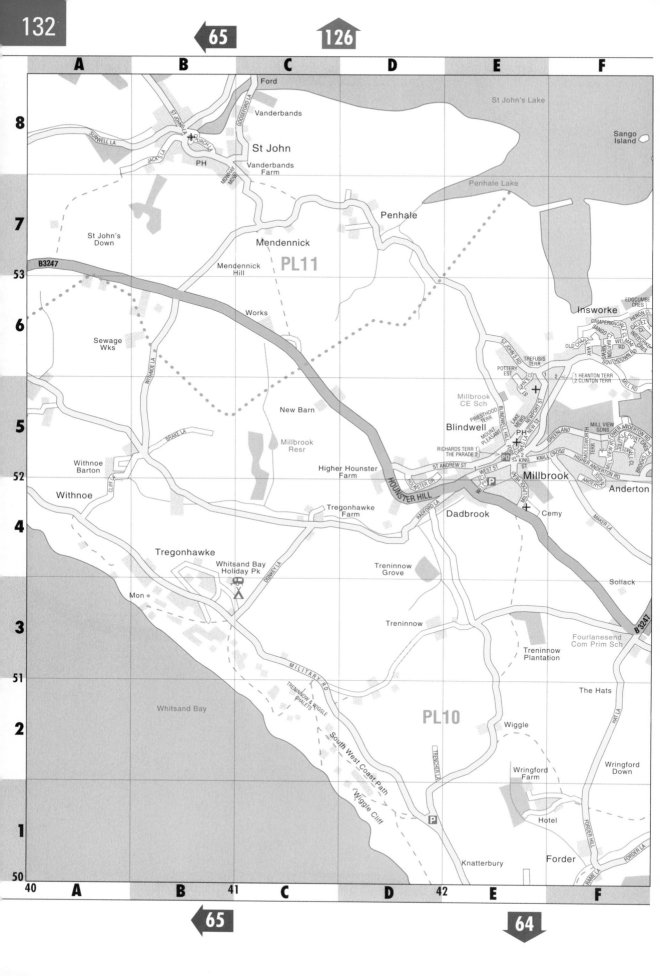

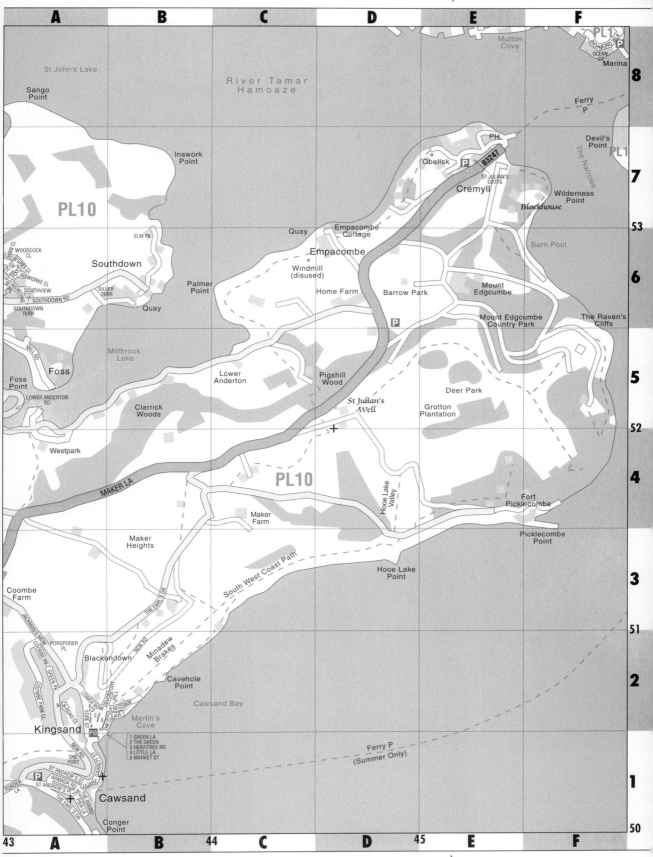

Mutton Cove

Marina

St John's Lake

River Tamar Hamoaze

Sango Point

Ferry P

Devil's Point

Inswork Point

PL1

PH

Obelisk

B3247

ST JULIAN'S COTTS

Cremyll

Wilderness Point

Blockhouse

PL10

ELM PK

Quay

Empacombe Cottage

Barn Pool

SWAN CL
WOODCOCK CL
EGRET CL
INSWORKE CL
SOUTHVIEW
SILVER TERR
SOUTHDOWN RD
SOUTHDOWN TERR

Southdown

Windmill (disused)

Empacombe

Home Farm

Barrow Park

Mount Edgcumbe

Quay

Palmer Point

P

Mount Edgcumbe Country Park

The Raven's Cliffs

MILL RD

Foss

Millbrook Lake

Lower Anderton

Pigshill Wood

Foss Point

LOWER ANDERTON RD

Clarrick Woods

Deer Park

Grotton Plantation

Westpark

St Julian's Well

MAKER LA

PL10

Hooe Lake Valley

Fort Picklecombe

Maker Farm

Picklecombe Point

Maker Heights

South West Coast Path

Hooe Lake Point

Coombe Farm

JACKMAN'S MDW
COOMBE PK
COTHER PARK CL
GREEN PK
NEW ROAD CL
PORSPODER PL

Blackendown

NEW RD

Minadew Brakes

Cavehole Point

Cawsand Bay

THE EARL'S DR
DEVONPORT HILL
LOWER ROW
THE CAVE
KINGSWAY
FORE ST

Kingsand

PO

Martin's Cove

1 GREEN LA
2 THE GREEN
3 HEAVITREE RD
4 LITTLE LA
5 MARKET ST

Ferry P (Summer Only)

NEW RD
FORDER LA
ST ANDREW'S ST
ARMADA RD
ST ANDREW'S PL
THE SQUARE
THE ROUND
ST THORN'S
THE FORT

P

Cawsand

Conger Point

43
44
45

133 ◀ 128 ▲

For full street detail of the highlighted area see pages 148 and 149.

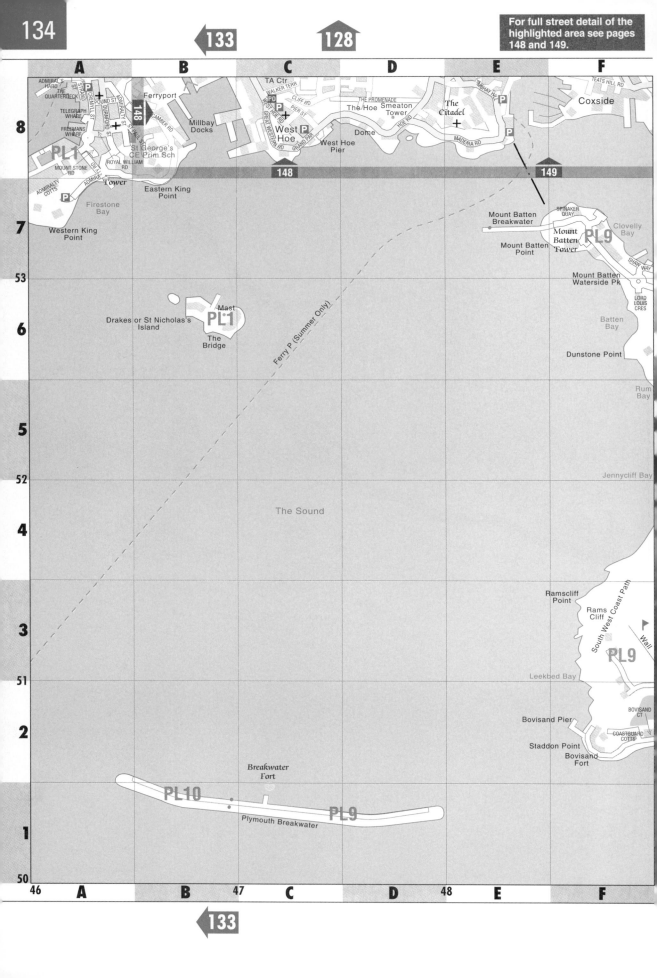

A B C D E F

8

ADMIRAL'S HARD
THE QUARTERDECK
TELEGRAPH WHARF
FREEMANS WHARF
PL1
MOUNT STONE RD
ADMIRALTY COTTS
Tower
Firestone Bay
Western King Point

Ferryport
Millbay Docks
St George's CE Prim Sch
Eastern King Point

TA Ctr
WALKER TERR
CLIFF RD
PIER ST
WEST HOE RD
GREAT WESTERN RD
GRAND PAR
West Hoe
West Hoe Pier

THE PROMENADE
The Hoe
Smeaton Tower
Dome
HOE RD
MADEIRA RD

LAMBHAY HILL
The Citadel

TEATS HILL RD
Coxside

148   149

7

Mount Batten Breakwater
Mount Batten Point
SPINAKER QUAY
Mount Batten Tower
PL9
Clovelly Bay
SHAW WAY

53

Mount Batten Waterside Pk
LORD LOUIS CRES

6

Drakes or St Nicholas's Island
Mast
PL1
The Bridge

Ferry P (Summer Only)

Batten Bay
Dunstone Point
Rum Bay

5

52

Jennycliff Bay

4

The Sound

3

Ramscliff Point
Rams Cliff
South West Coast Path
PL9
Wall

51

Leekbed Bay
BOVISAND CT

2

Breakwater Fort
Bovisand Pier
Staddon Point
Bovisand Fort
COASTGUARD COTTS

PL10
PL9
Plymouth Breakwater

1

50

46   A   B   47   C   D   48   E   F

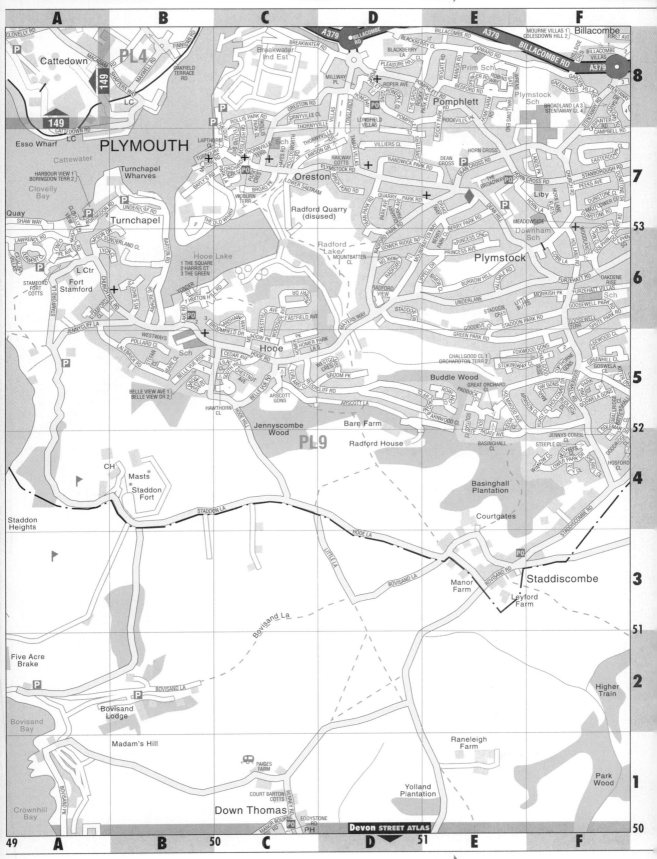

For full street detail of the highlighted area see page 149.

129

136

135

A B C D E F

8

7

53

6

5

52

4

3

51

2

1

50

Cattedown

PL4

149

149

LC

Esso Wharf

Cattewater

Clovelly Bay

Quay

Shaw Way

PLYMOUTH

Turnchapel Wharves

Turnchapel

Harbour View 1
Boringdon Terr 2

Lawrence Rd

Fort Stamford

Stamford Fort Cotts

L Ctr

Hooe Lake
1 THE SQUARE
2 HARRIS CT
3 THE GREEN

Hooe

Sch

Belle View Ave 1
Belle View Dr 2

Hawthorn Cl

Jennyscombe Wood

PL9

CH

Masts

Staddon Fort

Staddon Heights

Staddon La

Breakwater Ind Est

Breakwater Rd

A379

Billacombe Rd

Oreston

Radford Quarry (disused)

Radford Lake

Mountbatten Cl

Barn Farm

Radford House

Basinghall Plantation

Courtgates

Hooe La

Littlela

Bovisand La

Bovisand La

Five Acre Brake

Bovisand Lodge

Bovisand Bay

Madam's Hill

Crownhill Bay

Bovisand Pk

Paiges Farm

Court Barton Cotts

Down Thomas

Manor Bourne Rd

Eddystone Rd
PH

Pomphlett

Horn Cross

Plymstock

Buddle Wood

Great Orchard

Paddock

Challgood Cl 1
Orchardton Terr 2

Jennys Combe Cl

Steeple Cl

Hosford Cl

Basinghall Plantation

Manor Farm

Leyford Farm

Staddiscombe

Raneleigh Farm

Yolland Plantation

Higher Train

Park Wood

Billacombe

Mourne Villas 1
Colesdown Hill 2

Billacombe Villas

A379

Liby

Downham Sch

Meadowside

Prim Sch

Plymstock Sch

Broadland La 3
Stentaway Cl 4

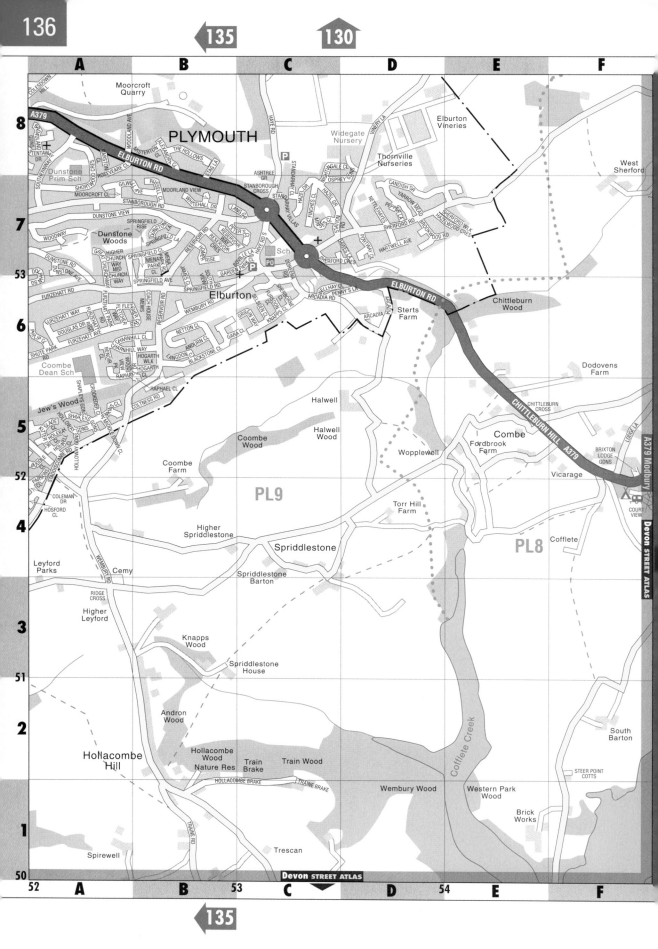

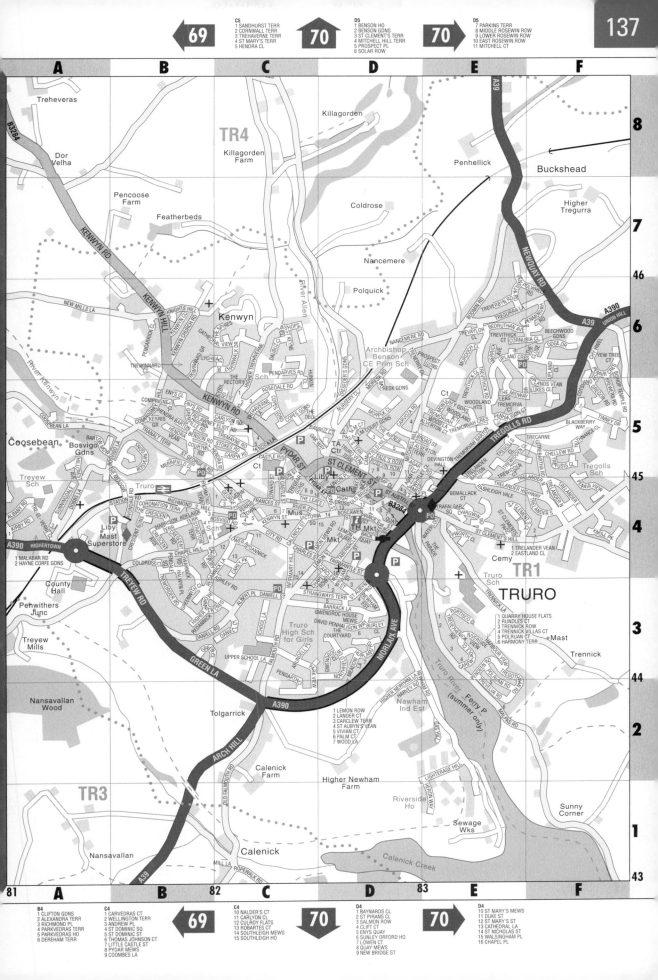

66 67

A B C D E F

8

Oak Wood
Home Farm
Magor Plantation

7
Magor Farm
Mount Whistle Farm
South Tehidy
Halgoss
Mount Whistle Rd

Kieve Mill Cottage
Magor Downs
Roscroggan
Tolvaddon Energy Pk

42
Kieve Hill Farm
Rosewarne Farm
Depot
Tolvaddon

6
Roskear Croft
Great Wheal Seton

Reskadinnick
North Rosewarne Farm
Rosewarne Terr
Rosewarne (Trng Ctr)

TR14

5
Higher Rosewarne
Forge Ind Pk
Rosemellin Com Prim Sch

41
Race Farm
Lower Rosewarne
Rosewarne Mews
Boiler Works Rd
Roskear Sch

4
New Downs Farm
Formal Ind Pk
Roskear
Pendarves St
A3047

Treswithian Farm
Treswithian
Cemy
Treswithian Rd
College St
Trelowarren St
Wesley St
Roskear
Roskear Sch
Dolcoath Rd

3
Camborne Sch & Com Coll
Crane
St Meriadoc CE Jun Sch
Church St
Trevenson St
Coll (Annexe)

40
Camborne
Liby
The Cross
South Terr
Trevithick Sch
Camborne
Pengegon

2
Cogegoes Ind Pk
Cogegoes Farm
Bounderven Farm
Pendarves Rd
Mount Pleasant Rd
Wheal Harriet

1
Penponds
Higher Penponds Rd
Pendarves View
Trevithick Sch
Mount Pleasant Farm
Beacon

39
63 A B 64 C D 65 E F

79 79

D3
1 ROSEWARNE RD
2 GURNEY'S LA
3 COMMERCIAL SQ
4 NEW CONNECTION ST
5 GODOLPHIN CT

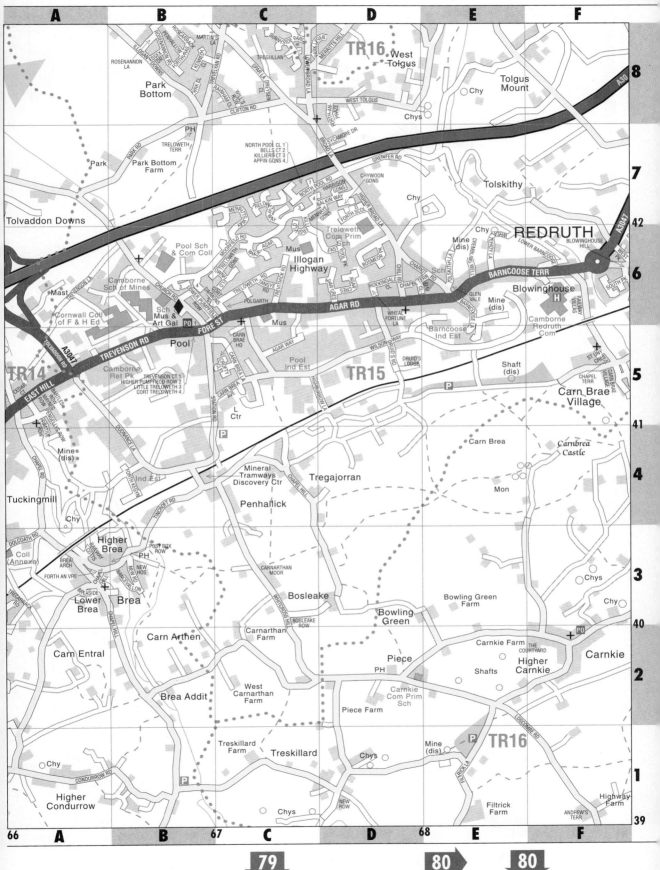

A B C D E F

8
7
42
6
5
41
4
3
40
2
1
39

A30

TR16
West Tolgus
Tolgus Mount
Chy
Chys

Park Bottom
ROSEACRACK
MARTIN'S LA
SUNNYSIDE PARK
KENNEDY
TREGULLAN
PARK LA KIEN
MERRITTS HILL
ROSENANNON LA
PENHALLOW RD
ILLOGAN DOWNS
RAVENHAM CL
PARK CL
THEVELAN RD
WILL'S ROW
SPAR LA DREYBEN CL

PH
TRELOWETH TERR
PARK RD
CLIFTON RD
Park
Park Bottom Farm

West Tolgus
NORTH POOL CL 1
BELLS CT 2
KILLIERS CT 3
APPIN GDNS 4
BROAD LA
SYCAMORE DR
POLPAN PRAZE

Tolskithy
GRENFER RD

CHYWOON GDNS
Chy

Tolvaddon Downs

NORTH POOL RD
HARRISON GDNS
BALKIN WAY
HIGHER BROAD LA
FORTH SCOL

Treloweth Com Prim Sch

REDRUTH
Mine (dis)
Chy
CREAMS WELL
LOWER BARNCOOSE
Blowinghouse Hill
POLSKITH LA

Mast
Camborne Sch of Mines

Pool Sch & Com Coll
MOORFIELD RD
MERRITTS WAY
KILLY WAY
AGAR RD
Mus
Illogan Highway
TRELOWETH
BOSMEOR
EAST POOL RD
AGAR CRES
ROEKINDALE CL
CHAPEL TERR
CHILI RD
CHARDY RD
Sch
GLEN VALE
Mine (dis)
Blowinghouse
H
Camborne Redruth Com
BARNCOOSE TERR
RAILWAY VILLAS
SOUTH PK
WEST PK

Cornwall Coll of F & H Ed
TREVENSON L
CHURCH RD
LOWER POW ROW
Sch
Mus & Art Gal
PO
FORE ST
Mus
POLGARTH
AGAR RD
TANGYE RD
TREVITHICK RD
SIMMONS CL
WHEAL FORTUNE LA
Barncoose Ind Est

A3047
TREVENSON RD
Pool
CARN BREA HO
Camborne Ret Pk
TREVENSON CT 1
HIGHER PUMPFIELD ROW 2
LITTLE TRELOWETH 3
CORT TRELOWETH 4
CARN BREA LA
AGAR WAY
Pool Ind Est
WILSON WAY
DRUID'S WAY
DRUID'S LODGE
Shaft (dis)
ST DAY CRES
CHAPEL TERR
Carn Brae Village

TR14
EAST HILL
TOLVADDON RD
CEDAR CT
BARTLES
MAIN RD
PENGELL'S ROW
PRIMITIVE ROW
Mine (dis)
DUDNANCE LA
L Ctr
STATION RD
P
HIGHROAD LA
TR15
P
Carn Brea
Carnbrea Castle
Mon

41

Tuckingmill
Chy
CHAPEL RD
FORTH KEGYN
Ind Est
TINCROFT RD
Mineral Tramways Discovery Ctr
CHAPEL HILL
Tregajorran
Penhallick
Chys
Chy

Coll (Annexe)
DOLCOATH RD
TRECARRACK RD
Higher Brea
RAILWAY
COTTS
BREA ARCH
FORTH AN VRE
NEW HOS
PH
POST BOX ROW
CARNARTHAN MOOR
Bowling Green Farm
Chys
Chy

Lower Brea
Brea
NANCE
NEW RD
KITTO
WHITCROSS LA
Bosleake
BOSLEAKE ROW
Bowling Green
PO
40
Carnkie

Carn Entral
Carn Arthen
Carnarthan Farm
Piece
PH
Carnie Farm
THE COURTYARD
Higher Carnkie
Shafts

Brea Addit
West Carnarthan Farm
Piece Farm
Carnkie Com Prim Sch
Mine (dis)
TR16
LOSCOMBE RD

Chy
CONDURROW RD
P
Treskillard Farm
Treskillard
Chys
NEW ROW
FILTRICK LA
Filtrick Farm
ANDREW'S TERR
Highway Farm

Higher Condurrow
Chys

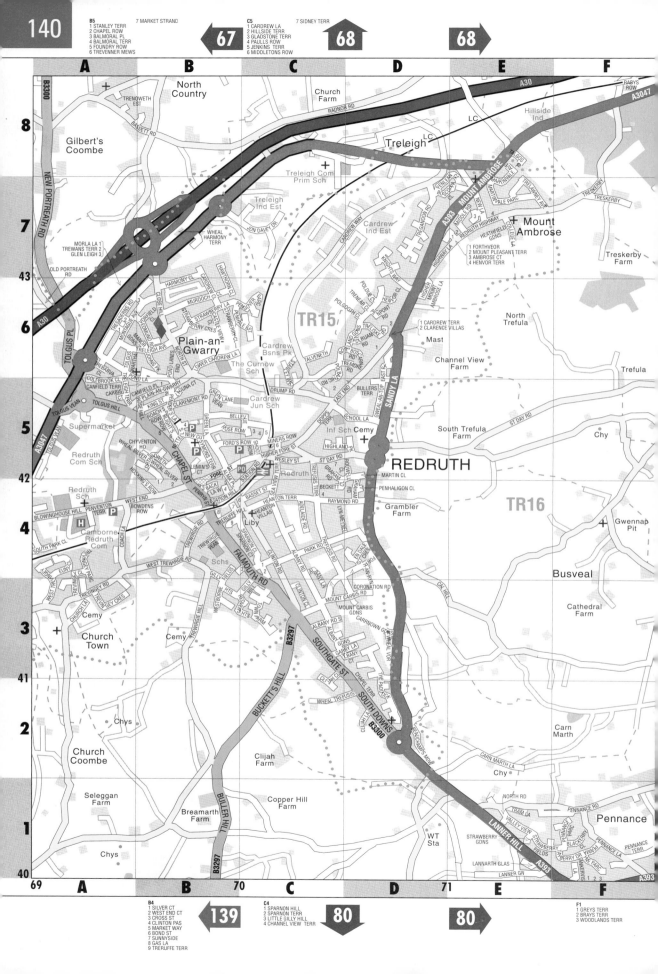

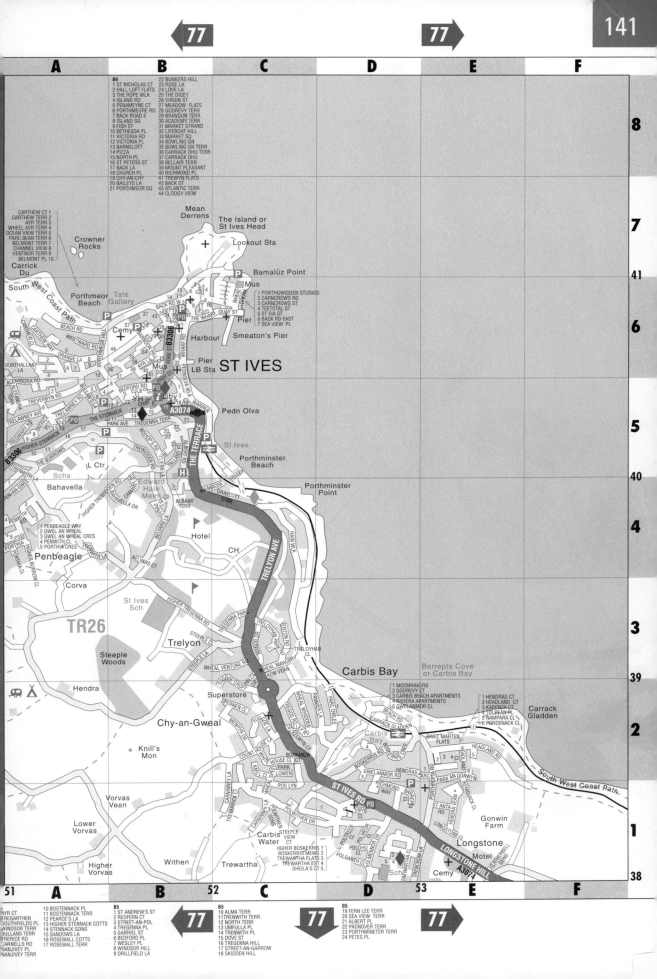

B6
1 ST NICHOLAS CT
2 HALL LOFT FLATS
3 THE ROPE WLK
4 ISLAND RD
5 PENAMEYNE CT
6 PORTHMEORE RD
7 BACK ROAD E
8 ISLAND SQ
9 FISH ST
10 BETHESDA PL
11 VICTORIA RD
12 VICTORIA PL
13 BARNSLOFT
14 PIZZA
15 NORTH PL
16 ST PETERS ST
17 BACK LA
18 CHURCH PL
19 CHY-AN-CHY
20 BAILEYS LA
21 PORTHMEOR SQ
22 BUNKERS HILL
23 ROSE LA
24 LOVE LA
25 THE DIGEY
26 VIRGIN ST
27 MEADOW FLATS
28 GODREVY TERR
29 BRANDON TERR
30 ACADEMY TERR
31 MARKET STRAND
32 LIFEBOAT HILL
33 MARKET SQ
34 BOWLING GN
35 BOWLING GN GN
36 CARRACK DHU TERR
37 CARRACK DHU
38 BELLAIR TERR
39 MOUNT PLEASANT
40 RICHMOND PL
41 TREWYN FLATS
42 BACK ST
43 ATLANTIC TERR
44 CLODGY VIEW

CARTHEW CT 1
CARTHEW TERR 2
AYR TERR 3
WHEEL AYR TERR 4
OCEAN VIEW TERR 5
PARC BEAN TERR 6
BELMONT TERR 7
CHANNEL VIEW 8
VENTNOR TERR 9
BELMONT PL 10

1 PORTHGWIDDEN STUDIOS
2 CARNCROWS RD
3 CARNCROWS ST
4 TEETOTAL ST
5 ST EIA ST
6 BACK RD EAST
7 SEA VIEW PL

ST IVES

1 PENBEAGLE WAY
2 GWEL AN WHEAL
3 GWEL AN WHEAL CRES
4 PENWITH CL
5 PORTHIA CRES

1 MOONRAKERS
2 GODREVY CT
3 CARBIS BEACH APARTMENTS
4 RIVIERA APARTMENTS
5 GWELANMOR CL

1 HENDRAS CT
2 HEADLAND CT
3 KABENZA CT
4 TOLPEAN PL
5 NAMPARA CL
6 BORDENACK CL

HIGHER BOSKERRIS 1
BOSKERRIS MEWS 2
TREWARTHA FLATS 3
TREWARTHA EST 4
SHEILA'S CT 5

AYR CT
TREGARTHEN
SOUTHFIELDS PL
WINDSOR TERR
BULLANS TERR
TRENICE RD
CARNELLS RD
NANJIVEY PL
NANJIVEY TERR
10 BOSTENNACK PL
11 BOSTENNACK TERR
12 PEARCE'S LA
13 HIGHER STENNACK COTTS
14 STENNACK GDNS
15 SANDOWS LA
16 ROSEWALL COTTS
17 ROSEWALL TERR

B5
1 ST ANDREW'S ST
2 REDFERN CT
3 STREET-AN-POL
4 TREGENNA PL
5 GABRIEL ST
6 BEDFORD PL
7 WESLEY PL
8 WINDSOR HILL
9 DRILLFIELD LA

B5
10 ALMA TERR
11 TRENWITH TERR
12 NORTH TERR
13 UMFULLA PL
14 TRENWITH PL
15 DOVE ST
16 TREGENNA HILL
17 STREET-AN-GARROW
18 SKIDDEN HILL

B5
19 FERN LEE TERR
20 SEA VIEW TERR
21 ALBERT PL
22 PADNOVER TERR
23 PORTHMINETER TERR
24 PETES PL

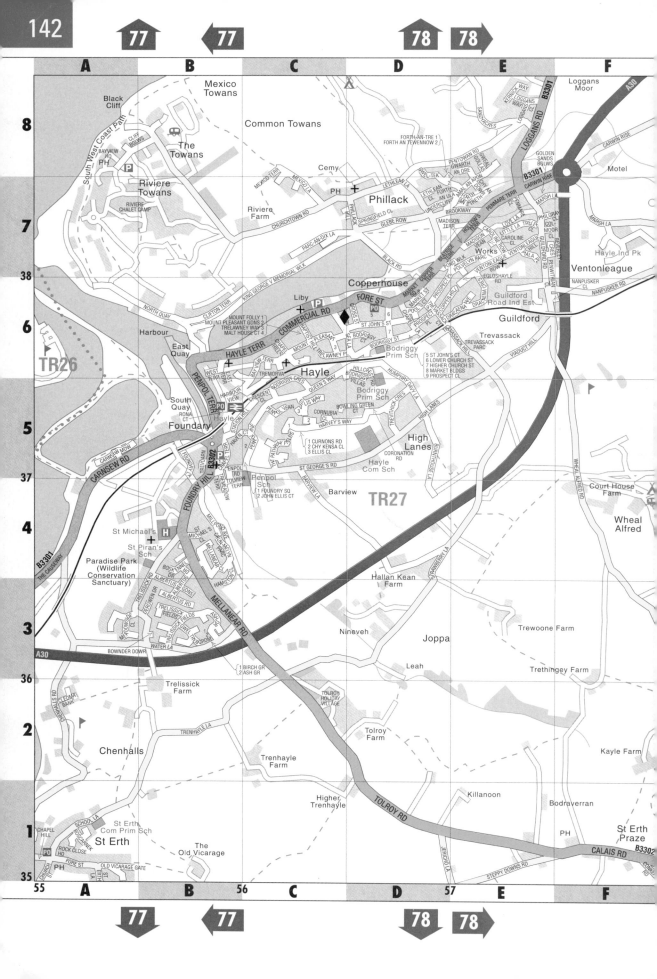

C7
1 ROSCADGHILL PARC
2 HEABROOK PARC
3 NICHOLAS PARC
4 MYTHYON CT
5 HEA COTTS
6 HAIG PL

7 POLTAIR TERR
8 BROOKWARD TERR
9 HOLLY TERR
10 CARMEN SQ
11 WESLEY ST
12 SYLVERTON ST
13 JAMAICA TERR

14 JAMAICA PL
15 PLEASANT PL
16 NEVADA PL
17 MELBOURNE TERR

D5
1 GREENBANK
2 HAWKINS CT

3 TREVEAN GDNS
4 ALVERTON TERR
5 WEETHES COTTS
6 CARMINOWE CRES
7 PENROSE TERR
8 LANDERYON GDNS

E5
1 TRENDEAL GDNS
2 CAMELOT CT
3 TAROVEER TERR
4 OLD BREWERY YD
5 ALMA PL
6 THE ARCADE
7 ST JOHNS CT
8 WHARFSIDE
9 WHARFSIDE VILLAGE
10 HANOVER CT
11 ST MICHAEL'S COTTS
12 PRINCESS CT
13 ST PIRANS CT
14 CHERRY GDNS
15 HARBOUR CT
16 CUSTOM HOUSE LA
17 KITTS CT
18 ST MICHAELS CT
19 ABBEY CT
20 VOUNDERVOUR LA
21 REGENT SQ
22 CHIRGWIN CT
23 CHANCERY LA
24 QUEEN'S SQ
25 MARKET PL
26 THE GREENMARKET
27 UNION ST
28 PARK CT
29 PARADE PASS
30 SIMPSONS CT
31 VICTORIA PL
32 BURITON ROW
33 SOUTH PAR
34 MORRAB PL
35 MORRAB TERR

E6
1 BARWISS TERR
2 PENARE GDNS
3 THE MEWS
4 ST HENRY ST
5 ST JOHN'S TERR
6 ST FRANCIS ST
7 ST WARREN ST
8 ST PHILIP ST
9 ST DOMINIC ST
10 GWAVAS ST
11 PENLEE CT
12 PENWITH ST
13 TREWARTHA TERR
14 CROSS ST
15 LESKINNICK PL
16 VICTORIA CT
17 VICTORIA SQ
18 VICTORIA MEWS
19 ALBERT TERR
20 ALBERT BLDGS
21 BELLE VUE TERR
22 MEDROSE TERR
23 ROSE TERR
24 EMPRESS AVE
25 GARLIDNA
26 PROSPECT PL
27 FOUNTAIN CT
28 BULLOCK MARKET TERR
29 WINDSOR PL
30 CLARENCE PL
31 CLARENCE TERR

E4
1 REDINNICK TERR
2 NORTH TERR
3 REDINNICK GDNS
4 SOUTH PLACE FOLLY
5 QUEEN'S CT
6 MARINE TERR
7 COULSON'S TERR
8 COULSON'S PL
9 COULSON'S BLDGS
10 CARNE'S BLDGS
11 SOUTH TERR

D3
1 MOUNT PROSPECT TERR
2 WEST TERR
3 TRENEGLOE TERR
4 CHARLES ST
5 FLORENCE PL
6 TOLCARNE TERR
7 ART GALLERY TERR

D4
1 UNDER CHAPEL YD
2 COINAGEHALL PL
3 GREEN ST
4 COINAGEHALL ST
5 BARBICAN LA

1 LESCUDJACK TERR
2 ROYALE CT
3 COASTGUARD CRES
4 LANNOWETH RD
5 PENROSE TERR
6 MABBOTS CT
7 LESKINNICK ST

1 REDINNICK TERR

1 MOUNT PROSPECT TERR

1 HIGHER GREEN ST
2 LOWER GREEN ST
3 PRIMROSE TERR
4 CARN GWAVAS TERR

BOSKERNICK CL 1
TREGLYN CL 2
GLOUBESTER CRES 3
PENKERNICK CL 4

JACK STEPHENS EST 1
PENDARVES FLATS 2
CHYANCLARE 3
ST CLARE FLATS 4
WINDSOR TERR 5

WILLOWFIELD FLATS 1
CASTLE HORNECK CL 2

1 POLWEATH CL
2 POLMEERE HO
3 TRANNACK TERR
4 PENMERE PL
5 HIGHER PEVERELL RD

RIDGEO MILL 1
HELPOWETH COTTS 2
CHYANDAUNCE CL 3
CHYANDAUNCE TERR 4
GULVAL ALMSHOUSES 5
SCHOOL LA 6
THE MEAD HO 7
CHYCORNICK TERR 8

CHYNOWETH GDNS 9
CHY-AN-HALL 10
TRYTHOGGA HILL 11
TRYTHOGGA RD 12
TREVARRACK PL 13
TREVARRACK TERR 14
TREVARRACK LA 15
PENDREA RD 16
PENDREA PL 17
GWEDHENNEK 18

THE COACH HO 2
CHYANDOUR SQ 3

C1
1 TREVENETH PL
2 TREWINCE TERR
3 HIGHER GWAVAS RD
4 GWAVAS BGLWS
5 BOWJEY TERR
6 SEA VIEW TERR
7 LYN TERR
8 MEADOW VILLAS
9 BOWJEY CT
10 NAVY INN CT
11 HARBOUR LIGHTS
12 EBENEZER PL
13 EDEN GDNS
14 CHURCH ST
15 FRANWILL TERR
16 PARC VILLAS
17 PARK RD
18 PARC TERR
19 JUBILEE BGLWS

C2
1 NORTH CNR
2 MALT HOUSE GDNS
3 THE MALT HOUSE
4 ANTOINE CL
5 WESLEY PL
6 STRICKLAND COTTS
7 GWAVAS QUAY
8 FARMERS MDW
9 CHAPEL ST
10 ORCHARD PL
11 ORCHARD HO
12 THE FRADGAN
13 THE BRIDGE HO
14 CLIFTON HILL
15 CLIFTON TERR
16 PENGWEL
17 BARLANDHU
18 ORCHARD TERR
19 LANE REDDIN TERR

20 HILLSIDE TERR
21 ANTOINE TERR
22 MOUNT VIEW TERR
23 ELMS CLOSE TERR
24 BAY VIEW TERR
25 GLOUCESTER PL

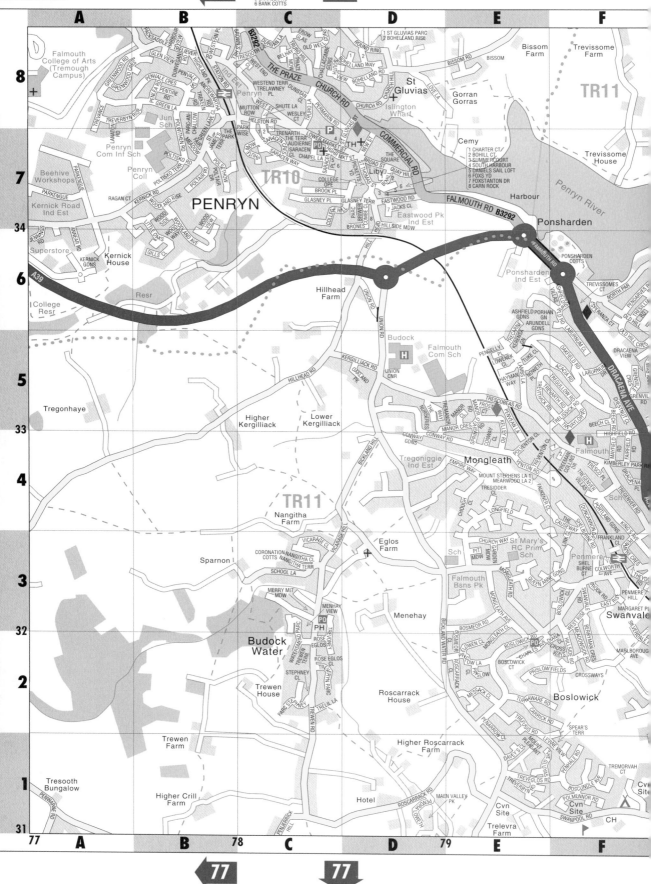

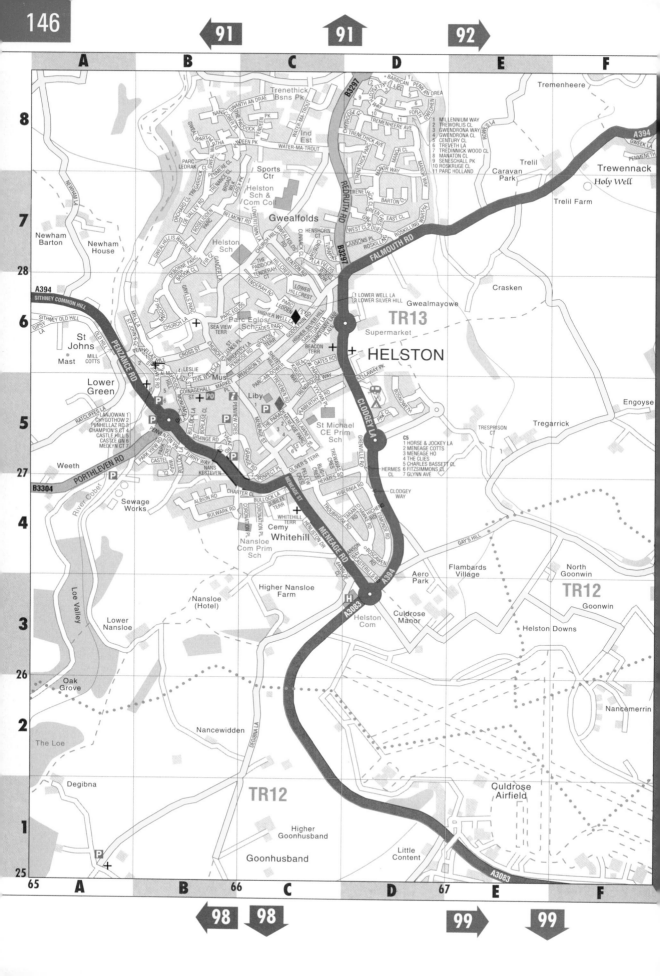

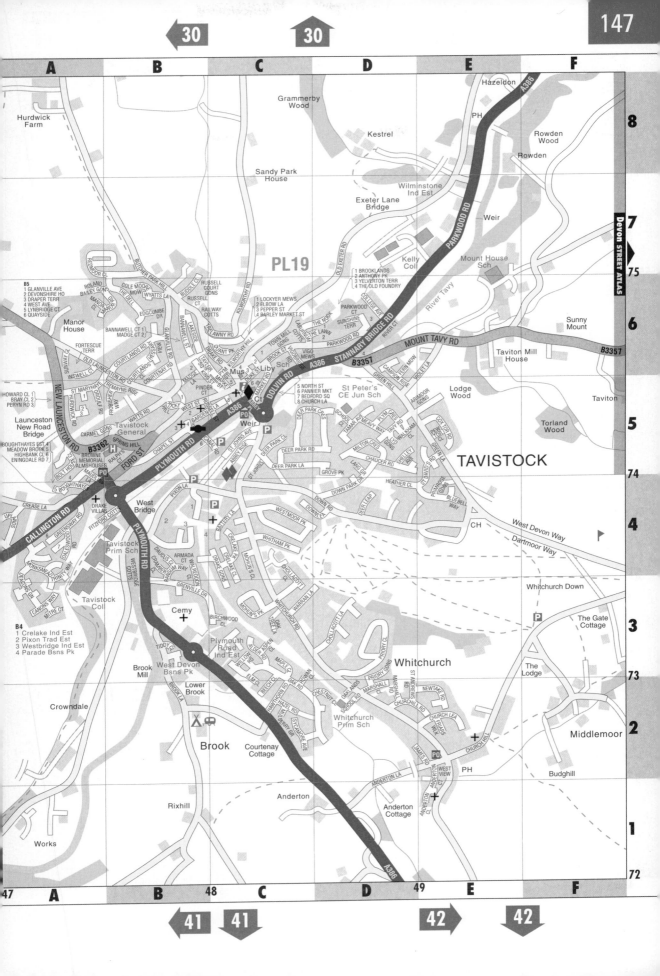

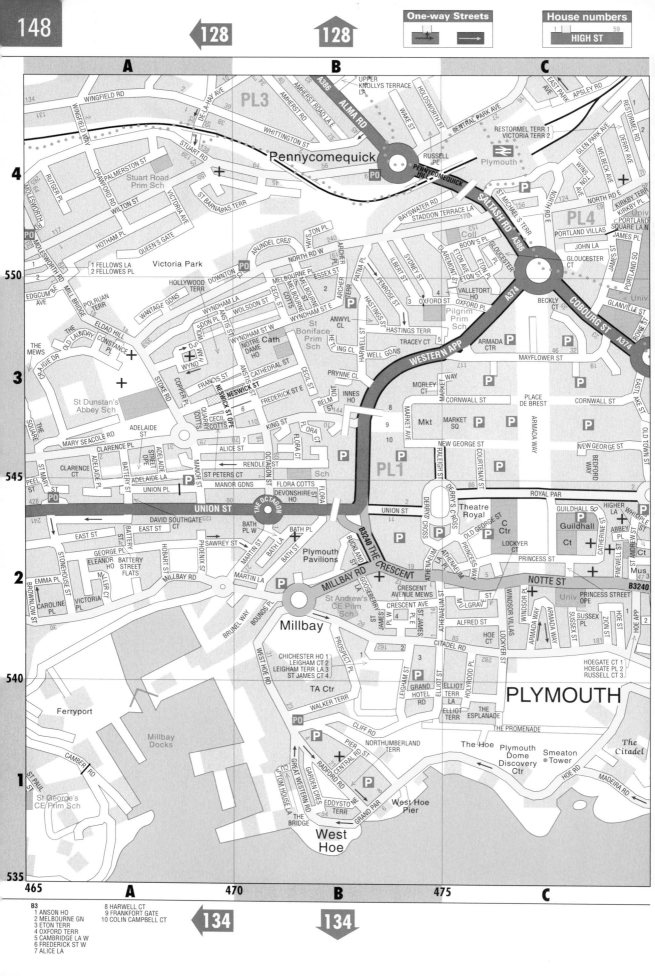

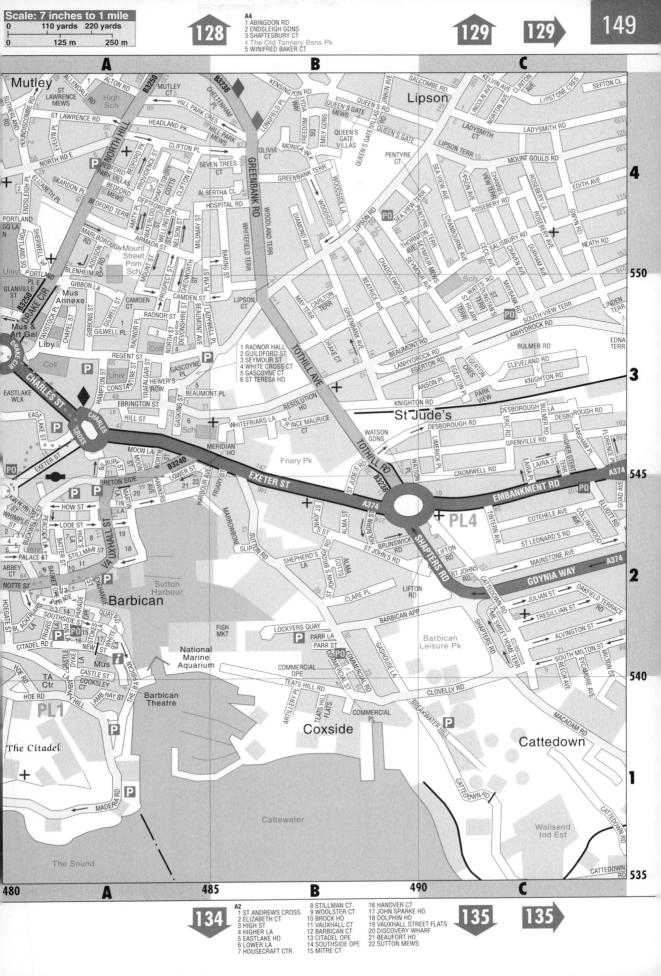

Index

Church Rd **6** Beckenham BR2..........**53** C6

Place name	Location number	Locality, town or village	Postcode district	Page and grid square
May be abbreviated on the map	Present when a number indicates the place's position in a crowded area of mapping	Shown when more than one place has the same name	District for the indexed place	Page number and grid reference for the standard mapping

Public and commercial buildings are highlighted in magenta   **Places of interest** are highlighted in blue with a star★

Abbreviations used in the index

Acad	Academy	Comm	Common	Gd	Ground	L	Leisure	Prom	Prom
App	Approach	Cott	Cottage	Gdn	Garden	La	Lane	Rd	Road
Arc	Arcade	Cres	Crescent	Gn	Green	Liby	Library	Recn	Recreation
Ave	Avenue	Cswy	Causeway	Gr	Grove	Mdw	Meadow	Ret	Retail
Bglw	Bungalow	Ct	Court	H	Hall	Meml	Memorial	Sh	Shopping
Bldg	Building	Ctr	Centre	Ho	House	Mkt	Market	Sq	Square
Bsns, Bus	Business	Ctry	Country	Hospl	Hospital	Mus	Museum	St	Street
Bvd	Boulevard	Cty	County	HQ	Headquarters	Orch	Orchard	Sta	Station
Cath	Cathedral	Dr	Drive	Hts	Heights	Pal	Palace	Terr	Terrace
Cir	Circus	Dro	Drove	Ind	Industrial	Par	Parade	TH	Town Hall
Cl	Close	Ed	Education	Inst	Institute	Pas	Passage	Univ	University
Cnr	Corner	Emb	Embankment	Int	International	Pk	Park	Wk, Wlk	Walk
Coll	College	Est	Estate	Intc	Interchange	Pl	Place	Wr	Water
Com	Community	Ex	Exhibition	Junc	Junction	Prec	Precinct	Yd	Yard

Index of localities, towns and villages

A

Altarnun 26 C8
Angarrack 78 C5
Antony 65 E5
Ashton 90 E3

B

Barripper 79 A5
Bere Alston 41 B1
Bere Ferrers 119 E3
Blackwater 68 D5
Blisland 35 D8
Bodmin 109 B5
Bolventor 25 E3
Boscastle 9 C1
Boyton 13 B2
Bray Shop 28 B1
Breage 90 F3
Bridgerule 8 A6
Buckland Monachorum .42 A3
Bude 104 E6
Budock Water 144 C2
Bugle 47 D1
Burras 80 A1

C

Callington 39 E5
Calstock 41 A3
Camborne 138 B2
Camelford 105 C4
Carbis Bay 141 D3
Cardinham 35 E3
Cargreen 119 A2
Carharrack 80 F8
Carnhell Green 78 F4
Carnkie 80 D1
Carnon Downs 82 A7
Cawsand 133 B1
Chacewater 68 F3
Coad's Green 27 D4
Common Moor 37 F4
Connor Downs 78 D5
Constantine 92 E3
Constantine Bay ...20 D1
Coombe 58 B2
Coppathorne 7 A3
Coverack 101 C4
Crackington Haven ..10 B7
Crafthole 65 B5
Crantock 43 D3
Crapstone 42 B2
Cross Lanes 99 C4
Crowlas 89 C8
Crumplehorn 62 D2
Cubert 55 D8
Cury 99 B4

D

Delabole 14 D3
Devoran 81 F6
Dobwalls 50 E8
Dousland 42 F3
Down Thomas 135 C1
Downderry 64 C5
Downgate 39 A7
Duloe 51 A1
Dunterton 28 F6

E

East Portholland ..84 E5
East Taphouse 50 B6
Edistone 2 F8
Egloskerry 18 A5

F

Falmouth 145 C4
Feock 82 C5
Flushing 145 C6

G

Four Lanes 80 A5
Fowey 116 B4
Foxhole 58 D5
Fraddam 78 D1
Fraddon 45 E1
Frogpool 81 C7

G

Gloweth 69 E3
Godolphin Cross ...90 E6
Golant 61 A5
Goldsithney 89 D5
Goonbell 68 D8
Goonhavern 55 E4
Gorran Haven 85 D5
Grampound 72 B7
Grampound Road ...57 E1
Grenofen 42 A6
Grimscott 5 A2
Gulval 88 E6
Gunnislake 40 F5
Gunwalloe 98 E5
Gweek 92 C1
Gwennap 80 F7
Gwinear 78 D4
Gwithian 66 B2

H

Harlyn 20 D2
Harrowbarrow 40 D5
Hatt 53 E4
Hayle 142 C6
Heamoor 143 B7
Helford 93 B1
Helston 146 D6
Helstone 24 B8
Herodsfoot 50 E3
Hessenford 64 C8
High Street 58 D4
Higher Town 74 C6
Holywell 43 B2
Horrabridge 42 C5
Horsebridge 29 C1
Hugh Town 74 C5

I

Illogan 67 E4
Indian Queens 45 E1

J

Jacobstow 11 B6

K

Kelly Bray 39 F6
Kilkhampton 5 A6

L

Ladock 57 C1
Lamerton 30 B3
Landrake 53 B3
Lane 111 B3
Langore 18 D5
Lanivet 47 F6
Lanjeth 58 E3
Lanlivery 48 C1
Lanner 80 D6
Lanreath 62 B1
Launceston 106 D5
Leedstown 78 E1
Lelant 77 E4
Lerryn 61 D8
Lewannick 27 B7
Lifton 19 F3
Linkinhorne 39 B8
Liskeard 113 E6
Little Petherick ...32 C6
Lizard 102 F2

M

Longrock 88 F6
Looe 117 D3
Lostwithiel 112 E1
Luckett 40 B8
Luxulyan 48 A1
Lynstone 104 D3

M

Mabe Burnthouse ..93 C8
Madron 143 A8
Maenporth 93 F4
Manaccan 101 A8
Marazion 89 B6
Marhamchurch 7 B6
Marshgate 10 C2
Mawgan 99 D7
Mawnan Smith 93 E3
Maxworthy 12 A3
Meavy 42 F2
Menheniot 52 A5
Merrymeet 38 C1
Metherell 40 D4
Mevagissey 73 D3
Middle Town 74 C6
Millbrook 132 E5
Milton Abbot 29 D6
Milton Combe 120 F8
Minions 38 B6
Mitchell 56 F5
Morwenstow 2 C2
Mount Hawke 68 C6
Mousehole 88 D1
Mullion 99 A1
Mylor Bridge 82 A3

N

Nancegollan 91 C7
Nancledra 76 F2
Nanpean 58 D7
Narkurs 64 C6
New Grimsby 74 B6
New Polzeath 21 E6
Newlyn 143 D2
Newquay 110 E7
North Brenton 30 E8
North Hill 27 B3
North Petherwin ...18 A8
Northward 74 B6

O

Old Grimsby 74 B6
Old Town 74 C5

P

Padstow 107 C4
Par 60 C4
Paul 88 C2
Pelynt 62 D5
Pendeen 75 A1
Pendoggett 23 A6
Penponds 138 B1
Penryn 144 B7
Pensilva 38 E5
Pentewan 73 C6
Penwithick 59 D7
Penzance 143 F5
Perranarworthal ...81 D6
Perranporth 55 A5
Perranuthnoe 89 D4
Perranwell Station .81 E6
Petherwin Gate 18 B7
Phillack 142 D7
Pillaton 53 B6
Playing Place 82 B8
Plymouth 148 C1
Polbathic 64 F8
Polgooth 59 A1
Polmassick 72 E4
Polperro 62 E1
Polruan 116 C2
Polyphant 17 F1
Polzeath 21 E5
Ponsanooth 81 B5

P

Pool 74 B6
Porkellis 92 B8
Port Isaac 22 D8
Porth Navas 93 B2
Porthleven 98 B8
Porthloo 74 C5
Porthtowan 68 A6
Portloe 84 B3
Portmellon 73 C3
Portreath 67 C6
Portscatho 83 C2
Portwrinkle 65 B4
Poughill 4 D2
Poundstock 6 E2
Praa Sands 90 C3
Praze-an-Beeble ...79 C2
Probus 71 C6
Pyworthy 8 E5

Q

Quethiock 52 C7
Quintrell Downs ...44 E3

R

Rame 64 B2
Reawla 78 E3
Redruth 140 D5
Relubbus 90 A7
Rilla Mill 38 E8
Roborough 121 D1
Roche 46 F3
Rock 21 D2
Rosudgeon 89 F4
Ruan Minor 103 B5
Rumford 32 A5

S

St Agnes 54 D1
St Austell 114 B5
St Blazey Gate ...115 F6
St Breock 24 B3
St Breward 24 B2
St Buryan 97 B6
St Cleer 37 F2
St Clether 17 A3
St Columb Major ...45 A6
St Columb Minor ..111 E7
St Columb Road 45 D2
St Day 68 E1
St Dennis 46 C1
St Dominick 40 D3
St Erme 142 A1
St Erth 142 A1
St Erth Praze 142 F1
St Eval 31 F3
St Germans 65 A8
St Giles-on-the-Heath .13 C1
St Hilary 89 E6
St Issey 32 E6
St Ive 38 F2
St Ives 141 C6
St John 132 C8
St Just 86 E6
St Just in Roseland .82 F2
St Keverne 101 C4
St Kew Highway 23 A2
St Martin 100 D6
St Mawes 95 B6
St Mawgan 45 A8
St Mellion 53 E8
St Merryn 31 F8
St Minver 22 A4
St Neot 36 F2
St Newlyn East 56 C7
St Stephen 58 B4
St Teath 23 E7
St Tudy 23 E3
St Wenn 46 D7
Saltash 122 B1
Seaton 64 B5
Sennen 96 B6
Sennen Cove 96 B7
Sheviock 65 B6
Shop 2 D1
Shortlanesend 69 F6
South Petherwin ...27 E8

S

South Tehidy 138 E7
Staddiscombe 135 F3
Stenalees 59 B8
Sticker 58 F1
Stithians 80 F3
Stoke Climsland ...28 C1
Stowford 5 E8
Stratton 4 E1
Summercourt 57 C7

T

Tavistock 147 E5
Tetcott 13 C7
Threemilestone 69 D4
Tideford 52 F2
Tintagel 14 D7
Torpoint 127 C3
Townshend 90 D7
Trebetherick 21 D4
Trebullett 28 A5
Treburley 28 C4
Tregadillett 18 C2
Tregony 71 F4
Tregurrian 44 E8
Trehan 65 F8
Treknow 14 C5
Trelights 22 C6
Tremar 38 A2
Trematon 53 E2
Trenance 31 C2
Trencreek 111 C4
Trenear 92 A6
Tresillian 70 F5
Trethurgy 59 F6
Trevone 20 F2
Trewellard 86 F8
Trewennack 146 F8
Trewoon 59 A3
Treworlas 83 D5
Troon 79 E5
Truro 137 E3

U

Upton Cross 38 D6

V

Venterdon 28 D2
Veryan 83 F6

W

Wadebridge 108 A6
Wainhouse Corner ..10 C4
Walkhampton 42 D4
Warbstow Cross 11 B2
Week St Mary 11 F8
Welcombe 2 D5
Whipsiderry 44 C6
Whitchurch 147 D3
White Cross 45 C2
Whitemoor 58 E8
Whitstone 7 F1
Widegates 63 F8
Widemouth Bay 6 F5
Woodford 4 D8

Y

Yelverton 42 D3
Yeolmbridge 18 F6

Z

Zelah 56 A2
Zennor 76 B5

A

Abbey Cl PL20 . . . . .42 B2
Abbey Ct
19 Penzance TR18 . . . . .143 E5
Plymouth PL1 . . . . .149 A2
Abbey Hill TR26 . . . . . . .77 E3
Abbey Mews PL31 . . . . .109 C4
Abbey Pl Plymouth PL1 . .148 C2
Tavistock PL19 . . . . . . .147 C5
Abbey Rise PL19 . . . . . .147 C5
Abbey St TR18 . . . . .143 E5
Abbots Cl PL31 . . . . . . .109 F4
Abbotsbury Way PL2 . . .127 F8
Abbotsfield Cl PL19 . . . .41 D8
Abbotsfield Cres PL19 . . .41 D8
Abbotts Rd PL3 . . . . . . .128 E6
Aberdeen Ave PL5 . . . . .124 D2
Aberdeen Cl PL24 . . . . . .60 B6
Aberfal Ho **1** TR11 . . . .145 C3
Abingdon Rd **1** PL4 . . .149 A4
Abney Cres PL6 . . . . . . .125 B6
Abscott La PL9 . . . . .135 C5
Acacia Rd TR11 . . . . . . .144 F5
Academy Terr **30** TR26 .141 B6
Acklington Pl PL5 . . . . . .123 E4
Acland Cl EX23 . . . . . . .104 E7
Acorn Dr PL25 . . . . .115 A3
Acre Pl PL1 . . . . .127 F3
Adams Cl Plymouth PL5 .123 F1
Torpoint PL11 . . . . .126 F3
Adams Cres PL11 . . . . . .126 E3
Addington Pl PL14 . . . . .113 D6
Addington S PL14 . . . . . .113 D6
Addison Rd PL4 . . . . . . .149 A4
Addison Terr PL22 . . . . .112 C2
Adela Rd PL11 . . . . .127 A3
Adelaide La PL1 . . . . . . .148 A2
Adelaide Pl PL1 . . . . . . .148 A3
Adelaide Rd TR15 . . . . .140 C4
Adelaide St
Camborne TR14 . . . . . .138 C4
Penzance TR18 . . . . . . .143 E6
Plymouth PL1 . . . . .148 A3
2 Plymouth, Ford PL2 .127 F5
Adelaide Street Ope
PL1 . . . . .148 A3
Adelaide Terr TR1 . . . . .137 B4
Adit La Newlyn TR18 . . .143 C1
Saltash PL12 . . . . .122 E3
Adits The PL18 . . . . .41 A3
Admiral's Hard PL1 . . . .134 A8
Admirals Quay TR11 . . .145 B5
Admiralty Cotts PL1 . . . .134 A7
Admiralty Rd
Plymouth, Millbay PL1 . .134 A8
Plymouth, St Bubeaux PL5 123 C2
Admiralty St
Plymouth, Keyham PL2 . .127 E6
Plymouth, Millbay PL1 . .134 A8
Admiralty Terr TR2 . . . . .83 B2
Agar Cres TR15 . . . . . . .139 D6
Agar Ct TR1 . . . . .137 D5
Agar Mdws **11** TR3 . . . .81 F7
Agar Rd Camborne TR15 .139 D6
Newquay TR7 . . . . .110 C5
St Austell PL25 . . . . . . .114 E6
Truro TR1 . . . . .137 E5
Agar Terr **4** PL31 . . . . .109 D5
Agar Way TR15 . . . . . . .139 C5
Agaton Rd PL5 . . . . .123 E3
Agnes Cl EX23 . . . . .104 F4
Ainslie Terr PL2 . . . . . . .127 E7
Aire Gdns PL3 . . . . .129 B5
Alamein Ct PL12 . . . . . .122 E2
Alamein Rd PL12 . . . . . .122 D2
Alan Harvey Cl **14** TR26 .77 A6
Alan Rd PL28 . . . . .107 D4
Alansmere Ct TR2 . . . . . .57 A1
Alanta Flats TR7 . . . . . .110 B5
Albany Cl TR5 . . . . .68 D8
Albany Ct TR15 . . . . . . .140 D3
Albany Gdns TR15 . . . . .140 C3
Albany La TR15 . . . . . . .140 C4
Albany Pl TR11 . . . . .145 A3
Albany Rd Falmouth TR11 145 A3
Newquay TR7 . . . . .110 F6
Redruth TR15 . . . . .140 C4
Truro TR1 . . . . .137 A4
Albany Rd S TR15 . . . . .140 C3
Albany St PL1 . . . . .127 E2
Albany Terr TR26 . . . . . .141 B4
Albemarle Villas PL1 . . .127 F3
Albert Bldgs **20** TR18 . .143 E6
Albert Cotts TR11 . . . . . .145 B4
Albert Pl Camborne TR14 .138 E3
21 St Ives TR26 . . . . . .141 B5
Truro TR1 . . . . .137 C4
Albert Rd Plymouth PL2 .127 F3
Saltash PL12 . . . . .123 A2
St Austell PL25 . . . . . . .114 D3
St Ives TR26 . . . . .141 B5
Albert St Camborne TR14 .138 E3
Penzance TR18 . . . . . . .143 F6
Albert Terr
Gunnislake PL18 . . . . . . .40 F5
19 Penzance TR18 . . . .143 E6
Albertha Cl PL4 . . . . . . .149 B4
Albertus Dr TR27 . . . . . .142 B3
Albertus Gdns TR27 . . . .142 B3
Albertus Rd TR27 . . . . . .142 B3

Albion Ct PL11 . . . . .127 B3
Albion Dr PL2 . . . . .128 E7
Albion Rd Helston TR13 .146 B4
Torpoint PL11 . . . . .127 B3
Albion Row TR16 . . . . . . .80 F8
Alcester Cl PL2 . . . . .127 E4
Alcester St PL2 . . . . .127 F4
Alden Wlk PL6 . . . . .129 B7
Alder Rd PL7 . . . . .147 C3
Aldercombe La EX23 . . . . .5 A6
Alderney Pl PL6 . . . . . . .124 F7
Aldersley Wlk PL6 . . . . .125 A1
Aldreath Cl PL20 . . . . . . .88 B7
Aldreath Rd PL20 . . . . . .88 B7
Alexander Ct PL26 . . . . . .85 D5
Alexandra Cl
5 Illogan TR16 . . . . . . .67 E4
Plymouth PL9 . . . . .136 B8
St Ives TR26 . . . . .77 A7
Alexandra Ct TR7 . . . . . .111 C8
Alexandra Dr PL20 . . . . . .41 C1
Alexandra Gdns TR18 . . .143 D4
Alexandra Pl
Penzance TR18 . . . . . . .143 D4
4 Plymouth PL4 . . . . .128 E4
St Ives TR26 . . . . .77 A7
Alexandra Rd
Bodmin PL31 . . . . .109 B5
Illogan TR16 . . . . .67 D4
Newquay TR7 . . . . .111 C8
Penzance TR18 . . . . . . .143 D4
Plymouth, Crownhill PL6 .124 F2
Plymouth, Ford PL2 . . . .127 F5
Plymouth, Mutley PL4 . .128 E4
St Austell PL25 . . . . . . .114 E3
St Ives TR26 . . . . .77 A7
Alexandra Sq PL12 . . . . .123 A2
Alexandra Terr
Mount Hawke TR4 . . . . . .68 C6
Penzance TR18 . . . . . . .143 D3
Plymouth PL2 . . . . .127 F5
St Ives TR26 . . . . .141 A5
Tremar PL14 . . . . .38 A4
2 Truro TR1 . . . . .137 B4
Alford Cl EX23 . . . . .104 F5
Alfred Pl PL2 . . . . .127 F5
Alfred Rd PL2 . . . . .127 F5
Alfred St PL1 . . . . .148 C2
Alger Wlk PL6 . . . . .124 E6
Alice La **7** PL1 . . . . . . .148 B3
Alice St PL1 . . . . .148 A3
All Saints Pk PL18 . . . . . .40 E5
Alldritt Cl TR7 . . . . .111 D7
Allen Pk PL30 . . . . .23 B2
Allen Vale PL14 . . . . . . .113 A5
Allenby Rd PL2 . . . . .128 A6
Allendale PL26 . . . . .58 C4
Allendale Rd PL4 . . . . . .149 A4
Allern La PL5 . . . . .120 C1
Allerton Wlk PL6 . . . . . .129 B7
Alley Hill PL20 . . . . .42 A1
Alleyne Gdns PL3 . . . . . .128 E8
Alma Cl TR5 . . . . .68 D8
Alma Cotts PL4 . . . . . . .149 B2
Alma Pl Heamoor TR18 . .143 C7
Newquay TR7 . . . . .110 D6
5 Penzance TR18 . . . .143 E5
Redruth TR15 . . . . .140 B5
Truro TR1 . . . . .69 F3
Alma St PL4 . . . . .149 B2
Alma Terr Carharrack TR16 .80 F8
Penzance TR18 . . . . . . .143 E5
10 St Ives TR26 . . . . . .141 B5
Almeria Ct PL7 . . . . .130 D4
Almond Dr PL7 . . . . .131 D6
Almshouse Hill TR13 . . .146 B5
Alton Pl PL4 . . . . .128 E4
Alton Rd PL4 . . . . .149 A4
Alverne Bldgs **7** TR18 . .143 E6
Alverton Com Prim Sch
TR18 . . . . .143 C4
Alverton Ct TR1 . . . . . . .137 C5
Alverton Rd TR18 . . . . . .143 D5
Alverton St TR18 . . . . . .143 D5
Alverton Terr
4 Penzance TR18 . . . .143 D5
Truro TR1 . . . . .137 D5
Alvington St PL4 . . . . . . .149 C2
Alwin Pk PL6 . . . . .125 A5
Alwyn Cl PL7 . . . . .111 E6
Amacre Dr PL9 . . . . .135 B6
Amados Cl PL7 . . . . .130 B4
Amados Dr PL7 . . . . .130 B4
Amados Rise PL7 . . . . . .130 C4
Amanda Way PL14 . . . . . .38 E4
Amble Rd **28** PL17 . . . . .39 F4
Ambrose Ct TR15 . . . . . .140 E7
Amelia Cl TR2 . . . . .71 C6
Amherst Rd PL3 . . . . . . .148 B4
Amherst Road La E PL3 .148 B4
Amity Pl PL4 . . . . .149 A4
An Bof Gdns PL31 . . . . .109 C4
Anderton Cl PL19 . . . . . .147 E1
Anderton Cl PL19 . . . . . .147 E2
Anderton La PL19 . . . . . .147 D2
Andrew Pl **3** TR1 . . . . .137 C4
Andrew's Terr TR16 . . . .139 F1
Andrewartha Rd TR10 . .144 B8
Andrews Way PL12 . . . . .53 C5
Aneray Rd TR14 . . . . . . .138 D4
Angarrack La TR27 . . . . .78 D5
Angarrack Mews TR27 . . .78 C5

Angavran Mdw TR8 . . . . .55 D8
Angel Hill **6** PL15 . . . . .106 C6
Angwin Ave **4** TR5 . . . . .54 C1
Anjardyn Pl PL24 . . . . . . .60 C5
Ankervin La TR16 . . . . . .140 F1
Ann's Pl PL3 . . . . .128 A4
Annear Rd TR10 . . . . . . .144 A6
Anson Ho **1** PL1 . . . . . .148 B3
Anson Pl
Plymouth, Devonport PL2 .127 F4
Plymouth, St Jude's PL4 .149 C3
Anson Rd PL2 . . . . .31 F3
Anson Way PL3 . . . . . . .146 D4
Anstis St Plymouth PL1 . .148 A3
Plymouth PL1 . . . . .148 B3
Anthony Cl EX23 . . . . .4 C3
Anthony Lowen PL28 . . .107 C4
Anthony Pk PL19 . . . . . .147 D6
Anthony Rd TR7 . . . . . . .110 C4
Antoine Cl **4** TR18 . . . . .143 C2
Antoine Terr **21** TR18 . .143 C2
Antony CE Jun & Inf Sch
PL11 . . . . .65 E5
Antony Gdns PL2 . . . . . .128 C8
Antony Hill PL11 . . . . . . .65 E5
Antony Ho★ PL11 . . . . . .126 D5
Antony Rd PL11 . . . . . . .127 B3
Antony Woodland Gdn★
PL11 . . . . .126 D6
Antron Hill TR10 . . . . . . .81 B1
Antron La TR10 . . . . .93 C8
Antron Way TR10 . . . . . .93 C8
Anvil Ct Camelford PL32 .105 D3
Venterdon PL17 . . . . . . .28 D1
Anvil Rd PL32 . . . . .105 D4
Anwyl Cl PL1 . . . . .148 B3
Anzac Ave PL5 . . . . .124 A4
Appin Gdns PL15 . . . . . .139 C7
Appletree La PL25 . . . . .115 D3
Apsley Rd PL28 . . . . . . .128 C4
Arbour The PL6 . . . . . . .124 E5
Arcade The **6** TR18 . . . .143 E5
Arcadia PL9 . . . . .136 D6
Arcadia Rd PL9 . . . . .136 C6
Arch Hill TR1 . . . . .137 C2
Arch La TR27 . . . . .77 D1
Archbishop Benson CE Prim
Sch TR1 . . . . .137 D6
Archer Pl PL1 . . . . .148 B4
Archer Terr PL1 . . . . .148 B3
Archway Ave PL4 . . . . . .129 B3
Arden Gr PL2 . . . . .128 C8
Arena Cres PL25 . . . . . .115 B4
Argal View TR10 . . . . . . .93 B6
Arimoor Gdns PL19 . . . .147 E5
Ark Royal Cl PL5 . . . . . .127 D8
Arkwright Gdns PL5 . . . .123 F2
Arley Cl PL6 . . . . .125 B6
Arlington Rd PL4 . . . . . .128 F4
Armada Ct PL19 . . . . . . .147 B4
Armada Ctr PL1 . . . . . . .148 C3
Armada Rd PL10 . . . . . . .133 A1
Armada St PL4 . . . . .149 A4
Armada Way
Plymouth PL1 . . . . .148 C2
Plymouth PL1 . . . . .148 C3
Armchair Cnr PL31 . . . . .109 C5
Arnheim Terr TR11 . . . . .145 B7
Arnison Ct PL9 . . . . .135 F5
Arnold's Point PL9 . . . . .129 C3
Arnside Ct PL6 . . . . .125 D3
Arrallas Barns TR2 . . . . . .57 B4
Arscott Gdns PL9 . . . . . .135 C5
Arscott La PL9 . . . . .135 D5
Art Gallery Terr PL11 . . .143 C3
Arthur Terr PL11 . . . . . . .127 B2
Arthurian Centre The★
PL32 . . . . .105 D8
Artillery Pl PL4 . . . . .149 B1
Arun Pl PL3 . . . . .129 C5
Arundel Cres PL1 . . . . . .148 B4
Arundel Ct TR27 . . . . . . .78 D6
Arundel Pk PL27 . . . . . . .78 D6
Arundel Terr Bude EX23 .104 D4
Plymouth PL2 . . . . .127 F4
Arundel Way
Connor Downs TR27 . . . .78 D6
Newquay TR7 . . . . .111 B7
Arundell Cl PL16 . . . . . . .19 F4
Arundell Gdns
Falmouth TR11 . . . . . . .144 E6
Lifton PL16 . . . . .19 F4
Arundell Pl TR1 . . . . . . .137 C3
Arundle Cl PL26 . . . . . . .58 C8
Arwenack Ave TR11 . . . .145 C3
Arwenack Ho **4** TR11 . .145 C3
Arwenack St TR11 . . . . .145 C4
Arworthal Mdws TR3 . . . .81 D6
Arwyn Cotts **5** TR11 . . .145 C3
Arwyn Pl **7** TR11 . . . . . .145 C3
Ash Cl **16** Par PL24 . . . . .60 B4
7 Yelverton PL20 . . . . . .42 C3
Ash Dr TR27 . . . . .142 B3
Ash Gr Hayle TR27 . . . . .142 B3
Par PL24 . . . . .60 B4
Plymouth PL2 . . . . .127 F7
Ash Vale PL16 . . . . .19 F4
Ashburgh Parc PL12 . . . .122 B3
Ashburnham Rd PL5 . . . .124 A3
Ashbury Cl PL14 . . . . . . .113 D7
Ashcombe Cl PL7 . . . . . .130 C7
Ashdown Cl
Plymouth PL6 . . . . .125 C3
Sticker PL26 . . . . .58 E1
Ashdown Wlk PL6 . . . . .125 C3
Ashery Dr PL9 . . . . .135 C6
Ashfield Gdns TR11 . . . .144 E6

Ashfield Rd TR11 . . . . . .144 F6
Ashfield Villas TR11 . . . .144 F6
Ashford Cl PL3 . . . . .129 A4
Ashford Cres PL3 . . . . . .129 A4
Ashford Hill PL4 . . . . . . .129 A4
Ashford Rd PL4 . . . . .128 F4
Ashleigh Cl PL5 . . . . . . .124 C7
Ashleigh La PL5 . . . . . . .120 D1
Ashleigh Way
Plymouth PL7 . . . . .131 C4
Probus TR2 . . . . .71 D6
Ashley Cl **9** PL26 . . . . . .59 D7
Ashley Rd
Shortlanesend TR4 . . . . .69 C6
Truro TR1 . . . . .137 C4
Ashmead **7** TR1 . . . . . . .57 E1
Ashridge Gdns PL5 . . . .124 C7
Ashton Cl PL6 . . . . .125 C6
Ashton Ct TR7 . . . . .111 D6
Ashton Way PL12 . . . . . .122 D3
Ashton Wlk EX23 . . . . . . .6 F5
Ashtree Cl PL6 . . . . .125 D7
Ashtree Gr PL9 . . . . .136 C8
Ashwood Cl PL7 . . . . . . .131 C6
Ashwood Park Rd PL7 . .131 C6
Aspen Cl PL19 . . . . .147 C3
Aspen Gdns PL7 . . . . . . .131 B5
Astor Dr PL4 . . . . .129 C3
Astwood Devopments
PL13 . . . . .63 D7
Athelstan Pk PL31 . . . . .109 F3
Athenaeum La PL1 . . . . .148 C2
Athenaeum Pl PL1 . . . . .148 C2
Athenaeum St PL1 . . . . .148 B2
Atherton Pl PL2 . . . . . . .127 E4
Atlantic Bay **1** TR6 . . . . .55 A5
Atlantic Coast Cvn Pk
TR27 . . . . .66 B1
Atlantic Cres PL19 . . . . . .96 C7
Atlantic Mews PL27 . . . . .21 D6
Atlantic Rd Delabole PL33 .14 D2
Newquay TR7 . . . . .110 C6
Tintagel PL34 . . . . .14 C7
Atlantic Terr
Camborne TR14 . . . . . .138 E2
New Polzeath PL27 . . . . .21 D6
48 St Ives TR26 . . . . . .141 B6
Atlantic Way
Porthtowan TR4 . . . . . . .68 A6
Tintagel PL34 . . . . .14 C7
Attery View PL15 . . . . . . .18 E6
Auckland Rd **3** PL2 . . . .128 A5
Audierne Rd TR10 . . . . .144 C7
Austin Ave PL2 . . . . .128 A6
Austin Cres PL6 . . . . . . .125 C1
Austin Farm Prim Sch
PL6 . . . . .129 C7
Automobilia Motor Mus★
PL6 . . . . .129 C7
Avalan Cl TR11 . . . . .82 A3
Avent Wlk PL7 . . . . .130 F7
Avenue Rd TR11 . . . . . . .145 C3
Avenue The St Hilary TR20 .89 F6
Truro TR1 . . . . .137 C4
Avery Ct PL22 . . . . .112 C2
Avery Way PL22 . . . . . . .122 C2
Avery's Row PL28 . . . . .107 D5
Avon Cl Plymouth PL3 . .129 C6
St Austell PL25 . . . . . . .115 A5
Avondale Rd TR1 . . . . . .137 B4
Avrack Cl TR19 . . . . .87 F3
Axe Cl PL3 . . . . .129 D6
Axford Hill PL17 . . . . . . .39 F2
Axtown La PL20 . . . . .42 C2
Aycliffe Gdns PL7 . . . . . .131 A3
Aylesbury Cres PL5 . . . .124 B5
Aylmer Pl **18** PL25 . . . .114 C3
Aylmer Sq **14** PL25 . . . .114 C3
Aylwin Cl PL7 . . . . .130 E6
Ayr Ct **1** TR26 . . . . .141 A5
Ayr La TR26 . . . . .141 A6
Ayr Terr TR26 . . . . .141 A6
Ayreville Rd PL2 . . . . . . .128 B2
Aysshton Gdns **15** PL17 .39 F4

B

Babbacombe Cl PL6 . . . .129 E8
Baber Cl PL12 . . . . .40 C2
Baber Ct PL12 . . . . .40 D2
Babis Farm Cl PL12 . . . .122 F1
Babis Farm Ct PL12 . . . .122 F1
Babis Farm Mews PL12 .122 F2
Babis Farm Row PL12 . .122 F1
Babis Farm Way PL12 . .122 F2
Babis La PL12 . . . . .122 F1
Baby Beach La PL27 . . . .21 D6
Back Hill Port Isaac PL27 .22 D7
Saltash PL12 . . . . .122 D2
Back La Angarrack TR27 . .78 C5
Callington PL17 . . . . . . .39 F4
Marazion TR17 . . . . .89 B5
Plymouth PL7 . . . . .130 E4
St Erth PL27 . . . . .77 D2
17 St Ives TR26 . . . . . .141 B6
Tintagel PL34 . . . . .14 D7
Tregony TR2 . . . . .71 F4
Veryan TR2 . . . . .83 F6
Back La W TR15 . . . . . . .140 B4
Back Quay TR1 . . . . .137 D4
Back Rd E **7** TR26 . . . . .141 B6
Back Rd W TR26 . . . . . .141 B6

Back St **42** TR26 . . . . . .141 B6
Badgers Wlk PL12 . . . . .122 D4
Bag La Polbathic PL12 . . .64 F8
St Germans PL12 . . . . . .65 A8
Bagbury Rd EX23 . . . . . .104 E3
Bahavella Dr TR26 . . . . .141 B4
Bailey Terr EX22 . . . . .8 A5
Baileys La **20** TR26 . . . . .141 B6
Bainbridge Ave PL3 . . . .128 F7
Bainbridge Ct PL7 . . . . . .130 F6
Baines Hill TR16 . . . . . . .67 C6
Bakehouse La **12** PL17 . .39 F4
Bakers Cl PL7 . . . . .131 C5
Bakers Pl PL1 . . . . .127 F1
Bakers Row TR13 . . . . . .90 F3
Bal Rd TR13 . . . . .91 E4
Bal-Jinjy Cl **19** PL24 . . . .60 B4
Balcoath TR16 . . . . .68 D1
Baldhu Row TR 20 . . . . . .76 F2
Balfield Rd **15** TR16 . . . .98 C8
Balfour Terr PL2 . . . . . . .127 E4
Balkin Way TR15 . . . . . .139 D7
Ball Terr PL27 . . . . .108 F2
Ballard Est TR16 . . . . . . .80 B5
Balmoral Ave PL2 . . . . . .127 F5
Balmoral Pl **3** TR15 . . . .140 B5
Balmoral Terr **4** TR15 . .140 B5
Balnoon Flats TR26 . . . . .77 A4
Bambry Cl TR20 . . . . . . .89 C5
Bampfylde Way PL6 . . . .124 D6
Bampfylde Way
Goldsithney TR20 . . . . . .89 C5
Plymouth PL6 . . . . .124 E6
Bampton Rd PL6 . . . . . . .125 E1
Band House La PL26 . . . .59 C7
Bangors Est EX23 . . . . . . .6 F2
Bangors Rd PL15 . . . . . . .18 E2
Bank Cotts **6** TR10 . . . . .144 C7
Bank Sq TR19 . . . . .86 F6
Bank St Newquay TR7 . .110 D6
St Columb Major TR9 . . .45 E4
Bannawell St PL19 . . . . .147 B6
Banns Rd TR4 . . . . .68 C6
Baptist Hill TR27 . . . . . .142 C6
Baptist St PL17 . . . . .41 A3
Bar La Connor Downs TR27 .78 C6
Falmouth TR11 . . . . . . .145 C3
Bar Mdws TR1 . . . . .70 C3
Bar Rd Falmouth TR11 . .145 C3
Mawnan Smith TR11 . . . .93 C2
Bar Terr **8** TR11 . . . . . .145 C3
Barbara Hepworth Mus★
TR26 . . . . .141 B6
Barbican App PL4 . . . . . .149 B2
Barbican Cl
Helston TR13 . . . . .146 D8
Looe PL13 . . . . .117 D5
Barbican Ct Looe PL13 . .117 D5
12 Plymouth PL1 . . . . .149 A2
Barbican Hill PL13 . . . . .117 D4
Barbican La TR18 . . . . . .143 F4
Barbican Leisure Pk
PL4 . . . . .149 C2
Barbican Rd Looe PL13 . .117 E6
Plymouth PL7 . . . . .130 E4
Barbican The PL1 . . . . . .149 A2
Barbican Theatre★ PL1 . .149 A1
Barbury Cres PL6 . . . . . .125 B8
Barcote Wlk PL6 . . . . . . .129 C8
Bardsey Cl PL6 . . . . .125 C7
Baring St PL4 . . . . .149 B4
Barker's Hill PL12 . . . . . .122 C1
Barkhouse La PL25 . . . . .115 B2
Barlandhu **17** TR18 . . . .143 C2
Barley Market St PL19 . .147 C6
Barlowena TR14 . . . . . . .138 D1
Barn Cl Plymouth PL7 . . .131 D4
Wainhouse Corner EX23 . .10 F6
Barn Crtyd TR27 . . . . . . .78 D6
Barn Hill Polbathic PL12 . .64 F8
Ruan Minor TR12 . . . . . .103 B4
Tideford PL12 . . . . .52 F1
Barn La Bodmin PL31 . . .109 C4
18 St Columb Major TR9 . .45 E4
Barn Meadow Pk PL13 . .117 B2
Barn Park La PL31 . . . . . .35 B2
Barn Park Rd PL3 . . . . . .128 D6
Barn Pk Lostwithiel PL22 .112 C2
Saltash PL12 . . . . .122 F3
Barn St PL14 . . . . .113 C5
Barncoose Com Prim Sch
TR15 . . . . .139 E6
Barncoose Ind Est TR15 .139 E6
Barncoose La TR15 . . . . .139 E6
Barncoose Terr TR15 . . .139 E6
Barndale Cres PL25 . . . .125 C6
Barne Barton Prim Sch
PL5 . . . . .127 D8
Barne Cl PL5 . . . . .123 D1
Barne La PL5 . . . . .127 C8
Barne Rd PL5 . . . . .127 C8
Barnecut Cl **6** PL14 . . . .38 A3
Barnfield Dr PL7 . . . . . . .131 C5
Barnfield Gdns TR18 . . . .88 E6
Barnfield Terr
3 Indian Queens TR9 . .45 E1
Liskeard PL14 . . . . .113 B4
Barningham Gdns PL6 . .125 A6
Barnoon Hill TR26 . . . . .141 B6
Barnpark Rd PL35 . . . . . . .9 C1
Barnsloft **13** TR26 . . . . .141 B6
Barnstaple Cl PL6 . . . . . .129 E7
Barnwood Cl PL9 . . . . . .135 E5
Barons Rd PL20 . . . . .42 E3
Barossa Rd PL11 . . . . . .127 B3
Barr's Cl PL23 . . . . .116 D5
Barrack La TR1 . . . . .137 D3
Barrack Pl PL1 . . . . .128 A1

Barrack St PL1 ....127 E2
Barrack's La TR16 ....68 E1
Barras Cross PL14 ......113 C6
Barras Pl PL14 ....113 C6
Barras St PL14 ....113 C6
Barrepta Cl TR26 ....141 D1
Barrie Cres PL31 ....109 E2
Barripper Rd
  Camborne TR14 ......138 C1
  Penponds TR14 ....79 C5
Barrow Down PL12 ......122 B3
Barry's La PL28 ....107 D5
Bartholomew Rd PL2 ....128 B5
Bartles Cl PL12 ....99 D7
Bartles Row TR14 ......139 A5
Barton Ave PL12 ....127 E5
Barton Cl
  6 Bodmin PL31 ....109 C6
  Heamoor TR18 ....143 D1
  Helston TR13 ....146 D7
  Landrake PL12 ....53 C3
  Plymouth,PL7 ....131 C5
Barton Ct PL26 ....58 A7
Barton La TR9 ....45 D1
Barton Mdw Pelynt PL13 .62 D6
  Truro TR1 ....137 A5
Barton Mdws PL12 ....53 B7
Barton Mews
  Landrake PL12 ....53 C3
  Millbrook PL10 ......132 F6
Barton Rd Plymouth PL9 .135 B6
  St Dennis PL26 ....58 A4
Barton The PL29 ....22 D6
Barview La TR27 ....142 C4
Barwis Hill TR18 ......143 E6
Barwis Terr 1 TR18 ...143 E6
Basinghall Cl PL9 .....135 E5
Basket Ope PL4 ....149 A2
Basset Rd TR14 ....138 E5
Basset St Camborne TR14 138 D2
  Falmouth TR11 ....145 A4
  Redruth TR15 ....140 C4
Bassett Cl PL26 ....47 A1
Bassett Pl 11 TR11 ....145 A4
Bassett Rd Illogan TR16 .67 C4
  Redruth TR15 ....140 B8
Bastville EX22 ....11 E8
Bath La PL1 ....148 A3
Bath Pl PL1 ....148 B2
Bath Pl W PL1 ....148 B2
Bath St PL1 ....148 B2
Batter St PL4 ....149 A2
Battershall Cl PL9 ....135 F5
Battery Hill TR16 ......67 C6
Battery La Polruan PL23 .116 C2
  Tavistock PL19 ......147 C4
Battery Mill La TR27 ...77 L3
Battery Pk PL23 ......116 C2
Battery Rd TR18 ......143 F4
Battery St PL1 ....148 A2
Battery Street Flats
  PL1 ....148 A2
Battery Terr PL26 ......73 C3
Battery The TR7 ......110 D7
Bawden Rd PL31 ....109 B3
Bay Apartments TR7 ...110 A6
Bay Ct TR11 ....145 C2
Bay Rd PL28 ....20 F2
Bay St PL13 ....117 D3
Bay The PL13 ....117 D3
Bay Tree Cotts 3 EX23 ..4 D1
Bay View Cres PL25 ...114 C6
Bay View Pk PL25 .....114 C6
Bay View Rd PL13 .....117 D4
Bay View Terr
  Hayle TR27 ....142 C6
  24 Newlyn TR18 .....143 C2
  Newquay TR7 ....110 C5
  Penzance TR18 ......143 D4
  15 Porthleven TR13 ..98 B8
Bay Villas TR20 ....88 F6
Baydon Cl PL6 ....125 C1
Baydown PL13 ....117 D5
Bayly's Rd PL9 ....135 B7
Baynards Cl 1 TR1 ....137 D4
Baynes Cl 3 PL14 .....38 C4
Bayswater Rd PL1 .....148 B4
Baytree Cl PL6 ....125 D6
Baytree Gdns PL2 .....128 A7
Baytree Hill PL14 ....113 C5
Bayview Dr PL13 ......117 E4
Bayview Ho TR27 .....142 A8
Beach Hill PL11 ....64 C4
Beach Rd
  Carbis Bay TR26 ....141 D2
  Crantock TR8 ....43 D3
  Mevagissey PL26 .....73 C4
  Newquay TR7 ....110 D6
  Newquay, Porth TR7 ..111 B8
  Perranporth TR6 .....55 A5
  Porthtowan TR4 ......68 A6
  St Austell PL25 .....115 D3
  St Ives PL26 ....141 A6
  Trevone PL28 ....20 F2
Beach View Cl TR7 ....111 C7
Beachfield Ave TR7 ...110 D6
Beachfield Ct TR18 ...143 D4
Beachside Ct TR4 ......68 A6
Beachside L Pk TR27 ...78 A6
Beachview Flats TR4 ...68 A6
Beacon Com Jun Sch
  TR11 ....145 A5
Beacon Cross 72 F4
Beacon Down Ave PL2 .128 B7
Beacon Dr TR5 ....54 B1

Beacon Est TR20 ....87 D4
Beacon Farm TR5 ......54 C1
Beacon Fields TR14 ...138 E2
Beacon Hill PL31 .....109 D4
Beacon Hill Mews PL31 109 D4
Beacon Ho PL3 ....129 D4
Beacon Inf Sch TR11 ..145 A5
Beacon Lanes PL31 ....109 D3
Beacon Parc TR13 ....146 C6
Beacon Park Rd PL2 ...128 B7
Beacon Pk Boyton PL15 .13 A2
  Pelynt PL13 ....62 D5
Beacon Rd Bodmin PL31 109 E3
  Falmouth TR11 ......145 A5
  Foxhole PL26 ....58 D5
  Marazion TR17 ....89 B5
  Newquay TR7 ....110 D7
  Porthleven TR13 .....98 B8
  St Agnes TR5 ....54 C1
  Summercourt TR8 .....57 B7
Beacon Sq TR14 ......138 F1
Beacon St TR11 ......145 B5
Beacon Terr
  Camborne TR14 ......138 E1
  5 Falmouth TR11 ....145 A4
  Foxhole PL26 ....58 D5
  Helston TR13 ....146 C6
  Lizard TR12 ....102 A3
Beacon The TR11 .....145 A5
Beacon View Pk 23 TR16 .67 E4
Beaconfield Rd PL2 ...128 B7
Beacons PL13 ....62 E5
Bealswood Cl PL18 .....41 A4
Bealswood Rd PL18 .....41 A6
Beam Rd PL26 ....47 C1
Beare Cl PL9 ....135 B5
Bears Terr TR16 ....80 E7
Bearsdown Cl PL6 ....129 C8
Bearsdown Rd PL6 ....129 C8
Beatrice Ave
  Plymouth Keyham PL2 .127 F5
  Plymouth St Jude's PL4 149 B3
  Saltash PL12 ....122 E2
Beatrice Gdns PL12 ...122 E1
Beatrice Rd PL5 ....48 D8
Beatrice Terr TR27 ...142 C7
Beattie Rd PL5 ....127 B8
Beatty Cl PL6 ....125 E7
Beauchamp Cres PL2 ..128 C7
Beauchamp Rd PL2 ....128 C7
Beauchamps Mdw TR15 140 D2
Beaudyn Wlk 5 PL6 ...129 C7
Beaufighter Ave PL27 ..31 F3
Beaufort Ave 8 PL27 ..31 F3
Beaufort Ho 21 PL4 ...149 A4
Beauly Cl PL7 ....131 A5
Beaumaris Gdns PL3 ..128 E8
Beaumaris Rd PL3 ....128 F7
Beaumont Ave PL4 ....149 A3
Beaumont Pl PL4 .....149 A3
Beaumont Rd PL4 .....149 A3
Beaumont St PL2 .....128 A5
Beaumont Terr PL12 ..122 F4
Beck Adams PL12 ......53 C3
Beckett Cl TR15 .....140 C4
Beckford Cl PL7 .....131 A5
Beckham Pl PL3 .....129 A6
Beckly Ct PL1 ....148 C3
Bede Gdns PL6 ....124 C1
Bede Haven Cl EX23 ..104 E4
Bederkese Ct PL31 ...109 D4
Bedford Cl PL18 ....40 F6
Bedford Mews PL4 ....149 A4
Bedford Park Villas PL4 149 A4
Bedford Pk
  10 Bere Alston PL20 ..41 B1
  Plymouth PL4 ....149 A4
Bedford Pl
  6 Bere Alston PL20 ..41 B1
  6 St Ives TR26 ......141 B5
Bedford Rd
  Horrabridge PL20 ....42 C4
  Plymouth PL9 ....135 E8
  St Ives PL26 ....141 B5
Bedford Sq PL19 .....147 C5
Bedford St
  Bere Alston PL20 .....41 B1
  Plymouth PL2 ....127 F4
Bedford Terr PL4 ....149 A4
Bedford Villas 7 PL20 ..41 B1
Bedford Way PL1 .....148 C3
Bedowan Mdws TR7 ...111 A5
Bedruthan Ave TR1 ...137 E6
Bee Ctr* PL27 ....22 A6
Beech Ave Liskeard PL14 113 B5
  Plymouth PL4 ......149 C2
Beech Cl Falmouth TR11 144 F5
  Tavistock PL19 .....147 C2
  Torpoint PL11 ......127 A3
Beech Ct PL6 ....125 C5
Beech Dr Bodmin PL31 .109 B4
  4 St Columb Major TR9 .45 D6
Beech Hall Flats 18 TR2 .95 A6
Beech La PL25 ....114 D3
Beech Rd
  17 Callington PL17 ...39 F4
  Falmouth TR11 .....144 F5
  St Austell PL25 ....114 D3
Beech Terr PL13 .....117 C6
Beechcroft Rd
  Plymouth Lower Compton
  PL3 ....129 A6
  Plymouth, Beacon Park
  PL2 ....128 B7

Beeches The 9 PL14 ...38 E4
Beechfield Ave PL20 ...42 D3
Beeching Pk PL17 .....39 F6
Beechwood Ave PL4 ..128 D4
Beechwood Cross PL7 .131 F7
Beechwood Gdns PL7 .131 E6
Beechwood Rise PL6 ..125 E1
Beechwood Terr PL4 ..128 D4
Beechwood Way PL7 ..131 E6
Beehive Workshops
  TR10 ....144 A7
Beeston Wlk 6 PL6 ...129 C7
Behenna Dr TR1 ....69 F3
Bekelege Dr TR14 ....138 F1
Belah Mdw PL32 ....16 A8
Belair Rd PL2 ....128 C4
Belair Villas PL2 ....128 C7
Belerion Rd TR16 ......67 C5
Belgrave La PL4 .....128 F4
Belgrave Rd PL4 .....128 F4
Belgrave Terr PL14 ..113 D6
Belgravia St PL18 ....143 D5
Belhay TR10 ....144 C8
Bell Cl PL7 ....130 F6
Bell Hill PL26 ....85 C5
Bell La Bodmin PL31 ..109 E5
  Lanner TR16 ....80 C6
Bell Veor TR16 ....80 E6
Bell Yd PL31 ....109 E6
Bell's Ct TR11 ......145 B4
Bell's Hill TR11 ......82 A3
Bella Vista Gdns TR10 ..81 E2
Bellair Rd TR20 .....143 A8
Bellair Terr 38 TR26 .141 B6
Bellamy Cl PL6 ......125 A1
Bellatt PL27 ....108 C3
Belle Acre Cl PL3 ...128 F6
Belle Vue Bude EX23 ..104 D6
  Newlyn TR18 ....143 C1
Belle Vue Ave
  Bude EX23 ....104 D6
  Plymouth PL9 ......135 B5
Belle Vue Dr PL9 ....135 B5
Belle Vue La EX23 ...104 D6
Belle Vue Rd
  Plymouth PL9 ......135 C5
  Saltash PL12 ......122 F2
Belle Vue Rise PL9 ..135 B5
Belle Vue Terr
  Gunnislake PL18 .....41 A6
  21 Penzance TR18 ..143 E6
Bellever Parc TR14 ..138 F4
Bellever Rd TR15 ....140 C5
Bellevue TR15 ......140 C5
Bellevue Cotts TR10 ..81 E2
Bellevue Sq PL11 ....127 B2
Bellingham Cres PL7 .131 C4
Belliver Ind Est PL6 .121 B1
Belliver Way PL6 ....121 B1
Bells Ct TR11 ....139 C7
Belmont Cl PL33 ......14 D2
Belmont Ct
  10 Plymouth PL3 ...128 A4
  11 Wadebridge PL27 108 B5
Belmont Mews PL14 ...38 D4
Belmont Pk PL14 ......38 D4
Belmont Pl Newquay TR7 110 D7
  Plymouth PL1 ......128 A4
  St Ives TR26 ....141 A6
Belmont Rd
  Falmouth TR11 .....145 A3
  Helston TR13 ......146 B7
  St Austell PL25 ....114 C4
Belmont St 8 Par PL24 .60 D5
  Plymouth PL1 ......148 B3
Belmont Terr Devoran TR3 81 F6
  St Ives TR26 ......141 A6
Belstone Cl PL5 .....124 A3
Belvedere La TR20 ....89 F5
Belvedere Rd PL4 ....129 B2
Belyars Ct TR26 .....141 B4
Belyars La TR26 .....141 B4
Bemallack Ct TR1 ....137 E4
Benbow St PL2 ......127 F4
Bencoolen Rd EX23 ..104 D5
Beneathway PL14 ......50 E7
Bennets La PL12 .....122 F3
Bennett St PL1 ......127 E1
Bennetts Cotts 3 TR10 144 C7
Benson Gdns 2 TR1 ..137 D5
Benson Ho 1 TR1 ....137 D5
Benson Rd TR1 ......137 D5
Bentley Dr 5 EX23 ....4 D1
Beramic Ct TR27 ......78 D6
Bere Alston Prim Sch
  PL20 ....41 B2
Bere Alston Sta PL20 ..41 B2
Bere Ferrers Sta PL20 119 E3
Berepper Cross TR12 ..98 C5
Beresford St PL2 ....128 A4
Berkeley Cl EX23 ......4 D1
Berkeley Cotts TR11 .145 A4
Berkeley Hill TR11 ..145 A4
Berkeley Mews 4 TR11 145 A4
Berkeley Path 3 TR11 145 A4
Berkeley Vale TR11 ..145 A4
Berkshire Dr PL2 ....127 F5
Bernice Cl PL4 ......129 A4
Bernice Terr PL4 ....129 A4
Berries Ave EX23 ....104 A4
Berries Mount EX23 ..104 A4
Berrow Park Rd PL3 ..128 C6
Berry La PL31 ....109 E5
Berry Park Rd PL9 ...135 E7
Berry Pk PL12 ....122 D4
Berry Rd TR7 ....110 E6

Berrycombe View 5
  PL31 ....109 D5
Berrycoombe Hill PL31 109 C5
Berrycoombe Prim Sch
  PL31 ....109 A4
Berrycoombe Rd PL31 .109 D5
Berrycoombe Vale PL31 109 C5
Berryfields Ho PL31 ..109 E5
Berryhill PL30 ....47 C6
Berryman Cres TR11 .144 F3
Berthon Rd PL5 ......127 C8
Berveth Cl TR3 ....69 D3
Berwick Ave PL5 .....124 E3
Bess Park Rd PL27 ...108 E6
Bethan Dr PL27 ......108 B5
Bethany Homes TR14 .138 C2
Bethany Pl TR19 ......86 F6
Bethel Rd PL25 ......114 C4
Bethesda Pl 10 TR26 .141 B6
Betjeman Wlk PL5 ...124 C3
Beverley Cres TR27 ..142 E7
Beverley Rd PL3 .....129 C4
Beverston Way PL6 ..125 B8
Beweys Pk PL12 .....122 C4
Beyrout Pl 6 PL1 ....127 F3
Bickern Rd PL11 ....127 B3
Bickford Cres TR13 ...91 B1
Bickford Rd PL15 ....106 C4
Bickham Park Rd PL3 .128 D7
Bickham Pl PL5 .....123 D2
Bickland Hill TR11 ..144 D4
Bickland Water Rd
  TR11 ....144 D2
Bickleigh Cl PL6 ....125 A1
Bickleigh Down CE Prim Sch
  PL6 ....125 D1
Bickleigh Down Rd PL6 121 D1
Bicton Cl PL6 ....125 D1
Biddick Dr PL2 .....127 F6
Biddick's Ct 5 PL25 .114 C4
Bideford Wlk PL6 ...129 C8
Big Gn PL13 ....62 D1
Bigbury Wlk PL6 ....129 E8
Biggin Hill PL5 .....123 F4
Bilbury St PL4 ......149 A3
Billacombe Rd PL9 ..129 E1
Billacombe Villas PL9 135 F8
Billing Cl PL6 ......124 D6
Billings Dr TR7 .....111 B5
Billington Cl PL6 ...129 B7
Binhamy Cl EX23 ....104 F4
Binhamy Rd EX23 .....7 B8
Binkham Hill PL20 ....42 D3
Birch Cl PL6 ....125 E7
Birch Gr TR27 ......142 B3
Birch Pond Rd PL9 ..135 D7
Bircham View PL6 ...125 C1
Birches The PL6 ....125 D6
Birchfield Ave PL2 ..128 B6
Birchill PL30 ....47 C6
Birchwood Cl PL19 ..147 C3
Birchwood Gdns PL7 .131 A7
Birkbeck Cl PL7 ....130 E7
Birkdale Cl PL12 ....122 C2
Biscombe Gdns PL12 .123 A2
Biscombes La 8 PL17 .39 E4
Biscovey Jun & Inf Schs
  PL24 ....60 B4
Biscovey Rd PL24 ....115 F5
Bishop Bronescombe CE Sch
  PL25 ....60 B4
Bishop Cornish CE Prim Sch
  PL12 ....122 C3
Bishop Temple Rd TR1 137 F6
Bishop's CE Prim Sch The
  TR7 ....110 F4
Bishop's Hill Rd PL27 .21 D6
Bishop's Rd TR26 ...141 B5
Bishops Cl TR1 .....137 C6
Bishops Cl PL7 ......81 F7
Bissoe Rd TR4 ....81 F7
Bissom TR10 ....144 E8
Bissom Rd
  Mylor Bridge TR11 ...82 A2
  Penryn TR10,TR11 ...81 F2
Black Rd TR27 ......142 D7
Blackall Gdns PL6 ..124 D6
Blackberry Cl PL9 ..135 E8
Blackberry La PL9 ..135 E8
Blackberry Way TR1 .137 F5
Blackbrook Cl PL20 ..42 E4
Blackerry Cl TR16 ..140 F1
Blackeven Cl PL6 ...121 D1
Blackeven Hill PL6 ..121 E1
Blackfriars La PL1 ..149 A2
Blackmore Cres PL6 .124 D6
Blacksmith La PL27 ..78 D6
Blackstone Cl PL9 ..136 B6
Blackthorn Cl
  Plymouth, Honicknowle
  PL5 ....124 B3
  Plymouth, Woolwell PL6 125 D8
Blackwater Com Prim Sch
  TR4 ....68 C5
Bladder La PL5 .....124 E2
Blagdon Cross EX21 ..13 F7
Blagdon Lodge Cross
  EX21 ....13 F8
Blairgowrie Rd PL5 ..123 F4
Blake Gdns PL5 .....124 E6
Blakes Pk PL14 .....113 D7
Blanchard Rd 2 PL7 .130 E6
Blanchdown Dr PL18 ..40 F7
Blanchminster Rd EX23 104 E5
Blandford Rd PL3 ...129 C6
Blatchborough Cross
  EX22 ....23 E1
Blaxton La PL5 .....120 C2
Blenheim Rd PL4 ...149 A4

Bligh Cres TR13 ....146 C3
Blight's Row TR15 ..140 B5
Blind La PL11 ....64 D6
Blindhole 7 PL15 ...106 C6
Blindwell Hill PL10 ..132 E5
Blisland Com Prim Sch
  PL30 ....35 D7
Bloom Fields TR13 ..143 C5
Bloomball Cl PL3 ...129 B6
Blowing House Cl PL25 114 B4
Blowing House Hill
  Crowlas TR20 ....89 B8
  Hayle TR20 ....77 A1
  St Austell PL25 ....114 C4
Blowing House La PL25 114 B4
Blowinghouse Hill TR15 140 A4
Blowinghouse La PL30 .109 D7
Blue Haze Cl PL6 ...125 D5
Bluebell Cl PL12 ....122 D4
Bluebell Way PL19 ..147 E4
Blunts La PL6 ....125 C3
Boaden Cl PL12 ......53 E5
Boakanza Ct TR26 ..141 C2
Boase St 1 TR18 ....143 C1
Bobs Rd PL24 ....60 B4
Bochym Hill TR12 ....99 C3
Boconnic La PL20 .....42 D3
Boconnoc Ave PL11 ..39 F3
Boconnoc Rd PL25 ..114 D2
Bodelva Rd PL24 ....115 E8
Bodgara Way PL14 ..113 D6
Bodgare Way Flats
  PL14 ....113 D6
Bodieve Rd PL27 ....108 D7
Bodinar Rd TR10 .....81 D2
Bodinel Rd PL31 ....109 C6
Bodinel Rd PL31 ....109 C6
Bodinnar Cl TR20 ....87 E6
Bodinnar La TR20 ....87 E6
Bodinnick Hts TR23 .116 E5
Bodinnick Parc PL30 ..23 E3
Bodinnick Rd PL30 ...23 E3
Bodmin & Wenford Rly*
  PL30,PL31 ....109 D2
Bodmin Bsns Ctr PL31 .35 B2
Bodmin Bsns Pk PL31 ..35 B2
Bodmin Com Coll PL31 109 E2
Bodmin General Sta*
  PL31 ....109 E3
Bodmin Hill PL22 ...112 B4
Bodmin Hospl PL31 ..109 B4
Bodmin Jail* PL31 ..109 D5
Bodmin Parkway Sta
  PL30 ....49 A7
Bodmin Rd Plymouth PL5 124 D3
  St Austell PL25 ....114 C6
  Truro TR1 ....137 E6
Bodmin Town Mus*
  PL31 ....109 E4
Bodrigan Rd PL13 ...117 D5
Bodriggy Cres TR27 .142 C5
Bodriggy Ct TR27 ...142 D6
Bodriggy Prim Sch
  Hayle TR27 ....142 D5
  Hayle TR27 ....142 D6
Bodriggy St TR27 ...142 D6
Bodriggy Villas TR27 142 D6
Body's Ct PL18 ....40 F6
Bohella Rd 19 TR2 ...95 A6
Bohelland Rd TR10 ..144 D8
Bohelland Rise TR10 144 D8
Bohelland Way TR10 144 D8
Bohill TR10 ....144 D7
Bohill Ct TR10 .....144 D7
Boiler Works Rd TR14 138 E5
Bojea Ind Est PL25 ..114 C7
Bojea Terr PL25 .....114 C6
Bojewyan Stennack TR19 75 B1
Bokenna Cross PL14 ..37 C1
Boldventure Ave PL25 115 B5
Boldventure Cl PL25 .115 B5
Boldventure Rd PL25 .115 B5
Bolenna La TR8 ......55 A4
Bolenowe Terr TR14 ..79 F4
Bolingey Chapel Flats
  TR6 ....55 B4
Bolingey Rd TR6 .....55 A4
Bolitho Rd TR18 ....143 C7
Bolitho Sch The TR18 143 C5
Bolowthas Cnr TR7 ..111 A7
Bolowthas Way TR7 ..111 C7
Bolster Ct 8 TR5 ....54 C1
Bolt House Ct PL19 ..147 A5
Boltern Rd TR17 .....89 C5
Bolventor La PL13 ...63 E8
Bon Cot Rd TR18 ...143 C2
Bonallack La TR12 ...92 D1
Bond St Plymouth PL6 124 E6
  6 Redruth TR15 ....140 B4
Bone Cellar Row TR2 ..70 F5
Bone Mill Rd TR6 ....55 B4
Bones La PL12 ....52 E4
Bonson Cl PL13 .....117 C4
Bonville Rd PL6 ....124 E6
Bonython Cl TR11 ....82 A3
Bonython Dr TR2 .....72 A7
Bonython Rd PL27 ..111 B7
Bonython Terr PL14 .113 B4
Boon's Pl PL1 ......148 C4
Borgwitha TR16 ......80 B5
Boringdon Ave PL5 ..127 D8
Boringdon Cl PL7 ...130 D7
Boringdon Hill PL7 ..130 E7

Boringdon Mill Bsns Ctr
PL7 . . . . .130 F6
Boringdon Prim Sch
PL7 . . . . .130 D7
Boringdon Rd
Plymouth, Plympton PL7 .130 D6
Plymouth, Turnchapel PL9 .135 A7
Boringdon Terr
Plymouth, Plympton PL7 .130 D6
Plymouth, Turnchapel PL9 .135 A7
Boringdon Villas PL7 . . .130 D6
Borlase Cl PL13 . . . . . . .146 B5
Borough Cross EX22 . . . . . .7 F5
Borough Ct PL11 . . . . . .126 E4
Borough Pk PL11 . . . . . .126 E4
Borrowdale Cl PL6 . . . . .124 D5
Bosawna Cl TR16 . . . . . . .68 E1
Boscarn Cl TR14 . . . . . . .79 B5
Boscarn Rd PL25 . . . . . .140 D6
Boscarne Cres PL25 . . . .114 F3
Boscarne Junction Sta★
PL30 . . . . .34 D2
Boscarne View PL30 . . . . .34 D2
Boscarnek TR27 . . . . . . .142 A1
Boscastle Com Prim Sch
PL35 . . . . .9 C1
Boscastle Gdns PL2 . . .128 C8
Boscastle Visitor Ctr★
PL35 . . . . .9 D2
Boscaswell Downs TR19 .75 A1
Boscaswell Est TR19 . . . .74 F1
Boscaswell Rd TR19 . . . .75 A1
Boscaswell Terr TR19 . . .75 A1
Boscathnoe La TR18 . . .143 B7
Boscathnoe Way TR18 . .143 B7
Boscawen Gdns **11** TR6 . .55 A4
Boscawen Pk PL26 . . . . . .58 B8
Boscawen Pl PL2 . . . . . .127 E4
Boscawen Rd
Chacewater TR4 . . . . .69 A3
Falmouth TR11 . . . . .145 B2
Helston TR13 . . . . .146 D4
Perranporth TR6 . . . . .55 A4
St Dennis PL26 . . . . .58 C8
Boscawen St TR1 . . . . . .137 D4
Boscean Cl TR14 . . . . . . .79 E4
Boscoppa Cl TR15 . . . . .140 D7
Boscoppa Rd
St Austell PL25 . . . . .115 A5
St Austell PL25 . . . . .115 B5
Boscundle Ave TR11 . . .144 F1
Boscundle Cl PL25 . . . . .115 D5
Boscundle Row PL12 . . .123 A2
Bosence Rd TR27 . . . . . . .90 C7
Bosillion La TR2 . . . . .72 A7
Bosinver La PL26 . . . . . . .59 A1
Boskear La PL31 . . . . . . .109 A4
Boskenna Cross TR19 . . . .97 C5
Boskenna Rd TR16 . . . . . .80 A5
Boskennal Barton TR19 . .97 B6
Boskennal La TR19 . . . . . .97 C5
Boskennel Dr TR27 . . . .142 B4
Boskenwyn Com Prim Sch
TR13 . . . . .92 A3
Boskernick Cl TR18 . . . .143 B1
Boskerris Cres TR26 . . . .141 D1
Boskerris Mews TR26 . . .141 D1
Boskerris Rd TR26 . . . . .141 D2
Boslanderew Hill TR19 . . .88 C2
Bosleake Row TR15 . . . .139 C3
Bosloggas Mews **9**
TR11 . . . . .145 C3
Boslowick Cl TR11 . . . . .144 F3
Boslowick Ct TR11 . . . . .144 F3
Boslowick Rd TR11 . . . .144 E2
Bosmeor Cl TR11 . . . . . .144 E2
Bosmeor Pk TR15 . . . . .139 D6
Bosmeor Rd TR11 . . . . .144 E3
Bosnoweth Helston TR13 146 D5
Probus TR2 . . . . .71 D6
Bosollow Vean TR20 . . . .87 D8
Bosorne Cl TR19 . . . . . . .86 E6
Bosorne Rd TR19 . . . . . .86 E6
Bosorne St TR19 . . . . . . .86 E6
Bosorne Terr TR19 . . . . .86 E6
Bosparva La
Leedstown TR27 . . . . .78 F2
Praze-an-Beeble TR14 . . . .79 A3
Bospolvans Rd **2** TR9 . .45 D6
Bospowis TR14 . . . . .138 C3
Bossiney Rd PL34 . . . . . . .14 D7
Bostennack Pl **10** TR26 .141 A5
Bostennack Terr **11**
TR26 . . . . .141 A5
Bosuen Rd TR7 . . . . .111 A7
Bosvean Gdns
11 Illogan TR16 . . . . . . .67 E4
Truro TR1 . . . . .137 B5
Bosvean Rd TR4 . . . . . . .69 F4
Bosvenna View PL31 . . .109 E4
Bosvenna Way TR18 . . .143 B7
Bosvenning Pl TR20 . . . .87 E6
Bosvigo Gdns★ TR1 . . .137 A5
Bosvigo La TR1 . . . . . . .137 B5
Bosvigo Rd TR1 . . . . . . .137 C4
Bosvigo Sch TR1 . . . . . .137 C4
Boswedden Pl TR19 . . . .86 E6
Boswedden Rd TR19 . . . .86 E6
Boswell Cl PL5 . . . . .124 B2
Boswergy TR18 . . . . . . .143 C5
Boswithian Rd TR14 . . . .138 F6
Bosworgey Cl **3** TR9 . . .45 D6
Bosworgy Rd TR27 . . . . . .90 B8
Botallack La TR19 . . . . . .86 E7

Botetoe Hill TR14 . . . . . .79 C4
Botetoe Rd TR14 . . . . . . .79 B4
Botha Rd **1** PL27 . . . . . .31 F3
Bothwicks Rd TR7 . . . . .110 C6
Boughthayes Est PL19 . .147 A5
Boulden Cl PL7 . . . . . . .131 C5
Boulter Cl PL6 . . . . .121 C1
Bound The PL10 . . . . . . .133 A1
Boundary Rd
Bodmin PL31 . . . . .109 A4
Dousland PL20 . . . . .42 E3
Bounder Treath TR12 . . .101 C1
Bounders La TR6 . . . . . . .55 B4
Boundervean La TR14 . . .138 E2
Bounds Cross EX22 . . . . . .8 B4
Bounds Pl PL1 . . . . .148 B2
Bounsall's La PL15 . . . . .106 C5
Bounsalls Ct PL15 . . . . .106 C5
Bourne Cl PL3 . . . . .129 D6
Boveway Dr PL14 . . . . . .113 E5
Boveway La PL14 . . . . . .113 D5
Boville La PL9 . . . . .136 C7
Bovisand Ct PL9 . . . . . . .134 F2
Bovisand La
Down Thomas PL9 . . . . . .135 B2
Staddiscombe PL9 . . . . . .135 D3
Bovisand Pk PL9 . . . . . .135 A1
Bovisand Rd PL9 . . . . . .135 E3
Bow La EX23 . . . . .4 D2
Bowden Park Rd PL6 . . .125 A1
Bowdens Row TR15 . . . .140 A4
Bowers Park Dr PL6 . . . .125 E7
Bowers Rd PL2 . . . . .128 B5
Bowglas PL20 . . . . .89 A8
Bowhays Wlk **2** PL6 . . .129 C7
Bowjey Cl TR18 . . . . . . .143 C1
Bowjey Hill TR18 . . . . . .143 C1
Bowjey Terr **5** TR18 . . .143 C1
Bowles Rd TR11 . . . . . . .145 A6
Bowling Gn
Menheniot PL14 . . . . .51 F3
34 St Ives TR26 . . . . . .141 B6
Bowling Gn Terr **35**
TR26 . . . . .141 B6
Bowling Gn The TR2 . . . .82 F2
Bowling Green Ct
Hayle TR27 . . . . .142 D5
Liskeard PL14 . . . . .113 B5
Bowling Green Rd TR18 . .92 F3
Bownder Dowr TR27 . . . .142 B3
Bownder Vean PL25 . . . .115 A5
Bowood Pk PL32 . . . . . . .24 B8
Box's Shop EX23 . . . . .7 A4
Boxhill Cl PL5 . . . . .124 B3
Boxhill Gdns PL2 . . . . . .128 C8
Boxwell Pk PL31 . . . . . .109 F4
Boyd Ave PL28 . . . . .107 C5
Boyton Com Prim Sch
PL15 . . . . .13 A3
Bracken Cl Bodmin PL31 .109 E5
Plymouth PL6 . . . . .125 D8
Bracken Terr PL7 . . . . . .110 E5
Brackenside PL13 . . . . . . .62 C1
Brackwell Pl PL7 . . . . . .108 B5
Braddock CE Prim Sch
PL22 . . . . .49 D6
Braddons Cl PL26 . . . . . .58 D6
Braddons Hill PL7 . . . . .130 B7
Bradfield Cl PL6 . . . . . . .125 E1
Bradford Cl PL6 . . . . . . .129 B7
Bradford Quay Rd PL27 .108 C6
Bradley Rd Newquay TR7 .111 C7
Plymouth PL4 . . . . .128 F4
Braeside Pk PL14 . . . . . . .50 E8
Braggs Hill PL15 . . . . . . .13 B3
Brake La PL10 . . . . .132 B5
Brake Rd PL5 . . . . .124 E2
Brake The PL7 . . . . .37 F4
Bramble Cl Newquay TR7 111 A4
Plymouth PL3 . . . . .129 D7
Bramble Hill EX23 . . . . .104 E5
Bramble Wlk **1** PL6 . . .129 C7
Bramblebank TR11 . . . . .145 B7
Brambles The PL14 . . . .113 E5
Bramfield Pl PL6 . . . . . .129 D7
Bramley Cl PL25 . . . . . .114 E4
Bramley Pk PL31 . . . . . .109 F5
Bramley Rd PL3 . . . . . . .129 C4
Brancker Rd PL2 . . . . . .128 C6
Brandon Rd PL2 . . . . . . .129 C4
Brandon Terr **29** TR26 .141 B6
Brandon Wlk EX23 . . . . . . .6 F5
Brandreth Rd **3** PL3 . . .128 F6
Brandy La PL20 . . . . .89 D4
Branksome Dr PL27 . . . .108 E5
Brannel Sch PL26 . . . . . .58 B3
Branscombe Gdns PL5 . .124 A3
Branson Ct **9** PL7 . . . . .131 C5
Branson Pk PL19 . . . . . . .42 A6
Branwell La PL18 . . . . . . .88 E6
Braunton Wlk PL6 . . . . .129 E8
Bray Cl PL19 . . . . .147 A5
Bray's Pl PL25 . . . . .114 F4
Brayford Cl PL5 . . . . . . .124 B3
Brays Terr **2** TR16 . . . .140 F1
Brazacott Cross PL15 . . . .12 B2
Brea Arch TR14 . . . . . . .139 A3
Brea Rd PL27 . . . . .21 D2
Bread St TR18 . . . . .143 E5
Breage CE Prim Sch
TR13 . . . . .90 F3
Break My Neck La TR20 . .88 B8
Breakwater Hill PL4 . . . .149 C1
Breakwater Ind Est PL9 135 C8
Breakwater Rd
Bude EX23 . . . . .104 D5

Breakwater Rd continued
Plymouth PL9 . . . . .135 C8
Brean Down Cl PL3 . . . .128 E6
Brean Down Rd PL3 . . . .128 E6
Breaside TR14 . . . . .139 A3
Brecon Cl Plymouth PL3 .129 A7
1 St Agnes TR5 . . . . . . .54 C1
Bree Shute La PL31 . . . .109 E5
Brent Knoll Rd **1** PL3 . .128 E6
Brentford Ave PL5 . . . . .124 B5
Brenton Rd PL11 . . . . . . .64 B5
Brentons Pk PL29 . . . . . .22 D6
Brentor Rd
Mary Tavy PL19 . . . . .30 F6
Plymouth PL4 . . . . .129 B2
Brentwartha PL13 . . . . . .62 E2
Breoke Hts PL27 . . . . . .108 A5
Brest Rd PL6 . . . . .125 A3
Brest Way PL6 . . . . .125 A3
Breton Side PL4 . . . . . . .149 A2
Brett Wlk PL7 . . . . .130 F7
Brewers Cl PL30 . . . . . . .47 F6
Brewers Hill PL26 . . . . . .58 C8
Brewers Rd TR1 . . . . . . .137 F5
Brewery Hill TR26 . . . . . .77 E4
Brewery La TR18 . . . . . .146 B6
Briansway PL12 . . . . . . .122 D2
Briar Cl Bude EX23 . . . . .104 E4
Plymouth PL3 . . . . .128 F7
Briar Tor PL20 . . . . .42 D3
Briardale Rd PL2 . . . . . .127 E6
Briarfield PL23 . . . . .116 D4
Briarleigh Cl PL6 . . . . . .125 F2
Briars Row PL12 . . . . . . .122 D4
Briars Ryn PL12 . . . . .53 B7
Briarwood PL14 . . . . . . .113 D5
Brickworks Hill TR16 . . . .68 D1
Bridals La PL13 . . . . .62 E2
Bridge Cl TR7 . . . . .111 A4
Bridge Ct PL25 . . . . . . .114 F4
Bridge Hill Illogan TR16 . .67 E4
St Columb Major TR9 . . . .45 E6
Bridge Ho The **13** TR18 .143 C7
Bridge La PL12 . . . . .53 A3
Bridge Pk EX22 . . . . .7 F7
Bridge Rd Goonhavern TR4 55 D4
Illogan TR16 . . . . .67 E4
St Austell PL25 . . . . .114 B3
Tideford PL12 . . . . .52 F2
Bridge Row TR16 . . . . . . .67 E5
Bridge St Par PL24 . . . . . .60 B6
7 Stratton EX23 . . . . .4 D1
Bridge The PL1 . . . . .148 B1
Bridge View PL25 . . . . . .108 C6
Bridgemead Cl PL26 . . . .114 C1
Bridgemoor Cross EX22 . .8 C6
Bridgerule CE Prim Sch
EX22 . . . . .8 A5
Bridgerule Ind Est EX22 . .7 F4
Bridges The PL12 . . . . . .122 E1
Bridgwater Cl PL6 . . . . .125 B1
Bridle Cl PL7 . . . . .131 B7
Bridle Way
Quintrell Downs TR8 . . . . .44 B3
Saltash PL12 . . . . .122 D4
Bridwell Cl PL5 . . . . . . .127 E8
Bridwell La N PL5 . . . . . .127 E8
Bridwell Rd PL5 . . . . . . .127 E8
Brillwater Rd TR11 . . . . . .92 E4
Brimford Cross EX39 . . . . .3 D4
Brimhill Cl PL7 . . . . .131 B3
Brisbane Terr PL14 . . . . .113 C5
Brismar Wlk **3** PL6 . . . .129 C7
Briston Orch PL12 . . . . . .53 E7
Britannia Pl PL4 . . . . . . .129 B2
British Cycling Mus★
PL32 . . . . .105 C8
British Rd TR5 . . . . .54 D1
Briton's Hill PL18 . . . . . .143 F6
Brixham Wlk PL6 . . . . . .129 E8
Brixton Lodge Gdns
PL8 . . . . .136 F5
Brixton Terr PL13 . . . . . .146 C5
Broad Cl EX22 . . . . .11 E7
Broad La Illogan TR15 . . .139 D7
Trematon PL12 . . . . .53 E2
Broad Mead PL17 . . . . . .39 E5
Broad Pk
Launceston PL15 . . . . . . .106 B7
Liskeard PL14 . . . . .51 B3
Plymouth PL9 . . . . .135 C7
Broad St
10 Launceston PL15 . . .106 C6
Lifton PL16 . . . . .19 F4
Newquay TR7 . . . . .110 D6
Padstow PL28 . . . . .107 D5
Penryn TR10 . . . . .144 C7
7 St Columb Major TR9 . .45 E6
Truro TR1 . . . . .137 E5
Broad View TR4 . . . . .56 D7
Broad Wlk Helston TR13 .146 B7
Saltash PL12 . . . . .122 C2
Broadclose Hill EX23 . . .104 E4
Broadland Gdns PL9 . . . .136 A6
Broadland La PL9 . . . . . .135 F8
Broadlands Cl PL7 . . . . .131 A3
Broadley Ct PL6 . . . . . . .121 B2
Broadley Ind Pk PL6 . . .121 B2
Broadley Park Rd PL6 . . .121 B2
Broads La TR11 . . . . .81 F3
Broads Yd PL11 . . . . .64 C5
Broadshell Cross EX22 . . . .8 E5
Broadway The PL9 . . . . .135 E7

Brock Ho **10** PL4 . . . . . .149 A2
Brockley Rd PL3 . . . . . . .129 C4
Brockstone Rd PL25 . . . .115 A5
Brockton Gdns PL6 . . . . .125 A8
Bromfield Cres TR2 . . . . .57 E1
Bromhead Ct PL6 . . . . . .129 A8
Bromley Pl **6** PL2 . . . . .128 A4
Bronescombe Cl TR10 . .144 D7
Bronte Pl PL5 . . . . .124 D1
Brook Cl Helston TR13 . .146 B7
Plymouth PL7 . . . . .131 A3
Brook Ct **6** TR11 . . . . .145 A4
Brook Dr EX23 . . . . .104 E2
Brook La PL19 . . . . .147 B2
Brook Pl Falmouth TR11 .145 A4
Penryn TR10 . . . . .144 C7
Brook Rd Falmouth TR11 .144 F3
Wadebridge PL27 . . . . . .108 B5
Brook St Falmouth TR11 .145 A4
16 Mousehole TR19 . . . .88 C1
Tavistock PL19 . . . . .147 C6
Brook The PL12 . . . . . . .122 D2
Brookdale Ct **12** PL27 . .108 B5
Brookdown Terr PL12 . . .122 D3
Brookdown Villas PL12 . .122 D3
Brooke Cl PL12 . . . . .123 A2
Brookfield Cl Lanjeth PL26 58 E3
Plymouth PL7 . . . . .131 B5
Brooking Way PL12 . . . .122 D2
Brookingfield Cl PL7 . . .130 C5
Brooklands
New Polzeath PL27 . . . . . .21 D6
Tavistock PL19 . . . . .147 D6
Brooklands Ct PL6 . . . . .124 E3
Brooklyn Flats **17** TR2 . .95 A6
Brooklyn Terr **16** TR2 . . .95 A6
Brooks PL22 . . . . .49 E3
Brooks La PL10 . . . . .132 B5
Brookside St Austell PL25 114 F4
Chacewater TR4 . . . . .68 F3
Brookside Cl PL15 . . . . .106 B8
Brookward Terr **8**
TR18 . . . . .143 C7
Brookway TR27 . . . . . . .142 E7
Brookwood Rd PL9 . . . . .136 D7
Broom Hill PL12 . . . . . . .122 D2
Broom Pk PL9 . . . . .135 D5
Broomfield Dr
Bodmin PL31 . . . . .109 B3
Plymouth PL9 . . . . .135 C5
Broomfield Rd PL27 . . . .108 D5
Broomhill Cross EX22 . . . .5 E3
Broomhill La EX23 . . . . . . .4 D2
Broughton Cl PL3 . . . . . .128 F7
Brown's Hill TR10 . . . . . .144 C8
Browne Meml Almshouses
PL19 . . . . .147 A5
Browning Dr PL31 . . . . .109 C3
Browning Rd PL2 . . . . . .128 A5
Brownlow Pl PL31 . . . . .109 D5
Brownlow St PL1 . . . . . .148 A3
Browns Hill PL23 . . . . . .116 C4
Broxton Dr PL9 . . . . .129 E1
Brunel Ave PL2 . . . . .127 F5
Brunel Prim Sch PL12 . .122 E2
Brunel Rd PL12 . . . . . . .122 C4
Brunel Terr **3** PL2 . . . . .127 F5
Brunel Way PL1 . . . . . . .148 A2
Brunswick Pl **10** PL2 . . .127 F4
Brunswick Rd PL4 . . . . .149 B2
Brush End TR26 . . . . .77 E4
Brynmoor Cl PL3 . . . . . .129 A7
Brynmoor Pk PL3 . . . . . .129 A6
Brynmoor Wlk PL3 . . . . .129 A6
Bryny Cl PL30 . . . . .23 E7
Buckett's Hill TR15 . . . .140 C2
Buckeys La TR2 . . . . .95 B6
Buckfast Cl PL2 . . . . . . .127 F4
Buckingham Nip TR4 . . . .68 F3
Buckingham Pl PL5 . . . .123 E2
Buckingham Terr TR16 . . .68 D1
Buckingham's Cl TR8 . . . .56 B7
Buckland Abbey★ PL20 .41 F1
Buckland Cl PL7 . . . . . . .130 D7
Buckland St PL1 . . . . . . .148 B2
Buckland Terr PL20 . . . . .42 C2
Bucklawren Rd PL13 . . . .63 E7
Buckler Village (Mobile
Homes Pk) PL25 . . . . . .115 B4
Bucklers La PL25 . . . . . .115 B4
Buckwell St PL1,PL4 . . . .149 A2
Buctor Pk PL19 . . . . .41 D8
Buddle Cl Plymouth PL9 .136 B6
Tavistock PL19 . . . . .147 B6
Bude Ind Est EX23 . . . . .104 F4
Bude Inf Sch EX23 . . . . .104 E5
Bude Jun Sch EX23 . . . .104 E5
Bude-stratton Mus★
EX23 . . . . .104 D5
Budehaven Com Sch
EX23 . . . . .104 F5
Budemeadows Cvn Site
EX23 . . . . .7 A4
Budge Mdws PL15 . . . . . .28 C4
Budleigh Cl PL9 . . . . . . .135 F5
Budnic Est TR6 . . . . .55 B5
Budnic Hill TR6 . . . . .55 B5
Budock Hospl TR11 . . . .144 D5
Budock Rd TR11 . . . . . . .145 A4
Budock Terr TR11 . . . . . .145 B3
Budock Vean La TR11 . . . .93 B2
Budshead Gn PL5 . . . . . .124 C4
Budshead Rd PL5 . . . . . .124 C4
Budshead Way PL6 . . . . .124 E2
Buena Vista Cl PL6 . . . . .125 D6
Buena Vista Dr PL6 . . . . .125 C6
Buena Vista Gdns PL6 . .125 C6
Buena Vista Way PL6 . . .125 C6

Bugle Prim Sch PL26 . . . .47 C1
Bugle Rural Workshops
PL26 . . . . .47 C1
Bugle Sta PL26 . . . . .47 C2
Buildings The TR20 . . . . .89 A6
Bull Hill PL23 . . . . .116 D4
Bull Point Prim Sch
PL5 . . . . .127 B8
Bullans Vale TR26 . . . . .141 A5
Bullans Terr **5** TR26 . . .141 A5
Bulleid Cl PL2 . . . . .127 F7
Bulleid Way **7** Plymouth PL7 .130 F4
Torpoint PL11 . . . . .127 A3
Buller Hill TR16 . . . . .80 B6
Buller Pk Liskeard PL14 .113 D5
Saltash PL12 . . . . .122 D3
Buller Rd PL11 . . . . .127 B3
Buller St PL13 . . . . .117 C3
Bullers Terr TR15 . . . . . .140 D5
Bullock La Helston TR13 .146 B5
Helston, Whitehill TR13 . .146 C4
Bullock Market Terr **28**
TR18 . . . . .143 E6
Bulmer Rd PL4 . . . . .149 C2
Bulteel Gdns PL6 . . . . . .124 E7
Bulwark Rd TR13 . . . . . .146 B4
Bungalows The PL13 . . .117 D6
Bunkers Hill
22 St Ives TR26 . . . . . .141 B6
Townshend TR27 . . . . . . .90 C8
Bunyan Cl PL5 . . . . .124 C1
Burden Cl PL31 . . . . . . .109 C4
Burgess Cl EX23 . . . . .4 D2
Burhos Row TR13 . . . . . .79 F1
Buriton Row **32** TR18 . .143 E5
Burleigh La PL3 . . . . . . .128 D7
Burleigh Manor PL3 . . . .128 D6
Burleigh Park Rd PL3 . . .128 D6
Burley Cl TR1 . . . . .137 D3
Burley Ct TR11 . . . . .145 B4
Burn La PL19 . . . . .30 E8
Burn View EX23 . . . . . . .104 D6
Burnard Cl PL6 . . . . .124 E7
Burnards Ct **3** PL31 . . .109 D5
Burnett Cl PL12 . . . . . . .122 D2
Burnett Rd PL6 . . . . .125 D8
Burnham Park Rd PL3 . .128 D6
Burnistone Cl PL7 . . . . . .131 A3
Burns Ave PL5 . . . . .124 C2
Burns View PL11 . . . . . . .65 B5
Burnthouse PL14 . . . . . . .37 C1
Burnthouse Cotts TR10 . .81 C1
Burnthouse La TR27 . . . .142 D5
Burraton Com Prim Sch
PL12 . . . . .122 C3
Burraton Rd PL12 . . . . . .122 C4
Burrator Rd PL20 . . . . . . .42 C2
Burrington Ind Est PL5 . .124 A1
Burrington Rd PL5 . . . . .124 A1
Burrington Way PL5 . . . .124 B1
Burrow Hill PL9 . . . . .135 G6
Burrows The TR26 . . . . .141 A5
Bursdon Moor Cross EX39 .3 B7
Burthallan La TR26 . . . . . .77 A7
Burton Cl PL6 . . . . .125 B6
Burwell Cl PL6 . . . . .125 E4
Bury Cl PL15 . . . . .11 B1
Bush Hill PL14 . . . . .51 C4
Bush Pk Launceston PL15 106 D5
Plymouth PL6 . . . . .125 C8
Butcher Park Hill PL19 . .147 B7
Bute Rd PL4 . . . . .129 A4
Butler Cl PL6 . . . . .125 B6
Butney Cnr TR14 . . . . . . .66 E3
Butt Park Rd PL5 . . . . . .124 B3
Butterdown PL12 . . . . . .122 B3
Buttlegate PL11 . . . . .64 D5
Butts La PL35 . . . . .9 D1
Butts Pk PL22 . . . . .112 D2
Butts The TR8 . . . . .56 B7
Buttsbear Cross EX22 . . . .7 F7
Byard Cl PL5 . . . . .123 E1
Byland Rd PL3 . . . . .129 A6
Byron Ave PL5 . . . . .124 C1

C

Cabot Cl PL12 . . . . .122 E2
Cades Parc TR13 . . . . . .146 C6
Cadoc Cl PL28 . . . . .20 D7
Cadogan Cl TR14 . . . . . .138 E1
Cadogan Rd TR14 . . . . . .138 E1
Cadover Cl PL6 . . . . .125 A1
Caernarvon Gdns PL2 . .128 B7
Cal Hill TR16 . . . . .140 D3
Calais Rd TR27 . . . . .142 F1
Calartha Rd TR19 . . . . . . .75 A1
Calartha Terr TR19 . . . . . .75 A1
Calder Cl PL3 . . . . .129 B6
Caldicot Gdns PL6 . . . . .125 C8
Caldwells Rd TR18 . . . . .143 E6
Caledonia Cl **1** PL7 . . .131 B5
Calenick St TR1 . . . . . . .137 C4
California Gdns PL3 . . . .129 D6
Callestick Cider Farm★
TR4 . . . . .55 B1
Callington Com Coll
PL17 . . . . .39 F5
Callington Mus★ PL17 . .39 E4
Callington Prim Sch
PL17 . . . . .39 E4
Callington Rd
Harrowbarrow PL17 . . . . . .40 C4
Liskeard PL14 . . . . .113 C2
Saltash PL12 . . . . .122 E3
Tavistock PL19 . . . . .147 A4

Calloose Farm Cvn Pk TR27 78 D2
Calloose La E TR27 78 D1
Calloose La W TR27 78 D1
Callywith Gate Ind Est PL31 35 B2
Calshot Cl TR7 111 E7
Calstock Com Prim Sch PL18 41 A3
Calstock Rd PL18 41 A6
Calstock Sta PL17 41 A3
Calvez Cl PL10 132 F6
Camaret Dr TR26 141 B4
Cambeak PL35 9 C1
Cambeak Cl EX23 10 C6
Cambeltown Way TR11 145 C3
Camber Rd PL1 148 A1
Camborne Cl PL5 124 A5
Camborne Geological Mus & Art Gal TR15 139 B6
Camborne Redruth Com Hospl
Redruth TR15 140 A4
Redruth, Blowinghouse TR15 139 F6
Camborne Ret Pk TR15 139 B5
Camborne Sch & Com Coll TR14 138 B3
Camborne Sch of Mines TR15 139 B6
Camborne Sta TR14 138 D2
Cambridge La W [5] PL1 148 B3
Cambridge Pl TR11 145 A3
Cambridge Rd PL2 127 F5
Camden Ct PL4 149 A3
Camden St PL4 149 A3
Camel Cl PL28 107 D4
Camel Ct PL30 109 C6
Camel Valley Vineyard★ PL30 34 B2
Camelford Prim Sch PL32 105 C3
Camelot Ct [2] TR18 143 E5
Camelot View PL32 105 C8
Camelside PL27 108 C5
Cameron Cl EX23 104 D7
Cameron Way PL6 125 B1
Camilla Terr PL2 128 D7
Camp Cross PL15 19 F7
Camp Hall Rd TR8 43 B1
Campbell Rd PL9 135 F7
Camperdown St PL2 127 F4
Camperknowle Cl PL10 132 F6
Campfield Hill TR1 137 D5
Campion Cl
[7] Plymouth PL7 131 C5
Saltash PL12 122 D4
Campion Rise PL19 147 D6
Campion View PL6 125 E8
Camullas Way TR7 110 A5
Canal Rd PL19 147 B5
Candish Dr PL9 136 D7
Canefields Ave PL7 131 B3
Canfield Pl TR15 140 A5
Canfield Terr TR15 140 A5
Canhaye Cl PL7 131 A3
Cann Gdns PL6 124 D6
Cann Wood View PL6 125 E7
Canna Pk★ PL15 18 D3
Cannamanning Rd [3] PL26 59 D7
Cannis Rd PL25 114 E6
Cannon Hill PL14 113 C5
Cannon St PL1 127 D2
Cannon Terr [2] PL14 113 C5
Cannons Pl TR13 146 D7
Canons Way PL19 147 A3
Canterbury Dr PL5 124 B4
Cantillion Cl PL27 21 E3
Canton PL26 85 D5
Canyke Rd PL31 48 D8
Cape Cl TR19 86 E6
Cape Cornwall Rd TR19 86 E6
Cape Cornwall Sch TR19 86 E6
Cape Cornwall St TR19 86 E6
Cape Terr TR19 86 E6
Cape Trelew TR19 86 E6
Captain's Wlk TR11 145 A2
Captains Gdns PL5 124 E1
Captains Ho PL26 73 C3
Caradon Bsns Ctr [8] PL14 113 C5
Caradon Cl
[9] Callington PL17 39 E4
[1] Pensilva PL14 38 E4
Plymouth PL6 125 A5
Caradon Ct [2] PL20 42 C4
Caradon Dr PL14 113 B6
Caradon Hts
Liskeard PL14 113 D7
Tremar PL14 38 B4
Caradon Terr PL12 122 E3
Caradon View PL14 37 F3
Carbeile Rd PL11 127 A2
Carbeile Sch PL11 127 A3
Carbes La PL22 112 C2
Carbis Bay Holiday Pk TR26 77 C4
Carbis Bay Sta TR26 141 D2
Carbis Beach Apartments TR26 141 D2
Carbis Ct TR15 140 A5
Carboth La PL15 106 B5
Carclaze Com Inf Sch PL25 114 E6
Carclaze Com Jun Sch PL25 114 E6
Carclaze Ind Est PL25 114 E7
Carclaze Rd PL25 114 E6
Carclew Ave TR7 110 E6
Carclew Rd TR11 81 F4
Carclew St TR1 137 D3
Carclew Terr Devoran TR3 81 F6
Truro TR1 137 D3
Cardell Rd PL31 109 D5
Cardell Way TR7 111 A5
Cardiff Cl PL7 131 B4
Cardigan Rd PL6 125 C1
Cardinal Ave PL5 127 D8
Cardinham Prim Sch PL30 35 F3
Cardinham Woods Forest Walks★ PL30 35 C1
Cardinnis Gn PL14 113 D6
Cardinnis Rd TR18 143 B5
Cardrew Bsns Pk TR15 140 C6
Cardrew Cl TR15 140 B6
Cardrew Ind Est TR15 140 D7
Cardrew Jun Sch TR15 140 C5
Cardrew La [1] TR15 140 C5
Cardrew Terr TR15 140 D6
Cardrew Way TR15 140 D7
Cardwen Est PL13 62 C6
Careswell Ave PL2 127 F8
Carew Ave PL5 124 B3
Carew Cl Crafthole PL11 65 B5
St Day TR16 68 E1
Carew Gdns
Plymouth PL5 124 B3
Saltash PL12 122 D3
Carew Gr PL5 124 B3
Carew Rd St Day TR16 68 D1
Truro TR1 137 C5
Carew Terr PL11 127 B2
Carew Wharf PL11 127 C2
Carew-Pole Cl TR1 137 E3
Carey Ct PL12 122 E3
Carey Pk Helston TR13 146 B7
Polperro PL13 62 E2
Truro TR1 137 C4
Cargoll Rd TR8 56 B7
Cargwyn PL26 59 D6
Carisbrooke Rd PL6 125 C1
Carkeek's Cl PL26 58 B3
Carland Cross TR8 56 D4
Carlidnack Cl TR11 93 D3
Carlidnack La TR11 93 D4
Carlidnack Rd TR11 93 E4
Carlisle Rd PL5 124 D3
Carloggas Cl TR8 45 A8
Carloggas Farm TR8 45 A8
Carloggas Gr [6] TR9 45 D6
Carloggas Way [10] TR9 45 D6
Carlton Cl PL3 129 B5
Carlton Terr
Plymouth, Lipson PL4 149 B3
Plymouth, Weston Mill PL5 127 E8
Carlton Vills PL12 53 E4
Carlyon Cl
Threemilestone TR3 69 D3
Torpoint PL11 126 F4
[11] Truro TR1 137 C4
Carlyon Ho TR1 69 E4
Carlyon Rd
Playing Place TR3 82 B8
St Austell PL25 114 E4
Truro TR1 137 C5
Carmarthen Rd PL4 129 B2
Carmel Gdns PL19 147 A5
Carmen Sq [10] TR18 143 C7
Carminow Cross PL30 48 D8
Carminow Rd PL31 48 D8
Carminow Road Ind Est PL31 48 D8
Carminow Way TR7 111 A7
Carminowe Cres [8] TR18 143 D5
Carmythen Ct TR7 111 B7
Carn Ave TR14 138 F2
Carn Bosavern TR19 86 F6
Carn Bosavern Cl TR19 86 F6
Carn Brae Ho TR15 139 C5
Carn Brae Village TR15 139 F5
Carn Brea Ave TR15 139 C5
Carn Brea La TR15 139 C5
Carn Cl TR27 78 E1
Carn Euny Settlement★ TR20 87 C3
Carn Gloose Rd TR19 86 D6
Carn Gwavas Terr TR18 143 D1
Carn Marth La TR16 140 E2
Carn Rock TR10 144 D7
Carn Ros TR19 74 F1
Carn View TR16 80 F6
Carn View Terr TR19 75 A1
Carnarthan Moor TR15 139 C3
Carnarthen Rd TR14 138 E3
Carnarthen St TR14 138 E2
Carncrows St TR26 141 C6
Carne Cross PL24 59 F7
Carne Ct PL26 58 C8
Carne Hill St Dennis PL26 46 C1
Trewoon PL25 58 F4
Carne Mdws TR2 70 F5
Carne View Cl TR14 138 F5
Carne View Rd TR2 71 D6
Carne's Bldgs [10] TR18 143 E4
Carnedon PL14 38 C7
Carnego La TR8 57 B6
Carnellis Rd [7] TR26 141 A5
Carnes Ct TR11 145 C2
Carneton Cl TR8 43 D3
Carnglaze Caverns★ PL14 36 F1
Carnhell Rd TR14,TR27 78 F4
Carninney La TR26 141 C1
Carnkie Com Prim Sch TR16 139 D2
Carnkief Cnr TR4 55 D4
Carnock Rd PL2 128 D8
Carnon Cres [13] TR3 81 F7
Carnon Terr TR3 81 F6
Carnoustie Dr PL12 122 C2
Carnsew Cl TR10 81 C1
Carnsew Cres TR10 81 C1
Carnsew Mdw TR27 142 A5
Carnsew Rd TR27 142 A5
Carnsmerry PL26 47 C1
Carnsmerry Cres PL25 114 E4
Carnstabba Rd [13] TR26 77 A6
Carntiscoe Workshops TR27 77 C2
Carnyorth Hill TR19 86 F8
Carnyorth Terr TR19 86 F8
Carolina Gdns PL2 127 F7
Caroline Cl TR27 142 E7
Caroline Pl PL1 148 A2
Caroline Row TR27 142 E7
Carpalla Rd PL26 58 D5
Carpalla Terr PL26 58 D5
Carpenter Rd PL9 135 F8
Carpenter St PL31 109 E5
Carpmael Ave TR8 111 B4
Carracawn Cross PL12 64 D8
Carrack Dhu [37] TR26 141 B6
Carrack Dhu Terr [36] TR26 141 B6
Carrack Gladden TR26 141 D2
Carradale Rd PL6 129 C7
Carrallack Mews TR19 86 E6
Carrallack Terr TR19 86 E5
Carriage Parc TR4 55 D4
Carrick Rd TR11 144 E2
Carrick Way TR2 95 A6
Carrickowel Cres [1] PL25 115 A5
Carrine Rd TR1 69 F3
Carrisbrooke Way PL12 122 B2
Carrnown Gdns TR15 140 D3
Carroll Rd PL5 124 C2
Carron La PL6 121 D1
Carsize La TR27 78 E1
Carter Cl TR7 111 A5
Carteret Rd EX23 104 E5
Carthew Cl
Liskeard PL14 113 D5
St Ives TR26 141 A6
Carthew Ct TR26 141 A6
Carthew La Burras TR13 80 A3
Praze-an-Beeble TR13 79 F2
Carthew Terr TR26 141 A6
Carthew Way TR26 141 A6
Carvath Ho PL25 114 D3
Carvedras Ct [1] TR1 137 C4
Carvosse Est TR20 89 B8
Carvoza Rd TR1 137 D5
Carvynick Cotts TR8 57 A7
Carwin La TR27 78 C5
Carwin Rise
Angarrack TR27 78 C5
Hayle TR27 142 E7
Carwinard Cl TR27 78 C5
Carwinion Rd TR11 93 E3
Carworgie Ct TR9 45 E2
Carworgie Manor Pk TR8 45 D3
Carworgie Way TR9 45 E2
Carwynnen Cl TR14 79 B3
Casey La PL13 62 D5
Castel Wary Cl TR13 146 B5
Casterills Rd TR13 146 D4
Castle Acre Gdns PL3 129 B5
Castle Bank Gdns PL3 129 B5
Castle Barbican PL7 130 E4
Castle Bldgs PL12 122 D4
Castle Canyke Rd PL31 109 F3
Castle Carey Gdns PL3 129 B5
Castle Cl TR11 145 E3
Castle Ct Praa Sands TR20 90 C3
Saltash PL12 122 C2
Castle Dr Bodmin PL31 109 F5
Falmouth TR11 145 F2
Praa Sands TR20 90 B3
St Mawes TR2 94 F5
Castle Dyke PL15 106 C6
Castle Dyke La PL1 149 A2
Castle Gdns PL14 113 C6
Castle Gn TR13 146 B5
Castle Hill Helston TR13 146 B5
[4] Liskeard PL14 113 C6
Lostwithiel PL22 112 C2
Saltash PL12 122 C1
Castle Hill Ct PL31 109 E5
Castle Hill Gdns PL31 109 F5
Castle Horneck Cl TR18 143 C5
Castle Horneck Rd TR18 143 C5
Castle Hts PL34 14 C7
Castle La Liskeard PL14 113 C6
Plymouth PL7 130 E4
Castle Mdws
Launceston PL15 106 A4
[2] St Agnes TR5 54 D1
Castle Meadows Ct [3] TR5 54 D1
Castle Rd
Crowlas TR20 89 A8
Longrock TR20 88 F8
Penzance TR18 143 E7
Tintagel PL34 14 C7
Castle Rise
Plymouth PL3 129 B4
Saltash PL12 122 D1
Truro TR1 137 C5
Castle St Bodmin PL31 109 F5
Launceston PL15 106 C6
Liskeard PL14 113 C6
Looe PL13 117 D3
Plymouth PL1 149 A2
Truro TR1 137 C4
Castle View Longrock TR20 88 F6
Lostwithiel PL22 112 E3
Saltash PL12 122 D1
Tintagel PL34 14 C7
Castle View Cl TR15 140 B6
Castle View Pk TR11 93 D3
Castlehayes Gdns PL7 130 E4
Castlemead Cl PL12 122 D3
Castlemead Dr PL12 122 D3
Castleton Cl PL3 129 A4
Caswarth Terr PL28 107 D5
Catalina Row PL27 31 F3
Catalina Villas PL9 135 A6
Cath of St Mary & St Boniface PL1 148 B3
Cathcart Ave PL4 129 B2
Cathebedron Rd
Carnhell Green TR14 78 F4
Praze-an-Beeble TR14 79 A3
Cathedral Church of the Blessed Virgin Mary★ TR1 137 D4
Cathedral La [13] TR1 137 D4
Cathedral St PL1 148 B3
Cathedral View TR1 137 C6
Catherine Cl EX23 104 F4
Catherine Pk PL13 62 E5
Catherine St PL1 148 C2
Catherine's Hill PL15 106 A6
Cattedown Rd PL4 149 C1
Catterick Cl PL5 123 E5
Cattewater Rd PL4 129 B1
Caudledown La PL26 59 C8
Caunter Rd PL14 113 D6
Causeland Sta PL14 51 B2
Causeway The
Falmouth TR11 144 F4
Hayle TR27 142 A4
Causewayhead TR18 143 E5
Causley Cl PL15 106 C7
Cavendish Rd PL4 129 B1
Caxton Gdns PL5 124 C1
Cayforth Flats TR16 67 C6
Cayley Way PL5 123 F2
Cecil Ave PL4 149 C4
Cecil Cotts PL1 148 A3
Cecil St PL1 148 B3
Cedar Ave PL9 135 C5
Cedar Cl
[21] Callington PL17 39 F4
Torpoint PL11 126 F2
Cedar Ct Camborne TR14 139 A5
Saltash PL12 122 F2
Cedar Dr PL11 126 F2
Cedar Gr EX23 104 E7
Cedar House Flats TR26 77 E4
Cedarcroft Rd PL2 128 B7
Celandine Gdns PL7 131 C5
Celia Hts PL31 109 F2
Celtic Rd PL17 39 F4
Cemetery Rd PL18 40 F5
Centenary Row Middle TR14 138 E3
Centenary Row W TR14 138 E2
Centenary St TR14 138 E3
Central Ave PL25 114 E5
Central Cl PL26 58 B4
Central Park Ave PL4 148 C4
Central Rd Holywell TR8 43 B1
Plymouth PL1 148 B1
Central Sq TR7 110 D6
Century Cl
Helston TR13 146 D8
St Austell PL25 114 F6
Century Ct TR7 111 C7
Century La TR2 83 F6
Century Sq [7] PL14 38 E4
Ceres Ct EX23 104 E1
Chacewater Hill TR4 69 A3
Chacewater Prim Sch TR4 69 A3
Chaddlewood Ave PL4 149 B3
Chaddlewood Cl PL7 131 A4
Chaddlewood Ho PL7 131 B5
Chaddlewood Inf Sch PL7 131 A5
Chaddlewood Prim Sch PL7 131 A5
Chagford Wlk PL6 129 E8
Chainwalk Dr TR1 137 C6
Challacombe Gdns TR10 144 C8
Challenger Quay [12] TR11 145 C3
Challgood Cl PL9 135 F5
Challgood Rise PL9 135 F5
Challis Ave TR8 45 A8
Challock Cl PL6 125 D4
Chamberlayne Dr PL7 130 E6
Champion's Ct TR13 146 B6
Chancery Cl TR4 70 D8
Chancery La [23] TR18 143 E5
Chandos Pl [12] PL25 114 C3
Channel Park Ave PL3 129 B5
Channel View
Polruan PL23 116 D2
St Ives TR26 141 A6
Channel View Terr
Plymouth PL4 149 C4
[4] Redruth TR15 140 C4
Channon Rd PL12 122 C4
Chantry Ct PL7 130 B5
Chantry La PL13 117 E4
Chantry Pk PL17 39 E4
Chapel Cl Camborne TR14 66 F1
Coad's Green PL15 27 D3
Connor Downs TR27 78 D6
Crantock TR8 110 A3
Gunnislake PL18 40 E5
[5] Horrabridge PL20 42 C4
St Just In Roseland TR2 82 F2
Chapel Cnr EX22 8 A5
Chapel Cotts EX23 4 C8
Chapel Cres TR4 56 A2
Chapel Ct
Camborne TR14 138 F4
Padstow PL28 107 D5
Chapel Farm TR14 79 E5
Chapel Field PL25 115 B5
Chapel Gn PL26 59 A1
Chapel Ground PL13 117 C3
Chapel Hill
Camborne, Brea TR14 139 A3
Camborne, Tregajorran TR15 139 C4
Gweek TR12 92 C2
Hayle TR27 142 C6
Lanner TR16 80 D6
Launceston PL15 106 B5
Newquay TR7 110 D6
Perranporth TR6 55 B4
Polgooth PL26 59 A1
Ponsanooth TR3 81 B4
Porthtowan TR4 68 A5
Redruth TR16 68 A4
St Erth TR27 142 A1
Sticker PL26 58 F1
Truro TR1 137 B4
Chapel La Bodmin PL31 109 D5
Goldsithney TR20 89 F5
Hayle TR27 142 D6
[4] Horrabridge PL20 42 C4
[2] Horrabridge PL20 42 C5
Penryn TR10 144 C7
Polruan PL23 116 D2
St Austell PL25 115 C6
St Teath PL30 23 F6
[5] Wadebridge PL27 108 B5
Wadebridge, St Mabyn PL30 34 D8
Chapel Mdw
Buckland Monachorum PL20 41 F3
Perranwell Sta TR3 81 D6
Chapel Park Terr PL15 106 B5
Chapel Pk PL15 106 B5
Chapel Pl Pillaton PL12 53 B7
[16] Truro TR1 137 D4
Chapel Point La PL26 73 C2
Chapel Rd
Camborne TR14 139 A4
Foxhole PL26 58 D5
Heamoor TR18 143 C8
Indian Queens TR9 45 E1
Leedstown TR27 78 E1
[2] Par PL24 60 C4
Roche PL26 46 F3
Saltash PL12 122 B3
St Just TR19 86 E6
St Tudy PL30 23 E3
Chapel Row
Praze-an-Beeble TR14 79 B2
[2] Redruth TR15 140 B5
Tremar PL14 38 A3
Truro TR1 137 D4
Widegates PL13 63 F8
Chapel Sq Crowlas TR20 89 B8
Mevagissey PL26 73 C3
Troon TR14 79 E5
Chapel St
[4] Bere Alston PL20 41 B1
[4] Callington PL17 39 F4
Camborne TR14 138 D2
Camelford PL32 105 C4
Grimscott EX23 5 B2
Gunnislake PL18 40 F6
Marazion TR17 89 B5
Mevagissey PL26 73 C3
[20] Mousehole TR19 88 C1
[9] Newlyn TR18 143 C2
Penzance TR18 143 E5
Plymouth PL4 149 A3
Plymouth, Mount Wise PL1 127 E2
Probus TR2 71 C6
Redruth TR15 140 B5
St Day TR16 68 D1
St Ives TR26 141 B5
St Just TR19 86 E6
Tavistock PL19 147 B5
Chapel Terr
Camborne TR15 139 D6
Devoran TR3 81 F6
Falmouth TR11 145 B4
Hayle TR27 142 B5
Par PL24 60 B6
[9] Porthleven TR13 98 B8
Redruth TR15 140 D2
Redruth, Carn Brae Village TR15 139 F5
Ruan Minor TR12 103 A5
St Day TR16 68 E1
[10] St Mawes TR2 95 A6
Trewellard TR19 86 F8
Chapel Town Cl TR11 93 D4
Chapel Way PL3 129 A6
Chapeldown Rd PL11 127 A2

Chapman Ct PL12 . . . . . .**122** B3
Chapmans Ope PL1 . . . . .**127** D2
Charaton Cross PL14 . . . . .**38** F4
Chard Barton PL5 . . . . . .**124** B3
Chard Rd PL5 . . . .**123** D2
Chard Terr 6 TR11 . . . . .**145** A4
Charfield Dr PL6 . . . .**129** A8
Chariot Rd TR15 . . . .**139** E6
Charles Ave TR11 . . . . . .**144** E2
Charles Bassett Cl 5
   TR13 . . . .**146** C5
Charles Cl PL25 . . . .**114** F3
Charles Cross PL4 . . . . . .**149** A3
Charles St
   Bugle PL26 . . . .**47** C1
   Newlyn TR18 . . . .**143** C3
   Plymouth PL1 . . . .**149** A3
   Truro TR1 . . . .**137** C4
Charles Terr PL3 . . . . . .**129** A6
Charlestown Prim Sch
   PL25 . . . .**115** C3
Charlestown Rd PL25 . . . .**115** B3
Charlestown Shipwreck,
   Rescue & Heritage Ctr★
   PL25 . . . .**115** B2
Charlotte Cl TR4 . . . .**68** C6
Charlotte St PL2 . . . .**127** E4
Charlton Cres PL6 . . . . . .**125** A2
Charlton Rd PL6 . . . .**125** A3
Charnhill Cl PL9 . . . .**136** A6
Charnhill Way PL9 . . . . . .**136** A6
Charter Cl TR13 . . . .**146** C4
Charter Ct TR10 . . . .**144** D7
Charter Way PL14 . . . . . .**113** C6
Chatsworth Gdns PL5 . . . .**123** F3
Chatsworth Way PL25 . . . .**115** C2
Chaucer Prim Sch PL5 . . . .**124** C2
Chaucer Rd PL19 . . . .**147** D5
Chaucer Way PL5 . . . .**124** C1
Chawleigh Cl PL18 . . . .**40** F5
Chedworth St PL4 . . . .**149** A3
Chegwins Hill PL26 . . . .**58** D5
Chegwyn Gdns 6 TR5 . . . . .**54** C1
Chegwyns PL26 . . . .**58** D5
Chelfham Sch PL20 . . . .**40** F3
Chellean Vean TR4 . . . .**81** C7
Chellew Rd TR1 . . . .**137** F5
Chelmer Cl PL7 . . . .**131** A5
Chelmsford Pl PL5 . . . . . .**124** C4
Chelson Gdns PL5 . . . . . .**125** E3
Cheltenham Pl
   Newquay TR7 . . . .**110** D6
   Plymouth PL4 . . . .**149** B4
Cheney Mill Farm Pk★
   TR27 . . . .**77** E1
Chenhalls Cl TR27 . . . .**77** E1
Chenhalls Rd TR27 . . . . . .**142** A2
Chenoweth TR14 . . . .**138** C4
Chepstow Ave PL6 . . . . . .**125** C8
Chequetts Cl 10 PL17 . . . . .**39** E4
Cheriton Cl PL5 . . . .**124** A3
Cherrill Gdns EX23 . . . . . .**104** E7
Cherry Cross EX22 . . . .**12** C3
Cherry Gdns 14 TR18 . . . .**143** E5
Cherry Pk PL7 . . . .**131** A4
Cherry Tree La PL7 . . . . . .**131** A4
Cherry Tree Mews PL25 . .**114** D3
Cheshire Dr PL6 . . . .**124** D6
Chester Ct TR7 . . . .**111** B4
Chester Pl 3 PL4 . . . .**128** E4
Chester Rd TR7 . . . .**111** A6
Chesterfield Rd PL3 . . . . .**129** B4
Chesterton Cl PL5 . . . . . .**124** C3
Chesterton Pl PL27 . . . . . .**108** A6
Chesterton Pl TR7 . . . . . .**111** A7
Chestnut Ave PL9 . . . . . .**135** C5
Chestnut Cl
   Callington PL17 . . . .**40** A4
   Falmouth TR11 . . . .**144** F5
   Lamerton PL19 . . . .**30** A4
   Saltash PL12 . . . .**122** D4
   St Tudy PL30 . . . .**23** E3
   Tavistock PL19 . . . .**147** D2
   Torpoint PL11 . . . .**126** F3
Chestnut Gr PL31 . . . .**109** B4
Chestnut Rd PL3 . . . .**128** D7
Chestnut Terr PL19 . . . . . .**30** A4
Cheviot Rd TR7 . . . .**110** E4
Chichester Cres
   Newquay TR7 . . . .**110** F4
   Saltash PL12 . . . .**122** E1
Chichester Ct PL20 . . . . . .**42** C4
Chichester Ho PL1 . . . . . .**148** B2
Childrey Gdns PL6 . . . . . .**125** C1
Childrey Wlk PL6 . . . .**125** C1
Chili Rd TR15 . . . .**139** D6
Chilton Cl PL6 . . . .**129** B7
Chings Alley 11 PL15 . . . . .**106** C6
Chippords Dr PL25 . . . . . .**114** A3
Chirgwin Ct 22 TR18 . . . .**143** E5
Chirgwin Rd TR1 . . . .**137** E4
Chisholme Cl PL25 . . . . . .**114** D3
Chisholme Ct PL25 . . . . . .**114** D3
Chittleburn Cross
   PL8 . . . .**136** E5
Chittleburn Hill PL8 . . . . .**136** E5
Chivenor Ave PL5 . . . .**123** D4
Chiverton Cross
   Blackwater TR4 . . . .**68** F5
   Rosudgeon TR20 . . . .**89** F4
Chiverton Greenacres
   TR5 . . . .**68** D8
Chiverton Way TR20 . . . . .**89** F4
Chollacott Cl PL19 . . . . . .**147** C4
Chollacott La PL19 . . . . . .**147** D3

Chough Cl
   Falmouth TR11 . . . .**144** E4
   Launceston PL15 . . . . . .**106** E4
Chough Cres PL25 . . . . . .**114** F4
Choughs Cl TR14 . . . .**138** B3
Christa Ct PL14 . . . .**38** D7
Christian Mill Bsns Pk
   PL6 . . . .**124** E4
Christian Way TR7 . . . . . .**111** C7
Chubb Dr PL3 . . . .**128** B4
Chudleigh Rd PL4 . . . . . .**129** A4
Church Cl Lelant TR26 . . . . .**77** E4
   Plymouth PL7 . . . .**130** B7
   St Erme TR4 . . . .**56** D1
Church Cove Rd TR12 . . . .**103** A2
Church End PL13 . . . .**117** D3
Church Gate 3 PL14 . . . . .**113** C5
Church Hill Calstock PL18 . . .**41** A3
   Chacewater TR4 . . . .**68** F2
   Crowlas TR20 . . . .**89** A8
   Golant PL23 . . . .**61** B6
   Helston TR13 . . . .**146** C7
   Herodsfoot PL14 . . . .**50** E3
   Hessenford PL11,PL12 . . . .**64** B8
   Milton Combe PL20 . . . . . .**41** F1
   Penryn TR10 . . . .**144** D8
   5 Pensilva PL14 . . . .**38** E4
   Plymouth PL6 . . . .**125** B1
   Port Isaac PL29 . . . .**22** D7
   St Day TR16 . . . .**68** E1
   7 St Mawes TR2 . . . .**95** A6
   Sticker PL26 . . . .**58** F1
   Tavistock PL19 . . . .**147** E2
   Tintagel PL34 . . . .**14** C7
Church Hill Rd PL9 . . . . . .**135** A6
Church La Bodmin PL31 . . .**109** E5
   Calstock PL18 . . . .**41** A3
   Camborne TR14 . . . .**138** D3
   Cargreen PL12 . . . .**119** A1
   Flushing TR11 . . . .**145** B7
   Helston TR13 . . . .**146** B6
   Lelant TR26 . . . .**77** E4
   Lostwithiel PL22 . . . .**112** C2
   Mevagissey PL26 . . . .**73** C4
   Padstow PL28 . . . .**107** D5
   Redruth TR15 . . . .**140** A3
   St Columb Minor TR7 . . . .**111** E7
   St John PL11 . . . .**132** B8
   Tavistock PL19 . . . .**147** C5
Church Lea
   Launceston PL15 . . . . . .**106** A7
   Tavistock PL19 . . . .**147** E2
Church Mews EX22 . . . . . .**11** E8
Church Park Ct PL6 . . . . .**125** E4
Church Park Mews
   PL27 . . . .**108** B4
Church Park Rd
   Crackington Haven EX23 . . .**10** C6
   Plymouth PL6 . . . .**125** E4
Church Path EX23 . . . . . .**104** C3
Church Pk Bodmin PL31 . . .**109** F5
   Horrabridge PL20 . . . .**42** C4
   Lerryn PL22 . . . .**61** D8
   St Mellion PL12 . . . .**53** D8
Church Pl Liskeard PL14 . . .**113** C5
   18 St Ives TR26 . . . .**141** B6
Church Rd
   Camborne, Pool TR15 . . . .**139** B6
   Camborne, Treswithian
      TR14 . . . .**138** B3
   Cury TR12 . . . .**99** A4
   Four Lanes TR16 . . . .**80** A5
   Heamoor TR18 . . . .**143** C7
   Illogan TR16 . . . .**67** E4
   Lanivet PL30 . . . .**47** E7
   Lelant TR26 . . . .**77** E4
   Mabe Burnthouse TR10 . . . .**93** C8
   Madron TR20 . . . .**143** A8
   Mount Hawke TR4 . . . .**68** C6
   Mylor Bridge TR11 . . . . . .**82** B2
   Pendeen TR19 . . . .**75** A1
   Penponds TR14 . . . .**138** B1
   Penryn TR10 . . . .**144** C8
   Perranarworthal TR3 . . . . .**81** D5
   Plymouth, Plympton PL7 . .**130** F4
   Plymouth, Plymstock PL9 . .**135** F7
   Saltash PL12 . . . .**122** D2
   Shortlanesend TR4 . . . . . .**69** F6
   St Austell PL25 . . . .**115** B3
   St Dennis PL26 . . . .**46** C1
   St Tudy PL30 . . . .**23** E3
   Stithians TR3 . . . .**80** F4
   Tideford PL12 . . . .**52** F2
Church Row
   Carharrack TR16 . . . .**80** C8
   Lanner TR16 . . . .**80** D6
   3 Porthleven TR13 . . . . . .**98** B8
   Sheviock PL11 . . . .**65** C6
Church Row La PL5 . . . . .**124** C6
Church Sq Bodmin PL31 . . .**109** E5
   Constantine TR11 . . . .**92** F4
   St Just TR19 . . . .**86** F6
   4 Stratton EX23 . . . .**4** E1
Church St Callington PL17 . . .**39** E4
   Calstock PL18 . . . .**41** A3
   Camborne TR14 . . . .**138** D3
   Carharrack TR16 . . . .**80** F8
   Falmouth TR11 . . . .**145** B4
   Gorran Haven PL26 . . . . . .**85** D5
   Helston TR13 . . . .**146** B6
   Landrake PL12 . . . .**53** C3
   Launceston PL15 . . . . . .**106** C6
   Liskeard PL14 . . . .**113** C5
   Looe, East Looe PL13 . . . .**117** D3
   Looe, West Looe PL13 . . . .**117** C3
   Mevagissey PL26 . . . .**73** C3
   14 Newlyn TR18 . . . .**143** C1
   Padstow PL28 . . . .**107** D5

Church St continued
   Par PL24 . . . .**60** B5
   Par, Tywardreath PL24 . . . .**60** D5
   Plymouth PL3 . . . .**128** A4
   Poughill EX23 . . . .**4** C2
   8 St Austell PL25 . . . . . .**114** C3
   St Columb Minor TR7 . . . .**111** D7
   St Erth TR27 . . . .**142** A1
   St Germans PL12 . . . .**65** A8
   St Just TR19 . . . .**86** F6
   5 Stratton EX23 . . . .**4** E1
Church St N PL14 . . . . . .**113** C5
Church St S PL14 . . . . . .**113** C5
Church Terr Devoran TR3 . . .**81** F6
   Grampound Road TR2 . . . . .**57** C1
Church Town Rd TR16 . . . .**67** E5
Church View St Neot PL14 . . .**36** F2
   Treburley PL15 . . . .**28** B5
   Walkhampton PL20 . . . . . .**42** E4
Church View Rd
   Camborne TR14 . . . .**138** F4
   Probus TR2 . . . .**71** D6
Church Way
   Falmouth TR11 . . . .**144** E3
   Plymouth PL5 . . . .**127** E8
   St Cleer PL15 . . . .**17** B2
Church Wlk PL15 . . . .**27** E8
Churchfield Cl TR20 . . . . . .**89** A8
Churchfields Rd TR8 . . . . .**55** D8
Churchill Rd PL19 . . . . . .**147** D2
Churchill Way PL3 . . . . . .**128** E6
Churchill Wlk PL12 . . . . .**122** E1
Churchlands PL13 . . . . . .**117** D5
Churchlands Cl PL6 . . . . .**125** E7
Churchlands Rd PL6 . . . . .**125** E8
Churchstow Wlk PL6 . . . . .**129** E8
Churchtown
   Cardinham PL30 . . . .**35** B7
   Gwinear TR27 . . . .**78** D4
   7 Mullion TR12 . . . .**99** A2
   5 St Agnes TR5 . . . .**54** C1
   St Minver PL27 . . . .**22** A4
   St Newlyn East TR8 . . . . . .**56** B7
Churchtown Mdws PL26 . . .**58** B4
Churchtown Rd
   Gwithian TR27 . . . .**66** B2
   Phillack TR27 . . . .**142** A2
   Portscatho TR2 . . . .**83** B2
   St Stephen PL26 . . . .**58** B4
Churchtown Vale PL12 . . . .**122** D1
Churchway Madron TR20 . .**143** A8
   11 Marazion TR17 . . . .**89** C5
Chute La PL26 . . . .**85** D5
Chy An Dowr TR27 . . . . . .**142** E7
Chy Hwel TR1 . . . .**137** F6
Chy Kensa Cl TR27 . . . . . .**142** C5
Chy Nampara 1 TR11 . . . .**145** A4
Chy-An-Chy 19 TR26 . . . . .**141** B6
Chy-An-Dour Cl 1 TR26 . . .**77** A6
Chy-An-Dour Rd TR20 . . . . .**90** C3
Chy-an-Gweal Est TR20 . . . .**89** A7
Chy-an-hall TR18 . . . . . .**143** F8
Chy-an-Mor TR20 . . . .**88** F6
Chyanclare TR18 . . . .**143** D6
Chyandaunce Cl TR18 . . . .**143** F7
Chyandaunce Terr TR18 . . .**143** F8
Chyandor Cl PL24 . . . .**60** C4
Chyandour Cl TR26 . . . . . .**77** A6
Chyandour Cliff TR18 . . . .**143** F6
Chyandour La TR18 . . . . . .**143** F7
Chyandour Sq TR18 . . . . .**143** F7
Chyandour Terr TR18 . . . .**143** F7
Chycoose Parc TR3 . . . . . .**82** A5
Chycornick Terr TR18 . . . .**143** F4
Chygothow TR13 . . . .**146** B6
Chylan Cres TR7 . . . .**111** C6
Chymeddon TR7 . . . .**110** E6
Chynance Penzance TR18 . .**143** D4
   Portreath TR16 . . . .**67** C6
Chynance Dr TR7 . . . .**110** D5
Chynowen La TR8 . . . .**43** D1
Chynowen Parc TR8 . . . . . .**43** D1
Chynoweth PL26 . . . .**59** C8
Chynoweth Gdns TR18 . . .**143** F8
Chynoweth La TR20 . . . . . .**89** C6
Chypons Est TR 20 . . . . . .**76** F3
Chypons Rd TR12 . . . .**99** B3
Chypraze Ct TR14 . . . . . .**138** B3
Chyreen La
   Carnon Downs TR3 . . . . . .**81** C1
   Playing Place TR3 . . . .**82** A8
Chyrn Dr PL30 . . . .**24** B3
Chyrose Rd TR14 . . . .**68** D1
Chysauster Settlement★
   TR 20 . . . .**76** D2
Chytodden Terr TR13 . . . . .**90** F5
Chytroose Cl TR13 . . . . . .**146** D8
Chyvelah Ope TR1 . . . .**69** E3
Chyvelah Rd TR3 . . . .**69** D4
Chyvelah Vale TR1 . . . .**69** E3
Chyvellas Cl TR18 . . . . . .**143** B1
Chyventon Cl TR19 . . . .**97** B6
Chyventon Ho TR15 . . . . .**140** B5
Chyverton Cl TR7 . . . .**110** D4
Chywoon Gdns TR15 . . . . .**139** D7
Chywoone Ave TR18 . . . . .**143** C1
Chywoone Cres TR18 . . . .**143** C1
Chywoone Hill TR18 . . . . .**143** C1
Chywoone Pl TR18 . . . . . .**143** C1
Chywoone Rural Workshops
   TR19 . . . .**87** A5
Citadel Ope 13 PL1 . . . . .**149** A2
Citadel Rd PL1 . . . .**148** C2
Citadel Rd E PL1 . . . .**149** A2
Citadel The★ PL1 . . . . . .**149** A1
City Bsns Pk PL3 . . . .**128** A4

City Mus & Art Gal★
   PL4 . . . .**149** A3
City Mus & Art Gal Annexe★
   PL4 . . . .**149** A3
City Rd TR1 . . . .**137** C4
Clairemont Pl 1 PL14 . . . . .**38** A3
Clampet La PL11 . . . .**65** E4
Clann Mdws PL30 . . . .**47** E7
Clann Rd PL30 . . . .**47** E7
Clare Pl PL4 . . . .**149** B2
Clare Terr PL11 . . . .**145** B4
Claremont Cotts 1
   TR11 . . . .**145** A5
Claremont Falls PL13 . . . . .**62** E2
Claremont Rd TR15 . . . . .**140** B5
Claremont St PL1 . . . .**148** C4
Claremont Terr 3 TR11 . . .**145** A5
Clarence Cl PL1 . . . .**148** A3
Clarence Pl
   30 Penzance TR18 . . . . . .**143** E6
   Plymouth, Morice Town
      PL2 . . . .**127** E4
   Plymouth, Stonehouse PL1 .**148** A3
Clarence Rd
   St Austell PL25 . . . .**114** B4
   Torpoint PL11 . . . .**127** B3
Clarence St TR18 . . . .**143** E5
Clarence Terr
   31 Penzance TR18 . . . . . .**143** E6
   7 Wadebridge PL27 . . . . .**108** B5
Clarence Villas TR15 . . . . .**140** D6
Clyde St PL2 . . . .**127** F5
Clarendon Ho 1 PL1 . . . . .**127** F3
Claybourne Cl PL25 . . . . .**114** F6
Claylands PL30 . . . .**24** A1
Clayton Pl PL4 . . . .**129** B2
Clayton Rd PL4 . . . .**129** B2
Clear View PL12 . . . .**122** E3
Clearbrook Ave PL5 . . . . .**123** E1
Clease Mdws PL32 . . . . . .**105** C3
Clease Rd PL32 . . . .**105** C4
Clease The PL32 . . . .**105** C3
Cleave Cres EX23 . . . .**4** B3
Cleave The PL10 . . . .**133** B2
Cleaveland PL27 . . . .**108** C4
Cleaverfield Mews
   PL15 . . . .**106** C7
Cleavewell PL27 . . . .**108** C4
Cledma Bank TR27 . . . . . .**142** A2
Cleers Hill St Dennis PL26 . .**46** E1
   Whitemoor PL26 . . . .**58** E8
Cleeve Gdns PL2 . . . .**128** A8
Clegg Ave PL11 . . . .**126** E3
Clemens Cl TR11 . . . .**145** B3
Clemens Rd PL14 . . . .**51** B3
Clemens Way TR27 . . . . . .**78** C6
Clement Rd PL7 . . . .**131** B5
Clements Rd TR18 . . . . . .**143** C1
Clemo Rd PL14 . . . .**113** E7
Clevedon Park Ave PL2 . . .**128** B6
Clevedon Rd TR7 . . . .**110** D5
Cleveland Ave PL13 . . . . .**117** D4
Cleveland Rd PL4 . . . .**149** C3
Clies The 4 TR13 . . . . . .**146** C5
Clifden Cl Mullion TR12 . . . .**99** A1
   Newquay TR7 . . . .**110** E5
Clifden Dr PL27 . . . .**21** D2
Clifden Rd PL25 . . . .**114** F4
Clifden Terr
   Bodmin PL31 . . . .**109** D5
   Lostwithiel PL22 . . . .**112** C2
Clifford Cl PL5 . . . .**123** E2
Clift Ct 4 TR1 . . . .**137** D4
Clifton Ave PL7 . . . .**130** E7
Clifton Cl PL7 . . . .**130** E7
Clifton Cres 16 TR11 . . . .**145** A4
Clifton Gdns 1 TR1 . . . . .**137** B4
Clifton Hill 14 TR18 . . . . .**143** C2
Clifton Pl
   14 Falmouth TR11 . . . . . .**145** A4
   Plymouth PL4 . . . .**149** A4
Clifton Rd TR15 . . . .**139** C8
Clifton St PL4 . . . .**149** A4
Clifton Terr
   15 Falmouth TR11 . . . . . .**145** A4
   Hayle TR27 . . . .**142** B6
   Liskeard PL14 . . . .**113** A5
   15 Newlyn TR18 . . . .**143** C2
   Portscatho TR2 . . . .**83** C2
Cligga Workshops
   TR6 . . . .**54** F4
Clijah Cl TR15 . . . .**140** C2
Clijah La TR15 . . . .**140** C2
Clinton Ave PL4 . . . .**129** A4
Clinton Cl Bude EX23 . . . .**104** C3
   Redruth TR15 . . . .**140** C3
Clinton Pas 4 TR15 . . . . .**140** B4

Clinton Rd
   Constantine TR11 . . . .**92** F3
   Redruth TR15 . . . .**140** C4
Clinton Terr PL10 . . . . . .**132** F6
Clittaford Rd PL6 . . . .**124** F7
Clittaford View PL6 . . . . .**124** E7
Cloake Pl PL12 . . . .**119** A2
Clodgey La TR13 . . . .**146** D5
Clodgey Way TR13 . . . . . .**146** D4
Clodgy View 44 TR26 . . . .**141** B6
Clonway 1 PL20 . . . .**42** C3
Clos Trevithick TR14 . . . . .**138** F2
Close Hill TR15 . . . .**140** B6
Close The
   14 Bere Alston PL20 . . . . .**41** B1
   Camelford PL32 . . . .**105** E5
   Lanner TR16 . . . .**80** C4
   Mylor Bridge TR11 . . . . . .**82** A3
   Penzance TR18 . . . .**143** D7
   Saltash PL12 . . . .**122** C3
   Trevone PL28 . . . .**20** D7
   Truro TR1 . . . .**137** F6
Clovelly Rd PL4 . . . .**149** C1
Clovelly View PL9 . . . . . .**135** A7
Clover Lane Ct 6 PL35 . . . . .**9** C1
Clover Rise PL6 . . . .**125** E8
Clover Wlk PL6 . . . .**122** C3
Clowance Cl PL1 . . . .**127** F1
Clowance La PL1 . . . .**127** F1
Clowance St PL1 . . . .**127** F1
Coach Ho The TR15 . . . . .**143** F7
Coach House La PL25 . . . .**114** C4
Coach House Mews PL9 . .**136** B6
Coach La TR15 . . . .**140** C4
Coaches Cnr TR13 . . . .**90** F3
Coachyard Mews PL28 . . .**107** D5
Coad's Green Prim Sch
   PL15 . . . .**27** D3
Coast Rd TR4 . . . .**68** A7
Coastguard Cotts
   Down Thomas PL9 . . . . . .**134** F2
   Mawnan Smith TR11 . . . . .**93** C1
   Mullion TR12 . . . .**98** F1
   Polperro PL13 . . . .**62** E2
   Rosudgeon TR20 . . . .**89** F4
Coastguard Cres PL13 . . . .**117** C3
Coastguard Hill PL29 . . . . .**22** D8
Coastguard Hos PL28 . . . . .**21** B4
Coastguard Sta Flats
   PL13 . . . .**117** C3
Coastguard Terr TR2 . . . . .**84** B3
Coastline Ct TR8 . . . .**44** C4
Cobb La PL9 . . . .**135** F6
Cobbett Rd PL5 . . . .**124** B2
Cobbs Well PL23 . . . .**116** C4
Cober Cres TR27 . . . .**78** C3
Cobourg St PL1 . . . .**148** C3
Cock's Lake La PL12 . . . . . .**53** D4
Cockington Cl PL6 . . . . . .**125** E1
Cockington Wlk PL6 . . . . .**125** E1
Cocklawelva PL27 . . . .**21** D2
Cockwells La TR26 . . . .**77** C1
Codiford Cres TR14 . . . . .**138** C4
Coffa Bridge Cl PL22 . . . .**112** D2
Coffeelake Mdw PL22 . . . .**112** C2
Cogegoes Ind Pk TR14 . . .**138** A2
Cogos Pk TR11 . . . .**82** A3
Coinagehall Pl TR18 . . . . .**143** F4
Coinagehall St
   Helston TR13 . . . .**146** B5
   Penzance TR18 . . . .**143** F4
Col-Moor Cl TR27 . . . . . .**142** E7
Colborne Ave TR16 . . . . . .**67** D4
Colborne Rd PL6 . . . .**125** A4
Coldrenick St PL5 . . . . . .**123** D1
Coldrose Ct TR1 . . . .**137** B4
Coldstyle Rd PL14 . . . . . .**113** C7
Coldwind Cross TR3 . . . . . .**81** D7
Cole Moore Mdw PL19 . . .**147** B6
Cole's Cotts PL7 . . . .**130** C6
Colebrook Cl TR15 . . . . . .**140** A5
Colebrook La PL7 . . . .**130** C7
Colebrook Rd
   Plymouth, Plympton PL7 . .**130** E6
   Plymouth, St Budeaux PL5 .**123** C1
Coleman Dr PL9 . . . .**135** F4
Colemans Cross PL15 . . . . .**19** C5
Colenso Cross TR20 . . . . . .**89** F5
Colenso Pl PL25 . . . .**114** D3
Coleridge Ave PL6 . . . . . .**124** F2
Coleridge Rd PL4 . . . .**129** A4
Colesdown Hill PL9 . . . . .**130** B1
Colesloggett Halt PL30 . . . .**48** F8
Colin Campbell Ct 10
   PL1 . . . .**148** B3
Colinsey Pl TR18 . . . .**143** D7
Colinsey Rd TR18 . . . . . .**143** D7
Coliza Hill PL26 . . . .**59** A2
Coll of St Mark & St John
   PL6 . . . .**125** C4
Collacombe Cross PL19 . . . .**29** F4
Collaford Cl PL7 . . . .**131** A4
Collan's Cross PL32 . . . . . .**15** D4
College Ave
   Plymouth PL3 . . . .**128** E5
   Tavistock PL19 . . . .**147** D6
College Cl TR2 . . . .**71** D6
College Dean Cl PL6 . . . . .**125** C5
College Gn Bodmin PL31 . .**109** E2
   St Austell PL25 . . . .**114** C3
College Hill TR10 . . . .**144** C7
College La Bodmin PL31 . . .**109** E2
   Plymouth PL4 . . . .**128** F4
   Redruth TR15 . . . .**140** E7
College of Falmouth The
   TR11 . . . .**145** A4
College Ope TR10 . . . . . .**144** C7

College Park Pl PL3 ....128 E5
College Rd
  Camelford PL32 ....105 D4
  Plymouth PL2 ....127 E5
College Road Prim Sch
  PL2 ....127 E5
College St TR14 ....138 C3
College View PL3 ......128 E4
College Way TR1 ....69 E3
Colliford Lake Pk★ PL14 .36 E8
Collin Cl PL5 ....123 D1
Collingwood Ave PL4 ..149 C2
Collingwood Rd PL1 ...128 A3
Collingwood Villas 5
  ....128 A3
Collins Parc TR3 ....80 F3
Collon Field PL22 ......61 D8
Collorian La TR26 ......77 C1
Collygree Parc TR20 ...89 C5
Colne Gdns PL3 ....129 B5
Colroger Cl TR12 ....99 B2
Colston Cl PL6 ....125 B6
Coltishall Cl PL5 ......123 F4
Coltness Rd PL9 ....136 B5
Coltsfield Cl PL6 ......129 B8
Colver Cl TR27 ....78 D6
Colvreath Rd TR7 .....110 F6
Colwill Rd PL6 ....125 E3
Colwill Wlk PL6 ....125 F3
Colworth Ave TR11 ....144 F3
Colwyn Rd PL11 ....127 A3
Combe La EX23 ....6 F4
Combley Dr PL6 ....125 D4
Comfort Rd TR11 ....82 A3
Comfort Wartha TR11 ..92 F4
Commercial Hill TR3 ...81 B4
Commercial Ope PL4 ..149 B2
Commercial Pl PL4 ....149 B1
Commercial Rd
  Calstock PL18 ....41 A3
  Hayle TR27 ....142 C6
  Horrabridge PL20 ......42 C4
  10 Mousehole TR19 ...88 C1
  Penryn TR10 ....144 D7
  Plymouth PL4 ....149 B2
  8 St Keverne TR12 ...101 C4
  5 St Mawes TR2 ......95 A6
Commercial Sq 3 TR14 138 D3
Commercial St
  Camborne TR14 ......138 D3
  Gunnislake PL18 ....41 A6
  Plymouth PL4 ....149 B2
Commercial Terr PL28 .107 D5
Commissioners Rd 1
  PL27 ....108 B5
Common La PL6 ....121 B5
Commons Cl 3 TR12 ...99 A2
Commons The TR12 .....99 A2
Comoran Ct TR17 ....89 C5
Compass Dr PL7 ....131 A4
Compass W PL15 ....18 C2
Comprigney Cl TR1 ...137 B5
Comprigney Hill TR1 ..137 B5
Compton Ave PL3 .....129 A5
Compton CE Prim Sch
  PL3 ....129 A6
Compton Knoll Cl PL3 .129 A6
Compton Leigh PL3 ...129 A6
Compton Park Rd PL3 .128 F5
Compton 2 PL17 ....39 E4
Compton Vale PL3 ....129 A5
Condurrow Rd TR14 ...139 A1
Congreve Gdns PL5 ...124 C1
Coniston Gdns PL4 ...124 F4
Conker Rd TR27 ....78 C1
Connaught Ave PL4 ...128 F4
Connaught La 2 PL4 ..128 E4
Connoc Cl PL14 ....113 C6
Connor Downs Prim Sch
  TR27 ....78 D6
Connor Hill TR27 ....78 D6
Conqueror Dr PL5 ....124 E1
Conrad Rd PL5 ....124 D1
Consols Rd TR16 ....80 F8
Consort Cl PL3 ....128 E7
Constable Cl PL5 .....124 D3
Constance Pl PL1 .....148 A4
Constantine Prim Sch
  TR11 ....92 C4
Constantine St PL4 ...149 A3
Convent Cl PL12 ......122 C3
Conway Cl TR11 ......144 E4
Conway Gdns
  Falmouth TR11 ......144 D4
  Plymouth PL2 ....128 B7
Conway Rd TR11 .....144 D4
Conyngham Ct PL6 ...129 A8
Cooban Ct PL6 ....129 A8
Cooks Level PL12 .....122 B3
Cooks Ct PL12 ....85 C5
Cooksland Ind Est PL31 .35 B2
Cooksland La PL31 .....35 B2
Cooksland Rd PL31 .....35 B1
Cooksley Ct PL1 ......149 A1
Cookworthy Rd PL2 ...127 F6
Coombe Cvn Pk TR14 ..66 F3
Coombe Dean Sch PL9 .136 A6
Coombe Dr PL12 ......119 A2
Coombe Hill PL26 ......58 C2
Coombe Junction Halt
  PL14 ....51 A6

Coombe La
  Cargreen PL12 ....119 A2
  Crafthole PL11 ....65 B5
  Penzance TR18 ....143 D7
  Plymouth PL5 ....124 D7
  Seaton PL11 ....64 B7
  Truro TR4 ....81 C8
Coombe Park Cl PL10 .133 A2
Coombe Park La PL5 ..124 A3
Coombe Pk
  Cawsand PL10 ....133 A2
  Penzance TR18 ....143 E6
  Saltash PL12 ....122 F2
Coombe Rd
  Callington PL17 ....39 F4
  Lanjeth PL26 ....58 D3
  Penzance TR18 ....143 E7
  Saltash PL12 ....123 A2
Coombe Sta PL14 ......51 A6
Coombe The
  Crumplehorn PL13 ......62 D2
  Newlyn TR18 ....143 B3
Coombe Vale TR18 ....143 B3
Coombe View
  15 Perranporth TR6 ...55 A4
  Plymouth PL2 ....127 F7
Coombe Way PL5 .....123 F1
Coombes La 9 TR1 ...137 C4
Cooper's La TR13 ......98 C8
Cooperage Rd PL25 ....59 A3
Coosebean La TR4 ....137 A5
Copes Gdns TR1 ......137 C5
Copleston Rd PL6 ....124 E5
Coppard Mdws PL7 ...130 B6
Copper Beech Way PL6 125 C7
Copper Hill TR27 .....142 D6
Copper Pl PL1 ....148 A3
Copper Terr TR27 ....142 D7
Copperfields PL20 .....42 B5
Coppers Pk PL6 ......125 E7
Coppice Gdns PL5 ....124 E2
Coppice Wood Dr PL6 .125 C7
Copse Cl PL7 ....130 D4
Copse Rd PL7 ....130 D4
Copse The PL25 ......114 F5
Copshorn Rd PL31 ...109 C7
Copthorne Cross PL15 .12 B2
Copthorne Gdns PL9 ..135 F5
Corea Terr PL1 ....128 A2
Corfe Ave PL3 ....128 E8
Coringdean Cl PL6 ....125 B6
Cormorant Dr PL25 ...115 A4
Corner Brake PL6 ....125 D7
Corner Gdns EX23 .....4 D1
Corner Pk TR15 ....26 C7
Cornfield Gdns PL7 ..131 B7
Cornhill Rd PL24 ......60 B5
Cornish Beam Engine Mus
  TR15 ....139 C6
Cornish Birds of Prey Ctr
  The★ TR9 ....32 C1
Cornish Cres TR1 ......69 E4
Cornish Engines Mus
  TR15 ....139 C6
Cornubia Cl Hayle TR27 .142 C5
  Truro TR1 ....137 C4
Cornwall Beach PL1 ..127 D2
Cornwall Coll of F & H Ed
  TR15 ....139 B6
Cornwall Coll of F & H Ed
  (Annexe)
  Camborne TR14 ......138 F3
  Camborne TR14 ......139 A3
Cornwall Geological Mus★
  TR18 ....143 E3
Cornwall Maritime Mus★
  TR11 ....145 A4
Cornwall St
  Bere Alston PL20 ......41 B1
  Plymouth PL1 ....148 C3
  Plymouth, Morice Town
  PL1 ....127 D2
Cornwall Terr
  Penzance TR18 ....143 E4
  2 Truro TR1 ....137 C5
Cornwood Rd PL7 ....131 B4
Cornworthy Cl PL2 ...128 A7
Coronation Ave TR14 .138 C3
Coronation Cl 2 PL17 ..39 F4
Coronation Cotts
  Budock Water TR11 ..144 C3
  Mabe Burnthouse TR10 ..81 C1
  St Keverne TR12 ....101 C4
Coronation Pl
  Helston TR13 ....146 C4
  Plymouth PL5 ....127 E8
Coronation Rd
  10 Callington PL17 ....39 F4
  Hayle TR27 ....142 D5
  1 Illogan TR16 ....67 E4
  Redruth TR15 ....140 D4
Coronation Terr
  Truro TR1 ....137 B4
  Veryan TR2 ....83 D7
  Blackwater TR4 ....68 E5
Coronation Way TR7 .111 C7
Corondale Rd PL2 ....128 B7
Corporation Rd
  Bodmin PL31 ....109 B4
  Plymouth PL2 ....128 D7
Corsham Cl PL6 ......125 B6
Cort Simmons TR15 ..139 C6
Cort Treloweth TR15 .139 B6
Corva Cl 11 TR26 ......77 A6
Corva Rd 9 TR26 ......77 A6
Cory Cl EX23 ....10 F6
Cosawes Est TR3 ......81 B4
Cosdon Pl PL6 ....124 F1

Coswinsawsin La TR14 ..79 A5
Cot Hill Plymouth PL7 ..130 B5
  Ponsanooth TR3 ....81 B4
  2 Stratton EX23 ......4 E1
Cot Hill Trad Est PL7 .130 B6
Cot Rd TR15,TR16 .....67 D4
Cot Wood TR3 ....81 B4
Cotehele Ave
  Plymouth, Keyham PL2 .127 F5
  Plymouth, Prince Rock PL4 149 C2
Cotehele Cl PL17 ......39 E3
Cotehele Ho★ PL12 ...40 F3
Cotehele Quay Mus★
  PL12 ....40 F3
Cotsland Rd TR1 ......137 F5
Cotswold Ave PL26 ....58 E1
Cotswold Cl PL26 .....58 E1
Cott Rd Lostwithiel PL22 .112 D2
  Lostwithiel PL22 .....112 D4
Cottage Gdn PL15 .....27 B7
Cottage Mews PL7 ...130 E4
Cotton Cl PL7 ....130 E4
Couchwell La PL22 ...112 C2
Coulson's Bldgs 9
  TR18 ....143 E4
Coulson's Pl 8 TR18 .143 E4
Coulson's Terr 7 TR18 143 E4
Coulthard Dr TR13 .....91 A3
Count House La TR26 .141 C2
Countess Bridge La TR27 90 A8
County Cl PL7 ....131 A5
County Rd EX23 ......104 E2
Court Barton Cotts PL9 135 C1
Court Barton Mews PL9 30 B4
Court Gdns PL25 .....114 C3
Court Mdw PL13 ....62 B7
Court The Plymouth PL6 .125 C7
  Saltash PL12 ....122 C2
Court View PL8 ....136 F4
Courtenay Rd PL19 ...147 B6
Courtenay St PL1 ....148 C3
Courtfield Rd PL3 ....128 F5
Courtland Cres PL7 ..130 D7
Courtlands PL12 ......122 E1
Courtlands Cl PL19 ..147 B6
Courtlands Cres 4
  PL25 ....115 A5
Courtlands Rd PL19 ..147 B6
Courtlands Sch PL6 ..124 F1
Courtney Cl PL13 ....117 D4
Courtney Rd
  Liskeard PL14 ....113 D6
  St Austell PL25 ......114 F5
  Truro TR1 ....137 B5
Courtyard Cotts TR4 ..70 C6
Courtyard The
  Redruth TR16 ....139 F2
  Truro TR1 ....137 D3
Cove Hill
  Perranarworthal TR3 ...81 D5
  Sennen Cove TR19 .....96 B7
Cove Mdw PL11 ......127 A6
Cove Rd TR19 ....96 C7
Coventry Rd TR11 ....145 B6
Coverack Prim Sch
  TR12 ....101 C1
Coverdale Pl PL5 .....124 C1
Cow Lard Cl PL15 ....106 A4
Cowdray Cl PL12 .....122 E2
Cowdray Terr PL12 ...122 E1
Cowley Rd PL5 ....124 C4
Cowling Gdns PL14 ...51 F6
Cowling Rd 2 TR3 ....81 F7
Cox Park Terr PL18 ...40 C6
Cox Tor Cl 6 PL20 ....42 C3
Cox Tor Rd PL19 .....147 E5
Cox's Cl PL6 ....125 B1
Coxs Mdw EX22 ......13 C7
Coypool Rd PL7 ......130 A6
Crabbs Cl PL15 ....13 F1
Crabtree Cl 3 PL14 ..113 B5
Crabtree Pk PL30,PL31 .109 D2
Crabtree Villas PL3 ..129 E5
Crackston Cl PL6 .....129 B7
Craigie Dr PL1 ....148 A3
Craigmore Ave PL2 ..127 F5
Cramber Cl
  Roborough PL6 ......125 C8
  Tavistock PL19 ......147 B4
Cranberry Rd TR14 ..138 B3
Cranbourne Ave PL4 .149 C4
Crane Rd Camborne TR14 138 C2
  Newlyn TR18 ....143 C3
Cranfield PL7 ....130 C7
Cranfield Rd TR14 ...138 B3
Cranmere Rd PL3 ....129 A6
Crantock St TR7 .....110 D6
Crantock Terr 7 PL2 .128 A5
Crapstone Terr PL20 ..42 B2
Crashaw Cl PL5 ......124 D3
Craven Ave PL4 .....149 C4
Crawford Rd PL1 ....148 A4
Creakavose PL26 ......58 A4
Creakavose Pk PL26 ..58 A4
Crease La PL19 ......147 A4
Creathorne Rd EX23 .104 E7
Creaz - An - Bre PL26 ..58 D5
Crediton Wlk PL6 ....129 E8
Creed La TR2 ....72 A7
Creedy Rd PL3 ....129 C5
Creekside View TR2 ...70 F4
Creeping La
  Newlyn TR18 ....143 C3
  Penzance TR18 ....143 C4
Crelake Cl PL19 ......147 C4
Crelake Ind Est 1 PL19 147 B4
Crelake Pk PL19 .....147 C4

Crellow Fields TR3 ....80 F3
Crellow Hill TR3 ......80 F3
Crellow La TR3 ....80 F3
Crellow Vale TR3 .....80 F3
Crembling Well TR15 .139 E6
Cremyll Rd PL11 .....127 B2
Cremyll St PL1 ....134 A8
Crescent Ave PL1 ....148 B2
Crescent Avenue Mews
  PL1 ....148 B2
Crescent Cl Hayle TR27 .142 E1
  Widemouth Bay EX23 ...6 F5
Crescent Gdns TR1 ..137 B4
Crescent Pl TR1 ......74 F1
Crescent Rd Bugle PL26 .47 C1
  Truro TR1 ....137 B4
Crescent Rise
  Constantine Bay PL28 ..20 C1
  Truro TR1 ....137 B4
Crescent The Bude EX23 104 C3
  Camborne TR14 ......138 D4
  Carbis Bay TR26 ......77 C4
  Common Moor PL14 ...37 F4
  Crapstone PL20 ....42 B3
  Gunnislake PL18 ......41 A6
  Landrake PL12 ....53 C3
  Lifton PL16 ....19 F4
  Liskeard PL14 ....113 C6
  Looe PL13 ....117 D1
  Newquay TR7 ....110 E6
  Plymouth PL1 ....148 A2
  Porthleven PL13 ......91 B1
  St Ives TR26 ....77 A7
  Truro TR1 ....137 B4
  Wadebridge PL30 ......34 D8
  Widemouth Bay EX23 ...6 F5
Cressbrook Cl PL6 ...125 C5
Cressbrook Dr PL6 ...125 C5
Cressbrook Wlk PL6 ..125 C2
Cresthill Rd PL2 .....128 B7
Creswell Terr TR19 ...86 F7
Cribbage Terr 7 PL31 109 C3
Cricket Ct EX23 ....7 B6
Cricketers Hollow PL27 .21 C3
Crift Cotts PL14 ......51 F7
Crift La PL12 ....64 F8
Criggan Mill Cvn Pk
  TR12 ....102 C7
Crinnick's Hill PL31 ..109 E4
Crinnis Cl PL25 ......115 E3
Crinnis Rd PL25 .....115 E3
Crinnis Wood PL25 ..115 E3
Crinnis Wood Ave PL25 115 D3
Crocker's Row PL18 ..41 A6
Crockers Way PL15 ...13 F1
Crockwell St PL31 ...109 E5
Croft Comm TR14 .....79 E5
Croft Parc 4 TR12 ...102 F2
Croft Pk PL6 ....125 C2
Croft Rd PL18 ....143 C4
Croft Row TR16 ....80 F8
Croftlands PL27 ....21 E3
Crofty Cl TR15 ......139 C5
Cromartie Rd PL4 ...129 B1
Cromer Cl PL6 ....125 A7
Cromer Wlk PL6 .....125 A7
Cromwell Gate PL6 ..125 C7
Cromwell Rd
  Plymouth PL4 ....149 C3
  St Austell PL25 ......114 F3
Crookeder Cl PL9 ....136 A5
Crookedor La PL11 ...65 D5
Crooklets EX23 ....104 C4
Crooklets Rd EX23 ..104 D6
Cross Cl TR7 ....111 C7
Cross Comm TR12 ...102 F2
Cross Gn PL15 ....19 F7
Cross Hill PL2 ....127 E4
Cross La Bodmin PL31 .109 E5
  Chacewater TR4 ......69 B1
  7 St Austell PL25 ...114 C3
Cross Lanes
  Cross Lanes TR12 .....99 C4
  Launceston PL15 .....106 C8
  Stratton EX23 ....4 F1
Cross Park Ave PL6 ..124 F1
Cross Park Rd PL6 ...124 F1
Cross Park Terr PL26 ..73 C4
Cross Park Way PL6 .124 F1
Cross Pk
  Buckland Monachorum PL20 42 A3
  Crafthole PL11 ....65 B5
Cross St Camborne TR14 .138 D2
  Hayle TR27 ....142 D6
  Helston TR13 ....146 B6
  Padstow PL28 ....107 D5
  14 Penzance TR18 ...143 E6
  3 Redruth TR15 .....140 B4
  Wadebridge PL27 ....108 B5
Cross Terr PL18 ....40 F5
Cross The
  Camborne TR14 ......138 D2
  St Dominick PL12 .....40 D2
  St Newlyn East TR8 ...56 B7
Crosswalla Fields TR13 146 C1
Crosswater EX23 ......2 C1
Crossway PL7 ....130 D7
Crossway Ave PL4 ...129 B3
Crossways TR11 .....144 F2
Crow Pk PL3 ....129 A6
Crowan Prim Sch TR14 .79 C2
Crowlas Ind Est TR20 ..89 B8
Crown Cl TR7 ....111 A4
Crown Cres TR8 ......56 B7
Crown Gdns PL6 .....125 C5
Crown Pk PL26 ....58 D8
Crown Terr PL26 ......58 D8
Crowndale Ave PL3 ..129 A6

Crownhill Ct PL6 .....124 F2
Crownhill Fort★ PL6 ..124 F3
Crownhill Fort Rd PL6 .124 F3
Crownhill Rd PL5 .....124 F2
Crows-An-Eglos 5 TR26 77 A6
Croydon Gdns PL5 ...123 E4
Crozier Rd 6 PL4 ....128 F4
Crun-Melyn Parc TR27 .142 B4
Cryben TR1 ....92 C1
Crylla Valley Cvn & Camping
  Pk PL12 ....53 D3
Cryon View TR1 ....69 D3
Cubert Prim Sch TR8 ..43 D1
Cuby Rd TR2 ....71 F4
Cuckoo La TR20 ....77 A3
Cuddenbeake Terr PL12 .65 B8
Cuffe Rd PL3 ....128 C4
Cul-Rian PL26 ....58 D7
Culdrose Airfield TR12 146 E1
Culdrose Cl PL5 .....123 E4
Cullen View TR1 ......71 C6
Culme Rd PL3 ....129 A5
Culroy Flats 12 TR1 ..137 C4
Culver Cl PL6 ....129 A8
Culver Ct PL12 ......122 F2
Culver Rd PL12 ......122 F2
Culver Way PL6 .....129 A7
Culverland Pk PL14 ..113 C4
Culvers Mdw PL15 ..106 B8
Culverwood Cl PL7 ..131 C5
Culverwood Rd PL14 .113 B8
Culvery The PL27 ....108 B4
Cumberland Rd PL1 .127 F1
Cumberland St PL1 .127 E2
Cumble Tor La PL12 ..53 D2
Cundy Cl PL7 ....130 A7
Cundy's La PL26 ......58 D4
Cunliffe Ave PL9 ....135 A6
Cunnack Cl TR13 ....146 C3
Cunningham Pk TR10 .81 C1
Cunningham Rd PL5 ..124 C3
Cunningham Way PL12 122 D3
Curlew Cl TR7 ....110 B5
Curlew Mews PL3 ...129 C4
Curlew Pk Ind Est TR4 .69 C3
Curnons Rd TR27 ...142 C5
Curnow Sch The TR15 .140 B8
Currian Hill PL26 .....58 D8
Currian Rd PL26 ......58 D7
Curtis Pl PL1 ....127 E4
Curtis VC Ct TR8 .....56 B7
Cury Prim Sch TR12 ..99 A4
Cusgarne Com Prim Sch
  ....81 C7
Cusgarne Hill TR4,TR16 .81 B8
Custom House Ct TR18 143 F5
Custom House La
  16 Penzance TR18 ...143 E5
  Plymouth PL1 ....148 B1
Customs House Hill
  PL23 ....116 D4
Cutcrew La PL12 ......52 E3
Cutmere Hill PL12 .....52 D3
Cutmere La PL12 ......52 D3
Cuxhaven Way TR20 ..88 F3
Cuxton Mdws PL20 ...41 F3
Cypress Ave PL25 ...115 F4
Cypress Cl 6 PL7 ...131 C5
Cyril Rd TR1 ....137 C5

D

Dabryn Way PL26 .....58 B4
Daglands Hill PL23 ..116 C4
Daglands Rd PL23 ...116 C4
Dairyland Farm World★
  TR8 ....44 F1
Dale Ave PL6 ....129 C7
Dale Cl TR7 ....111 A4
Dale Gdns PL4 ......128 D4
Dale Rd Newquay TR7 .111 A4
  Plymouth PL4 ....128 D4
Daleswood Rd PL19 .147 A4
Dalton Gdns PL5 ....123 E3
Damerel Cl PL1 ......127 F2
Dane Rd TR7 ....110 D7
Daniel Cl PL25 ......115 A4
Daniel Pl PL18 ......143 E4
Daniell Ct TR1 ......137 C3
Daniell Rd TR1 .....137 B3
Daniell St TR1 ......137 C3
Daniels La PL25 .....115 B4
Daniels Sail Loft TR10 .144 D7
Danmore Cl PL34 .....14 C7
Danum Dr PL7 ......131 B3
Daphne Du Maurier's
  Smuggler's Mus★ PL15 .25 E3
Darite Prim Sch PL14 .38 A4
Dark La Camelford PL32 .105 C4
  Liskeard PL14 ....113 D6
  Lostwithiel PL22 .....112 C1
Dark Street La PL7 ..130 E4
Darkey La PL16 ....19 F4
Darklake Cl PL6 .....125 E5
Darklake La PL6 .....125 D8
Darklake View PL6 ..125 E5
Darlington Rd TR20 ..88 F6
Darloe La PL13 ....62 D1
Darracott Hill EX39 ...2 E4
Dart Cl Plymouth PL3 .129 C7
  St Giles-On-The-Heath PL15 13 F1
Dartington Wlk PL6 .129 E8
Dartmeet Ave PL3 ..129 B6

Dartmoor View
　Plymouth PL4 ....129 C3
　Saltash PL12 ....122 E4
Dartmouth Wlk PL6 ......129 E8
Darwin Cres PL3 ....129 D5
Dashwood Ho TR11 ......145 A6
Daubuz Cl TR1 ....137 C6
Daubuz Ct TR1 ....137 D5
Daucus Cl PL19 ....147 B4
Davenham Cl PL6 ....125 B6
Davey's Cl TR11 ....144 E1
David Cl PL7 ....130 F6
David Penhaligon Way
　TR1 ....137 D3
David Southgate Ct PL1 148 A2
Davy Cl PL11 ....126 F3
Davy Rd PL6 ....125 C4
Davys Row PL14 ....37 C4
Daw's Mdw PL32 ....105 E4
Dawe Cres PL31 ....109 C3
Dawes Cl PL14 ....50 E7
Dawes La Looe PL13 .....117 C5
　Millbrook PL10 ....132 E5
　Plymouth PL9 ....136 D7
Dawlish Wlk PL6 ....129 E8
Dawn Rd PL13 ....117 D2
Dawnay Terr PL11 ....65 B5
Daws Ct PL12 ....123 A2
Dawson Cl PL5 ....123 E1
Daymer La PL27 ....21 D4
Daymond Rd PL5 ....123 D2
Dayton Cl PL6 ....124 E3
De Pass Gdns PL11 .....145 C3
De Pass Rd PL11 ....145 C2
De-La-Hay Ave PL3 .....148 A4
Deacon Dr PL12 ....122 F1
Deacons Cl PL19 ....147 A3
Dean Cross PL9 ....135 E7
Dean Cross Rd PL9 .....135 E7
Dean Hill Liskeard PL14 .113 B6
　Plymouth PL9 ....135 E7
Dean La PL14 ....113 B6
Dean Park Rd PL9 ......135 D7
Dean Rd PL7 ....130 D6
Dean St PL14 ....113 B6
Dean Terr PL14 ....113 B6
Debden Cl PL5 ....123 D4
Deeble Cl Plymouth PL7 .130 F7
　Threemilestone TR3 ....69 C3
Deep La PL7 ....131 C3
Deer Leap PL14 ....147 D4
Deer Park Cl PL19 .....147 C5
Deer Park Cres PL19 ...147 C5
Deer Park Dr PL3 ......129 D7
Deer Park La PL19 .....147 C5
Deer Park Rd PL19 .....147 C5
Deer Pk Newquay TR7 ...110 F5
　Saltash PL12 ....122 F3
Deerpark Forest Trail★
　PL14 ....50 D3
Defoe Cl PL5 ....124 C1
Degibna La TR12,TR13 ...146 C2
Delabole Prim Sch PL33 .14 D2
Delacombe Cl PL7 .....130 F7
Delamere Rd PL6 ......129 D7
Delavue Terr PL32 .....105 C3
Delaware Com Prim Sch
　PL18 ....40 F5
Delaware Cotts PL18 ....40 F6
Delaware Ct PL18 ....40 F5
Delaware Gdns PL2 ....127 F7
Delaware Rd PL18 ......40 F5
Dell Cl TR18 ....143 C3
Dell Mdw PL15 ....18 B8
Dell The Plymouth PL7 ..147 B6
　Tavistock PL19 ....147 B6
　Truro TR1 ....137 C5
Denas Water TR2 ....71 A5
Dengie Cl PL7 ....131 B5
Denham Cl PL5 ....124 C2
Dennis Cl PL5 ....127 C7
Dennis Gdns PL15 ......18 C2
Dennis La PL28 ....107 D4
Dennis Rd Liskeard PL14 113 D6
　Padstow PL28 ....107 D5
Dennison Ave PL25 ....115 A4
Dennison Rd PL31 .....109 D5
Dennybowl La
　Tideford PL12 ....52 E3
　Tideford PL12 ....52 F2
Denys View TR9 ....45 F2
Deptford Pl PL4 ....149 A4
Derby Rd PL5 ....124 C4
Derby's La PL26 ....85 C5
Dereham Terr **6** TR1 ...137 B4
Derowen Dr TR27 ......142 B3
Derriford Hospl PL6 ...125 B5
Derriford Rd PL6 ......125 B4
Derriton Rd EX22 ....8 F6
Derry Ave PL4 ....148 A4
Derry's Cross PL1 .....148 B2
Derwent Ave PL3 ......129 C5
Desborough La PL4 ....149 C3
Desborough Rd PL4 ....149 C3
Deveral Rd TR27 ....78 D2
Deveron Cl PL7 ....131 A5
Devington Ct TR11 ....145 C2
Devington Hall TR1 ...137 E5
Deviock Hill PL11 ......64 C5
Devon Terr PL3 ....128 E5
Devon Tors PL20 ....42 D3
Devon Tors Rd **9** PL20 .42 C3
Devonia Cl PL7 ....130 C4

Devonport High Sch for Boys
　PL1 ....128 A2
Devonport High Sch for Girls
　PL2 ....128 C6
Devonport Hill
　Cawsand PL10 ....133 A2
　Plymouth PL1 ....127 F1
Devonport Leat PL6 ....121 B5
Devonport Rd PL1 .....127 F3
Devonport Sta PL1 ....127 F3
Devonshire Ho
　Plymouth PL1 ....148 B2
　2 Tavistock PL19 ....147 B5
Devonshire St PL4 ....149 A3
Devoran La TR3 ....81 F6
Devoran St TR3 ....81 F6
Diamond Ave PL4 .....149 B4
Diana Cl TR1 ....144 E2
Dickens Rd PL5 ....124 B1
Dickiemoor La PL5 ....124 C2
Dickna St PL15 ....13 F1
Dicky La TR3 ....82 D6
Diddies La EX23 ....4 E1
Diddies Rd EX23 ....4 E1
Dieppe Cl PL1 ....127 F2
Digby Gr PL5 ....123 F5
Digey The **25** TR26 ....141 B6
Diggory's Field **4** PL14 .38 A3
Dinas Ct PL1 ....64 C5
Dinas Rd **1** TR9 ....45 D6
Dingle Cl PL17 ....28 D1
Dingle Rd
　Plymouth, North Prospect
　PL2 ....128 A6
　Plymouth, Plympton PL7 .130 C6
Dingles Cl TR3 ....81 B4
Dingwall Ave PL5 .....124 C1
Dipper Cl EX23 ....5 A6
Dipper La EX23 ....5 A7
Dirty La PL12 ....122 B5
Discovery Wharf **20** PL4 149 A2
Distine Cl PL3 ....129 B7
Dithmarschen Way
　PL25 ....114 B2
Dittisham Wlk PL6 ....129 E8
Ditton Ct PL6 ....129 A8
Dixon Pl PL2 ....127 E4
Dobbin Cl PL28 ....20 F2
Dobbin La PL28 ....20 F2
Dobbin Rd PL28 ....20 F2
Dobbs La TR1 ....137 A4
Dobell Rd PL5 ....114 E4
Dobwalls Family Adventure
　Pk★ PL14 ....50 E8
Dobwalls Prim Sch PL14 .50 E7
Dock La TR18 ....143 F5
Dockacre Rd PL15 .....106 C6
Dockey PL15 ....106 C5
Dockray Cl PL6 ....125 D4
Dockyard Halt PL1 ....127 E4
Doctor's La PL14 .....113 C6
Doctors Ho
　8 Boscastle PL35 ......9 C1
　5 St Keverne TR12 ...101 C4
Doctors La PL12 ....65 A8
Doddridge Cl PL9 .....135 F4
Dodson's Gap PL12 .....99 B7
Doidges Farm Cl PL6 ...129 B8
Dola La TR20 ....89 E5
Dolbeare Pk (Cvn Pk)
　PL12 ....53 B4
Dolcoath Ave TR14 ....138 F3
Dolcoath Cl TR14 .....138 F3
Dolcoath Rd TR14 .....138 F3
Dolgay Post PL27 ......32 A4
Dolphin Cl PL9 ....135 F6
Dolphin Court Rd PL9 .135 F6
Dolphin Ho **18** PL4 ....149 A2
Dolphin Sq PL9 ....135 F6
Dolphin St PL29 ....22 D7
Dolvin Rd PL19 ....147 C5
Domellick Cnr PL26 ....46 B1
Domellick Hill PL26 ....46 B1
Doniert's Cl PL14 .....113 B5
Donkey La
　Millbrook PL10 ....132 C4
　Portwrinkle PL11 ......65 A4
Donkey Pk PL28 ....31 F8
Donnington Dr PL3 ....129 C7
Donnington Rd TR18 ..143 C3
Dopps Terr TR15 ......140 C5
Dorchester Ave PL5 ...124 D4
Doreena Rd PL9 ......136 C7
Dormy Ave PL3 ....128 F5
Dorset Pk PL15 ....13 A2
Dorsmouth Terr PL14 ...40 D4
Doublebois Ind Est PL14 .50 D7
Doubletrees Ct **2** PL24 .60 B4
Doubletrees Sch PL24 ..60 B4
Douglas Cl PL26 ....47 A3
Douglas Dr PL9 ......136 A6
Douglass Rd PL3 ......129 C6
Doulton Rd PL25 .....115 A4
Dousland Ho PL20 ......42 E3
Dousland Rd PL20 ......42 D3
Dousland Terr PL20 ....42 E3
Dove Gdns PL3 ....129 D7
Dove St **15** TR26 .....141 B5
Dovedale Rd PL3 .....128 A7
Dover Rd PL6 ....125 E3
Down Cl PL12 ....122 C2
Down Park Dr PL19 ...147 D4
Down Parks EX23 ....5 B7
Down Rd Plymouth PL7 .131 C4
　Tavistock PL19 ....147 D4
Down The PL20 ....41 C1
Downfield Dr PL7 .....130 F5

Downfield Way PL7 ....130 F5
Downfield Wlk PL7 ....130 F5
Downgate Gdns PL2 ...128 D8
Downham Gdns PL5 ...124 C7
Downham Sch PL9 .....135 F7
Downlea PL19 ....147 D4
Downs La PL13 ....117 B3
Downs Lane Pk PL13 ..117 B3
Downs Rd PL13 ....117 C4
Downs The PL13 ......117 C3
Downs View Bude EX23 .104 D7
　Looe PL13 ....117 C3
Downside Ave PL6 ....129 C7
Downside Cl PL27 .....111 A4
Downstream Cl PL25 ..107 C5
Downton Cl PL1 ......148 A4
Dozmere TR3 ....82 A5
Dozmere Cl TR3 ....82 A5
Dracaena Ave
　Falmouth TR11 ....144 F5
　Hayle TR27 ....142 E6
Dracaena Cres TR27 ..142 E6
Dracaena Pl TR11 ....144 F4
Dracaena View TR11 ..144 F5
Drake Cir PL1,PL4 ....149 A3
Drake Ct PL4 ....149 B3
Drake Gdns PL19 .....147 C4
Drake Prim Sch PL2 ..127 E6
Drake Rd Padstow PL28 107 C5
　Tavistock PL19 ....147 C6
Drake Villas PL19 ....147 A4
Drake's Pk **3** PL20 ....41 B1
Drakefield Dr PL12 ...123 A3
Drakes Cl PL6 ....124 F4
Drakewalls Gdns PL18 ..40 F5
Drakewalls Pl PL18 ....40 F5
Drang The TR9 ....45 E1
Drannack La TR27 ......78 D4
Draper Terr **3** PL19 ..147 B5
Drax Gdns PL5 ....128 E8
Draycott Terr TR26 ...141 C4
Drayton Rd PL5 ......124 C1
Dreysen Cl TR15 .....139 C8
Drift Cl TR20 ....87 F3
Drift La PL14 ....49 C7
Drillhead La **9** TR26 ..141 B5
Drinnick Terr PL26 .....58 D6
Drive The PL3 ....128 E7
Driving La PL24 ....60 C6
Drogeada Cl PL15 ......27 D3
Droskyn Castle **12** TR6 ..55 A5
Droskyn Cl **15** TR6 .....55 A5
Droskyn Way TR6 ....55 A5
Druckham Terr PL15 ..106 D5
Druid's Lodge TR15 ..139 D5
Druid's Rd TR15 .....139 D5
Drummer's Hill PL26 ..114 C8
Drummond Pl PL2 .....127 F7
Drummond Pl PL1 ....127 F7
Drump Rd TR15 ......140 C5
Drunken Bridge Hill
　PL7 ....130 D4
Dryburgh Cres PL2 ...128 A8
Dryden Ave PL5 ......124 C1
Drym La Leedstown TR14 .78 F1
　Nancegollan TR14 .....91 A8
Drym Rd TR13 ....91 B7
Dualstone Cross EX22 ...8 B2
Ducane Wlk PL6 ......125 B1
Duchy Ave TR7 ....111 C7
Duchy Cl PL5 ....106 C7
Duchy Coll PL17 ....28 D1
Duchy Cotts PL17 ......28 D1
Duchy Hospl TR1 ......69 E4
Duchy Terr Minions PL14 .38 B6
　Upton Cross PL14 .....38 B7
Duck La PL12 ....53 E2
Duck St **9** TR19 ......88 C1
Duckworth St **3** PL2 ..128 A4
Ducky Cl PL17 ....53 C2
Ducky Row PL17 ......40 D4
Dudley Gdns PL6 .....129 B8
Dudley Rd PL7 ....130 B5
Dudman Rd TR1 ....69 F3
Dudnance La TR15 ...139 B4
Duke of Cornwall's Light
　Infantry Mus★ PL31 ..109 F3
Duke St Launceston PL15 106 A8
　Lostwithiel PL22 ......112 C2
　Padstow PL28 ....107 D5
　Plymouth PL1 ....127 E2
　St Austell PL25 ....114 C3
　Tavistock PL19 ....147 C6
　11 Truro TR1 ....137 D4
Duke's Way TR7 ......111 A5
Dukes Dr PL19 ....41 B4
Duloe Gdns PL2 ......128 C8
Duloe Prim Sch PL14 ..51 A1
Dumbarton Terr **7** TR19 .88 C1
Dumfries Rd PL25 ....124 D3
Dun Mere Cl **1** PL24 ..60 C4
Duncan St PL1 ....127 E1
Duncannon Dr TR11 ..144 F4
Dunclair Pk PL3 .....129 D5
Duncombe Ave PL5 ...124 D4
Dundas St **4** PL2 ....128 A4
Dunders Hill PL27 .....21 D5
Dundonald St PL2 ....127 F4
Dungarth Gn PL14 ....113 D6
Dungarth Rd PL14 ....113 D6
Dunhead View PL15 ....28 B6
Dunheved Fields PL15 106 C4
Dunheved Rd
　Launceston PL15 .....106 C5
　Saltash PL12 ....122 F2
Dunkeswell Cl PL2 ...127 E8
Dunley Wlk PL6 ......125 C1

Dunmere Rd PL31 .....109 B5
Dunn St PL35 ....9 C1
Dunnet Rd PL6 ....124 D7
Dunraven Dr PL6 .....125 A5
Dunsdon Cross EX22 ....5 F3
Dunstan Cl TR10 .....144 C8
Dunstan La PL12 ....40 A1
Dunstanville Terr **12**
　TR11 ....145 A5
Dunster Cl PL7 ....131 C4
Dunston Cl PL26 ....58 C8
Dunstone Ave PL9 ....136 A7
Dunstone Cl PL9 .....135 F7
Dunstone Dr PL9 .....135 F7
Dunstone La PL9 .....136 B7
Dunstone Prim Sch PL9 136 A8
Dunstone Rd
　Plymouth, Plymstock PL9 135 F7
　Plymouth, St Budeaux PL5 123 F3
Dunstone View PL9 ...136 A7
Duntz Hill PL16 ....19 F4
Dunvegan Rd TR10 ...144 B8
Dunveth Rd PL27 ....108 A5
Dupath La PL17 ....40 A4
Duporth Bay PL26 ....115 A1
Duporth Holiday Village
　PL26 ....115 A1
Duporth Rd PL25, PL26 115 A2
Dural Cross EX22 ......3 E3
Durban Rd PL3 ....128 D5
Durgan Crossroads TR11 93 D1
Durgan La TR10 ......144 C8
Durham Ave PL4 .....149 C4
Durley Dene PL26 .....77 E4
Durnford St PL1 .....128 A1
Durnford Street Ope
　PL1 ....128 A1
Durning Rd TR5 ....54 C1
Durrant Cl PL1 ....127 E1
Durris Cl PL6 ....125 D4
Durris Gdns PL6 .....125 D4
Durston Rd EX23 .....104 E7
Durwent Cl PL9 ......135 A6
Dutson Rd PL15 ......106 C7
Dutson Terr PL15 .....106 C7
Dux Cross EX22 ....8 C6
Duxford Cl PL5 ......123 E5
Dye House Cotts PL14 ..36 F2
Dynas-la Rd TR26 ....141 B4
Dynevor Cl PL3 ......128 F7

E

Eagle Rd PL7 ....131 C4
Earl's Acre PL3 ......128 C4
Earl's Dr The
　Cawsand PL10 ....133 A1
　Cawsand, Kingsand PL10 133 B3
　Rame PL10 ....64 C2
Earls Mill Rd PL7 ....130 E6
Earls Rise TR7 ....111 B5
Earls Wood Cl PL6 ...125 F3
Earls Wood Dr PL6 ...125 F3
East Bridge TR4 ....69 A3
East Camps Bay PL11 ..64 D3
East Charles St TR14 138 E2
East Cl TR13 ....146 E4
East Cliff PL13 ....117 D3
East Cliff La TR17 .....89 C5
East End TR15 ....140 C5
East Fairholme Rd EX23 104 F7
East Hill Camborne TR14 139 A5
　St Austell PL25 ......114 D3
East Mill PL15 ....106 D3
East Park Ave PL4 ...148 C4
East Pk Pensilva PL14 ..38 D4
　Redruth TR15 ....140 D6
East Pool Pk TR15 ...139 D6
East Rd Kilkhampton EX23 .5 A6
　Menheniot PL14 ....52 A5
　Quintrell Downs TR8 ...44 E3
　Stithians TR3 ....80 F3
East Rise TR11 ....144 F3
East Rosewin Row **10**
　TR1 ....137 D5
East St Newquay TR7 ..110 E6
　Plymouth PL1 ....148 A4
　Polruan PL23 ....116 D3
East Terr TR27 ....142 B6
East View PL14 ....51 F5
East Wharf PL26 ......73 C3
East Youlstone Cross
　EX23 ....3 C2
Eastbourne Cl PL25 ..114 D3
Eastbourne Rd PL25 ..114 D3
Eastbury Ave PL5 ....124 D4
Eastcliff TR4 ....68 A7
Eastcliff Avenue No 2
　TR4 ....68 A7
Eastcliffe Rd PL24 ....60 C5
Eastcote Cl PL6 .....125 B6
Eastcott Cross EX23 ....3 A2
Eastella Rd PL20 .....42 D3
Easterdown Cl PL9 ...135 F7
Eastern Ave PL14 ....113 D6
Eastern Gn Gulval TR18 .88 E6
　Penzance TR18 ......143 F7
Eastern La TR14 .....138 D4
Eastern Wood Rd PL7 131 D4
Eastfield Ave PL9 ....135 C6
Eastfield Way PL25 ..114 F5
Eastlake Ho **5** PL1 ..149 A2
Eastlake St PL1 ......149 A3
Eastlake Wlk PL1 ....149 A3
Eastland Cl TR1 .....137 F4

Eastwood Pk Ind Est
　TR10 ....144 A4
Eastwood Rd TR10 ...144 D7
Ebenezer Pl **12** TR18 143 C1
Ebrington St PL4 .....149 A3
Eddystone Cl PL3 ....129 C6
Eddystone Pl **3** PL27 .108 B5
Eddystone Rd
　Down Thomas PL9 ...135 C1
　St Austell PL25 ......114 E5
　Wadebridge PL27 ....108 B6
Eddystone Rise PL14 .113 D7
Eddystone Road Trad & Ind
　Est PL27 ....108 B6
Eddystone Terr
　2 Wadebridge PL27 ..108 B5
Eden Cl **11** PL24 ......60 B4
Eden Gdns **13** TR18 ..143 C1
Eden Project The★
　PL24 ....115 D8
Edgar Rd Jacobstow EX23 .11 A6
　Wainhouse Corner EX23 ..10 F6
Edgar Terr PL4 ....129 A4
Edgcumbe Ave
　Newquay TR7 ....110 F5
　Plymouth PL1 ....148 A3
Edgcumbe Cl PL18 .....41 A6
Edgcumbe Cres PL10 ..132 F6
Edgcumbe Ct **3** PL3 ..128 A3
Edgcumbe Dr PL19 ...147 B6
Edgcumbe Gdns TR7 ..110 F6
Edgcumbe Gn PL25 ...114 A3
Edgcumbe Park Rd PL3 128 D6
Edgcumbe Rd
　Lostwithiel PL22 .....112 C2
　Roche PL26 ....46 F3
　Saltash PL12 ....122 C5
　St Austell PL25 ......114 A3
Edgcumbe Terr **11** PL24 .60 B4
Edgcumbe Way PL18 ...40 E5
Edgcumbe Rd PL12 ....40 E5
Edgcumbe Terr **13** PL20 .41 B1
Edgemoor Cl PL14 ....38 A3
Edinburgh Cl PL25 ...115 C3
Edinburgh St **5** PL1 .127 E1
Edith Ave PL4 ....149 C4
Edith St PL5 ....123 D1
Edmonton **7** 33 B7
Edmund Rd TR15 .....140 B6
Edna Terr PL4 ....149 C3
Ednovean La TR20 .....89 E4
Edward Bolitho Ho (Hospl &
　Day Ctr) TR18 ......143 C1
Edward Hain Meml Hospl
　TR26 ....141 B5
Edward St
　Camborne TR14 ......138 F4
　Truro TR1 ....137 C4
Edwards Cl PL7 ......131 B4
Edwards Cres PL12 ..122 C2
Edwards Dr PL7 .....131 C4
Edwards Rd Devoran TR3 .81 F6
　St Giles-On-The-Heath PL15 13 F1
Effingham Cres PL3 ..128 D7
Efford Cres PL3 .....129 B6
Efford Down Pk EX23 104 C5
Efford Farm Bsns Pk
　EX23 ....104 C4
Efford La PL3 ....129 B5
Efford Pathway
　Plymouth PL3 ....129 C6
　Plymouth PL3 ....129 C5
Efford Rd PL3 ....129 B6
Efford Wlk PL3 ......129 B6
Egan's Way PL33 ......14 D2
Egerton Cres PL4 ....149 C3
Egerton Pl PL4 ......149 C3
Egerton Rd
　Padstow PL28 ....107 E4
　Plymouth PL4 ....149 C3
Eggbuckland Com Coll
　PL6 ....129 A8
Eggbuckland Rd PL3 .129 C7
Eggbuckland Vale Prim Sch
　PL6 ....129 A8
Eglos Ct PL30 ....23 E7
Eglos Mdw TR11 ....82 A3
Eglos Parc Mullion TR12 ..99 A2
　Wadebridge PL27 ....108 D5
Eglos Rd Crowlas TR20 ..89 A7
　Shortlanesend TR4 ....69 F6
　St Erme TR4 ....70 D8
Eglos View **2** PL35 .....9 D8
Egloshayle Rd
　Hayle TR27 ....142 E6
　Wadebridge PL27 ....108 D5
Egloskerry Prim Sch
　PL15 ....18 A5
Egret Cl PL10 ....133 A6
Eight Acre Cl **1** PL7 ..131 C5
Elaine Cl PL7 ....130 B5
Elbow La PL19 ......147 C6
Elburton Prim Sch PL9 136 C7
Elburton Rd PL9 .....136 B8
Eldad Hill PL1 ....148 A3
Elder Cl **2** PL7 .....131 B5
Elderfield Cl **7** PL24 ..60 D5
Eleanor Ho PL1 ......148 A2
Elerkey Cl TR2 ....83 F6
Elerkey La TR2 ......83 F6
Elford Cres PL7 .....130 E7
Elford Dr PL9 ....135 C7
Elford Pk PL20 ....42 D2
Elgin Cres PL5 ......124 E3
Elim Ct PL3 ....128 E5
Elim Terr PL3 ....128 E5

Eliot Cl PL15 ....18 C2
Eliot Ct TR7 ....110 F6
Eliot Dr PL12 ....65 B8
Eliot Gdns TR7 ....110 F6
Eliot Rd St Austell PL25 ..114 E4
  Truro TR1 ....137 C5
Eliot St PL5 ....127 E8
Elizabeth Cl
  Bodmin PL31 ....109 D4
  Threemilestone TR3 .....69 C3
Elizabeth Ct 2 PL1 ....149 A2
Elizabeth Pl PL4 ....149 A4
Elizabeth Rd Bude EX23 ..104 F5
  St Austell PL25 ....114 E3
Elizabeth Terr TR17 .....89 B5
Elizabethan House (Mus)
  The * PL1 ....149 A2
Ellen Cl TR4 ....68 C6
Ellenglaze Ct TR8 ....55 D8
Ellenglaze La TR8 ....55 D8
Ellenglaze Mdw TR8 .....55 D8
Elliot Sq PL11 ....127 B3
Elliot St PL1 ....148 B1
Elliot Terr PL1 ....148 C1
Elliot Terrace La PL1 .....148 C1
Elliott Cl PL12 ....122 D2
Elliott Rd PL4 ....129 B1
Ellis Cl TR27 ....142 C5
Ellis Way TR27 ....142 C5
Elliston Gdns 3 TR13 ..98 C8
Elm Cl Callington PL17 ....39 F4
  Camborne TR15 ....139 D6
  Newquay TR7 ....110 F4
  8 St Columb Major TR9 ..45 D6
  Tavistock PL19 ....147 C3
Elm Cotts PL12 ....122 C3
Elm Court Gdns PL12 ....137 D5
Elm Cres PL3,PL4 ....129 A4
Elm Ct TR1 ....137 D5
Elm Dr EX23 ....104 F5
Elm Gr Feock TR3 ....82 C5
  Plymouth PL7 ....130 E5
Elm Grove Cotts TR10 ..93 C6
Elm Lea EX23 ....104 F5
Elm Mdw TR3 ....82 C5
Elm Meadow Dr PL13 ..117 D4
Elm Pk PL10 ....133 B6
Elm Rd
  Plymouth, Glenholt PL6 ..125 D6
  Plymouth, Mannamead
  PL4 ....128 D6
Elm Terr 8 Mullion TR12 ..99 A2
  St Austell PL25 ....114 C4
Elm Tree Rd PL13 ....117 D4
EIMCroft PL2 ....128 B7
Elmgate Crossways PL12 65 E8
Elms Close Terr 23
  TR18 ....143 C2
Elms The
  Perranathnoe TR20 ....89 D4
  Plymouth PL3 ....128 A3
Elmsleigh Rd PL27 ....108 B6
Elmwood Cl PL6 ....125 D5
Elowen Cl TR11 ....144 E2
Elphinstone Rd PL2 ....128 C7
Elwell Rd PL12 ....123 A2
Elwick Gdns PL3 ....129 B5
Embankment La PL4 ....129 B2
Embankment Rd PL4 ....129 B2
Embankment Road La N
  PL4 ....129 B2
Emily Gdns PL4 ....149 B4
Emlyn Fields PL25 ....114 F6
Emma Pl PL1 ....128 A1
Emma Place Ope PL1 ....128 A1
Empire Way TR11 ....144 E4
Empress Ave 24 TR18 ..143 E6
Emslie Rd TR11 ....145 C2
Endleigh Dr PL15,PL19,
  PL17 ....28 F5
Endsleigh Gdns 2 PL4 ..149 A4
Endsleigh Park Rd PL3 ..128 D6
Endsleigh Pk EX23 ....7 B6
Endsleigh Pl PL4 ....149 A4
Endsleigh Rd PL9 ....135 C2
Endsleigh Terr PL14 ....113 C6
Energy Ctr * PL33 ....14 F4
Eningdale Rd PL19 ....147 A4
Ennerdale Gdns PL6 ....124 E5
Ennis Cl TR4 ....56 D1
Ennor's Rd TR7 ....110 D6
Enys Cl Carbis Bay TR26 ..141 D1
  Truro TR1 ....137 B5
Enys Cotts TR19 ....75 A2
Enys Quay 5 TR7 ....137 D4
Enys Rd Camborne TR14 ..138 D4
  Truro TR1 ....137 B5
Enys Redenek TR14 ....138 F5
Epping Cres PL6 ....129 D7
Epworth Cl TR1 ....137 E4
Epworth Terr 4 PL2 ....127 F7
Erdiston Ct EX23 ....104 D6
Ergue-Gaberic Way
  EX23 ....104 D5
Eric Rd Calstock PL18 .....41 B3
  Plymouth PL4 ....149 C3
Erisey Terr TR11 ....145 B4
Erith Ave PL2 ....127 E7
Erle Gdns PL7 ....130 E5
Ermington Terr PL4 ....128 C6
Ernesettle Cres PL5 ....123 E3
Ernesettle Gn PL5 ....123 E4
Ernesettle Jun & Inf Sch
  PL5 ....123 F4
Ernesettle La PL5 ....123 D4
Ernesettle Rd PL5 ....123 E3

Erow Glas TR10 ....144 C8
Esmonde Gdns PL5 ....127 B8
Esmonde Rd TR13 ....146 D4
Esperanza Ct TR11 ....144 F6
Esplanade PL23 ....116 C3
Esplanade Rd TR7 ....110 A6
Esplanade The PL1 ....148 C1
Essa Rd PL12 ....122 F2
Essex Dr TR15 ....139 B8
Essex St PL1 ....148 B4
Eston Cl TR10 ....93 C8
Estover Cl PL6 ....125 D2
Estover Com Coll PL6 ..125 D2
Estover Ind Est PL6 ....125 E2
Estover Prim Sch PL6 ..125 D2
Estover Rd PL6 ....125 C4
Estuary View
  Falmouth TR11 ....145 B5
  Lelant TR26 ....77 E3
  Newquay TR7 ....110 D5
Eton Ave PL1 ....148 C4
Eton Pl PL1 ....148 C4
Eton Rd PL25 ....115 A5
Eton St PL1 ....148 C4
Eton Terr 3 PL1 ....148 B3
Euny Cl TR15 ....140 A4
Eureka Vale 3 TR6 ....55 A5
Europa Ct TR8 ....31 C2
Evans Pl PL2 ....128 B5
Evans Way TR20 ....90 C4
Evea Cl TR1 ....69 F3
Evely Ct PL14 ....113 D7
Evelyn Pl PL4 ....149 A4
Evelyn St PL5 ....123 D1
Evenden Ct PL11 ....127 A3
Example Cross PL15 ....27 B6
Exchange St PL1 ....149 A2
Exe Gdns PL3 ....129 C7
Exeter Cl PL5 ....123 D4
Exeter Ct 5 PL15 ....106 C6
Exeter St
  Launceston PL15 ....106 C6
  Plymouth PL4 ....149 A3
  Plymouth PL4 ....149 B2
Exmouth Rd PL1 ....127 F3

F

Factory Cotts PL14 ....51 F5
Fair Cross TR2 ....72 C6
Fair Field TR2 ....89 B8
Fair Park View TR8 ....56 F5
Fair St TR9 ....45 E6
Fair View PL26 ....47 E4
Fair View Terr TR4 ....55 D8
Fairbourne Rd PL25 ....114 F4
Fairfax Rd TR2 ....70 F5
Fairfax Terr 5 PL2 ....127 E4
Fairfield Plymouth PL7 ..130 E7
  St Germans PL12 ....65 A8
Fairfield Ave PL2 ....128 C7
Fairfield Cl Lelant TR26 ..77 E4
  St Austell PL25 ....115 A4
Fairfield Pk PL15 ....26 C7
Fairfield Pl TR7 ....110 B5
Fairfield Rd Bude EX23 ..104 E5
  Falmouth TR11 ....144 F4
Fairfields PL13 ....117 D5
Fairlight PL14 ....113 D5
Fairmantle St TR1 ....137 D4
Fairmead Cl PL12 ....53 E4
Fairmead Mews PL12 ..122 C3
Fairmead Rd PL12 ....122 C2
Fairmeadow TR10 ....144 B7
Fairpark Rd
  Liskeard PL14 ....113 C5
  Wadebridge PL27 ....108 B5
Fairview Ave PL3 ....129 D5
Fairview Pk TR9 ....45 E2
Fairview Pl TR11 ....145 B4
Fairview Terr TR7 ....110 E6
Fairview Way PL3 ....129 C5
Fairway Saltash PL12 ..122 C3
  St Austell PL25 ....115 D3
Fairway The TR11 ....93 C8
Fairways The PL30 ....48 C7
Falcon Terr EX23 ....104 D5
Falmouth Bsns Pk TR11 144 E3
Falmouth College of Arts
  (Tremough Campus)
  TR10 ....144 A8
Falmouth College of Arts
  (Woodlane Campus)
  TR11 ....145 B3
Falmouth Com Sch (Lower)
  TR11 ....144 D5
Falmouth Com Sch (Upper)
  TR11 ....144 D5
Falmouth Docks Sta
  TR11 ....145 D3
Falmouth Hospl TR11 ..144 E4
Falmouth Rd
  Helston TR13 ....146 D7
  Penryn TR10 ....144 E7
  Redruth TR15 ....140 C4
  Truro TR1 ....137 C3
Falmouth Town (The Dell)
  Sta TR11 ....145 C3
Falmouth Wharves
  TR11 ....145 A6
Fanshawe Way PL9 ....135 C6
Faraday Mill Bsns Pk
  PL4 ....129 B1
Faraday Rd PL4 ....129 B1
Farm Cl PL7 ....130 C7
Farm La Plymouth PL5 ..124 B2
  Saltash PL12 ....122 D1

Farm Town TR15 ....140 C3
Farmer's La PL14 ....50 B6
Farmers Hill PL13 ....117 C4
Farmers Mdw 8 TR18 ..143 C2
Farnley Cl PL6 ....125 B6
Farrington Rd PL4 ....129 B3
Faugan La TR18 ....143 B1
Faugan Rd TR18 ....143 B1
Faukener Cl TR11 ....144 E4
Fayre View PL12 ....122 B3
Fearnside Way PL12 ....122 C3
Federation Rd PL3 ....129 C4
Fegan Rd PL5 ....123 B1
Feliskirk La TR17 ....89 B6
Felixstowe Ave TR7 ....111 E7
Fellowes Pl PL1 ....128 A2
Fellows La PL1 ....148 A4
Fenten Pk PL12 ....122 F3
Fenteroon Rd PL32 ....105 C3
Fentonluna La PL28 ....107 D6
Fenwick Rd PL1 ....145 B2
Fern Cl PL7 ....131 C5
Fern Lee Terr 19 TR26 ..141 B5
Fern Mdw PL19 ....147 D6
Ferndale Ave PL2 ....127 E7
Ferndale Cl PL6 ....125 D8
Ferndale Rd
  Falmouth TR11 ....145 A2
  Plymouth PL2 ....127 F7
Ferndale Terr PL14 ....113 B6
Fernhill Rd TR7 ....110 D6
Fernleigh Cres PL27 ....108 C4
Fernleigh Gdns PL27 ....108 C4
Fernleigh Rd
  Plymouth PL3 ....128 F5
  Wadebridge PL27 ....108 C5
Fernleigh Terr
  Gunnislake PL18 ....40 E5
  Nanpean PL26 ....58 C6
Fernside Pk PL14 ....38 A3
Fernside Rd TR14 ....138 B1
Ferrers Rd PL5 ....123 E1
Ferretts Cross EX23 ....11 A4
Ferris Town TR1 ....137 C4
Ferris Way PL23 ....116 E2
Ferry La PL11 ....126 D5
Ferry Rd PL1 ....127 E3
Ferry St PL11 ....127 C3
Festival Villas TR3 ....69 D3
Feversham Pl PL7 ....131 B6
Field Cl PL22 ....112 D2
Field Pl TR11 ....93 D3
Field The TR 20 ....76 F2
Fifield Ho PL26 ....58 B4
Fillace La PL20 ....42 C4
Filtrick La TR16 ....139 E1
Finch Cl PL3 ....129 C5
Finches Cl PL9 ....136 C7
Findon Gdns PL6 ....125 D4
Finewell St PL1 ....148 C2
Finn VC Est PL31 ....109 D5
Finnigan Rd PL4 ....129 B1
Finnygook La PL11 ....65 A4
Fir Cl Goonhavern TR4 ..55 D4
  Helston TR13 ....146 B7
  St Austell PL25 ....114 B3
Fir Gr 8 TR3 ....81 F7
Fircroft Rd PL2 ....128 B7
Firebeacon Cross EX39 ..2 F1
Firs The PL26 ....58 E8
Firsleigh Pk PL26 ....46 F3
First Ave
  Plymouth, Billacombe PL9 ..135 F8
  Plymouth, Stoke PL1 ....128 A2
Fisgard Way PL1 ....126 D3
Fish Mkt PL4 ....149 B2
Fish St 9 TR26 ....141 B6
Fish Strand Hill TR11 ..145 B4
Fish Strand Quay TR11 ..145 B4
Fisher Cl PL27 ....108 D6
Fisher Rd PL2 ....128 A5
Fistral Cl PL11 ....126 F4
Fistral Cres TR7 ....110 A5
Fistral Ct TR7 ....110 A5
Fitzford Cotts PL19 ....147 B4
Fitzroy Pl PL1 ....128 A3
Fitzroy Terr 7 PL1 ....128 A3
Fitzsimmons Cl 6 TR13 146 C5
Five Fields La TR11 ....145 A5
Five Wells La TR13 ....146 B5
Flamank Pk PL31 ....109 C4
Flambards Village*
  TR13 ....146 E4
Flamborough Rd PL6 ..125 B7
Flamborough Way PL6 ..125 A6
Flamsteed Cres PL5 ....123 E1
Flaxmoor Terr PL31 ....109 D5
Fleet St PL2 ....127 E6
Fletcher Cres PL9 ....136 B6
Fletcher Way PL9 ....136 A6
Fletemoor Rd PL5 ....123 E1
Flexbury Ave EX23 ....104 E7
Flexbury Mews EX23 ..104 E7
Flexbury Park Rd EX23 ..104 E6
Flexbury Pk EX23 ....104 E7
Flora Cotts PL1 ....148 B2
Flora Ct PL1 ....148 B3
Flora St PL1 ....148 B2
Florence Hill PL17 ....39 F5
Florence Pl
  Falmouth TR11 ....145 B3
  Newquay TR7 ....110 D6
  Plymouth PL4 ....149 C3
Florence Rd PL17 ....39 F6
Florence Road Ind Est
  PL17 ....39 F6
Florence St PL5 ....123 D1
Florence Terr TR11 ....145 B3

Florida Gdns PL3 ....129 C6
Floyd Cl PL2 ....127 F7
Flushing Sch TR11 ....145 B6
Folders La PL30 ....23 F6
Foliot Ave PL2 ....128 A6
Foliot Rd PL2 ....128 A6
Forbes Cl TR18 ....143 B1
Forbes Rd TR18 ....143 B1
Ford PL22 ....49 E3
Ford Hill PL2 ....128 A5
Ford Park La PL4 ....128 E4
Ford Park Rd PL4 ....128 D4
Ford Prim Sch PL2 ....128 A5
Ford St PL19 ....147 B5
Ford's Row TR15 ....140 B5
Forder Hill PL10 ....132 F1
Forder Hts PL6 ....125 B1
Forder La PL10 ....132 F1
Forder Valley Rd PL6 ..129 D8
Fords Hill TR12 ....100 D7
Fore St Ashton TR13 ....90 E3
  Barripper TR14 ....79 B5
  Bere Alston PL20 ....41 B1
  Bere Ferrers PL20 ....119 F3
  Bodmin PL31 ....109 D5
  Boscastle PL35 ....9 C1
  Bugle PL26 ....47 C1
  6 Callington PL17 ....39 E4
  Calstock PL18 ....41 A3
  Camborne TR14 ....138 D3
  Camborne, Beacon TR14 ..138 E1
  Camborne, Pool TR15 ..139 B6
  Camelford PL32 ....105 D4
  Cargreen PL12 ....119 A2
  Carharrack TR16 ....80 F8
  Cawsand PL10 ....133 A2
  Chacewater TR4 ....69 A3
  Constantine TR11 ....92 F4
  Crumplehorn PL13 ....62 D1
  Fowey PL23 ....116 D4
  Golant PL23 ....61 B5
  Goldsithney TR20 ....89 E5
  Grampound TR2 ....72 A7
  Grampound Road TR2 ..57 E5
  Gunnislake PL18 ....40 F5
  Gunnislake PL18 ....41 A6
  Hayle TR27 ....142 D6
  Herodsfoot PL14 ....50 E3
  Lelant TR26 ....77 E4
  Lerryn PL22 ....61 C7
  Lifton PL16 ....19 F4
  Liskeard PL14 ....113 C6
  Looe PL13 ....117 C3
  Lostwithiel PL22 ....112 C2
  Madron TR20 ....88 B7
  Marazion TR17 ....89 C5
  Mevagissey PL26 ....73 C3
  Millbrook PL10 ....132 E5
  Milton Abbot PL19 ....29 C6
  Mount Hawke TR4 ....68 C6
  13 Mousehole TR19 ....88 C1
  Nanpean PL26 ....58 D7
  Newlyn TR18 ....143 C1
  Newquay TR7 ....110 D6
  Par PL24 ....60 B5
  9 Par, Tywardreath PL24 ..60 D5
  Penponds PL14 ....138 B1
  Pensilva PL14 ....38 E4
  Plymouth, Devonport PL1 ..127 F2
  Plymouth, Plympton PL7 ..130 E4
  Plymouth, Tamerton Foliot
  PL5 ....124 B4
  Polgooth PL26 ....59 A1
  Polruan PL23 ....116 D2
  Port Isaac PL29 ....22 D2
  4 Porthleven TR13 ....98 B8
  Praze-an-Beeble TR14 ..79 B5
  Probus TR2 ....71 C6
  Redruth TR15 ....140 B5
  Roche PL26 ....46 F2
  Saltash PL12 ....122 F2
  St Austell PL25 ....114 C3
  St Cleer PL14 ....37 F3
  St Columb Major TR9 ..45 E6
  St Day TR16 ....68 D1
  St Dennis PL26 ....58 C8
  St Erth PL27 ....142 A1
  St Germans PL12 ....65 A8
  St Ives TR26 ....141 B6
  St Just TR19 ....86 F6
  St Stephen PL26 ....58 B4
  St Teath PL30 ....23 E7
  Sticker PL26 ....58 E1
  7 Stratton EX23 ....4 E1
  Tintagel PL34 ....14 C7
  Torpoint PL11 ....127 B3
  Tregony TR2 ....71 F3
  Troon TR14 ....79 E5
Foredown Pk PL14 ....38 C3
Forest Ave PL2 ....128 C4
Forest View PL6 ....125 D7
Foresters Rd PL9 ....135 D7
Forge Cl EX23 ....6 F1
Forge Ind Pk TR14 ....138 B5
Forge La PL12 ....122 C4
Forge The TR3 ....82 A7
Forge Way TR4 ....69 F6
Forlaze Rd PL27 ....21 D2
Formal Ind Pk TR14 ....138 B4
Forrabury Hill 5 PL35 ..9 C1
Forreglos Dr 10 TR17 ..89 C5
Forresters Rd PL9 ....125 D7
Forsythia Dr PL12 ....122 D3
Fort Austin Ave PL6 ....125 C1
Fort Terr PL4 ....124 F3
Fort The PL10 ....133 A1
Fortescue Cl PL26 ....58 D4

Fortescue Pl
  Lostwithiel PL22 ....112 D3
  Plymouth PL3 ....129 A6
Fortescue Terr PL19 ....147 A6
Forth An Cos TR3 ....81 B4
Forth An Streth TR27 ..142 E7
Forth An Tewennow
  TR27 ....142 D7
Forth An Vre TR14 ....142 E7
Forth An Vre TR14 ....139 A3
Forth Coth TR3 ....82 A7
Forth Dall 21 TR16 ....67 A4
Forth Gdns PL3 ....129 D6
Forth Gwedhen TR13 ..146 D8
Forth Kegyn TR15 ....139 B4
Forth Noweth 4 TR3 ..81 F7
Forth Scol
  Camborne TR15 ....139 D7
  6 Porthleven TR13 ....98 C8
Forth Vean TR13 ....90 E6
Forth-An-Nance TR16 ..67 C6
Forth-An-Praze
  Illogan TR15 ....139 D8
  St Day TR16 ....68 D1
Forth-An-Ryn TR15 ....140 D4
Forth-An-Tre TR27 ....142 D7
Forthcrom TR12 ....92 C1
Forthnoweth TR15 ....140 B5
Forthvean
  Camborne TR14 ....138 D1
  Portreath TR16 ....67 C5
Forthvean Cres TR4 ....68 A6
Forthvean Rd TR4,TR16 ..67 F7
Forthveor TR15 ....140 F7
Forthvras TR15 ....139 B8
Fosbrooke Ct 9 PL3 ....128 F6
Foster Dr PL31 ....109 C3
Fosters La PL34 ....14 C7
Fosters Way EX23 ....104 F6
Foulston Ave PL5 ....127 B8
Foundry Gdns PL15 ....106 C6
Foundry Hill TR27 ....142 B4
Foundry La Hayle TR27 ..142 B5
  Newlyn TR18 ....143 C2
Foundry Rd
  Camborne TR14 ....138 E3
  Stithians TR3 ....80 E7
Foundry Row 5 TR15 ..140 B5
Foundry Sq TR27 ....142 B5
Foundry St 6 PL27 ....108 B5
Foundry Terr PL27 ....108 B5
Fountain Ct 27 TR18 ..143 E6
Fountains Cres PL2 ....128 C8
Four Acres Rd TR2 ....83 F6
Four Lanes End TR19 ..88 B1
Four Lanes' End TR19 ..97 F6
Fourgates Est PL14 ....51 F5
Fourlanesend Com Prim Sch
  PL10 ....132 F3
Fowey Cres 27 PL17 ....39 F4
Fowey Gdns PL3 ....129 D6
Fowey Hospl PL23 ....116 D6
Fowey Mus * PL23 ....116 D4
Fowey Prim Sch PL23 ..116 C4
Fowlfield Row TR13 ....90 F3
Fox Field Cl PL3 ....129 C5
Fox's La TR11 ....145 B3
Foxdown PL27 ....108 C5
Foxes Field TR18 ....88 E6
Foxes La 5 TR19 ....88 C1
Foxglove Cl PL15 ....106 C4
Foxglove Way PL12 ....122 B3
Foxhole La PL26 ....85 D5
Foxhole Prim Sch PL26 ..58 D5
Foxs Yd TR10 ....144 D7
Foxstanton Dr TR10 ..144 D7
Foxtor Cl PL5 ....124 B3
Foxwood Gdns
  Plymouth, Plymstock PL9 ..135 F5
  Plymouth, Southway PL6 ..124 E5
Foyle Cl PL7 ....131 A5
Fraddam Rd TR27 ....78 D1
Fradgan Pl TR18 ....143 C2
Fradgan The 12 TR18 ..143 C2
Frances St TR1 ....137 C4
Francis La PL27 ....21 D5
Francis Rd PL27 ....21 D5
Francis St PL1 ....148 A3
Frankfort Gate 9 PL1 ..148 B3
Frankland Cl TR11 ....144 F3
Franklin Cl PL27 ....108 D6
Franklyn Cl PL25 ....114 F5
Franklyns Cl PL6 ....125 A4
Franklyns' PL6 ....125 A4
Franwill Terr 15 TR18 ..143 C1
Fraser Pl PL5 ....124 C7
Fraser Rd PL5 ....124 C7
Fraser Sq PL5 ....124 C7
Frederick St E PL1 ....148 B3
Frederick St W 6 PL1 ..148 B3
Fredington Gr PL2 ....128 B6
Freedom Sq PL4 ....149 B4
Freeman Collins Dr
  TR11 ....144 F4
Freemans Wharf PL1 ..134 A8
Fremantle Gdns 4 PL2 ..127 F4
Fremantle Pl PL2 ....127 F4
Frenchman's La PL12 ..53 C4
Frensham Ave PL6 ....125 C3
Frensham Gdns PL6 ....125 C2
Freshbrook Cl TR18 ....88 E6
Freshford Cl PL6 ....125 C1
Freshford Wlk PL6 ....125 C1
Freshwater La TR2 ....95 B6

Frewin Gdns PL6 . . . . . .125 B6
Friar's La Mullion TR12 . . .102 F6
Ruan Minor TR12 . . . . . . .103 B5
Friars Wlk PL19 . . . . .147 E2
Friars' La PL1 . . . . .149 A2
Friary Pk PL4 . . . . .149 B3
Friary St PL4 . . . . .149 B3
Frith Rd PL12 . . . . .122 D3
Frobisher App PL5 . . . . . .124 E2
Frobisher Dr PL12 . . . . . .122 E2
Frobisher Terr 9 PL11 . . .145 A5
Frobisher Way
  Tavistock PL19 . . . . .147 B5
  Torpoint PL11 . . . . .126 D3
Frog La TR2 . . . . .71 F3
Frogmore Ave
  Plymouth PL6 . . . . .129 B7
  Plymouth PL6 . . . . .129 C7
Frogmore Ct PL6 . . . . . . .129 B7
Frogwell Rd PL17 . . . . . . .39 E4
Frome Cl PL7 . . . . .131 A4
Front Rd PL11 . . . . .64 C4
Frontfield Cres PL6 . . . . .124 E5
Frost Ct TR11 . . . . .144 E5
Fuggoe Croft TR26 . . . . . .141 B5
Fuggoe La TR26 . . . . .141 C2
Fullaford Rd PL17 . . . . . . .40 A4
Fuller Rd TR6 . . . . .55 A5
Fuller-Tre Cl PL26 . . . . . . .46 F3
Fullerton Rd PL2 . . . . . . .128 A5
Furland Cl PL9 . . . . .135 C5
Furneaux Ave PL2 . . . . . .128 B5
Furneaux Rd PL2 . . . . . . .128 B6
Furry Way TR13 . . . . .146 B5
Fursdon Cl PL9 . . . . .136 C6
Furse Pk PL5 . . . . .127 C7
Furze Cross EX22 . . . . .8 B5
Furze Gdns EX23 . . . . .2 D1
Furze Hill PL31 . . . . .109 E5
Furze Pk Polruan PL23 . . .116 D2
  St Issey PL27 . . . . .32 D6
  Trelights PL29 . . . . .22 D6
Furzeacre Cl PL7 . . . . . . .131 A4
Furzedown Terr PL13 . . . .117 C4
Furzehatt Ave PL9 . . . . . .136 A6
Furzehatt Park Rd PL9 . .136 A6
Furzehatt Rd PL9 . . . . . . .135 F6
Furzehatt Rise PL9 . . . . . .136 A6
Furzehatt Villas PL9 . . . .135 F6
Furzehatt Way PL9 . . . . . .136 A6
Furzehill Rd PL4 . . . . .128 F4

G

Gabriel St 5 TR26 . . . . . .141 B5
Gains Cross EX22 . . . . .5 F3
Gainsborough Park Cvn Pk
  PL26 . . . . .58 D5
Galileo Cl PL7 . . . . .130 E6
Gallacher Way PL12 . . . . .122 B3
Galland Rd TR1 . . . . .69 F4
Gallant's Dr PL23 . . . . . . .116 B3
Galleon Ct TR7 . . . . .110 D4
Gallery La Landrake PL12 .53 A1
  St Germans PL12 . . . . .65 A8
Galligan Ct TR19 . . . . .97 A6
Galligan La TR19 . . . . .97 A6
Gallops The PL12 . . . . . . .122 D4
Galsworthy Cl PL5 . . . . . .124 C2
Galva Rd PL1 . . . . .131 C8
Gander La TR13 . . . . .146 B6
Ganges Cl TR11 . . . . .82 C2
Ganges Rd PL2 . . . . .128 A5
Ganna Park Rd PL3 . . . . .128 D6
Gannel Rd TR7 . . . . .110 C4
Gannel View Cl TR8 . . . . .111 B3
Gannet Dr PL25 . . . . .114 F4
Gara Cl PL9 . . . . .136 B6
Garby La TR15 . . . . .140 C3
Garcia Terr PL15 . . . . .106 D4
Garden Cl PL7 . . . . .131 D6
Garden Cres PL1 . . . . . . .148 B1
Garden La PL19 . . . . .147 B5
Garden Mdw TR11 . . . . . .144 C7
Garden Park Cl PL9 . . . . .136 C7
Garden Pk St PL2 . . . . . . .127 E4
Garden Village PL9 . . . . . .135 F8
Garden Way TR8 . . . . . . .111 F3
Gardeners Way PL27 . . . . .32 E6
Gards La PL5 . . . . .123 E2
Garfield Terr PL1,PL3 . . . .128 A3
Garland Pl TR14 . . . . .138 D4
Garlidna 25 TR18 . . . . . . .143 E6
Garras Com Prim Sch
  TR12 . . . . .99 D7
Garrett St PL10 . . . . .133 A1
Garrick Ct PL5 . . . . .124 C2
Garrison Cl PL1 . . . . .127 E1
Garro La TR12 . . . . .99 A1
Garston Cl PL9 . . . . .136 A8
Garth Morcom PL14 . . . . .113 B6
Garth Rd TR18 . . . . .143 B6
Garth-An-Creet TR26 . . . .77 A6
Gas Hill TR1 . . . . .137 E2
Gas La 8 TR15 . . . . .140 B4
Gas St TR14 . . . . .138 D3
Gascoyne Ct PL4 . . . . . . .149 A3
Gascoyne Pl PL4 . . . . . . .149 A3
Gashouse La PL4 . . . . . . .149 B2
Gasking St PL4 . . . . .149 A3
Gateway Ct TR27 . . . . .77 C6
Gatewynyack PL12 . . . . . .101 C1
Gavercoombe Pk PL34 . . .14 C7
Gay's Hill TR12,TR13 . . . .146 E4

Gays La PL12 . . . . .65 A8
Gdynia Way PL4 . . . . .149 C2
Gear Hill Madron TR20 . . .88 C8
  Mawgan TR20 . . . . .99 E8
  Mawgan TR20 . . . . .88 B8
Gears La
  Goldsithney TR17,TR20 . . .89 D6
  Goldsithney TR20 . . . . . . .89 E5
Geasons La PL7 . . . . .130 E5
Geever Cotts TR19 . . . . . .86 F1
Geevor Tin Mine★ TR19 . .74 F1
Geevor Tin Mine Mus★
  TR19 . . . . .74 F1
Geffery Cl PL12 . . . . .53 C3
Gendalls Way PL15 . . . . .106 B8
Gennys Cl PL18 . . . . .40 E6
George Ave PL7 . . . . .130 F6
George Cross PL7 . . . . . .130 F5
George Downing Ho
  PL6 . . . . .125 A1
George Fox Cl PL15 . . . . .106 A4
George La PL7 . . . . .130 F5
George Pl PL1 . . . . .148 A2
George Sq 5 Plymouth PL1 .127 F1
  Truro TR1 . . . . .137 C4
Georges La PL11 . . . . .65 C6
Georges Paddock PL15 . . .27 B3
Georgia Cres PL12 . . . . . .129 C6
Geraldine Terr PL12 . . . . .122 C1
Germoe Prim Sch TR20 . .90 C4
Gerrans Cl PL25 . . . . .115 B5
Gerrans Hill TR2 . . . . .83 B2
Gerrans Sch TR2 . . . . .83 B1
Gerrans Sq TR2 . . . . .83 B2
Ghost Hill TR20 . . . . .99 A1
Gibbon La PL4 . . . . .149 A3
Gibbons Fields 9 TR12 . . .99 A2
Gibbons St PL4 . . . . .149 A3
Gibby La PL35 . . . . .9 C1
Gibraltar Terr 6 TR2 . . . . .95 A6
Gibralter Sq 6 EX23 . . . . . .4 E1
Gibson Way TR13 . . . . . . .91 B1
Gifford Pl PL3 . . . . .128 D4
Gifford Terrace Rd PL3 . .128 E5
Gig La TR3 . . . . .82 A7
Gilbert Cl PL26 . . . . .58 B4
Gilbert Ct PL7 . . . . .131 B6
Gilbert La PL2 . . . . .128 C5
Gilbert Rd PL31 . . . . .109 F4
Gill Pk PL3 . . . . .129 B5
Gill-An-Creet TR26 . . . . . .77 A7
Gillbard Centenary Flats
  PL15 . . . . .106 B5
Gilley La PL26 . . . . .73 A4
Gills Cl TR18 . . . . .144 B6
Gilly Fields TR15 . . . . . . .140 B3
Gilly Gabben Ind Est
  TR12 . . . . .99 B7
Gilly Hill Cury TR12 . . . . . .99 B5
  Redruth TR15 . . . . .140 C3
Gilly La TR26 . . . . .77 C1
Gilston Rd PL12 . . . . .122 D4
Gilwell Ave PL9 . . . . .136 B7
Gilwell Pl PL4 . . . . .149 A3
Gilwell St PL4 . . . . .149 A3
Gipsy La Helston TR13 . . .91 C2
  Liskeard PL14 . . . . .113 A5
Gitchell La Crowlas TR20 .89 C8
  St Erth TR26 . . . . .77 C1
Glade The PL20 . . . . .42 B2
Gladstone Rd PL30 . . . . . .109 C2
Gladstone Terr
  Longrock TR20 . . . . .88 F6
  3 Redruth TR15 . . . . . . .140 C5
Gladwell Gdns 10 EX23 . . .4 D1
Glamis Dr TR7 . . . . .111 B6
Glantis Cres TR9 . . . . .45 E2
Glanville Ave 1 PL19 . . . .147 B5
Glanville Rd PL19 . . . . . . .147 B6
Glanville St PL1,PL4 . . . . .148 C3
Glanville Terr PL12 . . . . . .122 F3
Glasney Pl TR10 . . . . .144 C7
Glasney Rd TR11 . . . . . . .145 A5
Glasney Terr TR10 . . . . . .144 D7
Glebe Ave PL12 . . . . .122 F3
Glebe Cl Mawgan TR12 . . .99 D7
  6 St Columb Major TR9 . .45 E6
Glebe Cres PL27 . . . . .32 D6
Glebe Dr PL26 . . . . .46 F3
Glebe Mdw PL17 . . . . .39 E5
Glebe Parc PL30 . . . . .23 E3
Glebe Pl PL12 . . . . .103 B5
Glebe Row PL27 . . . . .142 D7
Glebe Terr
  Constantine TR11 . . . . . . .92 F4
  Ruan Minor TR12 . . . . . . .103 B5
Glebe The
  Camborne TR14 . . . . .138 C3
  Cubert TR8 . . . . .55 D8
  St Mellion PL12 . . . . .53 D8
  Week St Mary EX22 . . . . . .11 E8
Glebe View PL17 . . . . .39 E5
Glebelands
  Callington PL17 . . . . .39 E5
  Looe PL13 . . . . .117 D5
Glen Dale Cres TR15 . . . .140 D4
Glen Leigh TR15 . . . . .140 A6
Glen Park Ave PL4 . . . . . .148 C4
Glen Park Prim Sch
  PL7 . . . . .131 B5
Glen Pk PL14 . . . . .38 D4
Glen Rd
  Plymouth, Mannamead
    PL3 . . . . .128 F5
  Plymouth, Plympton PL7 . .130 F6
  Wadebridge PL27 . . . . . .108 B5
Glen Vale TR15 . . . . .139 E6

Glen View Par PL24 . . . . . .60 D5
  Penryn TR10 . . . . .144 B8
  Wadebridge PL27 . . . . . .108 B4
Glen-Dale Cl 3 PL25 . . . .115 A5
Glen-Dale Cres PL25 . . . .115 A5
Glenavon Rd PL3 . . . . . . .128 E6
Glenburn Cl PL3 . . . . .128 E7
Glendale Cres TR4 . . . . . . .68 C6
Glendale Terr PL26 . . . . . .58 E3
Glendower Rd PL3 . . . . . .128 D5
Gleneagle Ave 4 PL3 . . . .128 F6
Gleneagle Rd PL3 . . . . . . .128 F6
Gleneagle Villas 5 PL3 . .128 F6
Glenfeadon Terr TR16 . . . .67 C6
Glenfield Cl PL6 . . . . .125 D6
Glenfield Rd PL6 . . . . .125 D5
Glenfield Way PL6 . . . . . .125 D6
Glenholt Cl PL6 . . . . .125 D6
Glenholt Rd PL6 . . . . .125 D6
Glenhurst Rd 5 PL3 . . . . .128 E6
Glenmoor La TR12 . . . . . . .99 A1
Glenmore Ave PL2 . . . . . .127 F5
Glenmore Terr PL14 . . . . .113 D6
Glenthorne Rd TR3 . . . . . .69 C3
Glentor Rd PL3 . . . . .128 E7
Glentowan Rd PL26 . . . . . .73 C6
Glenview PL25 . . . . .114 B3
Glenwood Rd PL3 . . . . . . .128 E6
Globe Vale Cvn Pk TR16 . .68 B3
Globerdon Rd PL14 . . . . . .38 A4
Gloucester Ave PL25 . . . .115 C3
Gloucester Cres TR18 . . .143 B1
Gloucester Ct PL1 . . . . . .148 C4
Gloucester Pl
  25 Newlyn TR18 . . . . . . .143 C2
  Plymouth PL1 . . . . .148 B1
Gloucester Rd TR18 . . . . .143 C2
Gloweth View TR1 . . . . . . .69 E3
Gloweth Villas TR1 . . . . . .69 E3
Gluyas The TR11 . . . . . . .144 E1
Glyn Way TR3 . . . . .69 D3
Glynn Ave 7 TR13 . . . . . .146 C5
Glynn Rd Liskeard PL14 . .113 C6
  Padstow PL28 . . . . .107 D5
Goad Ave Plymouth PL4 . .149 C2
  Torpoint PL11 . . . . .126 E3
Goad Cl PL11 . . . . .126 E3
Godding Gdns PL6 . . . . . .124 E6
Godolphin Ave PL17 . . . . .89 B5
Godolphin Cl TR17 . . . . . .89 B6
Godolphin Cres TR11 . . . .90 E6
Godolphin Ct 5 TR14 . . . .138 D3
Godolphin Dr TR17 . . . . . .89 B5
Godolphin Ho★ TR13 . . . . .90 E6
Godolphin Pk 11 PL17 . . . .39 E4
Godolphin Pl TR17 . . . . . .89 B5
Godolphin Prim Sch
  TR13 . . . . .90 E6
Godolphin Rd
  Falmouth TR11 . . . . .144 F5
  Helston TR13 . . . . .146 C6
  Longrock TR20 . . . . .88 F6
Godolphin Terr TR17 . . . . .89 B5
Godolphin Way TR7 . . . . .111 B7
Godrevy Ct TR26 . . . . . . .141 D6
Godrevy Ho TR11 . . . . . . .69 E4
Godrevy Pk (Cvn Pk)
  TR27 . . . . .66 B1
Godrevy Terr 28 TR26 . . .141 B6
Goldbank Bglws PL30 . . . .34 C2
Golden Sands Bglws
  TR27 . . . . .142 E7
Goldfinch Cl PL15 . . . . . .106 E4
Goldfinch Cres PL12 . . . .122 E4
Goldfinch Gr PL12 . . . . . .122 D4
Goldmartin Cl TR11 . . . . . .93 D3
Goldsmith Gdns PL5 . . . .124 D3
Goldsworthy Way PL27 . .108 B5
Golf House Rd EX23 . . . . .104 D6
Golf Terr TR7 . . . . .110 C6
Golitha Falls★ PL14 . . . . . .37 B3
Gonvena Hill PL27 . . . . . .108 D6
Goodeve Cl PL9 . . . . .135 E6
Goodmans La PL14 . . . . . .38 D4
Goodmartin Sq TR11 . . . . .93 D3
Goodwin Ave PL6 . . . . . . .125 A6
Goodwin Cres PL2 . . . . . .128 A6
Goongumpas La TR16 . . . .68 E1
Goonhavern Prim Sch
  TR4 . . . . .55 D4
Goonhilly Earth Sta★
  TR12 . . . . .99 F4
Goonown La TR5 . . . . .54 D1
Goonown Rd
  Goonbell TR5 . . . . .68 D8
  St Agnes TR5 . . . . .54 D1
Goonrea PL13 . . . . .117 B4
Goonvrea TR3 . . . . .81 D5
Goonvrea Cl TR7 . . . . . . .110 F4
Goonvrea Rd TR5 . . . . . . .54 C1
Goonwartha Cl PL13 . . . .117 C4
Goonwartha Rd PL13 . . . .117 B3
Gooseberry La
  Pensilva PL14 . . . . .38 E4
  Plymouth PL1 . . . . .148 B2
Gooseford La PL11 . . . . . .132 C8
Goosewell Hill PL6 . . . . . .129 C8
Goosewell Park Rd PL9 . .135 F6
Goosewell Prim Sch
  PL9 . . . . .135 F6
Goosewell Rd PL9 . . . . . .135 F6
Goosewell Terr PL9 . . . . .135 F6
Gordon Ct PL12 . . . . .122 D2
Gordon Pl 8 TR9 . . . . .45 E6
Gordon Terr PL4 . . . . .128 E4

Gordons Cl TR3 . . . . .80 F3
Gorran Sch PL26 . . . . .85 B5
Gorse Cl TR7 . . . . .111 A4
Gorsey Cl PL5 . . . . .124 E2
Gorvin Cross EX39 . . . . . . .3 E6
Goswela Cl PL9 . . . . .135 F5
Goswela Gdns PL9 . . . . . .135 F5
Gotch Gdns PL14 . . . . .50 B6
Gothers Rd St Dennis PL26 .58 D6
  St Dennis, Gothers PL26 . .46 D1
Goudges La PL26 . . . . .58 E3
Gounce The 8 TR6 . . . . . . .55 A5
Gover Cl TR4 . . . . .68 C6
Gover La TR7 . . . . .110 D6
Gover Rd PL25 . . . . .114 B4
Goverseth Cvn Pk PL26 . .58 D6
Goverseth Hill PL26 . . . . .58 D6
Goverseth Rd PL26 . . . . . .58 D6
Goverseth Terr PL26 . . . . .58 D6
Gower Ridge Rd PL9 . . . .135 B6
Goyne's Field TR4 . . . . . . .68 A7
Gracca Terr PL26 . . . . .47 C1
Grade-Ruan Sch TR12 . . .103 B5
Grafton Rd PL4 . . . . .128 E4
Graham Ave PL5 . . . . .124 D1
Graham Rd Redruth TR15 140 C5
  Redruth TR15 . . . . .140 D4
Grainge Rd PL6 . . . . .125 A1
Grampound Rd Village CE
  Sch TR2 . . . . .57 E1
Grampound Road Ind Est
  TR2 . . . . .57 E1
Grampound-with-Creed CE
  Sch TR2 . . . . .72 A7
Granby Ct PL1 . . . . .127 E2
Granby Gn PL1 . . . . .127 E2
Granby Pl PL1 . . . . .127 E2
Granby St PL1 . . . . .127 E2
Granby Way PL1 . . . . .127 E2
Grand Hotel Rd PL1 . . . . .148 B1
Grand Par PL1 . . . . .148 B1
Grange Cotts PL7 . . . . . . .130 F4
Grange Rd Helston TR13 . .146 C6
  Plymouth PL6 . . . . .131 A4
  Yelverton PL20 . . . . .42 C3
Granite Way PL17 . . . . . . .39 E4
Grannery Ct EX23 . . . . . . .104 D5
Granny's Gn PL31 . . . . . . .109 E3
Granny's La TR6 . . . . .55 A4
Grant's Cl PL25 . . . . .114 C3
Grant's Wlk 4 PL25 . . . . .114 C3
Grantham Cl PL7 . . . . . . .130 B4
Grantley Gdns PL3 . . . . . .129 A5
Granville Terr EX23 . . . . .104 D5
Grasmere Cl PL6 . . . . . . .124 E5
Grasmere La PL14 . . . . . . .38 E5
Grass Valley Pk PL31 . . . .109 F4
Grassendale Ave PL2 . . . .127 F7
Grassmere Way PL12 . . . .122 D4
Gratton Cross PL20 . . . . . .42 D2
Gratton La PL20 . . . . .42 D2
Gravesend Gdns PL11 . . .127 B3
Gravesend Wlk PL5 . . . . .123 D4
Gray Cres PL5 . . . . .127 C8
Graybridge Rd PL20 . . . . . .42 C4
Great Berry Rd PL6 . . . . .124 F1
Great Charles Cl PL26 . . .58 D6
Great Churchway PL9 . . . .136 A4
Great Mdw PL14 . . . . .36 F2
Great Mis Tor Cl 5 PL20 . .42 C3
Great Orchard Cl PL9 . . . .135 E5
Great Park Cl 4 PL7 . . . . .131 C4
Great Western Commercial
  Village PL22 . . . . .112 D2
Great Western Rd PL1 . . .148 B1
Great Wheal Seton
  TR14 . . . . .138 F6
Great Woodford Dr PL7 . .130 B6
Greatfield Rd PL3 . . . . . . .129 B7
Greatlands Cres PL2 . . . .128 A6
Greatlands Pl 5 PL2 . . . . .128 A5
Greatwood TR11 . . . . .82 C3
Grebe Cl PL7 . . . . .130 F5
Greeb Way TR20 . . . . .89 D4
Green Acre PL15 . . . . .28 A5
Green Cl Feock TR3 . . . . . .82 C5
  Truro TR1 . . . . .137 B3
Green Cres TR13 . . . . .146 E6
Green Hill Lamerton PL19 .30 A3
  St Martin TR12 . . . . .100 D6
  Tavistock PL19 . . . . .147 D5
  Wadebridge PL27 . . . . . .108 C5
Green Hill Terr TR12 . . . . .100 D6
Green Hill Villas PL12 . . .100 D6
Green La Bodmin PL31 . . .109 F2
  Boscastle PL35 . . . . .9 C1
  Cawsand PL10 . . . . .133 A2
  Crantock TR8 . . . . .43 D3
  Fowey PL23 . . . . .116 C5
  Gwithian TR27 . . . . .66 B2
  Lelant TR26 . . . . .77 E4
  Marazion TR17 . . . . .89 B6
  Penryn TR10 . . . . .144 B8
  Porthleven TR13 . . . . .91 B1
  Portreath TR16 . . . . .67 C6
  Redruth TR15 . . . . .140 B5
  Redruth, Wheal Rose TR16 .68 C4
  Rock PL27 . . . . .21 D2
  Ruan Minor TR12 . . . . . . .103 A2
  Tavistock PL19 . . . . .147 E5
  Truro TR1 . . . . .137 B3
  Veryan TR2 . . . . .83 F6
  Yelverton PL20 . . . . .42 C1
Green La The TR27 . . . . . .77 F1
Green La W TR17 . . . . .89 A6
Green Lane Cl TR10 . . . . .144 B8
Green Lane Hill TR18 . . . .143 B6
Green Lane Vean TR15 . . .140 B5

Green Mdws PL32 . . . . . .105 C4
Green Park Ave PL4 . . . . .128 D4
Green Park Rd PL9 . . . . . .135 C5
Green Pk PL10 . . . . .133 A2
Green St Penzance TR18 .143 F4
  Truro TR1 . . . . .137 D4
Green The Bridgerule EX22 .8 A5
  Carnon Downs TR3 . . . . . .82 A5
  Cawsand PL10 . . . . .133 A2
  6 Horrabridge PL20 . . . . .42 C5
  Liskeard PL14 . . . . .113 B5
  Meavy PL20 . . . . .42 F2
  Milton Combe PL20 . . . . .120 F8
  Nancegollan TR13 . . . . . .91 B7
  Plymouth PL9 . . . . .135 B6
  Probus TR2 . . . . .71 C6
  Saltash PL12 . . . . .122 C3
  St Martin TR12 . . . . .100 D6
  6 Trewoon PL25 . . . . . . .59 A3
Greenacres Bodmin PL30 .34 C2
  Plymouth PL9 . . . . .135 F6
Greenbank
  Connor Downs TR27 . . . . .78 D6
  1 Penzance TR18 . . . . . .143 D5
  Polruan PL23 . . . . .116 D2
Greenbank Ave PL4 . . . . .149 B3
Greenbank Cl TR7 . . . . . . .57 E1
Greenbank Cres TR7 . . . .111 C7
Greenbank La PL14 . . . . .113 C6
Greenbank Rd
  Devoran TR3 . . . . .81 F6
  Liskeard PL14 . . . . .113 C6
  Plymouth PL4 . . . . .149 B4
Greenbank Terr
  1 Callington PL17 . . . . . .39 F4
  Plymouth PL4 . . . . .149 B4
  Yelverton PL20 . . . . .42 D3
Greenbanks Ct PL27 . . . . .21 E2
Greenbanks Rd PL27 . . . . .21 E2
Greendale Rd PL2 . . . . . .128 A7
Greenfield Cl 2 TR12 . . . .102 F2
Greenfield Rd PL12 . . . . .122 D2
Greenfield Terr TR16 . . . . .67 C6
Greenhill Cl PL9 . . . . .135 F5
Greenhills PL32 . . . . .105 C5
Greenland PL10 . . . . .132 F5
Greenlees Dr PL7 . . . . . . .131 B3
Greenmarket The 26
  TR18 . . . . .143 E5
Greens The Sennen TR19 . .96 C7
  Sennen Cove TR19 . . . . . .86 E1
Greensplat Rd PL25 . . . . .114 A6
Greensway Rd PL19 . . . . .147 A4
Greenway Ave PL7 . . . . . .130 B6
Greenway Cl 3 PL20 . . . . .42 C5
Greenwich Pl PL12 . . . . . .122 F3
Greenwith Cl TR1 . . . . . . .137 B3
Greenwith Cres TR3 . . . . .81 D6
Greenwith Hill TR3 . . . . . .81 D6
Greenwith Rd TR3 . . . . . . .81 D6
Greenwood Cres TR10 . . .144 A8
Greenwood Park Cl PL7 . .131 B6
Greenwood Park Rd
  PL7 . . . . .131 B6
Greenwood Rd TR10 . . . .144 A8
Gregor Rd TR1 . . . . .137 F5
Gregory's Ct 10 PL31 . . . .109 D5
Gregory's Mdw PL15 . . . .106 C3
Grenfell Ave PL12 . . . . . .122 D3
Grenfell Gdns PL12 . . . . .122 C3
Grenfell St 18 TR15 . . . . . .88 C1
Grenifer Rd TR15 . . . . . . .139 D7
Grenna La TR3 . . . . .81 D7
Grenofen Cl PL19 . . . . . . .42 A6
Grenville Cl 16 PL17 . . . . .39 F4
Grenville Cres TR11 . . . . .144 F5
Grenville Ct
  Plymouth PL7 . . . . .131 C6
  2 St Austell PL25 . . . . . .114 C3
Grenville Dr
  6 St Agnes TR5 . . . . .54 D1
  Tavistock PL19 . . . . .147 B3
Grenville Gdns TR14 . . . . .79 E5
Grenville Mdws PL12 . . . .112 C2
Grenville Pk PL20 . . . . . . .42 D2
Grenville Rd
  Falmouth TR11 . . . . .145 A5
  Helston TR13 . . . . .146 D5
  Lostwithiel PL22 . . . . . . .112 D2
  Padstow PL28 . . . . .107 C4
  Plymouth PL4 . . . . .149 C3
  Truro TR1 . . . . .137 B5
Grenville Road La S
  PL4 . . . . .129 B2
Grenville Wlk PL13 . . . . . .62 D2
Gresham Cl
  Newquay TR7 . . . . .110 F4
  Plymouth PL5 . . . . .124 C2
Greys Terr 1 TR16 . . . . . .140 F1
Greystoke Ave PL6 . . . . . .129 D7
Gribbas Cl TR3 . . . . .80 F3
Gribben Cl PL25 . . . . .114 E6
Gribben Rd PL25 . . . . .114 E6
Gribbin The PL14 . . . . . . .113 D6
Griffin Way PL9 . . . . .136 C6
Griffins The PL14 . . . . . . .113 D6
Griggs Cl PL7 . . . . .131 B4
Griggs Hill TR27 . . . . .77 E3
Grimscott Est EX23 . . . . . .5 B2
Grimspound Cl PL6 . . . . .129 E8
Grimstone Terr PL20 . . . . .42 B2
Grist La TR27 . . . . .78 C5
Grizedale Rd PL6 . . . . . . .129 D7
Grose Hill Cres 10 PL26 . .59 D7
Grose Mdws PL26 . . . . . . .58 B8
Grosvenor Ave TR7 . . . . .110 E6
Grosvenor Cotts 1 PL4 . .128 F4
Grosvenor Pl PL25 . . . . . .114 B4

Grosvenor Rd PL6 ....124 F2
Grove Cotts TR2 ....57 C1
Grove Dr 4 PL14 ......51 A7
Grove Hill
  Mawnan Smith TR11 .....93 D3
  St Mawes TR2 ....95 A6
Grove La TR20 ....89 F5
Grove Park Ct PL14 ...113 B4
Grove Pk Par PL24 ......60 C6
  Tavistock PL19 ....147 D5
  Torpoint PL11 ....126 E3
Grove Pl
  3 Falmouth TR11 .....145 C3
  Padstow PL28 ....107 D5
Grove Rd Par PL24 ....115 F6
  St Austell PL25 ....114 B4
Grove The
  Plymouth, Plymstock PL9 .135 D8
  Plymouth, Stoke PL3 ...128 A4
Grovehill Cres TR11 ...145 C3
Grovehill Dr TR11 .....145 C3
Grovehill Ho TR11 .....145 C3
Grylls Parc TR13 ......146 B6
Gue The 2 TR13 ....98 C8
Guildford Cl PL5 ......124 C3
Guildford Rd TR27 ....142 E7
Guildford Road Ind Est
  TR27 ....142 E6
Guildford St PL4 ......149 A3
Guildhall La PL22 .....112 C2
Guildhall Sq PL1 ......148 C2
Guineaport Parc PL27 .108 C5
Guineaport Rd PL27 ...108 C5
Guipavas Rd PL17 ......39 F4
Gulland Rd PL27 ....21 D6
Gully's La PL26 ....58 B8
Gulval Almshouses
  TR18 ....143 F8
Gulval Com Prim Sch
  TR18 ....88 E6
Gulworthy Cotts PL19 ..41 B7
Gulworthy Cross PL19 ..41 B7
Gulworthy Prim Sch
  PL19 ....41 B7
Gunnislake Prim Sch
  PL18 ....40 F6
Gunnislake Rural Workshops
  PL18 ....40 F6
Gunnislake Sta PL18 ...40 F5
Gunpool La 9 PL35 .....9 C1
Gunwennap PL32 ....10 B2
Gurlyn Hill TR20 ....90 A7
Gurnard Wlk PL3 ......129 C6
Gurney Cl Bude EX23 ..104 F2
  Torpoint PL11 ....126 F3
Gurney's La 2 TR14 ..138 D3
Gurnick Est TR18 .....143 B6
Gurnick Rd TR18 ......143 B1
Gurnick St 23 TR19 ....88 C1
Gustavus Rd TR14 .....138 D3
Gustory Rd PL28 ....43 D3
Guy Miles Way PL5 ....124 B3
Gwallon La TR17 ....89 C6
Gwallon Rd PL25 ......114 C5
Gwarnick Rd PL7 ......137 B4
Gwarth An Drae TR13 .146 C8
Gwarth An Ore TR27 ..142 E8
Gwavas Bglws 4 TR18 .143 C1
Gwavas La TR18 ....88 C2
Gwavas Quay 7 TR18 .143 C2
Gwavas Rd TR18 ....143 C1
Gwavas St 10 TR18 ....143 E6
Gweal Darras TR10 .....81 C1
Gweal Gollas TR27 ....142 E8
Gweal Wartha TR13 ...146 B8
Gweal-An-Top TR15 ...140 D5
Gweal-an-Top Inf Sch
  TR15 ....140 C5
Gwealdues TR13 ......146 D7
Gwealfolds Rd TR13 ..146 C7
Gwealhellis Warren
  TR13 ....146 B7
Gwedhennek TR18 .....143 F7
Gweek Dr Gweek TR12 ..92 C1
  Mawgan TR12 ....99 D8
Gweek La TR13 ....92 A3
Gwel An Garrek 2 TR12 .99 A1
Gwel An Wheal TR26 ..141 A4
Gwel An Wheal Cres
  TR26 ....141 A4
Gwel Avon Bsns Pk
  PL12 ....122 D4
Gwel Lewern TR18 ......88 E6
Gwel Marten Flats TR26 141 E2
Gwel Mengleth PL27 ..108 D5
Gwel Trencrom TR27 ..142 B3
Gwel-an-mor
  Marazion TR17 ....89 C5
  St Austell PL25 ......115 A5
  Trenance TR8 ....31 C2
Gwel-An-Nans Cl 2
  PL14 ....113 B5
Gwel-An-Scol TR3 ......82 C5
Gwel-Mor TR19 ....75 A1
Gwel-Tek TR27 ....142 D8
Gwelanmor Cl TR26 ...141 D2
Gwelanmor Rd TR26 ..141 D2
Gwelavon Cl PL27 .....108 C5
Gwelenys Rd 3 TR19 ...88 C1
Gwell-An-Nans TR2 ....71 C6
Gwelmeneth Pk 8 PL14 .38 A3
Gwelmor TR14 ....138 E2
Gwendra La PL26 ....58 E8
Gwendroc Cl TR1 ......137 D3
Gwendroc House Mews
  TR1 ....137 D3

Gwendrona Cl TR13 ...146 D8
Gwendrona Way TR13 .146 D8
Gwennap Pit* TR16 ...140 F4
Gwindra Ind Est PL26 ..58 C3
Gwindra Rd PL26 ....58 B4
Gwinear Com Prim Sch
  TR27 ....78 E4
Gwinear La TR27 ....78 E4
Gwinear Rd TR27 ......78 E5
Gwithian Cl PL11 .....126 F4
Gwithian Rd
  Connor Downs TR27 ....78 D6
  Gwithian TR27 ....66 C1
Gwithian Sands Chalet Pk
  TR27 ....66 B1
Gwyn Rd PL4 ....149 C4
Gwythian Way TR6 .....55 A4
Gyllyng Hall TR11 ....145 B3
Gyllyng St TR11 ......145 B4
Gyllyngvase Hill TR11 .145 B2
Gyllyngvase Rd TR11 ..145 B2
Gyllyngvase Terr TR11 .145 C2
Gypsy La PL33 ....14 C1

H

Haddington Rd PL2 ...127 F4
Haddon Way PL25 .....115 D3
Haig Pl 6 TR18 ....143 C7
Hain Wlk TR26 ....141 C4
Halcyon Ct PL2 ....128 A6
Halcyon Rd PL2 ....128 A6
Haldon Pl PL5 ....124 A3
Haley Barton 4 PL2 ..128 A5
Halgavor Pl PL31 .....109 F1
Halgavor Rd PL30,PL31 .109 D2
Halgavor View PL31 ..109 F2
Halifax Rd PL27 ....31 F3
Halimote Rd PL26 ......58 C8
Hall Loft Flats 2 TR26 141 B6
Hall Rd PL26 ....58 C8
Hall Terr PL23 ....116 C5
Hallan Vean TR19 ......96 A5
Hallane Rd PL25 ......115 A6
Hallaze Rd PL26 ....59 D7
Hallerton Cl PL15 ....126 E2
Hallett Cl PL12 ......122 B3
Hallett Way EX23 .....104 F7
Hallew Rd PL25 ....58 C7
Halley Gdns PL5 ......123 E1
Halloon Ave TR9 ....45 E2
Halt Rd Goonhavern TR4 ..55 D4
  St Newlyn East TR8 ....56 B7
Halvarras Pk TR3 ......82 B8
Halvarras Rd TR3 ......82 B8
Halveor Cl 5 TR9 ......45 E6
Halveor Ct TR6 ....55 B5
Halveor La TR9 ....45 D6
Halwin La TR13 ....92 B8
Halwin Prim Sch TR13 .92 C8
Halwyn Cl 12 TR3 ......81 F7
Halwyn Hill TR8 ......110 A3
Halwyn Pl TR1 ....137 B4
Halwyn Rd TR1 ....110 A3
Ham Cl PL2 ....128 B8
Ham Dr PL2 ....128 B8
Ham Gn PL2 ....128 A7
Ham Green Ct PL2 ....128 A7
Ham Green La PL2 ....128 A7
Ham Ho PL2 ....128 A8
Ham La PL2 ....128 A8
Hamble Cl PL3 ....129 D7
Hamilton Cl TR27 ....142 B4
Hamilton Gdns PL4 ...128 C4
Hamilton Pl TR11 ....145 D3
Hammill's Cl 13 TR13 ..98 C8
Hammills Dr 2 TR13 ...98 C8
Hamoaze Ave PL5 ....127 D8
Hamoaze Pl PL1 ......127 D2
Hamoaze Rd PL11 ....127 B2
Hampton St PL4 ......149 A3
Hancock Cl PL6 ......124 D6
Hancock La 14 TR2 ....95 A6
Hangmans Wlk TR11 ..145 A1
Hannaford Pl PL16 ....19 C3
Hannafore Cl PL13 ...117 C3
Hannafore La PL13 ...117 D2
Hannafore Rd PL13 ..117 D2
Hanover Cl
  10 Perranporth TR6 ...55 A5
  Plymouth PL3 ....129 B5
Hanover Ct
  Camborne TR14 ....138 E4
  12 Penzance TR18 ....143 E5
  16 Plymouth PL1 .....149 A2
Hanover Ho EX23 ....4 D4
Hanover Pk TR9 ....45 F2
Hanover Rd PL3 ......129 C4
Hanson Dr PL23 ......116 C3
Hanson Rd PL14 ......113 D6
Harbour Ave
  Plymouth PL4 ....149 A2
  Plymouth, Camels Head
  PL5 ....127 E8
Harbour Ct
  Falmouth TR11 ....145 B4
  15 Penzance TR18 ...143 E5
  Portreath TR16 ....67 C6
Harbour Ct Flats TR2 ..83 C2
Harbour Lights 11 TR18 143 C1
Harbour Rd Par PL24 ..60 C4
  Porthleven TR13 ......98 B4
  Wadebridge PL27 .....108 C5
Harbour St PL11 ......127 B3
Harbour Terr
  Falmouth TR11 ....145 B5
  Portreath TR16 ....67 C6

Harbour View
  Fowey PL23 ....116 C4
  Hayle TR17 ....142 B5
  Marazion TR17 ....89 B5
  Penryn TR10 ....144 B8
  Plymouth PL9 ....135 A7
  5 Porthleven TR13 ...98 B8
  Saltash PL12 ....122 C2
  Truro TR1 ....137 E3
Harbour View Cres
  TR18 ....143 E6
Harbourside 12 TR13 ..98 B8
Harcourt Cl TR1 ....69 F3
Hardisworthy Cross EX39 .2 C7
Hardy Cres PL5 ....124 E1
Hardy Ho TR3 ....80 F3
Harebell Cl PL12 .....122 D4
Harefield Cres TR14 .138 D4
Hareston Cl PL7 ......131 B3
Harewood Cl PL7 .....130 E5
Harewood Cres PL5 ..124 E4
Harewood Rd PL18 .....41 A3
Hargood Terr 6 PL2 ..127 F4
Hargreaves Cl PL5 ...123 F2
Harlech Cl PL3 ....129 A7
Harleigh Rd PL31 ....109 E3
Harleigh Terr PL31 ..109 E3
Harlyn Barton PL28 ...20 D2
Harlyn Cotts PL28 ....20 D2
Harlyn Rd PL28 ....20 D1
Harmer Cl PL31 ......109 D6
Harmony Cl
  Redruth TR15 ....140 B6
  Roche PL26 ....46 F3
Harmony Mdw PL26 ...46 F3
Harmony Rd PL26 ......46 F3
Harmony Terr
  4 Illogan TR16 ....67 E4
  Truro TR1 ....137 E2
Harnorlen Rd PL2 ....128 D7
Haroldsleigh Ave PL5 124 E2
Harriet Gdns PL7 ....130 B6
Harris Cl PL7 ....39 F6
  Plymouth PL9 ....135 B6
Harris Ct 1 Penryn TR10 144 C7
Harrison St 7 PL2 ...127 F4
Harrison Terr TR1 ...137 B4
Harrowbarrow Sch PL17 .40 D4
Harrowbeer La PL20 ...42 C3
Hartland Cl PL6 ......125 A7
Hartland Rd PL6 ......22 E7
Hartland Terr EX23 ..104 D6
Hartley Ave PL3 ......129 A6
Hartley Ct PL3 ....129 A6
Hartley Park Gdns PL3 128 F6
Hartley Rd PL3 ....128 E6
Hartmeade PL14 ....52 A5
Hartwell Ave PL9 ....136 D7
Harvenna Cl TR9 ......45 E1
Harvey Ave PL4 ......129 A4
Harvey Rd TR1 ....137 D2
Harvey's Way TR27 ..142 C5
Harwell Cl 8 PL1 ....148 B3
Harwell St PL1 ....148 B3
Harwood Ave PL5 ....124 C7
Hastings St PL1 ......148 B3
Hastings Terr PL1 ...148 B3
Haswell Cl PL6 ......129 A8
Hat La PL1 ....132 F2
Hatch's Hill TR27 .....78 C5
Havelock Terr PL2 ...127 F3
Haven Ct TR27 ....142 C5
Haven Pk PL14 ....39 A4
Haven Rd EX23 ....10 C6
Havett Cl PL14 ....50 E8
Hawarden Cotts PL4 .129 B1
Haweswater Cl PL6 ..124 E4
Hawk's Tor Dr PL15 ...27 B7
Hawke Rd TR13 ......146 B4
Hawkens Way 9 TR9 ..45 D6
Hawkers Ave PL4 ....149 A2
Hawkinge Gdns PL5 .123 E4
Hawkins Cl PL6 ......125 A5
Hawkins Ct 2 TR18 ..143 D5
Hawkins Dr TR7 ......110 E5
Hawkins Rd
  Padstow PL28 ....107 C5
  Penzance TR18 ....143 D5
Hawkins Way 12 TR11 145 A4
Hawks Pk PL12 ....122 C2
Hawthorn Ave
  Bude EX23 ....104 E4
  Torpoint PL11 ....126 F3
Hawthorn Cl Bude EX23 104 E4
  Plymouth, Hooe PL9 ..135 C5
  Plymouth, Woolwell PL6 125 D7
  Redruth TR15 ....140 B6
  St Austell PL25 .....114 F6
  7 St Columb Major TR9 45 D6
Hawthorn Gr PL2 .....128 C7
Hawthorn Rd PL19 ...147 C2
Hawthorn Way
  Plymouth PL3 ....129 B7
  Threemilestone TR3 ..69 C3
Hawthorns PL12 ....122 D2
Haxter Cl PL6 ....121 B1
Hay La Looe PL13 ....117 E4
  Sheviock PL11 ....65 B6
Haydon Gr PL5 ....123 C1
Haye Rd Callington PL17 .39 D4
  Plymouth PL7,PL9 ....130 C1
Haye Rd S PL9 ....136 C4
Hayes Rd PL9 ....135 C7
Hayle Com Sch TR27 142 D5
Hayle Ind Pk TR27 ...142 F7

Hayle Rd TR27 ....78 C1
Hayle Sta TR27 ......142 B5
Hayle Terr TR27 .....142 C6
Hayman Way TR11 ....144 B4
Hayne Corfe Gdns TR1 137 A4
Hayston Pl PL1 ......148 B3
Haytor Cl PL5 ....124 B3
Hazel Cl Plymouth PL6 125 B6
  St Austell PL25 .....115 A6
Hazel Dr PL9 ....136 C2
Hazel Gr Plymouth PL9 136 C7
  Yelverton PL20 ....42 D3
Hazel Rd PL19 ....147 C2
Hazelmead PL14 ......113 B5
Hazelwood Cres PL9 .136 D7
Hazelwood Dr PL6 ...125 D8
Hazelwood Rd PL17 ...39 C4
Hea Cl TR18 ....143 C7
Hea Cotts 5 TR18 ...143 B7
Hea Rd TR18 ....143 C7
Heabrook Parc 2 TR18 143 C7
Headland Cl TR26 ...141 E2
Headland Ct TR26 ...141 E2
Headland Pk PL4 ....149 A4
Headland Rd
  Carbis Bay TR26 .....141 E2
  Newquay TR7 ....110 C7
Headleigh Rd TR7 ...110 F5
Headon Cross EX23 ...11 A5
Healy Ct 9 PL4 ......127 E4
Healy Pl 2 PL4 ......127 F4
Heamoor Com Prim Sch
  TR18 ....143 B6
Heanton Terr
  Millbrook PL10 ......132 E6
  Redruth TR15 ....140 C4
Heanton Villas TR15 140 C4
Hearl Rd PL12 ....122 B3
Heath Terr PL18 ......40 F5
Heather Cl
  Heamoor TR18 ....143 B7
  Tavistock PL19 ......147 D4
Heather La 7 TR7 .....77 D2
Heather Mdw TR9 .....45 E1
Heather Way TR20 ....89 F4
Heatherbell Gdns PL26 141 E1
Heathers The PL6 ...125 D7
Heathfield Gdns TR15 140 E4
Heathfield Pk PL20 ...42 D3
Heathfield Rd PL4 ...129 B3
Heathlands Bsns Pk
  PL14 ....113 C5
Heathlands Ind Est 9
  PL14 ....113 C5
Heathlands Rd PL14 .113 C5
Heavitree Rd PL10 ..133 A2
Hedgerow Cl PL6 ....125 E8
Hedgerows The PL12 122 B3
Hedingham Cl PL7 ...131 C4
Hedingham Gdns PL6 125 B7
Helca Dr TR26 ....141 C3
Hele Cross PL15 ......13 C3
Hele Gdns PL7 ....131 A4
Hele La PL6 ....121 F2
Hele Rd PL12 ....7 A4
Hele's Sch PL7 ......130 C6
Hele's Terr PL7 .....129 B2
Helebridge Rd EX23 ...7 A5
Helena 7 PL26 ....59 D7
Helland Rd PL31 .....109 E6
Hellescott Way TR13 146 D8
Hellescott Rd PL15 ...18 B7
Hellesvean 2 TR26 ...77 A6
Hellesvean Ct 3 TR26 77 A6
Helleur Cl 4 PL24 ....60 B4
Helman Tor View PL31 109 E2
Helnoweth Cotts TR18 143 F8
Helnoweth Gdns TR18 143 F8
Helnoweth Hill TR18 143 F8
Helscott Rd EX23 ......7 A6
Helston Com Hospl
  TR13 ....146 D3
Helston Mus* TR13 ..146 B5
Helston Rd TR10 ....144 C8
Helston Sch & Com Coll
  TR13 ....146 C2
Hembal Cl 5 PL25 ....59 A3
Hembal La PL25 ......59 A3
Hembal Rd 4 PL25 ...59 A3
Hemerdon Hts PL7 ..131 A6
Hemerdon La PL7 ....131 C8
Hemerdon Way PL7 ..130 D6
Hen Wythva TR14 ....138 E2
Henders Cnr 6 PL3 ..128 F6
Henderson Pl PL2 ...127 F6
Hendra Barton TR1 ..137 B5
Hendra Cl Ashton TR13 90 E3
  Stithians TR3 ....80 E4
  5 Truro TR1 ....137 C5
Hendra Gdns PL15 ...106 B5
Hendra Holiday Pk TR8 111 C3
Hendra La Ashton TR13 90 D2
  Truro TR1 ....137 C5
Hendra Parc PL14 ...113 E7
Hendra Pk PL15 .....106 C5
Hendra Prazey PL26 ..58 B8
Hendra Rd St Dennis PL26 58 C8
  Stithians TR3 ....80 E4
  Truro TR1 ....137 C5
Hendra Terr TR3 ......80 E4
Hendra Tor View PL15 .26 C7
Hendra Vale PL15 ...106 B4
Hendra Vean
  Carbis Bay TR26 .....141 E1
  Truro TR1 ....137 B5
Hendras Ct TR26 ....141 E2
Hendras Parc TR26 .141 D2

Hendrawna La TR6 .....55 B4
Hendwell Cl PL6 .....124 E6
Henfor Cl 12 TR17 ....89 C5
Henfor Mews 6 TR17 ..89 C5
Henfor Terr 13 TR17 ..89 C5
Henfordh Grange PL14 113 A6
Hengar La PL30 ....23 F3
Henley Cl TR4 ....68 C6
Henley Cres TR4 .....68 C6
Henley Dr
  Mount Hawke TR4 .....68 C6
  Plymouth PL5 ....124 C7
Henliston Dr 3 TR13 146 C4
Henry Scott Tuke Ho 5
  TR11 ....145 A4
Hensbury La PL20 ....119 F4
Henscol TR16 ....80 D6
Henscol Vale PL14 ..113 A6
Henshorn Ct TR13 ...146 C2
Hental 3 PL4 ....55 A4
Hentervene Cvn & Camping
  Pk EX23 ....10 C5
Henver Cl TR27 ....78 E3
Henver Gdns TR27 ....78 E3
Henver La TR4 ....56 A3
Henver Rd TR7 ......111 B7
Henver Rd TR15 .....140 D6
Henvor Terr TR15 ...140 E7
Henwood Cres TR7 ..111 B7
Herbert Pl PL2 ......127 E4
Herbert St PL2 ......127 E4
Hereford Rd PL5 ....124 B5
Heritage Cl PL12 ....122 C3
Herland Hill TR27 ....78 D4
Herland Rd PL13 ......90 E6
Hermes Cl TR13 .....146 C4
Hermes Rd TR13 ....146 C4
Hermitage Rd
  Plymouth PL3 ....128 E5
  Roche PL26 ....46 F3
Heron Cl Millbrook PL10 132 F6
  Tresillian TR2 ....70 F5
Heron Way TR1 ......137 E1
Herons Ct 7 TR6 .....55 A5
Herring Cl PL14 .....113 C4
Herring Rd PL14 ....113 D7
Herschel Gdns PL5 ..123 E1
Hersham Cross EX23 ...5 B2
Hertland Wlk PL2 ...128 A7
Hessary Dr PL6 .....121 C1
Hessary Ho PL14 ...113 D6
Hessary View
  Saltash PL12 ....122 E4
  Tavistock PL19 ......147 B6
Hessenford Rd PL13,PL11 64 B6
Hetling Ct PL1 ......148 B3
Hewer's Row PL4 ....149 A3
Hewitt Cl PL12 ......122 C1
Hexham Pl PL2 ......128 A8
Hexton Hill Rd PL9 .135 B6
Heybrook Ave PL5 ..123 D1
Hgher Boskerris TR26 141 D1
Hibernia Rd TR13 ...146 B4
Hibernia Terr PL1 ..127 E8
Hichens La TR11 ....145 A5
Hichens Rd TR13 ...146 D4
Hick's La PL4 ....149 A2
Hickory Dr PL7 .....131 B5
Hicks Cl TR2 ....71 C6
Hidden Valley Adventure
  Pk* PL15 ....18 A3
High Cross Lanivet PL30 47 E5
  Porth Navas TR11 .....93 A4
  12 St Columb Major TR9 45 D6
  Truro TR1 ....137 D4
High Cross St PL25 .114 C4
High Field Rd TR4 ...68 C6
High Lanes Cubert TR8 55 E8
  Hayle TR27 ....142 C5
High St Boscastle PL35 .9 C1
  Camelford PL32 .....105 C3
  Chacewater TR4 ......68 F3
  Delabole PL33 ....14 D3
  Falmouth TR11 ......145 B5
  Launceston PL15 ....106 C6
  Padstow PL28 ....107 D5
  Penzance TR18 ......143 E5
  3 Plymouth PL1 .....149 A2
  Plymouth, Stonehouse PL1 128 A2
  Probus TR2 ....71 C6
  St Ives TR26 ....141 B6
  St Keverne TR12 ....101 C4
High Street & Waterloo
  Street Flats PL1 ...128 A1
High Street Ind Est PL26 58 D3
High Trip La
  Downgate PL17 ....39 F7
  Kelly Bray PL17 ......40 A8
Highbank Cl PL19 ...147 A4
Highburrow 24 TR13 ..98 C8
Highburrow La TR15 139 C5
Highbury PL17 ....38 E8
Highbury Cres PL7 ..130 C4
Highclere Gdns PL6 .125 B8
Highcliffe PL27 ......21 D3
Higher Albion Row TR16 80 F8
Higher Anderton Rd
  PL10 ....132 F5
Higher Beech Terr
  PL13 ....117 C4
Higher Bodiniel Rd
  PL31 ....109 C7
Higher Bolenna 14 TR6 55 A4
Higher Bore St PL31 109 C5
Higher Bridge Pk PL27 108 D5

Higher Broad La TR15 . .139 D7
Higher Bugle Bugle PL26 . .47 C1
Stenalees PL26 . . . . .59 C8
Higher Burrow TR2 . . . .141 A4
Higher Chapel St PL13 .117 D3
Higher Church St TR27 .142 D6
Higher Churchway PL9 .136 A7
Higher Cleaverfield
PL15 . . . . .106 C7
Higher Compton Rd
PL3 . . . . .128 F6
Higher Cotts TR2 . . . . .57 C1
Higher Cross La PL32 . .105 E4
Higher Daws La PL15 . . .18 E4
Higher East St **9** TR9 . .45 E6
Higher Efford Rd PL3 . .129 B5
Higher Elms TR27 . . . .21 F3
Higher Fernleigh Rd
PL27 . . . . .108 C4
Higher Fore St
Marazion TR17 . . . . .89 C5
Redruth TR15 . . . . .140 C5
Higher Glen Pk PL14 . . .38 D4
Higher Goongumpas La
TR16 . . . . .68 F1
Higher Green St TR18 . .143 D1
Higher Gwavas Rd **3**
TR18 . . . . .143 C1
Higher Kelly PL18 . . . .41 A3
Higher La Ashton TR13 . . .90 E3
Mawgan TR12 . . . . .99 D7
Plymouth PL1 . . . . . . .148 C2
Wadebridge PL27 . . . . .108 E4
Wadebridge PL27 . . . . .108 E5
Higher Larigan TR18 . .143 D4
Higher Lavorrick PL26 . .73 C4
Higher Lidden Rd TR15 .143 C3
Higher Lux PL14 . . . . .113 C6
Higher Market St
Looe PL13 . . . . .117 D3
Penryn TR10 . . . . .144 C7
Higher Mdw PL14 . . . . .50 E7
Higher Medrose PL33 . . .14 E3
Higher Middle Hill PL14 . .38 D4
Higher Mount Ambrose La
TR15 . . . . .140 D6
Higher Mowles PL3 . . .129 B6
Higher Newham TR1 137 D2
Higher Park Cl PL7 . . .131 B3
Higher Park Stenak TR16 80 F8
Higher Pengegon TR14 .138 F2
Higher Penponds Rd
TR14 . . . . .79 B5
Higher Peverell Rd
TR18 . . . . .143 E7
Higher Polsue Way TR2 . .70 F5
Higher Port View PL12 .122 F2
Higher Pumpfield Row
TR15 . . . . .139 B6
Higher Rd Breage TR13 . .90 F3
Pensilva PL14 . . . . .38 D4
Higher Redannick TR1 .137 B3
Higher Row TR13 . . . . .90 D3
Higher Silver Hill TR15 .146 C6
Higher Stennack TR26 .141 A5
Higher Stennack Cotts **13**
TR26 . . . . .141 A5
Higher Stert Terr PL4 . .148 C4
Higher Tamar Terr PL18 . .41 A7
Higher Terr 81 B4
Higher Tower Rd TR7 . .110 C6
Higher Tregenna Rd
TR26 . . . . .141 C3
Higher Trehaverne TR1 .137 C6
Higher Tremena TR1 . .114 C4
Higher Tresavean Terr
TR16 . . . . .80 E6
Higher Trewidden Rd
TR26 . . . . .141 B4
Higher Trezaise PL26 . . .47 A1
Higher Tristram PL27 . .21 D5
Higher Vicarage La **7**
TR12 . . . . .99 A1
Higher Well La TR13 . .146 C6
Higher Well Pk PL26 . . .73 C3
Higher West End PL26 . .73 C3
Higher Whiterock PL27 .108 B5
Higher Woodford La
PL7 . . . . .130 C7
Higher Woodside PL25 .114 A4
Highermoor Cross EX22 . .5 E1
Highertown TR1 . . . . . .69 F3
Highertown Pk PL12 . . .53 C3
Higherwell Cl TR7 . . . .111 A4
Highfield Ave
St Austell PL25 . . . . . . .114 D3
13 St Columb Major TR9 . .45 D6
Highfield Cl
Plymouth PL3 . . . . .129 C5
St Austell PL25 . . . . . . .114 D3
Highfield Est **3** PL14 . . .38 E4
Highfield Park Rd PL15 .106 A5
Highfield Pk PL12 . . . .122 B3
Highfield Prim Sch PL3 .129 C5
Highfield Rd
Camelford PL32 . . . . . . .105 C3
Falmouth TR11 . . . . . . .144 F4
Highfield Rd Ind Est
PL32 . . . . .105 C3
Highgate Hill **1** TR9 . . .45 E1
Highglen Dr PL7 . . . . .131 B7
Highgrove PL15 . . . . . .27 A6
Highland Pk
Penryn TR10 . . . . .144 B8
Redruth TR15 . . . . . . .140 C5

Highview TR4 . . . . .68 E5
Highview Cl PL14 . . . . . .38 A2
Highview Cres TR4 . . . . . .68 E5
Highway PL14 . . . . .50 B6
Highway La TR15 . . . . .140 D7
Higman Cl PL14 . . . . . . .50 E7
Hilgrove Rd TR7 . . . . . .111 A6
Hill Church TR4 . . . . .68 F2
Hill Cl Heamoor TR18 . .143 B7
Plymouth PL7 . . . . .130 D4
St Breward PL30 . . . . . . .24 B3
Hill Crest PL13 . . . . . . .128 E5
Hill Gdns PL12 . . . . . . .119 A2
Hill Hay Cl PL14 . . . . . .116 A4
Hill Head TR10 . . . . . . .144 D6
Hill La PL3 . . . . .128 F7
Hill Park Cres
Plymouth PL4 . . . . .149 A4
St Austell PL25 . . . . . . .114 A2
Hill Park Mews PL4 . . .149 B4
Hill Path PL5 . . . . .123 F5
Hill Pk PL27 . . . . .108 D6
Hill Rd PL27 . . . . .108 C5
Hill St Padstow PL28 . .107 D5
Plymouth PL4 . . . . .149 A3
Hill Top Crest PL5 . . . .123 E2
Hill View PL20 . . . . .41 F3
Hillcrest Helston TR13 .146 C7
Shortlanesend TR4 . . . . . .69 F6
Hillcrest Ave TR1 . . . . .137 A5
Hillcrest Cl Plymouth PL7 131 A5
14 St Columb Major TR9 . .45 E6
Hillcrest Dr PL7 . . . . . .131 A4
Hillcrest Rd TR27 . . . .142 D6
Hilldale PL9 . . . . .135 E6
Hilldean Cl PL5 . . . . . .124 C7
Hillhead TR2 . . . . .95 A6
Hillhead Gdns PL32 . . .105 D4
Hillhead Rd TR11 . . . .144 C5
Hillocks The PL13 . . . .117 D4
Hillpark Cotts PL15 . . .106 C6
Hillsborough **2** PL4 . . .128 E7
Hillsborough Cross EX22 . .8 D7
Hillsdunne Rd PL3 . . . .128 E6
Hillside
Grampound Road TR2 . . . .57 E1
Portreath TR16 . . . . .67 C6
St Austell PL25 . . . . . . .115 B3
Hillside Ave Par PL24 . . .60 B4
Plymouth PL4 . . . . .128 A4
Saltash PL12 . . . . .122 F3
Hillside Bglws TR13 . . . .90 F5
Hillside Cl PL20 . . . . . . .41 F3
Hillside Cres TR18 . . . .143 B7
Bodmin PL31 . . . . .109 C5
Hillside Gdns PL22 . . . .112 C2
Hillside Ind Est 140 E8
Hillside Mdw TR10 . . . .144 D7
Hillside Parc TR20 . . . . .88 B7
Hillside Pk PL31 . . . . . .109 D5
Hillside Rd
Falmouth TR11 . . . . . . .144 F4
Saltash PL12 . . . . .122 F3
St Austell PL25 . . . . . . .114 D5
Hillside Sch PL5 . . . . .124 B4
Hillside Terr
Carharrack TR16 . . . . . . .80 E8
Downderry PL11 . . . . .64 C5
Looe PL13 . . . . .117 D4
20 Redruth TR18 . . . . . .143 C2
2 Redruth TR15 . . . . . .140 C5
Hillson Cl PL27 . . . . . . .22 E7
Hillsview PL13 . . . . .62 D2
Hilton Ave PL5 . . . . . .124 D1
Hilton Rd EX23 . . . . .7 B6
Hingston Ct PL6 . . . . .129 A8
Hirmandale Rd PL5 . . .123 F3
Hobart St PL1 . . . . . . .148 A2
Hobbacott La EX23 . . . . . .7 B6
Hobbs Cres PL12 . . . . .122 C3
Hockens La PL23 . . . . .116 C2
Hodders Way PL12 . . . .119 A2
Hodge Cl PL12 . . . . . .122 C2
Hoe App PL1 . . . . .148 C2
Hoe Ct PL1 . . . . .148 C1
Hoe Rd PL1 . . . . .148 C1
Hoe St PL1 . . . . .148 C1
Hoe The PL1 . . . . .148 C1
Hoegate Cl PL1 . . . . . .148 C2
Hoegate Pl PL1 . . . . . .148 C2
Hoegate St PL1 . . . . . .149 A2
Hogarth Cl PL9 . . . . . .136 B6
Hogarth Wlk PL9 . . . . .136 B6
Holborn Pl PL7 . . . . . .130 E6
Holborn St PL4 . . . . . .149 B2
Holcombe Dr PL9 . . . . .135 F5
Holcroft Cl PL12 . . . . .122 D2
Holdsworth St PL4 . . . .148 B4
Hole Cross PL20 . . . . .119 E7
Holebay Gr PL9 . . . . . .136 A5
Hollabury Rd EX23 . . . .104 F7
Hollacombe Brake PL9 .136 C1
Holland Rd
Plymouth, Chaddlewood
PL7 . . . . .131 D5
Plymouth, Peverell PL3 . . .128 E6
Plymouth, Plymstock PL9 .135 F6
Widegates PL13 . . . . .63 E7
Hollies Rd PL14 . . . . . .106 A7
Hollow's Terr TR27 . . .142 E7
Holloway Gdns PL9 . . .136 A5
Hollowgutter La PL11 . .126 C2
Hollows The PL9 . . . . .136 B8
Holly Cl TR3 . . . . .69 C3
Holly Ct PL6 . . . . .129 C7
Holly Park Cl PL5 . . . .124 A5

Holly Park Dr PL5 . . . .124 A5
Holly Pk TR14 . . . . . . .138 B3
Holly Terr **9** TR18 . . . .143 C7
Hollycroft Rd PL3 . . . .129 A7
Hollywell Bay Fun Pk*
TR8 . . . . .43 C1
Hollywood Terr PL1 . . .148 A3
Holman Ave TR14 . . . .138 C4
Holman Ct PL2 . . . . . .128 C8
Holman Rd PL14 . . . . .113 E6
Holman's Pl **1** TR13 . . .98 C8
Holman's Terr TR16 . . . .80 B5
Holmans Bldgs PL1 . . .127 D2
Holmans Mdw PL15 . . . .19 C1
Holmbush Arch Rd
PL25 . . . . .115 B3
Holmbush Hill PL17 . . . .39 F7
Holmbush Ind Est PL25 .115 B4
Holmbush Rd PL25 . . . .115 C4
Holmer Down PL6 . . . .125 D7
Holmes Ave PL3 . . . . .129 B5
Holmwood Ave PL9 . . .135 C5
Holne Chase PL6 . . . . .125 B7
Holnicote Rd EX23 . . . .104 E5
Holt Cres TR7 . . . . . . .110 D5
Holtwood Rd PL6 . . . . .125 D6
Holwell Cl PL9 . . . . . . .136 A5
Holy Cross RC Prim Sch
PL4 . . . . .149 A3
Holyrood Pl PL1 . . . . . .148 C2
Holyway Cross PL15 . . . .18 A1
Holywell Ct TR3 . . . . . . .82 B8
Holywell Rd Cubert TR8 . .55 D8
Holywell TR8 . . . . .43 B1
Liskeard PL14 . . . . .113 C6
Newquay TR7 . . . . .110 F6
Playing Place TR3 . . . . . .82 B8
Home Farm Rd PL9 . . . .135 F7
Home Park (Plymouth Argyle
Fc) PL2 . . . . .128 C5
Home Park Ave PL3 . . .128 E6
Home Park Rd PL12 . . .123 A3
Home Pk Landrake PL12 . .53 C3
Plymouth PL2 . . . . .127 F4
Home Sweet Home Terr
PL4 . . . . .149 C2
Homefield PL31 . . . . . .109 F3
Homer Park La S PL9 . .135 C5
Homer Park Rd PL28 . . .20 F2
Homer Pk Plymouth PL9 .135 C5
Saltash PL12 . . . . .122 D3
Homer Rise PL9 . . . . . .136 B7
Homer Water Pk PL26 . .58 D4
Homeyard Homes The
TR2 . . . . .83 F6
Honcray PL9 . . . . .135 D8
Honey St PL31 . . . . . . .109 E5
Honeysuckle Cl
Plymouth PL6 . . . . .125 E7
Saltash PL12 . . . . .122 D4
Honicknowle Gn PL5 . . .124 B2
Honicknowle La PL5 . . .124 B1
Honicombe Cnr PL17 . . .40 C5
Honicombe Manor Holiday
Village PL17 . . . . .40 C5
Honiton Wlk PL5 . . . . .124 D4
Hood Hill TR14 . . . . . . .79 A6
Hooe Hill PL9 . . . . .135 C5
Hooe La PL9 . . . . .135 D3
Hooe Prim Sch PL9 . . .135 B6
Hooe Rd PL9 . . . . .135 C5
Hooksbury Ave PL7 . . .131 B3
Hooper Ct PL14 . . . . . .113 C8
Hooper La TR14 . . . . . .138 D2
Hooper St PL11 . . . . . .127 C3
Hoopers Cl PL12 . . . . . .53 C3
Hoopers La PL18 . . . . . .40 F6
Hope Terr TR7 . . . . . . .110 D6
Hopton Cl PL6 . . . . . . .128 E8
Horn Cross PL9 . . . . . .135 E7
Horn Cross Rd PL9 . . . .135 F7
Horn La PL9 . . . . .135 F7
Horn Lane Flats PL9 . . .135 F7
Hornapark Cl PL16 . . . . .19 E3
Hornbrook Gdns PL6 . . .124 D6
Hornby St **2** PL2 . . . . .127 F4
Hornchurch La PL5 . . . .123 E4
Hornchurch Rd PL5 . . . .123 E5
Hornick Hill PL26 . . . . . .58 E4
Horrabridge Prim Sch
PL20 . . . . .42 C4
Horse & Jockey La **1**
TR13 . . . . .146 C5
Horse Whim Dr PL25 . .115 B5
Horsepool La PL11 . . . . .65 B6
Horsepool Rd
Connor Downs TR27 . . . . .78 E6
Sheviock PL11 . . . . .65 B6
Horseshoe Cl PL26 . . . . .47 A3
Horsham La
Plymouth, Honicknowle
PL5 . . . . .124 C2
Plymouth, Tamerton Foliot
PL5 . . . . .124 C7
Horsley Rise PL25 . . . .114 D3
Horswell Cl PL7 . . . . . .131 B5
Horton Cross EX22 . . . . . .3 F7
Hosford Cl PL9 . . . . . .136 A4
Hosken's Mdw TR19 . . . .97 A6
Hosking's Row TR15 . . .140 B4
Hospital Rd
Plymouth PL4 . . . . .149 B4
Stratton EX23 . . . . .4 D1
Hotham Pl PL1 . . . . . . .148 A4
Houldsworth Rd PL9 . . .135 C7
Houndiscombe Rd PL4 . .128 E4
Hounster Dr PL10 . . . . .132 D4
Hounster Hill PL10 . . . .132 D4

Housecraft Ctr **7** PL4 . .149 A2
Housel Bay Rd TR12 . . .102 F2
Housman Cl PL5 . . . . .124 D3
How St PL4 . . . . .149 A2
Howard Cl Plymouth PL5 .123 F2
Saltash PL12 . . . . .122 D3
Tavistock PL19 . . . . . . .147 A5
Howard La EX23 . . . . .7 C8
Howard Rd PL9 . . . . . .135 E8
Howards Way EX23 . . . .104 C5
Howe Downs TR14 . . . . .79 A2
Howell's Rd **10** EX23 . . . .4 E1
Hudson Cross EX22 . . . . .5 E4
Hudson Rd PL7 . . . . . . .31 F3
Hughville St TR14 . . . . .138 D4
Hugus Rd TR3 . . . . .69 D3
Hull's La TR11 . . . . . . .145 C3
Humber Cl PL3 . . . . . .129 D6
Humphrey's Cl PL14 . . . .37 D3
Humphry Davy La PL17 142 D5
Humphry Davy Sch The
TR18 . . . . .143 E6
Hungerford Rd PL2 . . . .128 B5
Hunkin Cl TR1 . . . . . . .137 C5
Hunter Cl PL6 . . . . . . .124 F2
Hunters's Oak PL20 . . . .41 D2
Huntersfield TR14 . . . . .138 F7
Huntingdon Gdns PL5 . .124 D4
Huntley Pl PL3 . . . . . . .129 C4
Hunts Crossing* PL15 . .18 E3
Hurdon Rd PL15 . . . . . .106 D2
Hurdon Way PL15 . . . . .106 C3
Hurdwick Rd PL19 . . . .147 A5
Hurland Rd PL19 . . . . .137 D3
Hurlers The* PL14 . . . . .38 A4
Hurrabrook Cl PL6 . . . .125 E2
Hurrabrook Gdns PL6 . .125 E2
Hurrell Cl PL6 . . . . . . .124 D6
Hurrell Ct PL3 . . . . . . .129 C5
Hursley Bsns Pk PL6 . .121 D1
Hurst Cl PL9 . . . . .135 F5
Hustyns PL27 . . . . .33 D3
Hutchings Cl PL6 . . . . .124 D6
Huthnance Cl TR1 . . . .137 F5
Hutton Hts PL3 . . . . . . .69 D2
Huxham Cl PL6 . . . . . .129 A8
Huxley Cl PL7 . . . . . . .130 F7
Hyde Park Jun & Inf Schs
PL3 . . . . .128 E5
Hyde Park Rd PL3 . . . .128 E5

I

Idless La TR4 . . . . .69 F6
Ilbert Cotts PL7 . . . . . .130 E4
Ilbert St PL1 . . . . .148 B4
Illogan Downs TR15 . . .139 B8
Illogan Pk **8** TR16 . . . . .67 E4
Illogan Sch TR16 . . . . . .67 D5
Ince Cl PL11 . . . . .126 F4
Inchkeith Rd PL6 . . . . .124 F4
Indian Queens Com Prim Sch
TR9 . . . . .45 E1
Indian Queens Workshops
TR9 . . . . .45 E2
Infirmary Hill TR1 . . . . .137 C4
Ingra Rd PL3 . . . . .129 A6
Ingra Tor Cl **2** PL20 . . . .42 C3
Ingra Wlk PL6 . . . . . . .125 B8
Innes Ho PL1 . . . . .148 B3
Inney Cl PL17 . . . . .39 F4
Inny Vale Holiday Village
PL32 . . . . .16 A5
Inow Terr TR11 . . . . . . .93 A2
Instow Wlk PL5 . . . . . .124 A3
Inswell Ct PL19 . . . . . .147 A6
Insworke Cl PL10 . . . . .133 A4
Insworke Cres PL10 . . .132 F6
Insworke Pl PL10 . . . . .133 A6
Inverdene PL3 . . . . . . .128 D5
Ipswich Cl PL5 . . . . . .124 A4
Iron Mine La PL6 . . . . . .42 E3
Isacombe Oaks PL17 . . . .39 E7
Island Cres TR7 . . . . . .110 E6
Island Lanes PL31 . . . .109 F1
Island Rd **4** TR26 . . . . .141 B6
Island Sq **8** TR26 . . . .141 B6
Islington Wharf TR10 . .144 D8
Ivanhoe Rd PL5 . . . . . .123 D2
Ivey Terr PL14 . . . . . . .113 D7
Ivy Cotts PL18 . . . . . . .40 F6
Ivy La TR18 . . . . .143 C5
Ivydale PL15 . . . . .106 B6
Ivydale Rd PL4 . . . . . . .128 F4
Ivydene Flats TR7 . . . . .111 D7

J

Jack Bice Cl PL14 . . . . .113 C5
Jack La TR18 . . . . .143 E5
Jack Stephens Est
TR18 . . . . .143 D6
Jack's La TR11 . . . . . . .132 B8
Jackett's Stps TR11 . . .145 B5
Jackman's Mdw PL10 . .133 A3
Jacks Cl TR10 . . . . . . .144 D7
Jackson Cl PL5 . . . . . .127 F8
Jackson Pl PL2 . . . . . .127 F4
Jackson Way PL12 . . . .122 F3
Jacob's Ladder TR11 . . .145 B4
Jacobstow Com Prim Sch
EX23 . . . . .11 A6
Jago Ave PL11 . . . . . . .127 B3
Jago Pl PL31 . . . . .109 B3
Jake's La TR4 . . . . .69 A3
Jamaica Pl **14** TR18 . . . .143 C7

Jamaica Terr **13** TR18 . .143 C7
Jame's Cross EX23 . . . . . .2 C2
James Cl PL9 . . . . .136 B6
James Pl Plymouth PL4 . .148 C4
Truro TR1 . . . . .137 D4
James Rd PL19 . . . . . . .147 E3
James St Plymouth PL4 . .148 C4
Plymouth, Mount Wise PL1 127 C1
Jane's Ct TR11 . . . . . . .145 B5
Jasmine Gdns
Plymouth, Chaddlewood
PL7 . . . . .131 B5
Plymouth, Glenholt PL6 . .125 E6
Jasper Parc PL14 . . . . . .37 F3
Jays Cross PL15 . . . . . .19 C5
Jean Cres PL3 . . . . . . .129 B6
Jeanne Rees Ct **9** PL14 113 C6
Jedburgh Cres PL2 . . . .128 A8
Jeffery Cl PL6 . . . . . . .124 D4
Jelbert Way TR18 . . . . . .88 C6
Jellicoe Rd PL5 . . . . . .124 C1
Jenkins Cl PL9 . . . . . . .136 A5
Jenkins Cl TR7 . . . . . . .110 E6
Jenkins Terr **5** TR15 . .140 C5
Jennings Rd TR10 . . . . .144 A6
Jennings St TR18 . . . . .143 C5
Jenns Cross EX22 . . . . . .5 F7
Jennycliff La PL9 . . . . .135 A6
Jennys Combe Cl PL9 . .135 F4
Jephson Rd PL4 . . . . . .129 B3
Jericho La TR27 . . . . . .142 D1
Jeryon Cl PL25 . . . . . .114 E6
Jessops PL7 . . . . .130 D7
Jethan Dr PL14 . . . . . .138 B4
Jetty St PL26 . . . . .73 C3
Jewel's Cross EX22 . . . . . .7 F6
Jewell's Terr TR16 . . . . .80 B5
Jinkin Ave PL4 . . . . . . .149 B4
John Ellis Ct TR27 . . . .142 C4
John Kitto Com Coll
PL5 . . . . .124 C4
John La PL4 . . . . .148 C4
John Sparke Ho **17** PL1 .149 A2
John St Plymouth PL1 . .127 E3
Truro TR1 . . . . .137 C4
John's Cnr TR20 . . . . . . .89 C5
Johns Pk TR15 . . . . . . .140 B6
Johnson Cl **2** PL20 . . . .41 B1
Johnson Pk PL18 . . . . . .41 A3
Jon Davey Dr TR14 . . .140 C7
Jopes Cl **2** PL14 . . . . . .38 A3
Jordan La
Horrabridge PL20 . . . . . . .42 C5
Walkhampton PL20 . . . . . .42 C6
Jorys Mdw PL30 . . . . . .23 C3
Joseph's Ct **18** TR6 . . . .55 A5
Joseph's La TR18 . . . . .143 C1
Jubilee Bglws **19** TR18 .143 C1
Kilkhampton EX23 . . . . . .5 C5
Saltash PL12 . . . . .122 D2
Jubilee Cotts PL12 . . . . .53 C3
Jubilee Hill PL13 . . . . . .62 D5
Jubilee Mdw PL25 . . . .115 C5
Jubilee Pl **1** TR14 . . . . .138 E3
Jubilee Rd
Falmouth TR11 . . . . . . .145 A5
Pensilva PL14 . . . . .38 D4
Plymouth PL5 . . . . .123 F3
Threemilestone TR3 . . . . .69 C3
Wadebridge PL27 . . . . . .108 C3
Jubilee St TR7 . . . . . . .110 D6
Jubilee Terr
Bodmin PL31 . . . . .109 B5
Goonhavern TR4 . . . . . . .55 C5
Helston TR13 . . . . .146 C4
Plymouth PL4 . . . . .129 B2
Julian St PL4 . . . . .149 C2
Julian Wlk PL6 . . . . . . .125 E6
Jump Cl PL6 . . . . .121 C1
Juniper Way PL7 . . . . . .131 B5

K

Karenza Ct TR26 . . . . .141 E2
Kathleaven St PL5 . . . .123 D1
Kay Cl PL7 . . . . .130 F7
Kay Cres PL31 . . . . . . .109 B3
Kay Gdns PL27 . . . . . . .108 E5
Kea Com Prim Sch TR3 . .70 A1
Keason Est PL14 . . . . . .39 A2
Keason Hill PL12 . . . . . .53 C8
Keast Cl **2** TR9 . . . . . . .45 E1
Keat St PL2 . . . . .127 E1
Kedlestone Ave PL5 . . .124 A3
Keeble Pk TR3 . . . . .81 E6
Keep The PL12 . . . . . . .122 C2
Kehelland Village Sch
TR14 . . . . .66 F1
Keigwin Pl TR19 . . . . . .88 C3
Kellaway Pk TR13 . . . .146 D6
Kelley Rd TR11 . . . . . .144 E5
Kelliwith TR3 . . . . .82 B6
Kellow Hill PL13 . . . . . .62 D2
Kellow Pk PL11 . . . . . . .65 A7
Kellow Rd PL26 . . . . . . .58 C8
Kelly Cl PL5 . . . . .127 C7
Kelly Coll PL19 . . . . . .147 D7
Kelly Pk PL30 . . . . .34 C8
Kelvin Ave PL4 . . . . . .149 C4
Kelwyn Ct TR26 . . . . . .141 C2
Kemp Cl TR1 . . . . .137 D4
Kemp's Cl **7** TR5 . . . . .54 C1
Kempe Cl PL2 . . . . . . .127 F6
Kempton Terr PL11 . . . .127 B2
Kemyell Pl PL2 . . . . . .127 E1
Kendal Gn TR2 . . . . . . .57 C1

Kendal Pl PL5 ....124 E4
Kenidjack Ct TR26 ....141 E1
Kenilworth Rd PL2 ...128 B7
Kenley Gdns PL5 ......123 F4
Kenmare Dr PL7 ....131 A5
Kenn Cl PL5 ....124 B3
Kenna Pk TR1 ....69 F3
Kennall Vale TR3 .....81 B4
Kennall Vale Sch TR3 .81 B4
Kennedy Cl TR15 ......139 B8
Kennel Hill PL7 ......130 D4
Kennel Hill Cl PL7 ..130 C4
Kennerley Terr TR2 ...95 A6
Kennet Cl PL3 ....129 B6
Kensa Way TR27 ....78 E6
Kensey Pl 3 PL15 .....106 C6
Kensey View PL15 .....106 D5
Kensington Pl 8 PL4 ..128 E4
Kensington Rd PL4 ....149 B4
Kenstella Rd TR18 ....143 C2
Kent Ave PL25 ....115 C3
Kent Cl PL26 ....58 C8
Kent Rd PL2 ....127 F5
Kenwyn Church Rd TR1 .137 B6
Kenwyn Cl Bude EX23 ..104 D7
  Truro TR1 ....137 B6
Kenwyn Hill TR1 ......137 B6
Kenwyn Pk TR30 ....23 B2
Kenwyn Rd Truro TR1 ..137 C5
  Truro TR4,TR1 ....137 A7
Kenwyn St TR1 ....137 C4
Kenython La TR19 .....86 F7
Keppel Pl PL2 ....127 F4
Keppel St PL2 ....127 F4
Keppel Terr 8 PL2 ....127 F4
Ker Cl PL1 ....127 E1
Ker St Ope PL1 ....127 E2
Kerensa Gdns TR5 .....68 D8
Kerensa Gn TR11 ......144 E5
Kergilliack Rd TR11 ..144 D5
Kerley Gr TR1 ....69 F3
Kerley Hill TR4 ......69 A3
Kerley Vale TR4 ......69 A3
Kernhuon Ct PL31 .....109 D5
Kernick Gdns TR10 ....144 A6
Kernick Rd TR10 ......144 B7
Kernick Road Ind Est
  TR10 ....144 A7
Kernow Cl Bodmin PL31 109 F5
  Torpoint PL11 ....126 E3
  Wadebridge PL27 .....108 B5
Kernow Cres EX23 .....104 E4
Kernow Ct Newquay TR7 110 E6
  Torpoint PL11 ....126 E3
Kernow Mill* PL12 ....52 E1
Kernyk Lowen TR14 ....138 F5
Kerris Gr TR1 ....137 B5
Kersbrook Cross PL17 .27 F2
Kersey Cl TR11 ....145 C7
Kersey Rd TR11 ....145 B7
Keryor Cl PL25 ....114 F3
Kestle Dr TR1 ....69 F3
Kestral Units PL5 ....124 A1
Kestral Way 10 TR16 ..67 E4
Kestrel Cl Plymouth PL6 125 D1
  7 Porthleven TR13 ...98 B8
Keswick Cres PL6 .....125 D2
Keveral Gdns PL11 ....64 B5
Keveral La PL11 ......64 B4
Kew Cl TR7 ....111 A4
Kew Noweth TR14 ......138 D2
Kew Pendra TR1 ....97 A6
Kew Pendra Cl TR19 ...97 A6
Kew Vean TR26 ....141 C3
Keyes Cl PL1 ....127 F2
Keyham Barton RC Prim Sch
  PL2 ....127 E6
Keyham Rd PL2 ....127 E4
Keyham St PL2 ....127 E8
Keyham Sta PL2 ....127 E6
Khyber Cl PL11 ....54 C8
Kibbiscombe Terr PL14 63 A8
Kidwelly Cl PL7 ......131 C4
Kiel Pl PL3 ....129 D5
Kilhallon PL24 ....60 C4
Kilhallon Woodlands
  PL24 ....60 C5
Kilkhampton Jun & Inf Sch
  EX23 ....5 A6
Killarney Springs Leisure
  Pk* EX23 ....3 B1
Killatree Cross EX22 .8 F7
Killerton Rd EX23 ....104 D3
Killicourt TR3 ....82 A7
Killiers Ct TR15 .....139 C7
Killiersfield TR15 ...139 C6
Killigrew Rd PL12 ....122 D1
Killigrew Gdns TR4 ...70 D8
Killigrew Pl 9 TR11 ..145 A4
Killigrew Rd PL14 ....113 D6
Killigrew St TR11 ....145 A4
Killivose Gdns TR14 ..138 D1
Killivose Rd TR14 ....138 D1
Killyvarder Way PL25 .115 B6
Kilmar Cl PL14 ....37 F3
Kilmar Rd PL14 ....113 C6
Kilmar Way PL14 ......37 F3
Kilminorth Wood*
  PL13 ....117 A5
Kiln Cl Mevagissey PL26 73 C1
  Plymouth 127 C8
Kiln Mdws TR12 ....92 C1
Kilna La PL3 ....53 A2
Kilworthy Hill PL19 ..147 C6
Kilworthy Rd PL19 ....147 C6
Kimber Ct PL11 ....145 B4

Kimberley Ct TR7 .....110 D6
Kimberley Foster Cl
  PL11 ....65 B5
Kimberley Park Rd
  TR11 ....145 A4
Kimberley Pk PL14 ....38 A3
Kimberley Pl TR11 ....145 A4
Kimberly Cl TR7 ......110 D6
Kimberly Dr PL6 ......125 B1
Kiming EX23 ....104 E4
King Arthurs Terr PL34 14 C7
King Charles Prim Sch
  TR11 ....145 A3
King Edward Cres TR7 .110 D7
King Edward Rd PL12 ..122 F2
King George V Meml Wlk
  TR27 ....142 C6
King St Bude EX23 ....104 E5
  Gunnislake PL18 .....41 A6
  Millbrook PL10 ......132 E5
  Newquay TR7 ....110 D6
  Plymouth PL1 ....148 B3
  Redruth TR15 ....140 B5
  Tavistock PL19 ......147 B6
  Torpoint PL11 ....127 C3
  Truro TR1 ....137 D4
King's Ave Falmouth TR11 144 F4
  St Austell PL25 .....114 D3
King's Hill PL25 .....104 E4
King's Hill Ind Est
  EX23 ....104 F3
King's Tamerton Rd PL5 123 F7
Kingfisher Cl PL6 ....125 E6
Kingfisher Dr PL25 ...115 A4
Kings Cross EX39 .....2 E5
Kings Ct PL1 ....128 A3
Kings Hill EX23 ......104 E4
Kings Hill Mdw EX23 ..104 E3
Kings Mead PL7 ....21 E3
Kings Rd Marazion TR17 89 B5
  Plymouth, Devonport PL1 127 F2
  Plymouth, West Park PL5 123 F3
  4 St Mawes TR2 .....95 A6
Kings Sch PL3 ....128 E6
Kingsland Gardens Cl
  PL3 ....128 E6
Kingsley Ave PL11 ....127 B2
Kingsley Cl TR1 ......69 E3
Kingsley Cove TR4 ....68 A7
Kingsley Ct TR9 ......57 E8
Kingsley Meade TR8 ...111 E8
Kingsley Rd PL4 ......128 E4
Kingsley Way TR13 ....146 C5
Kingsley Terr TR16 ...67 C6
Kingsmill Rd PL12 ....122 C5
Kingston Cl PL7 ......131 A5
Kingston Dr PL7 ......131 B5
Kingston Rd PL17 .....28 E1
Kingsway PL10 ....133 B2
Kingsway Gdns PL6 ....124 F3
Kingswear Cres PL6 ...125 B1
Kingswood Park Ave
  PL3 ....128 D6
Kingswood Rd PL18 ....41 A6
Kinnaird Cres PL6 ....124 F7
Kinnard Cres PL6 .....124 F7
Kinross Ave PL4 ......129 A4
Kinsale Rd PL5 ....123 F3
Kinsman Est PL31 .....109 C3
Kinterbury Rd PL5 ....127 B8
Kinterbury St PL1 ....149 A2
Kinterbury Terr PL5 ..127 B8
Kinver Cl PL5 ....125 D4
Kipling Gdns PL5 .....124 D2
Kirby Rd TR1 ....137 A4
Kirkby Pl PL4 ....148 C4
Kirkby Terr PL4 ......148 C4
Kirkdale Gdns PL2 ....128 B7
Kirkella Rd PL20 .....42 D2
Kirkland Cl PL6 ......125 C7
Kirkstall Cl PL2 .....128 A8
Kirkwall Rd PL5 ......124 E3
Kirland Bower PL30 ...48 B7
Kirland Rd PL30 ......109 B2
Kirton Pl PL3 ....129 B5
Kit Hill Cres PL5 ....127 C8
Kitley Way PL5 ....123 D1
Kitter Dr PL9 ....136 A5
Kitts Ct 17 TR18 .....143 E5
Kleinfontein Terr PL14 38 D4
Knapmedown PL15 ......11 B1
Knapps Cl PL9 ....136 C6
Knave-Go-By TR14 .....79 D5
Kneele Gdns PL3 ......128 E8
Knight's Mdws TR3 ....81 F7
Knighton Rd PL4 ......149 C3
Knighton Terr 4 PL20 .42 C5
Knightor Cl PL25 .....59 E6
Knights Cl PL34 ......14 C7
Knights Ct PL22 ......112 B3
Knights Hill TR1 .....137 B6
Knights Way TR15 .....140 D7
Knill Cl PL1 ....127 E3
Knill Cross PL10 .....132 E5
Knoll Pk TR1 ....137 F4
Knoll The PL7 ....130 B6
Knowland Cl PL1 ......127 E3
Knowle Ave PL2 ....127 E6
Knowle Prim Sch PL5 ..124 D4
Knowle Terr PL20 .....42 E4
Kyl Cober Parc PL17 ..28 E1
Kynance Cl PL11 ......126 F4
Kynance Ho TR1 ....69 E4
Kynance Terr 7 TR12 ..102 C3

L

La Rochelle TR12 .....98 F1
La Vague TR3 ....82 C5
Labernum Terr EX23 ...5 A6
Laburnum Cl PL5 ......144 F5
Laburnum Cotts PL19 ..147 C6
Laburnum Dr TR11 .....144 F5
Lacey Cl TR14 ....79 E5
Ladock Rd Ladock TR2 .57 C1
  Probus TR2 ....71 C7
Lady Modifords CE Prim Sch
  PL20 ....42 E4
Lady St TR13 ....146 B5
Ladysmith Ct PL4 .....149 C4
Ladysmith St PL4 .....129 B3
Ladywell PL28 ....107 D5
Ladywell Pl PL4 ......149 B4
Laflouder Fields PL12 99 A2
Laflouder La TR12 ....99 A2
Laguna Ct TR15 ....140 B5
Laira Ave PL3 ....129 C4
Laira Bridge Rd PL4 ..129 B1
Laira Green Prim Sch
  PL3 ....129 C4
Laira Park Cres PL4 ..129 B4
Laira Park Pl PL4 ....129 B4
Laira Park Rd PL4 ....129 B4
Laira Pl PL4 ....149 C2
Laira St PL4 ....149 C3
Laity La TR26 ....77 C4
Laity Rd TR14 ....79 C4
Laity Wlk PL6 ....124 D6
Lake La Dousland PL20 42 E3
  Liskeard PL14 ....113 D5
Lake Mews PL10 ....132 E5
Lake Rd PL9 ....135 B6
Lake View PL12 ....53 C8
Lake View Cl PL5 .....124 B6
Lakeside PL11 ....147 B6
Lakeside Dr PL5 ......123 C5
Lakeview Dr PL5 ......124 B5
Lalebrick Rd PL9 .....135 B5
Lamanva Cl TR16 .....67 E4
Lamanva Rd 17 TR16 ...67 E4
Lamb Pk 5 PL24 ......60 C4
Lamb's Barn PL23 .....116 B4
Lambert Rd PL5 ....124 B6
Lambert Terr 4 TR11 ..145 A5
Lambhay Hill PL1 .....149 A1
Lambhay St PL1 ....149 A1
Lambourne Ave 7 TR5 .54 C1
Lambs La TR11 ....144 E5
Lameillion Hospl PL14 113 D5
Lamellyn Dr TR1 ......69 F3
Lamellyn Rd PL24 .....60 B4
Lamerhooe Cross PL19 .29 C1
Lamerhooe Dr
  Horsebridge PL19 ....29 C1
  Luckett PL19 ....40 C8
Lamerton Cl PL5 .....124 B3
Lametton Gn PL14 .....51 B4
Lamledra Hill PL26 ...85 D5
Lamorak Ct PL26 .....73 B3
Lamorna Ct TR16 .....67 D6
Lamorna Dr 11 PL17 ..39 F4
Lamorna Parc 12 PL17 .39 F4
Lamorna Pk PL11 .....126 E4
Lamorne Cl 4 TR6 ....55 A4
Lampen Rd PL14 ......36 F2
Lana Cotts PL22 .....13 C7
Lanadwell St PL28 ...107 D5
Lanaton Rd TR10 .....144 A8
Lancashire La TR20 ...89 F5
Lancaster Cres PL27 ..31 F3
Lancaster Gdns PL5 ...124 D4
Lanchard La PL14 .....113 B5
Lanchard Rd PL14 .....113 B5
Lanchard Rise PL14 ...113 B5
Land's End (St Just)
  Aerodrome TR19 .....86 F3
Landaviddy La PL13 ...62 D2
Lander Cl TR1 ....137 D3
Lander Rd PL12 ....122 F3
Landeryon Gdns 9
  TR18 ....143 D5
Landithy TR20 ....143 A8
Landlake Cross PL15 ..28 A8
Landlake Rd PL15 .....106 B2
Landrake Cl PL5 ......127 C8
Landreath Pl PL24 ....60 B5
Landrew Rd PL25 .....114 F6
Lands End* TR19 .....96 A5
Lands End Rd TR19 ...97 A6
Lands Pk PL9 ....135 F7
Landulph Cross PL12 ..118 F3
Landulph Gdns PL5 ...127 C8
Landuph Sch PL12 ....118 F1
Lane End Cross PL19 ..29 D2
Lane Reddin Terr 19
  TR18 ....143 C2
Lanepark La EX39 ....2 D5
Lang Gdns PL18 ......41 A3
Lang Gr Plymouth PL9 .136 C7
  Tavistock PL19 .....147 D5
Lang Rd PL14 ....113 B4
Langage Cross PL7 ...131 F6
Langage Ind Est PL7 .131 D6
Langage Pk PL7 ......131 C4
Langage Science Pk
  PL7 ....131 D5
Langarth Cl TR3 .....69 D4
Langdale Cl PL6 .....125 D1
Langdale Gdns PL6 ...125 D1
Langdon Cross PL15 ..18 D8

Langdon Ct PL9 ....136 B6
Langdon Down Way
  PL11 ....126 E3
Langerwell Cl PL12 ...122 C3
Langerwell La PL12 ...122 C3
Langfords Mdw 4 PL35 .9 C1
Langham Pl PL4 ....149 C3
Langhill Rd PL3 ......128 D5
Langley Cl PL6 ....125 A7
Langley Com Inf Sch
  PL6 ....125 A6
Langley Cres PL6 .....124 F7
Langmead Cl PL6 .....129 C8
Langmead Rd PL6 .....129 C8
Langmore Cl PL6 .....129 A7
Langorran Rd TR14 ...138 B3
Langreek Bglws PL13 ..62 C2
Langreek Rd PL13 .....62 C2
Langstone Rd PL2 ....128 C7
Langstone Terr PL2 ..128 C7
Langton Rd
  Falmouth TR11 ......145 A6
  8 Yelverton PL20 ...42 C3
Langton Terr 8 TR11 ..145 A5
Langurroc Rd TR8 ....110 A3
Langurtho Rd TR23 ...116 B4
Langweath Est TR12 ..99 D7
Langweath Gdns TR27 .77 E3
Langweath La TR12 ...99 D7
Langwedh TR16 ....67 D4
Lanhenvor Ave TR7 ...110 E5
Lanherne Ave TR8 ....45 A8
Lanheverne Parc 4
  TR12 ....101 C4
Lanhydrock Ho* PL30 .48 D6
Lanhydrock Rd PL4 ...129 B2
Lanhydrock View PL31 109 D3
Lanivet Com Prim Sch
  PL30 ....47 E7
Lanjowan TR13 ....146 B6
Lankelly La PL24 ....116 A4
Lanlivery Com Prim Sch
  PL30 ....48 D2
Lanlovie Mdw TR8 ....55 D8
Lanmoor St TR16 .....80 D6
Lannarth Glas TR16 ..140 E1
Lanner Gn TR16 ......140 E1
Lanner Hill TR16 ....140 E1
Lanner Moor Terr TR16 80 D6
Lanner Prim Sch TR16 80 D6
Lanner Sq TR16 ......80 D6
Lannoweth Rd TR18 ...143 F6
Lanoweth TR10 ....81 D2
Lanreath Farm & Folk Mus*
  PL13 ....62 B8
Lanreath Prim Sch PL13 62 A8
Lansallos St PL13 ...62 D1
Lansdown Cl TR18 ....104 D5
Lansdown Rd Bude EX23 104 D5
  Wadebridge PL27 ....108 B5
Lansdowne Cl TR18 ...143 C5
Lansdowne Ct TR18 ...143 C5
Lansdowne Ct TR18 ...143 C4
Lansdowne Rd
  Callington PL17 ....39 E4
  Falmouth TR11 ......145 C3
  Penzance TR18 ......143 C5
  Plymouth PL6 ....124 F2
Lantallack Cross PL12 53 A3
Lanuthnoe Est TR27 ..77 E3
Lanwithan Cl TR22 ...112 C2
Lanwithan Rd TR22 ...112 E1
Lanxon Cres PL30 ....48 C2
Lanyon Ct TR1 ....37 F3
Lanyon Rd TR3 ....82 B8
Lappa Valley Steam Rly*
  TR8 ....56 C7
Lapthorn Cl PL9 .....135 C7
Larch Cl PL12 ....122 C5
Larch Dr PL6 ....125 E7
Larcombe Rd PL25 ....115 A6
Laregan Hill TR18 ...143 D4
Lariggan Cres TR18 ..143 D4
Lariggan Rd TR18 ....143 D4
Lark Hill PL2 ....128 A6
Larkham Cl PL7 ......130 C6
Larkham La PL7 ......130 C6
Latham Cl PL6 ....129 A7
Latimer Cl PL7 ......131 B5
Latimer Wlk PL6 .....124 D7
Launcells Cross PL5 ..5 B1
Launceston Castle*
  PL15 ....106 C6
Launceston Cl
  Bodmin PL31 ....109 F4
  Plymouth PL6 ....125 D7
Launceston Coll PL15 106 C4
Launceston Com Prim Sch
  PL15 ....106 C5
Launceston Hospl PL15 106 C4
Launceston Rd
  Bodmin PL31 ....35 B1
  Callington PL17 ....39 E6
Launceston Ret Pk
  PL15 ....106 C6
Launceston Sta PL15 .106 B6
Launceston Steam Rly*
  PL15 ....18 E3
Laura Cl PL34 ....14 D7
Laura Dr PL25 ....115 A4
Laurel Cl PL2 ....128 A7
Laurel Dene PL2 .....128 A7
Laurel Rd PL2 ....128 A7
Lavington Cl PL7 ....131 B5
Lavinia Dr PL7 ......130 C5
Lavorrick Orchs PL26 .73 C4

Law Wlk PL6 ....124 D6
Lawn Cl 2 PL7 ....131 C5
Lawn Stps TR11 .....145 B4
Lawn The Par PL24 ...60 B5
Lawns The Plymouth PL5 124 E1
  Torpoint PL11 ......127 A4
Lawrence House Mus*
  PL15 ....106 C6
Lawrence Rd
  Plymouth PL9 ....135 A6
  St Agnes TR5 ....54 C1
Lawry Cl 6 PL14 .....113 B5
Lawson Gr PL9 ....135 C7
Lawton Cl TR7 ....110 B5
Lea Way EX23 ....104 F6
Leader Rd TR7 ....111 E7
Leander Way PL5 .....124 D2
Leanway PL12 ....122 E2
Leap Pk TR3 ....69 C3
Leas The TR1 ....137 E5
Leat Cl PL20 ....42 E3
Leat Rd Lifton PL16 ..19 F3
  Pendeen TR19 ....75 A1
Leat The 9 EX23 .....4 D5
Leat View PL12 ......122 B3
Leat Wlk Plymouth PL3 128 E6
  Roborough PL6 ......121 D1
Leatfield PL26 ......73 C3
Leatfield Dr PL6 ....124 F4
Leather Cl PL6 ......124 F7
Leather Tor Cl 4 PL20 42 C3
Leats The TR1 ....137 C4
Leatside PL6 ....121 C1
Leaves Yd PL3 ....129 B7
Leburnick Cross PL15 .28 D8
Ledgate La PL7 ......131 F8
Ledra Cl TR12 ....103 A4
Ledra Gdns PL25 .....114 B3
Ledrah Rd PL25 ......114 B3
Leedstown Com Prim Sch
  TR27 ....78 C1
Legion La 3 PL24 ....60 C8
Legis Wlk PL6 ....125 B8
Leigh Ct PL6 ....129 A4
Leigh La Hatt PL12 ..53 D6
  Roborough PL6 ......121 D1
Leigham Ct PL1 ......148 B2
Leigham Inf & Jun Schs
  PL6 ....125 E1
Leigham St PL1 ......148 B1
Leigham Terrace La
  PL1 ....148 B2
Leighton Rd PL3 .....128 D7
Lelant Mdws TR26 ....77 E4
Lelant Saltings Sta TR26 77 E4
Lelant Sta TR26 .....77 E4
Lemellen Gdns PL30 ..23 D4
Lemin Parc TR27 .....78 E3
Lemin's Ct TR15 .....140 B5
Lemon Hill TR11 .....82 A3
Lemon Hill Gdns TR11 82 A3
Lemon Mews Rd TR1 ..137 C4
Lemon Quay TR1 .....137 D4
Lemon Row TR1 ......137 D4
Lemon St
  St Keverne TR12 ....101 D4
  Truro TR1 ....137 D4
Lender La 5 TR12 ....99 A2
Lendewednack Com Prim
  Sch TR12 ....102 F2
Lendra La PL7 ....39 D4
Lerryn CE Prim Sch PL22 61 D3
Lerryn View PL22 ....61 C8
Lerwick Rd PL27 .....31 F3
Lescudjack Cres TR18 143 F6
Lescudjack Rd TR18 ..143 E6
Lesingey La TR20 ....88 A5
Leskinnick Pl 15 TR18 143 E6
Leskinnick St TR18 ..143 F6
Leskinnick Terr TR18 143 F6
Leslie Ct TR13 ......146 B6
Lesnewth 18 PL24 ....60 C8
Lester Cl PL3 ....129 B6
Lestraynes La TR10 ..92 E8
Lethlean Cl 1 TR27 ..142 D7
Lethlean La 7 TR27 ..142 D7
Levant Beam Engine*
  TR19 ....74 E1
Levant Cl TR19 ......86 E3
Levant Rd TR19 ......86 E8
Leverlake Rd EX23 ...6 F4
Levine View TR11 ....144 E1
Lewannick Cl PL15 ...27 B7
Lewannick Com Prim Sch
  PL15 ....27 B7
Lewarne Cres TR7 ...111 C7
Lewarne Rd TR7 .....111 C8
Lewes Gdns PL5 .....124 C4
Lewis Way PL25 .....114 E6
Lewman Cl TR2 ......71 C6
Lewman Rd TR2 ......71 C6
Ley La PL20 ....119 D6
Leypark Dr PL6 .....125 E2
Leypark Wlk PL6 ....125 E2
Leys La TR17 ....89 C3
Liberator Row 4 PL27 31 F3
Lidden Cl TR18 .....143 C3
Lidden Cres TR18 ...143 C3
Lidden Rd TR18 .....143 C3
Liddicoat Rd PL22 ..112 D3
Lifeboat Hill 32 TR26 141 B6
Lifton Prim Sch PL16 19 F4

Lifton Rd PL4 ....149 C2
Liftondown Cross PL16 .19 D4
Lighterage Hill TR1 ....137 E2
Lighthouse Hill PL16 ....67 C6
Lighthouse La TR12 ....102 F2
Lilac Cl PL9 ....135 C5
Lime Tree Way PL15 ....27 D4
Limerick Pl PL4 ....149 C3
Limes La PL14 ....113 B5
Limes The PL6 ....124 F2
Limetree Rd PL3 ......128 D7
Lincoln Ave PL4 ......149 C4
Lincoln Row **6** PL27 ..31 F3
Linden Ave TR7 ....110 E5
Linden Cres TR7 ......110 E5
Linden Terr PL4 ......149 C3
Lingard Cl PL14 ......113 A6
Lingfield Ave PL26 .....58 E1
Linhay Cl PL25 ....115 D6
Link Cl TR11 ....144 F4
Link Rd PL15 ....106 B3
Linkadells PL7 ....130 D6
Linketty La PL7 ......130 C5
Linketty La E PL6 .....125 A1
Linketty La W PL6 ....128 F8
Links View EX23 ......104 F6
Linley Cl TR3 ....69 D3
Linnet Ct PL12 ....122 C2
Linton Cl PL5 ....124 C8
Linton La EX39 ....2 E5
Linton Rd PL5 ....124 C7
Linton Sq PL5 ....124 C8
Lippell Dr PL9 ....135 E6
Lipson Ave PL4 ....149 C4
Lipson Com Coll PL4 ..129 C4
Lipson Ct PL4 ....149 B3
Lipson Rd PL4 ....149 C4
Lipson Terr PL4 ......149 C4
Lipson Vale PL4 ......129 A4
Lipson Vale Prim Sch
PL4 ....129 A4
Lipstone Cres PL4 ....149 C4
Lisbon Terr PL11 ......97 A6
Liscawn Terr PL11 ....127 B3
Liscombe Cl PL18 .....41 A7
Lishaperhill Cross EX22 ..5 E2
Liskeard (Looe Branch) Sta
PL14 ....113 B4
Liskeard Hill PL14 .....36 F2
Liskeard Inf Sch PL14 .113 B6
Liskeard Jun Sch PL14 .113 A6
Liskeard Rd
Callington PL17 ....39 E4
Saltash PL12 ....122 B3
Trematon PL12 ....53 E3
Liskeard Sch & Com Coll
PL14 ....113 C7
Liskeard Sta PL14 ....113 B4
Liskeard Town Mus★
PL14 ....113 C6
Liskerrett Rd PL14 ....113 D5
Liskey TR6 ....55 A4
Liskey Hill TR6 ....55 A4
Liskey Hill Cres **1** TR6 .55 A4
Lisson Gr PL4 ....128 F4
Lister Cl PL7 ....130 F6
Lister Hill **10** TR11 ...145 A4
Lister St TR11 ....145 A3
Listowel Dr PL13 .....117 D4
Listry Rd TR7 ....110 E5
Litchaton Cres PL7 ....130 B7
Litchaton Way PL7 ....130 B7
Litchfield Cl PL7 .....131 B6
Little Ash Gdns PL5 ...123 B1
Little Ash Rd PL5 .....123 B1
Little Bodieve Holiday Pk
PL27 ....108 D7
Little Bridge Pk PL27 .108 D6
Little Butts PL9 ......135 E6
Little Castle St **7** TR1 .137 C4
Little Dean PL14 .....113 A5
Little Dinas PL28 .....107 E4
Little Dock La PL5 ....124 B2
Little Down La PL6 ...121 E4
Little Down Pk TR7 ...111 A4
Little Fancy Cl PL6 ...125 C7
Little Gilly Hill **3** TR15 .140 C4
Little Gregwartha TR16 .80 A5
Little La Cawsand PL10 .133 A2
Hayle TR27 ....142 E7
Staddiscombe PL9 .....135 D3
Little Laney PL13 ......62 D1
Little Mdw PL31 ......109 D5
Little Mill La TR27 .....77 E2
Little Oaks TR10 .....144 B6
Little Orch PL12 ....53 C3
Little Point Cres PL10 .132 F5
Little Stark Cl PL26 ....58 B4
Little Treloweth TR15 .139 B6
Little Trelyn PL27 .....21 E2
Little Trethewey Est
TR19 ....96 E4
Little Trethiggey TR8 ..111 F2
Little Woburn Cl PL15 .106 C4
Littlebridge Mdw EX22 ..8 A5
Littleton Pl PL2 ......127 F4
Littlewood Cl PL7 ....131 A4
Lizard Cl PL6 ....124 F7
Lizard Head La TR12 ..102 E2
Lizard Nature Reserve The★
TR12 ....100 F2
Lizard Wlk PL6 ......125 A4
Llawnroc Cl TR14 ....138 C2
Llewellyn Cl PL32 ....105 C3

Lloyds Rd TR12 ......103 A2
Loatmead Cross EX22 ...3 E3
Lockeridge Rd PL20 ....41 B1
Lockington Ave PL3 ...128 F7
Locks Wlk PL1 ....127 E1
Lockyer Ct PL1 ......148 C2
Lockyer Mews PL19 ...147 C6
Lockyer Rd PL3 ......128 F5
Lockyer St PL1 ....148 C2
Lockyer Terr PL12 ....123 A3
Lockyers Quay PL4 ...149 B2
Lodenek Ave PL28 ....107 D4
Lodge Dr TR1 ....137 F6
Lodge Gdns PL6 .....124 E3
Lodge Hill PL14 ......113 A3
Lodge La PL8 ....136 F5
Lodge Way TR9 ....45 E2
Loe Bar Rd TR13 ......98 C8
Loe Valley Rd TR13 ...146 B7
Lofotten Cl PL1 ......127 E2
Loftus Gdns PL5 .....123 C2
Loggans Cl TR27 .....142 E8
Loggans Rd Hayle TR27 .78 B6
Phillack TR27 ....142 E8
Loggans Way TR27 ...142 E8
Lollabury Rd PL12 ...122 E3
Long Acre PL12 ......122 B4
Long Barn The TR20 ...89 A8
Long Cross PL29 ......22 C6
Long Down Gdns PL6 .125 C3
Long Orch PL20 ....41 B1
Long Park Cl PL9 .....135 F5
Long Park Dr PL6 ....125 D7
Long Park Rd PL12 ...122 D2
Long Rd PL12 ....122 B4
Long Row PL19 ....88 B1
Long Rowden PL3 ....128 E6
Long Stps PL23 ......116 C4
Long Terrace Cl **5** PL7 .131 C5
Long-A-Row Cl EX23 ...10 C6
Longacre
Harrowbarrow PL17 ....40 C4
Plymouth PL7 ....130 B7
Longbridge Cl PL6 ...129 F6
Longbridge Rd
Plymouth, Laira PL3 ..129 C4
Plymouth, Longbridge PL6 .129 E7
Longbrook Barton PL7 .130 D5
Longbrook St PL7 ....130 F4
Longcause PL7 ....130 F4
Longcause Com Specl Sch
PL7 ....130 F4
Longcoombe La PL13 ..62 D3
Longdowns Trad Est
TR10 ....81 A1
Longfield TR11 ......144 E4
Longfield Cl **25** PL17 ..39 F4
Longfield Dr PL32 ....105 C3
Longfield Pl PL4 .....149 B4
Longfield Rd PL32 ....105 C3
Longfield Villas PL9 ..135 D8
Longhouse La PL27 ....21 E3
Longlands PL9 ....135 D8
Longlands La PL12 ....122 B1
Longman's La **3** PL17 ..39 F4
Longmeadow Cl PL7 ..130 E7
Longmeadow Rd PL12 .122 C3
Longpark Dr EX23 .....6 F5
Longpark Way PL25 ..114 F5
Longrock Bsns Pk TR20 .88 F6
Longrock Ind Est TR20 ..88 F6
Longstone Ave PL6 ...125 A6
Longstone Cl TR26 ...141 E1
Longstone Hill TR26 ..141 E1
Longview Rd PL12 ....122 D3
Longview Terr PL3 ...129 B7
Longwood Cl PL7 ....131 A4
Longwool Mdw EX23 ...7 B6
Looe Aquarium★ PL13 .117 C3
Looe Bay Holiday Pk
PL13 ....117 F8
Looe Com Sch PL13 ..117 D6
Looe Hill Looe PL13 ...63 F7
Seaton PL13,PL11 ....64 A5
Looe Prim Sch PL13 ..117 D4
Looe St PL4 ....149 A2
Looe Sta PL13 ....117 C4
Looe Workshop Units
PL13 ....117 C5
Lookout The TR11 ....145 B5
Looseleigh Cl PL6 ....125 A4
Looseleigh La PL6 ....124 F5
Looseleigh Pk PL6 ...124 E5
Lopes Dr PL6 ....121 C4
Lopes Rd Dousland PL20 .42 E3
Plymouth PL2 ....128 B6
Lopwell Cl PL6 ......124 F5
Lord Louis Cres PL9 ..134 F6
Lords Mdw PL12 ......71 F3
Lorrimore Ave PL2 ...127 F5
Loscombe Cl TR16 ....80 A5
Loscombe La TR16 ....80 A5
Loscombe Rd TR16 ..139 E1
Lost Gdns of Heligan★
PL26 ....73 B5
Lostwithiel Sta PL22 .112 C2
Lostwithiel Mus★ PL22 .112 C2
Lostwithiel Rd PL30,PL31 .48 C2
Lostwithiel Sch PL22 .112 C2
Lostwithiel St PL23 ..116 C4
Lostwood Rd PL25 ...114 E4

Lotherton Cl PL7 .....131 B3
Loughboro Rd PL5 ...123 C1
Love La Bodmin PL31 .109 F5
Hayle TR27 ....142 E7
Mousehole TR19 ....88 C1
Penryn TR10 ....144 D8
Penzance TR18 ....143 C4
Saltash PL12 ....122 E2
24 St Ives TR26 .....141 B6
Lovell Rd PL3 ....128 F6
Lovely La PL12 ....65 A8
Loveny Cl PL14 ....36 F2
Loveny Rd PL14 ......36 F2
Lovibond Wlk PL27 ..108 C5
Low Lee Rd TR19 .....88 D1
Lowen Ct **7** TR1 ....137 D4
Lowen Way TR3 ....69 C3
Lowenac Cres TR27 ...78 E6
Lowenac Gdns TR14 ..138 C2
Lowenek Cl TR14 ....144 E5
Lower Anderton Rd
PL10 ....132 F5
Lower Aylmer Sq **15**
PL25 ....114 C3
Lower Barncoose TR15 .139 F6
Lower Biteford Cross
EX39 ....3 E6
Lower Bore St PL31 ..109 D5
Lower Boscaswell Parc
TR19 ....74 F1
Lower Broad La TR15,
TR16 ....139 C8
Lower Cardrew La TR15 140 B6
Lower Castle Rd TR2 ..95 A5
Lower Chapel St PL13 .117 D3
Lower Church St TR27 .142 D6
Lower Clicker Rd PL14 .51 F4
Lower Compton Rd PL3 128 F5
Lower Coronation Terr **9**
PL17 ....39 F4
Lower East St **1** TR9 ..45 E6
Lower Eastcliff TR4 ...68 A7
Lower Elms PL27 ......21 F3
Lower Fairfield PL12 ...65 A8
Lower Farm Rd PL7 ..131 A4
Lower Fore St PL12 ..123 A4
Lower Glen Pk PL14 ...38 D4
Lower Goongumpas La
TR16 ....68 F1
Lower Green St TR18 .143 E6
Lower Greenbanks PL21 .21 E2
Lower Gurnick Rd TR18 143 E5
Lower Hill TR13 .....146 C6
Lower Hillcrest
Helston TR13 ....146 C6
Perranporth TR6 ......55 A4
Lower Hillside PL14 ...50 B6
Lower Hugus Rd TR3 ..69 C3
Lower Kelly PL18 ......41 A3
Lower La Mawgan TR12 ..99 D7
6 Plymouth PL1 .....149 A2
Lower Lux St **3** PL14 .113 C6
Lower Market St
Looe PL13 ....117 D3
Penryn TR10 ....144 C7
Lower Mdw TR4 ....69 A3
Lower Merritts Hill **22**
TR16 ....67 E4
Lower Middle Hill PL14 .38 E4
Lower Molinnis PL26 ...47 D2
Lower Parc TR12 ......92 C2
Lower Pengegon TR14 .138 F3
Lower Peverell Rd TR18 143 E7
Lower Pk PL2 ....70 F5
Lower Polstain Rd TR3 ..69 D3
Lower Port View PL12 .122 F2
Lower Pumpfield Row
TR15 ....139 B6
Lower Rd PL11 ....64 C4
Lower Redannick TR1 .137 C4
Lower Ridings PL7 ...131 B7
Lower Rosewin Row **9**
TR1 ....137 D5
Lower Row PL13 .....133 A2
Lower Saltram PL9 ...135 C7
Lower Sheffield TR19 ..88 B1
Lower Sq EX22 ....11 E8
Lower St Looe PL13 ..117 D3
Plymouth PL4 ....149 A3
Lower Tamar Terr PL18 .41 A7
Lower Terr TR3 ....81 B4
Lower Tregongeeves
PL26 ....59 A1
Lower Tywarnhayle **11**
TR6 ....55 A5
Lower Well La TR13 ..146 C6
Lower Well Pk TR13 ...73 C3
Lower Wesley Terr PL14 .38 D4
Lower Woodside PL25 .114 A4
Lowerside PL2 ....128 A8
Lowertown Cl PL12 ...53 C3
Lowertown La TR13 ..146 C7
Lowery Cross PL20 ...42 F4
Lowley Rd PL15 ....18 E2
Lucas Cl PL31 ....109 E3
Lucas La PL7 ....130 D6
Lucas Terr PL4 ......129 B2
Lucknow Rd PL31 .....48 D8
Lucknow Rd S PL31 ...48 D8
Ludgvan Com Prim Sch
TR20 ....89 B8
Ludlow Rd **2** PL3 ...128 E6
Luffman Cl PL13 ......62 D6
Lugger The TR2 ....83 B2
Luke's La TR20 ....89 F6
Lukes Cl TR1 ....137 F5
Lulworth Dr PL6 .....125 B7

Lundy Cl PL6 ....124 F7
Lundy Dr EX23 ....10 C6
Lundy Rd PL27 ....22 C7
Lusart Dr **1** TR12 ...102 F2
Lusty Glaze Rd TR7 ..111 A7
Lutsford Cross EX39 ...3 A6
Lutyens Fold PL19 ....29 C6
Luxmore Cl PL6 .....125 E1
Luxon Dr TR7 ....110 F4
Luxstowe Dr **1** PL14 .113 C6
Luxstowe Gdns PL14 .113 C6
Luxulyan Rd PL24 ...115 F7
Luxulyan Sch PL30 ....48 A1
Luxulyan Sta PL30 ....47 F1
Lych Cl PL9 ....135 A6
Lychgate Dr TR1 ....137 C6
Lyd Gdns PL19 ......147 D5
Lydcot Wlk PL6 ......125 A1
Lydcott Cl PL13 ......63 F8
Lydcott Cres PL13 ....63 F8
Lydford Park Rd PL3 .128 D5
Lydia Way PL4 ......149 B4
Lympne Ave PL5 .....123 C5
Lyn Terr **7** TR18 ....143 C1
Lyn-Meynel TR15 ....140 C4
Lynbridge Ct **5** PL19 .147 B5
Lyndhurst Ave PL25 .115 A4
Lyndhurst Cl PL2 ....128 A4
Lyndhurst Rd PL2 ...128 C6
Lyndon Ct PL12 .....122 D4
Lyndrick Rd PL3 .....128 E2
Lynes Cotts **2** PL14 ..51 A7
Lynher Cl PL15 ....27 B3
Lynher Dr PL12 .....122 F1
Lynher St PL5 ....123 D2
Lynher View PL17 .....38 E8
Lynher Way
28 Callington PL17 ...39 F4
North Hill PL15 ....27 A4
Lynmouth Cl PL7 ....130 C7
Lynstone Rd EX23 ...104 D4
Lynwood Ave PL7 ...130 B6
Lynwood Cl PL31 ....109 C4
Lynwood Cotts **1** TR19 .88 C1
Lynwood Flats TR13 ..91 A1
Lyons Cl PL25 ....115 B4
Lytton Pl PL25 ......114 F4

M

Mabbots Ct TR18 ....143 F6
Mabe Com Prim Sch
TR10 ....81 C1
Mabena Cl PL30 ......34 C8
Macadam Rd PL4 ....149 C1
Macaulay Cres PL5 ..124 C1
Macey St PL11 ......127 C3
Mackenzie Pl PL5 ...123 C2
Madden Rd PL1 .....127 F2
Maddever Cres PL7 ..113 C5
Maddock Cl PL7 .....131 A4
Maddock Dr PL7 ....131 B4
Madeira Dr EX23 ......6 F5
Madeira Rd PL1 .....149 A1
Madeira Wlk TR11 ..145 A2
Madeirs Villas **1** PL20 .42 C5
Madford La PL15 ....106 C5
Madge Ct PL19 ......147 B6
Madge La PL19 .....147 B6
Madison Terr TR27 ..142 E7
Madison Vean TR27 ..142 E7
Madron Rd TR18 ....143 C7
Maen Valley Pk TR11 144 D1
Maenporth Est TR11 ..93 A4
Maenporth Rd TR11 ..93 A4
Maer Down Rd EX23 .104 C4
Maer La PL23 ....104 D8
Magdalen Gdns PL7 ..130 F3
Magnificent Music Machines
Mus★ PL14 ....51 C3
Magnolia Cl **3** PL7 ..131 B5
Magor Ave TR14 ......79 E5
Maida Vale Terr PL4 .128 F4
Maiden St **1** EX23 ....4 E1
Maidenwell Rd PL7 ..130 C5
Maidstone Pl PL5 ...123 E4
Main Rd Crumplehorn PL13 62 D2
Downderry PL11 ......64 C5
Main St TR18 ....143 E7
Maine Gdns PL2 .....127 F7
Mainstone Ave PL4 ..149 C2
Maitland Dr PL3 .....128 F8
Maker La PL10 ......133 B4
Maker Rd PL11 ......127 A2
Maker View PL3 .....128 B4
Malabar Rd TR1 ......69 F3
Mallard Cl PL7 ......130 F5
Malmesbury Cl PL2 ..128 B8
Malory Cl PL5 ......124 C1
Malpas Rd TR1 .....137 E2
Malt House Ct TR27 ..142 D6
Malt House Gdns **2**
TR18 ....143 C2
Malt House The **3**
TR18 ....143 C2
Malthouse La **1** TR13 .89 C5
Man Of War View **11**
TR12 ....102 F2
Manaccan Prim Sch
TR12 ....101 A8
Manadon Cl PL5 ....124 E1
Manadon Dr PL5 ....124 E1
Manadon Hill PL5,PL6 .124 E1
Manadon Vale Prim Sch
PL5 ....128 E8
Manaton Cl TR13 ...146 D8

Mandeley Cl PL33 .....14 D2
Manewas Way TR7 ...111 B7
Manfield Way PL25 ..115 C4
Manifold Gdns PL3 ..129 D5
Manley Cl PL14 .....113 B5
Manley Rd PL14 ....113 B5
Manley Terr **5** PL14 .113 B5
Mannamead Ave PL3 .128 F5
Mannamead Rd PL3 ..128 F4
Manor Bourne Rd PL9 .135 C1
Manor Cl Blisland PL30 ..34 C8
Crackington Haven EX23 ..10 C6
Falmouth TR11 ......144 E5
Heamoor TR18 ......143 D7
Helston TR13 ....146 D8
St Austell PL25 .....114 F5
Tavistock PL19 .....147 A6
Manor Cotts TR11 ...145 D3
Manor Cres TR11 ...144 E5
Manor Ct **1** TR2 .....95 A6
Manor Dr TR26 .....141 C3
Manor Farm PL20 ....42 E3
Manor Farm Cl **7** TR20 .89 B5
Manor Gdns
Camelford PL32 .....105 D4
Horrabridge PL20 .....42 B4
Plymouth PL2 ....148 B2
Redruth TR15 ....140 B6
Manor La PL3 ....129 C5
Manor Park Cl PL7 ..130 F5
Manor Park Dr PL7 ..131 A4
Manor Pk Dousland PL20 .42 E3
Duloe PL14 ....51 A1
Saltash PL12 ....122 D2
Manor Pl PL18 ......143 D7
Manor Rd Bude EX23 .104 E4
Camborne TR14 .....138 C2
Carharrack TR16 ......80 F8
Falmouth TR11 ......144 E5
Newquay TR7 ....110 D6
Plymouth PL9 ....135 E8
Tavistock PL19 .....147 B6
Manor St PL1 ....148 A3
Manor View PL24 .....60 B4
Manor Way
Heamoor TR18 ......143 D7
Helston TR13 ....146 D8
Manse Rd **6** TR3 .....81 B7
Manson PL26 ....58 C8
Manston Cl PL5 .....123 E5
Mantle Gdns PL5 ....127 D8
Maple Ave PL11 .....127 A3
Maple Cl Bodmin PL31 .109 B4
23 Callington PL17 ...39 F4
Plymouth PL6 ....125 E6
5 St Columb Major TR9 ..45 E6
Tavistock PL19 .....147 C3
Maple Gr
Plymouth, Mutley PL4 .128 D4
Plymouth, Plympton PL7 .130 B5
Maple Way PL6 .....125 E7
Marazion Prim Sch TR17 89 B5
Marazion Town Mus★
TR17 ....89 B5
Marbein Cotts TR8 ...44 D8
Marchant's Cross PL20 .42 F1
Marchant's Way PL20 .42 A4
Marconi Cl TR13 ....146 B6
Marcus Hill TR7 .....110 E6
Marcwheal **6** TR19 ...88 C1
Mardon Cl PL6 ......125 D4
Marett Rd PL5 ......123 F3
Margaret Ave PL25 ..114 E3
Margaret Cres PL31 .109 C4
Margaret Gdns PL27 .108 D5
Margaret Pk PL3 ....128 E8
Margaret Pl TR11 ...144 F3
Margate La PL30 ....107 F5
Marhamchurch CE Prim Sch
EX23 ....7 B6
Maria's La TR19 ......96 B7
Maribou Ct PL28 ......31 F7
Marina Rd PL5 ......123 F3
Marina Terr **7** PL4 ..128 F4
Marine Cres **5** TR11 ..145 C3
Marine Ct Falmouth TR11 145 D3
17 Perranporth TR6 ...55 A4
Torpoint PL11 ......127 B2
Marine Dr Looe PL13 .117 C3
Torpoint PL11 ......127 B2
Widemouth Bay EX23 ...6 E5
Marine Par TR2 ......95 A5
Marine Pk PL9 ......135 B7
Marine Terr Boscastle PL35 ..9 C2
6 Penzance TR18 ....143 E4
Maristow Ave PL2 ...127 F5
Maristow Cl PL6 ....124 F5
Market Ave PL1 .....148 B3
Market Bldgs TR27 ..142 D6
Market Cl PL1 ......128 A1
Market Hill PL25 ....114 C4
Market House Arc **8**
PL1 ....106 C6
Market Jew St TR18 .143 E5
Market Pl
Camelford PL32 .....105 D4
Helston TR13 ....146 B5
Marazion TR17 ......89 B5
Padstow PL28 ......107 D5
25 Penzance TR18 ...143 E5
St Columb Major TR9 ..45 E6
33 St Ives TR26 .....141 B6
Week St Mary EX22 ...11 E8
Market Rd Plymouth PL7 .130 D5
Tavistock PL19 .....147 C5
Market Sq Callington PL17 .39 E4
Hayle TR27 ....142 D6
Plymouth PL1 ......148 C3

Market Sq *continued*
St Day TR16 68 D1
St Just TR19 86 F6
Market St Bodmin PL31 109 E5
Cawsand PL10 133 A2
Devoran TR3 81 F6
Falmouth TR11 145 B4
Fowey PL23 116 D4
Hayle TR27 142 D6
9 Launceston PL15 106 C6
Liskeard PL14 113 C6
Plymouth PL1 128 A1
6 St Austell PL25 114 C3
St Just TR19 86 F6
3 Stratton EX23 4 E1
Tavistock PL19 147 C5
Market Strand
Falmouth TR11 145 B4
Padstow PL28 107 D5
7 Redruth TR15 140 B5
31 St Ives TR26 141 B6
Market Way
Plymouth PL1 148 C3
5 Redruth TR15 140 B4
Marks Dr PL31 109 E3
Markwell La PL12 53 C1
Marlborough Ave TR11 145 A3
Marlborough Cl
1 Falmouth TR11 145 A3
Saltash PL12 122 F1
Marlborough Cres TR11 145 A3
Marlborough Ct 5
TR11 145 A3
Marlborough Gr 2
TR11 145 A3
Marlborough Prim Sch
PL1 127 E2
Marlborough Rd
Falmouth TR11 145 B3
Plymouth PL4 149 A4
Marlborough Row PL1 127 E2
Marlborough Sch TR11 145 A3
Marlborough St PL1 127 E2
Marlborough Way PL26 58 E1
Marldon Cl PL5 124 B3
Marlow Gdns PL9 135 F5
Marriotts Ave TR14 138 B4
Marrowbone Slip PL4 149 B2
Marryat Gdns PL5 124 E1
Marsh Cl PL6 129 F6
Marsh La Angarrack TR27 142 F7
Calstock PL18 41 A3
Hayle TR27 142 E7
Marsh Mills PL6 129 F7
Marsh Mills Pk PL6 129 F6
Marsh Mills Ret Pk PL6 129 E7
Marshall Ave PL27 108 D5
Marshall Cl Roche PL26 46 F3
Tavistock PL19 147 D2
Marshall Rd
Bodmin PL31 109 D3
Bodmin, Nanstallon PL30 34 C2
Plymouth PL7 130 A5
Tavistock PL19 147 D2
Marshallen Rd TR4 68 C6
Marshalls Way PL29 22 D6
Marshfield View PL11 64 B5
Marshlands PL27 34 A6
Martin Cl TR15 140 D5
Martin La
Plymouth, Barbican PL4 149 A2
Plymouth, Millbay PL1 148 B2
Martin Sq 6 PL17 39 F4
Martin St PL1 148 B2
Martin's Ct 2 PL31 109 D5
Martin's La TR15 139 C8
Martins Cl PL14 113 E7
Martinvale Ave TR15 140 E7
Martinvale Parc TR15 140 E7
Martlesham Pl PL5 123 F4
Martyn's Cl TR4 55 D4
Mary Dean Ave PL5 124 C7
Mary Dean Cl PL5 124 C7
Mary Dean's CE Prim Sch
PL5 124 C7
Mary Moon Cl PL12 53 B7
Mary Newman's Cottage★
PL12 123 A2
Mary Seacole Rd PL1 148 A3
Maryland Cotts PL30 34 C5
Maryland Gdns PL2 127 F7
Marythorne Rd 15 PL20 41 B1
Masefield Gdns PL5 124 B1
Masons Row PL18 40 F6
Masterman Rd PL2 127 F4
Matela Cl 10 TR13 98 C8
Matthews Way PL14 51 F6
Maudlin Cl PL14 113 D5
Maudlins La PL19 147 A5
Maunsell Cl PL2 127 F7
Maurice Ct PL7 130 F4
Mawes Ct PL18 40 D5
Mawgan TR12 99 D6
Mawgan Cross TR12 99 D7
Mawgan-in-Pydar Com Prim
Sch TR8 45 A8
Mawnan Village CE Prim Sch
TR11 93 D3
Maxwell Rd PL4 135 B8
Maxworthy Cross PL15 12 B4
May Gdns TR16 80 D6
May La PL13 117 F5
May Terr PL4 149 B3
Maybank Rd PL4 149 C3
Maybrook Dr PL12 122 D2
Mayers Way PL9 135 D6
Mayfair Cres PL6 125 B1
Mayfield Cl Bodmin PL31 35 B2
Mayfield Cl *continued*
Port Isaac PL29 22 E7
St Austell PL25 115 A4
Mayfield Cres TR7 110 E5
Mayfield Dr
Port Isaac PL27 22 E7
Roche PL26 47 A3
Mayfield Rd
Falmouth TR11 144 F4
Newquay TR7 110 E5
Port Isaac PL29 22 E7
Mayflower Cl
18 Bere Alston PL20 41 B1
Plymouth PL9 135 F7
Mayflower Dr PL2 128 B5
Mayflower St PL1 148 C3
Maymear Terr PL30 23 E3
Mayna Parc PL15 18 B8
Maynard Pk PL20 41 B1
Maynarde Cl PL7 131 B5
Mayne Cl PL15 106 B7
Maynes Row TR14 139 A5
Mayon Farm TR19 96 B6
Mayon Green Cres TR19 96 B7
Mclean Dr PL26 58 D5
Mead Cnr EX39 2 D4
Mead Hos The TR18 143 F8
Mead The PL7 130 D7
Meadfoot Terr PL4 128 F5
Meadow Brook PL19 147 A4
Meadow Cl Gloweth TR1 69 E3
Newquay TR7 111 A4
Plymouth PL7 131 D4
Polruan PL23 116 D2
Saltash PL12 122 F3
St Austell PL25 114 F6
St Stephen PL26 58 B4
Meadow Ct
Mevagissey PL26 73 C3
Wadebridge PL30 34 C8
Meadow Dr Bude EX23 104 F6
Camborne TR14 138 C4
Looe PL13 117 D5
Par PL24 115 F5
Saltash PL12 122 D4
Meadow Flats 27 TR26 141 B6
Meadow La TR1 137 D3
Meadow Pk
7 Liskeard PL14 113 B5
Plymouth PL9 135 C5
Trewoon PL25 59 A3
Meadow Pl PL31 109 D4
Meadow Rd PL13 62 A7
Meadow Rise
1 Penwithick PL26 59 D7
Plymouth PL7 131 A4
12 St Columb Major TR9 45 E6
Meadow St PL26 73 C3
Meadow Terr PL14 37 F3
Meadow The Illogan TR16 67 D4
Truro TR1 137 B5
Meadow View
Camborne TR14 138 E1
8 Goldsithney TR20 89 E5
St Minver PL27 21 F3
Meadow View Rd PL7 130 D5
Meadow Villas 8 TR18 143 C1
Meadow Way
Plymouth PL7 130 D7
St Issey PL27 32 E6
Meadow Wlk PL23 116 D2
Meadowbank TR11 82 A3
Meadowbank Rd TR11 145 A6
Meadowfield Pl PL7 131 B3
Meadowhead PL27 108 C4
Meadowlands PL6 125 D7
Meadows The
St Dennis PL26 58 C8
St Dominick PL12 40 D2
St Teath PL30 23 E7
Torpoint PL11 126 E4
Meadowside
Launceston PL15 106 A4
Newquay TR7 111 A4
Plymouth PL9 135 F7
St Austell PL25 115 C6
Whitstone EX22 12 B8
Meadowside Cl
Hayle TR27 142 A3
St Kew Highway PL30 23 B2
Meadowside Rd TR11 144 F2
Meadowside Rise PL26 58 D6
Meadowsweet Pk PL12 122 C2
Meadway Looe PL13 117 E4
Saltash PL12 122 E1
St Austell PL25 114 F5
Mearwood La TR11 144 F4
Meaver Rd TR12 99 B1
Meavy Ave PL5 124 E2
Meavy Bourne PL20 42 D2
Meavy CE Prim Sch PL20 42 F2
Meavy La PL20 42 D2
Meavy Villas PL20 42 D2
Meavy Way Plymouth PL5 124 E2
Tavistock PL19 147 D5
Meddon Cross
Edistone EX39 3 C5
Welcombe EX39 3 C4
Meddy's Row PL14 39 A2
Medland Cres PL6 124 D6
Medland Gdns PL25 114 C4
Medlyn Ct TR13 146 B5
Medrose St PL33 14 E3
Medrose Terr 22 TR18 143 E6
Medrow PL15 27 A8
Medway Pl PL3 129 D6
Meeks Row PL18 41 A6
Melbourne Cotts PL1 148 B3
Melbourne Gn 2 PL1 148 B3
Melbourne Pl PL1 148 B4
Melbourne Rd PL14 113 B5
Melbourne St PL1 148 B3
Melbourne Terr 17
TR18 143 C7
Mellanear Cl TR27 142 B4
Mellanear Rd TR27 142 B3
Mellanvrane La TR7 110 F4
Melliars Way EX23 104 F6
Melrose Ave PL2 128 C8
Melrose Terr 6 TR9 45 E1
Melvill Cres TR11 145 B3
Melvill Ct TR11 145 B2
Melvill La TR11 145 B2
Melvill Rd TR11 145 C2
Melville Pl 1 PL2 128 A5
Melville Rd Plymouth PL2 128 A5
Threemilestone TR3 69 D3
Melville Terr PL22 112 C2
Mena Park Cl PL9 136 B7
Mena Park Rd PL9 136 B7
Menabilly Cl PL17 39 E3
Menabilly Rd PL25 114 E6
Menacuddle Hill PL25 114 C4
Menacuddle La PL25 114 C4
Menadue Ct TR27 78 E3
Menage St TR13 146 C5
Menague PL27 21 E3
Menakarne TR16 80 F8
Menallack Cheese Farm★
TR10 93 A6
Meneage Cotts 2 TR13 146 C5
Meneage Ho 3 TR13 146 C5
Meneage Parc TR13 146 C5
Meneage Rd TR13 146 C4
Meneage St TR13 146 C5
Meneage Villas PL25 114 B3
Menear Rd PL25 115 A6
Menefreda Way PL27 22 A4
Meneth TR12 92 C1
Meneth Rd TR14 138 F2
Menhay View TR11 144 C3
Menhaye Gdns TR15 139 D7
Menheniot Cres PL15 18 D5
Menheniot Prim Sch
PL14 52 A5
Menheniot Sta PL14 51 F4
Menhinick Cl PL12 53 C3
Menhyr Dr TR26 141 C2
Menna La TR2 57 E5
Mennaye Ct TR18 143 D4
Mennaye Rd TR18 143 D4
Merafield Cl PL7 130 B5
Merafield Dr PL7 130 C4
Merafield Farm Cotts
PL7 130 B4
Merafield Rd PL7 130 B4
Merafield Rise PL7 130 C4
Merchants House (Mus)★
PL1 148 C2
Merchants Quay PL15 18 E2
Meredith Rd PL2 128 C6
Meres Valley TR12 99 A2
Meridian Ho PL4 149 A3
Merlin Cl PL6 125 E8
Merlins Way PL34 14 D7
Mermaid Ct TR7 111 C8
Merrick Ave TR1 137 E6
Merrifield Cl TR1 137 B5
Merrifield Cross EX22 7 F4
Merrill Pl TR11 145 A3
Merritts Hill TR16 67 E4
Merritts Way TR15 139 C7
Merrivale Rd
Plymouth, Ham PL2 128 B7
Plymouth, Honicknowle
PL5 124 B3
Merrivale View Rd PL20 42 E3
Merry Mit Mdw TR11 144 C3
Mersey Cl PL3 129 D6
Merther Cl TR13 91 B4
Messack Cl TR11 144 E2
Metha Pk TR8 56 C7
Metha Rd TR8 56 C7
Methleigh Bottoms TR13 91 A1
Methleigh Parc TR13 91 A1
Mevagissey Aquarium★
PL26 73 C3
Mevagissey Com Prim Sch
PL26 73 C4
Mevagissey Ho TR1 69 E4
Mevagissey Mus★ PL26 73 C3
Mews Ct PL14 51 F5
Mews The Par PL24 60 B5
3 Penzance TR18 143 E6
Plymouth, Devonport PL1 128 A3
Plymouth, Stonehouse PL1 148 A3
Mexico La TR27 142 C7
Mexico Terr TR27 142 C8
Michael Rd PL3 129 A5
Michaelstow Holiday Village
PL30 23 F5
Michell Ave TR7 110 E6
Michigan Way PL3 129 C6
Mid Churchway PL9 136 A7
Mid Cornwall Bsns Ctr
PL25 115 E4
Mid Moor PL14 38 B6
Middle Down Cl PL9 136 A5
Middle Market St PL13 117 D3
Middle Rd TR15 140 E7
Middle Rosewin Row 8
TR1 137 D5
Middle Row TR13 90 E3
Middle St Padstow PL28 107 D5
Port Isaac PL29 22 D7
Middle Wharf PL26 73 C3
Middlefield Rd PL6 124 D6
Middlefield Cl PL12 122 B2
Middlegates 5 TR5 54 D1
Middleton Cres TR7 110 F4
Middleton Wlk PL5 123 D4
Middletons Row 6
TR15 140 C5
Middleway PL24 60 B5
Middlewell Parc PL27 108 B4
Midella Rd PL20 42 D2
Midway Dr TR1 137 E5
Midway Rd PL31 109 A5
Miers Cl PL5 127 C8
Mildmay St PL4 149 A4
Mile End TR12 102 F4
Milehouse Rd PL2 128 A5
Miles Mitchell Ave PL6 125 A1
Miles Mitchell Village
PL6 125 A1
Milford La PL5 124 B5
Military Rd
Millbrook PL10 132 C3
Plymouth PL3 129 E6
Rame PL10 64 C2
St Mawes TR2 95 B4
Mill Ball Hill EX23 10 B7
Mill Bridge PL1 148 A3
Mill Cl Porthleven TR13 91 A1
Wadebridge PL27 108 E5
Mill Cotts TR13 146 A6
Mill Ford Sch PL5 123 F4
Mill Gdns PL22 112 C2
Mill Hill Crumplehorn PL13 62 D1
Lelant TR27 77 E3
Lostwithiel PL22 112 D2
St Just In Roseland TR2 82 F3
Mill La Camelford PL32 105 D5
Coad's Green PL15 27 C1
Grampound TR2 72 A7
Helston TR13 146 B6
19 Mousehole TR19 88 C1
Porthleven TR13 91 A1
St Breward PL30 24 B3
St Germans PL12 65 A8
Torpoint PL11 127 A2
Tregony TR2 71 F3
Truro TR3 137 C1
Mill Pool 15 TR19 88 C1
Mill Rd Millbrook PL10 133 A5
Padstow PL28 107 D5
Penponds TR14 79 B5
Perranporth TR6 55 B4
Tideford PL12 52 F2
Mill Rd Est PL12 52 F2
Mill Sq PL28 107 D5
Mill St PL31 109 E5
Mill View Gdns PL10 132 F5
Mill View Rd PL10 132 F5
Milladon La PL12 64 D8
Millbank Mdw TR27 78 E1
Millbay Rd PL1 148 A2
Millbrook CE Sch PL10 132 E5
Millendreath Holliday Vill
PL13 117 F5
Millenium Appartments
TR10 81 D2
Millennium Way TR13 146 D8
Miller Bsns Pk PL14 113 B4
Miller Ct PL1 148 A2
Miller Way PL6 125 E3
Millet Cl TR17 89 D5
Millfield TR18 88 E6
Millham La PL22 112 E3
Millhill PL19 30 B1
Millhouse Pk PL11 127 A2
Millpond Ave TR27 142 B4
Millpool PL22 112 F3
Millpool Head PL10 132 E4
Millpool Rd PL10 133 A6
Mills Rd PL1 127 F2
Mills' St TR16 68 E1
Milltown Gdns PL15 18 E6
Millway Pl PL9 135 D8
Millwood Dr PL6 125 E1
Milne Pl PL1 127 F3
Milton Abbott Sch PL19 29 D5
Milton Cl PL5 124 D2
Milton Cres PL19 147 D5
Milton Ct Plymouth PL4 129 B1
Plymouth PL4 149 C2
Minack Theatre★ TR19 96 E2
Mine Hill PL14 51 F6
Mine La PL30 47 E7
Mineral Tramways Discovery
Ctr TR15 139 B4
Miners Ct TR6 55 A4
Miners Row TR15 140 C5
Miners Way PL14 113 D7
Minerva Cl PL7 131 A6
Minions Row PL14 38 B6
Minnie Pl TR11 145 B3
Minorca La PL26 47 D2
Minses Cl PL9 136 C7
Minster Ave EX23 104 F4
Minster Mdw TR12 101 A8
Minster Terr TR12 101 A8
Minton Cl PL25 115 A4
Mirador Pl PL4 129 C3
Misterton Cl PL9 136 B8
Mitchell Cl 3 TR12 102 F2
Mitchell Ct 11 TR1 137 D5
Mitchell Hill TR1 137 D5
Mitchell Hill Terr 4
TR1 137 D5
Mitchell La
Camborne TR14 138 E3
Mitchell TR8 56 E5
Mitchell Rd
Camborne TR14 138 C3
St Austell PL25 114 F4
Mitchell's Boatyard
PL26 73 C2
Mithian Jun & Inf Sch
TR5 54 E1
Mitre Ct 15 Plymouth PL1 149 A2
Tavistock PL19 147 A3
Modbury Cl PL5 124 B3
Modus La PL26 58 E1
Modyford Wlk PL20 41 F3
Mohun's Cl PL19 147 C4
Mohun's Pk PL19 147 C3
Molenick La PL12 52 E3
Molesworth Ct 4 PL27 108 B5
Molesworth Rd
Plymouth, Plympton PL7 130 C6
Plymouth, Stoke PL1,PL3 128 A3
Molesworth St
Tintagel PL34 14 C7
Wadebridge PL27 108 B5
Molesworth Terr PL10 132 F5
Molinnis PL26 47 C2
Molinnis Rd PL26 47 C2
Mollison Rd PL5 123 E2
Molyneaux Pl 10 PL1 127 F3
Monastery Cl TR12 101 D4
Mongleath Ave TR11 144 E3
Mongleath Cl TR11 144 E3
Mongleath Rd TR11 144 E3
Monica Wlk PL4 149 B4
Monks Hill PL15 28 C4
Monks Park Cotts PL15 106 D6
Monksmead PL19 147 A4
Monmouth Gdns PL5 124 C4
Monmouth La PL22 112 D2
Montacute Ave PL5 124 B2
Montague Ave TR15 140 A6
Monterey Cl EX23 104 E4
Monterey Gdns TR1 137 E5
Montgomery Cl PL12 122 D3
Montgomery Rd 2 PL26 59 D7
Montpelier Jun & Inf Schs
PL2 128 B6
Montpelier Rd PL2 128 C7
Monument Rd TR13 146 B5
Monument St PL1 127 E1
Monument Way PL31 109 C4
Moon La PL4 149 A3
Moon St PL4 149 A3
Moonrakers TR26 141 D2
Moonsfield 5 PL17 39 F4
Moor La PL5 123 E1
Moor Parc TR12 100 D6
Moor St TR14 138 D3
Moor View Bodmin PL31 109 F2
Plymouth, Keyham PL2 127 F5
Plymouth, Laira PL3 129 C4
Torpoint PL11 127 B3
Moor View Terr
Plymouth PL4 128 E4
Yelverton PL20 42 D2
Moorcroft Cl PL9 136 A7
Moorfield PL16 19 F4
Moorfield Ave 4 PL6 129 C7
Moorfield Rd
Camborne TR15 139 C6
St Giles-On-The-Heath PL15 13 F1
Moorlan Mdws PL26 47 A3
Moorland Ave PL7 130 F6
Moorland Cl
Liskeard PL14 113 D7
Pendeen TR19 74 F1
Yelverton PL20 121 D8
Moorland Ct
1 St Austell PL25 114 C3
Yelverton PL20 42 C2
Moorland Dr PL7 130 E6
Moorland Gdns PL7 130 F6
Moorland Rd
Indian Queens TR9 45 F2
Launceston PL15 106 A4
Par PL24 60 C4
Plymouth PL7 130 E5
St Austell PL25 114 C3
Moorland View
Linkinhorne PL17 39 B6
Liskeard PL14 113 D7
Plymouth, Derriford PL6 125 A5
Plymouth, Plymstock PL9 136 B7
Saltash PL12 122 F4
Moorland Way PL18 40 F5
Moorlands La PL12 122 C4
Moorlands Trad Est
PL12 122 C4
Moorview Terr PL14 38 D7
Morcom Cl PL25 115 A5
Moresk Cl TR1 137 D5
Moresk Gdns TR1 137 D5
Moresk Rd TR1 137 D5
Moreton Ave PL6 124 F1
Morice Sq PL1 127 E2
Morice St PL1 127 E2
Morice Town Prim Sch
PL2 127 E4
Morla La TR15 140 A6
Morlaix Ave TR1 137 D3
Morlaix Dr PL6 125 B4
Morleigh Cl PL25 114 F3
Morley Cl PL7 130 A5
Morley Ct PL1 148 B3
Morley Dr PL20 42 A2
Morley View Rd PL7 130 C6
Morrab Ct TR7 110 F6

Morrab Pl 34 TR18 ....143 E5
Morrab Rd
Camborne TR14 ....138 C3
Penzance TR18 ....143 E5
Morrab Terr 35 TR18 ...143 E5
Morrish Pk PL9 ....135 F6
Morshead Rd PL6 ....124 F2
Mortain Rd PL12 ....122 D4
Mortimore Cl PL12 ....122 D2
Morvan Trad Est PL14 ..114 F3
Morven Rd PL25 ....114 F3
Morview Rd PL18 ....63 F8
Morwell Gdns PL2 ....128 A6
Morwellham Quay★
PL19 ....41 B4
Morwenna Gdns TR26 ..55 B5
Morwenna Rd EX23 ....2 D1
Moses Cl PL6 ....124 E7
Moses Ct PL6 ....124 E7
Mosquito Cres 3 PL27 ..31 F3
Moss Side Ind Est PL17 ..39 F4
Moss Terr PL23 ....116 C3
Mostyn Ave PL4 ....129 A4
Mote Pk PL12 ....122 D4
Mothecombe Wlk PL6 ..125 E1
Moulton Cl PL7 ....131 B5
Mount Agar Rd TR3 .....81 F7
Mount Ambrose TR15 ..140 E7
Mount Batten Waterside Pk★
PL9 ....134 F7
Mount Bennett Rd 5
PL24 ....60 D5
Mount Bennett Terr 4
PL24 ....60 D5
Mount Camel PL32 ....105 C4
Mount Carbis Gdns
TR15 ....140 C3
Mount Carbis Rd TR15 .140 D3
Mount Charles Jun & Inf Sch
PL25 ....114 C4
Mount Charles Rd PL25 114 F3
Mount Cres PL24 ....60 C4
Mount Edgcumbe Country
Pk★ PL10 ....133 E6
Mount Edgcumbe Terr
TR11 ....145 B4
Mount Folly TR27 ....142 C6
Mount Gould Ave PL4 .129 B2
Mount Gould Cres PL4 .129 B3
Mount Gould Hospl PL4 129 B3
Mount Gould Rd PL4 ..129 B3
Mount Gould Way PL4 .129 B3
Mount Hawke Chalet Pk
TR4 ....68 B6
Mount Hawke Com Prim Sch
TR4 ....68 C6
Mount House Sch PL19 .147 E7
Mount Lidden TR18 ....143 C4
Mount Pleasant
Bodmin PL31 ....109 E5
Boscastle PL35 ....9 C1
Falmouth TR11 ....144 E1
Hayle TR27 ....142 C6
Lelant TR26 ....77 E3
Millbrook PL10 ....132 E5
Newlyn TR18 ....143 C4
Par PL24 ....60 B6
Plymouth PL5 ....124 B2
39 St Ives TR26 ....141 B6
Mount Pleasant Cl PL18 138 E1
Mount Pleasant Gdns
TR27 ....142 C6
Mount Pleasant Pl PL22 112 C3
Mount Pleasant Rd
Camborne TR14 ....138 D1
11 Porthleven TR13 ....98 B3
Threemilestone TR3 ....69 D3
Mount Pleasant Terr
TR15 ....140 E7
Mount Pleasure TR14 .138 E1
Mount Prospect Terr
TR18 ....143 C3
Mount Rd PL24 ....60 C4
Mount St Mevagissey PL26 73 C3
Penzance TR18 ....143 E6
Plymouth, Mount Wise PL1 127 E1
Plymouth, Mutley PL4 ..149 A4
Mount Stamper Rd
PL25 ....114 D7
Mount Stephens La
TR11 ....144 F4
Mount Stone Rd PL1 ..134 A8
Mount Street Prim Sch
PL4 ....149 A4
Mount Tamar Cl PL5 ..123 A4
Mount Tamar Sch PL5 .123 E2
Mount Tavy Rd PL19 ..147 E6
Mount Terr 9 PL24 .....60 B4
Mount View Lane TR8 ..111 B3
Madron TR20 ....88 A7
Mount View Cotts TR20 .89 A7
Mount View Terr
5 Marazion TR17 ....89 C5
22 Newlyn TR18 ....143 C2
Mount Whistle Rd TR14 138 F7
Mount Wise
Launceston PL15 ....106 C5
Newquay TR7 ....110 D3
Mount Wise Cotts TR7 .110 E5
Mount Wise Ct 1
PL1 ....127 F1
Mount Wise Prim Sch
PL1 ....127 C1
Mount's Bay Hol Flts
TR18 ....88 E6
Mount's Bay Sch TR18 .143 B7

Mount's Bay Terr 21
TR13 ....98 C8
Mount's Rd 20 TR13 ...98 C8
Mountbatten Cl
Plymouth PL9 ....135 D6
St Columb Minor TR7 ..111 E7
Mountbatten Rd 5 PL26 .59 D7
Mountbatten Way PL9 .135 E6
Mountfield Terr 6 PL24 .60 C4
Mountlea PL24 ....60 B4
Mounts Bay Rd PL13 ..143 C4
Mounts Bay Terr TR13 ..90 D3
Mountstephen Cl PL25 .114 B3
Mourne Villas PL9 .....135 F8
Mousehole Com Prim Sch
TR19 ....88 C1
Mousehole La TR19 ....88 C1
Mowbray Mews PL32 ...10 B2
Mowhay Cl TR7 ....111 A4
Mowhay La 1 PL17 ....39 E4
Mowhay Mdw
St John PL11 ....132 B8
Wadebridge PL27 ....108 B4
Mowhay Rd
Plymouth PL5 ....123 F1
Plymouth PL5 ....124 A2
Moyle Rd PL28 ....107 E4
Mr Potter's Mus of
Curiosity★ PL15 ....25 E3
Mudge Way PL7 ....130 E5
Mudges Terr PL18 ....41 A6
Mulberry Cl PL6 ....125 E7
Mulberry Ct TR11 .....145 B5
Mulberry Gr PL19 .....147 C2
Mulberry Quay TR11 ..145 B5
Mulberry Rd PL12 .....122 E1
Mulgrave St PL1 ....148 C2
Mullet Ave PL3 ....129 C4
Mullet Cl PL3 ....129 C4
Mullet Rd PL3 ....129 C4
Mullion Cl PL11 ....126 F4
Mullion Comp Sch TR12 .99 A1
Mullion Jun & Inf Sch
TR12 ....99 A1
Mullion Rural Workshops
TR12 ....99 A1
Mundys Field TR12 ....103 A5
Murdoch Cl
Redruth TR15 ....140 B6
Truro TR1 ....137 E6
Murdock Rd PL11 .....126 F3
Murrey Villas TR19 .....86 E6
Murtons Terr TR16 .....80 E7
Mus of Witchcraft★ PL35 .9 C2
Museum of Submarine
Telegraphy★ TR19 ....96 E3
Mutley Ct PL4 ....149 A4
Mutley Plain PL4 ....128 E4
Mutley Plain La PL4 ..128 E4
Mutley Rd PL3 ....128 E5
Mutton Hill TR27 ....78 D6
Mutton Row TR10 .....144 C8
My Lords Rd TR9 ....57 E8
Mylor Cl PL2 ....128 D8
Mylor Com Prim Sch
TR11 ....82 A3
Myrtle Cl PL20 ....42 E3
Myrtle Ct PL26 ....73 C3
Myrtles Ct PL12 ....122 D4
Myrtleville PL2 ....128 A6
Mythyon Ct 4 TR18 ...143 C7

N

Nailzee Ho PL13 ....117 D2
Nalder's Ct 10 TR1 ...137 C4
Nampara Ct 7 TR6 .....55 A4
Nancarrows PL12 ....122 C2
Nancealverne TR18 ....143 D6
Nancealverne Sch TR20 143 C6
Nancedden Farm TR20 .89 A8
Nancegollan Ind Est
TR13 ....91 B7
Nancemere Rd TR1 ....137 D6
Nancevallon TR14 .....139 B3
Nancherrow Hill TR19 ..86 F6
Nancherrow Row TR19 .86 F6
Nangitha Cl TR11 .....144 C3
Nangitha Terr TR11 ...144 C3
Nanhayes Row TR8 .....56 B7
Nanjivey Pl 8 TR26 ...141 A5
Nanjivey Terr 9 TR26 .141 A5
Nanpean Prim Sch PL26 .58 D6
Nanpusker Cl TR27 ....142 E6
Nanpusker Rd TR27 ....78 C4
Nans Kestenen TR13 ..146 B5
Nansale Ct TR7 ....111 A6
Nansavallon Rd TR1 ...69 F3
Nanscober Pl TR13 ....146 B8
Nansloe Cl TR13 ....146 C4
Nansloe Com Prim Sch
TR13 ....146 C4
Nansmellyon Rd TR12 ..99 A1
Nanstallon Com Prim Sch
PL30 ....34 C1
Nanterrow La TR27 .....66 D1
Nanturras Parc TR20 ...89 F5
Nanturras Row TR20 ...89 E5
Napier St PL1 ....127 F3
Napier Terr PL4 ....128 E4
Narkurs Cross PL11 ....64 D7
Narrow La Saltash PL12 122 C7
Summercourt TR8 ....57 C8
Narrowcliff TR7 ....111 A7
Nash Cl PL7 ....131 A5

Nathan Cl TR7 ....111 B5
National Marine Aquarium★
PL4 ....149 A2
National Seal Sanctuary
The★ TR12 ....92 C1
National Seal Sanctuary
Visitor Ctr★ TR12 ....92 D1
Navy Inn Ct 10 TR18 ..143 C1
Neal Cl PL7 ....131 B4
Neath Rd PL4 ....149 C4
Neeham Rd TR8 ....56 B7
Nelson Ave PL1 ....127 F3
Nelson Gdns 5 PL1 ...127 F3
Nelson St PL4 ....149 A4
Nelson Terr PL6 ....125 E6
Nepean St PL2 ....127 F5
Neptune Ave PL27 ....31 F3
Neswick St PL1 ....148 B3
Neswick Street Ope
PL1 ....148 A3
Nethercott Cross EX21 ..13 F7
Netherton St PL20 .....42 A3
Netherton Rd PL28 ....107 D4
Nettell's Hill TR15 ....140 B5
Nettlehayes PL9 ....136 D7
Netton Cl PL3 ....136 B6
Nevada Cl PL3 ....129 D6
Nevada Pl 16 TR18 ....143 C7
Nevada St TR18 ....143 C7
Nevada Villas 8 PL24 .60 C4
New Barn Hill PL7 .....130 F3
New Bglws PL30 ....36 B3
New Bridge St 9 TR1 .137 D4
New Connection St 4
TR14 ....138 D3
New Cotts
Gunnislake PL18 ....41 A6
Kilkhampton EX23 ....5 A6
New Ct TR11 ....145 B4
New Cut TR15 ....140 B5
New Dairy La TR17 .....89 B6
New George St PL1 ...148 C3
New Hill Est TR2 ....72 A7
New Hos TR14 ....139 B3
New La TR15 ....140 E7
New Launceston Rd
PL19 ....147 A5
New Mills Farm Pk★
PL15 ....18 C4
New Mills La TR1,TR4 .137 A6
New Molinnis PL26 .....47 C2
New Northernmays 2
PL15 ....106 C6
New Park Rd
Plymouth PL7 ....131 A4
Wadebridge PL27 ....108 C5
New Passage Hill PL1 .127 E3
New Pk Horrabridge PL20 .42 C4
Wadebridge PL27 ....108 A4
New Portreath Rd
Illogan TR16 ....67 F5
Redruth TR16 ....140 A7
New Rd Barripper TR14 .79 B5
Bere Alston PL20 ....41 B2
Boscastle PL35 ....9 C4
Callington PL17 ....39 E4
Camborne TR14 ....139 B3
Cawsand PL10 ....133 A1
Cawsand, Kingsand PL10 .133 B2
Lifton PL16 ....19 F4
Liskeard PL14 ....113 B5
Newlyn TR18 ....143 C3
Perranporth TR6 ....55 B4
Port Isaac PL29 ....22 D7
Roborough PL6 ....121 D2
Ruan Minor TR12 .....103 A4
Saltash PL12 ....122 E3
St Columb Major TR9 ..45 E6
St Hilary TR20 ....89 F6
St Just TR19 ....86 F6
Stithians TR3 ....80 F3
Stratton EX23 ....4 D1
Summercourt TR8 .....57 D7
Tregony TR2 ....71 F3
Troon TR14 ....79 E4
New Road Cl PL10 ....133 A2
New Road Hill PL23 ..116 C4
New Road Terr PL12 ...53 C3
New Row Gweek TR12 ..92 C1
Mylor Bridge TR11 .....82 A3
Nancledra TR 20 ....76 F2
Redruth TR16 ....139 D1
New St Bugle PL26 .....47 C1
Falmouth TR11 ....145 B4
Millbrook PL10 ....132 E5
Padstow PL28 ....107 D5
Penryn TR10 ....144 D7
Penzance TR18 ....143 E5
Plymouth PL1 ....149 A2
Troon TR14 ....79 E4
New Town La TR18 ....143 E5
New Windsor Terr 11
TR11 ....145 A4
New Wood Cl PL6 .....125 E8
New Zealand Ho PL3 .128 B4
Newacott Cross EX22 ...7 F5
Newbridge Hill PL18 ...41 A6
Newbridge La TR1,TR3 .69 F3
Newbridge Way TR1 ...69 F3
Newbury Cl PL5 ....124 B4
Newcastle Gdns PL5 ..124 B5
Newham Est TR1 ....137 D3
Newham Ind Est TR1 ..137 D2
Newham La
Helston TR13 ....146 A7
Lostwithiel PL22 ....49 A1
Newham Rd TR1 ....137 E2

Newhouses PL17 ....38 E8
Newlyn Art Gall★ TR18 .143 C3
Newlyn Rd TR19 ....97 B6
Newlyn Sch TR18 .....143 C1
Newman Rd
Plymouth PL5 ....123 E2
Saltash PL12 ....122 F3
Newmills 5 ....18 D4
Newnham Ind Est PL7 .130 F7
Newnham Rd PL7 .....130 F7
Newnham Way PL7 ....130 F6
Newport PL12 ....65 A8
Newport Cl 8 PL17 .....39 F4
Newport Ind Est PL15 .106 C6
Newport Sq PL15 .....106 B7
Newport St
Millbrook PL10 ....132 E5
Plymouth PL1 ....128 A1
Newport Terr 3 PL17 ..39 F4
Newquay Airport TR8 ..44 F8
Newquay Hospl TR7 ..110 F5
Newquay Jun Sch TR7 .110 F6
Newquay Rd
Goonhavern TR4 ....55 D4
St Columb Major TR9 ..45 D6
Truro TR1 ....137 F7
Newquay Sta TR7 .....110 F6
Newtake Rd TR19 .....147 E2
Newton Ave PL5 ....123 C4
Newton Cl PL14 ....50 E8
Newton Gdns PL5 .....123 F2
Newton Pk 13 TR2 .....95 A6
Newton Rd St Mawes TR2 .95 A6
Troon TR14 ....79 E5
Newtown PL23 ....60 F3
Newtown La TR17,TR20 .89 A7
Nicholas Ave TR16 .....80 A5
Nicholas Mdw PL17 ...40 E4
Nicholas Parc 3 TR18 .143 C7
Nicholson Rd PL14 ....124 E2
Nicolls Flats PL15 .....106 B5
Nightingale Cl PL9 ...136 C8
Nilch Pk PL12 ....122 C2
Nine Maidens Com Prim Sch
TR16 ....80 A4
Nine Oaks PL20 ....42 F3
No Go By Hill TR19 ....86 F7
No Mans' Land Rd TR11 .93 D5
Nook The PL19 ....147 E6
Norfolk Cl PL3 ....129 C5
Norfolk Rd
Falmouth TR11 ....145 B4
Plymouth PL3 ....129 C4
Norman Cotts PL15 ...106 C7
Norman's Way PL30 ....23 C3
Normandy Hill PL5 ....123 B2
Normandy Way
Bodmin PL31 ....109 F2
Camborne TR14 ....138 F3
Plymouth PL5 ....123 C3
North Cl EX23 ....5 A6
North Cliff 12 TR19 ....88 C1
North Cnr 1 TR18 .....86 C1
North Cornwall Mus & Gall★
PL32 ....105 C4
North Dimson PL18 .....40 F6
North Down Cres PL2 .127 B5
North Down Gdns PL2 .127 B6
North Down Rd PL2 ..128 B5
North Grange Ind Est
TR3 ....81 F4
North Hill Blackwater TR4 .68 C5
Carharrack TR16 ....80 F8
Chacewater TR4 ....68 F3
Plymouth PL4 ....149 A4
North Hill Pk PL25 ...114 D4
North Moor Cross EX22 ..3 F4
North Orchard Ct 1
TR20 ....89 E5
North Par
Camborne TR14 ....138 C3
Falmouth TR11 ....145 A6
Penzance TR18 ....143 E5
Portscatho TR2 ....83 B2
North Parade Rear
TR14 ....138 D3
North Park Villas PL12 .122 C4
North Petherwin Prim Sch
PL15 ....12 B1
North Pl 16 TR26 .....141 B6
North Pool Cl TR25 ...139 C7
North Pool Rd TR15 ..139 C7
North Prospect Prim Sch
PL2 ....128 A7
North Prospect Rd PL2 128 A6
North Quay Hayle TR27 142 B6
Padstow PL28 ....107 D6
North Quay Hill TR7 ..110 D7
North Quay Par PL28 .107 E6
North Rd Camborne TR14 138 D3
Goldsithney TR20 ....89 E5
Landrake PL12 ....53 C3
Lifton PL16 ....19 F4
Looe PL13 ....117 C3
Pentewan PL26 ....73 C6
Redruth TR16 ....140 E1
Saltash PL12 ....122 F3
St Teath PL30 ....23 C7
Torpoint PL11 ....127 B3
Whitemoor PL26 ....58 E8
Yelverton PL20 ....42 C3
North Rd E PL4 ....148 C4
North Rd W PL1 ....148 B4
North Roskear Rd TR14 138 F5
North Row TR16 ....86 F6
North St Fowey PL23 ..116 D4
Launceston PL15 ....106 A8

North St continued
Lostwithiel PL22 ....112 C2
Marazion TR17 ....89 B5
14 Mousehole TR19 ....88 C1
Par PL24 ....60 C5
Plymouth PL4 ....149 A3
Redruth TR15 ....140 B6
St Austell PL25 ....114 C4
Tavistock PL19 ....147 C5
North Terr
2 Penzance TR18 .....143 E4
Whitemoor PL26 ....58 E8
12 St Ives TR26 ....141 B5
North View PL13 ....117 B5
North Way PL11 ....111 F4
North Weald Gdns PL5 .123 B5
Northampton Cl PL5 ..124 B5
Northcott Mouth Rd
EX23 ....104 F8
Northesk St PL2 ....128 A4
Northey Cl TR4 ....69 E6
Northey Rd PL3 ....109 D4
Northfield Cl TR16 .....68 E1
Northfield Dr TR1 .....137 D3
Northgate Pl 1 PL15 ..106 C6
Northolt Ave PL5 .....123 D4
Northumberland St PL5 127 E8
Northumberland Terr
PL1 ....148 A1
Norton Ave PL4 ....149 C4
Norwich Ave PL5 .....124 B5
Notre Dame Cl PL6 ...124 F5
Notre Dame Ho PL1 ..148 B3
Notre Dame RC Sch
PL6 ....124 F5
Notte St PL1 ....148 C2
Notter Mill Holiday Village
PL12 ....53 D4
Novorossisk Rd PL6 ..125 E2
Noweth Pl TR11 ....144 E5
Nurseries The TR11 ...144 D5
Nursery Cl 11 Par PL24 .60 D5
Plymouth PL5 ....124 B7
Truro TR1 ....137 D5
Nut La TR27 ....77 E3
Nut Tree Hill PL12 .....65 B8

O

Oak Apple Cl PL12 ....122 D4
Oak Ave PL12 ....40 A1
Oak Dr 8 Liskeard PL14 .113 B5
Plymouth PL6 ....124 F3
Oak Ford PL30 ....48 C7
Oak La Truro TR1 ....69 E4
Whitstone EX22 ....7 F1
Oak Park Terr PL14 ...113 A6
Oak Rd St Tudy PL30 ...23 E3
Tavistock PL19 ....147 C2
Oak Ridge PL16 ....19 F4
Oak Tree Cl PL25 .....115 B3
Oak Tree Ct PL6 ....124 F1
Oak Tree La PL19 .....147 C3
Oak Tree Pk PL6 ....125 D6
Oak Vale TR2 ....72 A7
Oak Way TR1 ....137 D5
Oakapple Cl PL7 ....130 B7
Oakcroft Rd PL7 ....128 B6
Oakdene Rise PL9 .....135 F6
Oakdene Villas 7 TR9 ..45 E1
Oakey Orch PL17 ....40 D4
Oakfield Cl PL7 ....131 C6
Oakfield Pl PL1 ....129 B1
Oakfield Rd
Falmouth TR11 ....144 F5
Plymouth PL7 ....130 C6
Oakfield Terrace Rd
PL4 ....129 B1
Oakham Rd PL5 ....124 B5
Oakhill PL30 ....47 C6
Oakland Pk TR11 .....144 D5
Oaklands PL19 ....147 E2
Oaklands Bsns Pk PL13 .63 D8
Oaklands Cl PL6 ....125 D7
Oaklands Dr PL12 ....122 C3
Oaklands Gn PL12 ....122 C3
Oaklands Ind Est PL14 .113 E6
Oaklands Rd PL14 ....113 E6
Oakleigh Terr TR7 ....110 F6
Oakridge PL12 ....53 C7
Oaks The
Quintrell Downs TR8 ...111 F3
St Austell PL25 ....114 B3
Oakwood Cl PL6 ....125 D7
Oakwood Pk PL31 ....109 F4
Oates Rd Helston TR13 .146 C6
Marazion TR17 ....89 C5
Plymouth PL2 ....128 B5
Ocean Cres 22 TR13 ..98 C8
Ocean Ct Porthtowan TR4 .68 A7
Plymouth PL1 ....133 F8
Ocean St PL2 ....127 E6
Ocean View
Indian Queens TR9 .....45 E1
Polruan PL23 ....116 D2
Porthleven TR13 ....98 B8
Ocean View Rd EX23 ..104 D7
Ocean View Terr TR26 .141 A6
Octagon Cl PL1 ....148 B3
Octagon The PL1 .....148 B2
Okehampton Cl PL7 ..131 B4
Old Barn Ct TR7 ....110 D4
Old Barns The TR14 ...146 C6
Old Boat Yard The PL28 .107 E6
Old Boys Sch TR16 ....67 E5

Old Brewery Yd 4
TR18 ....143 E5
Old Bridge St TR1 ....137 D4
Old Callywith Rd PL31 ...35 B2
Old Canal Cl EX23 ....7 B6
Old Carnon Hill TR3 ....81 F6
Old Chapel Way PL10 ...132 F6
Old Chough TR7 ....111 C7
Old Church Rd TR11 ....93 E2
Old Coach Rd
Lanivet PL26,PL30 ....47 D6
Playing Place TR3 ....82 B8
Truro TR3 ....70 A1
Old Coastguard Cotts
PL11 ....65 A4
Old Corn Mill The TR12 ..92 C1
Old Dairy The PL3 ....129 B6
Old Drovers Way EX23 ....4 E1
Old Exeter Rd PL19 ....147 D7
Old Falmouth Rd TR1 ...137 C1
Old Farm Rd PL5 ....127 C8
Old Ferry Rd PL12 ....123 A3
Old Foundry Cl TR19 ....86 F6
Old Foundry The PL19 ..147 D6
Old George St PL1 ....148 C2
Old Grammer School Ct
PL22 ....112 C2
Old Greystone Hill PL15,
PL19 ....28 F6
Old Guildhall Mus*
PL13 ....117 D3
Old Hill Falmouth TR11 ...144 F6
Grampound TR2 ....72 A7
Helston TR13 ....146 A6
Old Hill Cres TR11 ....144 F5
Old La PL26 ....46 F3
Old Laira Rd PL3 ....129 C4
Old Launceston Rd
PL19 ....147 B6
Old Laundry The PL1 ...148 A3
Old Lawn School La
PL25 ....114 B3
Old Market Pl PL31 ....109 C4
Old Mill Cl PL15 ....27 B3
Old Mill Ct PL7 ....130 E5
Old Mill La Camborne TR14 78 F6
Penponds TR14 ....79 A6
Old Mine La PL18 ....40 E6
Old Nursery Cl TR13 ....91 A1
Old Orchard Cl EX23 ....7 B6
Old Park Rd PL3 ....128 D6
Old Paul Hill TR18 ....143 C2
Old Plymouth Rd PL3 ...129 E5
Old Portreath Rd
Illogan TR16 ....67 F5
Redruth TR15 ....67 F4
Old Post Office* PL34 ..14 C7
Old Post Office Hill 8
EX23 ....4 E1
Old Pound PL26 ....58 E6
Old Priory PL7 ....130 D5
Old Priory Jun Sch PL7 130 D5
Old Quarry Rd PL20 ....42 A3
Old Quay La PL12 ....65 B8
Old Rd Boscastle PL35 ....9 C2
Liskeard PL14 ....113 A6
Old Rectory Dr TR9 ....45 E6
Old Roselyon Cres PL24 .60 B5
Old Roselyon Rd PL24 ..60 C4
Old School Cl PL27 ....21 F3
Old School Ct
Padstow PL28 ....107 D5
Wadebridge PL27 ....108 B5
Old School La PL30 ....34 D4
Old School Rd PL5 ....127 C8
Old Schoolhouse The
TR11 ....145 B4
Old Smithy Cl 4 TR17 ...89 C5
Old Smithy Cotts EX39 ....2 E4
Old Station Rd
Horrabridge PL20 ....42 C4
1 Liskeard PL14 ....51 A7
Old Station The PL20 ....42 B4
Old Tannery Bsns Pk The 4
PL4 ....149 A4
Old Town Hall The PL24 ..60 B5
Old Town St PL1 ....148 C3
Old Tram Rd TR3 ....82 A5
Old Vicarage Cl TR3 ....80 F4
Old Vicarage Gate TR27 142 A1
Old Vicarage Pl 11 PL25 114 C3
Old Warleigh La PL5 ...124 B7
Old Well Gdns TR10 ...144 C8
Old Wharf The PL9 ....135 C7
Old Woodlands Rd PL5 .124 D3
Oldlands Cl PL6 ....125 B6
Oliver Ct PL12 ....40 A1
Oliver's Terr TR13 ....146 C5
Olivey Pl TR11 ....82 A3
Olivia Ct PL4 ....149 B4
Omaha Rd PL31 ....109 F3
Onslow Rd PL2 ....128 C7
Ope's Ct TR11 ....145 B5
Opie's Row TR16 ....80 B5
Opie's Terr TR16 ....80 A5
Opies La PL31 ....109 C5
Orange La TR26 ....141 A6
Orch The TR7 ....111 B7
Orchard Ave PL6 ....129 B7
Orchard Cl Helston TR13 .146 B7
3 Plymouth PL7 ....131 C5
Poughill EX23 ....4 D2
St Austell PL25 ....114 E4
St Giles-On-The-Heath PL15 13 F1
St Mellion PL12 ....53 C8
Tavistock PL19 ....41 D8
Tideford PL12 ....52 F2
Truro TR1 ....69 F3
Orchard Cotts PL19 ....30 B3
Orchard Cres PL9 ....135 C7
Orchard Ct Lamerton PL19 30 A3
Penzance TR18 ....143 C5
Orchard Gr PL25 ....114 B4
Orchard Ho 11 TR18 ....143 C2
Orchard La TR12 ....93 B1
Orchard Pl 10 TR18 ....143 C2
Orchard Rd PL2 ....128 B7
Orchard Terr 18 TR18 ...143 C2
Orchard The
Gunnislake PL18 ....41 A6
Lerryn PL22 ....61 D8
North Petherwin PL15 ....18 B8
St Erth TR27 ....77 E2
Orchard Vale TR11 ....145 C7
Orchard Way 6 TR20 ....89 E5
Orchardton Terr PL9 ...135 F5
Ordnance St PL1 ....127 E2
Ordulf Rd PL19 ....147 A5
Oregon Way PL3 ....129 D6
Oreston Prim Sch PL9 .135 C7
Oreston Rd PL9 ....135 C8
Orion Dr PL27 ....31 F3
Osborne Parc TR13 ....146 B7
Osborne Rd PL3 ....128 A3
Osborne Villas
10 Falmouth TR11 ....145 C3
2 Plymouth PL3 ....128 A3
Osprey Gdns PL9 ....136 C7
Otterham Com Prim Sch
PL32 ....10 C2
Otterham Pk PL32 ....16 A8
Ottery Cotts PL19 ....30 A2
Ottery Park Ind Est PL19 30 A2
Outland Rd PL2 ....128 C7
Overdale Rd PL2 ....128 A7
Overton Gdns PL3 ....128 F5
Overtonn Villas PL15 ...106 C5
Owen Sivell Cl PL14 ....113 E6
Oxford Ave PL3 ....128 E5
Oxford Gdns PL3 ....128 E5
Oxford Pl PL1 ....148 C3
Oxford St PL1 ....148 B3
Oxford Terr 4 PL1 ....148 B3
Oxland Rd TR16 ....67 E5

P

Paardeburg Rd PL31 ....48 D8
Packet La TR20 ....89 F5
Packington St PL2 ....128 A4
Packsaddle TR10 ....81 D2
Packsaddle Cl TR10 ....81 D2
Paddock Cl Plymouth PL9 135 E5
Saltash PL12 ....122 D4
Paddock The
Helston, Gwealfolds TR13 .146 C7
Helston, Lowertown TR13 .146 C8
Redruth TR15 ....140 D2
Padnover Terr 22 TR26 ..141 B5
Padstow Harbour Ind Est
PL28 ....107 E4
Padstow Jun & Inf Sch
PL28 ....107 C4
Padstow Workshop Units
PL28 ....107 B4
Page's Cross PL15 ....106 D4
Paiges Farm PL9 ....135 C1
Painton Water EX39 ....3 A8
Palace Rd PL25 ....114 D4
Palace St PL1 ....149 A2
Palm Ct TR1 ....137 D3
Palmers Terr PL34 ....14 C6
Palmers Way PL27 ....108 D6
Palmerston St PL1 ....148 A4
Pannier La TR26 ....141 C2
Pannier Mkt PL19 ....147 C5
Panson Cross PL15 ....13 E3
Par Gn PL24 ....60 C4
Par La PL24 ....60 B4
Par Moor Rd
Par PL24, PL25 ....60 B3
St Austell PL24, PL25 ....115 F4
Par Sta PL24 ....60 C5
Parade PL1 ....149 A2
Parade Bsns Pk 4 PL19 147 B4
Parade Hill TR19 ....88 D1
Parade Ope PL1 ....149 A2
Parade Pass 29 TR18 ....143 E5
Parade Rd PL5 ....124 A3
Parade Sq PL22 ....112 D2
Parade St TR18 ....143 E5
Parade The Helston TR13 146 C5
Liskeard PL14 ....113 C6
Lostwithiel PL22 ....112 D2
Millbrook PL10 ....132 E5
Milton Abbot PL19 ....29 C6
Mousehole TR19 ....88 D1
Truro TR1 ....137 E4
Paradise Park (Wildlife Conservation Sanctuary)*
TR27 ....142 A4
Paradise Pk EX22 ....7 F1
Paradise Rd Boscastle PL35 9 C1
Plymouth PL1 ....128 A2
Parc An Gate TR19 ....88 C1
Parc An Manns TR11 ....93 D3
Parc An Yorth TR19 ....86 F8
Parc Bean Terr TR26 ....141 A6
Parc Behan Ct TR2 ....83 F6
Parc Bowen TR13 ....92 A3
Parc Briwer TR10 ....144 D7
Parc Browse 10 TR12 ...102 F2
Parc Eglos Helston TR13 .146 B6
St Merryn PL28 ....31 F8
Parc Eglos Sch TR13 ...146 C6
Parc Enys TR12 ....99 B4
Parc Erissey Ind Est
TR16 ....68 A3
Parc Fer Cl EX23 ....4 E1
Parc Godrevy TR7 ....110 C5
Parc Holland TR13 ....146 D8
Parc Ledden TR13 ....146 C6
Parc Ledrak TR13 ....146 B8
Parc Letta TR18 ....143 C7
Parc Mellan TR18 ....143 D7
Parc Merys TR2 ....83 B2
Parc Monga Rd TR11 ....92 F3
Parc Morrep TR20 ....90 B3
Parc Owles TR26 ....141 D2
Parc Peneglos TR11 ....82 A3
Parc Shady TR26 ....77 C1
Parc Stephney TR11 ....144 C2
Parc Terr 18 TR18 ....143 C1
Parc Vean PL30 ....34 C1
Parc Venton Cl TR14 ...138 F2
Parc Villas 16 TR18 ....143 C1
Parc Wartha Ave TR18 .143 D6
Parc Wartha Cres TR18 .143 D6
Parc-Abnac TR20 ....88 B7
Parc-An-Bal Ct TR14 ...138 E4
Parc-An-Bre Dr PL26 ...58 C8
Parc-an-Cady Est TR19 .97 A6
Parc-An-Challow TR10 .144 B8
Parc-An-Creet TR26 ....77 A7
Parc-An-Dillon Rd TR2 ..83 B2
Parc-An-Dix La TR27 ...142 C7
Parc-An-Dower TR13 ...146 C6
Parc-An-Forth 6 TR26 ...77 A6
Parc-An-Gwarry 7 TR3 ..81 F7
Parc-An-Ithan 5 TR12 ..102 F2
Parc-An-Maen 11 TR13 ...98 C8
Parc-An-Peath TR19 ....97 A6
Parc-An-Stamps 4
TR26 ....77 A6
Parc-Askell Cl TR12 ....98 E5
Parc-Bracket St TR14 ...138 D3
Parcandowr TR2 ....57 E1
Pargolla Rd TR7 ....110 F6
Park An Gonwyn TR26 ..141 E2
Park An Gorsaf TR14 ...138 D2
Park Ave
Plymouth, Devonport PL1 .127 E3
Plymouth, Plymstock PL9 .135 D7
St Ives TR26 ....141 B5
Park Cl Illogan TR15 ....139 B8
Nancegollan TR13 ....91 B7
Plymouth PL7 ....130 B7
Park Cnr TR18 ....143 E5
Park Cres Falmouth TR11 145 A4
Helston TR13 ....146 B5
Plymouth PL9 ....135 C7
Ponsanooth TR3 ....81 B4
Park Ct 28 TR18 ....143 E5
Park Dr PL31 ....109 B4
Park Enskellaw 6 TR12 ..99 A2
Park Fenton PL14 ....113 D5
Park Gwyn PL26 ....58 B4
Park Hill TR11 ....145 A4
Park Ho PL25 ....114 B3
Park La
8 Bere Alston PL20 ....41 B1
Bugle PL26 ....47 C1
Camborne TR14 ....138 E2
Falmouth TR11 ....145 A4
Plymouth PL9 ....135 C7
Park Leven TR16 ....139 C8
Park Lowen TR26 ....141 C2
Park Pl
Grampound Road TR2 ....57 E1
Wadebridge PL27 ....108 B5
Park Place La 9 PL3 ...128 A4
Park Rd Camborne TR14 .138 E4
Fowey PL23 ....116 C4
Illogan TR15 ....139 B7
Lifton PL16 ....19 F3
Liskeard PL14 ....113 C6
17 Newlyn TR18 ....143 C1
Plymouth PL3 ....129 A6
Ponsanooth TR3 ....81 B4
Redruth TR15 ....140 C4
St Austell PL25 ....114 C3
St Dominick PL12 ....40 D2
Torpoint PL11 ....127 B3
Wadebridge PL27 ....108 B5
Whitemoor PL26 ....58 E8
Park Rd Hos PL22 ....112 C2
Park Rise TR11 ....145 A4
Park St PL3 ....128 A4
Park Stenak TR16 ....80 F8
Park Street Ope PL3 ...128 A4
Park Terr TR11 ....145 A4
Park The Penryn TR10 ...144 B7
Tregony TR2 ....71 F4
Park View Liskeard PL14 .113 C6
Plymouth PL4 ....149 C3
Pyworthy EX22 ....8 E5
Summercourt TR8 ....57 B7
Truro TR1 ....137 C3
Park View Cl TR3 ....82 A7
Park View Rd TR13 ....146 B5
Park View Terr PL27 ...108 B5
Park Way PL25 ....114 F5
Park Wise TR10 ....144 C8
Park Wood Rise PL16 ....19 F4
Park-An-Bans TR14 ....138 E1
Park-An-Pyth TR19 ....75 A1
Park-An-Tansys TR14 ...138 F2
Parka Rd TR9 ....45 E2
Parkancreeg 9 TR3 ....81 F7
Parkenbutts TR7 ....111 D7
Parkengear Vean TR2 ...71 D6
Parkengue TR10 ....144 A7
Parkenhead La PL28 ....20 F2
Parker Cl PL7 ....130 B5
Parker Rd PL2 ....128 B6
Parker's Gn PL18 ....40 F6
Parkesway PL12 ....122 D2
Parkfield Dr PL6 ....125 F1
Parkins Terr 7 TR1 ....137 D5
Parklands PL26 ....58 C7
Parklands Cl TR7 ....111 D6
Parknoweth TR12 ....99 A4
Parknoweth Cl TR8 ....56 B6
Parkryn Rd 4 TR19 ....88 C1
Parkside PL2 ....127 F5
Parkside Com Tech Coll
PL10 ....127 E3
Parkstone La PL7 ....130 F6
Parkvedras Ho 5 TR1 ..137 B4
Parkvedras Terr 4 TR1 .137 B4
Parkventon PL26 ....47 C2
Parkway Ct PL6 ....129 E7
Parkway Ho PL27 ....21 F3
Parkway Ind Est The
PL6 ....129 E7
Parkway The PL3,PL5,
PL6 ....124 B1
Parkwood Cl PL6 ....121 B2
Parkwood Ct PL19 ....147 D6
Parkwood Rd
Tavistock PL19 ....147 D6
Tavistock PL19 ....147 E7
Parkwoon Cl PL26 ....46 F3
Parnell Cl PL6 ....129 A8
Parr La PL4 ....149 B2
Parr St PL4 ....149 B2
Parsonage Ct PL16 ....19 F4
Parsons Cl PL9 ....136 A4
Parsons Gn PL17 ....39 E6
Partwayes PL19 ....30 A3
Pascoe Cl TR3 ....69 D4
Pasley St PL2 ....127 E4
Pasley St E PL2 ....127 F4
Passage Hill TR11 ....82 A3
Passage La PL23 ....116 B5
Passage St PL23 ....116 D5
Passmore Cl
Blackwater TR4 ....68 E5
Liskeard PL14 ....113 D6
Passmore Edwards Hospl
PL14 ....113 B6
Pathfields EX23 ....104 E5
Pathway Fields The
TR27 ....142 C5
Patna Pl PL1 ....148 B4
Patterdale Cl PL6 ....125 D3
Patterdale Wlk PL6 ....125 D3
Pattinson Cl PL6 ....125 E2
Pattinson Dr PL6 ....125 F2
Paul's Row TR1 ....137 D5
Paul's Terr TR1 ....137 D5
Paull Rd PL31 ....109 B4
Paulls Row 4 TR15 ....140 C5
Paviland Grange 6 PL1 128 A3
Pavilion Pk TR14 ....138 F4
Pavlova Cl PL14 ....113 C5
Pavlova Ct 6 PL14 ....113 C5
Paynter Wlk 5 PL7 ....131 B5
Paynter's Cross PL12 ...53 E7
Paynter's Lane End Est
TR16 ....67 D4
Paynters La TR16 ....67 E4
Peacock Ave PL11 ....127 A3
Peacock Cl PL7 ....130 F7
Peacock La PL4 ....149 A2
Pearce's La 12 TR26 ...141 A5
Pearce's Row 3 PL24 ...60 C4
Pearn Cotts 2 PL3 ....128 F6
Pearn Gdns PL3 ....129 A7
Pearn Rd PL3 ....129 A7
Pearn Ridge PL3 ....129 A7
Pearson Ave 3 PL4 ....128 F4
Pearson Rd PL4 ....128 F4
Pedlars Cl PL15 ....18 B8
Pedn-Moran TR2 ....95 B6
Pedn-y-ke 1 TR12 ....99 A1
Pednandrea TR19 ....86 E6
Pednolva Wlk TR26 ....141 B5
Peek Moor Cross EX22 ..13 E4
Peeks Ave PL9 ....135 F7
Peel St PL1 ....128 A1
Peguarra Cl PL28 ....20 E1
Peguarra Ct PL28 ....20 E1
Pelean Cross TR3 ....81 B5
Pelham Ct 11 TR11 ....145 C3
Pellew Cl
7 Falmouth TR11 ....145 A5
Padstow PL28 ....107 C5
Pellew Cres TR13 ....146 C4
Pellew Pl PL2 ....127 F4
Pellew Rd TR11 ....145 A5
Pellor Fields TR13 ....90 F3
Pelynt Prim Sch PL13 ...62 D6
Pembrey Wlk PL5 ....123 E4
Pembroke Cl 7 PL24 ....60 C4
Pembroke La PL1 ....127 E1
Pembroke Rd TR7 ....111 E7
Pembroke St
Plymouth PL1 ....127 E1
Plymouth PL1 ....127 F1
Pemros Rd PL5 ....123 C1
Pen Brea Cl TR2 ....95 B6
Pen Hallow Cl TR4 ....68 C6
Pen Porth Ave TR26 ....77 A7
Pen Tor PL30 ....35 C8
Pen y Bryn PL27 ....108 D6
Pen-An-Gwel TR26 ....141 A4
Pen-Egloe 8 TR2 ....95 A6
Pen-Tye TR27 ....78 E3
Penair Cres TR1 ....137 F6
Penair Sch TR1 ....70 D4
Penair View TR1 ....137 F4
Penally Ct PL35 ....9 D2
Penally Hill PL35 ....9 D2
Penally Terr PL35 ....9 C2
Penalverne Ave TR18 ..143 D5
Penalverne Cres TR18 ..143 D5
Penalverne Dr TR18 ...143 D5
Penalverne Pl TR18 ...143 D5
Penameyne Ct 5 TR26 .141 B6
Penare Gdns 2 TR18 ...143 E6
Penare Rd TR18 ....143 E6
Penare Terr TR18 ....143 E6
Penarrow Cl TR11 ....144 E2
Penarrow Rd TR11 ....145 C8
Penarth PL13 ....117 B3
Penarth Rd TR11 ....145 A5
Penarwyn Cres TR18 ...143 B7
Penarwyn Rd PL24 ....60 B4
Penarwyn Woods 6
PL24 ....60 B4
Penbeagle Cl TR26 ....77 A6
Penbeagle Cres 8 TR26 .77 A6
Penbeagle La TR26 ....77 A6
Penbeagle Terr 7 TR26 ..77 A6
Penbeagle Way TR26 ...141 A4
Penberthy Cross TR20 ...89 F7
Penberthy Rd
Helston TR13 ....146 C5
Portreath TR16 ....67 D6
Penbothidno TR11 ....92 F3
Penbrea Rd TR18 ....143 E7
Penbugle La PL31 ....109 E7
Pencair Ave PL11 ....126 E2
Pencalenick Sch TR1 ...70 E4
Pencantol TR4 ....81 C7
Pencarn Parc TR16 ....80 A5
Pencarrick Cl TR1 ....137 B6
Pencarrow* PL30 ....34 D6
Pencarrow Cl PL17 ....39 E3
Pencarrow Rd 13 TR16 ...67 E4
Pencavo Hill PL12 ....53 A3
Pencreber Rd 3 PL20 ...42 C4
Pendale Sq TR1 ....137 B4
Pendarves Flats TR18 ..143 D6
Pendarves Rd
Camborne TR14 ....138 C1
Falmouth TR11 ....144 F6
Penzance TR18 ....143 D6
Truro TR1 ....137 C6
Pendarves St
Camborne TR14 ....138 F4
Camborne, Beacon TR14 ..138 F1
Troon TR14 ....79 E4
Pendarves View TR14 ...138 C1
Pendean Ave PL14 ....113 B6
Pendean Cl PL14 ....113 B6
Pendean Ct PL14 ....113 B6
Pendean Dr PL14 ....113 B6
Pendeen Cl Plymouth PL6 124 F6
Threemilestone TR3 ....69 D3
Pendeen Cres
Plymouth PL6 ....125 A6
Threemilestone TR3 ....69 D3
Pendeen Ho TR1 ....69 E4
Pendeen Lighthouse Mus*
TR19 ....75 A1
Pendeen Pk TR13 ....146 C8
Pendeen Prim Sch TR19 .75 A1
Pendeen Rd
Porthleven TR13 ....91 B1
Threemilestone TR3 ....69 D3
Truro TR1 ....137 E3
Pendennis Castle*
TR11 ....145 E2
Pendennis Cl
Penzance TR18 ....143 E7
Plymouth PL3 ....128 F8
Torpoint PL11 ....126 F3
Pendennis Ct TR11 ....145 D3
Pendennis Pl TR18 ....143 F7
Pendennis Rd
Falmouth TR11 ....145 D3
Looe PL13 ....117 D5
Penzance TR18 ....143 E7
Pendennis Rise TR11 ...145 D3
Pender's La TR15 ....140 B5
Pendilly Ave PL11 ....126 F2
Pendour Pk PL22 ....112 E2
Pendower Ct TR2 ....83 D5
Pendower Rd Looe PL13 .117 E4
Veryan TR2 ....83 F6
Pendower Terr TR14 ...138 E1
Pendra Loweth TR11 ...144 D1
Pendragon Cres TR7 ...111 A4
Pendragon Ho TR11 ...145 D3
Pendragon Rd PL14 ....113 D6
Pendray Gdns PL14 ....50 E7
Pendrea Cl TR18 ....143 F7
Pendrea Pk TR14 ....138 F5
Pendrea Pl TR18 ....143 F7
Pendrea Rd TR18 ....143 F7
Pendrea Wood TR1 ....69 F3
Pendrim Rd PL13 ....117 D4
Pendruccombe Ct PL15 106 D5
Penforth TR14 ....138 E2
Penganne Cl TR7 ....110 D4
Pengarrock Hill TR12 ..101 D5
Pengarth 1 TR5 ....54 D1
Pengarth Cl TR1 ....137 C2
Pengarth Rd TR11 ....145 A3
Pengarth Rise TR11 ....145 A3
Pengegon Moor TR14 ..138 F2
Pengegon Parc TR14 ...138 F2
Pengegon Way TR14 ...138 F2

Pengelly
24 Callington PL17 ....39 F4
Delabole PL33 ....14 E2
Pengelly Cl PL11 ....126 F5
Pengelly Cross
Godolphin Cross TR27 ...90 F7
Wadebridge PL27 ......108 C1
Pengelly Hill PL11 .....127 A5
Pengelly Pk PL11 ......126 F5
Pengelly Pl PL11 ......144 E5
Pengelly Way TR3 ......69 D3
Pengellys Row TR14 ....139 A5
Pengeron Ave TR14 .....138 F7
Pengersick Est TR20 ...90 C3
Pengersick La TR20 ....90 C3
Pengersick Parc TR20 ..90 C3
Pengover Cl PL14 ......113 D6
Pengover Gn PL14 .....51 E8
Pengover Hts PL14 .....113 D6
Pengover Parc PL15 ....140 C4
Pengover Pk PL14 ......113 D6
Pengover Rd PL14 ......113 E6
Pengrowyn PL26 ....59 D6
Pengwarras Rd TR14 ...138 C3
Pengwel 16 TR18 ......143 C2
Penhale Cl PL14 ....37 F3
Penhale Est TR15 ......140 B6
Penhale Gdns TR9 .....57 D8
Penhale Mdw TR3 ......37 F3
Penhale Rd
Barripper TR14 ....79 A4
Carnhell Green TR14 ...78 F4
Falmouth TR11 ....144 F1
Penwithick PL26 ....59 D7
Penhaligon Ct TR15 ....140 D4
Penhaligon Ct TR1 ....137 E5
Penhaligon Way PL25 ..114 F4
Penhall La TR4 ....68 C6
Penhallow TR15 ....139 B8
Penhallow Cl TR2 ......83 C5
Penhallow Ct TR7 .....111 C7
Penhallow Parc PL33 ..14 D2
Penhallow Rd TR7 .....111 C7
Penhalls Way TR3 ......82 B8
Penhalt Farm Holiday Pk
EX23 ....6 E3
Penhaven Cl TR8 ......56 B7
Penhaven Ct TR7 ......110 C6
Penhellaz Hill TR13 ....146 B6
Penhellaz Rd TR13 ....146 B6
Penhole Cl PL15 ......27 D3
Penina Ave TR7 ....110 F4
Peninsular Pk PL12 ....122 C4
Penjerrick Hill
Budock Water TR11 ....144 C1
Falmouth TR11 ....93 E5
Penkenna Cl EX23 .....10 C6
Penkernick Cl TR18 ....143 B1
Penkernick Way TR9 ...45 E6
Penknight La PL22 .....112 A2
Penlea Rd TR10 ....144 B8
Penlean Ct TR15 ......140 D7
Penlee Cl
13 Callington PL17 ....39 F4
Praa Sands TR20 ......90 C3
Tregony TR2 ....71 F4
Penlee Cotts PL10 .....64 C2
Penlee Gdns PL3 ......128 A4
Penlee Ho TR1 ....69 E4
Penlee House Gall & Mus ★
TR18 ....143 E5
Penlee Manor Dr TR18 .143 E4
Penlee Pk PL11 ....126 F4
Penlee Pl 4 PL4 ......128 F4
Penlee Rd PL3 ....128 A4
Penlee St 11 TR18 ....143 E6
Penlee Villas TR3 .....82 B8
Penlee Way PL3 ....128 B4
Penlu Ho TR14 ....138 F5
Penluke Cl TR16 ......80 A5
Penlyne Woodland Trail ★
PL22 ....112 E5
Penmare Cl TR27 ......142 E7
Penmare Terr TR27 ....142 E7
Penmayne Parc TR16 ..140 F1
Penmayne Villas PL27 .21 E3
Penmead Rd PL33 .....14 E2
Penmelen PL32 ....105 C4
Penmeneth TR13 ......146 F8
Penmenner Est 7 TR12 .101 C4
Penmenner Rd TR12 ...102 F2
Penmere Cl
Helston TR13 ....146 B7
Penzance TR18 ....143 E7
Penmere Cres TR11 ...144 F3
Penmere Ct 4 TR11 ...145 A3
Penmere Dr TR7 ......110 C5
Penmere Hill 7 TR11 ..145 A3
Penmere Pl
3 Falmouth TR11 .....145 A3
Penzance TR18 ....143 E7
Penmere Rd
Penzance TR18 ....143 E7
St Austell PL25 ....115 A4
Penmere Sta TR11 ....144 F3
Penmerrin Ct TR7 .....110 E5
Penmeva View PL26 ...73 C3
Penmorvah TR11 ......82 A2
Penmorvah Pl TR14 ...138 E2
Penmorvah Rd TR1 ....137 F6
Penn An Drea TR13 ...146 D8
Pennance Hill TR11 ...93 F5
Pennance Ho TR11 ....145 A2
Pennance La TR16 ....140 F1
Pennance Parc TR16 ..140 F1

Pennance Rd
Falmouth TR11 ....145 A2
Lanner TR16 ....80 E7
Redruth TR16 ....140 F1
Pennance Terr TR16 ...140 F1
Pennard Villas PL27 ...33 B5
Pennkarn Parc PL33 ...14 E3
Pennor Dr PL25 ....114 D3
Penny's La PL9 ....136 D6
Pennycomequick Hill
PL1,PL3 ....148 B4
Pennycross Cl PL2 ....128 D8
Pennycross Park Rd
PL2 ....128 C7
Pennycross Prim Sch
PL2 ....128 C8
Pennygillam Ind Est
PL15 ....106 A4
Pennygillam Way PL15 .18 E2
Pennys La TR15 ......115 F5
Penoweth TR11 ....82 A2
Penpol Ave TR27 .....142 C5
Penpol Hill Crantock TR8 .110 B4
Devoran TR3 ....82 B6
Penpol Rd TR27 ......142 B5
Penpol Terr TR27 .....142 B5
Penpol Vean TR27 ....142 C5
Penponds Rd TR13 ....91 A1
Penponds Sch TR14 ...79 B5
Penpons Cl TR18 .....143 C4
Penpont Rd PL15 .....140 D6
Penpont View PL15 ...26 C7
Penquite Dr PL31 .....109 F5
Penrice Com Coll PL25 .115 A3
Penrice Hospl (Maternity &
Gastric) PL26 ....114 F1
Penrice Parc PL25 ....115 A3
Penrith Cl PL6 ....125 D3
Penrith Gdns PL6 .....125 D3
Penrith Wlk PL6 ......125 D3
Penrose Ct TR14 .....138 F7
Penrose Parc TR13 ...91 B1
Penrose Rd
Falmouth TR11 ....145 A4
Helston TR13 ....146 C6
Penrose St PL1 ....148 B3
Penrose Terr TR13 ....143 F6
Penrose Villas 5 PL4 .128 F4
Penrose Walks ★ TR12,
TR13 ....98 D8
Penruan La TR2 ......95 B6
Penryn Coll TR10 ....144 B7
Penryn Com Inf Sch
TR10 ....144 B7
Penryn Jun Sch TR10 .144 B8
Penryn St TR15 ......140 B4
Penryn Sta TR10 .....144 B8
Penscombe Cross PL15 .28 C6
Penscott La PL26 .....114 C1
Pensilva TR6 ....55 A4
Pensilva Prim Sch PL14 .38 E5
Pensilva Rural Workshop
PL14 ....38 E4
Penstowe Rd EX23 ...5 A6
Penstrasse Pl 1 PL24 .60 D5
Penstraze Bsns Ctr TR4 .69 A5
Penstraze La PL26 ....47 A4
Pensylva PL25 ....114 E3
Pentalek Rd TR14 ....138 D1
Pentamar St PL2 .....127 E4
Pentargon Rd 1 PL35 .9 C1
Pentewan Hill PL26 ...73 D6
Pentewan Rd PL25,PL26 .59 C1
Pentidna La TR27 ....66 B2
Pentillie PL26 ....73 C4
Pentillie Gdns 14 PL17 .39 E4
Pentillie Rd
Bere Alston PL20 .....41 B1
Plymouth PL4 ....128 E4
Pentillie Way PL26 ...73 C4
Pentillis Cres PL4 ....128 D4
Pentire Ave TR7 .....110 B5
Pentire Cres TR7 .....110 B5
Pentire Ct TR7 ....110 B5
Pentire Gn TR8 ......43 D3
Pentire Rd Newquay TR7 .110 C5
Penryn TR10 ....144 B8
Torpoint PL11 ....126 F3
Pentland Cl PL6 ......124 F7
Pentor Ct PL30 ......35 C8
Pentour 3 PL24 ......60 B4
Pentowan Rd TR27 ...142 E8
Pentre Ct EX23 ......4 D4
Pentreath Cl TR18 ...143 D7
Pentreath La Lizard TR12 .102 F2
Praa Sands TR20 .....90 B3
Pentreath Terr TR16 ..80 E7
Pentrevah Rd 8 PL26 .59 D7
Pentyre Ct PL4 ....149 C4
Pentyre Terr PL4 .....149 C4
Penvale 4 PL14 ......38 E4
Penvale Cres TR10 ...144 B8
Penvale Ct 8 TR11 ...145 A4
Penvale Dr TR10 .....144 B8
Penvean La TR11 .....144 E5
Penventinnie La TR1 ..69 E4
Penventinue La PL23 ..116 B7
Penventon Terr
Redruth TR15 ....140 A4
Redruth, Four Lanes TR16 .80 B6
Penventon View TR13 .146 B5
Penview Cres TR13 ...146 B5
Penvorder Cotts PL30 .24 B2
Penvorder La PL30 ...24 B2
Penware Parc TR14 ..138 C1
Penwarne Cl TR14 ...138 F7

Penwarne La PL26 ....73 C3
Penwarne Rd TR11 ...93 D5
Penwartha TR12 .....101 B2
Penwartha Cl
Constantine TR11 .....92 A3
St Columb Minor TR7 ..111 D7
Penwartha Ct TR11 ...92 F3
Penwartha Rd
15 Illogan TR16 ......67 E4
Perranporth TR6 ......55 B4
Penwartha Vean 14 TR16 .67 E4
Penwerris Cl TR11 ....145 A5
Penwerris La TR11 ...145 A6
Penwerris Rd TR1 ....69 F3
Penwerris Rise TR20 ..90 B3
Penwerris Terr 10 TR11 .145 A5
Penwethers La TR1 ...69 F3
Penwinnick Cl 9 TR5 ..54 C1
Penwinnick Parc 4 TR5 .54 D1
Penwinnick Rd
St Agnes TR5 ....68 D8
St Austell PL25 ....114 B3
Penwith Bsns Ctr TR20 .88 F6
Penwith Cl TR26 .....141 A4
Penwith Coll TR18 ....143 D7
Penwith Rd TR26 ....141 A4
Penwith St TR26 .....143 E6
Penwithian Cl TR27 ..142 E6
Penwithick Pk 6 PL26 .59 D7
Penworth Cl PL15 ....106 C5
Penwyth TR12 ....92 C1
Penzance Inf Sch TR18 .143 E7
Penzance Rd
Helston TR13 ....146 A6
St Buryan TR19 ......87 E1
Pepo La TR2 ....72 A7
Pepper Cl PL12 ......40 C2
Pepper La PL9 ....136 D7
Peppers St PL12 .....40 C2
Peppers Hill Cl PL15 ..18 F7
Peppers Park Rd PL14 .113 E6
Peppersfield Row TR13 .90 F3
Pepys Pl PL5 ....124 E1
Percuil View TR2 .....95 B6
Percy Davy Cl TR6 ...55 A5
Percy St PL5 ....123 E1
Percy Terr PL4 ....129 A4
Pergolla Ct TR7 ......110 F4
Perhaver Pk PL26 ....85 D5
Perhaver Way PL26 ..85 D5
Periwinkle Dr PL7 ....131 C5
Permarin Rd TR10 ...144 C8
Perran Cl TR3 ....81 F6
Perran Crossroads TR20 .89 E5
Perran Sands Holiday Ctr
TR6 ....55 B6
Perran View Holiday Park
TR5 ....54 E2
Perran-ar-worthal Com Prim
Sch TR3 ....81 D6
Perrancombe Garden Ct
TR6 ....55 A4
Perranporth Cl PL5 ...123 A4
Perranporth Jun & Inf Sch
TR6 ....55 A4
Perranwell Rd TR4 ...55 D4
Perranwell Sta TR3 ..81 E6
Perryman Cl PL7 .....130 E7
Perseverance Cotts 1
PL7 ....130 E7
Peryn Rd PL19 ......147 A5
Peter Hopper's Hill PL5 .120 C2
Peter's Cl PL9 ....136 C7
Peter's Park La PL5 ..123 E1
Peters Hill PL26 .....58 B4
Peters Park Cl PL5 ...123 E1
Peters Row PL19 ....75 A1
Petersfield Cl PL3 ....129 B6
Petes Pl 24 TR26 ....141 B5
Petherick Creek Holiday
Bglws PL27 ....32 C7
Petherick Rd EX23 ...104 E3
Pethericks Mill EX23 .104 E4
Pethick Cl PL6 ......124 D6
Pethill Cl PL6 ....125 D2
Pethybridge Dr PL31 .109 B3
Peverell Park Rd PL3 .128 D6
Peverell Rd
Penzance TR18 ......143 E7
7 Porthleven TR13 ...98 C8
Peverell Terr
Plymouth PL3 ....128 C5
Porthleven TR13 .....98 B8
Pew Tor Cl
Tavistock PL19 ......147 E5
3 Yelverton PL20 ...42 C3
Phernyssick Rd PL25 .114 F6
Philgray Cl TR27 ....142 E7
Philip Cl PL9 ....136 A6
Philip Gdns PL9 .....135 F6
Philip Rd TR27 ......142 D7
Phillack Hill TR27 ....142 D7
Phillimore St 3 PL2 ..127 E4
Phoenix Cl 9 PL20 ...42 C4
Phoenix St PL1 ......148 A2
Piala Pl PL27 ....142 E7
Pick Pie Dr PL6 .....125 E8
Pickard Way EX23 ...104 D7
Pickering Villas TR4 ..69 A3
Picketts Yd TR10 ....144 D7
Pier La PL10 ....133 A1
Pier St PL1 ....148 B1
Pigmeadow La PL14 ..113 C6
Pike Rd PL3 ....129 D5
Pike St PL14 ....113 C6
Pike's Hill PL11 ......145 B4
Pikes Hill PL23 ......116 C4

Pilchard Works The ★
TR18 ....143 C3
Pilgrim Cl PL2 ....128 B6
Pilgrim Ct 11 PL20 ...41 B1
Pilgrim Dr PL20 .....41 B1
Pilgrim Prim Sch PL1 .148 B3
Pilgrims Way TR27 ...78 C1
Pill La PL12 ....122 E4
Pillar Wlk PL6 ....124 E7
Pillars Cl TR8 ....56 F5
Pillars Rd Flushing TR11 .145 B8
Mylor Bridge TR11 ...82 A2
Pillmere Dr PL12 ....122 D4
Pilot Cotts PL28 .....21 B4
Pin La PL1 ....149 A2
Pinch Hill EX23 ......7 B7
Pinder Ct PL19 ......147 B5
Pine Cl TR26 ....141 B6
Pine Ct Par PL24 ....115 D5
Perranwell Sta TR3 ..81 D6
Pine Lodge Gdns ★
PL25 ....115 D4
Pine Rd PL18 ....143 B4
Pine Trees Camp Site ★
TR12 ....99 F5
Pine View PL18 .....41 A6
Pinewood Cl PL7 ....130 F6
Pinewood Dr PL6 ....125 F7
Pinewood Flats PL27 .21 D5
Pink Moors TR16 ....68 D1
Pinslow Cross PL15 ..19 C8
Pipers Cl PL15 ......18 E2
Pit Mdw TR11 ....144 E3
Pitick Terr TR11 .....145 B6
Pitland Cnr PL19 ....30 D4
Pityme Bsns Ctr PL27 .21 D3
Pityme Farm Rd PL27 .21 F3
Pityme Ind Est PL27 .21 D3
Pixieland Fun pk ★ EX23 .5 A6
Pixon La PL19 ......147 B4
Pixon Trad Est 2 PL19 .147 B4
Pizza 14 TR26 ....141 B6
Place de Brest PL1 ..148 C3
Place Parc TR7 ......111 D7
Place Rd PL23 ......116 C4
Place View PL23 ....116 C4
Place View Rd 15 TR2 .95 A6
Plaidy La PL13 ......117 E4
Plaidy Park Rd PL13 .117 E4
Plain-An-Gwarry TR15 .140 B5
Plaistow Cl PL5 .....123 E2
Plaistow Cres PL5 ...123 E2
Plaistow Hill Inf Sch
PL5 ....123 E2
Plas Newydd Terr PL31 .109 F5
Plash Mdw PL30 ....35 C8
Platt The PL27 ......108 C5
Pleasant Pl 15 TR18 .143 C7
Pleasant Terr TR19 ..86 E6
Pleasure Hill Cl PL9 .135 D8
Plestin Cl PL15 .....106 C7
Pleyber Christ Way
PL22 ....112 C2
Plintona View PL7 ...130 E7
Plougastel Dr PL12 ..122 E3
Plough Ct TR10 .....81 C2
Plough Gn PL12 .....122 C3
Plumer Rd PL6 ......124 F2
Plym Cres PL19 .....147 D5
Plym St PL4 ....148 A4
Plym Valley Rly ★ PL7 .130 A7
Plym View Prim Sch
PL3 ....129 D6
Plymbridge Gdns PL7 .130 C7
Plymbridge La PL6 ...125 B4
Plymbridge Rd
Plymouth, Estover PL6 .125 F5
Plymouth, Mainstone PL6 .125 F2
Plymouth, Plympton PL7 .130 C7
Plymouth PL6 ....125 A4
Plymouth City Airport
PL6 ....125 C5
Plymouth Coll PL4 ...128 E4
Plymouth Coll of Art &
Design PL4 ....149 A3
Plymouth Coll of Art &
Design (Sutton Annexe)
PL4 ....149 A3
Plymouth Coll of F Ed
PL1 ....128 A2
Plymouth Coll of F Ed
(Annexe) PL1 ....148 C4
Plymouth Coll Prep Sch
PL3 ....128 E6
Plymouth Dome Discovery
Ctr ★ PL1 ....148 C1
Plymouth High Sch for Girls
PL4 ....149 A4
Plymouth International Bsns
Pk PL6 ....125 A3
Plymouth Nuffield Hospl The
PL6 ....125 B4
Plymouth Pavilions PL1 .148 B2
Plymouth Rd
Liskeard PL14 ....113 D5
Plymouth PL7 ....130 B6
Tavistock PL19 ....147 B5
Plymouth Road Ind Est
PL19 ....147 C3
Plymouth Sta PL1,PL4 .148 C4
Plympton Hill PL7 ...130 D5
Plympton Hospl PL7 ..130 D5
Plympton St Mary CE Inf Sch
PL7 ....130 D5
Plympton St Maurice Prim
Sch PL7 ....130 F3
Plymstock Rd PL9 ...135 D7

Plymstock Sch PL9 ...135 F8
Plymtree Dr PL7 .....130 C7
Poad's Trust PL14 ...51 F5
Pocklington Rise PL7 .130 E5
Pocohontas Cres 4 TR9 .45 E1
Pode Dr PL7 ....131 B4
Point Curlew Country Holiday
Est PL28 ....31 A5
Point Rd TR3 ....82 A6
Polapit Tamar PL15 ..19 A8
Polbathic Rd PL11 ...140 C6
Polbreen Ave TR5 ...54 C1
Polbreen La TR5 ....54 C1
Poldark Gdns 7 PL24 .60 B4
Poldark Mine Heritage
Complex ★ TR13 ....92 A6
Poldark Rd 12 TR16 ..67 E4
Poldhu Cl TR26 ......141 A1
Poldhu Rd Liskeard PL14 .113 D6
Mullion TR12 ....99 A2
Poldice La TR16 .....68 E1
Poldice Terr TR16 ...68 E1
Poldrea PL24 ....60 D5
Poldrissick Hill PL12 .53 C2
Poldrissick La PL12 ..53 C2
Poldue Cl TR15 .....140 D6
Polean La PL13 .....117 B4
Polecoverack La TR12 .101 C1
Polgarth Camborne TR15 .139 C5
Newlyn TR18 ....143 B3
Polgarth Cl TR26 ....141 D1
Polgine Cl TR14 .....79 E5
Polgine La TR14 .....79 E5
Polglase Wlk TR4 ...70 D8
Polglaze Cl TR18 ....143 D7
Polgoon Cl TR18 ....143 C5
Polgooth Cl TR15 ...140 D6
Polgover Way 5 PL24 .60 B4
Polgrain Rd TR14 ...138 F6
Polgrean Pl PL24 ....60 B5
Polhigay Terr TR16 ..80 C2
Polhorman La TR12 ..99 A2
Police Ho TR11 .....145 B4
Polisken Way TR4 ...56 D1
Polkerris Rd TR16 ...80 F8
Polkirt Hill
Gorran Haven PL26 ..73 B1
Mevagissey PL26 ....73 C3
Polkyth Rd PL25 ....114 F4
Pollard Cl Plymouth PL9 .135 B2
Saltash PL12 ....122 B2
Pollard Rd 7 PL17 ..39 F4
Pollards Cl
Goonhavern TR4 .....55 D4
Pensilva PL14 ....38 E4
Pollards Way PL12 ..122 E3
Polmark Dr PL28 ....20 D2
Polmarth Cl PL25 ...114 F6
Polmassick Vineyard ★
PL26 ....72 E4
Polmear Ct 9 PL27 ..108 B5
Polmear Hill PL24 ...60 E4
Polmear Parc PL24 ..60 D4
Polmear Rd Par PL24 .60 D4
St Austell PL25 ......114 F3
Polmeere Ho TR18 ..143 E7
Polmeere Rd TR18 ..143 E7
Polmena Cl PL22 ....112 E1
Polmennor Dr TR26 ..141 D1
Polmennor Rd
Falmouth TR11 ......144 F1
Heamoor TR18 ......143 C8
Polmenor Downs N TR14,
TR27 ....78 F5
Polmenor Downs S TR14 .78 F4
Polmeor Cl TR26 ....141 D1
Polmewan Flats PL26 .59 A1
Polmor Rd TR20 ....89 B8
Polmorla Mews 10 PL27 .108 B5
Polmorla Rd PL27 ...108 B5
Polmorla Wlk PL27 ..108 C5
Polperro Heritage Mus ★
PL13 ....62 E2
Polperro Model Village ★
PL13 ....62 D1
Polperro Prim Sch PL13 .62 E2
Polperro Rd PL13 ...117 B4
Polpey La PL24 .....60 D5
Polruan Com Prim Sch
PL23 ....116 D2
Polruan Ct TR1 .....137 E2
Polruan Rd
Redruth TR15 ....140 D6
Truro TR1 ....137 E2
Polruan Terr PL1 ....148 A3
Polscoe Rd PL22 ....112 F3
Polsethow TR10 .....144 B7
Polstain Cres TR3 ...69 D3
Polstain Rd TR3 .....69 D3
Polstain Villas TR3 ..69 D3
Polsue Way TR2 .....70 F5
Poltair Ave PL25 ....114 E4
Poltair Cl TR3 ....143 E7
Poltair Com Sch & Sports
Coll PL25 ....114 D5
Poltair Ct PL25 .....114 E4
Poltair Dr TR10 .....144 B7
Poltair Hospl TR20 ..143 B8
Poltair Rd Penryn TR10 .144 B7
St Austell PL25 ......114 D4
Poltamar PL15 ......106 D5
Poltair Terr 7 TR18 ..143 C7
Poltesco La TR12 ...103 B5
Poltisko Rd TR10 ....144 B7
Poltisko Terr TR10 ..144 B7
Poltreen Cl TR26 ....141 D1

Polurrian Rd TR12 .....99 A1
Polvarth Est TR2 .....95 B6
Polvarth Rd TR2 .....95 A6
Polvean Cross PL14 .....51 A1
Polvean Terr PL14 .....51 A1
Polvella TR7 .....110 B5
Polvellan Terr PL13 .....117 C4
Polvelyn Parc TR27 .....142 E7
Polventon CI
  Falmouth TR11 .....144 E4
  Heamoor TR18 .....143 C7
Polventon Parc 6 TR12 101 C4
Polvillion Rd PL23 .....116 B4
Polweath CI TR18 .....143 E7
Polweath Rd TR18 .....143 E7
Polwhaveral Terr 6
  TR11 .....145 A5
Polwheal Rd TR14 .....138 C6
Polwhele House Sch TR4 70 C6
Polwhele Rd
  Newquay TR7 .....111 A3
  Truro TR1 .....137 F6
Polwithen Dr TR26 .....141 C1
Polwithen Gdns TR26 .141 C1
Polwithen Rd
  Falmouth TR11 .....145 A4
  Penryn TR10 .....144 B7
  Penzance TR18 .....143 D5
Polwrath Terr PL14 .....38 A4
Polwyn CI TR18 .....143 B7
Polyear CI PL14 .....59 A1
Polzeath Ct PL27 .....21 D6
Polzeath Gdns PL2 .....128 D8
Pomphlett CI PL9 .....135 D8
Pomphlett Farm Ind Est
  PL9 .....129 E1
Pomphlett Gdns PL9 .135 D8
Pomphlett Prim Sch
  PL9 .....135 E8
Pomphlett Rd PL9 .....135 E8
Pond La TR15 .....140 A6
Pond Lanes End TR15 ..140 B6
Pond View Terr PL26 ..58 D5
Pond Wlk TR27 .....142 D7
Pondbridge Hill 1
  PL14 .....113 C5
Pondfield Rd PL22 .....122 B3
Pondhu Cres PL25 .....114 B3
Pondhu Jun & Inf Sch
  PL25 .....114 B2
Pondhu Rd PL25 .....114 C3
Ponds Hill TR19 .....75 B1
Poniou La TR20 .....88 F6
Poniou Rd TR20 .....88 F6
Poniou Way TR20 .....88 F6
Ponsandane Farm Mews
  TR18 .....143 F7
Ponsharden Cotts TR11 .144 F6
Ponsharden Ind Est
  TR11 .....144 E6
Ponsmere Ct 4 TR6 ....55 A5
Ponsmere Rd TR6 .....55 A5
Ponsonby Rd PL3 .....128 B4
Ponstantual Hill TR12 ..99 D7
Ponsvale TR3 .....81 B4
Pontsmill Rd PL24 .....60 C6
Pool Hall PL14 .....51 F5
Pool Ind Est TR15 .....139 C5
Pool Sch & Com Coll
  TR15 .....139 B6
Pool St PL31 .....109 E5
Pool's Ct TR27 .....142 D6
Poole Park Rd PL5 .....127 C8
Poplar CI PL7 .....131 B5
Poplar Terr TR11 .....145 B7
Poplars Ct 9 TR6 .....55 A5
Porcupine PL24 .....60 C6
Pordenack CI TR26 .....141 E2
Porfell Animal Land★
  PL14 .....50 A2
Porhan Gn TR11 .....144 E6
Pork St TR12 .....100 D6
Porsham CI PL6 .....121 B1
Porsham La PL5 .....124 E8
Porspoder PL10 .....133 A2
Port Isaac Com Prim Sch
  PL29 .....22 E7
Port La PL15 .....27 E8
Portbyhan Rd PL13 ...117 C3
Porteous CI PL1 .....127 F3
Porter Way PL12 .....122 C3
Porth Bean Ct TR7 ...111 C7
Porth Bean Rd TR7 ...111 C7
Porth Par PL11 .....111 C8
Porth Sawle Flats TR2 .83 B2
Porth View TR7 .....95 B6
Porthcollum La TR27 ...78 A3
Portheast CI PL26 .....85 C5
Portheast Way PL26 ...85 C5
Porthellow Vineyard★
  TR12 .....101 D5
Portherras Cross TR19 .75 A1
Portherras Terr TR19 ...75 A1
Portherras Villas TR19 .75 A1
Porthgwidden Studios
  TR26 .....141 C6
Porthia CI TR26 .....141 A4
Porthia Cres TR26 .....141 A4
Porthia Rd TR26 .....141 A4
Porthilly La TR27 .....21 D2
Porthilly View PL28 ...107 E4
Porthkerris Water Sports
  Ctr★ TR12 .....101 E5
Porthleven Jun & Inf Sch
  TR13 .....91 B1
Porthleven Rd TR13 ...91 B1
Porthmellon Gdns PL17 .39 F4
Porthmeor Hill TR26 ..141 A6

Porthmeor Rd
  St Austell PL25 .....115 B3
  6 St Ives TR26 .....141 B6
Porthmeor Sq 21 TR26 .141 B6
Porthminster Terr 23
  TR26 .....141 B5
Porthpean Beach Rd
  PL26 .....59 E1
Porthpean Rd PL25,
  PL26 .....114 F2
Porthrepta Rd TR26 ..141 E1
Portisco CI TR1 .....137 E3
Portland CI PL14 .....113 D7
Portland Ct 9 PL1 ....127 F3
Portland Gdns PL14 ...144 F4
Portland PI 22 TR19 ...88 C1
Portland PI E PL4 .....149 A4
Portland Rd PL1 .....127 F3
Portland Sq
  Plymouth PL4 .....148 C4
  Plymouth PL4 .....149 A4
Portland Square La N
  PL4 .....149 A4
Portland Terr PL14 ...113 C7
Portland Villas PL4 ...148 C4
Portmellon Pk PL26 ...73 C3
Portreath Com Prim Sch
  TR16 .....67 D6
Portuan Rd PL13 .....117 C1
Portway PL9 .....136 D7
Posses La TR18 .....88 E6
Possession La PL12 ...53 C3
Post Box Row TR14 ...139 B3
Post Office Row PL26 ..58 D7
Potters La PL35 .....9 C1
Potters Way PL7 .....130 D6
Pottery Est PL10 .....132 E6
Pottery Rd PL1 .....127 D3
Poughill Rd EX23 .....104 F7
Poultney CI PL7 .....131 A5
Pound Dean PL13 .....113 A5
Pound Hill PL12 .....53 C3
Pound La Bodmin PL31 .109 E5
  Stoke Climsland PL17 ..28 E1
  Threemilestone TR3 ...69 E1
Pound Pk PL14 .....51 F5
Pound Rd PL20 .....42 B3
Pound St Liskeard PL14 .113 C6
  Plymouth PL1 .....134 A8
Pound's Cross PL6 ...120 C5
Poundfield CI 2 EX23 ..4 D1
Poundfield Hill 1 EX23 ..4 D1
Poundfield La EX23 .....4 D1
Pounds Park Rd
  1 Bere Alston PL20 ...41 B1
  Plymouth PL3 .....128 D7
Pounds Pk PL12 .....122 F3
Poundstock CI PL30 ...35 F3
Powderham Rd PL3 ...128 F7
Powis Gdns PL5 .....124 B2
Powisland Dr PL6 .....125 A5
Praed's La TR17 .....89 C5
Praze Mdw TR10 .....144 C8
Praze Rd Newquay TR7 .111 B7
  Porthleven TR13 .....91 B1
Praze The TR10 .....144 C8
Praze-An-Creet TR26 ..77 A7
Praze-An-Cronor TR27 .45 E5
Prazegooth La TR12 ..103 A4
Predannack Rd 4 TR12 .99 A1
Preeze Cross PL30 ....35 A6
Prestonbury CI PL6 ...125 B7
Prevenna Rd 2 TR19 ..88 C1
Prideaux CI PL12 .....122 C5
Prideaux PI★ PL28 ...107 C6
Prideaux Rd PL24 .....60 B6
Pridham La PL12 .....128 D7
Pridmouth Rd PL25 ...114 E6
Priestacott Pk EX23 ....5 A4
Priesthood Terr PL10 ..132 E5
Priestley Ave PL5 .....123 E2
Primitive Row TR14 ..139 C4
Primrose CI
  Camborne TR14 .....138 B4
  9 Goldsithney TR20 ..89 E5
  Roche PL26 .....47 A3
  Torpoint PL11 .....126 E4
Primrose Gdns
  Illogan TR16 .....67 D4
  Tavistock PL19 .....147 E4
Primrose Hill TR20 ....89 E5
Primrose La 4 TR20 ...89 E5
Primrose Rd EX23 ....104 F5
Primrose Terr
  Newlyn TR18 .....143 D1
  Portreath TR16 .....67 D6
  Tresillian TR2 .....70 F5
Primrose Valley TR26 .141 C4
Primrose Way
  Launceston PL15 .....106 E4
  Lewannick PL15 .....27 A6
Primrose Wlk PL12 ...122 D4
Prince Charles CI PL15 .106 C7
Prince Charles Ho PL25 114 E5
Prince Charles Pk PL25 114 E5
Prince Charles Rd PL25 114 E5
Prince Maurice Ct PL4 .149 B4
Prince Maurice Rd PL4 .128 F4
Prince Philip Rd PL15 .106 C7
Prince Rock Prim Sch
  PL4 .....129 B2
Prince's St TR1 .....137 D4
Princes Rd PL6 .....125 E6
Princes Row PL14 .....38 B6
Princes Sq PL13 .....117 C3
Princes St Bude EX23 .104 D5
  Looe PL13 .....117 C3

Princes St continued
  Penzance TR18 .....143 E5
  Plymouth PL1 .....127 E2
Princess Ave
  Plymouth, Plymstock PL9 .135 E6
  Plymouth, West Park PL5 .124 A3
Princess Ct PL9 .....135 E6
Princess Ct 12 TR18 ..143 E5
Princess Pk TR9 .....45 E1
Princess Rd PL14 .....38 C4
Princess St Plymouth PL1 148 C2
  St Just TR19 .....86 E6
Princess Terr 8 PL14 ..38 C4
Princess Villas PL17 ...28 B1
Princess Way PL1 .....148 C2
Priors CI 10 TR26 .....77 A6
Priors Row TR13 .....90 B3
Priory CI Par PL24 .....60 C5
  Tavistock PL19 .....147 D3
Priory Cotts PL15 .....106 B6
Priory Dr PL7 .....130 D5
Priory Gdns PL19 .....147 D3
Priory La PL15 .....106 B7
Priory Lawn Terr PL3 .129 A6
Priory Mill PL7 .....130 D5
Priory Park Rd PL15 ..106 B6
Priory Rd Bodmin PL31 .109 F4
  St Austell PL25 .....114 C4
  St Columb Minor TR7,TR8 .111 E7
Priory Ridge PL7 .....130 D5
Prislow CI TR11 .....144 E2
Prislow Fields TR11 ..144 E2
Prislow La TR11 .....144 E2
Probus Com Prim Sch
  TR2 .....71 C6
Promenade The PL1 ..148 C1
Prospect CI TR27 .....142 D6
Prospect Gdns TR1 ...137 F6
Prospect La PL12 .....122 C3
Prospect PI Ashton TR13 .90 E3
  Falmouth TR11 .....145 B5
  Hayle TR27 .....142 D6
  Helston TR13 .....146 C5
  Mevagissey PL26 .....73 C4
  26 Penzance TR18 ...143 E6
  8 Porthleven TR13 ..98 B8
  5 Truro TR1 .....137 D5
Prospect Row
  Ashton TR13 .....90 E3
  Plymouth PL4 .....127 E1
Prospect St PL4 .....149 A3
Prospect Terr
  Gunnislake PL18 .....41 A6
  Gunnislake, St Ann's Chapel
  PL18 .....40 E1
  Mevagissey PL26 .....73 C4
Prospect Wlk PL12 ...122 C3
Prosper CI PL26 .....47 A2
Prosper Hill TR27 .....66 B1
Prosper Rd PL26 .....47 A2
Prouse Cres PL2 .....128 C8
Prouse Rise PL12 .....122 E8
Prout's La TR27 .....78 D6
Prouts Ct 4 PL15 .....106 C6
Prouts Way PL15 .....18 C2
Providence PI
  Calstock PL18 .....41 A3
  Plymouth PL1 .....128 A3
Providence St PL4 ...149 A4
Provis Rd TR14 .....143 C4
Prynne CI PL1 .....148 B3
Puckator La PL14 .....38 A2
Puggis Hill TR14 .....138 C4
Pulla CI TR4 .....81 B6
Putnam CI TR14 .....113 D5
Pydar CI TR7 .....111 B5
Pydar Mews 8 TR1 ...137 C5
Pydar St TR1 .....137 C5
Pym St Plymouth PL1 .127 F3
  Tavistock PL19 .....147 C6
Pyramid CI PL25 .....58 F4
Pyworthy CE Prim Sch
  EX22 .....8 E5

Quakers Rd TR4,TR3 ...81 B6
Quant Pk PL19 .....147 C6
Quarry CI EX23 .....104 C7
Quarry Cotts
  Plymouth PL1 .....148 A4
  Plymouth, Honicknowle
  PL5 .....124 B2
Quarry Cres PL15 .....106 A3
Quarry Ct TR15 .....145 B4
Quarry Gdns TR18 ...143 D5
Quarry Hill
  Falmouth TR11 .....145 B4
  Gulval TR18 .....88 E7
Quarry House Flats TR1 137 A6
Quarry La Gunnislake PL18 40 F6
  Landrake PL12 .....53 D3
  Launceston PL15 .....18 E2
  Paul TR19 .....88 B1
  St Germans PL12 .....65 A8
Quarry Park Ave PL9 .135 D7
Quarry Park Rd
  Newquay TR7 .....110 F5
  Plymouth, Peverell PL3 .128 D5
  Plymouth, Plymstock PL9 .135 D7
Quarry Park Rd PL31 .109 C4
Quarry Rd Pensilva PL14 .38 C4
  Perranporth TR6 .....55 B4

Quarry St St Germans PL12 65 A8
  Torpoint PL11 .....127 C3
Quarry Trail★ PL34 ....14 C3
Quarterdeck The PL1 .134 A8
Quay Hill Falmouth TR11 145 C4
  Penryn TR10 .....144 D7
Quay La PL12 .....53 D1
Quay Mews 8 TR1 ...137 D4
Quay Rd Crumplehorn PL13 62 D1
  Devoran TR3 .....81 F6
  Landrake PL12 .....53 A2
  Looe PL13 .....117 C3
  Mylor Bridge TR11 ...82 B4
  Plymouth PL1 .....149 A2
  St Agnes TR5 .....54 D2
  St Germans PL12 .....65 B8
  Tideford PL12 .....52 F2
Quay St Falmouth TR11 .145 C4
  Looe PL13 .....117 C3
  Lostwithiel PL22 .....112 C2
  11 Mousehole TR19 ..88 C1
  Penzance TR18 .....143 F4
  St Ives TR26 .....141 C6
  Truro TR1 .....137 C4
Quay The Pentewan PL26 .73 C6
  Penzance TR18 .....143 F5
  Plymouth PL9 .....135 C4
  Polruan PL23 .....116 D3
  Portscatho TR2 .....83 B2
  St Germans PL12 .....65 B8
  St Mawes TR2 .....95 A6
Quayside 6 PL19 .....147 B5
Queen Anne Gdns TR11 144 E3
Queen Elizabeth Rd
  PL15 .....106 C7
Queen Mary Ct TR11 .145 B2
Queen Mary Rd TR11 .145 B2
Queen St Bude EX23 ..104 C5
  Goldsithney TR20 .....89 E5
  Lostwithiel PL22 .....112 C2
  Penzance TR18 .....143 E5
  Plymouth PL1 .....127 D2
  St Just TR19 .....86 E6
Queen Terr 40 C4
Queen's Cres PL31 ...109 B3
Queen's Ct 5 TR18 ...143 E4
Queen's Gate
  Plymouth, Lipson PL4 .149 B4
  Plymouth, Stoke PL3 .148 A4
Queen's Gate Mews PL4 149 B4
Queen's Gate Villas
  PL4 .....149 B4
Queen's Gate Villas Rd
  PL4 .....149 B4
Queen's Rd PL4 .....149 B4
Queen's Sq 24 TR18 ..143 E5
Queen's Way
  2 Goldsithney TR20 ..89 E5
  Hayle TR27 .....142 C5
Queens CI
  5 Indian Queens TR9 .45 E1
  Plymouth PL6 .....125 E6
Queens Pk PL21 .....108 C4
Queens Rd Plymouth PL5 .123 F3
  St Austell PL25 .....114 E3
Quenchwell Rd TR3 ....81 F7
Quethiock CE Prim Sch
  PL14 .....52 C7
Quillet Rd TR18 .....143 B3
Quilver CI PL26 .....85 D5
Quimperle Way PL14 .113 C6
Quintrell Downs Sta
  TR8 .....111 F3
Quintrell Gdns TR8 ....44 E3
Quintrell Rd TR7,TR8 .111 E5

Rabys Row TR16 .....140 F8
Race Hill
  Launceston PL15 .....106 C5
  Truro TR1 .....81 C8
Race Hill Terr PL15 ...106 C5
Rachel's Way 17 TR9 ..45 E6
Radcliffe CI PL6 .....124 E6
Radford Ave PL4 .....129 B1
Radford La PL10 .....132 D4
Radford Park Dr PL9 .135 D6
Radford Park Rd PL9 .135 D6
Radford Rd PL1 .....148 B1
Radford View PL9 .....135 D6
Radland Cross PL12 ...40 C3
Radnor CI PL31 .....109 F4
Radnor Hall PL4 .....149 A3
Radnor PI PL4 .....149 A3
Radnor Rd Redruth TR16 .140 C8
  Redruth TR16 .....68 C3
Radnor St PL4 .....149 A3
Ragan Ct TR10 .....144 A7
Raginnis Hill 24 TR19 ..88 C1
Raglan Ct PL1 .....127 F2
Raglan Gdns PL1 .....127 F2
Raglan Rd PL1 .....127 F2
Railway Cotts
  Camborne TR14 .....139 A3
  Falmouth TR11 .....145 B7
  6 Plymouth, Ford PL2 .127 F5
  Plymouth, Plymstock PL9 .135 D6
  Tavistock PL19 .....147 B6
Railway Cres PL14 .....38 A4
Railway Terr
  Bodmin PL31 .....109 D5
  Carharrack TR16 .....80 C8
Railway Villas PL15 ..139 F6
Rainham Terr TR15 ..139 C8
Rainy Fields CI PL28 ..107 D5

Rainyfields PL28 .....107 D5
Raleigh CI PL28 .....107 C4
Raleigh Ct PL7 .....131 B6
Raleigh PI 13 TR11 ...145 A4
Raleigh Rd PL28 .....107 C5
Raleigh St PL1 .....148 B3
Ralph's Ct PL19 .....147 B5
Ramage CI PL6 .....125 F3
Rame Croft PL10 .....80 E1
Rame La Cawsand PL10 .132 F1
  Rame PL10 .....64 B2
Rame View PL13 .....117 E5
Ramehead Cotts PL10 ..64 B1
Ramehead La PL10 .....64 B1
Ramillies Ave PL5 .....124 A4
Ramoth Way TR6 .....55 B5
Randwick Park Rd PL9 135 D7
Ranelagh Mews PL31 .109 D5
Ranelagh Rd PL25 .....114 F4
Ransum Way PL19 ...147 B4
Raphael CI PL9 .....136 B5
Raphael Dr PL9 .....136 A6
Raphael Rd PL13 .....62 C1
Rapson Rd PL14 .....113 D6
Rashleigh Ave
  Plymouth PL7 .....130 F7
  Saltash PL12 .....122 D1
Rashleigh Ct PL25 .....115 C3
Rashleigh La PL23 .....116 A4
Rashleigh Mews PL25 .115 A3
Rashleigh PI PL25 .....114 F4
Rashleigh Vale TR1 ...137 E4
Ratcliffes La PL26 .....146 A5
Rattle St PL26 .....85 D5
Rawley La TR7 .....110 E5
Rawlin CI PL6 .....129 C8
Rawlings La PL23 .....116 D5
Raymond Rd TR15 ...140 C4
Raymond Way PL7 ...130 D6
Raynham Rd PL3 .....128 B4
Reading Wlk PL5 .....124 C4
Readymoney Rd PL23 .116 B3
Reawla La TR27 .....78 E3
Rebecca CI PL24 .....60 B6
Recreation Rd PL2 ...128 C7
Rectory Gdns TR14 ..138 C2
Rectory Rd
  Camborne TR14 .....138 C2
  Lanivet PL30 .....47 F6
  Plymouth PL1 .....128 A2
  St Buryan TR19 .....97 B6
  St Dennis PL26 .....46 B1
  St Stephen PL26 .....58 B4
Rectory The TR1 .....137 C5
Red La Bugle PL26 .....47 C2
  Rosudgeon TR20 .....89 F5
Redannack 2 TR12 ....99 A2
Redannack N 1 TR12 ..99 A2
Redannick Cres TR1 ..137 B3
Redannick La TR1 .....137 B3
Redbrooke Rd TR14 ..138 C2
Redbrooke Terr TR14 .138 C2
Reddicliff CI PL9 .....135 E5
Reddicliff Rd PL9 .....135 D5
Reddington Rd PL3 ...129 B7
Redfern Ct 2 TR26 ...141 B5
Redhill CI PL5 .....123 E4
Redinnick Gdns 3
  TR18 .....143 E4
Redinnick PI TR18 ....143 D4
Redinnick Terr 1 TR18 143 E4
Redmoor CI
  Kelly Bray PL17 .....39 E6
  Tavistock PL19 .....147 A7
Redmoor Rd PL17 .....39 E6
Redruth CI PL5 .....124 C1
Redruth Com Sch TR15 140 A5
Redruth Highway TR15 140 E7
Redruth Rd TR13 .....146 D7
Redruth Sch TR15 ....140 C5
Redruth Sta TR15 .....140 C5
Redvale Rd PL30 .....23 E3
Redvers Gr PL7 .....130 E4
Redvers Hts PL7 .....140 B3
Redwing Dr PL6 .....125 D8
Redwood CI PL25 .....104 E5
Redwood Dr PL7 .....131 E5
Redwood Gr EX23 ...104 E5
Reeds Pk PL22 .....112 D2
Reeds Way TR7 .....110 D5
Reen Hill TR6 .....55 B4
Reens Cres TR18 .....143 D7
Reens Rd TR18 .....143 C7
Reeves CI TR13 .....91 B3
Regal Ct PL12 .....122 F2
Regent Sq 21 TR18 ..143 E5
Regent St PL4 .....149 A3
Regent Terr
  Penzance TR18 .....143 E4
  St Just TR19 .....86 E6
Reigate Rd PL9 .....135 E8
Relistian La TR27 .....78 E3
Relistian Pk TR27 .....78 E3
Relubbus Hill TR20 ....90 A6
Relubbus La TR20 .....90 A6
Rendle St Delabole PL33 ..14 E3
  Plymouth PL1 .....148 B3
Rendlesham Gdns PL6 125 E3
Renney Rd PL9 .....135 C1
Rennie Ave PL5 .....123 C1
Renoir CI PL9 .....136 A6
Renown St PL2 .....127 E6
Reperry Cross PL30 ...47 F6
Research Way PL6 ....125 C4
Reservoir Cres PL9 ...136 B7

Reservoir La **1** PL3 . . . .128 F6
Reservoir Rd
  Plymouth, Hartley PL3 . . . .128 F6
  Plymouth, Plymstock PL9 . .136 B7
Reservoir Way PL9 . . . . . .136 B7
Reskadinnick Rd TR14 . . . .138 B4
Resolution Ho PL4 . . . . . .149 B3
Respryn Ct PL14 . . . . .113 D6
Respryn Rd PL31 . . . . .48 D8
Restormel Castle★
  PL22 . . . . .112 C5
Restormel Ind Est PL22 112 D2
Restormel Rd Looe PL13 117 D4
  Lostwithiel PL22 . . . . .112 C4
  Newlyn PL18 . . . . .143 C3
  Plymouth PL4 . . . . .148 C4
Restormel Terr
  Falmouth TR11 . . . . .145 B3
  Plymouth PL4 . . . . .148 C4
Restronguet Hill TR11 . . . . .82 C6
Reswythen Wlk TR14 . . . . .138 F7
Retallack Gdns **3** TR20 . .89 E5
Retallick Mdws PL25 . . . . .115 B5
Retanna Cvn Pk TR13 . . . . .92 D7
Retanning La PL26 . . . . . . .58 E1
Retreat The
  Chacewater TR4 . . . . .69 A3
  Plymouth PL3 . . . . .129 B7
  St Columb Major TR9 . . . . .45 E6
Revel Rd PL3 . . . . .129 A6
Revell Park Rd PL7 . . . . . .130 E7
Reynolds Gr PL5 . . . . .127 C8
Reynolds Rd PL7 . . . . .130 C6
Rheola Gdns PL6 . . . . .125 D3
Rhind St PL31 . . . . .109 E5
Rhodes Cl PL7 . . . . .130 E7
Rhubarb Hill TR8 . . . . .43 B1
Rhude Cross EX23 . . . . .5 B3
Rialton Hts TR7 . . . . .111 E7
Rialton Rd TR7,TR8 . . . . . .111 E6
Ribble Gdns PL3 . . . . .129 D7
Rice La PL26 . . . . .85 C5
Richard Lander Sch TR1 . .69 F3
Richards Cres TR1 . . . . . . .69 F3
Richards Ct **9** PL31 . . . . .109 D5
Richards La TR16 . . . . .67 E4
Richards Row PL3 . . . . . . .128 F4
Richards Terr PL10 . . . . . .132 E5
Richmond Hill TR1 . . . . . .137 B4
Richmond Pl
  3 Truro TR1 . . . . .137 B4
  40 St Ives TR26 . . . . .141 B6
Richmond Rd Pelynt PL13 62 D6
  Plymouth PL6 . . . . .125 A2
Richmond St
  Heamoor TR18 . . . . .143 C7
  Penzance TR18 . . . . .143 E6
Richmond Terr
  Buckland Monachorum PL20 41 F3
  Truro TR1 . . . . .137 B4
Richmond Way TR26 . . . . .141 D1
Richmond Wlk PL1 . . . . . .127 F1
Rick Mdw PL15 . . . . .18 E6
Ricketts Rd PL26 . . . . .59 A1
Ride The PL7,PL9 . . . . .129 D2
Ridge Cross PL9 . . . . .136 A3
Ridge Ho PL4 . . . . .129 A4
Ridge Park Ave PL4 . . . . . .128 D4
Ridge Park Rd PL7 . . . . . .130 E5
Ridge Pk PL7 . . . . .130 E5
Ridge Rd PL7 . . . . .130 D6
Ridgegrove Hill PL15 . . . .106 D6
Ridgegrove La PL15 . . . . .106 C7
Ridgeo Mill PL18 . . . . .143 F8
Ridgevale Cl TR18 . . . . . . .143 F8
Ridgevale La TR18 . . . . . . .143 F8
Ridgeway
  19 Perranporth TR6 . . . . . .55 A5
  Plymouth PL7 . . . . .130 D5
  Plymouth PL7 . . . . .130 F5
  Probus TR2 . . . . .71 C6
  Saltash PL12 . . . . .122 D1
Ridgeway Sch PL7 . . . . . .130 E5
Ridgewell Terr TR9 . . . . . . .57 E8
Ridgewood Cl PL26 . . . . . .114 F1
Riga Terr PL13 . . . . .129 C4
Rigdale Cl PL6 . . . . .129 A7
Ringmore Way PL6 . . . . . .124 B3
Ringway Flats **8** PL31 . . .109 D5
Ringwell Holiday Pk TR3 81 F7
Rinsey La TR13 . . . . .90 D2
Risdon Pk PL4 . . . . .129 B1
Rivendell PL27 . . . . .108 C4
River Ct Saltash PL12 . . . . .122 D5
  Tavistock PL19 . . . . .147 D6
River St Mevagissey PL26 . .73 C3
  Portscatho TR2 . . . . .83 B2
  Truro TR1 . . . . .137 C4
River View Flushing TR11 .145 B7
  Gunnislake PL18 . . . . .40 E5
  Lerryn PL22 . . . . .61 C7
  Plymouth PL4 . . . . .129 B1
  Saltash PL12 . . . . .122 F3
  Tresillian PL27 . . . . .70 E4
River View La PL4 . . . . . . .129 B1
Riverford Cl PL6 . . . . .125 D7
Rivers The PL12 . . . . .122 E1
Riverside Angarrack TR27 . .78 C4
  Lanivet PL30 . . . . .47 E2
  Launceston PL15 . . . . .106 B7
  Lelant TR26 . . . . .77 C4
  Padstow PL28 . . . . .107 E5
Riverside Ave TR7 . . . . . . .110 A5
Riverside Bsns Pk PL1 . .127 E3
Riverside Cl **1** PL20 . . . . .42 C4

Riverside Cott PL12 . . . .122 C1
Riverside Cres TR7 . . . . . .110 A5
Riverside Ct PL22 . . . . . . .112 C2
Riverside Ho TR1 . . . . .137 D1
Riverside Holiday Pk
  TR8 . . . . .111 B1
Riverside Mews PL12 . . . .123 A3
Riverside Pl
  Plymouth PL1 . . . . .127 D2
  8 Wadebridge PL27 . . . . .108 B5
Riverside View TR1 . . . . . .137 E3
Riverside Wlk PL5 . . . . . . .124 B5
Riverview TR11 . . . . .145 A6
Riviera Apartments
  TR26 . . . . .141 D2
Riviera Est TR1 . . . . .70 C1
Riviera La TR2 . . . . .95 A6
Riviere Chalet Camp
  TR27 . . . . .142 A7
Riviere Sands Holiday Pk
  TR27 . . . . .142 B8
Riviere Towans TR27 . . . . .142 B7
Roach's Row TR15 . . . . . . .140 B5
Robartes Ct **13** TR1 . . . . .137 C4
Robartes Gardens Flats
  PL25 . . . . .114 E4
Robartes Gdns PL25 . . . . .114 E4
Robartes Jun Sch PL31 109 D4
Robartes Pl PL25 . . . . .114 E5
Robartes Rd
  Bodmin PL31 . . . . .109 D4
  Newquay TR7 . . . . .110 F5
  St Dennis PL26 . . . . .58 C8
Robartes Terr
  1 Illogan TR16 . . . . .67 E4
  Lostwithiel PL22 . . . . .112 C3
Robeclave Ct PL7 . . . . .131 C6
Robert Adams Cl PL7 . . . .130 E4
Robert Eliot Ct PL25 . . . . .114 B3
Robert Hichens Rd
  TR11 . . . . .145 A5
Roberts Ave PL11 . . . . . . .127 B3
Roberts Rd PL5 . . . . .127 D8
Robin Dr PL15 . . . . .106 E4
Robins Cl **13** PL24 . . . . . . .60 B4
Robins Way PL9 . . . . .135 E8
Roborough Ave PL6 . . . . . .125 B5
Roborough Cl PL6 . . . . . . .125 B5
Roborough Down La
  PL6 . . . . .121 F5
Roborough La PL5 . . . . . . .124 D8
Robyns Cl PL7 . . . . .131 B5
Roche Prim Sch PL26 . . . .46 F2
Roche Rd Bugle PL26 . . . . .47 C2
  Stenalees PL26 . . . . .59 C7
Roche Rural Workshops
  PL26 . . . . .47 A4
Roche Sta PL26 . . . . .47 A4
Rochester Rd **5** PL4 . . . .128 E4
Rochford Cres PL5 . . . . . . .123 F5
Rock Cl TR14 . . . . .138 F2
Rock Close Ho TR27 . . . . .142 A1
Rock Gdns PL9 . . . . .129 D1
Rock La PL31 . . . . .109 C4
Rock Rd Newlyn TR18 . . . .143 C3
  St Minver PL27 . . . . .21 E2
Rock Terr Heamoor TR18 . .143 C7
  Plymouth PL7 . . . . .130 D4
Rock Twrs PL12 . . . . .117 D2
Rock View Parc PL26 . . . . .47 B3
Rock Villas PL7 . . . . .21 D2
Rockfield Ave PL6 . . . . . . .124 F4
Rockhaven Gdns PL27 . . . .21 F3
Rockhead St PL33 . . . . .14 C3
Rockhill PL5 . . . . .124 C7
Rockingham Rd PL3 . . . . .129 A5
Rockville Pk PL9 . . . . .135 E8
Rockwood Rd PL25 . . . . . .125 E8
Rocky Hill PL19 . . . . .147 B5
Rocky La Praa Sands TR20 .90 C6
  St Agnes TR5 . . . . .54 C2
  Treworlas TR2 . . . . .83 D5
Rocky Park Ave PL9 . . . . . .135 E8
Rocky Park Rd PL9 . . . . . .135 E8
Rodda Cl PL18 . . . . .41 A7
Rodda's Rd TR4 . . . . .68 C6
Roddick Way **8** PL7 . . . .131 C5
Rodings The PL14 . . . . .51 F5
Rodney St PL5 . . . . .127 D8
Rodwell Cl PL15 . . . . .140 E5
Rodwell Ct TR27 . . . . .78 E1
Roebuck Villas TR11 . . . . .145 D3
Roekindale Ct TR15 . . . . . .139 D6
Roeselare Ave PL11 . . . . . .127 A3
Roeselare Cl PL11 . . . . . . .127 A3
Rogate Dr PL6 . . . . .125 D4
Rogate Wlk PL6 . . . . .125 D4
Rogers Dr PL12 . . . . .122 D4
Roland Bailey Gdns
  PL19 . . . . .147 A6
Rollis Park Cl PL9 . . . . . . .135 C8
Rollis Park Rd PL9 . . . . . . .135 C8
Rolston Cl PL6 . . . . .124 D6
Roma Cl TR7 . . . . .111 C7
Roman Bridge PL13 . . . . . .62 D1
Roman Dr PL31 . . . . .109 F2
Roman Rd PL5 . . . . .123 E2
Roman Way PL5 . . . . .123 E2
Romilly Gdns PL7 . . . . .130 B5
Romney Cl PL5 . . . . .124 B1
Rona Ct TR27 . . . . .142 B5
Ronald Terr PL2 . . . . .127 F5
Ronsdale Cl PL9 . . . . .135 E8
Roope Cl PL5 . . . . .127 C7
Rope Wlk
  Mount Hawke TR4 . . . . . . .68 C6
  Padstow PL28 . . . . .107 D5

Rope Wlk The
  3 St Ives TR26 . . . . .141 B6
  9 St Mawes TR2 . . . . .95 A6
Ropehaven Cl PL25 . . . . . .114 E6
Ropehaven Rd PL25 . . . . . .114 E6
Roper Ave PL5 . . . . .135 D8
Ropewalk Ct **2** TR11 . . . .145 C3
Ropewalk Rd TR3 . . . . .137 C1
Ropewalk The PL18 . . . . . .143 C4
Rorkes Cl PL5 . . . . .123 E2
Ros Lyn TR26 . . . . .141 C1
Roscadghill Parc **1**
  TR18 . . . . .143 C6
Roscadghill Rd TR18 . . . . .143 C6
Roscarrack Cl TR11 . . . . . .144 E2
Roscarrack Rd TR11 . . . . . .144 D1
Roscarrock Hill PL29 . . . . . .22 D7
Rose Cotts
  Camborne TR14 . . . . .138 E3
  Plymouth PL6 . . . . .129 B8
  Stithians TR3 . . . . .80 F3
Rose Eglos TR11 . . . . .144 C2
Rose Eglos Cl TR11 . . . . . .144 C2
Rose Gdns PL6 . . . . .125 E6
Rose Hill Alternun PL15 . . . .26 C8
  Fowey PL23 . . . . .116 C4
  Port Isaac PL29 . . . . .22 D7
  Porthtowan TR4 . . . . .68 A6
  Redruth TR15 . . . . .140 B5
  Sticker PL26 . . . . .58 F1
Rose Hill Cl PL22 . . . . .112 C2
Rose Hill Rd PL24 . . . . .60 B5
Rose Hill Terr PL17 . . . . . . .41 A3
Rose Hill Touring Pk
  TR4 . . . . .68 A6
Rose La **23** TR26 . . . . . . .141 B6
Rose Mdw TR3 . . . . .80 F3
Rose Mdws TR4 . . . . .55 D4
Rose Mullion Gdns PL17 .39 F5
Rose Row TR15 . . . . .140 B5
Rose Terr Gunnislake PL18 .40 E5
  Mitchell TR8 . . . . .56 F5
  23 Penzance TR18 . . . . . .143 E6
Rose Valley TR19 . . . . .75 B2
Roseannon TR11 . . . . .93 D3
Rosebery Ave PL4 . . . . . . .149 C4
Rosebery La PL4 . . . . .149 C4
Rosebery Rd PL4 . . . . .149 C4
Rosecliston Pk TR8 . . . . . .110 E1
Rosecott Pk EX23 . . . . .5 A4
Rosecraddoc Holiday Village
  PL14 . . . . .38 B2
Rosecraddoc Lodge Holiday
  Bglws PL14 . . . . .38 B2
Rosecraddoc View PL14 . .38 A2
Rosedale Ave PL2 . . . . . . .128 D7
Rosedale Gdns PL31 . . . . . .35 B2
Rosedale Rd TR1 . . . . .137 C5
Rosedown Ave PL2 . . . . . .128 A7
Rosehill Ladock TR2 . . . . . .57 C1
  Lanivet PL30 . . . . .47 C6
  Marazion TR17 . . . . .89 B5
  Mylor Bridge TR11 . . . . . . .82 A2
Rosehill Gdns TR18 . . . . . .143 B6
Rosehill Mdw TR18 . . . . . .143 B6
Rosehip Cl PL6 . . . . .125 E7
Roseland Cnr TR4 . . . . .69 A3
Roseland Com Sch The
  TR2 . . . . .72 A4
Roseland Cres TR2 . . . . . . .71 F3
Roseland Flats TR2 . . . . . . .95 A7
Roseland Gdns
  Bodmin PL31 . . . . .109 E6
  Redruth TR15 . . . . .140 D6
  Veryan TR2 . . . . .83 F6
Roseland Pk TR14 . . . . . . .138 D4
Roseland Terr TR4 . . . . . . .55 F2
Roselands Rd PL31 . . . . . .109 F6
Roselidden Parc TR13 . . . .146 B7
Roselyon Pl PL24 . . . . .60 C5
Roselyon Sch PL24 . . . . . .60 C4
Rosemellen Terr PL14 . . . .113 B4
Rosemellin TR14 . . . . .138 C4
Rosemellin Com Prim Sch
  TR14 . . . . .138 C4
Rosemullion Gdns TR14 138 F7
Rosemullion Ho TR1 . . . . . .69 A4
Rosemundy TR5 . . . . .54 D1
Rosenannon La TR15 . . . .139 B8
Rosenannon Rd TR15 . . . .139 B8
Rosevale TR18 . . . . .143 D4
Rosevale Cres TR14 . . . . . .138 C4
Rosevale Gdns PL30 . . . . . .59 F8
Rosevalley TR3 . . . . .69 D3
Rosevallon La PL31 . . . . . .109 C5
Rosevean Ave TR14 . . . . . .138 E3
Rosevean Cl TR14 . . . . . . .138 E3
Rosevean Ct **8** PL3 . . . . .128 E5
Rosevean Gdns PL3 . . . . . .128 E5
Rosevean Ho **7** PL3 . . . . .128 E5
Rosevean Rd TR18 . . . . . . .143 E6
Rosevean Terr TR18 . . . . . .143 E6
Rosevear Rd PL26 . . . . .47 C1
Roseveare Cl PL9 . . . . .136 A8
Roseveare Dr PL26 . . . . . . .46 D1
Rosevin Row TR1 . . . . .137 D5
Rosewall Cotts **16** TR26 . .141 A5
Rosewall Terr **17** TR26 . . .141 A5
Rosewarne TR13 . . . . .91 A1
Rosewarne (Trng Ctr)
  TR14 . . . . .138 D5
Rosewarne Cl TR14 . . . . . .138 D4
Rosewarne Gdns TR14 . . .138 D3
Rosewarne Manor Holiday
  Village TR27 . . . . .78 F5
Rosewarne Mdws TR14 . . .138 D5

Rosewarne Mews TR14 . . .138 D4
Rosewarne Rd
  1 Camborne TR14 . . . . . .138 D3
  Carnhell Green TR27 . . . . .138 D5
Rosewarne Terr TR14 . . . . .138 D5
Rosewin Mews **3** TR9 . . . .45 E6
Rosewin Row **2** TR9 . . . . .45 E6
Rosewithian Cl TR27 . . . . . .78 E6
Rosewood Cl PL9 . . . . .135 F5
Roseworthy Hill TR18 . . . . .78 F6
Roskear TR14 . . . . .138 E4
Roskear Fields TR14 . . . . . .138 E4
Roskear Parc TR14 . . . . . . .138 F5
Roskear Rd TR14 . . . . .138 E3
Roskear Sch TR14 . . . . . . .138 F3
Roskilling TR13 . . . . .146 D7
Roskilling Wartha TR13 146 D7
Roskilly Cotts TR19 . . . . . . .88 C2
Roskilly's Open Farm★
  TR12 . . . . .101 D3
Roskrow Cl TR16 . . . . .80 A5
Roskruge Cl TR13 . . . . . . .146 D8
Roslyn Cl PL25 . . . . .114 F5
Rosparc TR2 . . . . .71 D6
Rosparvah Gdns TR18 . . . .143 C7
Rospeath Cres PL2 . . . . . . .128 D8
Rospeath La TR20 . . . . .89 C7
Ross St PL2 . . . . .127 E4
Rossett Gdns PL31 . . . . . . .35 B1
Rosslyn Park Rd PL3 . . . . .128 D5
Rossventon TR4 . . . . .69 A1
Rostalek PL30 . . . . .24 B2
Rothbury Cl PL6 . . . . .125 E4
Rothbury Gdns PL6 . . . . . .125 D4
Rothesay Gdns PL5 . . . . . .124 D3
Rougemont Cl PL3 . . . . . . .129 B7
Rough La TR3 . . . . .81 B4
Rough St TR16 . . . . .80 D6
Roughtor Dr PL32 . . . . . . .105 C3
Roughtor Rd
  Camelford PL32 . . . . .15 D1
  Helstone PL32 . . . . .24 F8
Round Ring PL10 . . . . .144 D8
Round's La TR14 . . . . .14 D7
Roundhayes Farm Cotts
  EX23 . . . . .10 C5
Rous Rd PL12 . . . . .40 C2
Row La PL5 . . . . .123 E2
Row The PL12 . . . . .53 B7
Rowan Cl Bodmin PL31 . . .109 B4
  Plymouth PL7 . . . . .131 B5
  Tavistock PL19 . . . . .147 C3
Rowan Ct PL12 . . . . .122 C2
Rowan Way PL6 . . . . .125 E7
Rowans The Bude EX23 . . .104 E4
  Lifton PL16 . . . . .19 F4
  St Mellion PL12 . . . . .53 C8
Rowden St PL3 . . . . .128 E5
Rowdown Cl PL7 . . . . .131 D4
Rowe St
  Plymouth PL1,PL4 . . . . . . .148 C3
  Torpoint PL11 . . . . .127 B3
Rowe's La TR13 . . . . .146 E8
Rowes Terr PL26 . . . . .58 D5
Rowland Cl PL9 . . . . .135 E5
Rowse Gdns PL18 . . . . .41 A3
Royal Cornwall Hosp
  TR1 . . . . .69 E4
Royal Cornwall Mus★
  TR1 . . . . .137 C4
Royal Eye Infmy PL4 . . . . .128 E4
Royal Navy Ave PL2 . . . . . .127 F6
Royal Par PL1 . . . . .148 C3
Royale Ct TR18 . . . . .143 F6
Roydon Cl PL15 . . . . .106 B8
Roydon La PL15 . . . . .106 B8
Roydon Rd PL15 . . . . .106 B8
Ruby Terr TR13 . . . . .92 B8
Rudyerd Wlk PL3 . . . . .129 D6
Rufford Cl PL2 . . . . .128 A7
Rule Cross EX23 . . . . .2 E2
Ruminella View TR12 . . . . .103 A4
Rundle Cl PL14 . . . . .113 B4
Rundles Ct TR1 . . . . .137 E3
Runnymede Ct PL6 . . . . . .125 E2
Rush Park Terr PL18 . . . . . .40 F7
Ruskin Cres PL5 . . . . .124 D2
Ruskin Ct TR9 . . . . .45 D5
Russell Ave PL3 . . . . .128 F4
Russell Cl Gunnislake PL18 141 A7
  Plymouth PL9 . . . . .136 B7
  Saltash PL12 . . . . .122 C3
Russell Court Gdns
  PL19 . . . . .147 B6
Russell Ct Plymouth PL1 . .148 C2
  Saltash PL12 . . . . .122 C3
  Tavistock PL19 . . . . .147 B6
Russell Pl PL1 . . . . .148 B4
Russell St
  7 Liskeard PL14 . . . . .113 C5
  Tavistock PL19 . . . . .147 C5
Russell Way **4** TR10 . . . . .144 C7
Russet Wood PL5 . . . . .123 F4
Rutger Pl PL1 . . . . .148 A4
Ruthern Valley PL30 . . . . . .34 A1
Ruthven Cl PL6 . . . . .128 F8
Ruthy's La PL28 . . . . .107 C3
Rutland Rd PL4 . . . . .128 F4
Rydal Cl PL6 . . . . .125 D2
Ryder Rd PL2 . . . . .127 F4
Rydon La EX22 . . . . .8 F7
Rye Hill Ponsanooth TR3 . .81 B4
  Saltash PL12 . . . . .122 C2
Rylands Terr PL30 . . . . .24 B3

S

Saffron Cl PL23 . . . . .116 C4
St Agnes Mus★ TR5 . . . . . .54 C1
St Agnes Prim Sch TR5 . .54 C1
St Albans Pk PL20 . . . . . . .42 D2
St Ambrusca Rd TR8 . . . . .110 A3
St Andrew St
  Millbrook PL10 . . . . .132 E5
  Plymouth PL1 . . . . .148 C2
St Andrew's CE Prim Sch
  PL20 . . . . .41 F3
St Andrew's CE Prim Sch
  PL1 . . . . .148 B2
St Andrew's Cl PL18 . . . . . .41 B4
St Andrew's Cross **1**
  PL1 . . . . .149 A2
St Andrew's Pl PL10 . . . . .133 A1
St Andrew's Rd Par PL24 . .60 C5
  12 Stratton EX23 . . . . .4 D1
St Andrew's St
  Cawsand PL10 . . . . .133 A1
  1 St Ives TR26 . . . . .141 B5
St Andrew's Terr PL24 . . . . .60 C5
St Andrews Cl
  12 Bere Alston PL20 . . . . .41 B1
  Ponsanooth TR3 . . . . .81 B4
  Saltash PL12 . . . . .122 C2
St Andrews Rd PL19 . . . . .147 D2
St Ann's Hill EX23 . . . . . . .104 F3
St Anne's Rd
  Newquay TR7 . . . . .111 A7
  Plymouth PL6 . . . . .125 D6
  Saltash PL12 . . . . .122 E3
  3 Trewoon PL25 . . . . .59 A3
St Annes TR11 . . . . .93 D3
St Annes Cl EX22 . . . . .7 F1
St Annes Rd **17** PL24 . . . . .60 C4
St Anta Rd TR26 . . . . .141 E1
St Anthony Way TR11 . . . . .145 A2
St Aubyn Ave PL2 . . . . . . .127 F5
St Aubyn Cres TR7 . . . . . . .111 A6
St Aubyn Est TR14 . . . . . . .79 B2
St Aubyn Rd PL1 . . . . .127 E3
St Aubyn St PL1 . . . . .127 E3
St Aubyn's Rd TR1 . . . . . . .137 D3
St Aubyn's Vean TR1 . . . . .137 D3
St Aubyns TR20 . . . . .89 E5
St Austell Coll PL25 . . . . . .114 C4
St Austell Hosp PL25 . . . . .114 A4
St Austell Rd PL24 . . . . . . .115 F5
St Austell Row **2** TR2 . . . . .95 A6
St Austell Sta PL25 . . . . . .114 D4
St Austell St
  Summercourt TR8 . . . . .57 C6
  Truro TR1 . . . . .137 D4
St Barnabas Hosp PL12 122 F2
St Barnabas Terr PL1 . . . . .148 A4
St Benedicts Cl **13** PL24 . .60 D5
St Benets Cl PL30 . . . . .47 E6
St Blazey Rd PL24 . . . . .60 C4
St Boniface Cl PL2 . . . . . . .128 C7
St Boniface Dr PL2 . . . . . . .128 C7
St Boniface Prim Sch
  PL1 . . . . .148 B2
St Boniface's RC Coll
  PL5 . . . . .124 E1
St Breaca Cl TR13 . . . . .91 A1
St Breock Prim Sch
  PL27 . . . . .108 B5
St Breward Prim Sch
  PL30 . . . . .24 B3
St Bridget Ave PL6 . . . . . . .124 F1
St Budeaux Ferry Rd Sta
  PL5 . . . . .127 D8
St Budeaux Foundation Jun
  Sch PL5 . . . . .123 F2
St Buryan Hill TR19 . . . . . .96 F4
St Buryan Prim Sch TR19 96 B6
St Carantoc Way TR8 . . . . .43 D7
St Catherine's Castle★
  PL23 . . . . .116 B3
St Catherine's CE Prim Sch
  PL15 . . . . .106 A4
St Clare Flats TR18 . . . . . .143 D6
St Clare St TR18 . . . . .143 D6
St Cleer Dr PL27 . . . . .108 D6
St Cleer Prim Sch PL14 . .38 A3
St Cleer Rd PL14 . . . . .113 C7
St Clement St TR1 . . . . . . .137 D5
St Clement's Cl TR1 . . . . . .137 E4
St Clement's Hill TR1 . . . . .137 E4
St Clement's Terr **3**
  TR1 . . . . .137 D5
St Clements Parc TR1 . . . .137 E4
St Clements Terr **25**
  TR19 . . . . .88 C1
St Columb Major Com
  Sch TR9 . . . . .45 D5
St Columb Major Ind Est
  TR9 . . . . .45 D5
St Columb Minor Prim Sch
  TR7 . . . . .111 D8
St Columb Road Ind
  Workshops TR9 . . . . .45 D2
St Columb Road Sta TR9 45 D2
St Crewenna Terr TR8 . . . . .78 E1
St Cuthbert Cl PL15 . . . . . .106 B7
St Cuthbert's Rd TR7 . . . . .110 D6
St Cyriac PL30 . . . . .47 F1
St David's Rd PL19 . . . . . .147 E5
St Davids Cl EX23 . . . . .4 C3
St Day & Carharrack Com
  Prim Sch TR16 . . . . .68 C6
St Day Rd Redruth TR15 . .140 C5
  Redruth TR16 . . . . .140 E5
St Dennis Prim Sch PL26 58 C8

St Dominic Cl PL31 . . . .109 E5
St Dominic Sq **4** TR1 . .137 C4
St Dominic St
9 Penzance TR18 . . . . .143 E6
5 Truro TR1 . . . . .137 C4
St Dominick CE Sch
PL12 . . . . .40 D2
St Dunstan's Abbey Sch
PL1 . . . . .148 A3
St Dunstan's Terr PL4 . .149 C3
St Edmunds La PL28 . . .107 D5
St Edward Gdns PL6 . . .125 B1
St Edward's CE Prim Sch
PL6 . . . . .125 C1
St Eia St TR26 . . . . . . .141 C6
St Elizabeth Cl PL7 . . . .130 F3
St Elvan Cres TR13 . . . . .91 A1
St Enodoc Cl PL27 . . . . .108 D6
St Erme with Trispen Com
Prim Sch TR4 . . . . . . .70 D8
St Erth Com Prim Sch
TR27 . . . . .142 A1
St Erth Hill TR27 . . . . . . .77 F1
St Erth Ind Est TR27 . . . .77 E2
St Erth Rd PL2 . . . . . . .128 D7
St Erth Sta TR27 . . . . . . .77 E2
St Eval Pl PL5 . . . . .123 E4
St Fimbarrus Rd PL23 . .116 C3
St Francis CE Prim Sch
TR11 . . . . .144 E3
St Francis Cl PL5 . . . . . .124 B3
St Francis Rd TR9 . . . . . .45 C1
St Francis St **6** TR18 . . .143 E6
St Gabriel's Ave PL3 . . .128 D5
St George's Arc TR1 . . .145 B4
St George's Ave PL2 . . .128 C7
St George's CE Prim Sch
PL1 . . . . .148 A1
St George's Cres PL31 . .109 C4
St George's Hill TR26 . . . .55 A4
St George's Pk PL22 . . .112 C5
St George's Rd
Hayle TR27 . . . . .142 C5
Looe PL13 . . . . .117 D4
Newquay TR7 . . . . .110 D5
Saltash PL12 . . . . .122 E3
Truro TR1 . . . . .137 B5
St George's Terr
Perranporth TR6 . . . . . .54 F4
Plymouth PL2 . . . . .127 F4
St Georges Ct Looe PL13 117 D2
1 Plymouth PL2 . . . . .127 F4
St Georges Hill Cl **13**
TR6 . . . . .55 A4
St Georges Rd
Nanpean PL26 . . . . .58 D6
Saltash PL12 . . . . .122 D3
St Germans Prim Sch
PL12 . . . . .65 A8
St Germans Rd PL17 . . . .39 F3
St Giles Dr PL27 . . . . . .108 C6
St Giles Mews PL27 . . . .108 C6
St Giles on the Heath Prim
Sch PL15 . . . . .13 F1
St Gluvias Parc TR10 . . .144 D8
St Gluvias St TR10 . . . . .144 D7
St Golder Rd PL18 . . . . .143 B3
St Helens Wlk PL5 . . . . .124 C5
St Henry St **4** TR18 . . . .143 E4
St Hilary Prim Sch TR20 . .89 F6
St Hilary Terr PL4 . . . . .149 C3
St Ive Rd PL14 . . . . .38 E4
St Ives Bay Chalet & Cvn Pk
TR27 . . . . .78 B6
St Ives Bay Holiday Pk
TR27 . . . . .78 B6
St Ives Holiday Village
TR20,TR26 . . . . .77 C3
St Ives Jun & Inf Schs
TR26 . . . . .141 A5
St Ives La TR27 . . . . .66 B1
St Ives Mus★ TR26 . . . . .141 C6
St Ives Rd Lelant TR26 . .141 D1
Pendeen TR19 . . . . .75 A1
St Ives Sch TR26 . . . . . .141 B3
St Ives Sta TR26 . . . . . . .77 B7
St James Ct
Plymouth PL1 . . . . .148 B2
Torpoint PL11 . . . . .127 B3
St James Pl TR13 . . . . . .146 B6
St James Rd PL11 . . . . .127 B2
St James' Pl E PL1 . . . . .148 B2
St James' Pl W PL1 . . . .148 B2
St James' St TR18 . . . . .143 E5
St James's Terr TR10 . . .144 B7
St John's Bridge Rd
PL4 . . . . .149 B2
St John's Cl
Helston TR13 . . . . .146 A6
Millbrook PL10 . . . . . . .132 F6
St John's Ct
7 Falmouth TR11 . . . .145 A4
Hayle TR27 . . . . .142 D6
St John's Dr PL9 . . . . . .135 B6
St John's RC Prim Sch
TR14 . . . . .138 E2
St John's Rd
Helston TR13 . . . . .146 B6
Horrabridge PL20 . . . . . .42 C4
Millbrook PL10 . . . . . . .132 F6
Newquay TR7 . . . . .110 D5
Plymouth PL4 . . . . .149 B2
Plymouth, Turnchapel PL9 135 A6
St John's Hayle TR27 . . .142 D6
Plymouth PL4 . . . . .149 B2
St John's Terr
Devoran TR3 . . . . .81 F6
Pendeen TR19 . . . . .75 A1

St John's Terr continued
5 Penzance TR18 . . . . .143 E6
St Johns PL19 . . . . .147 C5
St Johns Ave PL19 . . . . .147 C5
St Johns Cl PL6 . . . . . . .125 D4
St Johns Ct **7** TR18 . . . .143 E5
St Johns Gdns TR11 . . . .145 B6
St Johns La PL11 . . . . . .132 B8
St Johns Rd
Launceston PL15 . . . . . .106 B4
Plymouth PL4 . . . . .149 C2
St Johns Wlk TR26 . . . . . .77 A7
St Joseph's Cl PL6 . . . . .124 F1
St Joseph's RC Prim Sch
PL1 . . . . .127 E2
St Joseph's Rd PL15 . . . .106 B8
St Joseph's Sch PL6 . . . .125 B7
St Jude's Rd PL4 . . . . . .149 B2
St Julian's Cotts PL10 . .133 E7
St Julitta PL30 . . . . .48 A1
St Just Prim Sch TR19 . . .86 E6
St Keri Ct PL15 . . . . .18 A5
St Keverne Pl PL2 . . . . .128 D8
St Keverne Prim Sch
TR12 . . . . .101 D4
St Keverne Rural Workshops
TR12 . . . . .101 D4
St Kew Com Prim Sch
PL30 . . . . .22 F3
St Keyne Cl TR1 . . . . . . .137 C6
St Keyne Sta PL14 . . . . . .51 C3
St Lawrence Mews PL4 149 A4
St Lawrence Rd
Bodmin PL30,PL31 . . . . .109 A4
Plymouth PL4 . . . . .149 A4
St Leo Pl PL2 . . . . .127 E4
St Leonard's Rd
Launceston PL15 . . . . . .106 B8
Plymouth PL4 . . . . .149 C2
St Leonards PL31 . . . . . .109 C5
St Levan Cl **8** TR17 . . . .89 C5
St Levan Com Prim Sch
TR19 . . . . .96 E5
St Levan Rd
7 Marazion TR17 . . . . .89 C5
Plymouth PL2 . . . . .127 F5
St Mabyn Holiday Pk
PL30 . . . . .34 E8
St Madderns CE Prim Sch
TR20 . . . . .143 A8
St Margarets Holiday Pk
PL26 . . . . .59 A1
St Margarets La TR26 . . . .59 A1
St Margarets Rd PL7 . . . .130 B7
St Mark's Prim Sch EX23 . .2 E2
St Marks Rd PL6 . . . . . .125 D5
St Marnach's PL13 . . . . . .62 B8
St Marnach's Rd PL13 . . . .62 B8
St Martin's Ave PL3 . . . .128 D7
St Martin's CE Prim Sch
PL14 . . . . .113 D5
St Martin's Cl TR14 . . . .138 C2
St Martin's Cres TR14 . . .138 C3
St Martin's Rd PL13 . . . .117 D6
St Martin's Terr TR14 . . .138 C4
St Martin-in-Meneage Prim
Sch TR12 . . . . .100 D6
St Martins Cl
Lewannick PL15 . . . . . . .27 B7
Looe PL13 . . . . .117 D5
St Martins Rd EX23 . . . . . .7 B8
St Marwenne Cl EX23 . . . .7 B6
St Mary St PL1 . . . . .148 A2
St Mary's PL13 . . . . .117 D3
St Mary's CE Prim Sch
TR18 . . . . .143 E4
St Mary's CE Sch TR1 . . .137 C6
St Mary's Cl PL31 . . . . . .109 C4
St Mary's Cres PL31 . . . .109 C4
St Mary's Ct TR7 . . . . . .110 D5
St Mary's Gdns PL31 . . . .109 C4
St Mary's Mews **10**
TR1 . . . . .137 C4
St Mary's RC Prim Sch
Bodmin PL31 . . . . .109 C4
Falmouth TR11 . . . . . . .144 E3
St Mary's RC Sch TR18 . .143 E7
St Mary's Rd
Bodmin PL31 . . . . .109 B3
Launceston PL15 . . . . . .106 C8
Newquay TR7 . . . . .110 D5
Plymouth PL7 . . . . .130 C6
St Mary's St
Penzance TR18 . . . . . . .143 E6
12 Truro TR1 . . . . .137 C4
St Mary's Terr TR18 . . . .143 E5
St Mary's Terr **4** TR1 . . .137 C4
St Maryhaye PL19 . . . . .147 A5
St Marys Ct PL7 . . . . . . .130 D5
St Marys Ct PL7 . . . . . . .130 D5
St Marys Rd PL24 . . . . . .60 B4
St Matthews Hill PL27 . . .108 D5
St Maurice Mews PL7 . . .130 E4
St Maurice Rd PL7 . . . . .130 F3
St Maurice View PL7 . . . .131 B4
St Mawes Prim Sch TR2 . .95 A6
St Mawes Terr **8** PL2 . . .127 F5
St Mawgan Ct PL31 . . . .109 F5
St Mellans Terr **5** TR1 . . .99 A1
St Meriadoc CE Inf Sch
TR14 . . . . .138 C2
St Meriadoc CE Jun Sch
TR14 . . . . .138 C3
St Meriadoc Rd TR14 . . .138 C3
St Merryn Holiday Village
PL28 . . . . .31 F7
St Merryn Prim Sch PL28 31 D8

St Mewan Com Prim Sch
PL26 . . . . .59 A2
St Mewan La PL25, PL26 . .59 A3
St Michael Ave PL2 . . . .127 F5
St Michael CE Prim Sch
TR13 . . . . .146 C5
St Michael's Cl
Hayle TR27 . . . . .142 B4
Plymouth PL1 . . . . .127 E1
St Michael's Cotts **11**
TR18 . . . . .143 E5
St Michael's Ct **7** PL1 . .127 E3
St Michael's Hospl
TR27 . . . . .142 B4
St Michael's Mount★
TR17 . . . . .89 B4
St Michael's Rd
Newquay TR7 . . . . .110 D5
Perranporth TR6 . . . . . . .55 A4
Ponsanooth TR3 . . . . . . .81 C4
9 Stratton EX23 . . . . . . .4 D1
St Michael's St TR18 . . . .143 E6
St Michael's Terr
Penzance TR18 . . . . . . .143 D6
Plymouth PL4 . . . . .148 C4
8 Plymouth, Devonport
PL1 . . . . .127 F3
St Michaels Cl PL15 . . . . .19 C1
St Michaels Ct
Mawnan Smith TR11 . . . .93 D3
18 Penzance TR18 . . . . .143 E6
St Minver House Holiday Est
PL27 . . . . .22 A3
St Minver Sch PL27 . . . . .21 F3
St Modwen Rd PL6 . . . . .129 F7
St Moritz Ct PL27 . . . . . .21 D5
St Nazaire App PL1 . . . . .127 E2
St Nazaire Cl PL1 . . . . . .127 E2
St Neot Com Prim Sch
PL14 . . . . .36 F2
St Newlyn East Prim Sch
TR8 . . . . .56 B7
St Nicholas Cl TR27 . . . . .78 C6
St Nicholas Ct **1** TR26 . .141 B6
St Nicholas Pk PL23 . . . .112 B3
St Nicholas St
Bodmin PL31 . . . . .109 E4
14 Truro TR1 . . . . .137 D4
St Nonna's Cl PL15 . . . . .26 C8
St Olaf's Rd **13** EX23 . . . . .4 D1
St Pancras Ave PL2 . . . .128 D8
St Paternus Cl PL15 . . . . .27 E8
St Paul St PL1 . . . . .134 A8
St Paul's RC Prim Sch
PL5 . . . . .123 D1
St Pauls Cl PL3 . . . . . . .129 C5
St Pauls Com Prim Sch
TR18 . . . . .143 D6
St Peter Cl PL7 . . . . .130 F4
St Peter's CE Jun Sch
PL19 . . . . .147 D5
St Peter's Hill TR18 . . . .143 C1
St Peter's RC Prim Sch
PL5 . . . . .124 B5
St Peters CE Prim Sch
PL1 . . . . .148 B3
St Peters Cl PL1 . . . . . . .148 A3
St Peters Rd
Plymouth PL1 . . . . .124 C2
11 Stratton EX23 . . . . . . .4 D1
St Peters St **16** TR26 . . . .141 B6
St Peters Way TR13 . . . . .98 C8
St Petroc's CE Prim Sch
PL31 . . . . .109 E4
St Petroc's Cl PL31 . . . . .109 E4
St Petroc's Sch EX23 . . . .104 D7
St Petrocs Mdw PL28 . . .107 C5
St Petry TR20 . . . . .89 E5
St Philip St **8** TR18 . . . .143 E6
St Piran Cl PL31 . . . . . . .109 B4
St Piran's Cl PL25 . . . . . .114 F6
St Piran's Hill TR3 . . . . . .81 D6
St Piran's Rd TR7 . . . . . .110 D6
St Piran's St TR27 . . . . . .142 B4
St Pirans Cl **2** TR1 . . . . .137 D4
St Pirans Ct **13** TR18 . . . .143 E5
St Pirans Par PL26 . . . . . .55 A5
St Pirans Parc **14** TR13 . . .98 C8
St Pirans Rd TR6 . . . . . . .55 A5
St Pirans Way TR20 . . . . .89 D4
St Pol-de-Leon View
TR19 . . . . .88 C2
St Rumon's CE Inf Sch
PL19 . . . . .147 C6
St Sampson's Terr PL23 . .61 B5
St Sampsons Cl **6** PL24 . .60 D5
St Saviour's Hill PL23 . . .116 D2
St Saviour's La PL28 . . . .107 D6
St Siliven TR18 . . . . .143 B5
St Simon's La PL14 . . . . .129 B3
St Smithwick Way TR11 145 C3
St Stephen Churchtown Prim
Sch PL26 . . . . .58 B4
St Stephen Rd PL7 . . . . .130 F3
St Stephen St PL1 . . . . . .127 F1
St Stephen's Hill
Launceston PL15 . . . . . .106 B7
Saltash PL12 . . . . .122 C1
St Stephen's Pl PL7 . . . .130 E5
St Stephen's Rd PL12 . . .122 C2
St Stephens Com Prim Sch
Launceston PL15 . . . . . .106 B8
Saltash PL12 . . . . .122 E2
St Stephens Ct PL15 . . . .106 B7
St Stephens Rd PL26 . . . .58 E1
St Sulien Luxulyan PL30 . . .60 A8

St Sulien continued
Luxulyan PL30 . . . . .48 A1
St Teresa Ho PL4 . . . . . .149 A3
St Therese Cl PL17 . . . . . .39 F4
St Therese's Ct PL1 . . . . .127 F2
St Thomas Cl PL7 . . . . . .130 F3
St Thomas Hill PL15 . . . .106 B6
St Thomas Rd PL15 . . . .106 B6
St Thomas St TR10 . . . . .144 D7
St Thomas' Rd TR7 . . . . .110 F5
St Tinney Farm PL32 . . . .10 D1
St Treath Com Prim Sch
PL30 . . . . .23 E7
St Tudy Com Prim Sch
PL30 . . . . .23 E3
St Uny CE Sch TR26 . . . .141 D1
St Uny Cl TR26 . . . . .77 E3
St Uny Cres TR15 . . . . . .139 F5
St Vincent St PL2 . . . . . .127 E4
St Warren St **7** TR18 . . . .143 E6
St Wenn Prim Sch PL30 . .46 D7
St Winnolls Pk PL13 . . . .117 E3
St Winnow Barton Farm
Mus★ PL22 . . . . .61 A8
St Winnow CE Sch PL22 112 F2
Salamanca St PL11 . . . . .127 B3
Salisbury Ope PL3 . . . . .128 B5
Salisbury Rd
Plymouth PL4 . . . . .149 C4
Truro TR1 . . . . .137 B4
Salisbury Road Jun Sch
PL4 . . . . .149 C3
Salmon Row **3** TR1 . . . .137 D4
Salt Cellar Hill **10** TR13 . . .98 B8
Salt Mill PL12 . . . . .122 F4
Saltash Bsns Pk PL12 . . .122 C4
Saltash Coll PL12 . . . . . .122 D2
Saltash Com Sch PL12 . .122 E1
Saltash Ctr (Coll of F Ed)
PL12 . . . . .122 C2
Saltash Ind Est PL12 . . .122 C4
Saltash Parkway Ind Est
PL12 . . . . .122 C4
Saltash Rd Callington PL17 39 F4
Plymouth PL3 . . . . .148 C4
Plymouth, Keyham PL2 . .127 C6
Saltash Sta PL12 . . . . . .123 A2
Saltbox Cl TR11 . . . . . . .82 A3
Saltbox Rd TR11 . . . . . . .82 A2
Saltings Cl TR26 . . . . . . .77 E3
Saltings The TR26 . . . . . .77 E3
Saltponds **20** TR19 . . . . .88 C1
Saltram Ho★ PL7 . . . . . .130 A4
Saltram Terr PL7 . . . . . .130 E5
Salts Mdw PL14 . . . . . . .50 B6
Sampford Cl PL20 . . . . . .42 D5
Sampford Terr **7** PL20 . . .42 C5
Sampson Cl PL18 . . . . . .40 D6
Sampson Gdns PL3 . . . . .81 B4
Sampson Way PL3 . . . . . .69 D3
Sampson's Ct TR27 . . . . .78 D6
Sampys Hill TR11 . . . . . .93 D3
Samuel Bone Cl PL14 . . .113 D6
Sanctuary Cl TR14 . . . . .138 C2
Sanctuary La
Helston TR13 . . . . .146 C6
12 Stratton EX23 . . . . . . .4 E1
Sanctuary Lane Flats
TR13 . . . . .146 C6
Sand Bay TR11 . . . . .145 C2
Sand Hill PL18 . . . . .41 A8
Sand Hill PL18 . . . . .41 A8
Sand-Bay Holiday Flats **2**
TR6 . . . . .55 A5
Sandbank Holiday Flats
TR27 . . . . .66 B1
Sandcock Cl PL17 . . . . . .39 F7
Sandfield Cres TR14 . . . .138 C2
Sandford Rd PL9 . . . . . .135 F8
Sandhole Cross EX39 . . . . .2 D8
Sandhurst Terr **1** TR1 . . .137 C5
Sandon Wlk PL6 . . . . . .125 A4
Sandows La **15** TR26 . . . .141 A5
Sandpiper Rd PL13 . . . . .63 B7
Sandplace Halt PL13 . . . . .63 B8
Sandplace Rd PL13 . . . . .117 C6
Sandra Way PL31 . . . . . .109 C5
Sandy Cl PL14 . . . . .51 B3
Sandy Cove Travel Lodge
TR4 . . . . .68 A6
Sandy Ct TR8 . . . . .31 B2
Sandy Hill PL25 . . . . . . .114 F4
Sandy Hill Com Prim Sch
PL25 . . . . .114 F4
Sandy La Harlyn PL28 . . . .20 D2
Redruth TR15, TR16 . . . .140 D5
Trevone PL28 . . . . .20 F2
Sandy Rd Plymouth PL7 . .131 C4
Porthtowan TR4 . . . . . . .68 A7
Sandyacres Hayle TR27 . . .78 B6
Phillack PL27 . . . . .142 E8
Sandyhills PL27 . . . . . . .21 E2
Sandylake La PL22 . . . . .112 F2
Sango Cl PL10 . . . . .132 F6
Sango Rd PL11 . . . . .127 A3
Saracen Cl TR10 . . . . . . .144 C7
Saracen Cres TR10 . . . . .144 C7
Saracen Rd **5** TR10 . . . .144 C7
Saracen Pl TR10 . . . . . . .144 C7
Saracen Way TR10 . . . . .144 C7
Sarah Cl PL20 . . . . .41 B1
Sarah's Ct PL28 . . . . . . .107 D4
Sarah's Gate PL27 . . . . . .32 C7
Sarah's La PL28 . . . . . . .107 D4
Sarah's Mdw PL28 . . . . .107 D4

Sarah's View PL28 . . . . .107 D4
Sarahs Cl PL28 . . . . . . .107 D4
Sargents Mdw EX23 . . . . . .2 D1
Sarum Cl PL3 . . . . .128 F7
Saunders La PL11 . . . . . .65 A5
Saunders Wlk PL6 . . . . .124 D6
Savage Rd PL5 . . . . .127 D7
Savoy Bldg **3** PL25 . . . .114 C3
Sawles Rd
St Austell PL25 . . . . . . .114 B2
St Austell PL25 . . . . . . .114 D2
Sawmills La TR16 . . . . . .68 D3
Sawrey St PL1 . . . . .148 A2
Sawyers Ct TR3 . . . . .92 A6
Scarlett's Well Rd PL31 . .109 B5
Scarletts Well Pk PL31 . .109 C5
Scarnes Well Rd PL31 . . .109 C5
Scarne Ind Est PL15 . . . .106 C3
Scholar's La TR13 . . . . . .91 C3
Scholars Cl PL14 . . . . . . .38 F2
School Cl Par PL24 . . . . . .60 B4
Plymouth PL7 . . . . .130 D7
St Columb Minor TR7 . . .111 E6
Tavistock PL19 . . . . . . .147 D5
School Dr PL6 . . . . .125 D7
School Hill Golant PL23 . . .61 B5
Herodsfoot PL14 . . . . . . .50 E3
Lanjeth PL26 . . . . .58 E4
Mevagissey PL26 . . . . . .73 C4
Padstow PL28 . . . . .107 D5
Perranwell Sta TR3 . . . . .81 D6
Shortlanesend TR4 . . . . .69 F6
South Petherwin PL15 . . . .27 E8
St Buryan TR19 . . . . . . .96 E5
St Keverne TR12 . . . . . .101 D4
St Keverne, Porthallow
TR12 . . . . .101 D4
St Neot PL14 . . . . .36 F2
School La
Budock Water TR11 . . . .144 C3
Gulval TR18 . . . . .88 E6
Jacobstow EX23 . . . . . . .11 A6
Marazion TR17 . . . . .89 C5
Plymouth PL7 . . . . .130 E4
Polruan PL23 . . . . .116 D3
Redruth TR15 . . . . .140 D5
St Austell PL25 . . . . . . .115 C6
St Erth TR27 . . . . .142 A1
Troon TR14 . . . . .79 E4
Truro TR1 . . . . .137 C3
School Rd Breage TR13 . . .90 F3
Landrake PL12 . . . . .53 C3
Pensilva PL14 . . . . .38 E5
Summercourt TR8 . . . . . .57 B7
Whitchurch PL19 . . . . . .147 D2
School Wlk PL27 . . . . . .108 D6
Sclerder La TR11 . . . . . . .62 E4
Scoble's Terr TR1 . . . . . .70 D1
Sconner Rd PL11 . . . . . .127 A3
Scoria Cl TR16 . . . . .68 D3
Scorrier St TR16 . . . . . . .68 E1
Scott Ave PL5 . . . . .127 C8
Scott Cl **2** PL14 . . . . . . .38 E4
Scott Hospl PL2 . . . . . . .128 A4
Scott Rd PL2 . . . . .128 B6
Scowbuds TR14 . . . . . . .138 F5
Scrations La PL22 . . . . . .112 C2
Screech Owl Sanctuary★
TR9 . . . . .46 A3
Sea La TR27 . . . . .142 D6
Sea Rd PL25 . . . . .115 D2
Sea View TR18 . . . . .40 E5
Sea View Ave PL4 . . . . . .149 C4
Sea View Cotts PL26 . . . . .73 C3
Sea View Cres **11** PL2 . . . .95 A4
Sea View Pl TR26 . . . . . .141 C6
Sea View Rd
Falmouth TR11 . . . . . . .145 B2
12 St Mawes TR2 . . . . .95 A6
Sea View Terr
Camborne TR14 . . . . . .138 E2
Helston TR13 . . . . .146 B6
6 Newlyn TR18 . . . . . .143 C1
Par TR24 . . . . .60 B6
11 Penwithick PL26 . . . .59 D7
Plymouth PL4 . . . . .149 B4
Redruth TR15 . . . . .140 C5
20 St Ives TR26 . . . . . .141 B5
Seabank TR11 . . . . .145 B2
Seacroft Rd PL5 . . . . . . .123 C2
Sealife Ctr★ TR7 . . . . . .110 D5
Seaspray Leisure Flats
TR4 . . . . .68 A7
Seaton Ave PL4 . . . . . . .128 E4
Seaton Bsns Pk PL6 . . . .125 B3
Seaton La PL4 . . . . .128 E4
Seaton Pk PL11 . . . . .64 B5
Seaton Pl PL2 . . . . .127 F5
Seaton Way PL20 . . . . . . .42 A2
Seaview Cotts TR11 . . . . .145 B5
Seaview Terr
Sennen Cove TR19 . . . . .96 A1
Summercourt TR8 . . . . . .57 E6
Seawell Rd EX23 . . . . . .104 F7
Second Ave
Plymouth, Billacombe PL9 .130 A1
Plymouth, Devonport PL1 .128 C4
Plymouth, Weston Mill PL2 127 C4
Sedgemoor Ctr (St Austin
Coll) PL25 . . . . .114 C4
Sedley Way PL5 . . . . . . .124 D3
Sefton Ave PL4 . . . . . . .129 B3
Sefton Cl PL4 . . . . .149 C4
Segrave Rd PL2 . . . . . . .128 B6
Seiners Ct **10** TR6 . . . . . .55 A4

Selkirk Pl PL5 . . . . . . .124 E2
Selsden Cl PL9 . . . . . . .136 C6
Sendall's Way PL6 . . . . .124 F4
Seneschall Pk TR13 . . . .146 D8
Sennen Cl PL11 . . . . . . .126 F4
Sennen Pl PL2 . . . . .127 E5
Sennen Prim Sch TR19 . .86 E1
Sentry Cl PL27 . . . . .32 D6
Sergeants Hill TR4 . . . . . .68 F3
Serpell Cl PL6 . . . . .124 E6
Serpells Mdw PL15 . . . . . .17 F1
Sethnoe Way TR13 . . . . . .91 A3
Seton Gdns TR14 . . . . . .138 B4
Seven Stars La PL5 . . . . .124 C6
Seven Trees Ct PL4 . . . . .149 B4
Severn Pl PL3 . . . . .129 C5
Sewell Ct PL3 . . . . .128 E5
Seymour Ave
  Newquay TR7 . . . . .110 E6
  Plymouth PL4 . . . . .149 B4
Seymour Cl TR3 . . . . .69 C3
Seymour Dr PL3 . . . . . . .128 E5
Seymour Mews PL4 . . . . .149 C4
Seymour Pk PL3 . . . . . . .129 A5
Seymour Rd
  Plymouth, Mannamead
   PL3 . . . . .128 E5
  Plymouth, Plympton PL7 . .130 E4
Seymour St PL4 . . . . . . .149 A3
Shackleton Cres [9] PL27 .31 F3
Shackleton Dr PL7 . . . . .111 B6
Shaft Downs La TR27 . . . .78 F3
Shaftesbury Cotts PL4 . . .149 A4
Shaftesbury Ct [3] PL4 . . .149 A4
Shakespeare Rd PL5 . . . .124 C2
Shaldon Cres PL5 . . . . . .124 B3
Shallowford Cl PL6 . . . . .129 C8
Shallowford Rd PL6 . . . . .129 C8
Shapleys Gdns PL9 . . . . .136 A5
Shapters Rd PL4 . . . . . . .149 C2
Shapters Way PL4 . . . . . .135 B8
Sharaman Cl PL25 . . . . . .115 A5
Sharlands Rd EX23 . . . . . . .7 B6
Sharon Way EX23 . . . . . .125 A5
Sharpitor Row PL20 . . . . .42 E4
Sharrose Rd PL9 . . . . . . .135 B5
Shaw Way PL9 . . . . .135 A7
Shearwood Cl PL7 . . . . . .130 C6
Sheep Fair Mdw [14] PL17 .39 F4
Sheepstor Rd PL6 . . . . . .125 D1
Sheila's Ct TR26 . . . . . . .141 D1
Shelburne Ct TR11 . . . . .144 F3
Shelburne Rd TR11 . . . . .144 F3
Shell Cl PL6 . . . . .125 E1
Shelley Ave PL19 . . . . . .147 D5
Shelley Rd PL25 . . . . . . .115 A4
Shelley Way PL5 . . . . . . .123 D1
Shepherd's La PL4 . . . . . .149 B2
Sherborne Cl PL9 . . . . . .136 C6
Sherford Cres
  Plymouth, Elburton PL9 . .136 C7
  Plymouth, West Park PL5 . .124 C4
Sherford Rd PL9 . . . . . . .136 D7
Sherford Wlk PL9 . . . . . .136 E7
Sheridan Rd PL5 . . . . . . .124 C1
Sherril Cl PL9 . . . . .135 F4
Sherwell La PL4 . . . . . . .149 A4
Sherwood Dr PL31 . . . . .109 C5
Sheviock La PL11 . . . . . . .65 B5
Shilla Pk PL32 . . . . .24 A8
Shilson Terr PL15 . . . . . .106 C5
Shipley Wlk PL6 . . . . . . .125 A1
Shirburn Rd PL6 . . . . . . .129 B8
Shire Horse Farm & Carriage
  Mus The ★ 79 F5
Shires Adventure Pk ★
  PL27 . . . . .32 M4
Shirley Gdns PL5 . . . . . .124 C1
Shoemakers Row PL13 . . .63 B7
Shoot Row TR15 . . . . . . .140 C5
Shop Hill [3] TR17 . . . . . .89 C5
Shop Pk PL14 . . . . .38 A2
Shoreline TR7 . . . . .111 B8
Shores La PL27 . . . . .21 E3
Short Cotts PL11 . . . . . . .127 A3
Short Cross Mews TR4 . . .68 C6
Short Cross Rd TR4 . . . . . .68 C6
Short Park Rd PL3 . . . . . .128 D5
Shortacross PL14 . . . . . . .38 A2
Shortlands EX22 . . . . .8 E5
Shortlanesend Prim Sch
  TR4 . . . . .69 F6
Shortwood Cres PL9 . . . .136 A7
Shrewsbury Rd PL5 . . . . .124 C4
Shrubberies Hill TR13 . . . .98 C8
Shute Hill Breage TR13 . . .90 F3
  Helston TR13 . . . . .146 C6
  Lostwithiel PL22 . . . . . .112 C2
  Mawnan Smith TR11 . . . . .93 D3
  Pelynt PL13 . . . . .63 D5
Shute La Penryn TR10 . . .144 C8
  Pensilva PL14 . . . . .38 E4
  [6] Porthleven TR13 . . . . .98 B8
Shute Mdw TR10 . . . . . .144 C7
Shute Park Rd PL9 . . . . . .135 F6
Shutta PL13 . . . . .117 C4
Sidings The PL33 . . . . . . .11 E5
Sidney Terr [7] TR15 . . . .140 C5
Silvanus Jenkin Ave
  PL14 . . . . .113 E5
Silver Birch Cl PL6 . . . . .125 C7
Silver Cl [1] TR15 . . . . . .140 B4
Silver Hill TR3 . . . . .81 D6

Silver St
  Bere Ferrers PL20 . . . . . .120 A3
  Saltash PL12 . . . . .123 A2
Silver Terr PL10 . . . . . . .133 A6
Silver Way TR3 . . . . .69 C3
Silverdale Ct TR7 . . . . . .110 E6
Silverdale Rd TR11 . . . . .145 A2
Silvershell Rd PL29 . . . . . .22 D7
Silvershell View PL29 . . . .22 D7
Silverton Cl EX23 . . . . . .104 E5
Silverton Rd EX23 . . . . . .104 E5
Simon Cl PL9 . . . . .135 E6
Simpsons Ct [30] PL18 . . .143 E5
Singlerose Rd PL26 . . . . . .59 C7
Sir James Smith's Sch
  PL32 . . . . .105 C4
Sir John Hunt Com Coll
  PL5 . . . . .124 D4
Sir Robert Geffery's CE Prim
  Sch PL18 . . . . .53 C3
Sir Williams Morles
  Almshouses PL12 . . . . . .65 A8
Sithney Com Prim Sch
  TR13 . . . . .91 B5
Sithney Common Hill
  TR13 . . . . .91 C2
Sithney Old Hill TR13 . . .146 A6
Sithney St PL5 . . . . .123 C1
Skardale Gdns PL6 . . . . .129 D8
Skardon Pl PL4 . . . . .149 A4
Skerries Rd PL6 . . . . . . .124 F7
Skidden Hill [18] TR26 . . .141 B5
Skinnard La PL18 . . . . . . .40 F5
Skitches Cnr EX23 . . . . . . .4 D1
Skyburriowe La TR12 . . . .99 C6
Skylark Rise PL6 . . . . . . .125 E8
Slade Cl PL9 . . . . .136 A5
Slade Park Rd PL14 . . . . . .38 E5
Slades La [2] TR10 . . . . . .144 C7
Slades Rd PL25 . . . . .114 C5
Slatelands Cl PL7 . . . . . .131 B5
Slipway PL27 . . . . .21 D2
Smallack Cl PL6 . . . . . . .124 F2
Smallack Dr PL6 . . . . . . .124 F2
Smallridge Cl PL9 . . . . . .135 F5
Smeaton Sq PL3 . . . . . . .129 D6
Smith's Cotts PL14 . . . . .113 C6
Smithfield Ct TR8 . . . . . .111 B3
Smithfield Dr PL12 . . . . .122 B3
Smithick Hill TR11 . . . . .145 B4
Smiths Way PL12 . . . . . .122 B3
Smithy Cl PL12 . . . . .122 C4
Smithy La PL32 . . . . .105 D3
Smithy La TR3 . . . . .81 F7
Smugglers Row TR11 . . . .145 B5
Snell Dr PL12 . . . . .122 B3
Snow's Pas TR11 . . . . . .145 B4
Snowdrop Cres PL15 . . . .106 E4
Socotra Dr [7] PL25 . . . . . .59 A3
Solar Row [6] TR1 . . . . . .137 D5
Somerset Cotts [7] PL3 . . .128 A4
Somerset Pl PL3 . . . . . . .128 A4
Somerset Place La [8]
  PL3 . . . . .128 A4
Somerville Rd TR6 . . . . . . .55 A4
Sonamerg Cl TR18 . . . . . .143 C7
Soper's Hill PL6 . . . . . . .120 E1
South Cliff [17] TR19 . . . . .88 C1
South Coombe La PL17 . . .39 F8
South Down Rd PL2 . . . . .128 B6
South Downs TR15 . . . . . .140 D2
South Dr TR14 . . . . .138 E8
South East Cornwall
  Discovery Ctr ★ PL13 . . .117 C4
South Harbour TR10 . . . .144 D7
South Hill
  Plymouth, Hooe PL9 . . . . .135 C5
  Plymouth, Stoke PL1 . . . .128 A3
South Hill Rd PL17 . . . . . .39 E5
South Milton St PL4 . . . . .149 C2
South Par [33] TR18 . . . . .143 E5
South Park Ct TR15 . . . . .140 C4
South Pl PL19 . . . . .86 E6
South Pk Jacobstow EX23 . .11 A6
  Redruth TR15 . . . . .139 F6
  [16] St Columb Major TR9 . .45 E6
South Petherwin Com Prim
  Sch PL15 . . . . .27 E8
South Pk Folly [4]
  TR18 . . . . .143 E4
South Place Gdns TR19 . . .86 E6
South Quay PL28 . . . . . .107 D5
South Quay Hill TR7 . . . .110 D6
South Rd Goldsithney TR20 89 C5
  Stithians TR3 . . . . .80 F3
South Roskear Terr
  TR14 . . . . .138 F4
South St Fowey PL23 . . . .116 D4
  Grampound Road TR2 . . . .57 E1
  Lostwithiel PL22 . . . . . .112 C2
  St Austell PL25 . . . . . . .114 C3
South Terr
  Camborne TR14 . . . . . . .138 D2
  [11] Penzance TR18 . . . . .143 E4
South Towan TR4 . . . . . . .68 A6
South Trelawny Prim Sch
  PL2 . . . . .128 A8
South View
  [10] Horrabridge PL20 . . . .42 C4
  Liskeard PL14 . . . . .113 D7
  Penryn TR10 . . . . .144 B8
  Plymouth, Crownhill PL5 . .124 E2
  Plymouth, Elburton PL9 . .136 B6
  Porthleven TR13 . . . . . . .91 A1
South View Cl PL7 . . . . . .130 D7
South View Parc TR4 . . . . .68 A6

South View Pk PL7 . . . . .130 D7
South View Terr
  Blackwater TR4 . . . . .68 E5
  Nancegollan TR13 . . . . . .91 B7
  Plymouth PL4 . . . . .149 C5
Southbourne Rd PL25 . . . .114 E2
Southcliff TR11 . . . . .145 C2
Southcott Mdws EX23 . . . .11 A6
Southdown Cl PL26 . . . . . .58 E1
Southdown Rd
  Millbrook PL10 . . . . .133 A6
  Sticker PL26 . . . . .58 E1
Southdown Terr PL10 . . . .133 A6
Southella Rd PL20 . . . . . . .42 D2
Southern Cl PL2 . . . . .127 F7
Southern Rd PL17 . . . . . . .39 F4
Southern Terr PL4 . . . . . .128 F4
Southern Way PL27 . . . . .108 C5
Southernhaye PL15 . . . . . .106 C5
Southernway PL9 . . . . . . .136 A8
Southfield PL12 . . . . .122 C3
Southfield Rd EX23 . . . . .104 E5
Southfields EX22 . . . . .8 A5
Southfields Pl [3] TR26 . . .141 A5
Southgate Ave PL9 . . . . . .135 E4
Southgate Cl PL9 . . . . . . .135 E4
Southgate St
  Launceston PL15 . . . . . .106 C5
  Redruth TR15 . . . . .140 C3
Southlea Terr TR3 . . . . . . .80 F3
Southleigh Ho [15] TR1 . . .137 C4
Southleigh Mews [14]
  TR1 . . . . .137 C4
Southpark Rd PL24 . . . . . .60 C5
Southside Ope [14] PL1 . . .149 A2
Southview PL10 . . . . .133 A6
Southview Dr PL31 . . . . . .109 A5
Southview Rd [15] PL24 . . .60 B4
Southview Terr [8] TR19 . . .88 C1
Southway PL28 . . . . .20 F2
Southway Com Coll PL6 . .124 F6
Southway Dr PL6 . . . . . . .124 C6
Southway La
  Plymouth, Southway PL6 . .125 B6
  Plymouth, Tamerton Foliot
   PL6 . . . . .124 C6
Southway Prim Sch PL6 . .124 E6
Southwell Rd PL6 . . . . . . .124 E1
Sovereign Ct PL7 . . . . . . .130 C5
Spar La TR15 . . . . .67 D4
Spargo Ct TR10 . . . . .93 C8
Sparkatown La PL20 . . . . . .42 E3
Sparke Cl PL7 . . . . .131 B4
Sparkwell CE Prim Sch
  PL7 . . . . .131 F8
Sparnon Cl Redruth TR15 .140 C4
  St Austell PL25 . . . . . . .114 B4
Sparnon Cross TR13 . . . . .90 F5
Sparnon Ct TR15 . . . . . . .140 C4
Sparnon Hill [1] TR15 . . . .140 C4
Sparnon Terr [2] TR15 . . .140 C4
Sparry La TR16 . . . . .80 F8
Spaven Mor TR14 . . . . . .138 F5
Spear's Terr TR11 . . . . . .144 F1
Speares The PL12 . . . . . .122 B2
Speech La TR3 . . . . .81 C4
Speedwell Cl Bude EX23 . .104 F5
  Millbrook PL10 . . . . .132 F5
Speedwell Cres PL6 . . . . .129 B7
Speedwell Wlk PL6 . . . . .129 B7
Spencer Gdns PL12 . . . . .122 F1
Spencer Rd PL9 . . . . .135 E8
Spernen Cl TR26 . . . . . . .141 C2
Spernen Wyn Rd TR11 . . .145 B2
Spicers Ct [11] EX23 . . . . . .4 E1
Spinaker Quay PL9 . . . . . .134 F7
Spinney The PL7 . . . . . . .131 A4
Spire Ct [3] TR1 . . . . . . .129 B5
Spire Hill Pk PL12 . . . . . .122 C2
Spires The TR1 . . . . .137 C6
Spirit of the West (Theme
  Pk) ★ TR9 . . . . .32 E1
Spitfire Row PL27 . . . . . . .31 F3
Sportsmans Rd PL32 . . . .105 C3
Spring Hill PL19 . . . . . . .147 B5
Spring Pk PL6 . . . . .125 C7
Springfield TR2 . . . . .83 B2
Springfield Ave PL9 . . . . .136 B6
Springfield Cl
  Dobwalls PL14 . . . . .50 E7
  Lostwithiel PL22 . . . . . .112 D2
  Phillack TR27 . . . . .142 D7
  Plymouth PL9 . . . . .136 B6
  Polgooth PL26 . . . . .59 A1
  St Austell PL25 . . . . . . .114 F5
Springfield Dr PL3 . . . . . .128 A4
Springfield La PL3 . . . . . .128 A4
Springfield Pk
  Barripper TR14 . . . . .79 B5
  Mylor Bridge TR11 . . . . . .82 A3
  Widegates PL13 . . . . .63 F3
Springfield Pl [15] TR9 . . . .45 E6
Springfield Rd
  Falmouth TR11 . . . . .144 E5
  Goldsithney TR20 . . . . . . .89 C5
  Liskeard PL14 . . . . .113 E6
  Looe PL13 . . . . .117 D5
  Newquay TR7 . . . . .110 F6
  Plymouth PL9 . . . . .136 B6
Springfield Rise PL9 . . . . .136 B7
Springfield Way
  Roche PL26 . . . . .46 F3
  Threemilestone TR3 . . . . .69 C3
Springfields Fun Pk & Pony
  Ctr ★ TR9 . . . . .45 E4
Springhill PL2 . . . . .128 C8
Springhill Gn PL2 . . . . . .128 C8

Springwell View PL31 . . .109 F5
Springwood Cl PL7 . . . . .131 A3
Spruce Gdns PL7 . . . . . . .131 B5
Spurway Rd PL14 . . . . . . .113 C6
Square The
  [16] Bere Alston PL20 . . . .41 B1
  Cawsand PL10 . . . . .133 A1
  Crowlas PL20 . . . . .89 A8
  Grampound Road TR2 . . . .57 E1
  Gunnislake PL18 . . . . . . .41 A6
  Kilkhampton EX23 . . . . . . .5 A6
  Landrake PL12 . . . . .53 C3
  Leedstown TR27 . . . . . . .78 E1
  [6] Lizard TR12 . . . . . . .102 F2
  Manaccan TR12 . . . . . . .101 A7
  Marazion TR17 . . . . .89 C5
  Pendeen TR19 . . . . .75 A1
  Penryn TR10 . . . . .144 D7
  Pentewan PL26 . . . . .73 C6
  Plymouth, Hooe PL9 . . . . .135 C5
  Plymouth, Stonehouse PL1 128 A2
  Portreath TR16 . . . . .67 C6
  Portscatho TR2 . . . . .83 B2
  Praze-an-Beeble TR14 . . . .79 B2
  Probus TR2 . . . . .71 C6
  Redruth TR15 . . . . .80 B5
  Saltash PL12 . . . . .122 C3
  St Keverne TR12 . . . . . . .101 D4
  [3] St Mawes TR2 . . . . . . .95 A6
  St Teath PL30 . . . . .23 E7
  Tregony TR2 . . . . .71 F3
  Veryan TR2 . . . . .83 F6
  Week St Mary EX22 . . . . . .11 E8
Squire La TR16 . . . . .80 F8
Squires La TR13 . . . . .91 C2
Stable Hobba Ind Est
  TR18 . . . . .143 B3
Stables The TR14 . . . . . . .67 B4
Staddiscombe Rd PL9 . . . .135 E6
Staddon Cres PL9 . . . . . .135 E6
Staddon Gn PL9 . . . . . . .135 D6
Staddon La PL9 . . . . .135 E4
Staddon Park Rd PL9 . . . .135 E6
Staddon Terrace La
  PL1 . . . . .148 B4
Stafford Cl TR7 . . . . .111 D6
Stag La
  Plymouth, Elburton PL9 . .136 B8
  Plymouth, Plympton PL9 . .130 B1
Staggy La TR3 . . . . .81 F7
Stamford Cl PL9 . . . . . . .135 A6
Stamford Fort Cotts
  PL9 . . . . .135 A6
Stamford Hill EX23 . . . . . . .4 D1
Stamford La PL9 . . . . . . .135 A6
Stamps Hill
  Indian Queens TR9 . . . . . .45 F4
  Summercourt PL26 . . . . . .57 F8
Stamps The PL17 . . . . . . .40 D5
Stanborough Cross PL9 . . .136 C7
Stanborough Rd PL9 . . . . .136 B7
Stanbury Ave PL6 . . . . . .124 F1
Stanbury Cl PL15 . . . . . . .13 F1
Stanbury Cross EX23 . . . . . .2 C1
Standarhay Cl PL9 . . . . . .136 C7
Standarhay Villas PL9 . . . .136 C7
Stanford Cl [5] TR18 . . . . .143 D5
Stanford Terr TR18 . . . . . .143 D5
Stangray Ave PL4 . . . . . . .128 D4
Stanharver Cl TR7 . . . . . .111 E6
Stanhope Rd PL5 . . . . . . .123 C1
Stanley Pl PL4 . . . . .129 B2
Stanley Terr [1] TR14 . . . .140 B5
Stanley Way TR15 . . . . . .140 C6
Stannary Bridge Rd
  PL19 . . . . .147 D6
Stannary Rd PL26 . . . . . . .59 C8
Stantons Row PL14 . . . . . .38 A3
Stanways Rd TR7 . . . . . . .111 D7
Staple Cl PL6 . . . . .121 C1
Stapleford Gdns PL5 . . . . .123 F5
Stapleton Rd EX23 . . . . . .104 F4
Star Pk PL18 . . . . .41 A6
Statham Rd PL31 . . . . . . .109 D4
Station App
  Newquay TR7 . . . . .110 F6
  St Columb Road TR9 . . . . .45 E2
  St Erth TR27 . . . . .77 E2
Station Hill Hayle TR27 . . .142 B5
  Lelant TR26 . . . . .77 E4
  Praze-an-Beeble TR14 . . . .79 B2
  Redruth TR15 . . . . .140 B4
Station La PL18 . . . . .41 A3
Station Par TR7 . . . . .110 F6
Station Rd
  Bere Alston PL20 . . . . . . .41 B1
  Bere Ferrers PL20 . . . . . .119 E3
  Bugle PL26 . . . . .47 C2
  Camborne TR15 . . . . . . .139 C5
  Carnhell Green TR14 . . . . .78 F4
  Chacewater TR4 . . . . .68 F4
  Fowey PL23 . . . . .116 D5
  Grampound Road TR2 . . . .57 E1
  Gunnislake PL18 . . . . . . .40 F6
  Helston TR13 . . . . .146 C7
  Horrabridge PL20 . . . . . . .42 C4
  Kelly Bray PL17 . . . . .39 F6
  Launceston PL15 . . . . . .106 C6
  Liskeard PL14 . . . . .113 B4
  Looe PL13 . . . . .117 C4
  Mary Tavy PL19 . . . . .30 F5
  North Brentor PL19 . . . . . .30 E8
  Padstow PL28 . . . . .107 D5
  Par PL24 . . . . .60 C5
  Penryn TR10 . . . . .144 B8
  Penzance TR18 . . . . . . .143 F6
  Perranporth TR6 . . . . .55 D5
  Perranwell Sta TR3 . . . . . .81 E6

Station Rd continued
  Plymouth, Elburton PL9 . .136 C7
  Plymouth, Keyham PL2 . . .127 E5
  Plymouth, Plympton PL7 . .130 E5
  Plymouth, Tamerton Foliot
   PL5 . . . . .124 A6
  Redruth TR15 . . . . .140 C5
  Saltash PL12 . . . . .123 A2
  St Columb Major TR9 . . . . .45 E5
  St Columb Road TR9 . . . . .45 E2
  St Newlyn East TR8 . . . . . .56 B7
  Truro TR1 . . . . .137 B4
  Wadebridge PL30 . . . . . . .34 C8
  Yelverton PL20 . . . . .42 D2
Station View PL19 . . . . . . .30 E8
Steamers Hill TR27 . . . . . .78 C5
Steamers Mdw TR27 . . . . .78 C5
Steeple Cl Plymouth PL9 . .135 F4
Steeple La TR26 . . . . .141 B3
Steeple View Ct TR26 . . . .141 C1
Steer Park Rd PL7 . . . . . .136 F2
Steer Point Cotts PL8 . . . .136 F2
Stefan Cl PL9 . . . . .135 B5
Stenalees Hill PL26 . . . . . .59 C7
Stenlake Pl PL4 . . . . .129 B2
Stenlake Terr PL4 . . . . . . .129 B2
Stennack Gdns [14] TR26 .141 A5
Stennack Parc TR19 . . . . . .86 F8
Stennack Rd PL25 . . . . . .115 B6
Stennack The TR26 . . . . . .141 B5
Stentaway Cl PL9 . . . . . . .135 F8
Stentaway Dr PL9 . . . . . . .136 A8
Stentaway Rd PL9 . . . . . . .135 F8
Stephens Rd PL14 . . . . . .113 E7
Stephney Cl TR11 . . . . . .144 C3
Steppy Downs Rd TR27 . . .78 A1
Stewarts Rd EX22 . . . . . . .11 E8
Stiles The TR8 . . . . .56 B7
Stillman Cl [8] PL4 . . . . . .149 A2
Stillman St PL4 . . . . .149 A2
Stirling Ct PL5 . . . . .123 C1
Stirling Rd PL5 . . . . .123 C1
Stithians Com Prim Sch
  TR3 . . . . .80 F4
Stithians Row TR16 . . . . . .80 B5
Stoggy La PL7 . . . . .131 A6
Stoke Climsland Prim Sch
  PL17 . . . . .39 E7
Stoke Damerel Bsns Ctr [5]
  PL3 . . . . .128 A4
Stoke Damerel Com Coll
  PL3 . . . . .128 B4
Stoke Damerel Prim Sch
  PL1 . . . . .128 A3
Stoke Hill La PL20 . . . . . . .42 B2
Stoke Rd Bray Shop PL17 . .28 A1
  Kelly Bray PL17 . . . . .39 E6
  Linkinhorne PL17 . . . . . . .39 A8
  Plymouth PL1 . . . . .148 A3
Stoke Terr PL17 . . . . .39 E6
Stokes La PL1 . . . . .149 A2
Stokes Rd TR1 . . . . .137 C5
Stokingway Cl PL9 . . . . . .135 E5
Stone Barton Cl PL7 . . . . .130 C6
Stone Barton Rd PL7 . . . . .130 C6
Stone Chair La TR19 . . . . .96 B7
Stone Cross PL16 . . . . . . .19 F5
Stone Hill EX23 . . . . .4 E2
Stonehall Flats PL1 . . . . . .128 A1
Stonehouse Bridge PL1 . . .128 A1
Stonehouse St PL1 . . . . . .148 A2
Stonewood Ct [4] TR9 . . . .45 E6
Stoney Cl PL25 . . . . .59 A4
Stoney La Polgooth PL26 . . .59 A1
  St Austell PL25 . . . . . . .114 C4
Stoney Lands PL12 . . . . . .53 C3
Stony La Bodmin PL31 . . . .34 D1
  Gunnislake PL18 . . . . . . .40 F5
Stopford Pl PL1 . . . . .127 F3
Stott Cl PL3 . . . . .129 C5
Stour Cl PL3 . . . . .129 D6
Stourscombe PL15 . . . . . .106 F3
Stourscombe Wood
  PL15 . . . . .106 F3
Stowe Gdns PL5 . . . . . . .124 C1
Stowford Cl PL20 . . . . . . .42 E3
Stowford Cross EX22 . . . . . .5 E8
Stracey Rd TR11 . . . . . . .145 B2
Strafford Cl EX23 . . . . . . .104 C3
Strand TR18 . . . . .143 C2
Strand St Padstow PL28 . . .107 D5
  Plymouth PL1 . . . . .134 A8
Strand The Bude EX23 . . . .104 D5
  Padstow PL28 . . . . .107 D5
Strangways Terr TR1 . . . . .137 D3
Stratton Hospl EX23 . . . . . .4 D1
Stratton Pl TR10 . . . . . . .144 A6
Stratton Prim Sch EX23 . . . .4 D1
Stratton Rd Bude EX23 . . .104 F4
  Stratton EX23 . . . . .4 D1
Stratton Terr
  Falmouth TR11 . . . . .145 A4
  Truro TR1 . . . . .137 B4
Stratton Wlk PL2 . . . . . . .128 C8
Strawberry Cl TR15 . . . . .140 B6
Strawberry Cres TR15 . . . .140 B6
Strawberry Fields TR16 . . .140 E1
Strawberry Gdns TR16 . . .140 E1
Strawberry La
  Hayle TR27 . . . . .142 D4
  Lelant TR26 . . . . .77 E4
  Redruth TR15 . . . . .140 B6
Stray Park Ct TR14 . . . . . .138 F2
Stray Park Rd TR14 . . . . . .138 E2
Stray Park Way TR14 . . . . .138 F2
Street-An-Garrow [17]
  TR26 . . . . .141 B5

Street-An-Pol 3 TR26 .141 B5
Stretyn 5 TR3 .81 F7
Strickland Cotts 6
TR18 .143 C2
Stringers Hill TR20 .88 A5
Strode Rd PL7 .130 F6
Stroma Cl PL6 .124 F7
Stroud Park Rd PL2 .128 C7
Stuart Rd PL3 .148 A4
Stuart Road Prim Sch
PL1 .148 A4
Stuarts Way PL12 .53 E5
Stucley Rd EX23 .4 D1
Sturdee Rd PL2 .128 A5
Sursdon Cross EX23 .5 A8
Sugar Mill Bsns Pk PL9 129 C1
Summer La PL13 .62 D6
Summer Lodge Holiday
Village TR8 .45 B2
Summercourt TR10 .144 D7
Summercourt Com Prim Sch
TR8 .57 C7
Summerfield Cl PL26 .73 B3
Summerfields PL12 .122 D1
Summerheath TR10 .81 C1
Summerhill Rd PL15 .106 A5
Summerlands Cl PL7 .131 C5
Summerlands Gdns PL7 131 C5
Summerlane Pk PL13 .62 D6
Summerleaze Ave EX23 104 D7
Summerleaze Cres
EX23 .104 D6
Summers Cl PL6 .129 B7
Summers St PL22 .112 C2
Summerville Cross EX39 .3 C6
Sun Girt La PL14 .113 C5
Suncrest PL14 .38 A4
Suncrest Est TR9 .45 E1
Sunderland Cl PL9 .135 A6
Sunderland Rd PL27 .31 F3
Sunland Holiday Est
TR16 .67 C5
Sunley Orford Ho 6
TR1 .137 D4
Sunningdale TR1 .137 A4
Sunningdale Rd PL12 .122 C2
Sunny Bank PL30 .48 E8
Sunny Cnr
Goldsithney TR20 .89 F5
Truro TR4 .81 B7
Sunny Corner La TR19 .96 C7
Sunny Dene PL5 .123 D1
Sunny Terr TR18 .143 B2
Sunnybank 23 TR13 .98 C8
Sunnybanks PL12 .53 E4
Sunnycroft PL13 .117 C3
Sunnyside Carnkie TR13 .80 D1
Menheniot PL14 .51 F5
Menheniot PL14 .52 B5
2 Perranporth TR6 .55 A4
Portscatho TR2 .83 B2
7 Redruth TR15 .140 B4
Sunnyside Mdw PL32 .105 D4
Sunnyside Parc TR15 .139 C8
Sunnyside Rd PL4 .129 B2
Sunnyvale Cl TR16 .67 C6
Sunnyvale Rd TR16 .67 D6
Sunrising Est PL13 .117 D5
Sunset Dr 8 TR13 .98 C8
Sunset Gdns 9 TR13 .98 C8
Sunway Cl PL19 .147 A6
Sunwell La Antony PL11 .65 E4
St John PL11 .132 A8
Surf View TR7 .110 A6
Sussex Pl PL1 .148 C2
Sussex Rd PL2 .127 F5
Sussex St PL1 .148 C2
Sussex Terr 5 PL2 .127 F5
Sutherland Rd PL4 .149 A4
Sutton Ct PL1 .127 F1
Sutton Mews 22 PL4 .149 A2
Sutton Rd PL4 .149 B2
Swaindale Rd 3 PL3 .128 E6
Swale Cl PL3 .129 B6
Swallow Cl EX23 .104 D5
Swallowfield Cl PL24 .60 D5
Swallows End PL9 .135 E8
Swan Cl PL10 .133 A6
Swan Gdns PL7 .130 F5
Swanpool Ct TR11 .145 A1
Swanpool Hill TR11 .145 A2
Swanpool Rd TR11 .144 F1
Swanpool St TR11 .145 C3
Swanvale Rd TR11 .144 F3
Sweet Brair Cres TR7 .111 A4
Swift Gdns PL5 .124 C2
Swinburne Gdns PL5 .124 C1
Swingate Cross EX22 .13 E8
Sycamore Ave
Plymouth PL4 .149 C2
St Austell PL25 .114 E5
Tavistock PL19 .147 C2
Sycamore Cl
Bodmin PL31 .109 B4
Polgooth PL26 .59 A1
Praze-an-Beeble TR14 .79 B2
Rock PL27 .21 E3
Sycamore Dr
Illogan TR15 .139 D7
Plymouth PL6 .125 C7
Torpoint PL11 .127 A3
Sycamore Gdns TR8 .57 B7
Sycamore Rd PL12 .122 B3
Sycamore The PL25 .114 C4
Sycamore Way PL6 .125 E6
Sydenham Cross PL19 .29 C2
Sydney Cl PL7 .130 E4
Sydney Rd Newquay TR7 .110 D6
Sydney Rd *continued*
Torpoint PL11 .127 B3
Sydney St PL1 .148 B4
Sylvan Cl PL25 .114 E6
Sylverton Pl 12 TR18 .143 C7
Symons Cl Blackwater TR4 68 E5
St Austell PL25 .115 A5
Symons Hill TR11 .145 A5
Symons Rd PL12 .122 F2
Symons Row PL14 .37 F3
Symons Terr TR15 .140 B5
Syra Cl PL30 .23 B2

T

Tabernacle St TR1 .137 D4
Tackbear Rd EX22,EX23 .7 E4
Tailyour Rd PL6 .124 F2
Talbot Gdns PL5 .127 D7
Talexandra Terr PL15 .106 D5
Talgos Cl TR16 .140 E8
Talland Hill PL13 .62 E2
Talland Rd TR26 .141 B5
Talmena Ave PL27 .108 A5
Talveneth
Camborne TR14 .138 F3
Pendeen TR19 .75 A1
Redruth TR15 .140 C6
Tamar Ave Plymouth PL2 .127 E5
Tavistock PL19 .147 D5
Tamar Bridge PL5 .123 A2
Tamar Cl
17 Bere Alston PL20 .41 B1
29 Callington PL17 .39 F4
Tamar Cotts PL19 .29 C1
Tamar St Plymouth PL1 .127 E3
Saltash PL12 .123 A2
Torpoint PL11 .127 C3
Tamar Terr Calstock PL17 .41 A3
Saltash PL12 .123 A2
Tamar Units PL15 .18 E2
Tamar Valley Donkey Pk*
PL18 .40 D5
Tamar View
Launceston PL15 .106 D5
Milton Abbot PL19 .29 C6
St Dominick PL12 .40 D2
Tamar View Ind Est
PL12 .122 D5
Tamar Villas PL9 .135 D7
Tamar Way PL18 .41 A6
Tamar Wharf PL1 .127 E3
Tamarisk La TR7 .111 A4
Tamarside Com Coll
PL5 .123 E1
Tamblin Ave PL14 .50 E7
Tamerton Ave PL5 .123 D1
Tamerton Cl PL5 .124 A6
Tamerton Foliot Rd
PL6 .124 D5
Tamerton Rd PL6 .121 B2
Tamerton Vale Prim Sch
PL6 .124 C6
Tangmere Ave PL5 .123 E5
Tangye Cl TR16 .67 E5
Tangye Rd TR15 .139 C6
Tanhouse Rd PL22 .112 C2
Tanwood View PL31 .109 C5
Tapson Dr PL9 .135 A6
Taranto Rd TR13 .146 D4
Taroveor Rd TR18 .143 E6
Taroveor Terr 3 TR18 .143 E5
Tarr PL22 .49 E3
Tarrandean La TR3 .81 E6
Tarten Cross PL12 .53 B4
Tate Gallery* TR26 .141 B6
Taunton Ave PL5 .124 B5
Taunton Pl PL5 .124 B5
Tavern Barn PL23 .116 C5
Tavistock Coll PL19 .147 A3
Tavistock Cross PL20 .41 C2
Tavistock General PL19 .147 B5
Tavistock Mus* PL19 .147 C6
Tavistock Pl PL4 .149 A3
Tavistock Prim Sch
PL19 .147 B4
Tavistock Rd
Callington PL17 .39 F4
Launceston PL15 .106 D5
Launceston, Stourscombe
PL15 .106 E3
Plymouth PL6 .125 B5
Plymouth, Manadon PL5 .124 E1
Yelverton PL20 .42 C3
Tavy Pl PL4 .128 F4
Tavy Rd Saltash PL12 .123 A3
Tavistock PL19 .147 D5
Taw Cl PL3 .129 D6
Tay Gdns PL3 .129 D7
Tayberry Dr TR16 .140 F1
Taylor Cl PL12 .122 C3
Taylor Rd PL12 .122 C4
Taylor Sq PL19 .147 B6
Taylor's Cross EX23 .5 B7
Teats Hill Flats PL4 .149 B1
Teats Hill Rd PL4 .149 B1
Tedder Rd 4 PL26 .59 D7
Tees Cl PL3 .129 C7
Teetotal St TR26 .141 C6
Tehidy Cl TR14 .138 F7
Tehidy Copse TR14 .67 B4
Tehidy Ctry Pk* TR14 .67 B4
Tehidy Gdns TR14 .138 F7
Tehidy Rd
Camborne TR14 .138 D4
Par PL24 .60 D5
Tehidy Terr TR11 .145 A6
Teign Rd PL3 .129 B6
Telcarne Cl TR27 .78 D6
Telegraph Hill TR16 .68 E1
Telegraph St TR16 .68 D1
Telegraph Wharf PL1 .134 A8
Telephone La PL26 .59 C8
Telford Cres PL5 .123 F2
Temeraire Rd PL5 .124 D2
Tenacres La PL14 .38 E4
Tenby Rd PL5 .123 C1
Tencreek Ave TR18 .143 E5
Tencreek Cvn & Camping Pk
PL13 .63 A3
Tenderah Ct TR13 .146 C7
Tenderah Rd TR13 .146 C6
Tennyson Gdns PL5 .124 B1
Tern Gdns PL7 .130 F5
Terr The Crafthole PL11 .65 B5
Portwrinkle PL11 .65 A4
Terra Nova Gn PL2 .128 B5
Terrace The
Chacewater TR4 .68 F3
Dobwalls PL14 .50 D7
Downderry PL11 .64 C5
East Portholland PL26 .84 E5
Harrowbarrow PL17 .40 D5
Penryn TR10 .144 C7
Pentewan PL26 .73 D6
Port Isaac PL29 .22 E7
Rock PL27 .21 D2
St Ives TR26 .141 B5
Yeolmbridge PL15 .18 E6
Terras Hill PL22 .112 C3
Terras Rd PL26 .58 A4
Tethadene PL30 .23 E7
Tewington Pl PL25 .114 B4
Tewkesbury Cl PL2 .128 A8
Thackeray Gdns PL5 .124 B1
Thames Gdns PL3 .129 D5
Thanckes Cl PL11 .127 A3
Thanckes Dr PL11 .127 A4
The Hillocks PL13 .117 D4
Theatre Ope PL1 .127 F1
Theatre Royal PL1 .148 C2
Therlow Rd PL3 .129 B6
Thetford Gdns PL6 .129 D8
Theydon Rd TR11 .144 F3
Third Ave
Plymouth, Billacombe PL9 .130 A1
Plymouth, Camels Head
PL2 .127 E7
Plymouth, Stoke PL1 .128 A2
Thirlmere Gdns PL6 .124 F4
Thistle Cl PL6 .125 E7
Thomas Bullock Cl PL30 .48 C2
Thomas Johnson Ct 6
TR1 .137 C4
Thomas St 4 TR13 .98 C8
Thomas Terr 5 TR13 .98 C8
Thorn Cl PL15 .26 C7
Thorn La PL12 .122 C3
Thorn Moor Cross PL15 .19 F7
Thorn Pk PL3 .128 F5
Thorn Terr PL14 .113 B5
Thornberry Terr TR18 .143 F6
Thornbury Park Ave
PL3 .128 D6
Thornbury Prim Sch
PL6 .125 D4
Thornbury Rd PL6 .125 E4
Thorndon Cross EX22 .8 F5
Thorne Cross EX23 .4 F2
Thornhill Rd PL3 .128 E6
Thornhill Way PL3 .128 E6
Thornpark Rd PL25 .114 E5
Thornton Ave PL4 .149 B4
Thornton Cl PL26 .46 F3
Thornville Terr PL9 .135 C7
Thornwell La PL12 .53 E2
Thornyville Cl PL9 .135 C8
Thornyville Dr PL9 .135 D8
Thornyville Villas PL9 .135 C8
Three Cross TR13 .91 F5
Three Holes Cross PL27 .34 A8
Threemilestone Ind Est
TR4 .69 C3
Threemilestone Prim Sch
TR3 .69 D3
Thurlestone Wlk PL6 .129 D8
Tiddy Cl St Germans PL12 .65 B8
Tavistock PL19 .147 B3
Tideford Cross La PL12 .52 F3
Tideford Dr
Landrake PL12 .53 A2
St Germans PL12 .65 B8
Tideford Rd PL12 .53 C3
Tides Reach TR7 .111 B7
Tillard Cl PL7 .131 C5
Tillie St 5 PL17 .39 E4
Tilly Cl PL9 .135 F4
Timber Cl PL25 .114 B4
Tin La PL4 .149 A2
Tincombe PL12 .122 C2
Tincroft Rd TR15 .139 B4
Tinners Dr PL27 .21 D6
Tinners Way
Callington PL17 .39 F5
New Polzeath PL27 .21 D6
Tinners Wlk TR11 .145 D3
Tinney Dr TR1 .137 F5
Tintagel Castle* PL34 .14 B8
Tintagel Cres PL2 .128 C8
Tintagel Hts PL34 .14 D6
Tintagel Prim Sch PL34 .14 C6
Tintagel Rd PL35 .9 C1
Tintagel Terr PL29 .22 D7
Tintagel Visitor Ctr*
PL34 .14 C7
Tintern Ave PL4 .149 C2
Tiny Mdws
Launceston PL15 .18 E1
South Petherwin PL15 .27 F8
Tipple Cross PL15 .19 C6
Tithe Rd PL7 .130 B7
Tiverton Cl PL6 .125 B8
Tobruk Rd PL12 .122 E3
Toby Way TR7 .110 D7
Tolcarne Cl PL25 .114 E3
Tolcarne Com Prim Sch
TR18 .143 C3
Tolcarne Mews TR7 .110 F6
Tolcarne Rd
Camborne TR14 .79 D5
Newquay TR7 .110 F6
St Day TR16 .68 D1
Tolcarne St TR14 .138 D2
Tolcarne Terr TR18 .143 C3
Tolgarrick Rd TR14 .138 F5
Tolgus Hill TR15 .140 A5
Tolgus Pl TR15 .140 A6
Tolgus Vean TR15 .140 A5
Tolgus Wartha TR15 .140 A6
Tollgate Cl PL14 .113 B4
Tollox Pl PL3 .129 B4
Tollyfrank Hill TR2 .83 F6
Tolpeon Flats TR26 .141 E2
Tolponds Rd TR13 .91 A1
Tolroy Holiday Village
TR27 .142 C2
Tolroy Rd TR27 .142 D1
Tolskithy La TR15 .139 E6
Tolticken Hill TR16 .67 E6
Toltuff Cres TR18 .143 C4
Toltuff Rd TR18 .143 C4
Tolvaddon Energy Pk
TR14 .138 F7
Tolvaddon Rd TR15 .139 A5
Tolvan Cross TR12 .92 C2
Tolver Pl TR18 .143 E6
Tolver Rd TR18 .143 E6
Tolview Terr TR27 .142 B4
Tom Lyon Rd PL14 .113 E5
Tom Nicolls Cl 7 PL14 .38 A3
Top Hill TR2 .57 E1
Top Of The Town Ctyd
PL12 .122 F2
Top Rd PL11 .64 C5
Tor Cl
Plymouth, Hartley PL3 .128 E7
Plymouth, Marsh Mills PL3 129 F5
Porthleven TR13 .91 B1
Tor La PL12 .122 B1
Tor Rd Newquay TR7 .110 E6
Plymouth PL3 .128 E7
Tor View Bugle PL26 .47 C2
8 Horrabridge PL20 .42 C4
Tregadillett PL15 .18 C2
Torbridge Cl PL12 .122 D2
Torbridge Rd
7 Horrabridge PL20 .42 C4
Plymouth PL7 .130 E6
Torbryan Cl PL6 .129 E8
Torland Rd PL3 .128 E7
Torleven Rd TR13 .91 B2
Torpoint Com Sch PL11 127 A4
Torpoint Inf Sch PL11 .127 B3
Torr Cres PL3 .128 E7
Torr La PL3 .128 E7
Torr Rd PL3 .128 E7
Torr View Ave PL3 .128 D7
Torridge Cl PL7 .131 A6
Torridge Rd PL7 .130 F6
Torridge Way PL3 .129 C5
Tors View Cl PL17 .39 F4
Torver Cl PL6 .125 D2
Torwood Cl PL31 .109 D4
Tory Brook Ave PL7 .130 E6
Tory Brook Ct PL7 .130 E6
Tory Way PL7 .130 D6
Tosberry Cross EX39 .3 B8
Tothill Ave PL4 .149 B3
Tothill Rd PL4 .149 B3
Totnes Cl PL7 .131 B4
Towan Blystra Rd TR7 .111 A5
Towan Ct PL28 .31 E8
Towan Prom TR7 .110 D6
Towan Rd Pentewan PL26 .73 D8
Porthtowan TR4 .68 A7
Towednack Rd TR26 .77 A6
Tower Cl Pelynt PL13 .62 D6
Sennen TR19 .96 B6
Tower Ct PL12 .122 C2
Tower Hill Looe PL13 .117 D3
Wadebridge PL27 .108 E5
Tower Ho PL1 .127 E1
Tower Mdws TR19 .97 A6
Tower Park Est PL13 .62 D6
Tower Park Rd PL13 .62 C6
Tower Pk Fowey PL23 .116 B3
Pelynt PL13 .62 D6
Tower Pk Cvn & Camping Pk
TR19 .87 C1
Tower Rd Newquay TR7 .110 D6
St Erme TR4 .70 D8
Tower St PL15 .106 C6
Tower View PL12 .122 D1
Towerfield Dr PL6 .125 C8
Towers Cl PL6 .125 F2
Town Arms Pas PL31 .109 E5
Town Farm TR15 .140 C3
Town Farm Cl 6 PL20 .42 C4
Town Hill TR5 .54 D1
Town Mill Gdns PL19 .147 C6
Town Mills PL15 .106 B7
Town Mills Flats PL15 .106 B7
Townfield TR15 .139 C6
Townsend PL23 .116 D2
Townshend Ave PL2 .127 E5
Townswell Cl PL12 .53 E2
Townswell La PL12 .53 E2
Traboe Cross TR12 .100 D3
Tracarus Ind Est PL28 .107 B4
Tracey Ct PL1 .148 B3
Trafalgar Cl PL5 .127 D8
Trafalgar Pl 3 PL1 .127 F3
Trafalgar Place La PL1 .127 F3
Trafalgar Sq TR1 .137 D4
Trafalgar St PL4 .149 A3
Traine Brake PL9 .136 C1
Traine Rd PL9 .136 B1
Traly Cl EX23 .104 F4
Tram La TR16 .140 E1
Tramway Rd PL6 .125 E7
Tranalt Terr TR1 .137 B5
Trannack Com Prim Sch
TR13 .91 E5
Trannack Mill Ind Est
TR13 .91 E5
Trannack Terr TR18 .143 E7
Tranquil La PL31 .109 C5
Transit Way PL5 .124 C3
Travellers Rest TR12 .99 B8
Travers Cl PL14 .113 A6
Tre-El- Verne Cl TR1 .137 A4
Tre-Pol PL26 .58 F1
Treago Gdns PL6 .125 C8
Trease TR19 .75 A1
Treassowe Rd TR18 .143 E6
Trebah Gdns* TR11 .93 C2
Treban Rd TR18 .143 C4
Trebartha Cl PL17 .39 E3
Trebartha Rd TR1 .137 F5
Trebarthen Terr TR4 .55 D5
Trebarva Cl TR15 .140 A6
Trebarvah La TR20 .89 E4
Trebarvah Rd TR11 .92 E4
Trebarwith Cres TR7 .110 E6
Trebarwith Rd PL33 .14 D4
Treberran Gdns TR14 .138 F6
Treboul Cross PL12 .64 F8
Treboul Way PL12 .65 B8
Treburdon Dr PL26 .46 F3
Treburley Cl PL15 .28 C4
Treburley Ind Est PL15 .28 C4
Treby Rd PL7 .130 F4
Trebyhan Parc TR3 .80 F3
Trecarn Cl PL15 .106 B5
Trecarne Falmouth TR11 .144 E5
Tremar PL14 .38 A3
Trecarne Cl Polgooth PL26 59 A1
St Austell PL25 .115 B5
Truro TR1 .137 E5
Trecarne Gdns PL33 .14 E3
Trecarne View PL14 .37 F3
Trecarrack Rd TR14 .138 F3
Trecarrel PL15 .106 C4
Trecarrell Cl PL15 .106 D4
Tredanek Cl PL31 .109 B5
Tredarrup Cross PL15 .11 A1
Tredarvah Dr TR18 .143 C5
Tredarvah Rd TR18 .143 C5
Tredavoe La TR18 .143 B1
Tredenham Cl 4 PL24 .60 C4
Tredenham Rd TR2 .95 B6
Tredethy Rd PL30 .34 F6
Tredinnick Cotts TR 20 .76 A1
Tredinnick La PL12 .53 B2
Tredinnick Lane-End
PL13 .64 A8
Tredinnick Way 12 TR6 .55 A4
Tredinnick Wood Cl
TR13 .146 D8
Tredour Rd TR7 .110 E4
Tredova Cres TR11 .145 B2
Tredragon Cl TR8 .31 C2
Tredragon Rd TR8 .31 C2
Tredrea Gdns TR3 .81 D5
Tredrea La TR27 .77 E2
Tredrizzick Cl PL27 .21 F3
Tredruston Rd PL27 .33 B6
Tredydan Rd PL15 .106 B6
Tredynas Rd TR11 .145 D3
Tredyson Pl TR11 .145 A3
Treen Flats TR14 .138 F3
Treen Hill TR19 .96 F4
Treetops Hill PL13 .117 A3
Treeve Farm Ind Units
TR27 .78 C6
Treeve La TR27 .78 C6
Treffry La PL30 .48 C6
Treffry Way 12 PL24 .60 B4
Trefinnick Rd PL17 .39 B8
Trefleur Cl 3 PL35 .9 C1
Trefloyd Cl PL17 .39 E6
Treforda Rd TR7 .110 F4
Treforest Rd PL27 .108 A6
Treforthlan 7 TR16 .67 E4
Treforthlan Cl 6 TR16 .67 E4
Trefrew Rd PL32 .105 D5
Trefusis Cl TR1 .137 F5
Trefusis Ct TR11 .145 A6
Trefusis Gdns PL3 .129 A4
Trefusis Rd
Falmouth TR11 .144 E2
Flushing TR11 .145 C6
Redruth TR15 .140 C4
Trefusis Terr
Millbrook PL10 .132 E6
Redruth TR15 .140 C5
Tregadillett Com Prim Sch
PL15 .18 C2

Tregaer TR11 ....145 C3
Tregainlands Pk PL30 ...34 D3
Tregalister Gdns PL12 ...65 B8
Tregaller La PL15 ....18 E1
Treganoon Rd TR15 .....140 D7
Tregargus View PL26 .....58 B4
Tregarland Cl
  Camborne TR14 ....138 E2
  Coad's Green PL15 .....27 D4
Tregarne Terr PL25 ....114 C4
Tregarrian Rd TR14 .....138 F7
Tregarrick PL13 ....117 B3
Tregarrick Cl TR13 .....146 B7
Tregarrick Ct PL13 .....117 B3
Tregarrick La PL13 ......62 D6
Tregarrick Rd PL26 .....46 F3
Tregarrick Way PL13 .....62 D6
Tregarth 12 PL26 ....59 D7
Tregartha Way PL14 ...113 D6
Tregarthen 2 TR26 ....141 A5
Tregassack Rd TR20 .....88 F7
Tregassick Rd TR2 ......83 B1
Tregavarras Row PL26 ...85 A5
Tregavethan View TR3 ...69 C4
Tregay La PL14 ....113 C7
Tregea Hill TR16 ....67 C6
Tregea Terr TR16 ....67 C6
Tregear Cl TR12 ....99 D6
Tregear Gdns TR1 ......137 C4
Tregease Rd TR5 ....54 C1
Tregellas Rd TR12 ....99 B1
Tregellast Cl TR12 ......101 D4
Tregellast Parc TR12 ...101 D4
Tregellast Rd TR12 .....101 D3
Tregembo Hill TR20 ......90 A7
Tregender La TR20 ....89 B8
Tregender Rd TR20 ....89 B8
Tregenna Cl
  Plymouth PL7 ....131 C4
  Wainhouse Corner EX23 ...10 F6
Tregenna Ct
  Camborne TR14 ....138 C2
  Falmouth TR11 ....145 C3
Tregenna Fields TR14 ...138 C2
Tregenna Hill 16 TR26 ...141 B5
Tregenna La TR14 ....138 C2
Tregenna Parc TR26 ....141 C3
Tregenna Pl 4 TR26 ...141 B5
Tregenna Rd PL30 ....35 C8
Tregenna Terr TR26 ....141 B5
Tregenver Rd TR11 .....144 F4
Tregenver Villas TR11 ...144 F4
Tregeseal Hill TR19 ......86 F7
Tregeseal Row TR19 .....86 F6
Tregeseal Terr TR19 .....86 F6
Tregew Cl TR11 ....145 B7
Tregew Rd Flushing TR11 145 B8
  Penryn TR10,TR11 ......81 F2
Treggodick Cotts TR20 .143 A8
Tregidden Hill TR12 ....100 F5
Tregie TR18 ....143 B3
Tregiskey Cotts PL26 ....73 C5
Tregisky La TR12 ....101 C1
Treglenwith Rd TR18 ...138 C4
Treglisson Rural Workshops
  TR27 ....78 C3
Treglyn Cl TR18 ....143 B1
Tregoddick Ct TR20 ......88 B7
Tregolds La PL28 ....31 F7
Tregolls Cl TR1 ....137 E5
Tregolls Rd TR1 ....137 E5
Tregolls Sch TR1 ....137 F5
Tregoney Hill PL26 ......73 C3
Tregongeeves La PL26 ...59 A2
Tregonhay PL14 ....38 C7
Tregonhayne Ct TR2 .....72 A4
Tregoniggie Ind Est
  TR11 ....144 D4
Tregoning Rd PL11 .....126 F2
Tregonissey Cl PL25 ...114 D5
Tregonissey Rd PL25 ...114 E5
Tregonissy La End PL25 114 E6
Tregonning Ct 5 TR6 ...55 A5
Tregonning Parc 9
  TR12 ....101 C4
Tregonning Rd TR3 ......80 C3
Tregonning Terr TR13 ...90 E3
Tregonning View 17
  TR13 ....98 C8
Tregony Com Prim Sch
  TR2 ....71 E4
Tregony Hill TR2 ....71 F3
Tregony Rd TR2 ....71 D6
Tregony Rural Workshops
  TR2 ....71 E3
Tregorrick Rd PL26 ....114 E1
Tregos Rd TR12 ....141 C2
Tregoss Rd TR7 ....110 F6
Tregothnan Rd
  Falmouth TR11 ....145 A5
  Truro TR1 ....137 E3
Tregowris Court Cotts
  TR12 ....101 B5
Tregrea TR14 ....138 E1
Tregrehan Gdns* PL24 .115 E6
Tregullan TR15 ....139 C8
Tregullan View PL31 ...109 D3
Tregullow Rd TR16 .....144 F6
Tregundy Cl 14 TR6 .....55 A5
Tregundy Ct 13 TR6 .....55 A5
Tregundy La TR6 ....55 A5
Tregundy Rd TR6 ....55 A5
Tregunna Cl TR13 ....91 B1

Tregunnel Cvn Pk TR7 ...110 D5
Tregunnel Hill TR7 .....110 D4
Tregunnick La PL11 ......64 B6
Tregunnus La PL11 ......64 D5
Tregunter Mews TR11 ...145 D3
Tregurra La TR1 ....137 E6
Tregurrian TR8 ....44 A4
Tregurrian Hill TR8 ......44 D8
Tregurtha Farm Cotts
  TR17 ....89 D6
Tregurtha View TR20 ....89 E5
Tregurthen Cl TR14 ....138 C2
Tregurthen Rd TR14 ....138 C2
Treguth Cl TR8 ....43 B1
Tregwary Rd TR26 .....141 A5
Tregye Campus (Truro Coll)
  TR3 ....82 A7
Tregye Rd TR3 ....82 A7
Trehaddle TR4 ....81 B7
Trehane Rd TR14 ....138 B3
Trehannick Cl PL30 ......23 E7
Trehaverne La TR1 .....137 C5
Trehaverne Terr 3 TR1 .137 C5
Trehawke La PL14 ....38 C1
Trehayes Mdw TR27 .....77 E2
Trehaze-Na Cl PL32 .....10 C3
Treheath Rd PL14 ....50 E7
Trehill Cross PL12 ....40 C2
Trehill La PL10 ....64 B2
Trehunsey Cl TR11 ......93 E2
Trekeen Rd TR10 ....144 B8
Trekenner Prim Sch
  PL15 ....28 C5
Trekenning Rd TR9 ......45 D5
Trekestle Pk PL15 ....18 C2
Trekye Cl TR16 ....80 B5
Trelake Rd PL25 ....114 B4
Trelander Barton TR1 ...137 E5
Trelander E TR1 ....137 F4
Trelander Highway TR1 137 E4
Trelander N TR1 ....137 F4
Trelander S TR1 ....137 F4
Trelander Vean TR1 ....137 F4
Trelantis Est PL28 ....31 F8
Trelaske La PL13 ....62 F4
Trelavour Rd PL26 ....58 C8
Trelavour Sq PL26 ....58 C8
Trelawne Cl 10 TR3 ......81 F7
Trelawne Cottage Gdns
  PL13 ....62 E4
Trelawne Gdns PL13 .....62 E5
Trelawne Rd TR3 ....81 F7
Trelawney Ave
  Falmouth TR11 ....145 B3
  Plymouth PL5 ....123 C4
  Poughill EX23 ....4 C3
  Redruth TR15 ....140 F7
  St Ives TR26 ....141 A5
Trelawney Cl
  Bodmin PL31 ....109 C4
  Maenporth TR11 ....93 E3
  Torpoint PL11 ....126 E3
  Warbstow Cross PL15 ...11 B1
Trelawney Cotts PL15 ...106 D5
Trelawney Est
  Madron TR20 ....143 A8
  Ponsanooth TR4 ....81 B7
Trelawney Gdns PL14 ...38 D4
Trelawney Hts 19 PL17 ...39 F4
Trelawney Parc
  St Columb Major TR9 ...45 D5
  Warbstow Cross PL15 ...11 B1
Trelawney Pl Hayle TR27 142 C6
  Penryn TR10 ....144 C8
  Plymouth PL5 ....123 D1
Trelawney Rd
  Bodmin PL31 ....109 C3
  Callington PL17 ....39 F4
  Camborne TR14 ....138 D3
  Chacewater TR4 ....69 A3
  Helston TR13 ....146 C5
  Newquay TR7 ....110 C5
  Padstow PL28 ....107 D4
  Plymouth PL3 ....128 D5
  Ponsanooth TR3 ....81 B4
  Saltash PL12 ....122 E2
  St Austell PL25 ....114 E5
  St Ives TR26 ....141 A5
  St Mawes TR2 ....95 A6
  Truro TR1 ....137 B5
Trelawney Rise
  18 Callington PL17 .....39 F4
  Torpoint PL11 ....126 E3
Trelawney Terr Cury TR12 .99 B4
  Looe PL13 ....117 C4
Trelawney Way
  Hayle TR27 ....142 C6
  Torpoint PL11 ....126 E3
Trelawny Ct TR14 ......138 C3
Trelawny Rd
  Falmouth TR11 ....145 B4
  Menheniot PL14 ....52 A6
  Plymouth PL7 ....130 C6
  St Agnes TR5 ....54 C1
  Tavistock PL19 ....147 C6
Treleaver Way TR1 ......69 F3
Trelee Cl TR27 ....142 E7
Treleigh Ave TR15 .....140 B6
Treleigh Com Prim Sch
  TR16 ....140 C8
Treleigh Ind Est TR16 ...140 C7
Treleigh Terr TR15 .....140 B5
Treleven Rd EX23 ......104 F4
Treliddon La PL11 ....64 C5
Treliever Cross TR10 ....81 C1
Treliever Rd
  Mabe Burnthouse TR10 ...81 C1
  Penryn TR10 ....144 B8

Treligga Downs Rd PL33 .14 D2
Trelil La TR11 ....144 C2
Trelindon PL15 ....27 E8
Trelinnoe Cl PL15 ....27 E8
Trelinnoe Gdns PL15 ....27 E8
Treliske Ind Est TR1 ....69 E4
Treliske Prep Sch TR1 ...69 F4
Treliske Rd TR15 ....140 D6
Trelispen Park Dr PL26 ...85 C5
Trelispen Pk PL26 ....85 C5
Trelissick Fields TR27 ..142 B3
Trelissick Gdns PL17 ....39 E3
Trelissick Rd
  Falmouth TR11 ....144 F5
  Hayle TR27 ....142 B3
Treloan La TR2 ....83 B1
Treloar Terr PL15 ......106 B6
Treloggan Ind Est TR7 ..111 B4
Treloggan La TR7 ......111 A5
Treloggan Rd TR7 .....111 A4
Trelowarren* TR12 ......99 F6
Trelowarren Ct 13 PL17 ...39 E4
Trelowarren St TR14 ...138 D3
Treloweth Cl
  Plymouth PL2 ....128 D8
  St Erth TR27 ....77 E2
Treloweth Com Prim Sch
  TR15 ....139 D6
Treloweth Gdns TR15 ...139 C6
Treloweth La TR27 ....77 E2
Treloweth Rd TR15 .....139 C6
Treloweth Terr TR15 ...139 B7
Treloweth Way TR15 ...139 C7
Treloyhan Cl TR26 .....141 C3
Treloyhan Park Rd
  TR26 ....141 C3
Trelyn PL27 ....21 E3
Trelyn Rd PL12 ....101 D4
Trelyon Ave TR26 ......141 C4
Trelyon Ct TR19 ....97 B6
Tremabe La PL14 ....50 E7
Tremabe Rd PL14 ....50 E7
Tremadart Cl PL14 ....51 A1
Tremaddock Cotts TR4 ...36 F3
Tremaddock Council Hos
  PL14 ....36 F3
Tremaine TR18 ....143 C7
Tremall Parc TR3 ....80 F3
Tremanor Way TR11 ....144 D5
Tremar Cl PL14 ....38 A2
Tremar La St Cleer PL14 .37 F3
  Tremar PL14 ....38 A3
Tremarle Home Pk
  TR14 ....138 F5
Tremarne Rd PL27 .....108 B5
Tremarren Rd PL27 ....108 B5
Trematon Cl PL11 ......126 E4
Trematon Terr PL4 .....128 E4
Tremayne Ct TR3 ....81 F6
Tremayne Pk TR14 .....138 F2
Tremayne Rd
  Carharrack TR16 ....80 C4
  St Austell PL25 ....114 E4
  Truro TR1 ....137 C5
Tremayne Rise PL19 ...147 B5
Tremayne Terr PL13 .....63 F8
Trembath Cres TR7 ....110 E5
Trembear Rd PL25 .....114 A4
Trembel Rd TR12 ....99 B2
Trembrase TR19 ....96 C7
Tremeadow Terr
  Hayle TR27 ....142 B4
  Liskeard PL14 ....113 D7
Tremear Gn TR9 ....45 E2
Tremearne Rd 16 TR13 ...98 C8
Tremeddan La PL14 ....113 C6
Tremeddan Terr PL14 ..113 B4
Tremeer La PL30 ....23 E3
Tremellin La PL27 ....77 F1
Tremena Gdns PL25 ...114 C4
Tremena Rd PL25 ......114 C4
Tremenheere Ave TR13 .146 D8
Tremenheere Rd TR18 ..143 E6
Tremewan 1 PL25 ......59 A3
Tremodrett Rd PL26 ....46 F3
Tremollett Cotts PL17 ...28 B1
Tremore Rd TR15 ......140 D6
Tremorva TR27 ....142 C6
Tremorva Ct TR1 ....137 E5
Tremorva Terr TR1 .....137 E5
Tremorvah Cres TR1 ...137 E5
Tremorvah Ct TR11 ....144 F1
Tremorvah Wood La
  TR1 ....137 E5
Trenance Ave TR7 .....110 F5
Trenance Ct TR13 ......146 B7
Trenance Cvn Pk TR7 ..110 E5
Trenance Hill PL25 .....114 A5
Trenance Inf Sch TR7 ..110 E5
Trenance La
  3 Mullion TR12 ....99 A1
  Newquay TR7 ....110 E4
Trenance Leisure Pk*
  TR7 ....111 A5
Trenance Pl TR25 ......114 B4
Trenance Rd
  Camborne TR14 ....138 E4
  Newquay TR7 ....110 E4
  St Austell PL25 ....114 B4
Trenance Stables* TR7 110 E4
Trenant PL14 ....68 D1
Trenant Cl PL27 ....21 E5

Trenant Cross PL14 ......63 A6
Trenant Ind Est PL27 ..108 D6
Trenant Rd Looe PL13 ..117 D5
  2 Par PL24 ....60 D5
Trenant Vale PL27 .....108 D6
Trenarren View PL25 ...115 A6
Trenarth TR10 ....144 C8
Trenarth Rd TR7 ....110 E5
Trenawin La TR27 ....78 E5
Trencher La PL10 ......132 D2
Trencreek Cl TR4 ....56 D1
Trencreek La TR8 ......111 B4
Trencreek Rd TR26,TR8 ..111 B4
Trencrom La TR26 .....141 D1
Trencrom Row TR20 .....77 B3
Trendeal Gdns 1 TR18 .143 E5
Trendlewood Rd PL6 ...125 D7
Trendreath Ct TR26 .....77 E3
Trenear TR15 ....140 D6
Treneere La TR18 ......143 E5
Treneere Rd TR18 .....143 E6
Trengloe Terr TR18 ....143 C3
Trenglos TR4 ....81 C7
Trenglos Terr TR18 .....88 E6
Trenery Cl TR1 ....137 D6
Trenerth Rd TR27 ....78 E2
Trengove PL26 ....47 C1
Trengove Cross TR11 ...92 D5
Trengrouse Ave PL11 ..126 F3
Trengrouse Way TR13 ..146 C5
Trenhaile Terr TR1 ......70 F2
Trenhayle La TR27 ....142 B2
Treningle View PL31 ...109 C3
Treninnick Hill TR7 .....111 F4
Treninnow & Wiggle Chalets
  PL10 ....132 C2
Trenithick Mdw TR4 .....68 C6
Trenithon La TR8 ....57 C6
Trennance Valley 6
  TR12 ....99 A1
Trennick La TR1 ....137 E3
Trennick Row TR1 .....137 E3
Trennick Villas Ct TR1 ..137 E3
Trenouth Cl 5 PL14 .....38 A3
Trenovissick Rd PL24 ...60 B4
Trenowah Rd PL25 .....115 C5
Trenoweth Ave TR18 ..138 B3
Trenoweth Cres TR18 ..143 B4
Trenoweth Ct 8 TR12 ..102 F2
Trenoweth Est TR15 ...140 A8
Trenoweth La TR10 .....93 B8
Trenoweth Mdw 9
  TR12 ....102 F2
Trenoweth Rd TR18 ....143 B5
Trenoweth Terr TR10 ...93 B8
Trenoweth Vean TR10 ...81 B1
Trenowth Terr TR2 ......57 E1
Trent Cl PL3 ....129 B6
Trentham Cl PL6 ....125 B6
Trentworthy Cross EX22 ...3 E2
Trenwith La TR26 ......141 A4
Trenwith Pl 14 TR26 ...141 B5
Trenwith Terr 11 TR26 .141 B5
Trenython Rd 10 PL24 ...60 B4
Treore Cl PL30 ....23 A6
Treovis Cross PL14 ......38 C8
Treraven La PL27 ......108 C3
Trerew Rd TR18 ....143 C4
Trerice Ct 15 PL17 ......39 E4
Trerice Dr TR7 ....111 B5
Trerice Fields TR14 .....79 B2
Trerice Pl TR26 ....141 A5
Trerice Rd 6 TR26 .....141 A5
Trerice Terr PL26 ....58 A8
Trerieve PL11 ....64 C5
Treroosel Rd PL30 ......23 D8
Treruffe Hill TR15 .....140 A6
Treruffe Terr 9 TR15 ..140 A6
Treryn Cl PL24 ....60 D5
Tresaderns Rd TR15 ...140 A6
Tresahar Rd TR11 .....145 A3
Tresamble Hill TR4,TR3 ...81 B6
Tresavean Est TR16 .....80 E6
Tresavean Terr TR16 ....80 E6
Tresaven Hill TR16 ......80 E6
Tresawla Ct TR14 ......138 F6
Tresawle Rd TR1 ......145 A6
Tresawls Ave TR1 ....69 F3
Tresawls Rd TR1,TR4 ....69 E3
Tresco Pl TR11 ....144 F4
Trescobeas Rd TR11 ...144 E5
Trescoe Rd TR20 ....88 F6
Trescol Vean Sch TR3 ...69 C2
Trescowe Rd TR20 ......89 F5
Tresdale Parc TR27 ......78 D6
Treseder's Gdns TR1 ...137 D5
Tresevern Hill TR3 ......80 D4
Tresidder TR1 ....144 F1
Tresillian Com Prim Inf Sch
  TR2 ....70 F5
Tresillian Ho TR1 ....69 E4
Tresillian Rd TR1 ......144 F1
Tresillian St PL4 ....149 C2
Tresithney Rd TR16 .....80 F8
Treskerby TR16 ....140 F7
Treskewes Est 1 TR12 .101 C4
Treskilling PL30 ....59 F8
Treslothan Rd TR14 .....79 D4
Tresluggan Rd PL5 ....123 D1

Tresooth La TR10 ......144 C
Tresowgar La TR2 ....71 B
Tresprison Ct TR13 ....146 E
Treswithian Park Rd
  TR14 ....138 B
Treswithian Rd TR14 ..138 B
Tretawn PL30 ....23 B
Trethannas Gdns TR14 ..79 B
Trethellan Hill TR7 .....110 C
Trethern Cl TR14 ....79 E
Tretherras Cl TR7 ......111 A
Tretherras Rd TR7 .....111 A
Tretherras Sch TR7 ....111 B
Trethevy Cl PL14 ....37 F
Trethevy Quoit* PL14 ...38 A
Trethew Gdns TR14 ....138 E
Trethewey Cl 10 TR9 ....45 E
Trethewey Way TR7 ...110 D
Trethiggey Cres TR8 ...111 F
Trethiggey Touring Pk
  TR8 ....111 F
Trethill La PL11 ....65 C
Trethorne Ct TR20 ......89 A
Trethorne Leisure Farm*
  PL15 ....18 B
Trethosa Rd PL26 ....58 B
Trethowan Hts TR1 ......69 F
Trethurffe Terr TR9 .....45 E
Trethurffe Villas TR2 ...57 C
Tretoil View PL31 ......109 E
Tretorvic TR18 ....143 C
Tretower Cl PL6 ....124 F
Trevadlock Hall Pk PL15 ...27 A
Trevail Cotts TR8 ....43 D
Trevale TR18 ....143 C
Trevalga Cl 5 TR6 ....55 A
Trevallack Parc 3
  TR12 ....101 C
Trevallack View 2
  TR12 ....101 C
Trevallion Pk TR3 ....82 B
Trevallyn Rd PL15 .....106 B
Trevance TR10 ....144 A
Trevance Pk PL24 ....60 D
Trevanion Cl PL27 .....108 B
Trevanion Ct TR1 ....69 F
Trevanion La PL25 ......59 A
Trevanion Pk PL27 ....108 C
Trevanion Rd
  Liskeard PL14 ....113 D
  St Austell PL25 ....114 D
  2 Trewoon PL25 ......59 A
  Wadebridge PL27 .....108 B
Trevannion Cl PL6 .....129 A
Trevanson Rd PL27 ....108 A
Trevanson St
  Wadebridge PL27 .....108 B
  Wadebridge PL27 .....108 B
Trevarner Way PL27 ...108 D
Trevarno Cl PL25 ....59 A
Trevarno La TR27 ....78 D
Trevarrack Cl TR18 ....143 F
Trevarrack La TR18 ....143 F
Trevarrack Pl TR18 ....143 F
Trevarrack Rd TR18 ...143 F
Trevarrack Row TR18 ...88 E
Trevarrick Cl TR1 ......141 C
Trevarrick Dr PL25 ....114 B
Trevarrick Rd PL25 ....114 B
Trevarth Est PL26 ......73 C
Trevarth Rd TR11 .....144 F
Trevarth Terr TR16 .....80 E
Trevarthian Rd
  St Austell PL25 ....114 C
  St Austell PL25 ....114 D
Trevarweneth Rd 8
  PL24 ....60 B
Trevassack Cl TR27 ....142 D
Trevassack Hill TR27 ..142 E
Trevassack Parc TR27 .142 E
Trevaunance Cl TR5 ....54 C
Trevaunance Rd TR5 ...54 C
Trevaylor Cl TR1 ......137 E
Trevaylor Rd TR11 .....144 F
Trevean Cl TR14 ....138 B
Trevean Gdns 3 TR18 .143 D
Trevean La TR20 ....89 C
Trevean Rd
  Penzance TR18 ....143 D
  Truro TR1 ....69 F
Trevean Way
  Newquay TR7 ....110 C
  Rosudgeon TR20 ....89 C
Trevear Cl PL25 ....114 D
Trevear Rd PL26 ....58 B
Trevecca Cotts PL14 ...113 C
Treveglos Rd TR11 ....144 E
Trevelga Cl TR7 ....111 A
Trevelgue Ct TR8 ....44 C
Trevelgue Holiday Pk
  TR8 ....44 D
Trevelgue Rd TR7,TR8 ..44 C
Trevella Pk TR8 ....110 C
Trevella Vean TR4 ......70 D
Trevellan Rd TR11 ......82 A
Trevelthan Rd 18 TR16 ..67 E
Trevelva Ct TR1 ....137 E
Trevelveth Rd TR8 .....110 B
Trevelyan Cl 10 TR20 ...67 F
Trevelyan Rd TR15,TR16 ..67 E
Trevelyan Way 5 TR20 ...67 F
Trevemper Rd TR7,TR8 .110 F
Treven La TR2 ....78 B
Trevena Cl TR18 ....143 C
Trevena Cross TR13 .....90 C

Trevena Dr PL34 ......14 C7
Trevena Gdns TR11 ....93 D3
Trevena Rd TR16 .....143 C4
Trevena Terr TR7 ....110 D6
Trevendon PL17 ......28 D1
Treveneague Gdns PL2 .128 D8
Treveneth Rd TR13 ...146 C5
Treveneth Cres TR18 ..143 C5
Treveneth Pl 1 TR18 ..143 C1
Trevenna Cross TR8 ...45 A8
Trevenner La TR17 ....89 C5
Trevenner Mews 6
  TR15 ....140 B5
Trevenson Sq TR17 ...89 C5
Trevenson Ct TR15 ...139 B6
Trevenson La
  Camborne TR14 .....138 D2
  Camborne, Pool TR15 .139 A6
Trevenson Rd
  Camborne TR15 .....139 B5
  Newquay TR7 ....111 B6
Trevenson St TR14 ...138 D2
Treventon Cl
  Falmouth TR1 ......144 E4
  Portscatho TR2 .....83 B2
Treventon Rd TR2 ....83 B2
Treventon Rise 11 TR9 ..45 E6
Treverby Com Prim Sch
  PL26 ....59 C8
Treverbyn Cl
  Liskeard PL14 ......113 C6
  Plymouth PL7 ......130 D6
Treverbyn Gdns PL25 .114 F4
Treverbyn Rd
  Falmouth TR1 ......144 E1
  Padstow PL28 ......107 E4
  Plymouth PL7 ......130 D6
  St Austell PL25 .....114 E7
  St Ives TR26 ....141 A5
  Stenalees PL26 .....59 C8
  Truro TR1 ....137 E6
Treverbyn Rise TR10 .144 A8
Trevere Cl TR27 ......78 C6
Treveryn Parc TR11 ...144 C2
Trevessa Cl PL2 ......128 D8
Treveth La TR13 .....146 D8
Trevethan Cl TR11 ...145 A4
Trevethan Ct 2 TR11 .145 A5
Trevethan Gdns 2
  TR11 ....145 A4
Trevethan Hill TR11 ..145 B5
Trevethan Pk PL20 ...119 F4
Trevethan Rd TR11 ...145 A4
Trevethan Rise TR11 ..145 A4
Trevethenick Rd TR1 ..137 E3
Trevia La PL32 ....105 B4
Trevia Pk Terr PL32 ..105 C3
Trevian Cl 6 TR6 .....55 A4
Treviglas Cl TR7 .....111 D7
Treviglas Com Coll TR7 .111 D7
Treviglas La TR2 .....71 C6
Treviglas Rise TR2 ...71 C6
Trevilley La PL30 ....23 E8
Trevillick La PL30 ....23 F6
Trevilling Rd PL27 ....108 B6
Trevillis Pk PL14 .....113 B4
Trevilson Cl TR8 .....56 C7
Trevince Parc TR16 ...80 F8
Trevingey Cl TR15 ....140 A3
Trevingey Cres TR15 ..140 A3
Trevingey Parc TR15 ..140 A4
Trevingey Rd TR15 ...140 A3
Trevisker Com Prim Sch
  PL27 ....31 F3
Treviskey Hill TR2 ...84 B3
Trevissomes Ct TR11 .144 F6
Trevithick PL28 ......31 F8
Trevithick Ave PL11 ..126 C4
Trevithick Cl
  Newquay TR7 ....110 F4
  St Merryn PL28 .....31 F8
  Truro TR1 ....137 E6
Trevithick Cres TR27 .142 D5
Trevithick Ct
  Camborne TR14 .....138 C3
  Truro TR1 ....137 E6
Trevithick Rd
  Camborne TR14 .....138 D3
  Camborne, Illogan Highway
    TR15 ....139 C6
  Chacewater TR4 ....69 A3
  Falmouth TR11 .....144 E6
  Plymouth PL5 ......123 E2
  St Austell PL25 .....114 E3
  Truro TR1 ....137 E5
Trevithick Sch TR14 ..138 D1
Trevoarn TR27 ....142 B5
Trevol Bsns Pk PL11 ..126 D3
Trevol Pl PL11 ....126 E3
Trevol Rd PL11 ......126 E3
Trevollard PL13 ......61 F7
Trevollard La PL12 ...53 D1
Trevone Cres PL25 ...114 A4
Trevone Gdns PL2 ....128 D8
Trevone Rd PL28 .....20 F2
Trevoney TR11 ....144 C2
Trevor Cl PL28 ....20 C1
Trevorder Cl PL11 ....126 F2
Trevorder Rd PL11 ...126 F2
Trevorgans Cross TR19 .87 B2
Trevose Ave TR7 .....110 C6
Trevose Cl TR5 ....54 C1
Trevose Ho TR1 ......69 E4
Trevose Rd TR1 ......69 E4
Trevose Way PL3 .....129 C6
Trevowah Rd TR8 ....43 D3

Trevozah Cross PL15 ..28 B8
Trevu Ho TR14 ......138 E1
Trevu Rd TR14 ......138 E2
Trevurvas La TR13 ....90 C3
Trewall Hill PL11 .....64 D5
Trewans Terr TR15 ...140 A6
Trewardreva Cross TR11 .92 E4
Trewarlett Cross PL15 .28 A7
Trewartha Cl TR26 ...141 D1
Trewartha Ct 2 PL14 .113 C6
Trewartha Est TR26 ..141 D1
Trewartha Flats TR26 .141 D1
Trewartha Rd TR26 ...90 C3
Trewartha Terr 18 TR18 .143 E6
Trewarton Rd TR10 ...81 D2
Trewarveneth Farm Cotts
  TR18 ....88 C2
Trewarveneth St TR18 .143 C2
Trewassa Flats PL32 ..15 F5
Trewavas Cres TR13 ..146 C5
Trewavas Rd TR18 ...143 C1
Treweath Rd TR18 ...143 D7
Treweege Row TR3 ...80 E4
Treweeks Rd TR19 ....75 A1
Treweese Cross PL14 .52 B7
Treweese Rd
  Menheniot PL14 .....52 B7
  Quethiock PL14 .....52 B8
Trewellard Hill TR19 ..87 A8
Trewellard Rd TR19 ..86 F8
Trewelloe Rd TR20 ...90 C3
Trewelm La TR16 .....68 E1
Trewen Rd TR11 .....144 C1
Trewen Terr TR11 ....144 C2
Trewern La TR20 .....87 E6
Trewetha Farm Lodges
  PL29 ....22 E7
Trewetha La PL29 ....22 E7
Trewey Hill TR 26 ....76 B4
Trewhella La TR20 ...89 F7
Trewhella Terr TR20 ..90 A6
Trewhiddle Rd PL25 ..114 C4
Trewidden Cl TR1 ....137 E5
Trewidden Ct TR1 ....137 E5
Trewidden Rd TR26 ..141 B5
Trewidland Prim Sch
  PL14 ....51 C3
Trewince TR11 ....93 B3
Trewince La
  Grampound Road TR2 ..57 E1
  Lostwithiel PL22 ....112 C3
  Porth Navas TR11 ...93 B3
Trewince Manor TR2 ..95 C6
Trewince Terr 2 TR18 .143 C1
Trewince Villas TR7 ...32 E6
Trewinnard Ct TR1 ...137 B6
Trewinnard Gr TR1 ...137 B6
Trewinnard La TR27 ..77 E1
Trewinnard Rd TR1 ...81 D5
Trewinnick Council Hos
  PL27 ....32 A5
Trewinnick Rd PL27 ..32 A5
Trewinnow Cross PL15 .27 D6
Trewint Cres PL13 ...117 D4
Trewint Est PL14 .....52 A5
Trewint La Landrake PL12 .53 B2
  Rock PL27 ....21 D3
Trewint Rd PL14 .....52 A6
Trewirgie Hill TR15 ..140 B3
Trewirgie Inf Sch TR15 .140 B4
Trewirgie Jun Sch TR15 .140 B4
Trewirgie Rd TR15 ...140 B4
Trewirgie Vean TR15 .140 B4
Trewiston La PL27 ....21 E3
Trewithan Gdns PL12 .112 C2
Trewithen Gdns* TR1 .71 E6
Trewithen Parc TR8 ..56 B7
Trewithen Rd TR18 ...143 D5
Trewithen Terr TR13 ..90 D5
Trewithy Dr PL6 .....124 F1
Trewollock Cl PL26 ...85 C5
Trewollock La PL26 ...85 C5
Trewoon Rd PL25 ....99 B2
Treworder Terr 6 PL14 .38 E4
Treworder Cl PL27 ...108 F5
Treworder Rd TR1 ....137 B3
Treworgan Ct TR4 ....56 D1
Treworlis Cl TR13 ....146 D8
Treworthal Rd TR3 ...81 D5
Treworvenneth Dr 9
  TR17 ....89 C5
Trewrickle La PL11 ...65 A5
Trewyn Flats 41 TR26 .141 B6
Treyarnon Bay YH*
  PL28 ....20 B1
Treyew Pl TR16 ......80 F8
Treyew Rd TR1 ......137 B3
Treyew Sch TR1 .....137 A4
Treza Rd TR13 ....91 A1
Trezaise Ave PL26 ...47 A2
Trezaise Cl PL26 .....47 A2
Trezaise Rd PL26 ....46 F2
Trezela Rd TR18 .....143 C2
Trinity Cl Bere Alston PL20 .41 B1
  Carnkie TR16 ....80 C2
Trinity House National
  Lighthouse Ctr* TR18 .143 F5
Trinity St PL25 ......114 C3
Trinity Way PL19 ....147 A4
Tripp Hill PL14 ......36 F2
Trispen Hill TR4 .....56 D1
Trolver Hill TR3 .....82 B6
Trolvus Vean TR10 ...81 A1
Troon Com Prim Sch
  TR14 ....79 E4
Troon Moor TR14 ....79 E4

Troon Row TR13 .....90 F3
Troubridge Rd TR13 ..146 C4
Trowbridge Cl PL5 ...124 C4
Troy Ct PL23 ....116 C4
Truck Hill TR2 ....71 B6
Trungle Parc TR19 ...88 C2
Trungle Terr TR19 ...88 C2
Trunglemoor Cotts TR19 .88 C2
Truro Coll TR1 ....69 E3
Truro Dr PL5 ....124 A5
Truro High Sch for Girls
  TR1 ....137 C3
Truro Rd TR10 ......144 C8
Truro La TR10 ......144 C8
Truro Rd Lanivet PL30 .47 F7
  St Austell PL25 .....114 A2
  St Austell PL25 .....114 B3
Truro Sch TR1 ......137 C3
Truro Sta TR1 ......137 B4
Truro Vean Terr TR1 .137 D5
Truthwall La TR19 ...86 F7
Tryhall Com Prim Sch
  TR 20 ....76 B1
Trythogga Hill TR18 ..143 F8
Trythogga Rd TR18 ..143 F8
Tubbon Hill TR3 .....81 A4
Tucker Cl PL5 ....127 F8
Tuckers Cl TR8 ......111 B4
Tuckingmill Terr TR13 .91 E4
Tudor Cl PL9 ....135 E5
Tudor Ct PL12 ......123 A2
Tudor Lodge Holiday Pk
  TR20 ....89 C7
Tuke Cl TR11 ....144 E5
Turbill Gdns 4 PL7 ..131 B5
Turf St PL31 ....109 C5
Turfdown Rd PL30 ...48 E8
Turnavean Rd PL25 ..114 A5
Turnaware Rd TR11 ..144 C2
Turnpike TR13 ......146 C7
Turnpike Hill 2 TR17 .89 C5
Turnpike Pl PL14 ....113 B4
Turnpike Rd
  Connor Downs TR27 ..78 C6
  Marazion TR17 ......89 C5
Turnpike The TR19 ...86 F6
Turnquay PL9 ....135 C7
Turret Gr PL4 ....128 F4
Tuxton Cl PL7 ....131 C3
Twelvewoods Cl PL14 .50 E8
Twelvewoods Pl PL14 .50 E8
Two Hills Pk PL12 ...122 C2
Two Trees PL27 ......108 B4
Two Trees Rd PL22 ..112 F1
Tyacke Rd TR13 .....146 B5
Tybesta TR2 ....72 A7
Tye Hill Cl PL25 .....59 A3
Tyland Rd PL32 .....105 F4
Tylney Cl PL6 ....125 B6
Tyndale Cl PL5 ......124 B1
Tyngham Pl TR26 ....77 E4
Tyngham Rd TR26 ...77 E4
Tyngham Row TR26 ..77 E4
Tyshute La PL14 .....59 A1
Tything Wlk 4 PL3 ...128 E6
Tywardreath Highway
  PL24 ....60 C6
Tywardreath Hill PL24 .60 C4
Tywardreath Sch PL24 .60 C6
Tywarnhale Way TR4 .68 A6
Tywarnhayle Rd TR6 ..55 A5

U

Uglow Cl TR14 ......138 C3
Ulalia Rd TR7 ....110 F6
Ullswater Cres PL6 ...124 E4
Umfulla Pl 13 TR26 ..141 B5
Under Chapel Yd TR18 .143 F4
Under La PL15 ......18 C3
Under Rd Boscastle PL35 ..9 C1
  Bridgerule EX22 .....8 A3
  Gunnislake PL18 ....41 A6
Undercliff TR27 ......142 D7
Undercliff Rd PL9 ...135 E4
Underhayes La PL15 ..106 A8
Underhill Rd PL3 ....128 A4
Underhill Villas PL3 ..128 A3
Underlane Boyton PL15 ..13 A3
  Marhamchurch EX23 ..7 B6
  Plymouth, Plympton PL7 .130 C4
  Plymouth, Plymstock PL9 .135 E6
Underways PL20 .....41 B1
Underwood Rd PL7 ..130 B6
Unicorn Cl PL7 ......130 B6
Union Cnr TR11 .....144 D5
Union Hill
  St Columb Major TR9 ..45 E6
  6 Stratton EX23 ....4 D1
  Truro TR1 ....70 C5
Union Pl Fowey PL23 .116 D4
  Plymouth PL1 ......148 A2
  Truro TR1 ....137 D5
Union Rd TR1 ....144 D6
Union Sq TR9 ....45 E6
Union St Camborne TR14 .138 D2
  27 Penzance TR18 ..143 E5
  Plymouth PL1 ......148 A2
  Truro TR1 ....137 C5
Unit Hos PL27 ......33 B5
United Downs Ind Pk
  TR16 ....81 A8
United Rd TR16 .....80 F8
Unity Cl PL6 ....125 D5
Unity Rd TR13 ......98 C8
Univ of Plymouth PL1,
  PL4 ....148 C3

Univ of Plymouth
  (Cookworthy Bldg)
  PL4 ....149 A3
Univ of Plymouth Bsns Sch
  PL4 ....148 C4
Univ of Plymouth The Hoe
  Ctr PL1 ....148 C2
Upcott Cross EX39 ....2 C1
Upland Cl TR1 ....137 F6
Upland Cres TR1 ....137 E6
Upland Dr PL6 ......125 A5
Uplands Saltash PL12 .122 E1
  Tavistock PL19 ......147 A4
Uplands Vean TR1 ...137 F5
Upper Castle Rd TR1 .95 A6
Upper Chapel PL15 ..106 A4
Upper Dobbin Cl PL28 .20 F2
Upper Dobbin La PL28 .20 F2
Upper Eastcliffe Rd PL24 60 D4
Upper Hillcrest 8 TR6 .55 A4
Upper Knollys Terrace La
  PL3 ....128 C4
Upper Ridings PL7 ...131 B7
Upper School La TR1 .137 C3
Upper Tredrea TR1 ...81 D5
Upperton La PL6 ....121 F3
Upton Cl PL3 ....129 B7
Upton Cross EX23 ...104 C2
Upton Cross Prim Sch
  PL14 ....38 C2
Upton Mdws EX23 ...104 C3
Upton Terr EX23 ....104 C3
Urban Terr PL17 ....39 F5
Uxbridge Dr PL5 ....123 E4
Uzella Pk PL22 ......112 C2

V

Vaagso Cl PL1 ......127 C1
Valency Row PL35 ....9 C2
Valentine Row 4 PL17 .39 E4
Valiant Ave PL5 .....124 A4
Vallard's La PL12 ....53 E4
Valletort Flats PL1 ..128 A2
Valletort Ho PL1 ....148 C3
Valletort La PL1 ....128 A3
Valletort Pl PL1 ....128 A2
Valletort Rd PL1 ....128 A3
Valley Cl Goonhavern TR4 .55 C3
  Truro TR1 ....69 F3
Valley Gdns 20 TR16 ..67 E4
Valley La TR3 ....81 F7
Valley Park La PL26 ..73 C3
Valley Rd Bude EX23 ..104 E5
  Carbis Bay TR26 ....141 C2
  Mevagissey PL26 ...73 C4
Valley The TR19 .....96 E3
Valley View Bodmin PL31 .109 C3
  19 Illogan TR16 ....67 E4
  Liskeard PL14 ......51 A4
  Plymouth PL6 ......125 D7
  Redruth TR16 ......140 E1
  St Teath PL30 ......23 E7
  Wadebridge PL27 ...108 C4
Valley View Cl PL3 ..129 B6
Valley View Dr TR1 ..69 F3
Valley View Rd PL3 ..129 B7
Valley View Terr TR3 .81 B5
Valley Wlk PL6 .....125 C6
Vanguard Cl PL5 ....124 D1
Vapron Rd PL3 ......128 F6
Vardun Terr PL14 ...113 B5
Varfell La TR20 .....89 A7
Varley La PL14 ......113 B5
Varley Terr 1 PL14 ..113 B5
Vauban Pl PL2 ......127 F4
Vaughan Cl PL2 .....128 C7
Vauxhall Ct 11 PL4 ..149 A2
Vauxhall St PL4 .....149 A2
Vauxhall Street Flats 19
  PL4 ....149 A2
Vean Rd PL14 ......138 E2
Vean Terr TR14 .....138 E2
Vear Ho TR14 ......138 D2
Vellan Cl TR14 .....79 B5
Vellan Parc Ave TR27 .78 C5
Vellan Vrane TR27 ...78 C5
Vellandrucia TR3 ....80 E7
Vellanhoggan Mews
  TR18 ....88 C6
Venland Cl 9 PL14 ...38 A3
Venn Cl 6 PL3 ......128 E6
Venn Cres PL3 ......128 E6
Venn Ct PL3 ....128 E6
Venn Gdns PL3 .....128 E6
Venn Gr PL3 ....128 E6
Venn Hill PL19 ......29 C6
Venn La PL2,PL3 ....128 E6
Venn Way PL3 ......128 E7
Venslooe Hill PL14 ..113 B7
Ventnor Terr TR26 ..141 A6
Venton Cl PL15 .....18 B8
Venton East Sq TR19 .86 F6
Venton Lace Rd TR2 ..57 C2
Venton Rd
  Falmouth TR11 .....144 C4
  St Ives TR26 ....141 C3
Ventonleague Hill TR27 142 E7
Ventonleague Row
  TR27 ....142 E7
Ventonraze TR16 ....67 E4
Ventonraze Terr 2 TR16 .67 E4
Veor Rd TR7 ....111 C2
Vermont Gdns PL2 ..127 F7
Verna Pl PL5 ....123 D2

Verna Rd PL5 ....123 C2
Vernigo Cross PL12 ..40 B1
Vernon Pl TR11 .....145 B4
Vernon Villas PL24 ..60 B4
Viaduct Hill TR27 ...142 E6
Viaduct La TR14 ....138 A1
Vicarage Cl
  Budock Water TR11 .144 C3
  Menheniot PL14 ....51 F5
Vicarage Gdns
  Milton Abbot PL19 ..29 C6
  Plymouth PL5 ......123 B1
Vicarage Hill
  Budock Water TR11 .144 C3
  Mevagissey PL26 ...73 C4
  10 St Austell PL25 ..114 C4
  St Day TR16 ....68 E1
  Tintagel PL34 ......14 C7
Vicarage La Lelant TR26 .77 E4
  Manaccan TR12 ....101 A8
  Poundstock EX23 ...6 F2
Vicarage Mdw PL23 ..116 C4
Vicarage Rd Bude EX23 .104 D5
  Par PL24 ....60 D5
  Plymouth PL7 ......130 C6
  Porthleven TR13 ...91 A1
  St Agnes TR5 ......54 D1
  Torpoint PL11 ......127 B2
Vicarage Row TR13 ..90 F3
Vicarage Terr TR11 ..92 F4
Victoria Ave PL1 ....148 A4
Victoria Bsns Pk PL26 .47 A4
Victoria Cl PL14 .....113 C6
Victoria Cotts
  Falmouth TR11 .....145 B3
  Plymouth PL6 ......129 B8
Victoria Ct 16 TR18 ..143 E6
Victoria Gdns
  St Columb Road TR9 .45 E2
  Threemilestone TR3 ..69 D3
Victoria La TR12 ....122 F2
Victoria Mews 18 TR18 .143 E6
Victoria Pk PL27 ....108 D6
Victoria Pl
  31 Penzance TR18 ..143 E5
  Plymouth PL1 ......148 A2
  9 St Austell PL25 ..114 C3
  12 St Ives TR26 ...141 B6
Victoria Quay
  Falmouth TR11 .....145 B5
  Truro TR1 ....70 D1
Victoria Rd Bude EX23 .104 D7
  Camelford PL32 ....105 E4
  Plymouth PL5 ......123 D2
  Roche PL26 ....46 F3
  St Austell PL25 .....114 C3
  11 St Ives TR26 ....141 B6
  Threemilestone TR3 ..69 D3
Victoria Road Prim Sch
  PL5 ....123 D1
Victoria Row TR16 ..86 E6
Victoria Sq Bodmin PL31 .109 F3
  17 Penzance TR18 ..143 E5
  Truro TR1 ....137 C4
Victoria St
  Camborne TR14 ....138 D2
  St Columb Major TR9 .45 E6
  Torpoint PL11 ......127 B3
Victoria Terr
  4 Liskeard PL14 ...113 B5
  Nanpean PL26 .....58 D6
  Plymouth PL4 ......148 C4
  Portscatho TR2 ....83 B2
  St Breward PL30 ...24 B3
Victory Rd EX22 ....13 A8
Victory St PL2 ......127 C6
Vigo Mews PL19 ....147 C6
Vigobridge Rd PL19 ..147 C6
Villa Marina TR17 ...89 B5
Village Dr PL6 ......121 C1
Village Farm Cl EX23 ..7 B6
Village The
  Buckland Monachorum PL20 41 F3
  Duloe PL14 ....51 A1
Villiers Cl PL9 ......135 D7
Vincent Way PL12 ...122 F2
Vine Cres PL2 ......128 B6
Vine Gdns PL2 .....128 B6
Vine Pl 10 PL24 .....60 D5
Vinefield Ct TR11 ...145 B7
Vinery La PL7,PL9 ...130 E1
Vineyard The TR3 ...80 F3
Vingoe's La TR20 ...88 B7
Vinstone Way PL5 ...123 D1
Violet Dr PL6 ....125 E8
Violet La PL19 ......147 E6
Virgin Hill TR17 ....89 C6
Virgin St 26 TR26 ...141 B6
Virginia Gdns PL2 ...127 F7
Visicks Works TR3 ...81 E6
Vivian Cl TR7 ....110 E5
Vivian Ct TR1 ....137 D3
Vivian Pk TR14 .....138 F2
Vivian Rd PL31 .....109 B4
Vixen Tor Cl PL20 ...42 C3
Vogue Hill TR16 ....68 D1
Vogue Terr TR16 ....68 D1
Vorfield Cl TR15 ....140 B6
Vosporth Hill TR8 ...110 A3
Voss Rd PL12 ....53 E1
Vounder Glaze TR19 .86 E6
Voundervour La 20
  TR18 ....143 E5

Vyvyan Dr TR8 ....44 E3
Vyvyan Pl TR13 ....146 C5
Vyvyan St TR14 ....138 D3
Vyvyan's Terr TR14 ...79 B2

W

Waddon Cl PL7 ....130 E7
Wadebridge Com Prim Sch
PL27 ....108 C6
Wadebridge Rd
St Tudy PL30 ....23 E3
Wadebridge PL30 ......34 C8
Wadebridge Sch PL27 .108 D6
Wadeland Terr 3 PL14 .51 A7
Wadham Cl 4 PL14 ...113 C5
Wadham Dr PL14 .....113 D5
Wadham Ho 5 PL14 ..113 C5
Wadham Rd PL14 .....113 D5
Wadham Terr 6 PL2 ..128 A5
Wagg La TR2 ....71 C6
Waggon Hill PL7 .....131 A4
Wain Pk PL7 ....130 F4
Wainsway TR6 ....55 A4
Wainways EX23 ....10 F6
Wake St PL4 ....148 B4
Wakefield Ave PL5 ...123 E1
Walcot Cl PL6 ....125 E3
Waldon Cl PL7 ....131 B6
Walk The PL15 ....106 C6
Walker Lines Ind Est
PL31 ....48 D8
Walker Terr PL1 .....148 B1
Walkham Bsns Pk PL5 .124 E1
Walkham Cl PL19 ....147 D5
Walkham Mdws PL2 ...42 C4
Walkhampton Rd PL20 .42 C4
Walkhampton Wlk PL6 125 E1
Wall Gdns TR27 ......78 E3
Wall Rd TR27 ....78 E3
Wall Vean TR27 ......78 E3
Wallace Mews 1 PL1 109 D5
Wallace Rd Bodmin PL31 109 D5
Plymouth PL7 ....131 A4
Wallpark Cl PL7 .....130 F7
Walnut Cl PL7 ....131 B5
Walnut Dr PL7 ....131 C5
Walnut Gdns PL7 ....131 C5
Walreddon Cl PL19 ..147 B4
Walsingham Ct PL7 ..131 B6
Walsingham Pl 15 TR1 137 D4
Walters La PL15 ......18 C1
Walters Rd PL5 ......123 C2
Waltham Pl PL2 .....128 A8
Walton Cres PL5 ....124 C1
Wandle Pl PL3 ....129 D5
Wansford Mdw PL26 ..85 C5
Wanstead Gr PL5 ....124 A4
Wantage Gdns PL1 ..148 A3
Warbstow Com Prim Sch
PL15 ....11 B1
Warburton Gdns PL5 123 C1
Ward Cl 4 EX23 ....4 D1
Ward Pl PL3 ....129 B5
Wardlow Cl PL6 .....128 F8
Wardlow Gdns PL6 ..128 F8
Warfelton Cres PL12 122 C2
Warfelton Gdns PL12 122 C2
Warfelton Terr PL12 122 C2
Waring Rd PL12 .....124 D7
Warleigh Ave PL2 ...127 C5
Warleigh Cres PL6 ..124 F5
Warleigh La PL2 .....127 C5
Warleigh Rd 1 PL4 ..128 E4
Warmwell Rd PL5 ...123 E4
Warne La PL19 ......147 C5
Warne Rd TR9 ....45 F2
Warne The PL13 ......62 E1
Warrens Field PL32 .105 D5
Warspite Gdns PL5 ..124 D2
Warton Cl PL5 ....124 D3
Warwick Ave Illogan TR16 67 D4
Plymouth PL5 ....124 D3
Warwick Cres 5 PL27 .31 C5
Warwick Orchard Cl
PL5 ....124 B3
Warwick Rd EX23 ...104 E4
Wasdale Cl PL6 .....125 D2
Wasdale Gdns PL6 ..125 D2
Washbourne Cl PL1 .127 E3
Water La Crantock TR8 .110 A3
Delabole PL33 ....14 E3
Golant PL23 ....61 B5
Hayle TR27 ....142 B3
St Agnes TR5 ....54 D1
Water's Edge PL28 ..107 E6
Water-Ma-Trout TR13 146 C8
Watergate Bay Holiday Pk
TR8 ....44 D8
Watergate La PL30 ...34 C8
Watergate Rd TR8 ...44 C6
Watering Hill Cl PL25 114 E3
Waterings Rd TR11 ...82 A2

Waterloo TR1 ....137 E4
Waterloo Cl
Plymouth PL1 ....128 A2
St Mawes TR2 ....95 A6
Waterloo Ct PL1 ....128 A2
Waterloo Rd TR11 ...145 B4
Waterloo St
Plymouth PL4 ....149 A4
Plymouth, Stoke PL1 .128 A3
Waterloo Yard Flats
PL1 ....128 A2
Waters Edge TR7 ....110 A6
Waterscape Cl PL25 .114 B4
Watersmead Parc TR11 144 C3
Watery La Bodmin PL31 109 D5
Milton Combe PL6 ...120 D6
Watson Gdns PL4 ...149 B3
Watson Pl PL4 ......149 B2
Watts Park Rd PL2 ..128 C7
Watts Rd PL19 ......147 B5
Watts' Rd PL4 ......149 C3
Waveney Gdns PL5 ..124 C3
Waverley Rd PL5 ....123 D2
Wavish Pk PL11 .....126 E3
Waycott Wlk PL6 ....124 D6
Wayfield Rd TR11 ....82 B2
Wayside Ct TR7 .....111 A4
Wayside Folk Mus ★
TR 26 ....76 B5
Wearde Rd PL12 ....122 E1
Webb St PL23 ....116 D4
Webber Hill TR11 ...145 B4
Webber St TR11 .....145 B4
Wedgewood Rd PL25 .115 A4
Weeth TR14 ....138 C3
Weeth Com Prim Sch
TR14 ....138 C4
Weeth La TR14 .....138 C3
Weeth Rd TR14 .....138 C4
Weethes Cotts 6 TR18 143 D5
Weir Cl PL6 ....125 F2
Weir Gdns PL6 ......125 F2
Weir Rd PL6 ....125 F2
Welaby Terr PL14 ....37 F3
Welbeck Ave PL4 ...148 C4
Welcome Cross EX39 ..3 B4
Welcome Cl TR4 ......56 D1
Well Gdns PL1 ......148 B3
Well La Constantine TR11 92 F4
Falmouth TR11 .....145 B4
Goldsithney TR20 ....89 C5
Liskeard PL14 ......113 C6
Looe PL13 ....117 C3
St Buryan TR19 ......97 E5
St Cleer PL14 ....37 F3
St Keverne TR12 ...101 D4
Tregony TR2 ....71 F3
Tremar PL14 ....38 A3
Welcombe EX39 ......2 E5
Well Mdw PL14 ......18 A5
Well Park Rd PL11 ..127 B3
Well St Callington PL17 .39 E4
Par PL24 ....60 D5
Tregony TR2 ....71 F3
Well Way TR7 ....111 C7
Welland Gdns PL3 ..129 C5
Weller Ct TR11 .....145 B3
Wellfield Cl
Coad's Green PL15 ...27 D3
Plymouth PL7 ....131 C5
Wellhay Cl PL9 .....136 C6
Wellington Ct TR14 138 C3
Wellington Gdns TR11 145 B4
Wellington Pl
Falmouth TR11 .....145 B4
Penzance TR18 .....143 D5
Wadebridge PL27 ...108 C5
Wellington Plantation
TR3 ....82 B7
Wellington Rd
Camborne TR14 ....138 D3
Porthleven TR13 .....91 B1
St Dennis PL26 ......58 C8
2 St Eval PL27 ....31 F3
Wellington St
Plymouth PL4 ....149 A4
Plymouth, Stoke PL1 .128 A3
Torpoint PL11 ......127 B3
Wellington Terr
Falmouth TR11 .....145 B4
Porthleven TR13 .....91 B1
Portscatho TR2 ......83 B2
2 Truro TR1 ....137 C4
Wellpark Rd PL18 ...40 F5
Wells Ct PL10 ......132 E4
Wellsbourne Pk PL3 129 A6
Welman Rd PL10 ....132 F6
Welsford Ave PL2 ..127 F5
Welway TR6 ....55 A4
Wembury Park Rd PL3 128 D6
Wembury Pl PL9 ....136 A4
Wendron CE Prim Sch
TR13 ....91 F5
Wendron St TR13 ...146 C6
Wenlock Gdns PL2 ..128 B8
Wensum Cl PL7 .....131 A4
Wentwood Gdns PL6 125 E3
Wentwood Pl PL6 ...125 E3
Wentworth Cl
Lynstone EX23 ......104 C3
Polzeath PL27 ....21 D5
Wentworth Pl PL14 .129 B2
Wentworth Way PL12 122 C2
Werrington Dr PL7 ..39 E4
Werrington Prim Sch
PL15 ....18 F7

Wesley Ave PL3 .....128 E5
Wesley Cl Kelly Bray PL17 .39 F6
Stenalees PL26 ......59 C8
Wesley Cottage ★ PL15 .26 B7
Wesley Ct Penryn TR10 144 C8
Pensilva PL14 ....38 D4
Torpoint PL11 ......127 C3
Wesley La PL12 .....122 F2
Wesley Pl
5 Newlyn TR18 .....143 C2
Plymouth, Mutley PL3 128 E5
1 Plymouth, Stoke PL2 .128 A4
St Austell PL25 .....114 C3
7 St Ives TR26 .....141 B5
Wesley Rd Cubert TR8 .55 D8
Pensilva PL14 ....38 D4
Saltash PL12 ....122 D4
Wesley St
Camborne TR14 ....138 E3
11 Heamoor TR18 ...143 C7
Redruth TR15 ......140 C5
Wesley Terr Bugle PL26 .47 C2
Looe PL13 ....117 D4
Wesley Way PL15 ...26 B7
Wesley Yd TR7 .....110 C6
West Ave 4 PL19 ...147 B5
West Beach Rd TR4 .68 A6
West Beckon Cl EX23 ..2 D1
West Bridge Rd PL15 106 B7
West Camps Bay PL11 .64 C4
West Charles St TR14 138 D2
West Cl TR13 ....146 D7
West Cliff TR4 ....68 A6
West Cnr 1 TR3 .....81 F7
West Cornwall Hospl
TR18 ....143 D6
West Ct TR7 ....110 C6
West Devon Bsns Pk
PL19 ....147 B3
West Down Cl PL13 .117 C4
West Down Rd PL2 ..128 B6
West End Goldsithney TR20 89 E5
Marazion TR17 ......89 B5
Pentewan PL26 ......73 C6
Redruth TR15 ......140 B4
St Day TR16 ....68 D1
West End Cl TR10 ...144 C8
West End Cotts PL11 .64 B8
West End Ct 2 PL11 .140 B4
West End Sq 7 PL17 .39 E4
West Fairholme Rd
EX23 ....104 E3
West Hill St Austell PL25 .114 C3
Wadebridge PL27 ...108 A6
West Hill Rd PL4 ...128 E4
West Hoe Rd PL1 ...148 B1
West Kitty TR5 ......54 C1
West La Crafthole PL11 .65 B5
Delabole PL33 ....14 E2
Landrake PL12 ......53 B3
West Looe Hill PL13 117 B3
West Looe Sq PL13 .117 C3
West Malling Ave PL5 123 E5
West Park Dr PL7 ...131 C5
West Park Est PL27 108 D5
West Park Hill PL7 ..131 B7
West Park Prim Sch
PL5 ....124 A2
West Park Rd EX23 .104 D7
West Pentire Rd TR8 .43 D3
West Pk Liskeard PL14 .51 C3
Perranwell Sta TR3 ..81 C6
Redruth TR15 ......139 F6
13 St Columb Major TR9 45 E6
Tideford PL12 ....52 F2
West Pl Falmouth TR11 145 A3
St Just TR19 ....86 E6
West Porthmear Cotts
PL25 ....115 B2
West Rd Looe PL13 .117 C4
Quintrell Downs TR8 .111 B3
West Rise TR11 .....144 F3
West St Grimscott EX23 ..5 B1
Liskeard PL14 ......113 B6
Millbrook PL10 .....132 E5
Penryn TR10 ....144 C8
Polruan PL23 ....116 C2
St Columb Major TR9 .45 E6
Tavistock PL19 .....147 B5
West Tehidy TR14 ..138 F7
West Terr Hayle TR27 142 B6
Newlyn TR18 ....143 C3
West Tolgus TR15 ..139 D8
West Trevingey TR15 140 A3
West Trewirgie Rd
TR15 ....140 B4
West View
Porthleven TR13 .....91 A1
Tavistock PL19 .....147 E2
Trevone PL28 ....21 E2
West View Rd 5 PL20 .41 B1
West Villas TR8 .....57 B7
West Week Cl EX22 ..11 E8
West Wharf PL26 ....73 C3
Westborne Hts TR11 140 B3
Westborne Rd TR14 138 B4
Westbourne Dr PL25 114 B3
Westbourne La PL14 113 B6
Westbourne Rd PL3 128 D5
Westbourne Terr
Fraddon TR9 ....57 D8
Saltash PL12 ....122 D4
Westbridge Cotts PL19 147 B4
Westbridge Rd PL19 .59 A3
Westbridge Ind Est 3
PL19 ....147 B4
Westbury Cl PL5 ....124 B4
Westby Rd EX23 ....104 E5

Westcombe Cres PL9 .135 D5
Westcott PL27 ......108 A6
Westcott Cl PL6 ....129 A8
Westcountry Cl PL2 127 F7
Westcroft Rd PL5 ...129 E5
Westdown Rd PL33 ...14 D2
Westella Rd PL20 ...42 D2
Westend Terr TR10 .144 C8
Westeria Terr PL12 ..128 C7
Westerlands Rd PL27 108 A6
Western App PL1 ...148 B2
Western Ave 6 PL14 .51 A7
Western College Rd
PL4 ....128 E5
Western Dr PL3 ....129 A4
Western Pl PL10 ...144 B8
Western Promenade Rd
TR18 ....143 E4
Western Rd PL15 ...106 A5
Western Terr
Falmouth TR11 .....145 A3
Launceston PL15 ...106 B5
Western Wood Way
PL7 ....131 D5
Westfield PL7 ....131 A6
Westfield Ave PL9 ..135 C6
Westgate St PL15 ...106 C5
Westground Way PL34 .14 C7
Westhampnett Pl PL5 123 F4
Westhays Cl PL9 ....135 F4
Westhead Rd PL10 ...64 B3
Westheath Ave PL30,
PL31 ....109 B3
Westheath Rd PL31 109 B3
Westlake Cl PL9 ....135 F4
Westlake Dr
Bere Alston PL20 ....41 B1
Plymouth PL9 ......136 B2
Westmoor Cl PL7 ...131 C6
Westmoor Cres TR3 ..81 D6
Westmoor Pk PL19 .147 C4
Weston Mill Com Prim Sch
PL2 ....127 E7
Weston Mill Dr PL5 127 F8
Weston Mill Hill PL5 123 F1
Weston Mill La PL5 124 A1
Weston Mill Rd PL5 123 E1
Weston Park Rd PL3 128 D6
Westover Rd PL17 ...39 E4
Westpark PL27 .....108 E4
Westward PL27 ......21 D5
Westward Rd TR26 141 A6
Westways PL9 ......135 B5
Westwinds PL32 ....16 A4
Westwood PL14 ....113 B6
Westwood Ave PL6 .125 C6
Wetherham La PL30 ..23 E3
Wharf Rd Penzance TR18 143 F5
St Ives TR26 ....141 B6
Wharf The
21 Mousehole TR19 ..88 C1
St Ives TR26 ....141 B6
Wharfside 8 TR18 ..143 E5
Wharfside Village 9
TR18 ....143 E5
Wheal TR6 ....55 B5
Wheal Agar TR15 ...139 C4
Wheal Alfred Rd TR27 142 F5
Wheal Bull PL26 .....58 D5
Wheal Busy La TR4 ..68 F3
Wheal Catherine Cl TR6 .55 B5
Wheal Dream TR26 .141 C6
Wheal Eliza Cl PL25 115 A5
Wheal Fortune La TR15 139 D6
Wheal Friendly La TR5 .54 C2
Wheal Gerry TR14 ..138 E4
Wheal Golden Dr TR8 .43 C1
Wheal Gorland Rd TR16 68 D1
Wheal Harmony Terr
TR15 ....140 B7
Wheal Jane Mdws TR3 .69 C3
Wheal Jewel (Gipsy Site)
TR16 ....68 E1
Wheal Kitty TR5 .....54 D1
Wheal Kitty La TR5 ..54 D1
Wheal Leisure TR6 ..55 A5
Wheal Leisure Cl 16 TR6 .55 A5
Wheal Margery TR26 141 C3
Wheal Maria Cotts PL19 .29 C1
Wheal Martyn Mus ★
PL26 ....59 B6
Wheal Northey PL25 115 B5
Wheal Quoit Ave TR5 .54 C1
Wheal Regent Pk PL25 115 A4
Wheal Rodney Holiday Bglws
TR17 ....89 C6
Wheal Rose 19 TR13 .98 C8
Wheal Silver TR15 .140 C5
Wheal Speed Rd TR26 141 C2
Wheal Tehidy La TR15 139 E6
Wheal Trefusis TR15 140 C6
Wheal Venture Rd TR26 141 C3
Wheal View PL26 ....58 B4
Wheal Vor TR15 ....140 D3
Wheal Vyvyan TR11 ..92 F4
Wheal Whidden TR26 141 C2
Wheal-An-Wens TR17 .89 C5
Wheatfield Cres TR7 .111 A4
Wheatridge PL7 ....130 B7
Wheel Ayr Terr TR26 141 A6
Wheeler Higman Cl PL26 59 C7
Wheelwright Ct PL20 .42 E4
Wherry Pl PL23 ....116 D2
Wherry Way PL14 ...50 E7
Whieldon Rd PL25 ..115 A4
Whimple St PL1 ....148 C2
Whin Bank Rd PL5 ..124 E2
Whipsiderry Cl PL27 .44 C6
Whistley Down PL20 .42 B2
Whitby Cres PL6 ...125 A1

Whitby Rd PL6 .....125 A1
Whitchurch Prim Sch
PL19 ....147 D2
Whitchurch Rd
Horrabridge PL20 ...42 C5
Tavistock PL19 .....147 C3
Whitcross Hill TR15 139 C3
White Cross Cury TR12 .99 A3
Redruth TR16 ....68 C3
White Cross Ct PL4 149 A3
White Hart Arc The
PL15 ....106 C5
White Horse TR13 ...91 A6
White House Cl TR26 141 C2
White La PL1 ....149 A2
White Lodge EX23 ..10 C7
White Smock Mdw 7
PL35 ....9 C1
White Walls Ct 16 TR6 .55 A5
White's Cl 3 TR5 ....54 C1
Whiteacres Holiday Pk
TR8 ....45 B3
Whitebarrow Cotts TR14 .37 A4
Whitecroft Way EX23 ..5 A6
Whitecross Blisland PL30 .35 D7
Fowey PL23 ....116 F6
Whitecross Ind Est TR8 ..45 B2
Whitefield Terr PL4 149 A4
Whiteford Rd PL3 ..128 C6
Whitefriars La PL4 .149 B3
Whitegate PL26 .....58 B8
Whitegate Mdws PL26 .58 B8
Whitegate Rd TR7 ..111 A6
Whitegate Sh Ctr TR7 111 A6
Whitehall Bgws PL30 ..23 B2
Whitehall Dr
9 Bere Alston PL20 ..41 B1
Plymouth PL9 ......136 B2
Whitehall Est PL30 ..23 B2
Whitehill Cross PL15 ..19 C6
Whitehill Terr TR13 146 C4
Whitemoor Prim Sch
PL26 ....58 E8
Whiterock Cl PL27 .108 B5
Whiterock Rd PL27 108 B5
Whiterock Terr PL27 108 B5
Whiterocks Pk PL18 ..40 D6
Whitestone Cres PL31 109 C3
Whitestone Rd PL31 109 C3
Whitham Pk PL19 ..147 C4
Whitleigh Ave PL5 ..124 E2
Whitleigh Cotts PL5 124 E2
Whitleigh Ct PL5 ...124 D4
Whitleigh Gn PL5 ..124 C4
Whitleigh Prim Sch
PL5 ....124 D4
Whitleigh Villas PL5 124 E2
Whitleigh Way PL5 124 C4
Whitley Cl TR1 .....137 D4
Whitley Grange PL14 113 A6
Whitpot Hill PL12 ...64 F8
Whitsam Cross PL20 .41 A1
Whitsand Bay View PL11 .65 A4
Whitson Cross PL5 ..124 C7
Whitsoncross La PL5 124 C7
Whitstone Com Prim Sch
EX22 ....7 F1
Whitstone Head Sch EX22 .7 F1
Whittington St PL3 148 B4
Whitworth Cl TR5 ...54 C1
Whity Cross PL12 ..122 A4
Widegate Nursery PL6 136 D8
Widemouth Bay Cvn Pk
EX23 ....6 E3
Widemouth Bay Holiday
Village EX23 ....6 F4
Widewell La PL6 ...125 C7
Widewell Prim Sch PL6 125 B7
Widewell Rd PL6 ...125 B7
Widey Court Prim Sch
PL6 ....124 F1
Widey Cross PL6 ...124 F1
Widey Ct PL6 ......124 F1
Widey La PL6 ......124 F1
Widey View PL3 ...128 E6
Wilcove La PL11 ...126 E5
Wildebeest Rd 7 PL27 .31 F3
Wilderness Rd PL3 .128 E5
Wildflower La
Newquay TR7 ......111 A6
Newquay TR7 ......111 B5
Wilkes Wlk TR1 ....137 D4
Wilkinson Rd PL5 ..127 D8
Will's Row TR15 ...139 C8
Willas Rd PL16 ......19 F4
William Edwards Cl
EX23 ....104 E6
William Evans Cl PL6 124 D5
William Laundry Cl PL14 .52 A5
William St
Camborne TR14 ....138 D2
Truro TR1 ....137 D4
William Young Mews
PL14 ....113 E5
Williams Ave PL4 ..129 B1
Willis Vean TR12 ....99 A1
Willoughby Pl PL17 ..39 E4
Willow Cl
22 Callington PL17 ..39 F4
Mylor Bridge TR11 ..82 A3
Plymouth PL3 ......129 E5
Quintrell Downs TR8 .44 E3
Willow Cotts PL7 ...130 D4
Willow Ct PL6 ......129 E7
Willow Dr TR14 ....138 B4
Willow Gn PL12 ....122 D2
Willow Rd PL19 ....147 C3
Willow Way PL14 ..113 B5

Willow Wlk PL6 ....125 D5
Willowby Pk PL20 ....42 D2
Willowfield Flats TR18 .143 C5
Willows The Bugle PL26 ..47 C1
  Whipsiderry TR7 ....44 C6
Wills Cl PL6 ....124 E7
Wills Moor PL26 ....85 C5
Wilminstone Ind Est
  PL19 ....147 E7
Wilmot Gdns PL5 ....124 D3
Wilsey View PL15 ......17 B7
Wilson Cres PL2 ....128 B5
Wilson Way
  Camborne TR15 ....139 D5
  14 Par PL24 ....60 B4
Wilsworthy Cross EX22 ..12 C7
Wilton Rd PL1 ....128 A3
Wilton St PL1 ....148 A4
Wilton Terr PL13 ....62 D6
Wiltshire Cl PL4 ....128 F4
Winchester Gdns PL5 ...124 A5
Windermere Cres PL6 ...124 F4
Winding Terr TR10 .....81 A1
Windmill PL23 ....116 C4
Windmill Hill
  Launceston PL15 ......106 C5
  Saltash PL12 ....122 E2
  St Just In Roseland TR2 ..82 F2
Windmill Hill Terr PL15 .106 C5
Windmill Ho PL23 ......116 C4
Windmill Ind Est PL23 ..116 C4
Windmill La PL15 ......106 C5
Windsor Ct
  Falmouth TR11 ....145 B4
  Newquay TR7 ....110 D5
Windsor Dr PL25 ......115 C3
Windsor Gr PL31 ......109 F5
Windsor Hill 8 TR26 ..141 B5
Windsor La
  Kelly Bray PL17 ....39 F6
  Saltash PL12 ....122 E2
Windsor Mews PL31 ...109 E5
Windsor Pl
  Liskeard PL14 ....113 C5
  29 Penzance TR18 .....143 E6
  Plymouth PL1 ....148 C2
Windsor Rd PL3 ....129 B7
Windsor Terr
  Falmouth TR11 ....145 B4
  Penzance TR18 ....143 D6
  4 St Ives TR26 ....141 A5
Windsor Villas PL1 ....148 C2
Wingfield PL31 ....35 B2
Wingfield Rd PL3 ......148 A4

Wingfield Way PL3 ....148 A4
Winifred Baker Ct 5
  PL4 ....149 A4
Winnard's Perch TR9 ...32 D1
Winnicott Cl PL6 ......124 E7
Winnow Cl PL9 ....135 F4
Winns Row TR13 ....146 C6
Winsbury Ct PL6 ......125 A1
Winsor Cotts PL15 ....106 B7
Winsor Est PL13 ....62 D5
Winstanley Wlk PL3 ...129 D6
Winston Ave PL4 ......148 C4
Winstowe Terr TR8 ....110 A3
Winwell Field PL27 ....108 D6
Witham Gdns PL3 .....129 C5
Withnoe La PL10 ......132 B6
Woburn Rd PL15 ......106 B4
Woburn Terr PL9 ......135 C7
Wodehouse Terr TR11 ..145 B4
Wolcocke Cl TR17 .....89 D5
Wollaton Gr PL5 ......123 F3
Wolrige Ave PL7 ......131 B5
Wolrige Way PL7 ......131 A5
Wolsdon Pl PL1 ....148 A3
Wolsdon St PL1 ....148 B3
Wolseley Bsns Pk 2
  PL2 ....128 A5
Wolseley Cl PL2 ......128 A5
Wolseley Rd
  Plymouth, Camels Head
    PL5 ....127 F6
  Plymouth, St Budeaux PL5 123 C1
Wolseley Road Flats
  PL2 ....127 F6
Wolverwood Cl PL7 ...131 C3
Wolverwood La PL7 ...131 B3
Wombwell Cres PL2 ...127 E7
Wood Acre PL12 ......122 B4
Wood Cl PL12 ....122 B3
Wood Dr PL12 ....53 C8
Wood La Landrake PL12 ..53 D2
  Par PL24 ....60 D5
  Truro TR1 ....137 D3
Wood View TR10 ......144 B7
Wooda La PL15 ....106 B6
Wooda Rd PL15 ....106 C6
Woodbine Cotts PL7 ..130 E4
Woodbine La TR16 .....67 D4
Woodbury Gdns PL5 ...124 A3
Woodchurch PL20 .....42 B3
Woodcock Cl PL10 ....133 A6
Woodend Rd PL6 .....125 D7
Woodfield Prim Sch
  PL5 ....124 C5

Woodfield Rd EX23 ....104 E7
Woodford Ave PL7 ....130 A7
Woodford Cl PL7 .....130 A7
Woodford Cres PL7 ...130 A6
Woodford Cross EX23 ...2 C1
Woodford Gn PL7 .....130 B6
Woodford Inf Sch PL7 .130 B6
Woodford Jun Sch PL7 .130 B7
Woodford Rd PL6 .....125 D6
Woodgate Rd PL14 ....113 A5
Woodgrove Pk PL26 ...59 A1
Woodhey Rd PL2 .....128 A7
Woodland Ave
  12 Par PL24 ....60 D5
  Penryn TR10 ....144 B6
  Plymouth PL9 ....136 A8
Woodland Cl Lanivet PL30 47 E7
  St Austell PL25 ....114 E3
Woodland Ct TR1 .....137 E5
Woodland Dr PL7 .....130 B4
Woodland Glade PL30 ..47 F7
Woodland Hts TR1 ....137 E5
Woodland Rd
  Plymouth PL7 ....130 C6
  St Austell PL25 ....114 E3
Woodland Rise
  Penryn TR10 ....144 B7
  Rilla Mill PL17 ....38 E8
Woodland Terr
  Plymouth PL4 ....149 B4
  St Columb Road TR9 ...45 E2
Woodland View
  Coombe PL26 ....58 C2
  Lanivet PL30 ....47 E6
Woodland Way
  Gunnislake PL18 ......41 A7
  Torpoint PL11 ....126 F3
Woodland Way Cl PL18 ..40 F6
Woodlands Dousland PL20 42 E3
  4 Mullion TR12 ....99 A2
  Plymouth PL9 ....135 F6
Woodlands Ct PL5 ....124 A3
Woodlands End PL6 ...125 D5
Woodlands La PL6 ....125 F1
Woodlands Sch PL5 ...124 B4
Woodlands Terr 3
  TR16 ....140 F1
Woodlands The TR14 ...67 B4
Woodlands View PL13 ..117 B4
Woodlane TR11 ....145 B3
Woodlane Cl TR11 ....145 B3
Woodlane Cres TR11 ..145 B3
Woodlane Dr TR11 ....145 B3
Woodley Cl 8 EX23 ....4 D1

Woodman's Cnr PL20 ..42 D3
Woodovis Holiday Pk
  PL19 ....29 F1
Woodridge Cl TR27 ....78 E1
Woods-Browning Ind Est
  PL31 ....109 F2
Woodside Crapstone PL20 .42 B2
  Penryn TR10 ....144 B7
  Plymouth PL4 ....149 B4
Woodside Ave PL9 ....135 C6
Woodside Ct PL7 .....130 E4
Woodside La PL4 .....149 B4
Woodstock Gdns PL5 ..123 D1
Woodvale Terr PL15 ...106 C5
Woodview Pk PL9 .....136 A6
Woodville Cl PL27 ....127 F7
Woodville Rd
  Morwenstow EX23 ......2 C1
  Plymouth PL2 ....127 F6
  Woodford EX23 ....4 D8
Woodway Penryn TR10 .144 B7
  Plymouth PL9 ....136 A7
Woolacombe Cross PL20 41 C1
Woolacombe Rd PL20 ..41 C1
Woollcombe Ave PL7 ..130 F4
Woolster Ct 9 PL4 ....149 A2
Woolwell Cres PL6 ....125 C8
Woolwell Dr PL6 ......125 C7
Woolwell Rd PL6 .....125 D7
Woon La 3 TR3 ....81 F7
Worcester Rd PL25 ...115 A4
Wordsworth Cres PL2 ..127 E7
Wordsworth Rd PL2 ...127 F7
Wotton Cross PL12 ....53 B4
Wreford Cl 11 TR9 ....45 D6
Wren Gdns PL7 ....130 C6
Wren Ind Est TR1 .....69 E4
Wrens Gate PL9 ......135 E8
Wrey Ave PL14 ....113 C7
Wright Cl PL1 ....127 E3
Wyatts La PL19 ....147 B6
Wych Hazel Way TR7 ..110 F4
Wycliffe Rd PL3 ......129 B4
Wye Gdns PL3 ....129 D7
Wykeham Dr PL2 .....128 A7
Wyleaf Holiday Pk EX23 ..4 F3
Wyndham La PL1 .....148 A3
Wyndham Sq PL1 .....148 A3
Wyndham St E PL1 ...148 B3
Wyndham St W PL1 ...148 B3
Wyndhurst Orch PL27 ..108 B6
Wyoming Cl PL3 ......129 C6
Wythburn Gdns PL6 ...125 D3

Y

Yardley Gdns PL6 .....125 E3
Yarg Cheese Farm ★
  PL14 ....38 D8
Yarrow Mead PL9 .....136 D7
Yealmpstone Cl PL7 ...131 B4
Yealmpstone Dr PL7 ..131 B3
Yealmpstone Farm Prim Sch
  PL7 ....131 B3
Yeats Cl PL5 ....124 C2
Yellow Tor Ct PL12 ...122 C2
Yellow Tor La PL12 ...122 C2
Yellow-wort TR16 .....80 C3
Yellowtor Rd PL12 ....122 B2
Yelverton Bsns Pk PL20 .42 B2
Yelverton Paperweight Mus ★
  PL20 ....42 C2
Yelverton Terr
  Tavistock TR19 ....147 D6
  Yelverton PL20 ....42 D2
Yeo Cl PL3 ....129 B5
Yeoland La PL20 ......42 C1
Yeomadon Cross EX22 ...8 E4
Yeomans Cl PL14 .....113 C5
Yeomans Way PL7 ....131 A4
Yew Tree Ct TR1 .....137 F6
Yewdale Gdns PL6 ....125 D2
Yonder St PL9 ....135 B6
York Pl PL2 ....127 F4
York Rd Plymouth PL5 ..127 E8
  Torpoint PL11 ....127 B3
York St Penzance TR18 .143 D6
  Plymouth PL1 ....127 E2
York Terr 7 PL2 .....127 F5
Youldon Way PL20 ....42 C4

Z

Zaggy La PL17 ....39 E4
Zion St PL1 ....148 C2
Zodiac Ho TR19 ......96 E3

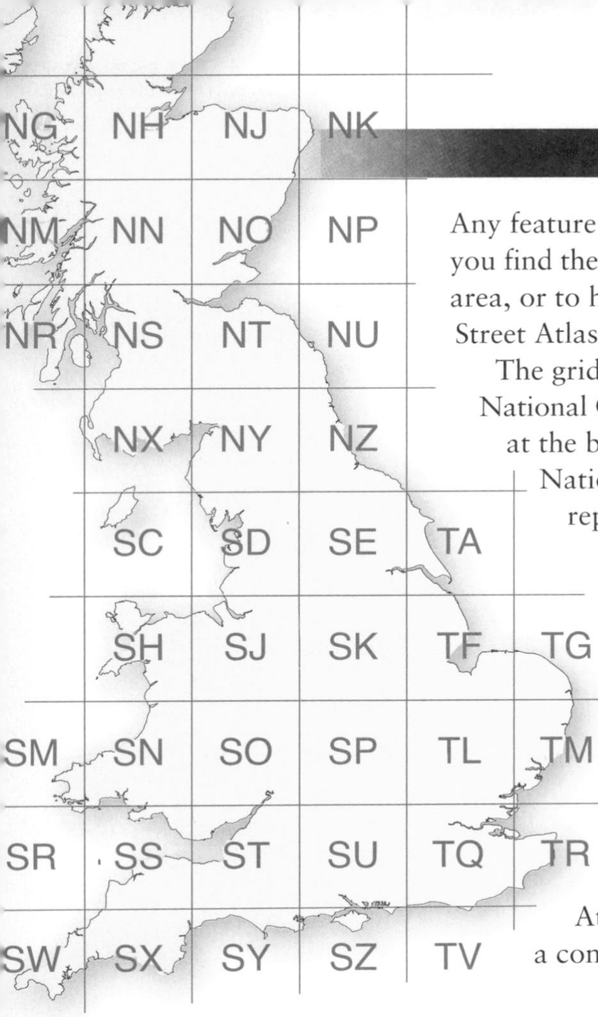

The grid of two-letter references map (left side):

NG NH NJ NK
NM NN NO NP
NR NS NT NU
NX NY NZ
SC SD SE TA
SH SJ SK TF TG
SM SN SO SP TL TM
SR SS ST SU TQ TR
SW SX SY SZ TV

Any feature in this atlas can be given a unique reference to help you find the same feature on other Ordnance Survey maps of the area, or to help someone else locate you if they do not have a Street Atlas.

The grid squares in this atlas match the Ordnance Survey National Grid and are at 500 metre intervals. The small figures at the bottom and sides of every other grid line are the National Grid kilometre values (**00** to **99** km) and are repeated across the country every 100 km (see left).

To give a unique National Grid reference you need to locate where in the country you are. The country is divided into 100 km squares with each square given a unique two-letter reference. Use the administrative map to determine in which 100 km square a particular page of this atlas falls.

The bold letters and numbers between each grid line (**A** to **F**, **1** to **8**) are for use within a specific Street Atlas only, and when used with the page number, are a convenient way of referencing these grid squares.

Example   The railway bridge over DARLEY GREEN RD in grid square B1

Step 1: Identify the two-letter reference, in this example the page is in **SP**

Step 2: Identify the 1 km square in which the railway bridge falls. Use the figures in the southwest corner of this square: Eastings **17**, Northings **74**. This gives a unique reference: **SP 17 74**, accurate to 1 km.

Step 3: To give a more precise reference accurate to 100 m you need to estimate how many tenths along and how many tenths up this 1 km square the feature is (to help with this the 1 km square is divided into four 500 m squares). This makes the bridge about **8** tenths along and about **1** tenth up from the southwest corner.

This gives a unique reference: **SP 178 741**, accurate to 100 m.

Eastings (read from left to right along the bottom) come before Northings (read from bottom to top). If you have trouble remembering say to yourself "Along the hall, THEN up the stairs"!

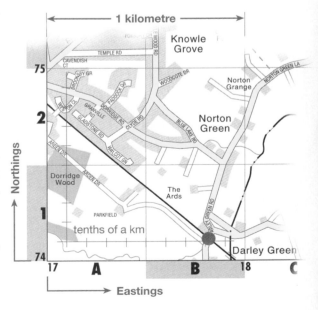

Name and Address	Telephone	Page	Grid reference

Addresses

Name and Address	Telephone	Page	Grid reference

Name and Address	Telephone	Page	Grid reference

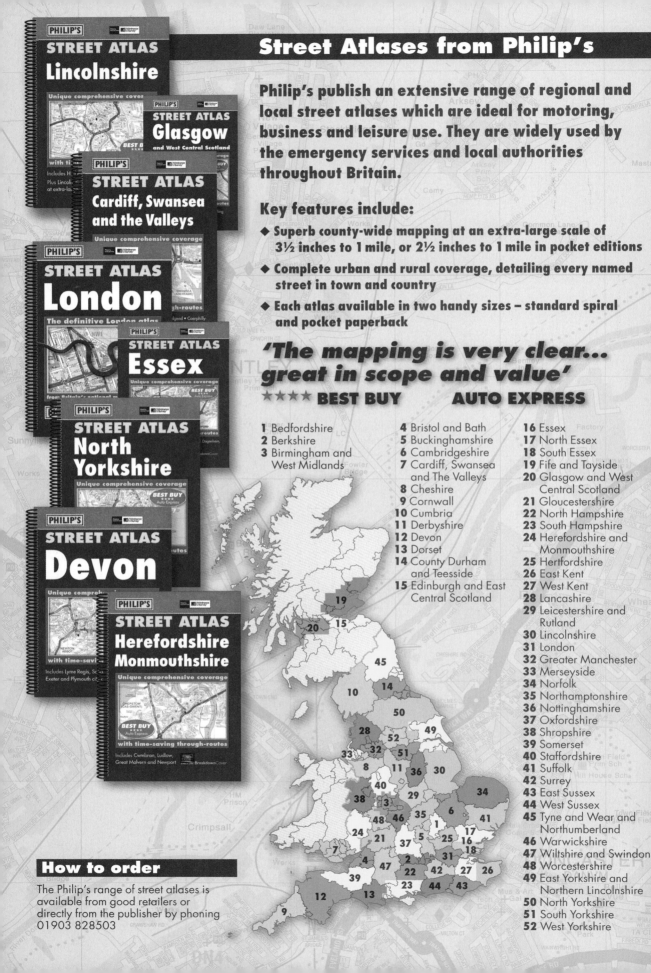